Aesthetic Theories:

Studies in the Philosophy of Art

THE FRONTISPIECE, *The Gathering of Nine Old Men at Lo-chung (or Hsiang-shan)*, *depicts a well-known gathering of literati in the year 845, a frequent subject of paintings. This work, reproduced here through the courtesy of the University of California, probably dates from the Ming dynasty (1368–1644).*

Aesthetic Theories:

Studies in the Philosophy of Art

Edited by

KARL ASCHENBRENNER
Department of Philosophy
University of California, Berkeley

ARNOLD ISENBERG

PRENTICE-HALL, INC. *Englewood Cliffs, New Jersey*

PRENTICE-HALL SERIES IN PHILOSOPHY
ARTHUR E. MURPHY, EDITOR

PRENTICE-HALL INTERNATIONAL, INC., *London*
PRENTICE-HALL OF AUSTRALIA, PTY., LTD., *Sydney*
PRENTICE-HALL OF CANADA, LTD., *Toronto*
PRENTICE-HALL OF INDIA (PRIVATE) LTD., *New Delhi*
PRENTICE-HALL OF JAPAN, INC., *Tokyo*

Second printing.....September, 1965

Library of Congress Catalog Card No.: 64–11554

Printed in the United States of America

C-01835

FOREWORD

The aim of the editors in arranging this volume is to present to their readers, academic and otherwise, the thoughts of philosophers on aesthetics and art. Writings abound on these subjects, and they derive from every conceivable source and standpoint—from historians, critics, artists, sociologists, psychologists, and a host of writers in other fields besides philosophy. Many of these writers have important things to say, and if we exclude their works, it is only because they are not essentially philosophical. Our own field is in itself extensive.

The historical orientation of this collection is apparent. What is not so apparent is that works drawn from the tradition (if we can call that which has lain unread and often despised "tradition") provide a better basis for beginning the study of aesthetic theories than do contemporary works alone. The readings we present must themselves be the test of the truth of this judgment. It is to be hoped that others will seek to verify this directly, and that if in the end they disagree, they do so not on the basis of pride in their ignorance of the subject but on the basis of first-hand knowledge of it.

We have not exhausted all of the standpoints and doctrines of western aesthetics. We emphasize the importance of the great modern tradition since the Renaissance. These writings seem to control and to limit the purview of their successors; their influence engulfs the present age; their scope usually extends beyond those of the current age; they are more likely to survive intense study. Besides, they are well (not to say better) written, well reasoned, well thought out and planned. Neglect of them seems the only likely explanation for the fact that our contemporaries so often innocently revive and present as discoveries certain doctrines that were once thoroughly sounded and justifiably dismissed. But many of the brilliant works to which we allude are, for one reason or another, currently unavailable. Hutcheson's treatise, for example, may be represented in a large university library by one precious copy of an eighteenth-century edition. Diderot's brilliant essay is buried in the collected *Oeuvres* and in the volumes of the *Encyclopédie*. The four volumes of Hegel's posthumous *Philosophy of Fine Art* contain much waste, much connective tissue, but also much that the present editors regret having to omit.

This collection is not a compendium or a work of scholarship. It is addressed primarily to students—indeed, to beginners—though we hope that aestheticians and knowledgeable critics will also find it useful. We draw on the history of aesthetics to the extent that it supplies the best treatment of living issues. Since we hope to advance aesthetics rather more than intellecual history, we have not been scrupulous to "cover" the history of our subject, and some works of historical importance have been omitted.

Many readers, confronted with no matter how good a collection, may feel uneasy if they suspect it of being unrepresentative or arbitrary in its selection. There are, however, many reasons for particular inclusions and omissions.

1. We have had limited space at our disposal. For a reader to say that we should have included this or that *in preference* to something will be a fair criticism, and one that may well be heeded in a later edition. But it would have been impossible to include *additional* readings.

2. We have omitted some famous, pertinent, and invaluable works that are available in low-priced editions—for example, the *Symposium* of Plato. Perhaps the only exception we have made to this rule is in reprinting the *Poetics* of Aristotle. Such works as the *Ion* and *Greater Hippias* have been accessible only in relatively expensive volumes, the larger parts of which are devoted to something other than aesthetics.

3. At the same time we have included certain works that are required by most instructors. We have, for example, reprinted the first chapter of Santayana's *Sense of Beauty,* even though it is widely reprinted and available at little cost. But it is a succinct summary of much that had gone before, and many instructors assign and lecture on it.

4. We have omitted any selection from certain fairly illustrious works that we believe to be duplicated by something better that we do include. The reader will perhaps note the absence of Burke's youthful and influential *Philosophical Inquiry into the Origin of Our Ideas on the Sublime and Beautiful* (1756). The introduction to that essay, "On Taste," has no consideration that is not better treated by Hume and a number of other authors. The body of the book is anticipated by a number of writers, and it is immeasurably surpassed by Kant's analysis some thirty years later.

5. We had intended to present at the end of the volume a series of short, but penetrating and suggestive, passages from a number of authors. This plan did not prove feasible. This is but one of many omissions. We have had to pass over any philosopher whose treatment of aesthetics is brief, diffuse, or fragmentary. The principal example is Shaftesbury, whom some regard as the founder of modern aesthetics. But unlike his disciple, Hutcheson, he has no special treatise or essay; his ideas on aesthetics are dispersed throughout the *Characteristics* and other works. He is quotable, but he is reprintable only *in toto.* The same thing is true in greater degree of a writer like Hobbes, whose opinions on humor and poetry, expressed in a sentence or two, contain each an aesthetic *impliciter,* but this would have to be spelled out by somebody other than Hobbes. St. Augustine and St. Thomas Aquinas are even greater names in philosophy, and there are those who consider that they held valuable and, indeed, authoritative views on beauty and art. But these opinions are not consecutive, detailed, and concentrated on the great issues. They constitute a doctrine only when they are pieced together and expounded, by a Gilson or a Maritain, in the light of theology and metaphysics. Perhaps this will serve in part to explain the omission of material between Plotinus and Hutcheson. The great medieval and Renaissance authors—Aquinas, Leonardo, Montaigne, Bacon, Descartes,

Pascal, and others—did not explicitly propound aesthetic theories, and it is not for a book of readings to supply the *implicit* doctrines of those ages.

A collection of shorter aesthetic doctrines and aperçus is afforded by Carritt's *Philosophies of Beauty*.[1] A most useful work embodying this sort of material is Wladyslaw Tatarkiewicz's extensive and masterful collection of excerpts from ancient and medieval writers, which contains both originals and Polish translations.[2] Professor Tatarkiewicz is preparing the same volume with English translations and will continue on the same plan through the Renaissance and later periods.

6. Another part of our apology will have to involve a brief consideration of "boundary disputes." Employing the customary figure of speech that conceives of any subject matter as a field, a province, or an area, we may say that aesthetics and the criticism of art are adjoining fields.[3] We may even concede that they interpenetrate. Yet the separation must be risked, since even though the edges may be indistinct or nonexistent, nobody will deny that the respective cores stand widely apart. Who would call the third *Critique* of Kant a work of criticism or say that Dryden, Johnson, or Arnold was an aesthetician? We have drawn the line wherever we have felt intuitively that it needed to be drawn. The result has been the elimination of many distinguished writers who constitute the background of the European "aesthetic consciousness": from Crousaz, Dubos, Addison, Young, Blair, Herder, Goethe, Schiller, and the Schlegels, through Ruskin, Tolstoy, Taine, Freud, and many of our own contemporaries. The omission, on the other hand, of such writers as Bergson, Croce, and Dewey has been due not to any doubt as to whether they qualify as aestheticians but often to considerations either of comparative merit or of space. The latter consideration has also led us to omit nearly every one of our immediate contemporaries.

But to return for a moment to the question of boundaries: The difference between Hume's essay on "The Standard of Taste" (included) and the much longer and fuller work *The Elements of Taste* (excluded) by his cousin and friend Henry Home, Lord Kames, is a case in point. Hume tries to write for gentlemen and critics; he affects literary discernment; and he betrays not only the tastes but the standards— more precisely, the notions concerning standards—of his time. Yet from the outset, in the very posing of his question (which we may paraphrase: If *A* says, "This work is good", and *B* says, "It is bad", what method, if any, can be found by which the issue can be resolved?), he is digging down to a philosophical level. Despite his bluff confidence, he is still a skeptic of sorts, aware of a deep-lying impasse that would yield only to the hardest thought combined with something like philosophical genius. Kames has no such theoretical sweep. From start to finish he is concerned with recommending various aesthetic preferences and proposing (as Hume also does in parts of his essay) all kinds of small techniques for reaching the right opinions. The choice between Hume and Kames was an easy one for us to make.

---

[1] E. F. Carritt, *Philosophies of Beauty* (New York: Oxford University Press, 1931).

[2] W. Tatarkiewicz, *Historia Estetyki* (Krakow: Wroclaw, 1960).

[3] The relation of aesthetics to criticism is controversial. Some have held that aesthetics stands to criticism as doctrine to subject matter (the "metacritical" conception of aesthetics), that it "rises out" of the criticism of art, in turn criticizing the concepts and propositions of that discipline; others have held that aesthetics "lies beyond" criticism but presupposes its existence as well as that of art and nature; still others, at the opposite pole, say that they are, if not "identical," at least "indistinguishable."

7. The exclusion of Schopenhauer demands a special apology, for it is something that we deeply regret. In a word, we saw no way of representing him fairly except at prohibitive length.

8. In the nineteenth century and down to the early part of this century, German production in aesthetics outweighed that of all other countries combined, and in terms of quality, this enormous output is not to be despised. There is no question in our minds but that the translation of works by Herbart, Fechner, Vischer, Lotze, Zimmermann, Lipps, Konrad Lange, Nicolai Hartmann, and others would be a boon to the study of aesthetics in the English-speaking world. But our reasons for leaving these authors nearly unrepresented is obvious. The size of some of these works would dwarf the present volume, and the labor of selection and translation would be prohibitive. (A translation of an essay by Lipps has, however, been prepared for this volume.) Besides, we know of nothing in the German literature (after Kant, Schiller, Hegel, and Schopenhauer) that ought to take precedence over the authors represented here. The same considerations apply to the more strictly contemporary French and Italian products. We do not claim that Moore, Lewis, and Prall are better than all their French or Italian contemporaries. We think they are as good, and they are at hand.

9. Finally, the omission of Baumgarten, who coined the term "aesthetic" in his *Meditationes* of 1735 (not his *Aesthetica* of 1750 as it is so often said), is owing to the lack of an available translation of his Latin *Aesthetica,* which alone has the requisite theoretical scope that we expect of a philosopher in this field. The *Meditationes* (an English translation appeared in 1954[4]) adumbrates the foundations of eighteenth-century rationalism in poetics.

It remains to explain the absence of an index. Our authors do not often use proper names, and a topical index would be useless unless it were expanded into what would amount to a philosophical disquisition. The same idea does not often appear in the same terminology, and different ideas do not always assume different labels. What Kant means by the phrase "as if it were a quality of the thing" Santayana sums up in the word "objectified"; and what Santayana understands by the word "expression" is not at all what many other aestheticians understand by the term. Nevertheless, it is no very formidable task for the reader to come to know when two authors are talking about the same or about different things.

In this foreword we have attempted to "place" the current body of selections in the sea of aesthetic theory. We make bold to say that the main line of aesthetic theory is more than represented in this volume; it is virtually given.

---

4 Alexander Baumgarten, *Reflections on Poetry,* Karl Aschenbrenner and William B. Holther, trans. (Berkeley: University of California Press, 1954).

CONTENTS

Aesthetic Theories:

Studies in the Philosophy of Art

PLATO

(427-347 B.C.)

Plato, whom many acclaim the greatest of all philosophers, came of a wealthy and distinguished Athenian family. Nearly all his works have survived, but we do not know very much about his life, especially the first thirty years of it. One thing that seems certain is that he was drawn into the circle of the aging Socrates, where he must have given much time to thought and argument on philosophical matters, for the earlier dialogues, although written when Plato was past thirty, show a command of dialectical method and a knowledge of various problems that could not have been picked up merely by the way. If the so-called Seventh Epistle is authentic (as most scholars now believe), then we know some of Plato's views on political events from 410 to 400 B.C. Surprising as it may seem, he was for a time more nearly sympathetic to the democratic than to the aristocratic faction in Athens, though the latter group was led by members of his own family. But we do not know whether or not he was actively involved in the Pëloponnesian War, during the later years of which he would have been of military age, or indirectly involved in its frightful repercussions at home. (The war lasted from 431 to 403.)

After the trial and execution of Socrates in 399, Plato seems to have embarked on a journey to foreign lands. In 388 he founded the Academy, usually regarded as the first university in history. The composition of the dialogues together with the labors of administering and teaching at the Academy account for most of the rest of his life. But he also paid three extensive visits to the court of Dionysius I and Dionysius II, the so-called "tyrants" of Syracuse, and he is believed to have visited Pythagorean colonies in Sicily and Italy. Accounts handed down of "experiments in statecraft" that he is supposed to have conducted at Syracuse are sketchy and not very reliable.

The aesthetics of Plato embraces such topics as the nature of art, the expression of character and feeling in the arts, the status and function of the figurative arts, the moral significance of fine art, the concept of beauty, the relation of beauty to love,

1

and the role of art and the beautiful in the state and in the education of men. Plato's ideas on these subjects can be fully understood only by seeing them in the setting of his metaphysics, his theory of knowledge, and his politics. A complete survey of the aesthetics would therefore take us through very nearly all of the dialogues. This body of thought could not be adequately represented by a diffuse selection of excerpts. In lieu of such a group of samples, we are giving almost the full text for each of two important though limited themes sometimes neglected by students of the *Symposium* and the *Republic,* together with a substantial selection from the latter.

The *Ion* is the earliest work we have dealing with the subject of the creative process in poetry. If the reader should feel that it is one-sided in its stress on inspiration, he is asked to consider whether in regard to that subject it leaves very much to be said.

The *Greater Hippias* is in a sense the first full-dress presentation of a philosophy of beauty or art. More obviously than perhaps any other passage in Plato, it belongs to the field of aesthetics in the modern sense of the word. The main proposal it puts forward (but in the end rejects or, at least, fails to find satisfactory), that beauty is identical with the pleasures of sight and of hearing, would seem to be opposed to those doctrines of Plato that presume the existence of a supersensible, absolute beauty. The *Greater Hippias* does not, in fact, literally contradict any thesis to be found elsewhere in the dialogues; but it is well to remember that it is not representative of Plato's typically metaphysical and absolutistic aesthetics. For these one should turn to the *Republic, Symposium,* and *Phaedrus.*

Considering these lines of Platonic thought and much more besides that culminates in the great doctrine of "ideas" or "forms" in all of the dialogues, we can begin to appreciate Plato's place as the prince of philosophers. Whitehead's apothegm that all philosophy is but a series of footnotes to Plato might well be true were it not for the great tradition of naturalism, now in ascendance, that has contested Platonism for some hundreds of years.

PLATO

Greater Hippias

(Translated by Benjamin Jowett)

From The Dialogues of Plato, *4th ed., Benjamin Jowett, trans. Oxford: The Clarendon Press, 1953. Reprinted by permission of The Clarendon Press.*

Persons of the Dialogue

§ SOCRATES/HIPPIAS

Socrates. Quite lately, my noble friend, 286 when I was condemning as ugly some things in certain compositions, and praising others as beautiful, somebody threw me into confusion by interrogating me in a most offensive manner, rather to this effect: "You, Socrates, pray how do *you* know what things are beautiful and what are ugly? Come now, can you tell me what beauty is?" In my incompetence I was confounded, and could find no proper answer to give him; so, leaving the company, I was filled with anger and reproaches against myself, and promised myself that the first time I met with one of you wise men, I would listen to him and learn, and when I had mastered my lesson thoroughly, I would go back to my questioner and join battle with him again. So you see that you have come at a beautifully appropriate moment, and I ask you to teach me properly what is beauty by itself, answering my questions with the utmost precision you can attain; I do not want to be made to look a fool a second time, by another cross-examination. Of course you know perfectly, and it is only a scrap of your vast learning.

Hippias. A scrap indeed, Socrates; and of no value, I may add.

Soc. Then I shall acquire it without trouble, and nobody will confound me again.

Hip. Nobody at all, if I am not a bun- 287 gling amateur in my profession.

Soc. Bravo, Hippias; how splendid, if we do defeat the adversary! Will it be a nuisance to you if I act as his understudy and fasten on your answers with my objections, so that you may put me through some vigorous practice? I have had a fair amount of experience of his objections. If, therefore, it makes no difference to you, I should like to play the critic; in this way I shall get a firmer grasp of what I learn.

Hip. Certainly; put your criticisms. As I said just now, it is not a big question; I might teach you to answer much more difficult ones with such cogency that no human being would be able to confute you.

Soc. How magnificent! Well now, on your invitation let me assume his role to the best of my ability, and try to interrogate you. If you were to deliver to him the discourse to which you refer—the discourse about beautiful practices—he would hear you to the end; and when you stopped, the very first question he would put would be about beauty—it is a kind of habit with him; he would say, "Stranger from Elis, is it not by justice that the just are just?" Would you answer, Hippias, as if he were asking the question?

Hip. I shall answer that it is by justice.

Soc. "Then this, namely justice, is definitely something."

Hip. Certainly.

Soc. "Again, it is by wisdom that the wise are wise, and by goodness that all things are good?"

Hip. Undoubtedly.

Soc. "That is, by really existent things—one could scarcely say, 'by things which have no real existence'?"

Hip. Quite so.

Soc. "Then are not all beautiful things beautiful by beauty?"

Hip. Yes, by beauty.

Soc. "Which has a real existence?"

Hip. Yes, what else do you think?

Soc. "Then tell me, stranger," he would say, "what is this thing, beauty?"

Hip. By putting this question he just wants to find out what is beautiful?

Soc. I do not think so, Hippias; he wants to know what is beauty—the beautiful.

Hip. What is the difference between them?

Soc. You think there is none?

Hip. There is no difference.

Soc. Obviously you know best. Still, my good sir, look at it again; he asks you not what is beautiful, but what is beauty.

Hip. I understand, my good sir, and I will indeed tell him what is beauty, defying anyone to refute me. I assure you, Socrates, if I must speak the truth, that a beautiful maiden is a beauty.

Soc. Upon my word, Hippias, a beautiful answer—very creditable. Then if I give that answer I shall have answered the question, 288 and answered it correctly, and I can defy anyone to refute me?

Hip. How can you be refuted when everyone thinks the same and everyone who hears you will testify that you are right?

Soc. Quite so. Now, Hippias, let me recapitulate to myself what you say. That man will question me something like this: "Come, Socrates, give me an answer. Returning to your examples of beauty, tell me what must beauty by itself be in order to explain why we apply the word to them?" And you want me to reply that if a beautiful maiden is a beauty, we have found why they are entitled to that name?

Hip. Do you imagine that he will then try to refute you by proving that you have not mentioned a beautiful thing, or that if he does attempt it he will not look a fool?

Soc. I am sure, my worthy friend, that he will try to refute me; the event will show whether the attempt will make him look a fool. But allow me to tell you what he will say.

Hip. Go on, then.

Soc. He will say, "How delicious you are, Socrates! Is not a beautiful mare a beauty

—the god himself praised mares in his oracle?" How shall we reply, Hippias? Must we not say that the mare, too, or at least a beautiful one, is a beauty? We can hardly be so audacious as to deny that beauty is beautiful.

Hip. Quite right; I may add that the god, too, spoke quite correctly; the mares we breed in our country are very beautiful.

Soc. He will now say, "Very well; but what about a beautiful lyre? Is that not a beauty?" Are we to agree, Hippias?

Hip. Yes.

Soc. Judging from his character, I feel pretty sure that he will then go on, "What about a beautiful pot, my dear sir? Is not that a beauty?"

Hip. Who is this fellow? What a boor, to dare to introduce such vulgar examples into a grave discussion!

Soc. He is that sort of person, Hippias; not at all refined, a common fellow caring for nothing but the truth. Still, he must have his answer and I give my own first; if the pot is the work of a good potter, smooth and round and properly fired, like some very beautiful pots I have seen, the two-handled ones that hold six choes,[1]—if he were to ask his question about a pot like that, we should have to admit that it is beautiful. How could we assert that what is a beautiful thing is not a beauty?

Hip. No, we could not.

Soc. "Then even a beautiful pot," he will say, "is a beauty?" Please answer.

Hip. Yes I suppose so. Even this utensil is beautiful when it is beautifully made, but generically it does not deserve to be judged beautiful in comparison with a mare or a maiden, or all the other things of beauty.

Soc. Very well. I understand, Hippias, that when he puts these questions I should answer, "Sir, you do not grasp the truth of Heracleitus' saying that the most beautiful of apes is ugly compared with the human race; and the most beautiful of pots is ugly

when grouped with maidens—so says Hippias the wise"—that is correct?

Hip. Quite the right answer.

Soc. Now mark my words, I am sure that he will then say. "Yes, Socrates, but if maidens are grouped with gods, will not the result be the same as when pots were grouped with maidens? Will not the most beautiful maiden appear ugly? Does not Heracleitus, whom you adduce, employ these very words, 'The wisest of men, when compared to a god, will appear but an ape in wisdom and beauty and all else'?" Shall we admit, Hippias, that the most beautiful maiden is ugly in comparison with the race of gods?

Hip. That no one can deny, Socrates.

Soc. If then we make this admission, he will laugh and say, "Socrates, do you remember what you were asked?" "Yes," I shall answer. "I was asked what beauty by itself is." He will rejoin, "Then when you are asked for beauty, do you offer in reply that which you yourself acknowledge to be no more beautiful than ugly?" "Apparently," I shall say; what do you advise me to reply?

Hip. As you do reply; for of course he will be right in saying that in comparison with gods the human race is not beautiful.

Soc. He will continue, "If I had asked you at the beginning what is both beautiful and ugly, and you had answered me as now, would not your answer have been correct? But do you still think that absolute beauty, by which all other things are ordered in loveliness, and appear beautiful when its form is added—do you think that that is a maiden, or a mare, or a lyre?"

Hip. But still, Socrates, if this is what he wants, it is the easiest thing in the world to tell him what is that beauty which orders all other things in loveliness and makes them appear beautiful when it is added to them. The fellow must be a perfect fool, knowing nothing about things of beauty; if you reply to him that this about which he is asking, beauty, is nothing else than gold,

289

---

1 [The χοῦς was about six pints.—TR. NOTE.]

he will be at a loss and will not attempt to refute you. For I suppose we all know that if anything has gold added to it, it will appear beautiful when so adorned even though it appeared ugly before.

Soc. You do not know what a ruffian he is; he accepts nothing without making difficulties.

Hip. What do you mean? He must accept 290 an accurate statement, on pain of ridicule.

Soc. Well, my friend, this answer of yours he will not only refuse to accept, but he will even scoff at me viciously, saying, "You blockhead! Do you reckon Pheidias a bad artist?" I suppose I shall answer, "Not in the least."

Hip. Quite right.

Soc. Yes, so I think. But when I agree that Pheidias is a good artist, he will say, "Then do you fancy that Pheidias was ignorant of this beauty of which you speak?" I shall reply, "What is the point?" and he will rejoin, "The point is that he did not give his Athena eyes of gold or use gold for the rest of her face, or for her hands, or for her feet, as he would have done if supreme beauty could be given to them only by the use of gold; he made them of ivory. Clearly he made this mistake through ignorance, not knowing that it is really gold that confers beauty on everything to which it is added." How are we to answer him then, Hippias?

Hip. Quite easy. We shall reply that Pheidias was artistically right; for ivory too is beautiful, I suppose.

Soc. "Why then," he will say, "did he not also make the eyeballs of ivory? He made them of stone, finding out stone as like as possible to ivory. Or is the stone that is beautiful itself a beauty?" Shall we say that it is?

Hip. Yes—it is beautiful, at least, whenever it is appropriate.

Soc. "But ugly when not appropriate?" Am I to agree?

Hip. Yes—when not appropriate.

Soc. He will go on, "Well then, O man of wisdom, do not ivory and gold cause a thing to appear beautiful when they are appropriate, and ugly when they are not?" Shall we deny it or admit that he is right?

Hip. We shall at any rate admit that whatever is appropriate to a particular thing makes that thing beautiful.

Soc. He will continue, "Then when a man boils the pot of which we spoke, the beautiful pot full of beautiful soup, which is the more appropriate to it—a ladle of gold or a ladle of fig-wood?"

Hip. Really, Socrates, what a creature! Please tell me who he is.

Soc. You would not know him if I told you his name.

Hip. I know enough about him at this moment to know that he is a dolt.

Soc. He is a terrible nuisance, Hippias; still, how shall we answer? Which of the two ladles are we to choose as appropriate to the soup and the pot? Obviously the one of fig-wood? For it gives the soup a better smell, I suppose; and moreover, my friend, it would not break our pot and spill the soup and put out the fire and deprive the guests at our dinner of a truly noble dish, whereas that golden ladle would do all this; and therefore, if you do not object, I think we should say that the wooden ladle is more 291 appropriate than the golden.

Hip. Yes, it is more appropriate; but I should not myself go on talking with the fellow while he asks such questions.

Soc. Quite right, my friend. It would not be appropriate for you to be contaminated by such language, you who are so well dressed, and wear such good shoes, and are renowned for wisdom throughout the Greek world. But to me it does not matter if I am mixed up with that fellow; so fortify me with your instruction, and for my sake answer the questions. He will say, "If indeed the wooden ladle is more appropriate than the golden, will it not also be more beautiful, since you, Socrates, have admitted that the appropriate is more beautiful than the inappropriate?" Can we then avoid the admission that the wooden ladle is more beautiful than the golden?

Hip. Would you like me to give you a definition of beauty by which you can save yourself from prolonged discussion?

Soc. Certainly, but first please tell me which of the two ladles I have just mentioned is appropriate, and the more beautiful?

Hip. Well, if you like, answer him that it is the one made of fig-wood.

Soc. Say now what a moment ago you were proposing to say; for following your answer, if I take the line that beauty is gold, I shall apparently have to face the fact that gold is no more beautiful than fig-wood. Now, once more, what according to you is beauty?

Hip. You shall have your answer. You are looking, I think, for a reply ascribing to beauty such a nature that it will never appear ugly to anyone anywhere?

Soc. Exactly; you catch my meaning admirably.

Hip. Now please attend; if anyone can find any fault with what I say, I give you full leave to call me an imbecile.

Soc. I am on tenterhooks.

Hip. Then I maintain that always, everywhere, and for every man it is most beautiful to be rich, healthy, honoured by the Greeks, to reach old age and, after burying his parents nobly, himself to be borne to the tomb with solemn ceremony by his own children.

Soc. Bravo, bravo, Hippias; those are words wonderful, sublime, worthy of you, and you have my grateful admiration for your kindness in bringing all your ability to my assistance. Still, our shafts are not hitting our man, and I warn you that he will now deride us more than ever.

Hip. A poor sort of derision, Socrates, for in deriding us when he can find no objection to our view, he will be deriding himself and will be derided by the company. 292

Soc. Perhaps so; perhaps, however, when he has the answer you suggest he may not be content just to laugh at me. So I forebode.

Hip. What do you mean?

Soc. If he happens to have a stick with him, he will attempt to get at me with it very forcibly, unless I escape by running away.

Hip. What? Is the fellow somehow your lord and master? Surely he will be arrested and punished for such behaviour? Or has Athens no system of justice, that she allows her citizens to commit wrongful assaults on one another?

Soc. She forbids it absolutely.

Hip. Then he will be punished for his wrongful assaults.

Soc. I do not think so, Hippias — emphatically not, if that were the answer I gave him; I think his assault would be justified.

Hip. Since that is your own opinion, well, I think so too.

Soc. But may I go on to explain why, in my own opinion, that answer would justify an assault upon me? Or will you too assault me without trial, refusing me a hearing?

Hip. No: such a refusal would be monstrous. But what have you to say?

Soc. I will continue on the same plan as a moment ago, pretending to be that fellow but not using to you the kind of offensive and grotesque words he would to me. He will say, I feel sure, "Do you not think, Socrates, that you deserve a thrashing after chanting so badly out of tune a dithyramb so long and so irrelevant to the question you were asked?" "What do you mean?" I shall say. "What do I mean? Are you incapable of remembering that I asked about beauty itself, that which gives the property of being beautiful to everything to which it is added—to stone and wood, and man, and god, and every action and branch of learning? I am asking, Sir, what is beauty itself, and for all my shouting I cannot make you hear me; you might be a stone sitting beside me, a real millstone with neither ears nor brain." Would not you, Hippias, be indignant if in terror I were to answer him, "But this is what Hippias declared beauty to be, although I kept on asking him, exactly as you do me, for that which is beautiful always and for everyone." Frankly, will not that answer make you indignant?

Hip. I am quite sure, Socrates, that what I specified is beautiful to all, and will so appear to all.

Soc. He will reply, "And will be so in the future? For beauty, I take it, is always beautiful?"

Hip. Certainly.

Soc. "And it was beautiful, too, in the past?"

Hip. It was.

Soc. Then he will go on, "So this stranger from Elis asserted that it would have been beautiful for Achilles to be buried after his parents, and similarly for his grandfather Aeacus, and for the other children of gods, and for the gods themselves?"

Hip. What is this? Tell him to go to—glory! These questions of his are irreverent, Socrates.

Soc. Surely it is not exactly irreverent to say that these things are so, when someone else has asked the question?

Hip. Well, presumably not.

Soc. Presumably he will then say, "It is you who affirm that it is beautiful always and for everyone to bury his parents and be buried by his children. Does not 'everyone' include Heracles and all the others we mentioned a moment ago?"

Hip. I did not mean to include the gods.

Soc. "Nor the heroes either, apparently."

Hip. Not if they were the children of gods.

Soc. "But if they were not?"

Hip. Certainly.

Soc. "Then from your own argument, it now appears that the fate which is terrible and impious and shameful for Tantalus and Dardanus and Zethus is beautiful for Pelops

and the other heroes of similar parentage?"

Hip. I think so.

Soc. He will go on, "Then you think, contrary to what you said just now, that to bury one's parents and be buried by one's children is sometimes, and for some persons, shameful; and it looks more than ever impossible that it should become, or be, beautiful to everyone. So this definition meets the same fate as those we discussed earlier—the maiden and the pot; it is an even more ludicrous failure, offering us that which is beautiful to some men, and not to others. And to this very day, Socrates, you cannot answer the question you were asked—beauty, what is it?" These and other like reproaches he will hurl at me with some justice, if I give him this answer. For the most part he talks to me something after this fashion; but sometimes, as if in pity for my inexperience and lack of education, he himself proffers a question, and asks whether I think beauty is such and such; or it may be on some other subject—whatever he happens to be thinking about, and we are discussing.

Hip. What do you mean, Socrates?

Soc. I will explain. "My worthy Socrates," he says, "don't give answers of that kind, and in that way—they are silly, easily torn to rags; but consider this suggestion. In one of our answers a little while ago we got hold of, and expressed, the idea that gold is beautiful or not beautiful according as it is placed in an appropriate setting; and similarly with everything else to which this qualification can be added. Now consider this appropriateness, and reflect on the general nature of the appropriate, and see whether it might not be beauty." Myself, I am in the habit of invariably agreeing to such surmises, for I can never think of anything to say; but you, do you think that the appropriate is beautiful?

Hip. Certainly, Socrates.

Soc. Let us consider, and make sure that there is no deception.

293

Hip. So we ought.

Soc. Come on then. Do we define the appropriate as that which by its presence 294 causes the things in which it becomes present to *appear* beautiful, or causes them to *be* beautiful, or neither?

Hip. In my own opinion, that which causes things to appear beautiful; for example, a man may be a figure of fun, but when he wears clothes or shoes that fit well he does seem a finer man.

Soc. But then if the appropriate really makes things more beautiful than they are, the appropriate is a kind of fraud in relation to beauty, and would not be that for which we are looking, would it? We were looking, I think, for that by which all beautiful things are beautiful—corresponding to that by which all great things are great, namely, excess; by this all great things are great, and great they must certainly be if they exceed, even though they do not appear so: similarly we ask about beauty, by which all beautiful things are beautiful whether they appear so or not—what can that be? It cannot be the appropriate, for on your own view this causes things to appear more beautiful than they are, and does not leave them to appear such as they are in reality. We ought to take that which causes things to be beautiful, as I said just now, whether they appear so or not, and try to define it; this is what we are looking for, if we are looking for beauty.

Hip. But, Socrates, the appropriate causes things both to be and to appear beautiful, when it is present.

Soc. Then it is impossible for things that are in fact beautiful not to appear beautiful, since by hypothesis that which makes them appear beautiful is present in them?

Hip. It is impossible.

Soc. Then it is our conclusion, Hippias, that all established usages and all practices which are in reality beautiful are regarded as beautiful by all men, and always appear so to them? Or do we think the exact oppo-site, that ignorance of them is prevalent, and that these are the chief of all objects of contention and fighting, both between individuals and between states?

Hip. The latter, I think; ignorance prevails.

Soc. It would not, if the appearance of beauty were but added to them; and it would be added if the appropriate were beautiful and moreover caused them to *appear* as well as *be* beautiful. It follows that if the appropriate is that which causes things to be in fact beautiful, then it would be that beauty for which we are looking, but still it would not be that which causes them to appear beautiful; if, on the other hand, that which causes things to appear beautiful is the appropriate, it is not that beauty for which we are looking. That for which we are looking makes things beautiful, but the same cause never could make things both appear and be either beautiful or anything else. We have then these alternatives; is the appropriate that which causes things to appear beautiful, or that which causes them to be so?

Hip. To appear, I think.

Soc. Oh dear! Then the chance of finding out what the beautiful really is has slipped through our fingers and vanished, since the appropriate has proved to be something other than beautiful.

Hip. Upon my word, Socrates, I should never have thought it!

Soc. But still, my friend, do not let us 295 give up yet; I have still a sort of hope that the nature of beauty will reveal itself.

Hip. Yes indeed, it is not hard to discover. I am sure that if I were to retire into solitude for a little while and reflect by myself, I could define it for you with superlative precision.

Soc. Hippias, Hippias, don't boast. You know what trouble it has already given us, and I am afraid it may get angry with us and run away more resolutely than ever. But what nonsense I am talking; for you, I suppose, will easily discover it when once you are alone. Still, I beg you most earnestly to discover it with me here; or, if you please, let us look for it together as we are now doing. If we find it, well and good; if not, I imagine I shall resign myself to my fate, and you will go away and discover it easily. Of course, if we find it now, you will not be annoyed by inquiries from me about the nature of your private discovery: so please look at your conception of beauty by itself. I define it as—pray give me your whole attention and stop me if I talk nonsense—well, let us assume that whatever is useful is beautiful. My ground for the proposition is as follows: we do not say that eyes are beautiful when they appear to be without the faculty of sight; we do when they have that faculty and so are useful for seeing. Is that correct?

Hip. Yes.

Soc. Similarly we say that the whole body is beautifully made, sometimes for running, sometimes for wrestling; and we speak in the same way of all animals. A beautiful horse, or cock, or quail, and all utensils, and means of transport both on land and on sea, merchant vessels and ships of war, and all instruments of music and of the arts generally, and, if you like, practices and laws— we apply the word "beautiful" to practically all these in the same manner; in each case we take as our criterion the natural constitution or the workmanship or the form of enactment, and whatever is useful we call beautiful, and beautiful in that respect in which it is useful and for the purpose for which and at the time at which it is useful; and we call ugly that which is useless in all these respects. Is not this your view also, Hippias?

Hip. Yes, it is.

Soc. Then we are now right in affirming that the useful is pre-eminently beautiful.

Hip. We are.

Soc. And that which has the power to achieve its specific purpose is useful for the purpose which it has the power to achieve, and that which is without that power is useless?

Hip. Certainly.

Soc. Then power is a beautiful thing, and the lack of it ugly?

Hip. Very much so. We have evidence of that fact from public life, among other sources; for in political affairs generally, and 296 also within a man's own city, power is the most beautiful of things, and lack of it the most ugly and shameful.

Soc. Good! Does it then follow — a momentous consequence—that wisdom is the most beautiful, and ignorance the most shameful of all things?

Hip. What do you think, Socrates?

Soc. A moment's quiet, my dear friend; I have misgivings about the line we are taking now.

Hip. Why these misgivings again? This time your argument has proceeded magnificently.

Soc. I could wish it were so; but let us consider together this point. Could a man do something which he had neither the knowledge nor the least atom of power to do?

Hip. Of course not; how could he do what he had not the power to do?

Soc. Then those who by reason of some error contrive and work evil involuntarily —surely they would never do such things if they were without the power to do them?

Hip. Obviously not.

Soc. And those who have the power to do a thing do it through power, not of course by being powerless?

Hip. Certainly not.

Soc. Those who do what they do, all have the power to do it?

Hip. Yes.

Soc. And evil is done much more abundantly than good by all men from childhood upwards, erring involuntarily?

Hip. That is so.

Soc. Well then, are we to say that this power, and these useful things—I mean any things useful for working some evil—are we to say that these are beautiful, or that they are far from being so?

Hip. Far from it, in my opinion.

Soc. Then the powerful and the useful are not, it appears, the beauty we want.

Hip. They are, Socrates, if they are powerful for good and are useful for such purposes.

Soc. Still the theory that that which is powerful and useful without qualification is beautiful has vanished away. Do you think, however, that what we really had in mind to say was that beauty is that which is both useful and powerful for some good purpose?

Hip. I think so.

Soc. But this is equivalent to "beneficial," is it not?

Hip. Certainly.

Soc. So we reach the conclusion that beautiful bodies, and beautiful rules of life, and wisdom, and all the things we mentioned just now, are beautiful because they are beneficial?

Hip. Evidently.

Soc. Then it looks as if beauty is the beneficial, Hippias.

Hip. Undoubtedly.

Soc. Now the beneficial is that which produces good?

Hip. Yes.

Soc. And that which produces is identical with the cause?

Hip. That is so.

Soc. Then the beneficial is the cause of the good?

Hip. It is.

Soc. But surely, Hippias, the cause and that of which it is the cause are different; for the cause could scarcely be the cause of the cause. Look at it in this way. The cause was defined as something that produces, was it not?

Hip. Certainly.

Soc. And that which produces produces only that which is coming into existence; it does not produce that which produces.

Hip. That is so.

Soc. And that which is coming into existence, and that which produces it, are two different things?

Hip. Yes.

Soc. Then the cause is not the cause of the cause, but of that which is coming into existence through it?

Hip. Certainly.

Soc. If then beauty is the cause of good, then the good would be brought into existence by beauty; and it would appear that we devote ourselves to the pursuit of wisdom and of all other beautiful things for the reason that their product and offspring, the good, is worthy of devotion; and from our explorations it looks as though beauty is metaphorically a kind of father of the good.

Hip. Certainly; you say well, Socrates.

Soc. Do I not say this also well, that the father is not his son, nor the son his father?

Hip. Quite well.

Soc. And that the cause is not that which it brings into existence, nor vice versa?

Hip. True.

Soc. Then most certainly, my good sir, beauty is not good nor the good beautiful. Do you think that possible after our discussion?

Hip. No. I most certainly do not.

Soc. Then does it please us, and should we be willing to say, that the beautiful is not good, nor the good beautiful?

Hip. Most certainly not; it does not please me at all.

Soc. Most certainly I agree, Hippias; it pleases me least of any of the theories we have discussed.

Hip. Very likely.

Soc. Then it looks as if the view which a little while ago we thought the finest result of our discussions, the view that the beneficial, and the useful, and the power to produce something good, is beautiful, is in fact wrong; but it is, if possible, more open to ridicule than those first definitions according to which the maiden was the beautiful, and so was a succession of other things.

Hip. Apparently.

Soc. For myself, Hippias, I don't know where to turn, and am completely at a loss; have you anything to say?

Hip. Not at the moment; but as I said a little while ago, I feel sure I shall find a way out after some reflection.

Soc. But I do not feel that I can wait for the issue of your reflection, I am so eager for this knowledge; and indeed, I fancy I have just hit on something. Come now: if we were to say that whatever we enjoy— I do not mean to include all pleasures, but only what we enjoy through our senses of hearing and sight—if we were to say that this is beautiful, how should we fare in our struggle? Surely beautiful human beings, and all decorative work, and pictures, and plastic art, delight us when we see them if they are beautiful; and beautiful sounds, and music as a whole, and discourses, and tales of imagination, have the same effect; so that if we were to reply to that blustering fellow: "My worthy sir, beauty is the pleasant which comes through the senses of hearing and sight," do you not think that we should stop his bluster?

Hip. At last, Socrates, I think we have a good definition of beauty.

Soc. Well, but are we then to say that those practices which are beautiful, and the laws, are beautiful as giving pleasure through our senses of sight and hearing, or that they are in some other category?

Hip. Perhaps these cases might escape our man.

Soc. No, Hippias, they would certainly not escape the man by whom I should be most ashamed to be caught talking pretentious nonsense.

Hip. Whom do you mean?

Soc. The son of Sophroniscus,[2] who would no more allow me to hazard these assertions while they are unexplored than to assert what I do not know as though I knew it.

Hip. Well, now you have raised the point,

---

2 [That is, Socrates himself.—TR. NOTE.]

I must say that I too think this question about the laws is on a different footing.

Soc. Gently, Hippias; we may quite well be imagining that we see our way clearly, when we have really fallen into the same difficulty about beauty as that in which we were caught a moment ago.

Hip. What do you mean, Socrates?

Soc. This is what strikes me—there may be something in it. These matters of law and practice might perhaps prove after all to be within the range of the perceptions of hearing and sight; however, let us hold fast to the statement that the pleasant which comes through these senses is beautiful, leaving the question of the laws altogether on one side. But if we were asked by the person to whom I refer, or by anyone else: "Why, Hippias and Socrates, have you picked out within the class of the pleasant that which is pleasant in the way you affirm to be beautiful, while you deny the designation 'beautiful' to that which is pleasant according to the other senses, that is, the senses which have to do with food, and drink, and sexual intercourse, and all such things? Or do you deny that these are pleasant, and claim that in such things there is no pleasure whatever, or in anything except seeing and hearing?" What shall we say?

Hip. Obviously we shall reply that these other things also offer very great pleasures.

Soc. "Why then," he will say, "do you take away this designation and refuse to allow them beauty when they are pleasures no less than the others?" We shall answer: "Because everyone would laugh at us if we said that it is not pleasant to eat, but beautiful, or that a pleasant smell is not pleasant, but beautiful; and as to sexual intercourse, everyone would contend against us that it is most pleasant, while admitting that it ought to be enjoyed only where there is none to see because it is a disgraceful and repulsive sight." When we say this, Hippias, he would probably rejoin: "I too understand that you are and have been ashamed to say that these pleasures are beautiful, because that is not the common view; but my question was, what is beautiful, not what the mass of men think it to be." I imagine we shall re-state our original proposition. "In our view that part of the pleasant which comes by sight and hearing is beautiful." However, can you suggest any other way of dealing with the question, or any addition to that reply?

Hip. As the argument now stands, we are bound to give that answer, and that only.

Soc. "Admirable," he will reply. "If then the pleasant which comes by sight and hearing is beautiful, is it not obvious that any pleasant thing outside that category could not be beautiful?" Shall we agree?

Hip. Yes.

Soc. He will go on: "Then is that which is pleasant through sight, pleasant through sight and through hearing, or is that which is pleasant through hearing, pleasant through hearing and through sight?" We shall reply: "By no means; the pleasant which comes by either sense would certainly not be pleasant through both—that seems to be your meaning; our statement was that either of these pleasant things would be beautiful just by itself, and also both of them together." Shall that be our answer?

Hip. Certainly.

Soc. "Well, then," he will say, "does any pleasant thing whatever differ from any other pleasant thing in respect of its pleasantness? The question is not whether a particular pleasure is greater or smaller, or exists in a higher or lower degree, but whether there can be a difference between pleasures in this particular respect, that one is, and another is not, a pleasure?" We do not think so, do we?

Hip. No.

Soc. He will continue: "It follows that you chose out these from among the other pleasures for some other reason than that they are pleasures. Since there is some difference between them and the others, you saw in both of them some quality capable of providing a criterion by which you judge them to be beautiful; for the pleasure that comes through sight, I take it, is not beautiful just because it comes through sight. If that were the reason why it is beautiful, the other pleasure, the one which comes through hearing, would never be beautiful; it is emphatically not pleasure through sight." Shall we reply that his reasoning is correct?

Hip. Yes.

Soc. "Nor again is the pleasure that comes through hearing beautiful because it is through hearing; for again, in that case the pleasure through sight would never be beautiful since it is emphatically not pleasure through hearing." Shall we agree that he argues correctly?

Hip. He does.

Soc. "But yet both are beautiful, you affirm?" We do affirm it?

Hip. Yes.

Soc. "Then they have something identical which makes them to be beautiful, a common quality which appertains to both of them in common and to each singly; otherwise they could not, I take it, both of them be beautiful as a pair, and also each separately?" Answer me as though you were answering him.

Hip. I answer that what you say is my opinion also.

Soc. If then these pleasures are both of them as a pair conditioned in some way, but neither singly is so conditioned, they could not be beautiful by reason of this particular condition?

Hip. And how is it possible, Socrates, that when neither of them singly has been conditioned in some way—any way you like to think of—yet both as a pair should be conditioned in the way in which neither singly has been conditioned?

Soc. You think it impossible?

Hip. I do: not being entirely unacquainted either with the nature of the subject, or with the terminology of our present discussion.

Soc. Very nice, Hippias. But still I fancy perchance I see an example of what you say to be impossible, though really I may see nothing.

Hip. It is not a case of "perchance"; you see wrong, of good set purpose.

Soc. Indeed, many such examples rise up before my mind's eye; but I distrust them because they are visible to me, who have never earned a penny by wisdom, while they do not appear to you who have earned more in that way than anyone else alive; and, my friend, I am pondering whether you are not playing with me and deceiving me on purpose, so clearly and in such numbers do I see them.

Hip. Nobody will know better than you whether I am playing with you or not, when you start to describe these visions of yours; your description of them will be plain nonsense. You will never find both of us together conditioned in a way in which neither has been conditioned separately.

Soc. What's that, Hippias? You may be talking sense and I do not grasp it, but please let me explain more clearly what I mean. It appears to me that there are attributes which cannot, and do not now, belong to either of us singly, but can belong to both together; and, conversely, that there are attributes of which both together are capable, but neither singly.

Hip. Here indeed, Socrates, are absurdities even more monstrous than those of your answer a little while ago. Only consider: If we are both just men, is not each of us individually just? If each of us is unjust, are not both so? If both are well, is not each of us well also? Or if each of us were tired, or were wounded, or struck, or conditioned in any other way, then should we not both of us as a pair be conditioned in that way? Similarly, if both of us were made of gold, or silver, or ivory, or if you prefer it, were noble or wise or honoured, or, for that matter, old men or young, or had any other human attribute you like to mention, must it not follow inevitably that each of us singly is that same?

Soc. Most certainly.

Hip. You see, Socrates, the fact is that you yourself do not consider things as a whole, nor do those with whom you habitually converse; you test beauty and each general concept by taking it separately and mentally dissecting it, with the result that you fail to perceive the magnitude and continuity of the substances of which reality is composed. And now this failure has gone so far that you imagine that there is something, an attribute or substantive nature, which appertains to two of them together but not to each singly, or conversely to each singly but not to the two together; that is the state of mind to which you and your friends are reduced—how unreasoning, and superficial, and stupid, and uncomprehending!

Soc. Such is the lot of us mortals, Hippias —a man does what he can, not what he wishes, according to the oft-quoted proverb; however, your constant admonitions are a great help. Just now, before your admonition of our stupidity in these matters, I had some further thoughts about them which perhaps I might explain to you—or shall I refrain?

Hip. I know what you are going to say, Socrates; I know the mind of every school of dialecticians. But say your say, if you prefer it.

Soc. Well, I do prefer it. Before you said what you did, my honoured friend, we were so uninstructed as to hold the opinion that each of us two, you and myself, is one, but that, taken together, we cannot be that which each of us is singly—for we are two and not one; such was our folly. Now, however, we have been taught by you that if together we are two, each of us singly must also be two, and if each is one, so must we both be; for on the continuous theory of reality according to Hippias it cannot be otherwise—whatever two entities are together, each is singly, and whatever each is, both are. Here I sit, fixed by you in this belief. But first, Hippias, remind me; are you and I both one, or are you two, and I two?

Hip. What do you mean, Socrates?

Soc. Exactly what I say; you frighten me out of plain speech, because you get angry with me whenever you think that you have made a good point. Still, let me ask you this further question; is not each of us two one, possessing the attribute of being one?

Hip. Certainly.

Soc. Then if each of us is one, each is also an odd number; you hold that one is an odd number, do you not ?

Hip. I do.

Soc. Are we then both together an odd number, being two?

Hip. Impossible.

Soc. Both together would be an even number?

Hip. Assuredly.

Soc. Since then both together are even, does it follow that each of us singly is even?

Hip. Certainly not.

Soc. It is not then absolutely inevitable that, as you said just now, each individual should be what both are together, and that both should be what each is?

Hip. Not in such cases, but it is inevitable in the kind of case I mentioned earlier.

Soc. That suffices. Hippias; even that reply is to be accepted, as it is an acknowledgement that sometimes it is so, and sometimes not. If you recall the starting-point of our discussion, you will remember that I was arguing that the pleasures which come through sight and hearing are beautiful not because each of them was so conditioned as to be beautiful but not both together, nor because both of them together were similarly conditioned but not each singly; they were beautiful by virtue of something which conditions both together and also each singly, and so you agreed that both together were beautiful and each singly. Accordingly I thought that if both together are beautiful, they must be beautiful because of an essen-

tial character belonging to both and not of a character which is lacking in one or other; and I still think so. But start again as from the beginning. If pleasure through sight and pleasure through hearing are beautiful both together and each singly, does not that which makes them beautiful belong to both together and to each singly?

Hip. Certainly.

Soc. Then can they be beautiful because each singly and both together are pleasures? On this reasoning, would not all other pleasures be beautiful just as much, for, if you remember, they were acknowledged to be just as much pleasures?

Hip. Yes, I remember.

Soc. These particular ones, however, were stated to be beautiful because they came through sight and hearing.

Hip. Yes, that was the statement.

Soc. Now consider whether I am right on this point. According to my recollection, it was said that part of the category of the pleasant was beautiful—not every "pleasant," but that which comes through hearing and sight.

Hip. That is correct.

Soc. And this quality belongs to both together but not to each singly, does it not? As we said earlier, each of them singly does not come through both senses; both together come through both but not each singly. Is that so?

Hip. Yes.

Soc. Then each of them singly is not beautiful by that which does not belong to each (for that which is of both does not belong to each); and it follows that while from our agreed propositions we may rightly say that both together are beautiful, we may not say it of each singly. Is not this the necessary conclusion?

Hip. It appears so.

Soc. Are we to say then that both together are beautiful, but not each?

Hip. I see no objection.

Soc. I do, my friend. We certainly had examples of attributes appertaining to individual entities in such a way that if they appertained to two together they appertained also to each singly, and if to each, then to both—all the attributes which were specified by you.

Hip. Yes.

Soc. But on the other hand those which I specified did not; and among those were the concept "each," and the concept "both." Is that right?

Hip. Yes.

Soc. To which category, Hippias, do you think the beautiful belongs? To the category of those you mentioned? If I am strong and you are too, we are both strong, and if I am just and you too, we are both just, and if both, then each singly; in the same way, if I am beautiful and you too, are we also both beautiful and if both, then each singly? Or may the same principle apply as in mathematics, when for instance the two components of even numbers may severally be odd, but may also be even; and, again, when quantities which are irrational if taken singly may be either rational or irrational if taken together; and there are innumerable other such examples, as indeed I told you occurred to my mind? In which category do you place beauty? Do you take the same view of it as I do? To me it seems a gross absurdity to hold that while both of us together are beautiful, neither is so singly, or that each singly is beautiful but not both together, or anything else of that kind? Do you choose my alternative, or the other?

Hip. Yours.

Soc. Quite right, if we wish to be spared further inquiry; for if this category includes beauty, it can no longer be maintained that the pleasant which comes through sight and hearing is beautiful; the description "which comes through sight and hearing" makes both together beautiful but not each singly 304 —which was impossible, as I think, and you too.

Hip. Yes, we think the same.

Soc. Then it is impossible for the pleasant which comes through sight and hearing to be beautiful, since when we equate it with beauty an impossible result is produced.

Hip. Quite so.

Soc. My questioner will say: "Now start again from the beginning since you have missed the mark this time. What according to you is this 'beautiful' which appertains to both these pleasures, and by reason of which you have honoured them above the others and called them beautiful?" I think, Hippias, we are bound to reply that these are the most harmless of pleasures and the best, both taken together and taken singly. Can you suggest any other reason why they are superior to the others?

Hip. None; they really are the best.

Soc. "This then," he will say, "is your definition of beauty; beneficial pleasure." "Apparently," I shall reply; and you?

Hip. I too.

Soc. He will go on: "Well then, is not the beneficial that which produces the good, and that which produces and that which is produced were shown a little while ago to be different, and so our discussion has ended up in the old discussion, has it not? For the good cannot be beautiful, nor beauty good, if the two are not identical with one another." "Nothing is more certain," we shall reply, if we are honest; there can be no justification for demurring to truth.

Hip. But I must ask you, Socrates, what do you suppose is the upshot of all this? As I said a little while ago, it is the scrapings and shavings of argument, cut up into little bits; what is both beautiful and most precious is the ability to produce an eloquent and beautiful speech to a law-court or a council-meeting or any other official body whom you are addressing, to convince your audience, and to depart with the greatest of all prizes, your own salvation and that of your friends and property. These then are the things to which a man should hold fast, abandoning these pettifogging arguments of yours, unless he wishes to be accounted a complete fool because he occupies himself, as we are now doing, with trumpery nonsense.

Soc. You, my dear Hippias, are blissfully fortunate because you know what way of life a man ought to follow, and moreover have followed it with success—so you tell me. I, however, am subject to what appears to be some supernatural ill fortune. I wander about in unending perplexity, and when I lay my perplexity before you wise men, you turn on me and batter me with abuse as soon as I have explained my plight. You all say just what you, Hippias, are now saying, how foolish and petty and worthless are the matters with which I occupy myself; but when in turn I am convinced by you and repeat exactly what you tell me, that the height of excellence is the ability to produce an eloquent and beautiful speech and win the day in a law-court or any other assembly, I am called every kind of bad name by some of the audience, including especially that man who is always cross-questioning me. He is a very close relative of mine and lives in the same house, and when I go home and he hears me give utterance to these opinions he asks me whether I am not ashamed of my audacity in talking about a beautiful way of life, when questioning makes it evident that I do not even know the meaning of the word "beauty." "And yet," he goes on, "how can you know whose speech is beautiful or the reverse (and the same applies to any action whatsoever) when you have no knowledge of beauty? And so long as you are what you are, don't you think that you might as well be dead?" It is my lot, you see, to be reviled and abused alike by you gentlemen, and by him. However, I suppose all this must be endured; I may get some good from it—stranger things have happened. And indeed, Hippias, I do think I have got some good out of my conversation with the two of you; I think now I appreciate the true meaning of the proverb, "All that is beautiful is difficult."

PLATO

Ion

(Translated by Benjamin Jowett)

From The Dialogues of Plato, *4th ed., Benjamin Jowett, trans. Oxford: The Clarendon Press, 1953. Reprinted by permission of The Clarendon Press.*

Persons of the Dialogue

§ SOCRATES/ION

Socrates. Welcome, Ion. Are you from 530 your native city of Ephesus?

Ion. No, Socrates; but from Epidaurus, where I attended the festival of Aesculapius.

Soc. Indeed! Do the Epidaurians have a contest of rhapsodes in his honour?

Ion. O yes; and of other kinds of music.

Soc. And were you one of the competitors —and did you succeed?

Ion. I—we—obtained the first prize of all, Socrates.

Soc. Well done; now we must win another victory, at the Panathenaea.

Ion. It shall be so, please heaven.

Soc. I have often envied the profession of a rhapsode, Ion; for it is a part of your art to wear fine clothes and to look as beautiful as you can, while at the same time you are obliged to be continually in the company of many good poets, and especially of Homer, who is the best and most divine of them, and to understand his mind, and not merely learn his words by rote; all this is a thing greatly to be envied. I am sure that no man can become a good rhapsode who does not understand the meaning of the poet. For the rhapsode ought to interpret the mind of the poet to his hearers, but how can he interpret him well unless he knows what he means? All this is much to be envied, I repeat.

Ion. Very true, Socrates; interpretation has certainly been the most laborious part of my art; and I believe myself able to speak about Homer better than any man; and that neither Metrodorus of Lampsacus, nor Stesimbrotus of Thasos, nor Glaucon, nor anyone else who ever was, had as good ideas about Homer as I have, or as many.

Soc. I am glad to hear you say so, Ion; I see that you will not refuse to acquaint me with them.

Ion. Certainly, Socrates; and you really ought to hear how exquisitely I display the beauties of Homer. I think that the Homeridae should give me a golden crown.[1]

Soc. I shall take an opportunity of hearing your embellishments of him at some other time. But just now I should like to ask you a question: Does your art extend to Hesiod and Archilochus, or to Homer only?

Ion. To Homer only; he is in himself quite enough.

Soc. Are there any things about which Homer and Hesiod agree?

Ion. Yes; in my opinion there are a good many.

Soc. And can you interpret what Homer says about these matters better than what Hesiod says?

Ion. I can interpret them equally well, Socrates, where they agree.

Soc. But what about matters in which they do not agree? for example, about divination, of which both Homer and Hesiod have something to say,—

Ion. Very true.

Soc. Would you or a good prophet be a better interpreter of what these two poets say about divination, not only when they agree, but when they disagree?

Ion. A prophet.

Soc. And if you were a prophet, and could interpret them where they agree, would you not know how to interpret them also where they disagree?

Ion. Clearly.

Soc. But how did you come to have this skill about Homer only, and not about Hesiod or the other poets? Does not Homer speak of the same themes which all other poets handle? Is not war his great argument? and does he not speak of human society and of intercourse of men, good and bad, skilled and unskilled, and of the gods conversing with one another and with mankind, and about what happens in heaven and in the world below, and the generations of gods and heroes? Are not these the themes of which Homer sings?

Ion. Very true, Socrates.

Soc. And do not the other poets sing of the same?

Ion. Yes, Socrates; but not in the same way as Homer.

Soc. What, in a worse way?

Ion. Yes, in a far worse.

Soc. And Homer in a better way?

Ion. He is incomparably better.

Soc. And yet surely, my dear friend Ion, where many people are discussing numbers, and one speaks better than the rest, there is somebody who can judge which of them is the good speaker?

Ion. Yes.

Soc. And he who judges of the good will be the same as he who judges of the bad speakers?

Ion. The same.

Soc. One who knows the science of arithmetic?

Ion. Yes.

Soc. Or again, if many persons are discussing the wholesomeness of food, and one speaks better than the rest, will he who recognizes the better speaker be a different person from him who recognizes the worse, or the same?

Ion. Clearly the same.

Soc. And who is he, and what is his name?

Ion. The physician.

531

---

1 [Or: "I think I have well deserved the golden crown given me by the Homeridae."—TR. NOTE.]

Soc. And speaking generally, in all discussions in which the subject is the same and many men are speaking, will not he who knows the good know the bad speaker also? For obviously if he does not know the bad, neither will he know the good, when the same topic is being discussed. 532

Ion. True.

Soc. We find, in fact, that the same person is skilful in both?

Ion. Yes.

Soc. And you say that Homer and the other poets, such as Hesiod and Archilochus, speak of the same things, although not in the same way; but the one speaks well and the other not so well?

Ion. Yes; and I am right in saying so.

Soc. And if you know the good speaker, you ought also to know the inferior speakers to be inferior?

Ion. It would seem so.

Soc. Then, my dear friend, can I be mistaken in saying that Ion is equally skilled in Homer and in other poets, since he himself acknowledges that the same person will be a good judge of all those who speak of the same things; and that almost all poets do speak of the same things?

Ion. Why then, Socrates, do I lose attention and have absolutely no ideas of the least value and practically fall asleep when anyone speaks of any other poet; but when Homer is mentioned, I wake up at once and am all attention and have plenty to say?

Soc. The reason, my friend, is not hard to guess. No one can fail to see that you speak of Homer without any art or knowledge. If you were able to speak of him by rules of art, you would have been able to speak of all other poets; for poetry is a whole.

Ion. Yes.

Soc. And when anyone acquires any other art as a whole, the same may be said of them. Would you like me to explain my meaning, Ion?

Ion. Yes, indeed, Socrates; I very much

wish that you would: for I love to hear you wise men talk.

Soc. O that we were wise, Ion, and that you could truly call us so; but you rhapsodes and actors, and the poets whose verses you sing, are wise; whereas I am a common man, who only speak the truth. For consider what a very commonplace and trivial thing is this which I have said—a thing which any man might say: that when a man has acquired a knowledge of a whole art, the inquiry into good and bad is one and the same. Let us consider this matter; is not the art of painting a whole?

Ion. Yes.

Soc. And there are and have been many painters good and bad?

Ion. Yes.

Soc. And did you ever know anyone who was skilful in pointing out the excellences and defects of Polygnotus the son of Aglaophon, but incapable of criticizing other 533 painters; and when the work of any other painter was produced, went to sleep and was at a loss, and had no ideas; but when he had to give his opinion about Polygnotus, or whoever the painter might be, and about him only, woke up and was attentive and had plenty to say?

Ion. No indeed, I have never known such a person.

Soc. Or take sculpture—did you ever know of anyone who was skilful in expounding the merits of Daedalus the son of Metion, or of Epeius the son of Panopeus, or of Theodorus the Samian, or of any individual sculptor; but when the works of sculptors in general were produced, was at a loss and went to sleep and had nothing to say?

Ion. No indeed; no more than the other.

Soc. And if I am not mistaken, you never met with anyone among flute-players or harp-players or singers to the harp or rhapsodes who was able to discourse of Olympus or Thamyras or Orpheus, or Phemius the rhapsode of Ithaca, but was at a loss when he came to speak of Ion of Ephesus, and had no notion of his merits or defects?

Ion. I cannot deny what you say, Socrates. Nevertheless I am conscious in my own self, and the world agrees with me, that I do speak better and have more to say about Homer than any other man; but I do not speak equally well about others. After all, there must be some reason for this; what is it?

Soc. I see the reason, Ion; and I will proceed to explain to you what I imagine it to be. The gift which you possess of speaking excellently about Homer is not an art, but, as I was just saying, an inspiration; there is a divinity moving you, like that contained in the stone which Euripides calls a magnet, but which is commonly known as the stone of Heraclea. This stone not only attracts iron rings, but also imparts to them a similar power of attracting other rings; and sometimes you may see a number of pieces of iron and rings suspended from one another so as to form quite a long chain: and all of them derive their power of suspension from the original stone. In like manner the Muse first of all inspires men herself; and from these inspired persons a chain of other persons is suspended, who take the inspiration. For all good poets, epic as well as lyric, compose their beautiful poems not by art, but because they are inspired and possessed. And as the Cory- 534 bantian revellers when they dance are not in their right mind, so the lyric poets are not in their right mind when they are composing their beautiful strains: but when falling under the power of music and metre they are inspired and possessed; like Bacchic maidens who draw milk and honey from the rivers when they are under the influence of Dionysus but not when they are in their right mind. And the soul of the lyric poet does the same, as they themselves say; for they tell us that they bring songs from honeyed fountains, culling them out of the gardens and dells of the Muses; they, like the bees, winging their way from flower to flower. And this is true. For the poet is a light and winged and holy thing, and

there is no invention in him until he has been inspired and is out of his senses, and reason is no longer in him: no man, while he retains that faculty, has the oracular gift of poetry.

Many are the noble words in which poets speak concerning the actions of men; but like yourself when speaking about Homer, they do not speak of them by any rules of art: they are simply inspired to utter that to which the Muse impels them, and that only; and when inspired, one of them will make dithyrambs, another hymns of praise, another choral strains, another epic or iambic verses, but not one of them is of any account in the other kinds. For not by art does the poet sing, but by power divine; had he learned by rules of art, he would have known how to speak not of one theme only, but of all; and therefore God takes away reason from poets, and uses them as his ministers, as he also uses the pronouncers of oracles and holy prophets, in order that we who hear them may know them to be speaking not of themselves, who utter these priceless words while bereft of reason, but that God himself is the speaker, and that through them he is addressing us. And Tynnichus the Chalcidian affords a striking instance of what I am saying: he wrote no poem that anyone would care to remember but the famous paean which is in everyone's mouth, one of the finest lyric poems ever written, simply an invention of the Muses, as he himself says. For in this way God would seem to demonstrate to us and not to allow us to doubt that these beautiful poems are not human, nor the work of man, but divine and the work of God; and that the poets are only the interpreters of the gods by whom they are severally possessed. Was not this the lesson which God intended to teach 535 when by the mouth of the worst of poets he sang the best of songs? Am I not right, Ion?

Ion. Yes, indeed, Socrates, I feel that you are; for your words touch my soul, and I am persuaded that in these works the good poets, under divine inspiration, interpret to us the voice of the gods.

Soc. And you rhapsodists are the interpreters of the poets?

Ion. There again you are right.

Soc. Then you are the interpreters of interpreters?

Ion. Precisely.

Soc. I wish you would frankly tell me, Ion, what I am going to ask of you: When you produce the greatest effect upon the audience in the recitation of some striking passage, such as the apparition of Odysseus leaping forth on the floor, recognized by the suitors and shaking out his arrows at his feet, or the description of Achilles springing upon Hector, or the sorrows of Andromache, Hecuba, or Priam,—are you in your right mind? Are you not carried out of yourself, and does not your soul in an ecstasy seem to be among the persons or places of which you are speaking, whether they are in Ithaca or in Troy or whatever may be the scene of the poem?

Ion. That proof strikes home to me, Socrates. For I must frankly confess that at the tale of pity my eyes are filled with tears, and when I speak of horrors, my hair stands on end and my heart throbs.

Soc. Well, Ion, and what are we to say of a man who at a sacrifice or festival, when he is dressed in an embroidered robe, and has golden crowns upon his head, of which nobody has robbed him, appears weeping or panic-stricken in the presence of more than twenty thousand friendly faces, when there is no one despoiling or wronging him;—is he in his right mind or is he not?

Ion. No indeed, Socrates, I must say that, strictly speaking, he is not in his right mind.

Soc. And are you aware that you produce similar effects on most of the spectators?

Ion. Only too well; for I look down upon them from the stage, and behold the various emotions of pity, wonder, sternness, stamped upon their countenances when I am speaking: and I am obliged to give my very best attention to them; for if I make them cry I

myself shall laugh, and if I make them laugh I myself shall cry, when the time of payment arrives.

Soc. Do you know that the spectator is the last of the rings which, as I am saying, receive the power of the original magnet from one another? The rhapsode like yourself and the actor are intermediate links, 536 and the poet himself is the first of them. Through all these God sways the souls of men in any direction which He pleases, causing each link to communicate the power to the next. Thus there is a vast chain of dancers and masters and under-masters of choruses, who are suspended, as if from the stone, at the side of the rings which hang down from the Muse. And every poet has some Muse from whom he is suspended, and by whom he is said to be possessed, which is nearly the same thing; for he is taken hold of. And from these first rings, which are the poets, depend others, some deriving their inspiration from Orpheus, others from Musaeus; but the greater number are possessed and held by Homer. Of whom, Ion, you are one, and are possessed by Homer; and when anyone repeats the words of another poet you go to sleep, and know not what to say; but when anyone recites a strain of Homer you wake up in a moment, and your soul leaps within you, and you have plenty to say; for not by art or knowledge about Homer do you say what you say, but by divine inspiration and by possession; just as the Corybantian revellers too have a quick perception of that strain only which is appropriated to the god by whom they are possessed, and have plenty of dances and words for that, but take no heed of any other. And you, Ion, when the name of Homer is mentioned have plenty to say, and have nothing to say of others. You ask, "Why is this?" The answer is that your skill in the praise of Homer comes not from art but from divine inspiration.

Ion. That is good, Socrates; and yet I doubt whether you will ever have eloquence enough to persuade me that I praise Homer only when I am mad and possessed; and if you could hear me speak of him I am sure you would never think this to be the case.

Soc. I should like very much to hear you, but not until you have answered a question which I have to ask. On what part of Homer do you speak well?—not surely about every part?

Ion. There is no part, Socrates, about which I do not speak well; of that I can assure you.

Soc. Surely not about things in Homer of which you have no knowledge?

Ion. And what is there in Homer of which I have no knowledge?

Soc. Why, does not Homer speak in 537 many passages about arts? For example, about driving; if I can only remember the lines I will repeat them.

Ion. I remember, and will repeat them.

Soc. Tell me then, what Nestor says to Antilochus, his son, where he bids him be careful of the turn at the horse-race in honour of Patroclus.

Ion. "Bend gently," he says, "in the polished chariot to the left of them, and urge the horse on the right hand with whip and voice; and slacken the rein. And when you are at the goal, let the left horse draw near, so that the nave of the well-wrought wheel may appear to graze the extremity; but have care not to touch the stone."[2]

Soc. Enough. Now, Ion, will the charioteer or the physician be the better judge of the propriety of these lines?

Ion. The charioteer, clearly.

Soc. And will the reason be that this is his art, or will there be any other reason?

Ion. No, that will be the reason.

Soc. And every art is appointed by God to have knowledge of a certain work; 'for that which we know by the art of the pilot we shall not succeed in knowing also by the art of medicine?

Ion. Certainly not.

---

[2] [*Iliad,* XXIII, 335.—TR. NOTE.]

Soc. Nor shall we know by the art of the carpenter that which we know by the art of medicine?

Ion. Certainly not.

Soc. And this is true of all the arts;—that which we know with one art we shall not know with the other? But let me ask a prior question: You admit that there are differences of arts?

Ion. Yes.

Soc. You would argue, as I should, that if there are two kinds of knowledge, dealing with different things, these can be called different arts?

Ion. Yes.

Soc. Yes, surely; for if the object of knowledge were the same, there would be no meaning in saying that the arts were different,—since they both gave the same knowledge. For example, I know that here are five fingers, and you know the same. And if I were to ask whether I and you became acquainted with this fact by the help of the same art of arithmetic, you would acknowledge that we did?

Ion. Yes.

Soc. Tell me, then, what I was intending 538 to ask you,—whether in your opinion this holds universally? If two arts are the same, must not they necessarily have the same objects? And if one differs from another, must it not be because the object is different?

Ion. That is my opinion, Socrates.

Soc. Then he who has no knowledge of a particular art will have no right judgement of the precepts and practice of that art?

Ion. Very true.

Soc. Then which will be the better judge of the lines which you were reciting from Homer, you or the charioteer?

Ion. The charioteer.

Soc. Why, yes, because you are a rhapsode and not a charioteer.

Ion. Yes.

Soc. And the art of the rhapsode is different from that of the charioteer?

Ion. Yes.

Soc. And if a different knowledge, then a knowledge of different matters?

Ion. True.

Soc. You know the passage in which Hecamede, the concubine of Nestor, is described as giving to the wounded Machaon a posset, as he says, "Made with Pramnian wine; and she grated cheese of goat's milk with a grater of bronze, and at his side placed an onion which gives a relish to drink."[3] Now would you say that the art of the rhapsode or the art of medicine was better able to judge of the propriety of these lines?

Ion. The art of medicine.

Soc. And when Homer says, "and she descended into the deep like a leaden plummet, which, set in the horn of ox that ranges the fields, rushes along carrying death among the ravenous fishes,"[4] will the art of the fisherman or of the rhapsode be better able to judge what these lines mean, and whether they are accurate or not?

Ion. Clearly, Socrates, the art of the fisherman.

Soc. Come now, suppose that you were to say to me: "Since you, Socrates, are able to assign different passages in Homer to their corresponding arts, I wish that you would tell me what are the passages of which the excellence ought to be judged by the prophet and prophetic art"; and you will see how readily and truly I shall answer you. For there are many such passages, particularly in the *Odyssey;* as, for example, the passage in which Theoclymenus the prophet of the house of Melampus says to the suitors:

> Wretched men! what is happening to 539 you? Your heads and your faces and your limbs underneath are shrouded in night; and the voice of lamentation bursts forth, and your cheeks are wet with tears. And the vestibule is full, and the court is full, of ghosts descending into the darkness of Erebus, and the sun has perished out of

heaven, and an evil mist is spread abroad.[5]

And there are many such passages in the *Iliad* also; as for example in the description of the battle near the rampart, where he says:

> As they were eager to pass the ditch, there came to them an omen: a soaring eagle, skirting the people on his left, bore a huge blood-red dragon in his talons, still living and panting; nor had he yet resigned the strife, for he bent back and smote the bird which carried him on the breast by the neck, and he in pain let him fall from him to the ground into the midst of the multitude. And the eagle, with a cry, was born afar on the wings of the wind.[6]

These are the sort of things which I should say that the prophet ought to consider and determine.

Ion. And you are quite right, Socrates, in saying so.

Soc. Yes, Ion, and you are right also. And as I have selected from the *Iliad* and *Odyssey* for you passages which describe the office of the prophet and the physician and the fisherman, do you, who know Homer so much better than I do, Ion, select for me passages which relate to the rhapsode and the rhapsode's art, and which the rhapsode ought to examine and judge of better than other men.

Ion. All passages, I should say, Socrates.

Soc. Not all, Ion, surely. Have you already forgotten what you were saying? A rhapsode ought to have a better memory.

Ion. Why, what am I forgetting? 540

Soc. Do you not remember that you declared the art of the rhapsode to be different from the art of the charioteer?

Ion. Yes, I remember.

Soc. And you admitted that being different they would know different objects?

Ion. Yes.

Soc. Then upon your own showing the rhapsode, and the art of the rhapsode, will not know everything?

---

3 [*Iliad*, XI, 639–640.—TR. NOTE.]
4 [*Iliad*, XXIV, 80.—TR. NOTE.]

5 [*Odyssey*, XX, 351.—TR. NOTE.]
6 [*Iliad*, XII, 200.—TR. NOTE.]

Ion. I should exclude such things as you mention, Socrates.

Soc. You mean to say that you would exclude pretty much the subjects of the other arts. As he does not know all of them, which of them will he know?

Ion. He will know what a man and what a woman ought to say, and what a freeman and what a slave ought to say, and what a ruler and what a subject.

Soc. Do you mean that a rhapsode will know better than the pilot what the ruler of a sea-tossed vessel ought to say?

Ion. No; the pilot will know best.

Soc. Or will the rhapsode know better than the physician what the ruler of a sick man ought to say?

Ion. Again, no.

Soc. But he will know what a slave ought to say?

Ion. Yes.

Soc. Suppose the slave to be a cowherd; the rhapsode will know better than the cowherd what he ought to say in order to soothe infuriated cows?

Ion. No, he will not.

Soc. But he will know what a spinning-woman ought to say about the working of wool?

Ion. No.

Soc. At any rate he will know what a general ought to say when exhorting his soldiers?

Ion. Yes, that is the sort of thing which the rhapsode will be sure to know.

Soc. What! Is the art of the rhapsode the art of the general?

Ion. I am sure that I should know what a general ought to say.

Soc. Why, yes, Ion, because you may possibly have the knowledge of a general as well as that of a rhapsode; and you might also have a knowledge of horsemanship as well as of the lyre, and then you would know when horses were well or ill managed. But suppose I were to ask you: By the help of which art, Ion, do you know whether horses are well managed, by your skill as a horseman or as a performer on the lyre— what would you answer?

Ion. I should reply, by my skill as a horseman.

Soc. And if you judged of performers on the lyre, you would admit that you judged of them as a performer on the lyre, and not as a horseman?

Ion. Yes.

Soc. And in judging of the general's art, do you judge as a general, or as a good rhapsode?

Ion. To me there appears to be no difference between them.

Soc. What do you mean? Do you mean 541 to say that the art of the rhapsode and of the general is the same?

Ion. Yes, one and the same.

Soc. Then he who is a good rhapsode is also a good general?

Ion. Certainly, Socrates.

Soc. And he who is a good general is also a good rhapsode?

Ion. No; I do not agree to that.

Soc. But you do agree that he who is a good rhapsode is also a good general.

Ion. Certainly.

Soc. And you are the best of Hellenic rhapsodes?

Ion. Far the best, Socrates.

Soc. And are you also the best general, Ion?

Ion. To be sure, Socrates; and Homer was my master.

Soc. But then, Ion, why in the name of goodness do you, who are the best of generals as well as the best of rhapsodes in all Hellas, go about reciting rhapsodies when you might be a general? Do you think that the Hellenes are in grave need of a rhapsode with his golden crown, and have no need at all of a general?

Ion. Why, Socrates, the reason is that my countrymen, the Ephesians, are the servants and soldiers of Athens, and do not need a general; and that you and Sparta are not likely to appoint me, for you think that you have enough generals of your own.

Soc. My good Ion, did you never hear of Apollodorus of Cyzicus?

Ion. Who may he be?

Soc. One who, though a foreigner, has often been chosen their general by the Athenians: and there is Phanosthenes of Andros, and Heraclides of Clazomenae, whom they have also appointed to the command of their armies and to other offices, although aliens, after they had shown their merit. And will they not choose Ion the Ephesian to be their general, and honour him, if they deem him qualified? Were not the Ephesians originally Athenians, and Ephesus is no mean city? But, indeed, Ion, if you are correct in saying that by art and knowledge you are able to praise Homer, you do not deal fairly with me, and after all your professions of knowing many glorious things about Homer, and promises that you would exhibit them, you only deceive me, and so far from exhibiting the art of which you are a master, will not, even after my repeated entreaties, explain to me the nature of it. You literally assume as many forms as Proteus, twisting and turning up and down, until at last you slip away from me in the disguise of a general, in order that you may escape exhibiting 542 your Homeric lore. And if you have art, then, as I was saying, in falsifying your promise that you would exhibit Homer, you are not dealing fairly with me. But if, as I believe, you have no art, but speak all these beautiful words about Homer unconsciously under his inspiring influence, then I acquit you of dishonesty, and shall only say that you are inspired. Which do you prefer to be thought, dishonest or inspired?

Ion. There is a great difference, Socrates, between the two alternatives; and inspiration is by far the nobler.

Soc. Then, Ion, I shall assume the nobler alternative; and attribute to you in your praises of Homer inspiration, and not art.

PLATO

Republic X

(Translated by Benjamin Jowett)

From The Dialogues of Plato, *4th ed., Benjamin Jowett, trans. Oxford: The Clarendon Press, 1953. Reprinted by permission of The Clarendon Press.*

[*The* Republic *is a narration by Socrates of earlier conversations between himself and others. In Book X, his companion is Glaucon, a brother of Plato.*]

Of the many excellences which I perceive 595 in the order of our State, there is none which upon reflection pleases me better than the rule about poetry.

To what do you refer?

To our refusal to admit the imitative kind of poetry, for it certainly ought not to be received. . . .

What do you mean?

Speaking in confidence, for you will not denounce me to the tragedians and the rest of the imitative tribe, all poetical imitations are ruinous to the understanding of the hearers, unless as an antidote they possess the knowledge of the true nature of the originals.

Explain the purport of your remark.

Well, I will tell you, although I have always from my earliest youth had an awe and love of Homer which even now makes the words falter on my lips, for he seems to be the great captain and teacher of the whole of that noble tragic company; but a man is not to be reverenced more than the truth, and therefore I will speak out.

Very good, he said.

Listen to me then, or rather, answer me.

Put your question.

Can you give me a general definition of

imitation? for I really do not myself understand what it professes to be.

A likely thing, then, that I should know.

There would be nothing strange in that, for the duller eye may often see a thing sooner than the keener.

Very true, he said; but in your presence, even if I had any faint notion, I could not muster courage to utter it. Will you inquire yourself?

Well then, shall we begin the inquiry at this point, following our usual method: Whenever a number of individuals have a common name, we assume that there is one corresponding idea or form:[1]—do you understand me?

I do.

Let us take, for our present purpose, any instance of such a group; there are beds and tables in the world—many of each, are there not?

Yes.

But there are only two ideas or forms of such furniture—one the idea of a bed, the other of a table.

True.

And the maker of either of them makes a bed or he makes a table for our use, in accordance with the idea—that is our way of speaking in this and similar instances—but no artificer makes the idea itself: how could he?

Impossible.

And there is another artificer,—I should like to know what you would say of him.

Who is he?

One who is the maker of all the works of all other workmen.

What an extraordinary man!

Wait a little, and there will be more reason for your saying so. For this is the craftsman who is able to make not only

596

furniture of every kind, but all that grows out of the earth, and all living creatures, himself included; and besides these he can make earth and sky and the gods, and all the things which are in heaven or in the realm of Hades under the earth.

He must be a wizard and no mistake.

Oh! you are incredulous, are you? Do you mean that there is no such maker or creator, or that in one sense there might be a maker of all these things but in another not? Do you see that there is a way in which you could make them all yourself?

And what way is this? he asked.

An easy way enough; or rather, there are many ways in which the feat might be quickly and easily accomplished, none quicker than that of turning a mirror round and round—you would soon enough make the sun and the heavens, and the earth and yourself, and other animals and plants, and furniture and all the other things of which we were just now speaking, in the mirror.

Yes, he said; but they would be appearances only.

Very good, I said, you are coming to the point now. And the painter too is, as I conceive, just such another—a creator of appearances, is he not?

Of course.

But then I suppose you will say that what he creates is untrue. And yet there is a sense in which the painter also creates a bed? Is there not?

Yes, he said, but here again, an appearance only.

And what of the maker of the bed? were you not saying that he too makes, not the idea which according to our view is the real object denoted by the word bed, but only a particular bed?

Yes, I did.

Then if he does not make a real object he cannot make what *is*, but only some semblance of existence; and if any one were to say that the work of the maker of the bed, or of any other workman, has real

597

1 [Or (probably better): "We have been accustomed to assume that there is one single idea corresponding to each group of particulars; and to these we give the same name (as we give the idea)." See J. A. Smith, *Classical Review*, XXXI (1917), 69–71.—TR. NOTE.]

existence, he could hardly be supposed to be speaking the truth.

Not, at least, he replied, in the view of those who make a business of these discussions.

No wonder, then, that his work too is an indistinct expression of truth.

No wonder.

Suppose now that by the light of the examples just offered we inquire who this imitator is?

If you please.

Well then, here we find three beds: one existing in nature, which is made by God, as I think that we may say—for no one else can be the maker?

No one, I think.

There is another which is the work of the carpenter?

Yes.

And the work of the painter is a third?

Yes.

Beds, then, are of three kinds, and there are three artists who superintend them: God, the maker of the bed, and the painter?

Yes, there are three of them.

God, whether from choice or from necessity, made one bed in nature and one only; two or more such beds neither ever have been nor ever will be made by God.

Why is that?

Because even if He had made but two, a third would still appear behind them of which they again both possessed the form, and that would be the real bed and not the two others.

Very true, he said.

God knew this, I suppose, and He desired to be the real maker of a real bed, not a kind of maker of a kind of bed, and therefore He created a bed which is essentially and by nature one only.

So it seems.

Shall we, then, speak of Him as the natural author or maker of the bed?

Yes, he replied; inasmuch as by the natural process of creation He is the author of this and of all other things.

And what shall we say of the carpenter—is not he also the maker of a bed?

Yes.

But would you call the painter an artificer and maker?

Certainly not.

Yet if he is not the maker, what is he in relation to the bed?

I think, he said, that we may fairly designate him as the imitator of that which the others make.

Good, I said; then you call him whose product is third in the descent from nature, an imitator?

Certainly, he said.

And so if the tragic poet is an imitator, he too is thrice removed from the king and from the truth; and so are all other imitators.

That appears to be so.

Then about the imitator we are agreed. And what about the painter?—Do you think he tries to imitate in each case that which originally exists in nature, or only the creations of artificers? 598

The latter.

As they are or as they appear? you have still to determine this.

What do you mean?

I mean to ask whether a bed really becomes different when it is seen from different points of view, obliquely or directly or from any other point of view? Or does it simply appear different, without being really so? And the same of all things.

Yes, he said, the difference is only apparent.

Now let me ask you another question: Which is the art of painting designed to be —an imitation of things as they are, or as they appear—of appearance or of reality?

Of appearance, he said.

Then the imitator is a long way off the truth, and can reproduce all things because he lightly touches on a small part of them, and that part an image. For example: A painter will paint a cobbler, carpenter, or any other artisan, though he knows nothing of their arts; and, if he is a good painter, he may deceive children or simple persons when he shows them his picture of a carpenter from a distance, and they will fancy that, they are looking at a real carpenter.

Certainly.

And surely, my friend, this is how we should regard all such claims: whenever any one informs us that he has found a man who knows all the arts, and all things else that anybody knows, and every single thing with a higher degree of accuracy than any other man—whoever tells us this, I think that we can only retort that he is a simple creature who seems to have been deceived by some wizard or imitator whom he met, and whom he thought all-knowing, because he himself was unable to analyse the nature of knowledge and ignorance and imitation.

Most true.

And next, I said, we have to consider tragedy and its leader, Homer; for we hear some persons saying that these poets know all the arts; and all things human; where virtue and vice are concerned, and indeed all divine things too; because the good poet cannot compose well unless he knows his subject, and he who has not this knowledge can never be a poet. We ought to consider whether here also there may not be a similar illusion. Perhaps they may have come across imitators and been deceived by them; they may not have remembered when they saw their works that these were thrice removed 599 from the truth, and could easily be made without any knowledge of the truth, because they are appearances only and not realities? Or, after all, they may be in the right, and good poets do really know the things about which they seem to the many to speak so well?

The question, he said, should by all means be considered.

Now do you suppose that if a person were able to make the original as well as the image, he would seriously devote himself to the image-making branch? Would he allow imitation to be the ruling principle of his life, as if he had nothing higher in him?

I should say not.

But the real artist, who had real knowledge of those things which he chose also to imitate, would be interested in realities and not in imitations; and would desire to leave as memorials of himself works many and fair; and, instead of being the author of encomiums, he would prefer to be the theme of them.

Yes, he said, that would be to him a source of much greater honour and profit.

Now let us refrain, I said, from calling Homer or any other poet to account regarding those arts to which his poems incidentally refer: we will not ask them, in case any poet has been a doctor and not a mere imitator of medical parlance, to show what patients have been restored to health by a poet, ancient or modern, as they were by Asclepius; or what disciples in medicine a poet has left behind him, like the Asclepiads. Nor shall we press the same question upon them about the other arts. But we have a right to know respecting warfare, strategy, the administration of States and the education of man, which are the chiefest and noblest subjects of his poems, and we may fairly ask him about them. "Friend Homer," then we say to him, "if you are only in the second remove from truth in what you say of virtue, and not in the third—not an image maker, that is, by our definition, an imitator—and if you are able to discern what pursuits make men better or worse in private or public life, tell us what State was ever better governed by your help? The good order of Lacedaemon is due to Lycurgus, and many other cities great and small have been similarly benefited by others; but who says that you have been a good legislator to them and have done them any good? Italy and Sicily boast of Charondas, and there is Solon who is renowned among us; but what city has anything to say about you?" Is there any city which he might name?

I think not, said Glaucon; not even the Homerids themselves pretend that he was a legislator.

Well, but is there any war on record 600 which was carried on successfully owing to his leadership or counsel?

There is not.

Or is there anything comparable to those clever improvements in the arts, or in other operations, which are said to have been due to men of practical genius such as Thales the Milesian or Anacharsis the Scythian?

There is absolutely nothing of the kind.

But, if Homer never did any public service, was he privately a guide or teacher of any? Had he in his lifetime friends who loved to associate with him, and who handed down to posterity an Homeric way of life, such as was established by Pythagoras, who was especially beloved for this reason and whose followers are to this day conspicuous among others by what they term the Pythagorean way of life?

Nothing of the kind is recorded of him. For surely, Socrates, Creophylus, the companion of Homer, that child of flesh, whose name always makes us laugh, might be more justly ridiculed for his want of breeding, if what is said is true, that Homer was greatly neglected by him in his own day when he was alive?

Yes, I replied, that is the tradition. But can you imagine, Glaucon, that if Homer had really been able to educate and improve mankind—if he had been capable of knowledge and not been a mere imitator—can you imagine, I say, that he would not have attracted many followers, and been honoured and loved by them? Protagoras of Abdera, and Prodicus of Ceos, and a host of others, have only to whisper to their contemporaries: "You will never be able to manage either your own house or your own State until you appoint us to be your ministers of education"—and this ingenious device of theirs has such an effect in making men love them that their companions all but carry them about on their shoulders. And is it conceivable that the contemporaries of Homer, or again of Hesiod, would have allowed either of them to go about as rhapsodists, if they had really been able to help mankind forward in virtue? Would they not have been as unwilling to part with them as with gold, and have compelled them to stay at home with them? Or, if the master would not stay, then the disciples would have followed him about everywhere, until they had got education enough?

Yes, Socrates, that, I think, is quite true.

Then must we not infer that all these poetical individuals, beginning with Homer, are only imitators, who copy images of virtue and the other themes of their poetry, but have no contact with the truth? The poet is like a painter who, as we have already observed, will make a likeness of a 601 cobbler though he understands nothing of cobbling; and his picture is good enough for those who know no more than he does, and judge only by colours and figures.

Quite so.

In like manner the poet with his words and phrases[2] may be said to lay on the colours of the several arts, himself understanding their nature only enough to imitate them; and other people, who are as ignorant as he is, and judge only from his words, imagine that if he speaks of cobbling, or of military tactics, or of anything else, in metre and harmony and rhythm, he speaks very well—such is the sweet influence which melody and rhythm by nature have. For I am sure that you know what a poor appearance the works of poets make when stripped of the colours which art puts upon them, and recited in simple prose. You have seen some examples?

Yes, he said.

They are like faces which were never really beautiful, but only blooming, seen when the bloom of youth has passed away from them?

Exactly.

Come now, and observe this point: The imitator or maker of the image knows noth-

---

[2] [Or: "with his nouns and verbs."—TR. NOTE.]

ing, we have said, of true existence; he knows appearances only. Am I not right?

Yes.

Then let us have a clear understanding, and not be satisfied with half an explanation.

Proceed.

Of the painter we say that he will paint reins, and he will paint a bit?

Yes.

And the worker in leather and brass will make them?

Certainly.

But does the painter know the right form of the bit and reins? Nay, hardly even the workers in brass and leather who make them; only the horseman who knows how to use them—he knows their right form.

Most true.

And may we not say the same of all things?

What?

That there are three arts which are concerned with all things: one which uses, another which makes, a third which imitates them?

Yes.

And the excellence and beauty and rightness of every structure, animate or inanimate, and of every action of man, is relative solely to the use for which nature or the artist has intended them.

True.

Then beyond doubt it is the user who has the greatest experience of them, and he must report to the maker the good or bad qualities which develop themselves in use; for example, the flute-player will tell the flute-maker which of his flutes is satisfactory to the performer;[3] he will tell him how he ought to make them, and the other will attend to his instructions?

Of course.

So the one pronounces with knowledge

about the goodness and badness of flutes, while the other, confiding in him, will make them accordingly?

True.

The instrument is the same, but about the excellence or badness of it the maker will possess a correct belief, since he associates with one who knows, and is compelled to hear what he has to say; whereas the user will have knowledge?

602

True.

But will the imitator have either? Will he know from use whether or no that which he paints is correct or beautiful? or will he have right opinion from being compelled to associate with another who knows and gives him instructions about what he should paint?

Neither.

Then an imitator will no more have true opinion than he will have knowledge about the goodness or badness of his models?

I suppose not.

The imitative poet will be in a brilliant state of intelligence about the theme of his poetry?

Nay, very much the reverse.

And still he will go on imitating without knowing what makes a thing good or bad, and may be expected therefore to imitate only that which appears to be good to the ignorant multitude?

Just so.

Thus far then we are pretty well agreed that the imitator has no knowledge worth mentioning of what he imitates. Imitation is only a kind of play or sport, and the tragic poets, whether they write in iambic or in heroic verse, are imitators in the highest degree?

Very true.

And now tell me, I conjure you,—this imitation is concerned with an object which is thrice removed from the truth?

Certainly.

And what kind of faculty in man is that to which imitation makes its special appeal?

What do you mean?

---

3 [Or, to avoid the repetition of ὑπηρετεῖν in a different sense: "will make a report to the flute-maker, *who assists him in his playing*, about the flutes."—TR. NOTE.]

I will explain: The same body does not appear equal to our sight when seen near and when seen at a distance?

True.

And the same objects appear straight when looked at out of the water, and crooked when in the water; and the concave becomes convex, owing to the illusion about colours to which the sight is liable. Thus every sort of confusion is revealed within us; and this is that weakness of the human mind on which the art of painting in light and shadow, the art of conjuring, and many other ingenious devices impose, having an effect upon us like magic.

True.

And the arts of measuring and numbering and weighing come to the rescue of the human understanding—there is the beauty of them—with the result that the apparent greater or less, or more or heavier, no longer have the mastery over us, but give way before the power of calculation and measuring and weighing?

Most true.

And this, surely, must be the work of the calculating and rational principle in the soul?

To be sure.

And often when this principle measures and certifies that some things are equal, or that some are greater or less than others, it is, at the same time, contradicted by the appearance which the objects present?

True.

But did we not say that such a contradiction is impossible—the same faculty cannot have contrary opinions at the same time about the same thing?

We did; and rightly.

Then that part of the soul which has an opinion contrary to measure can hardly be the same with that which has an opinion in accordance with measure? 603

True.

And the part of the soul which trusts to measure and calculation is likely to be the better one?

Certainly.

And therefore that which is opposed to this is probably an inferior principle in our nature?

No doubt.

This was the conclusion at which I was seeking to arrive when I said that painting or drawing, and imitation in general, are engaged upon productions which are far removed from truth, and are also the companions and friends and associates of a principle within us which is equally removed from reason, and that they have no true or healthy aim.

Exactly.

The imitative art is an inferior who from intercourse with an inferior has inferior offspring.

Very true.

And is this confined to the sight only, or does it extend to the hearing also, relating in fact to what we term poetry?

Probably the same would be true of poetry.

Do not rely, I said, on a probability derived from the analogy of painting; but let us once more go directly to that faculty of the mind with which imitative poetry has converse, and see whether it is good or bad.

By all means.

We may state the question thus:—Imitation imitates the actions of men, whether voluntary or involuntary, on which, as they imagine, a good or bad result has ensued, and they rejoice or sorrow accordingly. Is there anything more?

No, there is nothing else.

But in all this variety of circumstances is the man at unity with himself—or rather, as in the instance of sight there was confusion and opposition in his opinions about the same things, so here also is there not strife and inconsistency in his life? Though I need hardly raise the question again, for I remember that all this has been already admitted; and the soul has been acknowledged by us to be full of these and ten thousand similar oppositions occurring at the same moment?

And we were right, he said.

Yes, I said, thus far we were right; but there was an omission which must now be supplied.

What was the omission?

Were we not saying that a good man, who has the misfortune to lose his son or anything else which is most dear to him, will bear the loss with more equanimity than another?

Yes, indeed.

But will he have no sorrow, or shall we say that although he cannot help sorrowing, he will moderate his sorrow?

The latter, he said, is the truer statement.

Tell me: will he be more likely to struggle 604 and hold out against his sorrow when he is seen by his equals, or when he is alone in a deserted place?

The fact of being seen will make a great difference, he said.

When he is by himself he will not mind saying many things which he would be ashamed of any one hearing, and also doing many things which he would not care to be seen doing?

True.

And doubtless it is the law and reason in him which bids him resist; while it is the affliction itself which is urging him to indulge his sorrow?

True.

But when a man is drawn in two opposite directions, to and from the same object, this, as we affirm, necessarily implies two distinct principles in him?

Certainly.

One of them is ready to follow the guidance of the law?

How do you mean?

The law would say that to be patient under calamity is best, and that we should not give way to impatience, as the good and evil in such things are not clear, and nothing is gained by impatience; also, because no human thing is of serious importance, and

grief stands in the way of that which at the moment is most required.

What is most required? he asked.

That we should take counsel about what has happened, and when the dice have been thrown, according to their fall, order our affairs in the way which reason deems best; not, like children who have had a fall, keeping hold of the part struck and wasting time in setting up a howl, but always accustoming the soul forthwith to apply a remedy, raising up that which is sickly and fallen, banishing the cry of sorrow by the healing art.

Yes, he said, that is the true way of meeting the attacks of fortune.

Well then, I said, the higher principle is ready to follow this suggestion of reason?

Clearly.

But the other principle, which inclines us to recollection of our troubles and to lamentation, and can never have enough of them, we may call irrational, useless, and cowardly?

Indeed, we may.

Now does not the principle which is thus inclined to complaint, furnish a great variety of materials for imitation? Whereas the wise and calm temperament, being always nearly equable, is not easy to imitate or to appreciate when imitated, especially at a public festival when a promiscuous crowd is assembled in a theatre. For the feeling represented is one to which they are strangers.

Certainly.

Then the imitative poet who aims at being 605 popular is not by nature made, nor is his art intended, to please or to affect the rational principle in the soul; but he will appeal rather to the lachrymose and fitful temper, which is easily imitated?

Clearly.

And now we may fairly take him and place him by the side of the painter, for he is like him in two ways: first, inasmuch as his creations have an inferior degree of truth—in this, I say, he is like him; and he is also like him in being the associate of an inferior part of the soul; and this is enough to show that we shall be right in refusing to admit him into a State which is to be well ordered, because he awakens and nourishes this part of the soul, and by strengthening it impairs the reason. As in a city when the evil are permitted to wield power and the finer men are put out of the way, so in the soul of each man, as we shall maintain, the imitative poet implants an evil constitution, for he indulges the irrational nature which has no discernment of greater and less, but thinks the same thing at one time great and at another small—he is an imitator of images and is very far removed from the truth.

Exactly.

But we have not yet brought forward the heaviest count in our accusation:—the power which poetry has of harming even the good (and there are very few who are not harmed), is surely an awful thing?

Yes, certainly, if the effect is what you say.

Hear and judge: The best of us, as I conceive, when we listen to a passage of Homer or one of the tragedians, in which he represents some hero who is drawling out his sorrows in a long oration, or singing, and smiting his breast—the best of us, you know, delight in giving way to sympathy, and are in raptures at the excellence of the poet who stirs our feelings most.

Yes, of course I know.

But when any sorrow of our own happens to us, then you may observe that we pride ourselves on the opposite quality—we would fain be quiet and patient; this is considered the manly part, and the other which delighted us in the recitation is now deemed to be the part of a woman.

Very true, he said.

Now can we be right in praising and admiring another who is doing that which any one of us would abominate and be ashamed of in his own person?

No, he said, that is certainly not reasonable.

Nay, I said, quite reasonable from one point of view.   606

What point of view?

If you consider, I said, that when in misfortune we feel a natural hunger and desire to relieve our sorrow by weeping and lamentation, and that this very feeling which is starved and suppressed in our own calamities is satisfied and delighted by the poets;—the better nature in each of us, not having been sufficiently trained by reason or habit, allows the sympathetic element to break loose because the sorrow is another's; and the spectator fancies that there can be no disgrace to himself in praising and pitying any one who while professing to be a brave man, gives way to untimely lamentation; he thinks that the pleasure is a gain, and is far from wishing to lose it by rejection of the whole poem. Few persons ever reflect, as I should imagine, that the contagion must pass from others to themselves. For the pity which has been nourished and strengthened in the misfortunes of others is with difficulty repressed in our own.

How very true!

And does not the same hold also of the ridiculous? There are jests which you would be ashamed to make yourself, and yet on the comic stage, or indeed in private, when you hear them, you are greatly amused by them, and are not at all disgusted at their unseemliness;—the case of pity is repeated;—there is a principle in human nature which is disposed to raise a laugh, and this, which you once restrained by reason because you were afraid of being thought a buffoon, is now let out again; and having stimulated the risible faculty at the theatre, you are betrayed unconsciously to yourself into playing the comic poet at home.

Quite true, he said.

And the same may be said of lust and anger and all the other affections, of desire and pain and pleasure, which are held to be inseparable from every action—in all of them poetry has a like effect; it feeds and waters the passions instead of drying them up; it lets them rule, although they ought to be controlled if mankind are ever to increase in happiness and virtue.

I cannot deny it.

Therefore, Glaucon, I said, whenever you meet with any of the eulogists of Homer declaring that he has been the educator of Hellas, and that he is profitable for education and for the ordering of human things, and that you should take him up again and again and get to know him and regulate your whole life according to him, we may love and honour those who say these things —they are excellent people, as far as their lights extend; and we are ready to acknowledge that Homer is the greatest of poets and first of tragedy writers; but we must remain firm in our conviction that hymns to the gods and praises of famous men are the only poetry which ought to be admitted into our State. For if you go beyond this and allow the honeyed Muse to enter, either in epic or lyric verse, not law and the reason of mankind, which by common consent have ever been deemed best,[4] but pleasure and pain will be the rulers in our State.

That is most true, he said.

And now since we have reverted to the subject of poetry, let this our defence serve to show the reasonableness of our former judgement in sending away out of our State an art having the tendencies which we have described; for reason constrained us. But that she may not impute to us any harshness or want of politeness, let us tell her that there is an ancient quarrel between philosophy and poetry; of which there are many proofs, such as the saying of "the yelping hound howling at her lord," or of one "mighty in the vain talk of fools," and "the mob of sages circumventing Zeus," and the "subtle thinkers who are beggars after all";[5] and there are innumerable other signs of ancient enmity between them. Notwith-

standing this, let us assure the poetry which aims at pleasure, and the art of imitation, that if she will only prove her title to exist in a well-ordered State we shall be delighted to receive her—we are very conscious of her charms; but it would not be right on that account to betray the truth. I dare say, Glaucon, that you are as much charmed by her as I am, especially when she appears in Homer?

Yes, indeed, I am greatly charmed.

Shall I propose, then, that she be allowed to return from exile, but upon this condition only—that she make a defence of herself in some lyrical or other metre?

Certainly.

And we may further grant to those of her defenders who are lovers of poetry and yet not poets the permission to speak in prose on her behalf: let them show not only that she is pleasant but also useful to States and to human life, and we will listen in a kindly spirit; for we shall surely be the gainers if this can be proved, that there is a use in poetry as well as a delight?

Certainly, he said, we shall be the gainers.

If her defence fails, then, my dear friend, like other persons who are enamoured of something, but put a restraint upon themselves when they think their desires are opposed to their interests, so too must we after the manner of lovers give her up, though not without a struggle. We too are inspired by that love of such poetry which the education of noble States has implanted in us, and therefore we shall be glad if she appears at her best and truest; but so long as she is unable to make good her defence, this argument of ours shall be a charm to us, which we will repeat to ourselves while we listen to her strains; that we may not fall away into the childish love of her which captivates the many. At all events we are well aware[6] that poetry, such as we have

---

4 [Or: "law, and the principle which the community in every case has pronounced to be the best."—TR. NOTE.]

5 [Reading and sense uncertain. The origin of all these quotations is unknown.—TR. NOTE.]

6 [Or, if we accept Madvig's ingenious but unnecessary emendation ᾀσόμεθα, "At all events we will sing, that," etc.—TR. NOTE.]

described, is not to be regarded seriously as attaining to the truth; and he who listens to her, fearing for the safety of the city which is within him, should be on his guard against her seductions and make our words his law.

Yes, he said, I quite agree with you.

Yes, I said, my dear Glaucon, for great is the issue at stake, greater than appears, whether a man is to be good or bad. And what will any one be profited if under the influence of honour or money or power, aye, or under the excitement of poetry, he neglect justice and virtue?

Yes, he said; I have been convinced by the argument, as I believe that anyone else would have been.

ARISTOTLE

(384-322 B.C.)

Aristotle was born at Stagira in Thrace, the son of the Macedonian court physician, Nicomachus. At the age of eighteen he went to Athens and apparently became a pupil in the Academy of Plato. On the death of Plato in 347 or 348 B.C., he left Athens and for some years sojourned in cities of Asia Minor, where he married and had a son. From about the year 342 he served in Macedonia as tutor to the future Alexander the Great. Aristotle returned to Athens in 335 and founded a school of his own, the Lyceum. In the last year of his life he retired to Chalcis in Euboea, where he died in 322.

We do not possess all, nor perhaps even the greater part, of Aristotle's writings, and the text of some of them has suffered much more than the ordinary vicissitudes that befell ancient documents. A number of his empirical studies have survived. The most famed of his strictly philosophical works is the *Organon,* a series of treatises on logic and the methods and problems of acquiring knowledge, and the *Metaphysics,* which is a study of first principles and the concepts underlying all other knowledge. The latter work also comprises Aristotle's theology, the doctrine of the Prime Mover, who he thinks must be presupposed as setting things in motion, since their natural state is rest or immobility.

Aristotle has been roundly condemned for some five centuries for his static view of nature and knowledge. Although he set an example of empirical awareness, he believed that the sciences could be "completed" fairly readily. The modern scientist, on the other hand, is committed to a perpetual revision of assumptions and conclusions, and investigation is never regarded as wholly terminated. In Aristotle, science leads to, and culminates in, a definition, a statement of the essence of a thing. This essence is thought of as a species, which is a genus qualified by a differentiating characteristic. (Man, for example, is an animal with the differentia of rationality.) The followers of Aristotle, impressed by his vast learning, too often acquiesced in his definitions instead of developing their own. The modern reaction against him was inevitable.

Aristotle's static view has been replaced by a dynamic view of nature and science. Modern scientists ask how does *this* vary, given an alteration in *that,* and by exactly *how much.* The end we seek is more often the practical use of knowledge to produce change rather than aesthetic contemplation of truth as an end in itself. Since our aims are so different, it is by no means obvious that Aristotelian science is "false," ours "true."

The *Poetics,* a mere fragment of a larger work that is lost, is nevertheless complete in itself. For the many kinds of plays and the many kinds of feelings and states of mind evoked by them, Aristotle offers a scheme of classification (a characteristic Aristotelian procedure). We are told why tragedy is the most sublime and moving of dramatic genres and what makes it different from others. The definition of tragedy in the sixth chapter may well be the most famed aesthetic observation ever made. The treatise as a whole is by far the most influential of all writings on the general subject of the arts, even though it does not directly treat "aesthetics"—a science unknown to a man who invented so many. Although it is only in short passages and incidental remarks that the *Poetics* impinges on what can be called aesthetics in a strict sense, its indirect influence on modern aesthetic theory is immense. From Aristotle's specific observations on drama, we can readily generalize (though we should be wary of doing so) about other arts. We are on more certain ground when we try to excogitate the generalizations of an aesthetic or artistic nature that he presupposes.

The famed doctrine of *catharsis* in tragedy must inevitably be compared with Plato's severe strictures on the exploitation and expression of emotion in drama (cf. the third, and especially the tenth, book of the *Republic*). Nowhere is the contrast between two great minds so evident as here. Aristotle believes that in tragedy we experience a purgation of the soul through pity and fear. Plato is scandalized at the systematic mass indulgence of emotions promoted by drama. Since he thinks that artists do not address themselves to the supreme philosophical task of developing the good man in the good society, he will not permit drama or any other art complete liberty of expression. Clearly, both of these philosophers regard art as an enterprise that is to be taken with utmost seriousness. As theorists of the arts they are powers to be reckoned with now, as in every bygone age.

ARISTOTLE

Poetics

(Translated by Ingram Bywater)

From The Works of Aristotle, *Vol. XI, W. D. Ross, ed. Oxford: The Clarendon Press, 1952. Reprinted by permission of The Clarendon Press.*

Preliminary Discourse on Tragedy, Epic Poetry, and Comedy, as the Chief Forms of Imitative Poetry

Our subject being Poetry, I propose to 1447ᵃ speak not only of the art in general but also of its species and their respective capacities; of the structure of plot required for a good poem; of the number and nature of the constituent parts of a poem; and likewise of any other matters in the same line of inquiry. Let us follow the natural order and begin with the primary facts.

Epic poetry and Tragedy, as also Comedy, Dithyrambic poetry, and most flute-playing and lyre-playing, are all, viewed as a whole, modes of imitation. But at the same time they differ from one another in three ways, either by a difference of kind in their means, or by differences in the objects, or in the manner of their imitations. . . .

Chapter One

§ THE POETIC ARTS DISTINGUISHED BY THE MEANS THEY USE

Just as colour and form are used as means by some, who (whether by art or constant practice) imitate and portray many things by their aid, and the voice is used by others; so also in the above-mentioned group of

41

arts, the means with them as a whole are rhythm, language, and harmony—used, however, either singly or in certain combinations. A combination of harmony and rhythm alone is the means in flute-playing and lyre-playing, and any other arts there may be of the same description, e.g. imitative piping. Rhythm alone, without harmony, is the means in the dancer's imitations; for even he, by the rhythms of his attitudes, may represent men's characters, as well as what they do and suffer. There is further an art which imitates by language alone, without harmony, in prose or in verse, and if in verse, either in some one or in a plurality of metres. This form of imitation 1447b is to this day without a name. We have no common name for a mime of Sophron or Xenarchus and a Socratic conversation; and we should still be without one even if the imitation in the two instances were in trimeters or elegiacs or some other kind of verse—though it is the way with people to tack on "poet" to the name of a metre, and talk of elegiac poets and epic poets, thinking that they call them poets not by reason of the imitative nature of their work, but indiscriminately by reason of the metre they write in. Even if a theory of medicine or physical philosophy be put forth in a metrical form, it is usual to describe the writer in this way; Homer and Empedocles, however, have really nothing in common apart from their metre so that, if the one is to be called a poet, the other should be termed a physicist rather than a poet. We should be in the same position also, if the imitation in these instances were in all the metres, like the *Centaur* (a rhapsody in a medley of all metres) of Chaeremon; and Chaeremon one has to recognize as a poet. So much, then, as to these arts. There are, lastly, certain other arts, which combine all the means enumerated, rhythm, melody, and verse, e.g., Dithyrambic and Nomic poetry, Tragedy and Comedy; with this difference, however, that the three kinds of means are in some of them all employed together, and in others brought in separately, one after the other. These elements of difference in the above arts I term the means of their imitation.

Chapter Two

§ THE POETIC ARTS DISTINGUISHED
  BY THEIR OBJECT

The objects the imitator represents are actions, with agents who are necessarily either 1448a good men or bad—the diversities of human character being nearly always derivative from this primary distinction, since the line between virtue and vice is one dividing the whole of mankind. It follows, therefore, that the agents represented must be either above our own level of goodness, or beneath it, or just such as we are; in the same way as, with the painters, the personages of Polygnotus are better than we are, those of Pauson worse, and those of Dionysius just like ourselves. It is clear that each of the above-mentioned arts will admit of these differences, and that it will become a separate art by representing objects with this point of difference. Even in dancing, flute-playing, and lyre-playing such diversities are possible; and they are also possible in the nameless art that uses language, prose, or verse without harmony, as its means; Homer's personages, for instance, are better than we are; Cleophon's are on our own level; and those of Hegemon of Thasos, the first writer of parodies, and Nicochares, the author of the *Diliad,* are beneath it. The same is true of the Dithyramb and the Nome: the personages may be presented in them with the difference exemplified in the. . .Cyclopses of Timotheus and Philoxenus. This difference it is that distinguishes Tragedy and Comedy also; the one would make its personages worse, and the other better, than the men of the present day.

Chapter Three

§ THE POETIC ARTS DISTINGUISHED
BY THE MANNER OF THEIR
IMITATIONS

A third difference in these arts is in the manner in which each kind of object is represented. Given both the same means and the same kind of object for imitation, one may either (1) speak at one moment in narrative and at another in an assumed character, as Homer does; or (2) one may remain the same throughout, without any such change; or (3) the imitators may represent the whole story dramatically, as though they were actually doing the things described.

As we said at the beginning, therefore, the differences in the imitation of these arts come under three heads, their means, their objects, and their manner.

So that as an imitator Sophocles will be on one side akin to Homer, both portraying good men; and on another to Aristophanes, since both present their personages as acting and doing. This in fact, according to some, is the reason for plays being termed dramas, because in a play the personages act the story. Hence too both Tragedy and Comedy are claimed by the Dorians as their discoveries; Comedy by the Megarians—by those in Greece as having arisen when Megara became a democracy, and by the Sicilian Megarians on the ground that the poet Epicharmus was of their country, and a good deal earlier than Chionides and Magnes; even Tragedy also is claimed by certain of the Peloponnesian Dorians. In support of this claim they point to the words "comedy" and "drama." Their word for the outlying hamlets, they say, is *comae*, whereas Athenians call them *demes*—thus assuming that comedians got the name not from their *comoe* or revels, but from their strolling from hamlet to hamlet, lack of appreciation keeping them out of the city. 1448b

Their word also for "to act," they say, is *dran*, whereas Athenians use *prattein*.

So much, then as to the number and nature of the points of difference in the imitation of these arts.

Chapter Four

§ ORIGIN AND DEVELOPMENT OF
POETRY AND ITS KINDS

It is clear that the general origin of poetry was due to two causes, each of them part of human nature. Imitation is natural to man from childhood, one of his advantages over the lower animals being this, that he is the most imitative creature in the world, and learns at first by imitation. And it is also natural for all to delight in works of imitation. The truth of this second point is shown by experience: though the objects themselves may be painful to see, we delight to view the most realistic representations of them in art, the forms for example of the lowest animals and of dead bodies. The explanation is to be found in a further fact: to be learning something is the greatest of pleasures not only to the philosopher but also to the rest of mankind, however small their capacity for it; the reason of the delight in seeing the picture is that one is at the same time learning—gathering the meaning of things, e.g., that the man there is so-and-so; for if one has not seen the thing before, one's pleasure will not be in the picture as an imitation of it, but will be due to the execution or colouring or some similar cause. Imitation, then, being natural to us —as also the sense of harmony and rhythm, the metres being obviously species of rhythms—it was through their original aptitude, and by a series of improvements for the most part gradual on their first efforts, that they created poetry out of their improvisations.

Poetry, however, soon broke up into two kinds according to the differences of character in the individual poets; for the graver among them would represent noble actions, and those of noble personages; and the meaner sort the actions of the ignoble. The latter class produced invectives at first, just as others did hymns and panegyrics. We know of no such poem by any of the pre-Homeric poets, though there were probably many such writers among them; instances, however, may be found from Homer downwards, e.g., his *Margites,* and the similar poems of others. In this poetry of invective its natural fitness brought an iambic metre into use; hence our present term "iambic," because it was the metre of their "iambs" or invectives against one another. The result was that the old poets became some of them writers of heroic and others of iambic verse. Homer's position, however, is peculiar: just as he was in the serious style the poet of poets, standing alone not only through the literary excellence, but also through the dramatic character of his imitations, so too he was the first to outline for us the general forms of Comedy by producing not a dramatic invective, but a dramatic picture of the Ridiculous; his *Margites* in fact stands in the same relation to our comedies as the *Iliad* and *Odyssey* to our tragedies. As soon, 1449ª however, as Tragedy and Comedy appeared in the field, those naturally drawn to the one line of poetry became writers of comedies instead of iambs, and those naturally drawn to the other, writers of tragedies instead of epics, because these new modes of art were grander and of more esteem than the old.

If it be asked whether Tragedy is now all that it need be in its formative elements, to consider that, and decide it theoretically and in relation to the theatres, is a matter for another inquiry.

It certainly began in improvisations—as did also Comedy; the one originating with the authors of the Dithyramb, the other with those of the phallic songs, which still survive as institutions in many of our cities. And its advance after that was little by little, through their improving on whatever they had before them at each stage. It was in fact only after a long series of changes that the movement of Tragedy stopped on its attaining to its natural form. (1) The number of actors was first increased to two by Aeschylus, who curtailed the business of the Chorus, and made the dialogue, or spoken portion, take the leading part in the play. (2) A third actor and scenery were due to Sophocles. (3) Tragedy acquired also its magnitude. Discarding short stories and a ludicrous diction, through its passing out of its satyric stage, it assumed, though only at a late point in its progress, a tone of dignity; and its metre changed then from trochaic to iambic. The reason for their original use of the trochaic tetrameter was that their poetry was satyric and more connected with dancing than it now is. As soon, however, as a spoken part came in, nature herself found the appropriate metre. The iambic, we know, is the most speakable of metres, as is shown by the fact that we very often fall into it in conversation, whereas we rarely talk hexameters, and only when we depart from the speaking tone of voice. (4) Another change was a plurality of episodes or acts. As for the remaining matters, the superadded embellishments and the account of their introduction, these must be taken as said, as it would probably be a long piece of work to go through the details.

Chapter Five

§ COMEDY AND EPIC POETRY

As for Comedy, it is (as has been observed) an imitation of men worse than the average; worse, however, not as regards any and every sort of fault, but only as regards one particular kind, the Ridiculous, which is a species of the Ugly. The Ridiculous may be

defined as a mistake or deformity not productive of pain or harm to others; the mask,
for instance, that excites laughter, is something ugly and distorted without causing
pain.

Though the successive changes in Tragedy
and their authors are not unknown, we
cannot say the same of Comedy; its early
stages passed unnoticed, because it was not
as yet taken up in a serious way. It was 1449b
only at a late point in its progress that a
chorus of comedians was officially granted
by the archon; they used to be mere volun-
teers. It had also already certain definite
forms at the time when the record of those
termed comic poets begins. Who it was supplied it with masks, or prologues, or a
plurality of actors and the like, has remained unknown. The invented Fable, or
Plot, however, originated in Sicily, with
Epicharmus and Phormis; of Athenian poets
Crates was the first to drop the Comedy of
invective and frame stories of a general and
non-personal nature, in other words, Fables
or Plots.

Epic poetry, then, has been seen to agree
with Tragedy to this extent, that of being
an imitation of serious subjects in a grand
kind of verse. It differs from it, however,
(1) in that it is in one kind of verse and
in narrative form; and (2) in its length—
which is due to its action having no fixed
limit of time, whereas Tragedy endeavours to
keep as far as possible within a single circuit
of the sun, or something near that. This,
I say, is another point of difference between
them, though at first the practice in this
respect was just the same in tragedies as in
epic poems. They differ also (3) in their
constituents, some being common to both
and others peculiar to Tragedy—hence a
judge of good and bad in Tragedy is a judge
of that in epic poetry also. All the parts of
an epic are included in Tragedy; but those
of Tragedy are not all of them to be found
in the Epic.

Chapter Six

§ DEFINITION OF A TRAGEDY AND THE
  RULES FOR ITS CONSTRUCTION;
  DEFINITION AND ANALYSIS INTO
  QUALITATIVE PARTS

Reserving hexameter poetry and Comedy for
consideration hereafter[1] let us proceed now
to the discussion of tragedy; before doing
so, however, we must gather up the definition resulting from what has been said. A
tragedy, then, is the imitation of an action
that is serious and also, as having magnitude, complete in itself; in language with
pleasurable accessories, each kind brought
in separately in the parts of the work; in
a dramatic, not in a narrative form; with
incidents arousing pity and fear, wherewith
to accomplish its catharsis of such emotions.
Here by "language with pleasurable accessories" I mean that with rhythm and harmony or song superadded; and by "the
kinds separately" I mean that some portions
are worked out with verse only, and others
in turn with song.

As they act the stories, it follows that in
the first place the Spectacle (or stage appearance of the actors) must be some part of
the whole; and in the second Melody and
Diction, these two being the means of their
imitation. Here by "Diction" I mean merely
this, the composition of the verses; and by
"Melody," what is too completely understood to require explanation. But further:
the subject represented also is an action;
and the action involves agents, who must
necessarily have their distinctive qualities
both of character and thought, since it is
from these that we ascribe certain qualities 1450a
to their actions. There are in the natural
order of things, therefore, two causes,
Thought and Character, of their actions,
and consequently of their success or failure

---

[1] [For hexameter poetry, cf. Chapters 23f.;
comedy was treated of in the lost Second Book.—
TR. NOTE.]

in their lives. Now the action (that which was done) is represented in the play by the Fable or Plot. The Fable, in our present sense of the term, is simply this, the combination of the incidents, or things done in the story; whereas Character is what makes us ascribe certain moral qualities to the agents; and Thought is shown in all they say when proving a particular point or, it may be, enunciating a general truth. There are six parts consequently of every tragedy, as a whole (that is) of such or such quality, viz., a Fable or Plot, Characters, Diction, Thought, Spectacle, and Melody; two of them arising from the means, one from the manner, and three from the objects of the dramatic imitation; and there is nothing else besides these six. Of these, its formative elements, then, not a few of the dramatists have made due use, as every play, one may say, admits of Spectacle, Character, Fable, Diction, Melody, and Thought.

The most important of the six is the combination of the incidents of the story. Tragedy is essentially an imitation not of persons but of action and life, of happiness and misery. All human happiness or misery takes the form of action; the end for which we live is a certain kind of activity, not a quality. Character gives us qualities, but it is in our actions—what we do—that we are happy or the reverse. In a play accordingly they do not act in order to portray the Characters; they include the Characters for the sake of the action. So that it is the action in it, i.e., its Fable or Plot, that is the end and purpose of the tragedy and the end is everywhere the chief thing. Besides this, a tragedy is impossible without action, but there may be one without Character. The tragedies of most of the moderns are characterless—a defect common among poets of all kinds, and with its counterpart in painting in Zeuxis as compared with Polygnotus; for whereas the latter is strong in character, the work of Zeuxis is devoid of it. And again: one may string together a series of characteristic speeches of the utmost finish as regards Diction and Thought, and yet fail to produce the true tragic effect; but one will have much better success with a tragedy which, however inferior in these respects, has a Plot, a combination of incidents, in it. And again: the most powerful elements of attraction in Tragedy, the Peripeties and Discoveries, are parts of the Plot. A further proof is in the fact that beginners succeed earlier with the Diction and Characters than with the construction of a story; and the same may be said of nearly all the early dramatists. We maintain, therefore, that the first essential, the life and soul, so to speak, of Tragedy is the Plot; and that the Characters come second—compare the parallel in 1450b painting, where the most beautiful colours laid on without order will not give one the same pleasure as a simple black-and-white sketch of a portrait. We maintain that Tragedy is primarily an imitation of action, and that it is mainly for the sake of the action that it imitates the personal agents. Third comes the element of Thought, i.e., the power of saying whatever can be said, or what is appropriate to the occasion. This is what, in the speeches in Tragedy, falls under the arts of Politics and Rhetoric; for the older poets make their personages discourse like statesmen, and the moderns like rhetoricians. One must not confuse it with Character. Character in a play is that which reveals the moral purpose of the agents, i.e., the sort of thing they seek or avoid, where that is not obvious—hence there is no room for Character in a speech on a purely indifferent subject. Thought, on the other hand, is shown in all they say when proving or disproving some particular point, or enunciating some universal proposition. Fourth among the literary elements is the Diction of the personages, i.e., as before explained, the expression of their thoughts in words, which is practically the same thing with verse as with prose. As for the two remaining parts, the Melody is the greatest of the pleasurable accessories of Tragedy.

The Spectacle, though an attraction, is the least artistic of all the parts, and has least to do with the art of poetry. The tragic effect is quite possible without a public performance and actors; and besides, the getting-up of the Spectacle is more a matter for the costumer than the poet.

Chapter Seven

§ THE PLOT: ARRANGEMENT AND
  LENGTH OF THE PLAY

Having thus distinguished the parts, let us now consider the proper construction of the Fable or Plot, as that is at once the first and the most important thing in Tragedy. We have laid it down that a tragedy is an imitation of an action that is complete in itself, as a whole of some magnitude; for a whole may be of no magnitude to speak of. Now a whole is that which has beginning, middle, and end. A beginning is that which is not itself necessarily after anything else, and which has naturally something else after it; an end is that which is naturally after something itself, either as its necessary or usual consequent, and with nothing else after it; and a middle, that which is by nature after one thing and has also another after it. A well-constructed Plot, therefore, cannot either begin or end at any point one likes; beginning and end in it must be of the forms just described. Again: to be beautiful, a living creature, and every whole made up of parts, must not only present a certain order in its arrangement of parts, but also be of a certain definite magnitude. Beauty is a matter of size and order, and therefore impossible either (1) in a very minute creature, since our perception becomes indistinct as it approaches instantaneity; or (2) in a creature of vast size—one, say, 1,000 miles long— as in that case, instead of the object being seen all at once, the unity and wholeness of it is lost to the beholder. Just in the same way, then, as a beautiful whole made up of parts, or a beautiful living creature, must

be of some size, but a size to be taken in by the eye, so a story or Plot must be of some length, but of a length to be taken in by the memory. As for the limit of its length, so far as that is relative to public performances and spectators, it does not fall within the theory of poetry. If they had to perform a hundred tragedies, they would be timed by water-clocks, as they are said to have been at one period. The limit, however, set by the actual nature of the thing is this: the longer the story, consistently with its being comprehensible as a whole, the finer it is by reason of its magnitude. As a rough general formula, "a length which allows of the hero passing by a series of probable or necessary stages from misfortune to happiness, or from happiness to misfortune," may suffice as a limit for the magnitude of the story.

Chapter Eight

§ THE PLOT: UNITY OF ACTION

The Unity of a Plot does not consist, as some suppose, in its having one man as its subject. An infinity of things befall that one man, some of which it is impossible to reduce to unity; and in like manner there are many actions of one man which cannot be made to form one action. One sees, therefore, the mistake of all the poets who have written a *Heracleid*, a *Theseid*, or similar poems; they suppose that, because Heracles was one man, the story also of Heracles must be one story. Homer, however, evidently understood this point quite well, whether by art or instinct, just in the same way as he excels the rest in every other respect. In writing an *Odyssey*, he did not make the poem cover all that ever befell his hero— it befell him, for instance, to get wounded on Parnassus and also to feign madness at the time of the call to arms, but the two incidents had no necessary or probable connection with one another—instead of doing that, he took as the subject of the *Odyssey*, as also of the *Iliad,* an action with a Unity of the kind we are describing. The truth is that, just as in the other imitative arts one imitation is always of one thing, so in poetry the story, as an imitation of action, must represent one action, a complete whole, with its several incidents so closely connected that the transposal or withdrawal of any one of them will disjoin and dislocate the whole. For that which makes no perceptible difference by its presence or absence is no real part of the whole.

Chapter Nine

§ THE PLOT: THE POET MUST DEPICT THE PROBABLE AND THE UNIVERSAL

From what we have said it will be seen that the poet's function is to describe, not the thing that has happened, but a kind of thing that might happen, i.e., what is possible as being probable or necessary. The distinction between historian and poet 1451b is not in the one writing prose and the other verse—you might put the work of Herodotus into verse, and it would still be a species of history; it consists really in this, that the one describes the thing that has been, and the other a kind of thing that might be. Hence poetry is something more philosophic and of graver import than history, since its statements are of the nature rather of universals, whereas those of history are singulars. By a universal statement I mean one as to what such or such a kind of man will probably or necessarily say or do— which is the aim of poetry, though it affixes proper names to the characters; by a singular statement, one as to what, say, Alcibiades did or had done to him. In Comedy this has become clear by this time; it is only when their plot is already made up of probable incidents that they give it a basis of proper names, choosing for the purpose any names that may occur to them, instead of writing like the old iambic poets about particular persons. In Tragedy, however, they still adhere to the historic names; and for this reason: what convinces is the possible; now whereas we are not yet sure as to the possibility of that which has not happened, that which has happened is manifestly possible, else it would not have come to pass. Nevertheless even in Tragedy there are some plays with but one or two known names in them, the rest being inventions; and there are some without a single known name, e.g., Agathon's *Antheus,* in which both incidents and names are of the poet's invention; and it is no less delightful on that account. So that one must not aim at a rigid adherence to the traditional stories on which tragedies are based. It would be absurd, in fact, to do so, as even the known stories are only known to a few, though they are a delight none the less to all.

It is evident from the above that the poet must be more the poet of his stories or Plots than of his verses, inasmuch as he is a poet by virtue of the imitative element in his work, and it is actions that he imitates. And if he should come to take a subject from actual history, he is none the less a poet for that; since some historic occurrences may very well be in the probable and possible order of things; and it is in that aspect of them that he is their poet.

Of simple Plots and actions the episodic are the worst. I call a Plot episodic when there is neither probability nor necessity in the sequence of its episodes. Actions of this sort bad poets construct through their own fault, and good ones on account of the players. His work being for public performance, a good poet often stretches out a Plot beyond its capabilities, and is thus obliged to twist the sequence of incident.

Tragedy, however, is an imitation not 1452a only of a complete action, but also of incidents arousing pity and fear. Such incidents have the very greatest effect on the mind when they occur unexpectedly and at the same time in consequence of one another; there is more of the marvelous in them then than if they happened of themselves or by mere chance. Even matters of chance seem most marvelous if there is an appearance of design as it were in them; as for instance the statue of Mitys at Argos killed the author of Mitys' death by falling down on him when a looker-on at a public spectacle; for incidents like that we think to be not without a meaning. A Plot, therefore, of this sort is necessarily finer than others.

Chapter Ten

§ THE PLOT: SIMPLE AND COMPLEX PLOTS

Plots are either simple or complex, since the actions they represent are naturally of this twofold description. The action, proceeding in the way defined, as one continuous whole, I call simple, when the change in the hero's fortunes takes place without Peripety or Discovery; and complex, when it involves one or the other, or both. These should each of them arise out of the structure of the Plot itself, so as to be the consequence, necessary or probable, of the antecedents. There is a great difference between a thing happening *propter hoc* and *post hoc*.

Chapter Eleven

§ THE PLOT: PERIPETY, DISCOVERY, AND SUFFERING

A Peripety is the change of the kind described from one state of things within the play to its opposite, and that too in the way we are saying, in the probable or necessary sequence of events; as it is for instance in *Oedipus*: here the opposite state of things is produced by the Messenger, who, coming to gladden Oedipus and to remove his fears as to his mother, reveals the secret of his birth.[2] And in *Lynceus*:[3] just as he is being led off for execution, with Danaus at his

side to put him to death, the incidents preceding this bring it about that he is saved and Danaus put to death. A Discovery is, as the very word implies, a change from ignorance to knowledge, and thus to either love or hate, in the personages marked for good or evil fortune. The finest form of Discovery is one attended by Peripeties, like that which goes with the Discovery in *Oedipus*. There are no doubt other forms of it; what we have said may happen in a way in reference to inanimate things, even things of a very casual kind; and it is also possible to discover whether some one has done or not done something. But the form most directly connected with the Plot and the action of the piece is the first-mentioned. This, with a Peripety, will arouse either pity 1452b or fear—actions of that nature being what Tragedy is assumed to represent; and it will also serve to bring about the happy or unhappy ending. The Discovery, then, being of persons, it may be that of one party only to the other, the latter being already known; or both the parties may have to discover themselves. Iphigenia, for instance, was discovered to Orestes by sending the letter;[4] and another Discovery was required to reveal him to Iphigenia.

Two parts of the Plot, then, Peripety and Discovery, are on matters of this sort. A third part is Suffering; which we may define as an action of a destructive or painful nature, such as murders on the stage, tortures, woundings, and the like. The other two have been already explained.

Chapter Twelve

§ THE QUANTITATIVE PARTS OF TRAGEDY

The parts of Tragedy to be treated as formative elements in the whole were mentioned in a previous Chapter.[5] From the

---

2 [*Oedipus Tyrannus*, 911-1085.—TR. NOTE.]
3 [By Theodectes.—TR. NOTE.]

4 [*Iphigenia in Tauris*, 727 ff.—TR. NOTE.]
5 [Chapter 6.—TR. NOTE.]

point of view, however, of this quantity, i.e., the separate sections into which it is divided, a tragedy has the following parts: Prologue, Episode, Exode, and a choral portion, distinguished into Parode and Stasimon; these two are common to all tragedies, whereas songs from the stage and *Commoe* are only found in some. The Prologue is all that precedes the Parode of the chorus; an Episode all that comes in between two whole choral songs; the Exode all that follows after the last choral song. In the choral portion the Parode is the whole first statement of the chorus; a Stasimon, a song of the chorus without anapests or trochees; a *Commos,* a lamentation sung by chorus and actor in concert. The parts of Tragedy to be used as formative elements in the whole we have already mentioned; the above are its parts from the point of view of its quantity, or the separate sections into which it is divided.

Chapter Thirteen

§ HOW THE PLOT CAN BEST PRODUCE
THE EMOTIONAL EFFECT OF
TRAGEDY: THE TRAGIC HERO

The next points after what we have said above will be these: (1) What is the poet to aim at, and what is he to avoid, in constructing his Plots? and (2) What are the conditions on which the tragic effect depends?

We assume that, for the finest form of Tragedy, the Plot must be not simple but complex; and further, that it must imitate actions arousing fear and pity, since that is the distinctive function of this kind of imitation. It follows, therefore, that there are three forms of Plot to be avoided. (1) A good man must not be seen passing from happiness to misery, or (2) a bad man from misery to happiness. The first situation is not fear-inspiring or piteous, but simply odious to us. The second is the most un-

tragic that can be; it has no one of the requisites of Tragedy; it does not appeal either to the human feeling in us, or to our pity, or to our fears. Nor, on the other hand, should (3) an extremely bad man be seen falling from happiness into misery. Such a story may arouse the human feeling in us, but it will not move us to either pity or fear; pity is occasioned by undeserved misfortune, and fear by that of one like ourselves; so that there will be nothing either piteous or fear-inspiring in the situation. There remains, then, the intermediate kind of personage, a man not pre-eminently virtuous and just, whose misfortune, however, is brought upon him not by vice and depravity but by some error of judgement, of the number of those in the enjoyment of great reputation and prosperity; e.g., Oedipus, Thyestes, and the men of note of similar families. The perfect Plot, accordingly, must have a single, and not (as some tell us) a double issue; the change in the hero's fortunes must be not from misery to happiness, but on the contrary from happiness to misery; and the cause of it must lie not in any depravity, but in some great error on his part; the man himself being either such as we have described, or better, not worse, than that. Fact also confirms our theory. Though the poets began by accepting any tragic story that came to hand, in these days the finest tragedies are always on the story of some few houses, on that of Alcmeon, Oedipus, Orestes, Meleager, Thyestes, Telephus, or any others that may have been involved, as either agents or sufferers, in some deed of horror. The theoretically best tragedy, then, has a Plot of this description. The critics, therefore, are wrong who blame Euripides for taking this line in his tragedies, and giving many of them an unhappy ending. It is, as we have said, the right line to take. The best proof is this: on the stage, and in the public performances, such plays, properly worked out, are seen to be the most truly tragic; and Euripides, even if his execution be faulty in every other point, is seen to be nevertheless the most tragic certainly of the dramatists. After this comes the construction of Plot which some rank first, one with a double story (like the *Odyssey*) and an opposite issue for the good and the bad personages. It is ranked as first only through the weakness of the audiences; the poets merely follow their public, writing as its wishes dictate. But the pleasure here is not that of Tragedy. It belongs rather to Comedy, where the bitterest enemies in the piece (e.g., Orestes and Aegisthus) walk off good friends at the end, with no slaying of any one by any one.

Chapter Fourteen

§ THE TRAGIC DEED

The tragic fear and pity may be aroused by 1453b the Spectacle; but they may also be aroused by the very structure and incidents of the play—which is the better way and shows the better poet. The Plot in fact should be so framed that, even without seeing the things take place, he who simply hears the account of them shall be filled with horror and pity at the incidents; which is just the effect that the mere recital of the story in *Oedipus* would have on one. To produce this same effect by means of the Spectacle is less artistic, and requires extraneous aid. Those, however, who make use of the Spectacle to put before us that which is merely monstrous and not productive of fear, are wholly out of touch with Tragedy; not every kind of pleasure should be required of a tragedy, but only its own proper pleasure.

The tragic pleasure is that of pity and fear, and the poet has to produce it by a work of imitation; it is clear, therefore, that the causes should be included in the incidents of his story. Let us see, then, what kinds of incident strike one as horrible, or rather as piteous. In a deed of this description the parties must necessarily be either friends, or enemies, or indifferent to one another. Now when enemy does it on enemy, there is nothing to move us to pity either in his doing or in his meditating the deed, except so far as the actual pain of the sufferer is concerned; and the same is true when the parties are indifferent to one another. Whenever the tragic deed, however, is done within the family—when murder or the like is done or meditated by brother on brother, by son on father, by mother on son, or son on mother—these are the situations the poet should seek after. The traditional stories, accordingly, must be kept as they are, e.g., the murder of Clytemnestra by Orestes and of Eriphyle by Alcmeon. At the same time even with these there is something left to the poet himself; it is for him to devise the right way of treating them. Let us explain more clearly what we mean by "the right way." The deed of horror may be done by the doer knowingly and consciously, as in the old poets, and in Medea's murder of her children in Euripides.[6] Or he may do it, but in ignorance of his relationship, and discover that afterwards, as does the Oedipus in Sophocles. Here the deed is outside the play; but it may be within it, like the act of the Alcmeon in *Astydamas,* or that of the Telegonus in *Ulysses Wounded.*[7] A third possibility is for one meditating some deadly injury to another, in ignorance of his relationship, to make the discovery in time to draw back. These exhaust the possibilities, since the deed must necessarily be either done or not done, and either knowingly or unknowingly.

The worst situation is when the personage is with full knowledge on the point of doing the deed, and leaves it undone. It is odious and also (through the absence of suffering) untragic; hence it is that no one is made to act thus except in some few instances, e.g., Haemon and Creon in 1454a

---

6 [*Medea,* 1236.—TR. NOTE.]
7 [Perhaps by Sophocles.—TR. NOTE.]

Antigone.[8] Next after this comes the actual perpetration of the deed meditated. A better situation than that, however, is for the deed to be done in ignorance, and the relationship discovered afterwards, since there is nothing odious in it, and the Discovery will serve to astound us. But the best of all is the last; what we have in *Cresphontes*,[9] for example, where Merope, on the point of slaying her son, recognizes him in time; in *Iphigenia,* where sister and brother are in a like position; and in *Helle*,[10] where the son recognizes his mother, when on the point of giving her up to her enemy.

This will explain why our tragedies are restricted (as we said just now) to such a small number of families. It was accident rather than art that led the poets in quest of subjects to embody this kind of incident in their Plots. They are still obliged, accordingly, to have recourse to the families in which such horrors have occurred.

On the construction of the Plot, and the kind of Plot required for Tragedy, enough has now been said.

Chapter Fifteen

§ RULES FOR THE CHARACTER OF THE TRAGIC PERSONAGES: NOTE ON THE USE OF STAGE-ARTIFICE

In the Characters there are four points to aim at. First and foremost, that they shall be good. There will be an element of character in the play, if (as has been observed) what a personage says or does reveals a certain moral purpose; and a good element of character, if the purpose so revealed is good. Such goodness is possible in every type of personage, even in a woman or a slave, though the one is perhaps an inferior, and the other a wholly worthless being. The second point is to make them

appropriate. The Character before us may be, say, manly; but it is not appropriate in a female Character to be manly, or clever. The third is to make them like the reality, which is not the same as their being good and appropriate, in our sense of the term. The fourth is to make them consistent and the same throughout; even if inconsistency be part of the man before one for imitation as presenting that form of character, he should still be consistently inconsistent. We have an instance of baseness of character, not required for the story, in the Menelaus in *Orestes*; of the incongruous and unbefitting in the lamentation of Ulysses in *Scylla*,[11] and in the (clever) speech of Melanippe;[12] and of inconsistency in *Iphigenia at Aulis*,[13] where Iphigenia the suppliant is utterly unlike the later Iphigenia. The right thing, however, is in the Characters just as in the incidents of the play to endeavour always after the necessary or the probable; so that whenever such-and-such a personage says or does such-and-such a thing, it shall be the necessary or probable outcome of his character; and whenever this incident follows on that, it shall be either the necessary or the probable consequence of it. From this one sees (to digress for a moment) that the Dénouement also should arise out of the plot itself, 1454b and not depend on a stage-artifice, as in *Medea*,[14] or in the story of the (arrested) departure of the Greeks in the *Iliad*.[15] The artifice must be reserved for matters outside the play—for past events beyond human knowledge, or events yet to come, which require to be foretold or announced; since it is the privilege of the Gods to know everything. There should be nothing improbable among the actual incidents. If it be unavoidable, however, it should be outside the tragedy, like the improbability in

---

8 [Line 1231.—TR. NOTE.]
9 [By Euripides.—TR. NOTE.]
10 [Authorship unknown.—TR. NOTE.]

11 [A dithyramb by Timotheus.—TR. NOTE.]
12 [By Euripides.—TR. NOTE.]
13 [Lines 1211 ff.; 1368 ff.—TR. NOTE.]
14 [Line 1317.—TR. NOTE.]
15 [Book II, 155.—TR. NOTE.]

the *Oedipus* of Sophocles. But to return to the Characters. As Tragedy is an imitation of personages better than the ordinary man, we in our way should follow the example of good portrait-painters, who reproduce the distinctive features of a man, and at the same time, without losing the likeness, make him handsomer than he is. The poet in like manner, in portraying men quick or slow to anger, or with similar infirmities of character, must know how to represent them as such, and at the same time as good men, as Agathon and Homer have represented Achilles.

All these rules one must keep in mind throughout, and, further, those also for such points of stage-effect as directly depend on the art of the poet, since in these too one may often make mistakes. Enough, however, has been said on the subject in one of our published writings. . . .[16]

Chapter Twenty-Three

§ RULES FOR THE CONSTRUCTION OF AN EPIC; IT MUST PRESERVE UNITY OF ACTION

As for the poetry which merely narrates, or imitates by means of versified language (without action), it is evident that it has several points in common with Tragedy.

The construction of its stories should clearly be like that in a drama; they should be based on a single action, one that is a complete whole in itself, with a beginning, middle, and end, so as to enable the work to produce its own proper pleasure with all the organic unity of a living creature. Nor should one suppose that there is anything like them in our usual histories. A history has to deal not with one action, but with one period and all that happened in that to one or more persons, however disconnected the several events may have been. Just as two events may take place at the same time, e.g., the sea-fight off Salamis and the battle with the Carthaginians in Sicily, without converging to the same end, so too of two consecutive events one may sometimes come after the other with no one end as their common issue. Nevertheless most of our epic poets, one may say, ignore the distinction.

Herein, then, to repeat what we have said before,[17] we have a further proof of Homer's marvelous superiority to the rest. He did not attempt to deal even with the Trojan War in its entirety, though it was a whole with a definite beginning and end— through a feeling apparently that it was too long a story to be taken in in one view, or if not that, too complicated from the variety of incident in it. As it is, he has singled out one section of the whole; many of the other incidents, however, he brings in as episodes, using the Catalogue of the Ships, for instance, and other episodes to relieve the uniformity of his narrative. As for the other epic poets, they treat of one man, or one period; or else of an action which, although one, has a multiplicity of parts in it. This last is what the authors of the 1459b *Cypria*[18] and *Little Iliad*[19] have done. And the result is that whereas the *Iliad* or *Odyssey* supplies materials for only one, or at most two tragedies, the *Cypria* does that for several and the *Little Iliad* for more than eight: for an *Adjudgment of Arms,* a *Philoctetes,* a *Neoptolemus,* a *Eurypylus,* a *Ulysses as Beggar,* a *Laconian Women,* a *Fall of Ilium,* and a *Departure of the Fleet;* as also a *Sinon,* and a *Women of Troy.*

Chapter Twenty-Four

§ POINTS OF RESEMBLANCE AND OF DIFFERENCE BETWEEN EPIC POETRY AND TRAGEDY

Besides this, Epic poetry must divide into

---

16 [In the lost dialogue, *On Poets.*—TR. NOTE.]

17 [See Chapter Eight, above.—TR. NOTE.]
18 [Authorship unknown.—TR. NOTE.]
19 [Authorship unknown.—TR. NOTE.]

the same species as Tragedy; it must be either simple or complex, a story of character or one of suffering. Its parts, too, with the exception of Song and Spectacle, must be the same, as it requires Peripeties, Discoveries and scenes of suffering just like Tragedy. Lastly, the Thought and Diction in it must be good in their way. All these elements appear in Homer first; and he has made due use of them. His two poems are each examples of construction, the *Iliad* simple and a story of suffering, the *Odyssey* complex (there is Discovery throughout it) and a story of character. And they are more than this, since in Diction and Thought too they surpass all other poems.

There is, however, a difference in the Epic as compared with Tragedy, (1) in its length, and (2) in its metre. (1) As to its length, the limit already suggested will suffice: it must be possible for the beginning and end of the work to be taken in in one view—a condition which will be fulfilled if the poem be shorter than the old epics, and about as long as the series of tragedies offered for one hearing. For the extension of its length epic poetry has a special advantage, of which it makes large use. In a play one cannot represent an action with a number of parts going on simultaneously; one is limited to the part on the stage and connected with the actors. Whereas in epic poetry the narrative form makes it possible for one to describe a number of simultaneous incidents; and these, if germane to the subject, increase the body of the poem. This then is a gain to the Epic, tending to give it grandeur, and also variety of interest and room for episodes of diverse kinds. Uniformity of incident by the satiety it soon creates is apt to ruin tragedies on the stage. (2) As for its metre, the heroic has been assigned it from experience; were any one to attempt a narrative poem in some one, or in several, of the other metres, the incongruity of the thing would be apparent. The heroic in fact is the gravest and weightiest of metres—which is what makes it more tolerant than the rest of strange words and metaphors, that also being a point in which the narrative form of poetry goes beyond all others. The iambic and trochaic, on the other hand, are metres of movement, the one representing that of life and action, the other that of the dance. Still 1460a more unnatural would it appear, if one were to write an epic in a medley of metres, as Chaeremon did.[20] Hence it is that no one has ever written a long story in any but heroic verse; nature herself, as we have said, teaches us to select the metre appropriate to such a story.

Homer, admirable as he is in every other respect, is especially so in this, that he alone among epic poets is not unaware of the part to be played by the poet himself in the poem. The poet should say very little *in propria persona,* as he is no imitator when doing that. Whereas the other poets are perpetually coming forward in person, and say but little, and that only here and there, as imitators, Homer after a brief preface brings in forthwith a man, a woman, or some other character—no one of them characterless, but each with distinctive characteristics.

The marvelous is certainly required in Tragedy. The Epic, however, affords more opening for the improbable, the chief factor in the marvelous, because in it the agents are not visibly before one. The scene of the pursuit of Hector would be ridiculous on the stage—the Greeks halting instead of pursuing him, and Achilles shaking his head to stop them;[21] but in the poem the absurdity is overlooked. The marvelous, however, is a cause of pleasure, as is shown by the fact that we all tell a story with additions, in the belief that we are doing our hearers a pleasure.

Homer more than any other has taught the rest of us the art of framing lies in the right way. I mean the use of paralogism.

---

20 [*Centaur.* Cf. 1447b.—TR. NOTE.]
21 [*Iliad,* XXIII, 205.—TR. NOTE.]

Whenever, if A is or happens, a consequent, B, is or happens, men's notion is that, if the B is, the A also is—but that is a false conclusion. Accordingly, if A is untrue, but there is something else, B, that on the assumption of its truth follows as its consequent, the right thing then is to add on the B. Just because we know the truth of the consequent, we are in our own minds led on to the erroneous inference of the truth of the antecedent. Here is an instance, from the *Bath-story* in the *Odyssey*.[22]

A likely impossibility is always preferable to an unconvincing possibility. The story should never be made up of improbable incidents; there should be nothing of the sort in it. If, however, such incidents are unavoidable, they should be outside the piece, like the hero's ignorance in *Oedipus* of the circumstances of Laius' death; not within it, like the report of the Pythian games in *Electra*,[23] or the man's having come to Mysia from Tegea without uttering a word on the way, in *The Mysians*.[24] So that it is ridiculous to say that one's Plot would have been spoilt without them, since it is fundamentally wrong to make up such Plots. If the poet has taken such a Plot, however, and one sees that he might have put it in a more probable form, he is guilty of absurdity as well as a fault of art. Even in the *Odyssey* the improbabilities in the setting-ashore of Ulysses[25] would be clearly intolerable in the hands of an inferior poet. As it is, the poet conceals them, his other excellences veiling their absurdity. Elaborate Diction, however, is required only in places where there is no action, and no Character or Thought to be revealed. Where there is Character or Thought, on the other hand, an over-ornate Diction tends to obscure them.

---

22 [XIX, 164-260.—TR. NOTE.]
23 [Sophocles, *Electra*, 660 ff.—TR. NOTE.]
24 [Probably by Aeschylus.—TR. NOTE.]
25 [XIII, 116 ff.—TR. NOTE.]

Chapter Twenty-Five

§ POSSIBLE CRITICISMS OF AN EPIC OR TRAGEDY AND THE ANSWERS TO THEM

As regards Problems and their Solutions, one may see the number and nature of the assumptions on which they proceed by viewing the matter in the following way. (1) The poet being an imitator just like the painter or other maker of likenesses, he must necessarily in all instances represent things in one or other of three aspects, either as they were or are, or as they are said or thought to be or to have been, or as they ought to be. (2) All this he does in language, with an admixture, it may be, of strange words and metaphors, as also of the various modified forms of words, since the use of these is conceded in poetry. (3) It is to be remembered, too, that there is not the same kind of correctness in poetry as in politics, or indeed any other art. There is, however, within the limits of poetry itself a possibility of two kinds of error, the one directly, the other only accidentally connected with the art. If the poet meant to describe the thing correctly, and failed through lack of power of expression, his art itself is at fault. But if it was through his having meant to describe it in some incorrect way (e.g., to make the horse in movement have both right legs thrown forward) that the technical error (one in 1460b a matter of, say, medicine or some other special science), or impossibilities of whatever kind they may be, have got into his description, his error in that case is not in the essentials of the poetic art. These, therefore, must be the premises of the Solutions in answer to the criticisms involved in the Problems.

As to the criticisms relating to the poet's art itself, any impossibilities there may be in his descriptions of things are faults. But from another point of view they are justifiable, if they serve the end of poetry itself—if (to assume what we have said of that end) they make the effect of either that very portion of the work or some other portion more astounding. The Pursuit of Hector is an instance in point. If, however, the poetic end might have been as well or better attained without sacrifice of technical correctness in such matters, the impossibility is not to be justified, since the description should be, if it can, entirely free from error. One may ask, too, whether the error is in a matter directly or only accidentally connected with the poetic art; since it is a lesser error in an artist not to know, for instance, that the hind has no horns, than to produce an unrecognizable picture of one.

If the poet's description be criticized as not true to fact, one may urge perhaps that the object ought to be as described—an answer like that of Sophocles, who said that he drew men as they ought to be, and Euripides as they were. If the description, however, be neither true nor of the thing as it ought to be, the answer must be then, that it is in accordance with opinion. The tales about Gods, for instance, may be as wrong as Xenophanes thinks, neither true nor the better thing to say; but they are certainly in accordance with opinion. Of other statements in poetry one may perhaps say, not that they are better than the truth, but that the fact was so at the time; e.g. the description of the arms: 'their spears stood upright, butt-end upon the ground';[26] for that was the usual way of fixing them then, as it is still with the Illyrians. As for the question whether something said or done in a poem is morally right or not, in dealing with that one should consider not only the intrinsic quality of the actual word or deed, but also the person who says or does it, the person to whom he says or does it, the time, the means, and the motive of the agent —whether he does it to attain a greater good, or to avoid a greater evil.

26 [*Iliad,* X, 152.—TR. NOTE.]
27 [Line 663.—TR. NOTE.]

Speaking generally, one has to justify (1) the Impossible by reference to the requirements of poetry, or to the better, or to opinion. For the purposes of poetry a convincing impossibility is preferable to an unconvincing possibility; and if men such as Zeuxis depicted be impossible, the answer is that it is better they should be like that, as the artist ought to improve on his model. (2) The Improbable one has to justify either by showing it to be in accordance with opinion, or by urging that at times it is not improbable; for there is a probability of things happening also against probability. (3) The contradictions found in the poet's language one should first test as one does an opponent's confutation in a dialectical argument, so as to see whether he means the same thing, in the same relation, and in the same sense, before admitting that he has contradicted either something he has said himself or what a man of sound sense assumes as true. But there is no possible apology for improbability of Plot or depravity of character, when they are not necessary and no use is made of them, like the improbability in the appearance of Aegeus in *Medea*[27] and the baseness of Meneiaus in *Orestes*.

The objections, then, of critics start with faults of five kinds: the allegation is always that something is either (1) impossible, (2) improbable, (3) corrupting, (4) contradictory, or (5) against technical correctness. . . .

Chapter Twenty-Six

§ TRAGEDY ARTISTICALLY SUPERIOR TO EPIC POETRY

The question may be raised whether the epic or the tragic is the higher form of imitation. It may be argued that, if the less vulgar is the higher, and the less vulgar is always that which addresses the better public, an art addressing any and every one is of a very vulgar order. It is a belief that their public cannot see the meaning, unless they add something themselves, that causes the perpetual movements of the performers—bad flute-players, for instance, rolling about, if quoit-throwing is to be represented, and pulling at the conductor, if Scylla is the subject of the piece. Tragedy, then, is said to be an art of this order—to be in fact just what the later actors were in the eyes of their predecessors; for Mynniscus used to call Callippides "the ape," because he thought he so overacted his parts; and a similar view was taken of 1462a Pindarus also. All Tragedy, however, is said to stand to the Epic as the newer to the older school of actors. The one, accordingly, is said to address a cultivated audience, which does not need the accompaniment of gesture; the other, an uncultivated one. If, therefore, Tragedy is a vulgar art, it must clearly be lower than the Epic.

The answer to this is twofold. In the first place, one may urge (1) that the censure does not touch the art of the dramatic poet, but only that of his interpreter; for it is quite possible to overdo the gesturing even in an epic recital, as did Sosistratus, and in a singing contest, as did Mnasitheus of Opus. (2) That one should not condemn all movement, unless one means to condemn even the dance, but only that of ignoble people—which is the point of the criticism passed on Callippides and in the present day on others, that their women are not like gentlewomen. (3) That Tragedy may produce its effect even without movement or action in just the same way as Epic poetry; for from the mere reading of a play its quality may be seen. So that, if it be superior in all other respects, this element of inferiority is no necessary part of it.

In the second place, one must remember (1) that Tragedy has everything that the Epic has (even the epic metre being admissible), together with a not inconsiderable addition in the shape of the Music (a very real factor in the pleasure of the drama) and the Spectacle. (2) That its reality of presentation is felt in the play as read, as well as in the play as acted. (3) That the tragic imitation requires less space for the attainment of its end; which is a great 1462b advantage, since the more concentrated effect is more pleasurable than one with a large admixture of time to dilute it— consider the *Oedipus* of Sophocles, for instance, and the effect of expanding it into the number of lines of the *Iliad*. (4) That there is less unity in the imitation of the epic poets, as is proved by the fact that any one work of theirs supplies matter for several tragedies; the result being that, if they take what is really a single story, it seems curt when briefly told, and thin and waterish when on the scale of length usual with their verse. In saying that there is less unity in an epic, I mean an epic made up of a plurality of actions, in the same way as the *Iliad* and *Odyssey* have many such parts, each one of them in itself of some magnitude; yet the structure of the two Homeric poems is as perfect as can be, and the action in them is as nearly as possible one action. If, then, Tragedy is superior in these respects, and also, besides these, in its poetic effect (since the two forms of poetry should give us, not any or every pleasure, but the very special kind we have mentioned), it is clear that, as attaining the poetic effect better than the Epic, it will be the higher form of art.

So much for Tragedy and Epic poetry— for these two arts in general and their species; the number and nature of their constituent parts; the causes of success and failure in them; the Objections of the critics, and the Solutions in answer to them.

PLOTINUS

(205-270)

Plotinus is the principal figure of the Neoplatonic school and (unless Augustine is reckoned as an ancient) the last great philosopher of antiquity. Born somewhere in Egypt, he came at the age of twenty-seven to Alexandria to study philosophy. Twelve years later, after having accompanied the Emperor Gordian on a military expedition to the East, he settled in Rome. There he wrote the treatises that were subsequently collected by his disciple and editor, Porphyry, and were issued as a single work entitled *Enneads* (composed of six sets of nine treatises each). Porphyry's *Life* is the main source of information concerning Plotinus. The influence of his work upon modern thought commences in 1492 with the Latin translation by Ficino.

The two treatises presented here are like an extract of those passages from the *Symposium* and *Phaedrus* of Plato that epitomize what might be called the subdivision on aesthetics of the theory of ideas. They are no substitute for Plato but as a restatement could hardly be surpassed. Plato's idea of love and its relation to beauty is perhaps not unfolded in sufficient detail by Plotinus; but every other element is represented—notably, the ascent from the senses to the pure intellect and from earthly to "heavenly" beauty upon the ladder whose rungs are lower and higher grades of perfection.

Plotinus gives us our main example (the other is by Hegel) of metaphysical aesthetics. But the problem with which he starts off in the first few paragraphs (what gives beauty to material forms) is similar to the one we find discussed by many authors who have no thought of appealing, like Plotinus, to transcendent, metaphysical entities for its solution. They hold that this appeal does not solve the problem, and they would regard the fervid, almost mystical, tone and the mood of exaltation of the *Enneads* as only obscuring the issues. But there can be no doubt as to the power and influence that this kind of approach has had throughout history, especially among those who are not philosophers. And whatever our loyalties, we ought to concede that aesthetic problems must be looked at from all sides, including this one, on which Plato's mark is so deeply graven.

PLOTINUS

On Beauty

(Translated by Stephen MacKenna)

From The Enneads, *Stephen MacKenna,
trans. New York: Pantheon Books, 1956.
Reprinted by permission of Pantheon Books,
a division of Random House, Inc.*

FIRST ENNEAD

Sixth Tractate

§ ONE

Beauty addresses itself chiefly to sight; but there is a beauty for the hearing too, as in certain combinations of words and in all kinds of music, for melodies and cadences are beautiful; and minds that lift themselves above the realm of sense to a higher order are aware of beauty in the conduct of life, in actions, in character, in the pursuits of the intellect; and there is the beauty of the virtues. What loftier beauty there may be, yet, our argument will bring to light.

What, then, is it that gives comeliness to material forms and draws the ear to the sweetness perceived in sounds, and what is the secret of the beauty there is in all that derives from Soul?

Is there some One Principle from which all take their grace, or is there a beauty peculiar to the embodied and another for the bodiless? Finally, one or many, what would such a Principle be?

Consider that some things, material shapes for instance, are gracious not by anything inherent but by something communicated, while others are lovely of themselves, as, for example, Virtue.

The same bodies appear sometimes beautiful, sometimes not; so that there is a good deal between being body and being beautiful.

What, then, is this something that shows itself in certain material forms? This is the natural beginning of our inquiry.

What is it that attracts the eyes of those to whom a beautiful object is presented, and calls them, lures them, towards it, and fills them with joy at the sight? If we possess ourselves of this, we have at once a standpoint for the wider survey.

Almost everyone declares that the symmetry of parts towards each other and towards a whole, with, besides, a certain charm of colour, constitutes the beauty recognized by the eye, that in visible things, as indeed in all else, universally, the beautiful thing is essentially symmetrical, patterned.

But think what this means.

Only a compound can be beautiful, never anything devoid of parts; and only a whole; the several parts will have beauty, not in themselves, but only as working together to give a comely total. Yet beauty in an aggregate demands beauty in details: it cannot be constructed out of ugliness; its law must run throughout.

All the loveliness of colour and even the light of the sun, being devoid of parts and so not beautiful by symmetry, must be ruled out of the realm of beauty. And how comes gold to be a beautiful thing? And lightning by night, and the stars, why are these so fair?

In sounds also the simple must be proscribed, though often in a whole noble composition each several tone is delicious in itself.

Again since the one face, constant in symmetry, appears sometimes fair and sometimes not, can we doubt that beauty is something more than symmetry, that symmetry itself owes its beauty to a remoter principle?

Turn to what is attractive in methods of life or in the expression of thought; are we to call in symmetry here? What symmetry is to be found in noble conduct, or excellent laws, in any form of mental pursuit?

What symmetry can there be in points of abstract thought?

The symmetry of being accordant with each other? But there may be accordance or entire identity where there is nothing but ugliness: the proposition that honesty is merely a generous artlessness chimes in the most perfect harmony with the proposition that morality means weakness of will; the accordance is complete.

Then again, all the virtues are a beauty of the Soul, a beauty authentic beyond any of these others; but how does symmetry enter here? The Soul, it is true, is not a simple unity, but still its virtue cannot have the symmetry of size or of number: what standard of measurement could preside over the compromise or the coalescence of the Soul's faculties or purposes?

Finally, how by this theory would there be beauty in the Intellectual-Principle, essentially the solitary?

§ TWO

Let us, then, go back to the source, and indicate at once the Principle that bestows beauty on material things.

Undoubtedly this Principle exists; it is something that is perceived at the first glance, something which the Soul names as from an ancient knowledge and, recognizing, welcomes it, enters into unison with it.

But let the Soul fall in with the Ugly and at once it shrinks within itself, denies the thing, turns away from it, not accordant, resenting it.

Our interpretation is that the Soul—by the very truth of its nature, by its affiliation to the noblest Existents in the hierarchy of Being—when it sees anything of that kin, or any trace of that kinship, thrills with an immediate delight, takes its own to itself, and thus stirs anew to the sense of its nature and of all its affinity.

But, is there any such likeness between the loveliness of this world and the splendours in the Supreme? Such a likeness in the particulars would make the two orders alike: but what is there in common between beauty here and beauty There?

We hold that all the loveliness of this world comes by communion in Ideal-Form.

All shapelessness whose kind admits of pattern and form, as long as it remains outside of Reason and Idea, is ugly by that very isolation from the Divine-Thought. And this is the Absolute Ugly: an ugly thing is something that has not been entirely mastered by pattern, that is by Reason, the Matter not yielding at all points and in all respects to Ideal-Form.

But where the Ideal-Form has entered, it has grouped and co-ordinated what from a diversity of parts was to become a unity: it has rallied confusion into co-operation: it has made the sum one harmonious coherence: for the Idea is a unity and what it moulds must come to unity as far as multiplicity may.

And on what has thus been compacted to unity, Beauty enthrones itself, giving itself to the parts as to the sum: when it lights on some natural unity, a thing of like parts, then it gives itself to that whole. Thus, for an illustration, there is the beauty, conferred by craftsmanship, of all a house with all its parts, and the beauty which some natural quality may give to a single stone.

This, then, is how the material thing becomes beautiful—by communicating in the thought that flows from the Divine.

§ THREE

And the Soul includes a faculty peculiarly addressed to Beauty—one incomparably sure in the appreciation of its own, when Soul entire is enlisted to support its judgement.

Or perhaps the Soul itself acts immediately, affirming the Beautiful where it finds something accordant with the Ideal-Form within itself, using this Idea as a canon of accuracy in its decision.

But what accordance is there between the material and that which antedates all Matter?

On what principle does the architect, when he finds the house standing before him correspondent with his inner ideal of a house, pronounce it beautiful? Is it not that the house before him, the stones apart, is the inner idea stamped upon the mass of exterior matter, the indivisible exhibited in diversity?

So with the perceptive faculty: discerning in certain objects the Ideal-Form which has bound and controlled shapeless matter, opposed in nature to Idea, seeing further stamped upon the common shapes some shape excellent above the common, it gathers into unity what still remains fragmentary, catches it up and carries it within, no longer a thing of parts, and presents it to the Ideal-Principle as something concordant and congenial, a natural friend: the joy here is like that of a good man who discerns in a youth the early signs of a virtue consonant with the achieved perfection within his own soul.

The beauty of colour is also the outcome of a unification: it derives from shape, from the conquest of the darkness inherent in Matter by the pouring-in of light, the unembodied, which is a Rational-Principle and an Ideal-Form.

Hence it is that Fire itself is splendid beyond all material bodies, holding the rank of Ideal-Principle to the other elements, making ever upwards, the subtlest and sprightliest of all bodies, as very near to the unembodied; itself alone admitting no other, all the others penetrated by it: for they take warmth but this is never cold; it has colour primally; they receive the Form of colour from it: hence the splendour of its light, the splendour that belongs to the Idea. And all that has resisted and is but uncertainly held by its light remains outside of beauty, as not having absorbed the plenitude of the Form of colour.

And harmonies unheard in sound create the harmonies we hear and wake the Soul to the consciousness of beauty, showing it the one essence in another kind: for the measures of our sensible music are not arbitrary but are determined by the Principle whose labour is to dominate Matter and bring pattern into being.

Thus far of the beauties of the realm of sense, images and shadow-pictures, fugitives that have entered into Matter—to adorn, and to ravish, where they are seen.

§ FOUR

But there are earlier and loftier beauties than these. In the sense-bound life we are no longer granted to know them, but the Soul, taking no help from the organs, sees and proclaims them. To the vision of these we must mount, leaving sense to its own low place.

As it is not for those to speak of the graceful forms of the material world who have never seen them or known their grace —men born blind, let us suppose—in the same way those must be silent upon the beauty of noble conduct and of learning and all that order who have never cared for such things, nor may those tell of the splendour of virtue who have never known the face of Justice and of Moral-Wisdom beautiful beyond the beauty of Evening and of Dawn.

Such vision is for those only who see with the Soul's sight—and at the vision, they will rejoice, and awe will fall upon them and a trouble deeper than all the rest could ever stir, for now they are moving in the realm of Truth.

This is the spirit that Beauty must ever induce, wonderment and a delicious trouble, longing and love and a trembling that is all delight. For the unseen all this may be felt as for the seen; and this the Souls feel for it, every Soul in some degree, but those the more deeply that are the more truly apt to this higher love—just as all take delight in the beauty of the body but all are not stung as sharply, and those only that feel the keener wound are known as Lovers.

§ FIVE

These Lovers, then, lovers of the beauty outside of sense, must be made to declare themselves.

What do you feel in presence of the grace you discern in actions, in manners, in sound morality, in all the works and fruits of virtue, in the beauty of Souls? When you see that you yourselves are beautiful within, what do you feel? What is this Dionysiac exultation that thrills through your being, this straining upwards of all your soul, this longing to break away from the body and live sunken within the veritable self?

These are no other than the emotions of Souls under the spell of love.

But what is it that awakens all this passion? No shape, no colour, no grandeur of mass: all is for a Soul, something whose beauty rests upon no colour, for the moral wisdom the Soul enshrines and all the other hueless splendour of the virtues. It is that you find in yourself, or admire in another, loftiness of spirit; righteousness of life; disciplined purity; courage of the majestic face; gravity, modesty that goes fearless and tranquil and passionless; and, shining down upon all, the light of god-like Intellection.

All these noble qualities are to be reverenced and loved, no doubt, but what entitles them to be called beautiful?

They exist: they manifest themselves to us: anyone that sees them must admit that they have reality of Being; and is not Real-Being really beautiful?

But we have not yet shown by what property in them they have wrought the

Soul to loveliness: what is this grace, this splendour as of Light, resting upon all the virtues?

Let us take the contrary, the ugliness of the Soul, and set that against its beauty: to understand, at once, what this ugliness is and how it comes to appear in the Soul will certainly open our way before us.

Let us then suppose an ugly Soul, dissolute, unrighteous: teeming with all the lusts; torn by internal discord; beset by the fears of its cowardice and the envies of its pettiness; thinking, in the little thought it has, only of the perishable and the base; perverse in all its impulses; the friend of unclean pleasures; living the life of abandonment to bodily sensation and delighting in its deformity.

What must we think but that all this shame is something that has gathered about the Soul, some foreign bane outraging it, soiling it, so that, encumbered with all manner of turpitude, it has no longer a clean activity or a clean sensation, but commands only a life smouldering dully under the crust of evil; that, sunk in manifold death, it no longer sees what a Soul should see, may no longer rest in its own being, dragged ever as it is towards the outer, the lower, the dark?

An unclean thing, I dare to say; flickering hither and thither at the call of objects of sense, deeply infected with the taint of body, occupied always in Matter, and absorbing Matter into itself; in its commerce with the Ignoble it has trafficked away for an alien nature its own essential Idea.

If a man has been immersed in filth or daubed with mud, his native comeliness disappears and all that is seen is the foul stuff besmearing him: his ugly condition is due to alien matter that has encrusted him, and if he is to win back his grace it must be his business to scour and purify himself and make himself what he was.

So, we may justly say, a Soul becomes ugly—by something foisted upon it, by sinking itself into the alien, by a fall, a descent into body, into Matter. The dishonour of the Soul is in its ceasing to be clean and apart. Gold is degraded when it is mixed with earthy particles; if these be worked out, the gold is left and is beautiful, isolated from all that is foreign, gold with gold alone. And so the Soul; let it be but cleared of the desires that come by its too intimate converse with the body, emancipated from all the passions, purged of all that embodiment has thrust upon it, withdrawn, a solitary, to itself again—in that moment the ugliness that came only from the alien is stripped away.

§ SIX

For, as the ancient teaching was, moral-discipline and courage and every virtue, not even excepting Wisdom itself, all is purification.

Hence the Mysteries with good reason adumbrate the immersion of the unpurified in filth, even in the Nether-World, since the unclean loves filth for its very filthiness, and swine foul of body find their joy in foulness.

What else is Sophrosyny,[1] rightly so-called, but to take no part in the pleasures of the body, to break away from them as unclean and unworthy of the clean? So too, Courage is but being fearless of the death which is but the parting of the Soul from the body, an event which no one can dread whose delight is to be his unmingled self. And Magnanimity is but disregard for the lure of things here. And Wisdom is but the Act of the Intellectual-Principle withdrawn from the lower places and leading the Soul to the Above.

The Soul thus cleansed is all Idea and Reason, wholly free of body, intellective, entirely of that divine order from which the wellspring of Beauty rises and all the race of Beauty.

---

[1] [This term is usually rendered into English as "temperance" or "self-control."—ED. NOTE.]

Hence the Soul heightened to the Intellectual-Principle is beautiful to all its power. For Intellection and all that proceeds from Intellection are the Soul's beauty, a graciousness native to it and not foreign, for only with these is it truly Soul. And it is just to say that in the Soul's becoming a good and beautiful thing is its becoming like to God, for from the Divine comes all the Beauty and all the Good in beings.

We may even say that Beauty *is* the Authentic-Existents and Ugliness is the Principle contrary to Existence: and the Ugly is also the primal evil; therefore its contrary is at once good and beautiful, or is Good and Beauty: and hence the one method will discover to us the Beauty-Good and the Ugliness-Evil.

And Beauty, this Beauty which is also The Good, must be posed as The First: directly deriving from this First is the Intellectual-Principle which is pre-eminently the manifestation of Beauty; through the Intellectual-Principle Soul is beautiful. The beauty in things of a lower order—actions and pursuits for instance—comes by operation of the shaping Soul which is also the author of the beauty found in the world of sense. For the Soul, a divine thing, a fragment as it were of the Primal Beauty, makes beautiful to the fullness of their capacity all things whatsoever that it grasps and moulds.

§ SEVEN

Therefore we must ascend again towards the Good, the desired of every Soul. Anyone that has seen This, knows what I intend when I say that it is beautiful. Even the desire of it is to be desired as a Good. To attain it is for those that will take the upward path, who will set all their forces towards it, who will divest themselves of all that we have put on in our descent: so, to those that approach the Holy Celebrations of the Mysteries, there are appointed purifications and the laying aside of the garments worn before, and the entry in nakedness—until, passing, on the upward way, all that is other than the God, each in the solitude of himself shall behold that solitary-dwelling Existence, the Apart, the Unmingled, the Pure, that from Which all things depend, for Which all look and live and act and know, the Source of Life and of Intellection and of Being.

And one that shall know this vision—with what passion of love shall he not be seized, with what pang of desire, what longing to be molten into one with This, what wondering delight! If he that has never seen this Being must hunger for It as for all his welfare, he that has known must love and reverence It as the very Beauty; he will be flooded with awe and gladness, stricken by a salutary terror; he loves with a veritable love, with sharp desire; all other loves than this he must despise, and disdain all that once seemed fair.

This, indeed, is the mood even of those who, having witnessed the manifestation of Gods or Supernals, can never again feel the old delight in the comeliness of material forms: what then are we to think of one that contemplates Absolute Beauty in Its essential integrity, no accumulation of flesh and matter, no dweller on earth or in the heavens—so perfect Its purity—far above all such things in that they are nonessential, composite, not primal but descending from This?

Beholding this Being—the Choragus of all Existence, the Self-Intent that ever gives forth and never takes—resting, rapt, in the vision and possession of so lofty a loveliness, growing to Its likeness, what Beauty can the Soul yet lack? For This, the Beauty supreme, the absolute, and the primal, fashions Its lovers to Beauty and makes them also worthy of love.

And for This, the sternest and the uttermost combat is set before the Souls; all our labour is for This, lest we be left without part in this noblest vision, which to attain is to be blessed in the blissful sight, which to fail of is to fail utterly.

For not he that has failed of the joy that is in colour or in visible forms, not he that has failed of power or of honours or of kingdom has failed, but only he that has failed of only This, for Whose winning he should renounce kingdoms and command over earth and ocean and sky, if only, spurning the world of sense from beneath his feet, and straining to This, he may see.

§ EIGHT

But what must we do? How lies the path? How come to vision of the inaccessible Beauty, dwelling as if in consecrated precincts, apart from the common ways where all may see, even the profane?

He that has the strength, let him arise and withdraw into himself, foregoing all that is known by the eyes, turning away for ever from the material beauty that once made his joy. When he perceives those shapes of grace that show in body, let him not pursue: he must know them for copies, vestiges, shadows, and hasten away towards That they tell of. For if anyone follow what is like a beautiful shape playing over water—is there not a myth telling in symbol of such a dupe, how he sank into the depths of the current and was swept away to nothingness? So too, one that is held by material beauty and will not break free shall be precipitated, not in body but in Soul, down to the dark depths loathed of the Intellective-Being, where, blind even in the Lower-World, he shall have commerce only with shadows, there as here.

"Let us flee then to the beloved Fatherland": this is the soundest counsel. But what is this flight? How are we to gain the open sea? For Odysseus is surely a parable to us when he commands the flight from the sorceries of Circe or Calypso—not content to linger for all the pleasure offered to his eyes and all the delight of sense filling his days.

The Fatherland to us is There whence we have come, and There is The Father.

What then is our course, what the manner of our flight? This is not a journey for the feet; the feet bring us only from land to land; nor need you think of coach or ship to carry you away; all this order of things you must set aside and refuse to see: you must close the eyes and call instead upon another vision which is to be waked within you, a vision, the birth-right of all, which few turn to use.

§ NINE

And this inner vision, what is its operation?

Newly awakened—it is all too feeble to bear the ultimate splendour. Therefore the Soul must be trained—to the habit of remarking, first, all noble pursuits, then the works of beauty produced not by the labour of the arts but by the virtue of men known for their goodness: lastly, you must search the souls of those that have shaped these beautiful forms.

But how are you to see into a virtuous Soul and know its loveliness?

Withdraw into yourself and look. And if you do not find yourself beautiful yet, act as does the creator of a statue that is to be made beautiful: he cuts away here, he smoothes there, he makes this line lighter, this other purer, until a lovely face has grown upon his work. So do you also: cut away all that is excessive, straighten all that is crooked, bring light to all that is overcast, labour to make all one glow of beauty and never cease chiselling your statue, until there shall shine out on you from it the godlike splendour of virtue, until you shall see the perfect goodness surely established in the stainless shrine.

When you know that you have become this perfect work, when you are self-gathered in the purity of your being, nothing now remaining that can shatter that inner unity, nothing from without clinging to the authentic man, when you find yourself wholly true to your essential nature, wholly that only veritable Light which is not measured by space, not narrowed to any circumscribed form nor again diffused as a thing void of term, but ever unmeasurable as something greater than all measure and more than all quantity—when you perceive that you have grown to this, you are now become very vision: now call up all your confidence, strike forward yet a step—you need a guide no longer—strain, and see.

This is the only eye that sees the mighty Beauty. If the eye that adventures the vision be dimmed by vice, impure, or weak, and unable in its cowardly blenching to see the uttermost brightness, then it sees nothing even though another point to what lies plain to sight before it. To any vision must be brought an eye adapted to what is to be seen, and having some likeness to it. Never did eye see the sun unless it had first become sunlike, and never can the Soul have vision of the First Beauty unless itself be beautiful.

Therefore, first let each become godlike and each beautiful who cares to see God and Beauty. So, mounting, the Soul will come first to the Intellectual-Principle and survey all the beautiful Ideas in the Supreme and will avow that this is Beauty, that the Ideas are Beauty. For by their efficacy comes all Beauty else, by the offspring and essence of the Intellectual-Being. What is beyond the Intellectual-Principle we affirm to be the nature of Good radiating Beauty before it. So that, treating the Intellectual-Cosmos as one, the first is the Beautiful: if we make distinction there, the Realm of Ideas constitutes the Beauty of the Intellectual Sphere; and The Good, which lies beyond, is the Fountain at once and Principle of Beauty: the Primal Good and the Primal Beauty have the one dwelling place and, thus, always, Beauty's seat is There.

PLOTINUS

On Intellectual Beauty

(Translated by Stephen MacKenna)

From The Enneads, *Stephen MacKenna, trans. New York: Pantheon Books, 1956. Reprinted by permission of Pantheon Books, a division of Random House, Inc.*

FIFTH ENNEAD

Eighth Tractate

§ ONE

It is a principle with us that one who has attained to the vision of the Intellectual Beauty and grasped the beauty of the Authentic Intellect will be able also to come to understand the Father and Transcendent of that Divine Being. It concerns us, then, to try to see and say, for ourselves and as far as such matters may be told, how the Beauty of the Divine Intellect and of the Intellectual Cosmos may be revealed to contemplation.

Let us go to the realm of magnitudes:— suppose two blocks of stone lying side by side: one is unpatterned, quite untouched by art; the other has been minutely wrought by the craftsman's hands into some statue of god or man, a Grace or a Muse, or if a human being, not a portrait but a creation in which the sculptor's art has concentrated all loveliness.

Now it must be seen that the stone thus brought under the artist's hand to the beauty of form is beautiful not as stone— for so the crude block would be as pleasant —but in virtue of the Form or Idea introduced by the art. This form is not in the material; it is in the designer before ever it enters the stone; and the artificer holds it not by his equipment of eyes and hands but by his participation in his art. The beauty, therefore, exists in a far higher state in the art; for it does not come over integrally into the work; that original beauty is not transferred; what comes over is a derivative and a minor: and even that shows itself upon the statue not integrally and with entire realization of intention but only in so far as it has subdued the resistance of the material.

Art, then, creating in the image of its own nature and content, and working by the Idea or Reason-Principle of the beautiful object it is to produce, must itself be beautiful in a far higher and purer degree since it is the seat and source of that beauty, indwelling in the art, which must naturally be more complete than any comeliness of the external. In the degree in which the beauty is diffused by entering into matter, it is so much the weaker than that concentrated in unity; everything that reaches outwards is the less for it, strength less strong, heat less hot, every power less potent, and so beauty less beautiful.

Then again every prime cause must be, within itself, more powerful than its effect can be: the musical does not derive from an unmusical source but from music; and so the art exhibited in the material work derives from an art yet higher.

Still the arts are not to be slighted on the ground that they create by imitation of natural objects; for, to begin with, these natural objects are themselves imitations; then, we must recognize that they give no bare reproduction of the thing seen but go back to the Reason-Principles from which Nature itself derives, and, furthermore, that much of their work is all their own; they are holders of beauty and add where nature is lacking. Thus Pheidias wrought the Zeus upon no model among things of sense but by apprehending what form Zeus must take if he chose to become manifest to sight.

§ TWO

But let us leave the arts and consider those works produced by Nature and admitted to be naturally beautiful which the creations of art are charged with imitating, all reasoning life and unreasoning things alike, but especially the consummate among them, where the moulder and maker has subdued the material and given the form he desired. Now what is the beauty here? It has nothing to do with the blood or the menstrual process: either there is also a colour and form apart from all this or there is nothing unless sheer ugliness or (at best) a bare recipient, as it were the mere Matter of beauty.

Whence shone forth the beauty of Helen, battle-sought; or of all those women like in loveliness to Aphrodite; or of Aphrodite herself; or of any human being that has been perfect in beauty; or of any of these gods manifest to sight, or unseen but carrying what would be beauty if we saw?

In all these is it not the Idea, something of that realm but communicated to the produced from within the producer, just as in works of art, we held, it is communicated from the arts to their creations? Now we can surely not believe that, while the made thing and the Idea thus impressed upon Matter are beautiful, yet the Idea not so alloyed but resting still with the creator— the Idea primal, immaterial, firmly a unity —is not Beauty.

If material extension were in itself the ground of beauty, then the creating principle, being without extension, could not be beautiful: but beauty cannot be made to depend upon magnitude since, whether in a large object or a small, the one Idea equally moves and forms the mind by its inherent power. A further indication is that as long as the object remains outside us we know nothing of it; it affects us by entry; but only as an Idea can it enter through the eyes which are not of scope to take an extended mass: we are, no doubt, simultaneously possessed of the magnitude which, however, we take in not as mass but by an elaboration upon the presented form.

Then again the principle producing the beauty must be, itself, ugly, neutral, or beautiful: ugly, it could not produce the opposite; neutral, why should its product be the one rather than the other? The Nature, then, which creates things so lovely must be itself of a far earlier beauty; we, undisciplined in discernment of the inward, knowing nothing of it, run after the outer, never understanding that it is the inner which stirs us; we are in the case of one who sees his own reflection but not realizing whence it comes goes in pursuit of it.

But that the thing we are pursuing is something different and that the beauty is not in the concrete object is manifest from the beauty there is in matters of study, in conduct and custom; briefly, in soul or mind. And it is precisely here that the greater beauty lies, perceived whenever you look to the wisdom in a man and delight in it, not wasting attention on the face, which may be hideous, but passing all appearance by and catching only at the inner comeliness, the truly personal; if you are still unmoved and cannot acknowledge beauty under such conditions, then looking to your own inner being you will find no beauty to delight you and it will be futile in that state to seek the greater vision, for you will be questing it through the ugly and impure.

This is why such matters are not spoken of to everyone; you, if you are conscious of beauty within, remember.

§ THREE

Thus there is in the Nature-Principle itself an Ideal archetype of the beauty that is found in material forms and, of that archetype again, the still more beautiful archetype in Soul, source of that in Nature. In the proficient soul this is brighter and of more advanced loveliness: adorning the soul and bringing to it a light from that greater light which is Beauty primally, its immediate presence sets the soul reflecting upon the quality of this prior, the archetype which has no such entries, and is present nowhere but remains in itself alone, and thus is not even to be called a Reason-Principle but is the creative source of the very first Reason-Principle which is the Beauty to which Soul serves as Matter.

This prior, then, is the Intellectual-Principle, the veritable, abiding and not fluctuant since not taking intellectual quality from outside itself. By what image, thus, can we represent it? We have nowhere to go but to what is less. Only from itself can we take an image of it; that is, there can be no representation of it, except in the sense that we represent gold by some portion of gold—purified, either actually or mentally, if it be impure—insisting at the same time that this is not the total thing gold, but merely the particular gold of a particular parcel. In the same way we learn in this matter from the purified Intellect in ourselves or, if you like, from the gods and the glory of the Intellect in them.

For assuredly all the gods are august and beautiful in a beauty beyond our speech. And what makes them so? Intellect; and especially Intellect operating within them (the divine sun and stars) to visibility. It is not through the loveliness of their corporeal forms: even those that have body are not gods by that beauty; it is in virtue of Intellect that they, too, are gods, and as gods beautiful. They do not veer between wisdom and folly: in the immunity of Intellect unmoving and pure, they are wise always, all-knowing, taking cognizance not of the human but of their own being and of all that lies within the contemplation of Intellect. Those of them whose dwelling is in the heavens are ever in this meditation—what task prevents them?—and from afar they look, too, into that further heaven by a lifting of the head. The gods belonging to that higher Heaven itself, they whose station is upon it and in it, see and know in virtue of their omnipresence to it. For all There is heaven; earth is heaven, and sea heaven; and animal and plant and man; all is the heavenly content of that heaven: and the gods in it, despising neither men nor anything else that is there where all is of the heavenly order, traverse all that country and all space in peace.

§ FOUR

To "live at ease" is There; and to these divine beings verity is mother and nurse, existence and sustenance; all that is not of process but of authentic being they see, and themselves in all: for all is transparent, nothing dark, nothing resistant; every being is lucid to every other, in breadth and depth; light runs through light. And each of them contains all within itself, and at the same time sees all in every other, so that everywhere there is all, and all is all and each all, and infinite the glory. Each of them is great; the small is great; the sun, There, is all the stars; and every star, again, is all the stars and sun. While some one manner of being is dominant in each, all are mirrored in every other.

Movement There is pure (as self-caused), for the moving principle is not a separate thing to complicate it as it speeds.

So, too, Repose is not troubled, for there is no admixture of the unstable; and the Beauty is all beauty since it is not resident in what is not beautiful. Each There walks upon no alien soil; its place is its essential self; and, as each moves, so to speak, towards what is Above, it is attended by the very ground from which it starts: there is no distinguishing between the Being and the Place; all is Intellect, the Principle and the ground on which it stands, alike. Thus we might think that our visible sky (the ground or place of the stars), lit as it is, produces the light which reaches us from it, though of course this is really produced by the stars (as it were, by the Principles

of light alone, not also by the ground as the analogy would require).

In our realm all is part rising from part and nothing can be more than partial; but There each being is an eternal product of a whole and is at once a whole and an individual manifesting as part but, to the keen vision There, known for the whole it is.

The myth of Lynceus seeing into the very deeps of the earth tells us of those eyes in the divine. No weariness overtakes this vision which yet brings no such satiety as would call for its ending; for there never was a void to be filled so that, with the fullness and the attainment of purpose, the sense of sufficiency be induced: nor is there any such incongruity within the divine that one Being There could be repulsive to another: and of course all There are unchangeable. This absence of satisfaction means only a satisfaction leading to no distaste for that which produces it; to see is to look the more, since for them to continue in the contemplation of an infinite self and of infinite objects is but to acquiesce in the bidding of their nature.

Life, pure, is never a burden; how then could there be weariness There where the living is most noble? That very life is wisdom, not a wisdom built up by reasonings but complete from the beginning, suffering no lack which could set it inquiring, a wisdom primal, unborrowed, not something added to the Being, but its very essence. No wisdom, thus, is greater; this is the authentic knowing, assessor to the divine Intellect as projected into manifestation simultaneously with it; thus, in the symbolic saying, Justice is assessor to Zeus.

[Perfect wisdom:] for all the Principles of this order, dwelling There, are as it were visible images projected from themselves, so that all becomes an object of contemplation to contemplators immeasurably blessed. The greatness and power of the wisdom There we may know from this, that it embraces all the real Beings, and has made all and all follow it, and yet that it is itself those beings, which sprang into being with it, so that all is one and the essence There is wisdom. If we have failed to understand, it is that we have thought of knowledge as a mass of theorems and an accumulation of propositions, though that is false even for our sciences of the sense-realm. But in case this should be questioned, we may leave our own sciences for the present, and deal with the knowing in the Supreme at which Plato glances where he speaks of "that knowledge which is not a stranger in something strange to it"—though in what sense, he leaves us to examine and declare, if we boast ourselves worthy of the discussion. This is probably our best starting-point.

§ FIVE

All that comes to be, work of nature or of craft, some wisdom has made: everywhere a wisdom presides at a making.

No doubt the wisdom of the artist may be the guide of the work; it is sufficient explanation of the wisdom exhibited in the arts; but the artist himself goes back, after all, to that wisdom in Nature which is embodied in himself; and this is not a wisdom built up of theorems but one totality, not a wisdom consisting of manifold detail co-ordinated into a unity but rather a unity working out into detail.

Now, if we could think of this as the primal wisdom, we need look no further, since, at that, we have discovered a principle which is neither a derivative nor a "stranger in something strange to it." But if we are told that, while this Reason-Principle is in Nature, yet Nature itself is its source, we ask how Nature came to possess it; and, if Nature derived it from some other source, we ask what that other source may be; if, on the contrary, the principle is self-sprung, we need look no further: but if (as we assume) we are referred to the Intellectual-Principle we must make clear whether the Intellectual-Principle engendered the wisdom: if we learn that it did, we ask whence: if from itself, then inevitably it is itself Wisdom.

The true Wisdom, then (found to be identical with the Intellectual-Principle), is Real Being; and Real Being is Wisdom; it is wisdom that gives value to Real Being; and Being is Real in virtue of its origin in wisdom. It follows that all forms of existence not possessing wisdom are, indeed, Beings in right of the wisdom which went to their forming, but, as not in themselves possessing it, are not Real Beings.

We cannot, therefore, think that the divine Beings of that sphere, or the other supremely blessed There, need look to our apparatus of science: all of that realm (the very Beings themselves), all is noble image, such images as we may conceive to lie within the soul of the wise—but There not as inscription but as authentic existence. The ancients had this in mind when they declared the Ideas (Forms) to be Beings, Essentials.

§ SIX

Similarly, as it seems to me, the wise of Egypt—whether in precise knowledge or by a prompting of nature—indicated the truth where, in their effort towards philosophical statement, they left aside the writing-forms that take in the detail of words and sentences—those characters that represent sounds and convey the propositions of reasoning—and drew pictures instead, engraving in the temple-inscriptions a separate image for every separate item: thus they exhibited the absence of discursiveness in the Intellectual Realm.

For each manifestation of knowledge and wisdom is a distinct image, an object in itself an immediate unity, not an aggregate of discursive reasoning and detailed willing. Later from this wisdom in unity there appears, in another form of being, an image, already less compact, which announces the original in terms of discourse and seeks the causes by which things are such that the wonder rises how a generated world can be so excellent.

For, one who knows must declare his wonder that this Wisdom, while not itself containing the causes by which Being exists and takes such excellence, yet imparts them to the entities produced in Being's realm. This excellence, whose necessity is scarcely or not at all manifest to search, exists, if we could but find it out, before all searching and reasoning.

What I say may be considered in one chief thing, and thence applied to all the particular entities.

§ SEVEN

Consider the universe: we are agreed that its existence and its nature come to it from beyond itself; are we, now, to imagine that its maker first thought it out in detail— the earth, and its necessary situation in the middle; water and, again, its position as lying upon the earth; all the other elements and objects up to the sky in due place and order; living beings with their appropriate forms as we know them, their inner organs and their outer limbs—and that having thus appointed every item beforehand, he then set about the execution?

Such designing was not even possible; how could the plan for a universe come to one that had never looked outward? Nor could he work on material gathered from elsewhere as our craftsmen do, using hands and tools; feet and hands are of the later order.

One way, only, remains: all things must exist in something else; of that prior—since there is no obstacle, all being continuous within the realm of reality—there has suddenly appeared a sign, an image, whether given forth directly or through the ministry of soul or of some phase of soul, matters nothing for the moment: thus the entire aggregate of existence springs from the divine world, in greater beauty There because There unmingled but mingled here.

From the beginning to end all is gripped by the Forms of the Intellectual Realm: Matter itself is held by the Ideas of the elements and to these Ideas are added other Ideas and others again, so that it is hard to work down to crude Matter beneath all that sheathing of Idea. Indeed since Matter itself is, in its degree, an Idea—the lowest —all this universe is Idea and there is nothing that is not Idea as the archetype was. And all is made silently, since nothing had part in the making but Being and Idea— a further reason why creation went without toil. The Exemplar was the Idea of an All and so an All must come into being.

Thus nothing stood in the way of the Idea, and even now it dominates, despite all the clash of things: the creation is not hindered on its way even now; it stands firm in virtue of being All. To me, moreover, it seems that if we ourselves were archetypes, Ideas, veritable Being, and the Idea with which we construct here were our veritable Essence, then our creative power, too, would toillessly effect its purpose: as man now stands, he does not produce in his work a true image of himself: become man, he has ceased to be the All; ceasing to be man —we read—"he soars aloft and administers the Cosmos entire"; restored to the All he is maker of the All.

But—to our immediate purpose—it is possible to give a reason why the earth is set in the midst and why it is round and why the ecliptic runs precisely as it does, but, looking to the creating principle, we cannot say that because this was the way therefore things were so planned; we can say only that because the Exemplar is what it is, therefore the things of this world are good; the causing principle, we might put it, reached the conclusion before all formal reasoning and not from any premisses, not by sequence or plan but before either, since all of that order is later, all reason, demonstration, persuasion.

Since there is a Source, all the created

must spring from it and in accordance with it; and we are rightly told not to go seeking the causes impelling a Source to produce, especially when this is the perfectly sufficient Source and identical with the Term: a Source which is Source and Term must be the All-Unity, complete in itself.

§ EIGHT

This then is Beauty primally: it is entire and omnipresent as an entirety; and therefore in none of its parts or members lacking in beauty; beautiful thus beyond denial. Certainly it cannot be anything (be, for example, Beauty) without being wholly that thing; it can be nothing which it is to possess partially or in which it utterly fails (and therefore it must entirely be Beauty entire).

If this principle were not beautiful, what other could be? Its prior does not deign to be beautiful; that which is the first to manifest itself—Form and object of vision to the intellect—cannot but be lovely to see. It is to indicate this that Plato, drawing on something well within our observation, represents the Creator as approving the work he has achieved: the intention is to make us feel the lovable beauty of the archetype and of the Divine Idea; for to admire a representation is to admire the original upon which it was made.

It is not surprising if we fail to recognize what is passing within us: lovers, and those in general that admire beauty here, do not stay to reflect that it is to be traced, as of course it must be, to the Beauty There. That the admiration of the Demiurge is to be referred to the Ideal Exemplar is deliberately made evident by the rest of the passage: "He admired; and determined to bring the work into still closer likeness with the Exemplar": he makes us feel the magnificent beauty of the Exemplar by telling us that the Beauty sprung from this world is, itself, a copy from That.

And indeed if the divine did not exist, the

transcendently beautiful, in a beauty beyond all thought, what could be lovelier than the things we see? Certainly no reproach can rightly be brought against this world save only that it is not That.

§ NINE

Let us, then, make a mental picture of our universe: each member shall remain what it is, distinctly apart; yet all is to form, as far as possible, a complete unity so that whatever comes into view, say the outer orb of the heavens, shall bring immediately with it the vision, on the one plane, of the sun and of all the stars with earth and sea and all living things as if exhibited upon a transparent globe.

Bring this vision actually before your sight, so that there shall be in your mind the gleaming representation of a sphere, a picture holding all the things of the universe moving or in repose or (as in reality) some at rest, some in motion. Keep this sphere before you, and from it imagine another, a sphere stripped of magnitude and of spatial differences; cast out your inborn sense of Matter, taking care not merely to attenuate it: call on God, maker of the sphere whose image you now hold, and pray Him to enter. And may He come bringing His own Universe with all the gods that dwell in it —He who is the one God and all the gods, where each is all, blending into a unity, distinct in powers but all one god in virtue of that one divine power of many facets.

More truly, this is the one God who is all the gods; for, in the coming to be of all those, this, the one, has suffered no diminishing. He and all have one existence, while each again is distinct. It is distinction by state without interval: there is no outward form to set one here and another there and to prevent any from being an entire identity; yet there is no sharing of parts from one to another. Nor is each of those divine wholes a power in fragment, a power totalling to the sum of the measurable segments: the divine is one all-power, reaching out to infinity, powerful to infinity: and so great is God that his very members are infinites. What place can be named to which He does not reach?

Great, too, is this firmament of ours and all the powers constellated within it, but it would be greater still, unspeakably, but that there is inbound in it something of the petty power of body; no doubt the powers of fire and other bodily substances might themselves be thought very great, but in fact, it is through their failure in the true power that we see them burning, destroying, wearing things away, and slaving towards the production of life; they destroy because they are themselves in process of destruction, and they produce because they belong to the realm of the produced.

The power in that other world has merely Being and Beauty of Being. Beauty without Being could not be, nor Being voided of Beauty: abandoned of Beauty, Being loses something of its essence. Being is desirable because it is identical with Beauty; and Beauty is loved because it is Being. How then can we debate which is the cause of the other, where the nature is one? The very figment of Being needs some imposed image of Beauty to make it passable, and even to ensure its existence; it exists to the degree in which it has taken some share in the beauty of Idea; and the more deeply it has drawn on this, the less imperfect it is, precisely because the nature which is essentially the beautiful has entered into it the more intimately.

§ TEN

This is why Zeus, although the oldest of the gods and their sovereign, advances first (in the Phaedrus myth) towards that vision, followed by gods and demigods and such souls as are of strength to see. That Being appears before them from some unseen place and rising loftily over them pours its light upon all things, so that all gleams in its radiance; it upholds some beings, and they see; the lower are dazzled and turn away, unfit to gaze upon that sun, the trouble falling the more heavily on those most remote.

Of those looking upon that Being and its content, and able to see, all take something but not all the same vision always: intently gazing, one sees the fount and principle of Justice, another is filled with the sight of Moral Wisdom, the original of that quality as found, sometimes at least, among men, copied by them in their degree from the divine virtue which, covering all the expanse, so to speak, of the Intellectual Realm is seen, last attainment of all, by those who have known already many splendid visions.

The gods see, each singly and all as one. So, too, the souls; they see all There in right of being sprung, themselves, of that universe and therefore including all from beginning to end and having their existence There if only by that phase which belongs inherently to the Divine, though often too they are There entire, those of them that have not incurred separation.

This vision Zeus takes and it is for such of us, also, as share his love and appropriate our part in the Beauty There, the final object of all seeing, the entire beauty upon all things; for all There sheds radiance, and floods those that have found their way thither so that they too become beautiful; thus it will often happen that men climbing heights where the soil has taken a yellow glow will themselves appear so, borrowing colour from the place on which they move. The colour flowering on that other height we speak of is Beauty; or rather all There is light and beauty, through and through, for the beauty is no mere bloom upon the surface.

To those that do not see entire, the immediate impression is alone taken into account; but those drunken with this wine, filled with the nectar, all their soul penetrated by this beauty, cannot remain mere gazers: no longer is there a spectator outside gazing on an outside spectacle; the clear-eyed hold the vision within themselves, though, for the most part, they have no idea that it is within but look towards it as to something beyond them and see it as an object of vision caught by a direction of the will.

All that one sees as a spectacle is still external; one must bring the vision within and see no longer in that mode of separation but as we know ourselves; thus a man filled with a god—possessed by Apollo or by one of the Muses—need no longer look outside for his vision of the divine being; it is but finding the strength to see divinity within.

§ ELEVEN

Similarly any one, unable to see himself, but possessed by that God, has but to bring that divine-within before his consciousness and at once he sees an image of himself, himself lifted to a better beauty: now let him ignore that image, lovely though it is, and sink into a perfect self-identity, no such separation remaining; at once he forms a multiple unity with the God silently present; in the degree of his power and will, the two become one; should he turn back to the former duality, still he is pure and remains very near to the God; he has but to look again and the same presence is there.

This conversion brings gain: at the first stage, that of separation, a man is aware of self; but retreating inwards, he becomes possessor of all; he puts sense away behind him in dread of the separated life and becomes one in the Divine; if he plans to see in separation, he sets himself outside.

The novice must hold himself constantly under some image of the Divine Being and seek in the light of a clear conception; knowing thus, in a deep conviction, whither he is going—into what a sublimity he penetrates—he must give himself forthwith to the inner and, radiant with the Divine Intellections (with which he is now one),

be no longer the seer, but, as that place has made him, the seen.

Still, we will be told, one cannot be in beauty and yet fail to see it. The very contrary: to see the divine as something external is to be outside of it; to become it is to be most truly in beauty: since sight deals with the external, there can here be no vision unless in the sense of identification with the object.

And this identification amounts to a self-knowing, a self-consciousness, guarded by the fear of losing the self in the desire of a too wide awareness.

It must be remembered that sensations of the ugly and evil impress us more violently than those of what is agreeable and yet leave less knowledge as the residue of the shock: sickness makes the rougher mark, but health, tranquilly present, explains itself better; it takes the first place, it is the natural thing, it belongs to our being; illness is alien, unnatural, and thus makes itself felt by its very incongruity, while the other conditions are native and we take no notice. Such being our nature, we are most completely aware of ourselves when we are most completely identified with the object of our knowledge.

This is why in that other sphere, when we are deepest in that knowledge by intellection, we are aware of none; we are expecting some impression on sense, which has nothing to report since it has seen nothing and never could in that order see anything. The unbelieving element is sense; it is the other, the Intellectual-Principle, that sees; and if this too doubted, it could not even credit its own existence, for it can never stand away and with bodily eyes apprehend itself as a visible object.

§ TWELVE

We have told how this vision is to be procured, whether by the mode of separation or in identity: now, seen in either way, what does it give to report?

The vision has been of God in travail of a beautiful offspring, God engendering a universe within himself in a painless labour and—rejoiced in what he has brought into being, proud of his children—keeping all closely by Him, for the pleasure He has in his radiance and in theirs.

Of this offspring—all beautiful, but most beautiful those that have remained within —only one has become manifest without; from him (Zeus, sovereign over the visible universe), the youngest born, we may gather, as from some image, the greatness of the Father and of the Brothers that remain within the Father's house.

Still the manifested God cannot think that he has come forth in vain from the father; for through him another universe has arisen, beautiful as the image of beauty, and it could not be lawful that Beauty and Being should fail of a beautiful image.

This second Cosmos at every point copies the archetype: it has life and being in copy, and has beauty as springing from that diviner world. In its character of image it holds, too, that divine perpetuity without which it would only at times be truly representative and sometimes fail like a construction of art; for every image whose existence lies in the nature of things must stand during the entire existence of the archetype.

Hence it is false to put an end to the visible sphere as long as the Intellectual endures, or to found it upon a decision taken by its maker at some given moment.

That teaching shirks the penetration of such a making as is here involved: it fails to see that as long as the Supreme is radiant there can be no failing of its sequel but, that existing, all exists. And—since the necessity of conveying our meaning compels such terms—the Supreme has existed for ever and for ever will exist.

§ THIRTEEN

The God fettered (as in the Kronos Myth)

to an unchanging identity leaves the ordering of this universe to his son (to Zeus), for it could not be in his character to neglect his rule within the divine sphere, and, as though sated with the Authentic-Beauty, seek a lordship too recent and too poor for his might. Ignoring this lower world, Kronos (Intellectual-Principle) claims for himself his own father (Ouranos, the Absolute, or One) with all the upward-tending between them: and he counts all that tends to the inferior, beginning from his son (Zeus, the All-Soul), as ranking beneath him. Thus he holds a mid-position determined on the one side by the differentiation implied in the severance from the very highest and, on the other, by that which keeps him apart from the link between himself and the lower: he stands between a greater father and an inferior son. But since that father is too lofty to be thought of under the name of Beauty, the second God remains the primally beautiful.

Soul also has beauty, but is less beautiful than Intellect as being its image and therefore, though beautiful in nature, taking increase of beauty by looking to that original. Since then the All-Soul—to use the more familiar term—since Aphrodite herself is so beautiful, what name can we give to that other? If Soul is so lovely in its own right, of what quality must that prior be? And since its being is derived, what must that power be from which the Soul takes the double beauty, the borrowed and the inherent?

We ourselves possess beauty when we are true to our own being; our ugliness is in going over to another order; our self-knowledge, that is to say, is our beauty; in self-ignorance we are ugly.

Thus beauty is of the Divine and comes Thence only.

Do these considerations suffice to a clear understanding of the Intellectual Sphere or must we make yet another attempt by another road?

FRANCIS
HUTCHESON

(1694-1746)

Starting out as a schoolmaster and a licensed Presbyterian clergyman, Hutcheson was in 1729 elected to the chair of moral philosophy at the University of Glasgow, a post in which he remained until his death. In 1725 and 1728 he had published his *Four Essays,* including a work originally entitled "An Inquiry into the Original of Our Ideas of Beauty and Virtue, in Two Treatises, in Which the Principles of the Late Lord Shaftesbury Are Explained and Defended against the Author of the 'Fable of the Bees'; and the 'Ideas of Moral Good and Evil' Are Established According to the Sentiments of the Ancient Moralists, with an Attempt to Introduce a Mathematical Calculation on Subjects of Morality." The first of the two treatises is reprinted here.

The aesthetical notions of Shaftesbury are not to be found concentrated in any one place; and the opinions of Addison do not traverse but only touch on topics of aesthetics. We may say, then, that Hutcheson's was the first formal English essay on aesthetics that made an orderly review of the subject. It is, along with Baumgarten's *Reflections on Poetry* (1735) and *Aesthetica* (1750, 1758), one of the twin fountainheads of modern aesthetic theory—and very nearly a perfect handbook of the ideas that have figured in the development of aesthetics since Hutcheson's day. Beyond its larger themes—the disinterested character of the sense of beauty and the immediacy of its object, uniformity in variety as a principle of form, and one or two others—there is a more than cursory presentation, in a clear and simple style, of eight or ten issues that are still, at this day, very much alive: a "subjectivist" theory of value, for example, in Section I, and the kind of aesthetic relativism that

79

often goes along with it; the momentous distinction between absolute ("abstract," "geometrical") and representative beauty; "associationism"; "intentionalism" (Section IV); an influential analysis, in Section VI, of the concept of ugliness; and so on. What is conspicuously absent in Hutcheson (apart from opinions and solutions that were to be proposed by others) is perhaps only a full statement of the problems presented by conflicting judgments of taste. Neoclassical preferences, if not prejudices, of the age are visible at some points in the argument and must be allowed for.

We have omitted the long section (V) on beauty and the sense of beauty as a basis for inferences concerning God and creation, which—though Hutcheson's aesthetic is not complete without it—may be passed over by those not presently concerned about "natural religion."

In the early pages of the selection from Diderot there is a critical summary of Hutcheson's aesthetic.

FRANCIS HUTCHESON

An Inquiry Concerning Beauty

(First published: 1725.)

§ 1. CONCERNING SOME POWERS OF PERCEPTION, DISTINCT FROM WHAT IS GENERALLY UNDERSTOOD BY SENSATION

To make the following observations understood, it may be necessary to premise some definitions and observations either universally acknowledged, or sufficiently proved by many writers both ancient and modern, concerning our perceptions, called sensations, and the actions of the mind consequent upon them.

1. Those ideas that are raised in the mind upon the presence of external objects, and their acting upon our bodies, are called sensations. We find that the mind in such cases is passive, and has not power directly to prevent the perception or idea, or to vary it at its reception, as long as we continue our bodies in a state fit to be acted upon by the external object.

2. When two perceptions are entirely different from each other, or agree in nothing but the general idea of sensation, we call the powers of receiving those different perceptions, different senses. Thus seeing and hearing denote the different powers of receiving the ideas of colours and sounds. And although colours have vast differences among themselves, as also have sounds, yet there is a greater agreement among the most opposite colours than between any colour

and a sound; hence we call all colours perceptions of the same sense. All the several senses seem to have their distinct organs, except feeling, which is in some degree diffused over the whole body.

3. The mind has a power of compounding ideas that were received separately, of comparing their objects by means of the ideas, and of observing their relations and proportions; of enlarging and diminishing its ideas at pleasure, or in any certain ratio, or degree; and of considering separately each of the simple ideas, which might perhaps have been impressed jointly in the sensation. This last operation we commonly call abstraction.

4. The ideas of substances are compounded of the various simple ideas jointly impressed when they presented themselves to our senses. We define substances only by enumerating these sensible ideas; and such definitions may raise an idea clear enough of the substance in the mind of one who never immediately perceived the substance; provided he has separately received by his senses all the simple ideas that are in the composition of the complex one of the substance defined; but if he has not received any of these ideas, or wants the senses necessary for the perception of them, no definition can ever raise in him any idea of that sense in which he is deficient.

5. Many of our sensitive perceptions are pleasant, and many painful, immediately, and that without any knowledge of the cause of this pleasure or pain, or how the objects excite it or are the occasions of it; or without seeing to what further advantage or detriment the use of such objects might tend; nor would the most accurate knowledge of these things vary either the pleasure or pain of the perception, however it might give a rational pleasure distinct from the sensible; or might raise a distinct joy, from prospect of further advantage in the object, or aversion, from apprehension of evil.

6. Hence it follows that when instruction, education, or prejudice of any kind,

raises any desire or aversion toward an object, this desire or aversion must be founded upon an opinion of some perfection, or of some deficiency in those qualities for perception, of which we have the proper senses. Thus if beauty be desired by one who has not the sense of sight, the desire must be raised by some apprehended regularity of figure, sweetness of voice, smoothness or softness, or some other quality perceivable by the other senses, without relation to the ideas of colour.

7. The ideas raised in different persons by the same object are probably different, when they disagree in their approbation or dislike; and in the same person, when his fancy at one time differs from what it was at another. This will appear from reflecting on those objects to which we have now an aversion, though they were formerly agreeable. And we shall generally find that there is some accidental conjunction of a disagreeable idea, which always recurs with the object; as in those wines which men acquire an aversion to after they have taken them in an emetic preparation. In this case we are conscious that the idea is altered from what it was when that wine was agreeable, by the conjunction of the ideas of loathing and sickness of stomach. The like change of idea may be insensibly made by the change of our bodies as we advance in years, which may occasion an indifference toward meats we were fond of in our childhood.

We shall not find it perhaps so easy to account for the diversity of fancy in our dress, and some other affairs; and yet this may arise from a like accidental conjunction of ideas: as for instance, if either from anything in nature, or from the opinion of our country or acquaintance, the fancying of glaring colours be looked upon as an evidence of levity, or of any other evil quality of mind; or if any colour or fashion be commonly used by rustics, or by men of any disagreeable profession, employment, or temper; these additional ideas may recur constantly with that of the colour or fashion, and cause a constant dislike to them in those who join the additional ideas, although the colour or form be no way disagreeable of themselves, and actually do please others who join no such ideas to them. But there does not seem to be any ground to believe such a diversity in human minds, as that the same idea or perception should give pleasure to one and pain to another, or to the same person at different times; not to say that it seems a contradiction that the same idea should do so. ·

8. The only pleasure of sense that our philosophers seem to consider is that which accompanies the simple ideas of sensation. But there are vastly greater pleasures in those complex ideas of objects which obtain the names of beautiful, regular, harmonious. Thus everyone acknowledges he is more delighted with a fine face, a just picture, than with the view of any one colour, were it as strong and lively as possible; and more pleased with a prospect of the sun rising among settled clouds and colouring their edges, with a starry hemisphere, a fine landscape, a regular building, than with a clear blue sky, a smooth sea, or a large open plain, not diversified by woods, hills, waters, buildings. And yet even these latter appearances are not quite simple. So in music the pleasure of fine composition is incomparably greater than that of any one note, how sweet, full, or swelling soever.

9. Let it be observed that, in the following papers, the word beauty is taken for the idea raised in us, and a sense of beauty for our power of receiving this idea. Harmony also denotes our pleasant ideas arising from composition of sounds, and a good ear (as it is generally taken) a power of perceiving this pleasure. In the following sections, an attempt is made to discover what is the immediate occasion of these pleasant ideas, or what real quality in the objects ordinarily excites them.

10. It is of no consequence whether we call these ideas of beauty and harmony perceptions of the external senses of seeing and hearing or not. I should rather choose to call our power of perceiving these ideas an internal sense, were it only for the convenience of distinguishing them from other sensations of seeing and hearing, which men may have without perception of beauty and harmony. It is plain from experience that many men have, in the common meaning, the senses of seeing and hearing perfect enough; they perceive all the simple ideas separately, and have their pleasures; they distinguish them from each other, such as one colour from another, either quite different, or the stronger or fainter of the same colour; they can tell in separate notes the higher, lower, sharper, or flatter, when separately sounded; in figures they discern the length, breadth, wideness of each line, surface, angle; and may be as capable of hearing and seeing at great distances as any men whatsoever. And yet perhaps they shall relish no pleasure in musical compositions, in painting, architecture, natural landscape; or but a very weak one in comparison of what others enjoy from the same objects. This greater capacity of receiving such pleasant ideas we commonly call a fine genius or taste. In music we seem universally to acknowledge something like a distinct sense from the external one of hearing, and call it a good ear; and the like distinction we would probably acknowledge in other affairs, had we also got distinct names to denote these powers of perception by.

11. There will appear another reason perhaps afterward for calling this power of perceiving the ideas of beauty an internal sense, from this, that in some other affairs, where our external senses are not much concerned, we discern a sort of beauty, very like, in many respects, to that observed in sensible objects, and accompanied with like pleasure. Such is that beauty perceived in theorems, or universal truths, in general causes, and in some extensive principles of action.

12. Let everyone here consider how dif-

ferent we must suppose the perception to be with which a poet is transported upon the prospect of any of those objects of natural beauty, which ravish us even in his description; from that cold, lifeless conception which we imagine to be in a dull critic, or one of the virtuosi, without what we call a fine taste. This latter class of men may have greater perfection in that knowledge, which is derived from external sensation; they can tell all the specific differences of trees, herbs, minerals, metals; they know the form of every leaf, stalk, root, flower, and seed of all the species, about which the poet is often very ignorant. And yet the poet shall have a vastly more delightful perception of the whole; and not only the poet, but any man of a fine taste. Our external sense may by measuring teach us all the proportions of architecture to the tenth of an inch, and the situation of every muscle in the human body; and a good memory may retain these; and yet there is still something further necessary, not only to make a complete master in architecture, painting, or statuary, but even a tolerable judge in these works; or to receive the highest pleasure in contemplating them. Since then there are such different powers of perception, where what are commonly called the external senses are the same; since the most accurate knowledge of what the external senses discover often does not give the pleasure of beauty or harmony, which yet one of a good taste will enjoy at once without much knowledge; we may justly use another name for these higher and more delightful perceptions of beauty and harmony, and call the power of receiving such impressions an internal sense. The difference of the perceptions seems sufficient to vindicate the use of a different name.

13. This superior power of perception is justly called a sense, because of its affinity to the other senses in this, that the pleasure does not arise from any knowledge of principles, proportions, causes, or of the usefulness of the object; but strikes us at first with the idea of beauty; nor does the most accurate knowledge increase this pleasure of beauty, however it may super-add a distinct rational pleasure from prospects of advantage, or from the increase of knowledge.[1]

14. And further, the ideas of beauty and harmony, like other sensible ideas, are necessarily pleasant to us, as well as immediately so; neither can any resolution of our own, nor any prospect of advantage or disadvantage, vary the beauty or deformity of an object. For as in the external sensations, no view of interest will make an object grateful, nor detriment, distinct from immediate pain in the perception, make it disagreeable to the sense; so propose the whole world as a reward, or threaten the greatest evil, to make us approve a deformed object, or disapprove a beautiful one; dissimulation may be procured by rewards or threatenings, or we may in external conduct abstain from any pursuit of the beautiful, and pursue the deformed; but our sentiments of the forms, and our perceptions, would continue invariably the same.

15. Hence it plainly appears that some objects are immediately the occasions of this pleasure of beauty, and that we have senses fitted for perceiving it, and that it is distinct from that joy which arises from self-love upon prospect of advantage. Nay, do not we often see conveniency and use neglected to obtain beauty, without any other prospect of advantage in the beautiful form than the suggesting the pleasant ideas of beauty? Now this shows us that however we may pursue beautiful objects from self-love, with a view to obtain the pleasures of beauty, as in architecture, gardening, and many other affairs; yet there must be a sense of beauty, antecedent to prospects of even this advantage, without which sense these objects would not be thus advantageous, nor excite in us this pleasure which constitutes them advantageous. Our sense

---

[1] See Article 5, above.

of beauty from objects, by which they are constituted good to us, is very distinct from our desire of them when they are thus constituted. Our desire of beauty may be counterbalanced by rewards or threatenings, but never our sense of it; even as fear of death, or love of life, may make us choose and desire a bitter potion, or neglect those meats which the sense of taste would recommend as pleasant; and yet no prospect of advantage, or fear of evil, can make that potion agreeable to the sense, or meats disagreeable to it that were not so antecedently to this prospect. Just in the same manner as to the sense of beauty and harmony; that the pursuit of such objects is frequently neglected, from prospects of advantage, aversion to labour, or any other motive of self-love, does not prove that we have no sense of beauty, but only that our desire of it may be counterbalanced by a stronger desire. So gold outweighing silver is never adduced as a proof that the latter is void of gravity.

16. Had we no such sense of beauty and harmony, houses, gardens, dress, equipage might have been recommended to us as convenient, fruitful, warm, easy; but never as beautiful. And in faces I see nothing that could please us but liveliness of colour and smoothness of surface. And yet nothing is more certain than that all these objects are recommended under quite different views on many occasions. And no custom, education, or example could ever give us perceptions distinct from those of the senses which we had the use of before, or recommend objects under another conception than grateful to them.[2] But of the influence of custom, education, example upon the sense of beauty we shall treat below.[3]

17. Beauty is either original or comparative; or if any like the terms better, absolute or relative. Only let it be noted that by absolute or original beauty is not under-

stood any quality supposed to be in the object, that should of itself be beautiful without relation to any mind which perceives it. For beauty, like other names of sensible ideas, properly denotes the perception of some mind; so cold, heat, sweet, bitter denote the sensations in our minds, to which perhaps there is no resemblance in the objects that excite these ideas in us, however we generally imagine that there is something in the object just like our perception. The ideas of beauty and harmony being excited upon our perception of some primary quality, and having relation to figure and time, may indeed have a nearer resemblance to objects than these sensations that seem not so much any pictures of objects as modifications of the perceiving mind; and yet were there no mind with a sense of beauty to contemplate objects, I see not how they could be called beautiful. We therefore by absolute beauty understand only that beauty which we perceive in objects without comparison to anything external, of which the object is supposed an imitation, or picture; such as that beauty perceived from the works of nature, artificial forms, figures, theorems.[4] Comparative or relative beauty is that which we perceive in objects, commonly considered as imitations or resemblances of something else. These two kinds of beauty employ the three following sections.

§ 2. OF ORIGINAL OR ABSOLUTE BEAUTY

1. Since it is certain that we have ideas of beauty and harmony, let us examine

---

[2] See Article 6, above.

[3] Section 7.

[4] This division of beauty is taken from the different foundations of pleasure as to our sense of it, rather than from the objects themselves; for most of the following instances of relative beauty have also absolute beauty, and many of the instances of absolute beauty have also relative beauty in some respect or other. But we may distinctly consider these two fountains of pleasure, uniformity in the object itself, and resemblance to some original.

what quality in objects excites these ideas or is the occasion of them. And let it be here observed that our inquiry is only about the qualities that are beautiful to men, or about the foundation of their sense of beauty; for, as was above hinted, beauty has always relation to the sense of some mind; and when we afterwards show how generally the objects that occur to us are beautiful, we mean agreeable to the sense of men; for as there are not a few objects which seem no way beautiful to men, so we see a variety of other animals who seem delighted with them; they may have senses otherwise constituted than those of men, and may have the ideas of beauty excited by objects of a quite different form. We see animals fitted for every place; and what to men appears rude and shapeless, or loathsome, may be to them a paradise.

2. That we may more distinctly discover the general foundation or occasion of the ideas of beauty among men, it will be necessary to consider it first in its simpler kinds, such as occur to us in regular figures; and we may perhaps find that the same foundation extends to all the more complex species of it.

3. The figures that excite in us the ideas of beauty seem to be those in which there is uniformity amidst variety. There are many conceptions of objects that are agreeable upon other accounts, such as grandeur, novelty, sanctity, and some others, that shall be touched at afterwards.[5] But what we call beautiful in objects, to speak in the mathematical style, seems to be in a compound ratio of uniformity and variety; so that where the uniformity of bodies is equal, the beauty is as the variety; and where the variety is equal, the beauty is as the uniformity. This will be plain from examples.

First, the variety increases the beauty in equal uniformity. The beauty of an equilateral triangle is less than that of the square;

which is less than that of a pentagon; and this again is surpassed by the hexagon. When indeed the number of sides is much increased, the proportion of them to the radius, or diameter of the figure, is so much lost to our observation that the beauty does not always increase with the number of sides; and the want of parallelism in the sides of heptagons, and other figures of odd numbers, may also diminish their beauty. So in solids, the icosahedron surpasses the dodecahedron, and this the octahedron, which is still more beautiful than the cube; and this again surpasses the regular pyramid. The obvious ground of this is greater variety with equal uniformity.

The greater uniformity increases the beauty amidst equal variety, in these instances: An equilateral triangle, or even an isosceles, surpasses the scalene; a square surpasses the rhomb or lozenge, and this again the rhomboid, which yet is still more beautiful than the trapezium, or any figure with irregularly curved sides. So the regular solids vastly surpass all other solids of equal number of plane surfaces. And the same is observable not only in the five perfectly regular solids, but in all those which have any considerable uniformity, as cylinders, prisms, pyramids, obelisks; which please every eye more than any rude figures, where there is no unity or resemblance among the parts.

Instances of the compound ratio we have in comparing circles or spheres with ellipses or spheroids not very eccentric; and in comparing the compound solids, the hexoctahedron and icosadodecahedron, with the perfectly regular ones of which they are compounded. And we shall find that the want of that most perfect uniformity observable in the latter is compensated by the greater variety in the others, so that the beauty is nearly equal.

4. These observations would probably hold true for the most part, and might be confirmed by the judgement of children in

the simpler figures, where the variety is not too great for their comprehension. And however uncertain some of the particular aforesaid instances may seem, yet this is perpetually to be observed, that children are fond of all regular figures in their little diversions, although they be no more convenient, or useful for them, than the figures of our common pebbles. We see how early they discover a taste or sense of beauty, in desiring to see buildings, regular gardens, or even representations of them in pictures of any kind.

5. It is the same foundation which we have for our sense of beauty in the works of nature; in every part of the world which we call beautiful, there is vast uniformity amidst almost infinite variety. Many parts of the universe seem not at all designed for the use of man; nay, it is but a very small spot with which we have any acquaintance. The figures and motions of the great bodies are not obvious to our senses, but found out by reasoning and reflection, upon many long observations. And yet as far as we can by sense discover, or by reasoning enlarge our knowledge, and extend our imagination, we generally find the structure, and order, and motion, agreeable to our sense of beauty. Every particular object in nature does not indeed appear beautiful to us; but there is a vast profusion of beauty over most of the objects which occur either to our senses or reasonings upon observation. For not to mention the apparent situation of the heavenly bodies in the circumference of a great sphere, which is wholly occasioned by the imperfection of our sight in discerning distances, the forms of all the great bodies in the universe are nearly spherical, the orbits of their revolutions generally elliptical, and without great eccentricity in those which continually occur to our observation, and these are figures of great uniformity, and therefore pleasing to us. Further, to pass by the less obvious uniformity in the proportion of their quantities of matter, distances, times of revolving, to each other,

what can exhibit a greater instance of uniformity amidst variety than the constant tenor of revolutions in nearly equal times, in each planet around its axis, and the central fire or sun, through all the ages of which we have any records, and in nearly the same orbit? By which, after certain periods, all the same appearances are again renewed; the alternate successions of light and shade, or day and night, constantly pursuing each other around each planet, with an agreeable and regular diversity in the times they possess the various hemispheres, in the summer, harvest, winter, and spring; and the various phases, aspects, and situations, of the planets, to each other, their conjunctions and oppositions, in which they suddenly darken each other with their conic shades in eclipses, are repeated to us at their fixed periods with invariable constancy. These are the beauties which charm the astronomer, and make his tedious calculations pleasant. *Molliter austerum studio fallente laborem.*[6]

6. Again, as to the dry part of the surface of our globe, a great part of which is covered with a very pleasant, inoffensive colour, how beautifully is it diversified with various degrees of light and shade, according to the different situations of the parts of its surface, in mountains, valleys, hills, and open plains, which are variously inclined toward the great luminary!

7. If we descend to the minuter works of nature, what vast uniformity among all the species of plants and vegetables in the manner of their growth and propagation! What exact resemblance among all the plants of the same species, whose numbers surpass our imagination! And this uniformity is not only observable in the form in gross; nay, in this it is not so very exact in all instances, but in the structure of their minutest parts, which no eye unassisted

6 Horace, *Satires,* II, ii, 12 [While eagerness softens and prevents your perceiving the severity of the game].

with glasses can discern. In the almost infinite multitude of leaves, fruit, seed, flowers of any one species, we see an exact uniformity in the structure and situation of the smallest fibres. This is the beauty which charms an ingenious botanist. Nay, what vast uniformity and regularity of figure is found in each particular plant, or leaf, or flower! In all trees and most smaller plants, the stalks or trunks are either cylinders nearly, or regular prisms; the branches similar to their several trunks, arising at nearly regular distances, when no accidents retard their natural growth. In one species the branches arise in pairs on the opposite sides; the perpendicular plane of direction of the immediately superior pair intersecting the plane of direction of the inferior, nearly at right angles. In another species, the branches shall spring singly, and alternately, all around in nearly equal distances. And the branches in other species shall sprout all in knots around the trunk, one for each year. And in every species, all the branches in the first shoots preserve the same angles with their trunk; and they again sprout out into smaller branches exactly after the manner of their trunks. Nor ought we to pass over that great unity of colours in all the flowers of the same plant or tree, and often of a whole species; and their exact agreement in many shaded transitions into opposite colours, in which all the flowers of the same plant generally agree, nay, often all the flowers of a species.

8. Again, as to the beauty of animals, either in their inward structure, which we come to the knowledge of by experiment and long observation, or their outward form, we shall find vast uniformity among all the species which are known to us, in the structure of those parts, upon which life depends more immediately. And how amazing is the unity of mechanism, when we shall find that almost infinite diversity of motions, all their actions in walking, running, flying, swimming; all their serious efforts for self-preservation, all their freakish contortions when they are gay and sportful, in all their various limbs, performed by one simple contrivance of a contracting muscle, applied with inconceivable diversities to answer all these ends! Various engines might have obtained the same ends; but then there had been less uniformity, and the beauty of our animal systems, and of particular animals, had been much less, when this surprising unity of mechanism had been removed from them.

9. Among animals of the same species, the unity is very obvious, and this resemblance is the very ground of our ranking them in such classes or species, notwithstanding the great diversities in bulk, colour, shape, which are observed even in those called of the same species. And then in each individual, what vast beauty arises from the exact resemblance of all the external double members to each other, which seems the universal intention of nature, when no accident prevents it! We see the want of this resemblance never fails to pass for an imperfection, and want of beauty, though no other inconvenience ensues; as when the eyes are not exactly alike, or one arm or leg is a little shorter or smaller than its fellow.

10. There is a further beauty in animals, arising from a certain proportion of the various parts to each other, which still pleases the sense of spectators, though they cannot calculate it with the accuracy of a statuary [sculptor]. The statuary knows what proportion of each part of the face to the whole face is most agreeable, and can tell us the same of the proportion of the face to the body, or any parts of it, and between the diameters and lengths of each limb. When this proportion of the head to the body is remarkably altered, we shall have a giant or a dwarf. And hence it is that either the one or the other may be represented to us even in miniature, without relation to any external object, by observing

how the body surpasses the proportion it should have to the head in giants, and falls below it in dwarfs. There is a further beauty arising from that figure, which is a natural indication of strength; but this may be passed over, because probably it may be alleged that our approbation of this shape flows from opinion of advantage, and not from the form itself.

The beauty arising from mechanism, apparently adapted to the necessities and advantages of any animal, which pleases us, even though there be no advantage to ourselves ensuing from it, will be considered under the head of relative beauty, or design.[7]

11. The peculiar beauty of fowls can scarce be omitted, which arises from the vast variety of feathers, a curious sort of machine adapted to many admirable uses, which retain a vast resemblance in their structure among all the species, and a perfect uniformity in those of the same species in the corresponding parts, and in the two sides of each individual; besides all the beauty of lively colours and gradual shades, not only in the external appearance of the fowl, resulting from an artful combination of shaded feathers, but often visible even in one feather separately.

12. If our reasonings about the nature of fluids be just, the vast stores of water will give us an instance of uniformity in nature above imagination, when we reflect upon the almost infinite multitude of small, polished, smooth spheres, which must be supposed formed in all the parts of this globe. The same uniformity there is probably among the parts of other fluids as well as water; and the like must be observed in several other natural bodies, as salts, sulfurs, and such like, whose uniform properties do probably depend upon a uniformity in the figures of their parts.

13. Under original beauty we may include harmony, or beauty of sound, if that expression can be allowed, because harmony is not usually conceived as an imitation of anything else. Harmony often raises pleasure in those who know not what is the occasion of it. And yet the foundation of this pleasure is known to be a sort of uniformity. When the several vibrations of one note regularly coincide with the vibrations of another, they make an agreeable composition; and such notes are called chords. Thus the vibrations of any one note coincide in time with every second vibration of its octave; and two vibrations of any note coincide with three of its fifth; and so on in the rest of the chords. Now good compositions, besides the frequency of these chords, must retain a general unity of key, a uniformity among the parts, in bars, risings, fallings, closes. The necessity of this will appear, by observing the dissonance which would arise from tacking parts of different tunes together as one, although both were separately agreeable. A greater uniformity is also observable among the basses, tenors, trebles of the same tune. Some other powers of music may be considered afterwards.[8]

14. But in all these instances of beauty let it be observed that the pleasure is communicated to those who never reflected on this general foundation; and that all here alleged is this, that the pleasant sensation arises only from objects in which there is uniformity amidst variety. We may have the sensation without knowing what is the occasion of it; as a man's taste may suggest ideas of sweets, acids, bitters, though he be ignorant of the forms of the small bodies, or their motions, which excite these perceptions in him.

§ 3. OF THE BEAUTY OF THEOREMS

1. The beauty of theorems, or universal truths demonstrated, deserves a distinct consideration, because of a nature pretty

---

[7] See Section 4, Article 7.

[8] See Section 6, Article 12.

different from the former kinds of beauty; and yet there is none in which we shall see such an amazing variety with uniformity; and hence arises a very great pleasure distinct from prospects of any further advantage.

2. For in one theorem we may find included, with the most exact agreement, an infinite multitude of particular truths; nay, often an infinity of infinites; so that although the necessity of forming abstract ideas, and universal theorems, arises perhaps from the limitation of our minds, which cannot admit an infinite multitude of singular ideas or judgments at once, yet this power gives us an evidence of the largeness of the human capacity above our imagination. Thus, for instance, the forty-seventh proposition of the first book of Euclid's *Elements* [the Pythagorean theorem] contains an infinite multitude of truths, concerning the infinite possible sizes of right-angled triangles, as you make the area greater or less; and in each of these sizes you may find an infinite multitude of dissimilar triangles, as you vary the proportion of the base to the perpendicular; all which infinities of infinites agree in the general theorem. Thus also one fluxional calculation shall determine the tangents of all algebraic curves; of these curves there are infinite orders and species possible, of each species infinite sizes, or magnitudes of areas, of each size infinite individuals, of each individual curve an infinity of points, from which tangents may be drawn. But all these infinities of infinites are exactly comprehended in the general theorem, which fixes the lengths of the subtangents, or their proportion to the abscissa.

3. That we may the better discern this agreement, or unity of an infinity of objects in the general theorem, to be the foundation of the beauty or pleasure attending their discovery, let us compare our satisfaction in such discoveries with the uneasy state of mind which we are in, when we can only measure lines, or surfaces, by a scale, or are

making experiments which we can reduce to no general canon, but only heaping up a multitude of particular incoherent observations. Now each of these trials discovers a new truth, but with no pleasure or beauty, notwithstanding the variety, till we can discover some sort of unity, or reduce them to some general canon.

4. Again, let us take a metaphysical axiom, such as this: Every whole is greater than its part; and we shall find no beauty in the contemplation; because however this proposition does contain many infinities of particular truths, yet the unity is inconsiderable, since they all agree only in a vague, undetermined conception of whole and part, and in an indefinite excess of the former above the latter, which is sometimes great and sometimes small. So, should we hear that the cylinder is greater than the inscribed sphere, and this again greater than the cone of the same altitude and diameter of the base, we shall find no pleasure in this knowledge of a general relation of greater and less, without any precise difference or proportion. But when we see the universal exact agreement of all possible sizes of such systems of solids, that they preserve to each other the constant ratio of 3, 2, 1; how beautiful is the theorem, and how are we ravished with its first discovery!

5. There is another beauty in propositions, which cannot be omitted, which is this: When one theorem shall contain a vast multitude of corollaries easily deducible from it. Thus that theorem which gives us the equation of a curve, whence perhaps most of its properties may be deduced, does some way please and satisfy our mind above any other proposition. Such a theorem also is the thirty-fifth of the first book of Euclid, from which the whole art of measuring right-lined areas is deduced, by resolution into triangles, which are the halves of so many parallelograms; and these are each respectively equal to so many rectangles of the base into the perpendicular altitude. The forty-seventh of the first is another

of like beauty, and so are many others. In the search of nature there is the like beauty in the knowledge of some great principles, or universal forces, from which innumerable effects do flow. Such is gravitation, in Sir Isaac Newton's scheme; such also is the knowledge of the original of rights, perfect and imperfect, and external; alienable and unalienable, with their manner of translations; from whence the greatest part of moral duties may be deduced in the various relations of human life.

It is easy to see how men are charmed with the beauty of such knowledge, besides its usefulness; and this sets them upon deducing the properties of each figure from one genesis, and demonstrating the mechanic forces from one theorem of the composition of motion; even after they have sufficient knowledge and certainty in all these truths from distinct, independent demonstrations. And this pleasure we enjoy even when we have no prospect of obtaining any other advantage in life from such manner of deduction, besides the immediate pleasure of contemplating the beauty. Nor could love of fame excite us to such regular methods of deduction, were we not conscious that mankind is pleased with them immediately by this internal sense of their beauty.

It is no less easy to see into what absurd whimsies men have been led by this sense of beauty, and a silly affectation of obtaining it in the other sciences as well as mathematics. 'Twas this probably which set Descartes on that hopeful project of deducing all human knowledge from one proposition, viz., *cogito, ergo sum* [I think, therefore I am]; while others with as little sense contended that *impossibile est idem simul esse et non esse* [it is impossible for the same thing at once to be and not to be] had much fairer pretensions to the style and title of *principium humanae cognitionis absolute primum* [an absolutely primary princicple of human knowledge]. Leibniz had an equal affection for his favorite principle of a sufficient reason for everything in nature, and bragged

to Dr. Clarke of the wonders he had wrought in the intellectual world by its assistance; but his learned antagonist seems to think he had not sufficient reason for his boasting. If we look into particular sciences, we may see, in the systems learned men have given us of them, the inconveniences of this love of uniformity. Dr. Cumberland has taken a great deal of needless pains to reduce the laws of nature to one general practical proposition; and how awkwardly is Puffendorf forced to deduce the several duties of men to God, themselves, and their neighbors, from his single fundamental principle of *sociableness to the whole race of mankind.* As if they had not been better drawn, each respectively, from their immediate sources, viz., religion, self-love, and sociableness. This observation might easily be extended further, were it necessary, and is a strong proof that men have a sense of beauty in uniformity in the sciences, notwithstanding the contortions of common sense they may be led into by pursuing it.

6. This delight which accompanies sciences, or universal theorems, may really be called a kind of sensation; since it necessarily accompanies the discovery of any proposition, and is distinct from bare knowledge itself, being most violent at first, whereas the knowledge is uniformly the same. And however knowledge enlarges the mind, and makes us more capable of comprehensive views and projects in some kinds of business, whence advantage may also arise to us; yet we may leave it in the breast of every student to determine whether he has not often felt this pleasure without any such prospect of advantage from the discovery of his theorem. All that can thence be inferred is only this, that as in our external senses, so in our internal ones, the pleasant sensations generally arise from those objects which calm reason would have recommended, had we understood their use, and which might have engaged our pursuits from self-interest.

As to the works of art, were we to run

through the various artificial contrivances or structures, we should find the foundation of the beauty which appears in them to be constantly some kind of uniformity, or unity of proportion among the parts, and of each part to the whole. As there is a vast diversity of proportions possible, and different kinds of uniformity, so there is room enough for that diversity of fancies observable in architecture, gardening, and such like arts in different nations; they all may have uniformity, though the parts in one may differ from those in another. The Chinese or Persian buildings are not like the Grecian and Roman, and yet the former has its uniformity of the various parts to each other, and to the whole, as well as the latter. In that kind of architecture which the Europeans call regular, the uniformity of parts is very obvious, the several parts are regular figures, and either equal or similar at least in the same range; the pedestals are parallelepipedons, or square prisms; the pillars, cylinders nearly; the arches circular, and all those in the same row equal; there is the same proportion everywhere observed in the same range between the diameters of pillars and their heights, their capitals, the diameters of arches, the heights of the pedestals, the projections of the cornice, and all ornaments in each of our five orders. And though other countries do not follow the Grecian or Roman proportions; yet there is even among them a proportion retained, a uniformity, and resemblance of corresponding figures; and every deviation in one part from that proportion which is observed in the rest of the building is displeasing to every eye, and destroys or diminishes at least the beauty of the whole.

7. The same might be observed through all other works of art even to the meanest utensil, the beauty of every one of which we shall always find to have the same foundation of uniformity amidst variety, without which they shall appear mean, irregular, and deformed.

§ 4. OF RELATIVE OR COMPARATIVE BEAUTY

1. If the preceding thoughts concerning the foundation of absolute beauty be just, we may easily understand wherein relative beauty consists. All beauty is relative to the sense of some mind perceiving it; but what we call relative is that which is apprehended in any object, commonly considered as an imitation of some original. And this beauty is founded on a conformity or a kind of unity between the original and the copy. The original may be either some object in nature, or some established idea; for if there be any known idea as a standard, and rules to fix this image or idea by, we may make a beautiful imitation. Thus a statuary, painter, or poet may please us with a Hercules, if his piece retains that grandeur, and those marks of strength and courage, which we imagine in that hero. And further, to obtain comparative beauty alone, it is not necessary that there be any beauty in the original; the imitation of absolute beauty may indeed in the whole make a more lovely piece, and yet an exact imitation shall still be beautiful, though the original were entirely void of it. Thus the deformities of old age in a picture, the rudest rocks or mountains in a landscape, if well represented, shall have abundant beauty, though not perhaps so great as if the original were absolutely beautiful, and as well represented.

2. The same observation holds true in the descriptions of the poets either of natural objects or persons; and this relative beauty is what they should principally endeavor to obtain, as the peculiar beauty of their works. By the *moratae fabulae,* or the $\tilde{\eta}\theta\eta$ of Aristotle, we are not to understand virtuous manners in a moral sense, but a just representation of manners or characters as they are in nature;[9] and that the actions

---

[9] [The reference is to Horace, *De Arte Poetica,* 319–20. *Morata recte fabula*...(A tale in which the characters are well drawn).—ED. NOTE.]

and sentiments be suited to the characters of the persons to whom they are ascribed in epic and dramatic poetry. Perhaps very good reasons may be suggested from the nature of our passions to prove that a poet should not out of choice draw the finest characters possible for virtue; these characters indeed abstractly considered might give more pleasure, and have more beauty, than the imperfect ones which occur in life with a mixture of good and evil. But it may suffice at present to suggest against this choice that we have more lively ideas of imperfect men with all their passions than of morally perfect heroes, such as really never occur to our observation, and of which consequently we cannot judge exactly as to their agreement with the copy. And further, through consciousness of our own state, we are more nearly touched and affected by the imperfect characters, since in them we see represented, in the persons of others, the contrasts of inclinations, and the struggles between the passions of self-love and those of honour and virtue, which we often feel in our own breasts. This is the perfection of beauty for which Homer is justly admired, as well as for the variety of his characters.

3. Many other beauties of poetry may be reduced under this class of relative beauty. The probability is absolutely necessary to make us imagine resemblance; it is by resemblance that the similitudes, metaphors, and allegories are made beautiful, whether either the subject or the thing compared to it have beauty or not; the beauty indeed is greater, when both have some original beauty or dignity as well as resemblance. And this is the foundation of the rule of studying decency in metaphors and similes as well as likeness. The measures and cadence are instances of harmony, and come under the head of absolute beauty.

4. We may here observe a strange proneness in our minds to make perpetual comparisons of all things which occur to our observation, even those which would seem very remote. There are certain resemblances in the motions of all animals upon like passions, which easily found a comparison; but this does not serve to entertain our fancy. Inanimate objects have often such positions as resemble those of the human body in various circumstances; these airs or gestures of the body are indications of dispositions in the mind, so that our very passions and affections as well as other circumstances obtain a resemblance to natural inanimate objects. Thus a tempest at sea is often an emblem of wrath; a plant or tree drooping under the rain, of a person in sorrow; a poppy bending its stalk, or a flower withering when cut by the plow, resembles the death of a blooming hero; an aged oak in the mountains shall represent an old empire; a flame seizing a wood shall represent a war. In short, everything in nature, by our strange inclination to resemblance, shall be brought to represent other things, even the most remote, especially the passions and circumstances of human nature in which we are more nearly concerned; and to confirm this, and furnish instances of it, one need only look into Homer or Virgil. A fruitful fancy would find in a grove or a wood an emblem for every character in a commonwealth, and every turn of temper, or station in life.

5. Concerning that kind of comparative beauty which has a necessary relation to some established idea, we may observe that some works of art acquire a distinct beauty by their correspondence to some universally supposed intention in the artificer, or the persons who employed him. And to obtain this beauty, sometimes they do not form their works so as to attain the highest perfection of original beauty separately considered; because a composition of this relative beauty, along with some degree of the original kind, may give more pleasure than a more perfect original beauty separately. Thus we see that strict regularity in laying out of gardens in parterres, vistas, parallel walks, is often neglected to obtain an imita-

tion of nature even in some of its wildnesses. And we are more pleased with this imitation, especially when the scene is large and spacious, than with the more confined exactness of regular work. So likewise in the monuments erected in honour of deceased heroes; although a cylinder, or prism, or regular solid may have more original beauty than a very acute pyramid or obelisk, yet the latter pleases more, by answering better the supposed intentions of stability, and being conspicuous. For the same reason cubes, or square prisms, are generally chosen for the pedestals of statues, and not any of the more beautiful solids, which do not seem so secure from rolling. This may be the reason too why columns or pillars look best when made a little taper from the middle, or a third from the bottom, that they may not seem top-heavy and in danger of falling.

6. The like reason may influence artists, in many other instances, to depart from the rules of original beauty, as above laid down. And yet this is no argument against our sense of beauty being founded, as was above explained, on uniformity amidst variety, but only an evidence that our sense of beauty of the original kind may be varied and over-balanced by another kind of beauty.

7. This beauty arising from correspondence to intention would open to curious observers a new scene of beauty in the works of nature, by considering how the mechanism of the various parts known to us seems adapted to the perfection of that part, and yet in subordination to the good of some system or whole. We generally suppose the good of the greatest whole, or of all beings, to have been the intention of the author of nature; and cannot avoid being pleased when we see any part of this design executed in the systems we are acquainted with. The observations already made on this subject are in everyone's hand, in the treatises of our late improvers of mechanical philosophy. We may only

here observe the pleasure which anyone shall receive from seeing any design well executed by curious mechanism, even when his own advantage is no way concerned; as also that pleasant sensation he shall have in discovering the design to which any complex machine is adapted, when he has perhaps had a general knowledge of the machine before, without seeing its correspondence or aptness to execute any design. . . .

§ 6. OF THE UNIVERSALITY OF THE SENSE OF BEAUTY AMONG MEN

1. We before insinuated "that all beauty has a relation to some perceiving power"; and consequently since we know not the variety of senses which may be among animals, there is no form in nature concerning which we can pronounce "that it has no beauty"; for it may still please some perceiving power.[10] But our inquiry is confined to men; and before we examine the universality of this sense of beauty, or their agreement in approving uniformity, it may be proper to consider "if, as the other senses which give us pleasure do also give us pain, so this sense of beauty does make some objects disagreeable to us, and the occasion of pain." That many objects give no pleasure to our sense is obvious, many are certainly void of beauty. But then there is no form which seems necessarily disagreeable of itself, when we dread no other evil from it, and compare it with nothing better of the kind. Many objects are naturally displeasing, and distasteful to our external senses, as well as others pleasing and agreeable; as smells, tastes, and some separate sounds. But for our sense of beauty, no composition of objects which give not unpleasant simple ideas seems positively unpleasant or painful of itself, had we never observed anything better of the kind. Deformity is only the absence of beauty, or

10 See Section 1, Article 17; Section 4, Article 1.

deficiency in the beauty expected in any species. Thus bad music pleases rustics who never heard any better, and the finest ear is not offended with tuning of instruments if it be not too tedious, where no harmony is expected. And yet much smaller dissonancy shall offend amidst the performance, where harmony is expected. A rude heap of stones is no way offensive to one who shall be displeased with irregularity in architecture, where beauty was expected. And had there been a species of that form which we call now ugly or deformed, and had we never seen or expected greater beauty, we should have received no disgust from it, although the pleasure would not have been so great in this form as in those we now admire. Our sense of beauty seems designed to give us positive pleasure, but not positive pain or disgust, any further than what arises from disappointment.

2. There are indeed many faces which at first view are apt to raise dislike; but this generally not from any positive deformity which of itself is positively displeasing, but either from want of expected beauty, or much more from their carrying some natural indications of morally bad dispositions, which we all acquire a faculty of discerning in countenances, airs, and gestures. That this is not occasioned by any form positively disgusting, will appear from this, "that if upon long acquaintance we are sure of finding sweetness of temper, humanity, and cheerfulness, although the bodily form continues, it shall give us no disgust or displeasure"; whereas what were naturally disagreeable, or the occasion of pain, or positive distaste, would always continue so, even although the aversion we might have toward it were counterbalanced by other considerations. There are horrors raised by some objects which are only the effect of fear for ourselves, or compassion toward others, when either reason or some foolish association of ideas makes us apprehend danger, and not the effect of anything in the form itself. For we find that most of

these objects which excite horror at first, when experience or reason has removed the fear, may become the occasions of pleasure; as in ravenous beasts, a tempestuous sea, a craggy precipice, a dark shady valley.

3. We shall see afterwards "that associations of ideas make objects pleasant, and delightful, which are not naturally apt to give any such pleasures; and the same way the casual conjunctions of ideas may give a disgust, where there is nothing disagreeable in the form itself."[11] And this is the occasion of many fantastic aversions to figures of some animals, and to some other forms. Thus swine, serpents of all kinds, and some insects really beautiful enough are beheld with aversion by many people, who have got some accidental ideas associated to them. And for distastes of this kind there is no other account can be given.

4. But as to the universal agreement of mankind in their sense of beauty from uniformity amidst variety, we must consult experience. And as we allow all men reason, since all men are capable of understanding simple arguments, though few are capable of complex demonstrations, so in this case it must be sufficient to prove this sense of beauty universal "if all men are better pleased with uniformity in the simpler instances than the contrary, even when there is no advantage observed attending it; and likewise if all men, according as their capacity enlarges so as to receive and compare more complex ideas, do further extend their delight in uniformity, and are pleased with its more complex kinds, both original and relative."

Now let us consider if ever any person was void of this sense in simpler instances. Few trials have been made in the simplest instances of harmony, because as soon as we find an ear not capable of relishing complex compositions, such as our tunes are, no further pains are employed about such. But in figures, did ever any man make choice of

---

11 See Articles 11 and 12, below.

a trapezium, or any irregular curve, for the ichnography of his house without necessity, or some great motive of conveniency? Or to make the opposite walls not parallel or unequal in height? Were ever trapezia, irregular polygons or curves chosen for the forms of doors or windows, though these figures might have answered the uses as well, and would have often saved a great part of the time and labor and expense to workmen, which is now employed in suiting the stones and timber to the regular forms? Among all the fantastic modes of dress, none was ever quite void of uniformity, if it were only in the resemblance of the two sides of the same robe, and in some general aptitude to the human form. The Pictish painting had always relative beauty by resemblance to other objects, and often those objects were originally beautiful, however justly we might apply Horace's censure of impertinent descriptions in poetry, *sed non erat hic locus*.[12] But never were any so extravagant as to affect such figures as are made by the casual spilling of liquid colours. Who was ever pleased with an inequality of heights in windows of the same range, or dissimilar shapes of them? With unequal legs or arms or eyes or cheeks in a mistress? It must be however acknowledged "that interest often may counterbalance our sense of beauty in this affair as well as in others, and superior good qualities may make us overlook such imperfections."

5. Nay further, it may perhaps appear "that regularity and uniformity are so copiously diffused through the universe, and we are so readily determined to pursue this as the foundation of beauty in works of art, that there is scarcely anything ever fancied as beautiful where there is not really something of this uniformity and regularity." We are indeed often mistaken in imagining that there is the greatest possible beauty, where it is but very imperfect; but still it

is some degree of beauty which pleases, although there may be higher degrees which we do not observe; and our sense acts with full regularity when we are pleased, although we are kept by a false prejudice from pursuing objects which would please us more. A Goth, for instance, is mistaken, when from education he imagines the architecture of his country to be the most perfect; and a conjunction of some of the hostile ideas may make him have an aversion to Roman buildings, and study to demolish them, as some of our reformers did the popish buildings, not being able to separate the ideas of the superstitious worship from the forms of the buildings where it was practiced. And yet it is still real beauty which pleases the Goth, founded upon uniformity amidst variety. For the Gothic pillars are uniform to each other, not only in their sections, which are lozenge-formed, but also in their heights and ornaments. Their arches are not one uniform curve, but yet they are segments of similar curves, and generally equal in the same ranges. The very Indian buildings have some kind of uniformity, and many of the eastern nations, though they differ much from us, yet have great regularity and beauty in their manner, as well as the Romans in theirs. Our Indian screens, which wonderfully supply the regular imagination of our ladies with ideas of deformity, in which nature is very churlish and sparing, do want indeed all the beauty arising from proportion of parts, and conformity to nature; and yet they cannot divest themselves of all beauty and uniformity in the separate parts. And this diversifying the human body into various contortions may give some wild pleasure from variety, since some uniformity to the human shape is still retained.

6. There is one sort of beauty which might perhaps have been better mentioned before, but will not be impertinent here, because the taste or relish of it is universal in all nations, and with the young as well as the old, and that is the beauty of history.

---

12 Horace, *De Arte Poetica,* 19 [But this was not the place for it].

Everyone knows how dull a study it is to read over a collection of gazettes, which shall perhaps relate all the same events with the historian. The superior pleasure then of history must arise, like that of poetry, from the manners; as when we see a character well drawn, wherein we find the secret causes of a great diversity of seemingly inconsistent actions; or an interest of state laid open, or an artful view nicely unfolded, the execution of which influences very different and opposite actions, as the circumstances may alter. Now this reduces the whole to a unity of design at least. And this may be observed in the very fables which entertain children, otherwise we cannot make them relish them.

7. What has been said will probably be assented to if we always remember in our inquiries into the universality of the sense of beauty "that there may be real beauty, where there is not the greatest, and that there are an infinity of different forms which shall all have some unity, and yet differ from each other." So that men may have different fancies of beauty, and yet uniformity be the universal foundation of our approbation of any form whatsoever as beautiful. And we shall find that it is so in the architecture, gardening, dress, equipage, and furniture of houses, even among the most uncultivated nations, where uniformity still pleases, without any other advantage than the pleasure of the contemplation of it.

8. It will deserve our consideration on this subject, how, in like cases, we form very different judgments concerning the internal and external senses. Nothing is more ordinary among those who after Mr. Locke have shaken off the groundless opinions about innate ideas than to allege "that all our relish for beauty, and order, is either from advantage, or custom, or education," for no other reason but the variety of fancies in the world. And from this they conclude "that our fancies do not arise from any natural power of perception, or sense." And yet all allow our external senses to be natural, and "that the pleasures or pains of their sensations, however they may be increased, or diminished, by custom, or education, and counterbalanced by interest, yet are really antecedent to custom, habit, education, or prospect of interest." Now it is certain "that there is at least as great a variety of fancies about their objects, and the objects of beauty." Nay, it is much more difficult, and perhaps impossible, to bring the fancies or relishes of the external senses to any general foundation at all, or to find any rule for the agreeable or disagreeable. And yet we all allow "that these are natural powers of perception."

9. The reason of this different judgment can be no other than this, "that we have got distinct names for the external senses, and none, or very few, for the internal." And by this are led, as in many other cases, to look upon the former as some way more fixed, and real and natural, than the latter. The sense of harmony has got its name, a good ear; and we are generally brought to acknowledge this a natural power of perception, or a sense some way distinct from hearing. Now it is certain "that there is as necessary a perception of beauty upon the presence of regular objects, as of harmony upon hearing certain sounds."

10. But let it be observed here once for all "that an internal sense no more presupposes an innate idea, or principle of knowledge, than the external." Both are natural powers of perception, or determinations of the mind to receive necessarily certain ideas from the presence of objects. The internal sense is a passive power of receiving ideas of beauty from all objects in which there is uniformity amidst variety. Nor does there seem anything more difficult in this matter than "that the mind should be always determined to receive the idea of sweet, when particles of such a form enter the pores of the tongue; or to have the idea of sound upon any quick undulation of the air." The one seems to have as little connection with its idea as the other. And the same power

could with equal ease constitute the former the occasion of ideas as the latter.

11. The association of ideas above hinted at is one great cause of the apparent diversity of fancies in the sense of beauty, as well as in the external senses, and often makes men have an aversion to objects of beauty, and a liking to others void of it, but under different conceptions than those of beauty or deformity.[13] And here it may not be improper to give some instances of some of these associations. The beauty of trees, their cool shades, and their aptness to conceal from observation have made groves and woods the usual retreat to those who love solitude, especially to the religious, the pensive, the melancholy, and the amorous. And do not we find that we have so joined the ideas of these dispositions of mind with those external objects that they always recur to us along with them? The cunning of the heathen priests might make such obscure places the scene of the fictitious appearances of their deities; and hence we join ideas of something divine to them. We know the like effect in the ideas of our churches, from the perpetual use of them only in religious exercises. The faint light in Gothic buildings has had the same association of a very foreign idea, which our poet shows in his epithet—"A dim religious light."[14]

In like manner it is known "that often all the circumstances of actions or places, or dresses of persons, or voice, or song, which have occurred at any time together, when we were strongly affected by any passion, will be so connected that any one of these will make all the rest recur." And this is often the occasion both of great pleasure and pain, delight and aversion to many objects, which of themselves might have been perfectly indifferent to us. But these approbations, or distastes, are remote from the ideas of beauty, being plainly different ideas.

12. There is also another charm in music to various persons, which is distinct from the harmony, and is occasioned by its raising agreeable passions. The human voice is obviously varied by all the stronger passions; now when our ear discerns any resemblance between the air of a tune, whether sung or played upon an instrument, either in its time or key, or any other circumstance, to the sound of the human voice in any passion, we shall be touched by it in a very sensible manner, and have melancholy, joy, gravity, thoughtfulness excited in us by a sort of sympathy or contagion. The same connection is observable between the very air of a tune and the words expressing any passion which we have heard it fitted to, so that they shall both recur to us together, though but one of them affects our senses. Now in such a diversity of pleasing or displeasing ideas which may be conjoined with forms of bodies, or tunes, when men are of such different dispositions, and prone to such a variety of passions, it is no wonder "that they should often disagree in their fancies of objects, even although their sense of beauty and harmony were perfectly uniform"; because many other ideas may either please or displease, according to persons, tempers, and past circumstances. We know how agreeable a very wild country may be to any person who has spent the cheerful days of his youth in it, and how disagreeable very beautiful places may be if they were the scenes of his misery. And this may help us in many cases to account for the diversities of fancy, without denying the uniformity of our internal sense of beauty.

13. Grandeur and novelty are two ideas different from beauty, which often recommend objects to us. The reason of this is foreign to the present subject. See [Addison] *Spectator,* No. 412.

---

13 See Article 3, above.
14 John Milton, "Il Penseroso," Line 160.

§ 7. OF THE POWER OF CUSTOM,
EDUCATION, AND EXAMPLE AS TO
OUR INTERNAL SENSES

1. Custom, education, and example are
so often alleged in this affair, as the occasion of our relish for beautiful objects, and
for our approbation of, or delight in a certain conduct in life in a moral sense, that it
is necessary to examine these three particularly, to make it appear "that there is a
natural power of perception, or sense of
beauty in objects, antecedent to all custom,
education, or example."

2. Custom, as distinct from the other
two, operates in this manner. As to actions,
it only gives a disposition to the mind or
body more easily to perform those actions
which have been frequently repeated, but
never leads us to apprehend them under any
other view than what we were capable of
apprehending them under at first; nor gives
us any new power of perception about them.
We are naturally capable of sentiments of
fear, and dread, of any powerful presence;
and so custom may connect the ideas of
religious horror to certain buildings. But no
custom could have made a being naturally
incapable of fear receive such ideas. So had
we no other power of perceiving, or forming
ideas of actions, but as they were advantageous or disadvantageous, custom could
only have made us more ready at perceiving
the advantage or disadvantage of actions.
But this is not to our present purpose.

As to our approbation of, or delight in,
external objects, when the blood or spirits
of which anatomists talk are roused, quick-
ened, or fermented as they call it, in any
agreeable manner by medicine or nutri-
ment; or any glands frequently stimulated
to secretion; it is certain that to preserve
the body easy, we will delight in objects of
taste, which of themselves are not immediately pleasant to the taste, if they promote
that agreeable state, which the body had
been accustomed to. Further, custom will

so alter the state of the body that what at
first raised uneasy sensations will cease to
do so, or perhaps raise another agreeable
idea of the same sense; but custom can
never give us any idea of a different sense
from what we had antecedent to it. It will
never make the blind approve objects as
coloured, or those who have no taste approve
meats as delicious, however they might like
such as proved strengthening or exhilarating. Were our glands and the parts about
them void of feeling, did we perceive no
pleasure from certain brisker motions in the
blood, no custom would make stimulating
or intoxicating fluids or medicines agreeable, when they were not so to the taste.
So by like reasoning, had we no natural
sense of beauty from uniformity, custom
could never have made us imagine any
beauty in objects; if we had had no ear,
custom could never have given us the pleasures of harmony. When we have these
natural senses antecedently, custom may
make us capable of extending our views
further, and of receiving more complex
ideas of beauty in bodies, or harmony in
sounds, by increasing our attention and
quickness of perception. But however custom may increase our power of receiving or
comparing complex ideas, yet it seems
rather to weaken than strengthen the ideas
of beauty, or the impressions of pleasure
from regular objects; else how were it possible that any person could go into the open
air on a sunny day, or clear evening, without the most extravagant raptures, such as
Milton represents our ancestor in upon his
first creation?[15] For such any person would
certainly fall into, upon the first representation of such a scene.

Custom in like manner could make it
easier for any person to discern the use of
a complex machine, and approve it as advantageous; but he would never have imagined it beautiful, had he no natural sense

---

15 John Milton, *Paradise Lost,* Book VIII.

of beauty. Custom may make us quicker in apprehending the truth of complex theorems, but we all find the pleasure of beauty of theorems as strong at first as ever. Custom makes us more capable of retaining and comparing complex ideas, so as to discern more complicated uniformity, which escapes the observation of novices in any art; but all this presupposes a natural sense of beauty in uniformity. For had there been nothing in forms which was constituted necessarily the occasion of pleasure to our senses, no repetition of indifferent ideas as to pleasure or pain, beauty or deformity, could ever have made them grow pleasing or displeasing.

3. The effect of education is this, that thereby we receive many speculative opinions, sometimes true and sometimes false, and are often led to believe that objects may be naturally apt to give pleasure or pain to our external senses, when in reality the object has no such qualities. And further, by education there are some strong associations of ideas, without any reason, by mere accident sometimes, as well as by design, which it is very hard for us ever after to break asunder. Thus aversions are raised to darkness, and to many kinds of meats, and to certain innocent actions. Approbations without ground are raised in like manner. But in all these instances, education never makes us apprehend any qualities in objects which we have not naturally senses capable of perceiving. We know what sickness of the stomach is, and may without ground believe that very healthful meats will raise this; we by our sight and smell receive disagreeable ideas of the food of swine, and their sties, and perhaps cannot prevent the recurring of these ideas at table. But never were men naturally blind prejudiced against objects as of a disagreeable colour, or in favour of others as of a beautiful colour. They hear perhaps men dispraise one colour; they imagine this colour to be some quite different sensible quality of the other senses. And the same

way a man naturally void of taste could by no education receive the ideas of taste, or be prejudiced in favor of meats as delicious. So, had we no natural sense of beauty and harmony, we never could be prejudiced in favor of objects or sounds as beautiful or harmonious. Education may make an unattentive Goth imagine that his countrymen have attained the perfection of architecture; and an aversion to their enemies the Romans may have joined some disagreeable ideas to their very buildings, and excited them to their demolition; but he had never formed these prejudices, had he been void of a sense of beauty. Did ever blind men debate whether purple or scarlet were the finer colour? Or could any education prejudice them in favour of either as colours?

Thus education and custom may influence our internal senses, where they are antecedently, by enlarging the capacity of our minds to retain and compare the parts of complex compositions. And if the finest objects are presented to us, we grow conscious of a pleasure far superior to what common performances excite. But all this presupposes our sense of beauty to be natural. Instruction in anatomy, observation of nature, and of those airs of the countenance and attitudes of body which accompany any sentiment, action, or passion may enable us to know where there is a just imitation. But why should an exact imitation please upon observation, if we had not naturally a sense of beauty in it, more than the observing the situation of fifty or a hundred pebbles thrown at random? And should we repeat our attention to them ever so often, we shall never dream of their growing beautiful.

4. There is something worth our observation as to the manner of rooting out the prejudices of education, not quite foreign to the present purpose. When the prejudice arises from associations of ideas without any natural connection, we must frequently force ourselves to bear representations of those objects, or the use of them when sepa-

rated from the disagreeable idea. And this may at last disjoin the unreasonable association, especially if we can join new agreeable ideas to them. Thus opinions of superstition are best removed by pleasant conversation of persons we esteem for their virtue, or seeing them despise such opinions. But when the prejudice arises from an apprehension or opinion of natural evil, as the attendant, or consequent, of any object or action; if the evil be apprehended to be the constant and immediate attendant, a few trials without receiving any damage will remove the prejudice, as in that against meats. But where the evil is not represented as the perpetual concomitant, but as what may possibly or probably at some time or other accompany the use of the object, there must be frequent reasoning with ourselves, or a long series of trials without any detriment, to remove the prejudice. Such is the case of our fear of spirits in the dark, and in churchyards. And when the evil is represented as the consequence perhaps a long time after, or in a future state, it is then hardest of all to remove the prejudice. And this is only to be effected by slow processes of reason, because in this case there can be no trials made; and this is the case of superstitious prejudices against actions apprehended as offensive to the Deity; and hence it is that they are so hard to be rooted out.

5. Example seems to operate in this manner. We are conscious that we act very much for pleasure, or private good; and hence are led to imagine that others do so too. Hence we conclude there must be some perfection in the objects which we see others pursue, and evil in those which we observe them constantly shunning. Or, the example of others may serve to us as so many trials to remove the apprehension of evil in objects which we had an aversion to. But all this is done upon an apprehension of qualities perceivable by the senses which we have; for no example will induce the blind or deaf to pursue objects as coloured or

sonorous; nor could example any more engage us to pursue objects as beautiful or harmonious, had we no sense of beauty or harmony naturally.

Example may make us without examination conclude that our countrymen have obtained the perfection of beauty in their works, or that there is less beauty in the orders of architecture or painting used in other nations, and so content ourselves with very imperfect forms. And often fear of contempt as void of taste or genius makes us join in approving the performances of the reputed masters in our country, and restrains those who have naturally a fine genius, or the internal senses very acute, from studying to obtain the greatest perfection. It makes also those of a bad taste pretend a perception of ideas of beauty when they do not perceive them. But all this presupposes some natural power of receiving ideas of beauty and harmony. Nor can example effect anything further, unless it be to lead men to pursue objects by implicit faith for some perfection which the pursuer is conscious he does not know, or which perhaps is some very different quality from the idea perceived by those of a good taste in such affairs.

§ 8. OF THE IMPORTANCE OF THE INTERNAL SENSES IN LIFE AND THE FINAL CAUSES OF THEM

1. The busy part of mankind may look upon these things as airy dreams of an inflamed imagination, which a wise man should despise who rationally pursues more solid possessions independent of fancy. But a little reflection will convince us "that the gratifications of our internal senses are as natural, real, and satisfying enjoyments as any sensible pleasure whatsoever"; and "that they are the chief ends for which we commonly pursue wealth and power." For how is wealth or power advantageous? How do they make us happy, or prove good to us? No otherwise than as they supply grati-

fications to our senses or faculties of perceiving pleasure. Now, are these senses or faculties only the external ones? No. Everybody sees that a small portion of wealth or power will supply more pleasures of the external senses than we can enjoy. We know that scarcity often heightens these perceptions more than abundance, which cloys that appetite which is necessary to all pleasure in enjoyment. And hence the poet's advice is perfectly just: "...*tu pulmentaria quaere sudando.*"[16] In short, the only use of a great fortune above a very small one (except in good offices and moral pleasures) must be to supply us with the pleasures of beauty, order, and harmony.

This is confirmed by the constant practice of the very enemies to these senses. As soon as they think they are got above the world, or extricated from the hurries of avarice and ambition, banished nature will return upon them and set them upon pursuits of beauty and order in their houses, gardens, dress, table, equipage; they are never easy without some degree of this. And were their hearts open to our view, we should see regularity, decency, beauty, as what their wishes terminate upon, either to themselves or their posterity, and what their imagination is always presenting to them as the possible effect of their labours; nor without this could they ever justify their pursuits to themselves.

There may perhaps be some instances of human nature perverted into a thorough miser, who loves nothing but money, and whose fancy arises no higher than the cold dull thought of possession. But such an instance in an age must not be made the standard of mankind against the whole body.

If we examine the pursuits of the luxurious, who in the opinion of the world is wholly devoted to his belly, we shall generally find that the far greater part of

his expense is employed to procure other sensations than those of taste, such as fine attendants, regular apartments, services of plate, and the like. Besides, a large share of the preparation must be supposed designed for some sort of generous, friendly purposes, as to please acquaintance, strangers, parasites. How few would be contented to enjoy the same sensations alone, in a cottage, or out of earthen pitchers? To conclude this point, however these internal sensations may be overlooked in our philosophical inquiries about the human faculties, we shall find in fact "that they employ us more, and are more efficacious in life, either to our pleasure, or uneasiness, than all our external senses taken together."

2. As to the final causes of this internal sense, we need not inquire "whether to an almighty and all-knowing Being there be any real excellence in regular forms, in acting by general laws, in knowing by theorems." We seem scarce capable of answering such questions any way; nor need we inquire "whether other animals may not discern uniformity and regularity in objects which escape our observation, and may not perhaps have their senses constituted so as to perceive beauty, from the same foundation which we do, in objects which our senses are not fitted to examine or compare." We shall confine ourselves to a subject where we have some certain foundations to go upon, and only inquire "if we can find any reasons worthy of the great author of nature for making such a connection between regular objects and the pleasure which accompanies our perceptions of them"; or "what reasons might possibly influence him to create the world as it at present is, as far as we can observe, everywhere full of regularity and uniformity." Let it be here observed, that as far as we know of any of the great bodies of the universe, we see forms and motions really beautiful to our senses; and if we were placed in any planet, the apparent courses

---

16 Horace, *Satires* II, ii, 20 [...let exercise be your relish].

would still be regular and uniform, and consequently beautiful to our sense. Now this gives us no small ground to imagine that if the senses of their inhabitants are in the same manner adapted to their habitations and the objects occurring to their view, as ours are here, their senses must be upon the same general foundation with ours.

But to return to the questions: What occurs to resolve them may be contained in the following propositions.

1. The manner of knowledge by universal theorems, and of operation by universal causes, as far as we can attain to this manner, must be most convenient for beings of limited understanding and power, since this prevents distraction in their understandings through the multiplicity of propositions, and toil and weariness to their powers of action. And consequently their reason, without any sense of beauty, must approve of such methods when they reflect upon their apparent advantage.

2. Those objects of contemplation in which there is uniformity amidst variety are more distinctly and easily comprehended and retained than irregular objects, because the accurate observation of one or two parts often leads to the knowledge of the whole. Thus we can, from a pillar or two with an intermediate arch and cornice, form a distinct idea of a whole regular building, if we know of what species it is, and have its length and breadth. From a side and solid angle we have the whole regular solid; the measuring one side gives the whole square; one radius the whole circle pretty nearly; two diameters an oval; one ordinate and abscissa the parabola; and so on in more complex figures which have any regularity, which can be entirely determined and known in every part from a few data. Whereas it must be a long attention to a vast multiplicity of parts which can ascertain or fix the idea of any irregular form, or give any distinct idea of it, or make us capable of retaining; as appears in the forms of rude rocks, and pebbles, and confused heaps, even when the multitude of sensible parts is not so great as in the regular forms. For such irregular objects distract the mind with variety, since for every sensible part we must have a quite different idea.

3. From the last two propositions it follows "that beings of limited understanding and power, if they act rationally for their own interest, must choose to operate by the simplest means, to invest general theorems, and to study regular objects if they be but equal in use with irregular ones, that they may avoid the endless toil of producing each effect by a separate operation, of searching each different truth by a different inquiry, and of imprinting the endless variety of dissimilar ideas in irregular objects."

4. But then, besides this consideration of interest, there does not appear to be any necessary connection, antecedently to the constitution of the Author of nature, between the regular forms, actions, theorems, and that sudden sensible pleasure excited in us upon observation of them, even when we do not reflect upon the advantage mentioned in the former proposition. And possibly the Deity could have formed us so as to have received no pleasure from such objects, or connected pleasure to those of a quite contrary nature. We have a tolerable presumption of this in the beauties of various animals; they give some small pleasure indeed to everyone who views them, but then every one in its own species seems vastly more delighted with their peculiar beauties than with the beauties of a different species, which seldom raise any desire but among animals of the same species with the one admired. This makes it probable that the pleasure is not the necessary result of the form itself, otherwise it would equally affect all apprehensions in what species soever. This present constitution is much more adapted to preserve the regularity of the universe, and is probably not the effect of necessity but choice in the supreme agent who constituted our senses.

5. Now from the whole we may conclude "that supposing the Deity so kind as to connect sensible pleasure with certain actions or contemplations, besides the rational advantage perceivable in them, there is a great moral necessity, from his goodness, that the internal sense of men should be constituted as it is at present so as to make uniformity amidst variety the occasion of pleasure." For were it not so, but on the contrary, if irregular objects, particular truths, and operations pleased us, besides the endless toil this would involve us in, there must arise a perpetual dissatisfaction in all rational agents with themselves, since reason and interest would lead us to simple general causes, while a contrary sense of beauty would make us disapprove them. Universal theorems would appear to our understanding the best means of increasing our knowledge of what might be useful, while a contrary sense would set us on the search after singular truths. Thought and reflection would recommend objects with uniformity amidst variety, and yet this perverse instinct would involve us in labyrinths of confusion and dissimilitude. And hence we see "how suitable it is to the sagacious bounty which we suppose in the Deity to constitute our internal senses in the manner in which they are, by which pleasure is joined to the contemplation of those objects which a finite mind can best imprint and retain the ideas of with the least distraction; to those actions which are most efficacious, and fruitful in useful effects; and to those theorems which most enlarge our minds."

As to the other question, "What reason might influence the Deity, whom no diversities of operation could distract or weary, to choose to operate by simplest means and general laws, and to diffuse uniformity, pro-portion, and similitude through all the parts of nature which we can observe"; perhaps there may be some real excellence in this manner of operation, and in these forms, which we know not. But this we may probably say, that since the divine goodness, for the reasons above mentioned, has constituted our sense of beauty as it is at present, the same goodness might determine the great Architect to adorn this vast theatre in that manner which should be agreeable to the spectators, and that part which is exposed to the observation of men so as to be pleasant to them; especially if we suppose that he designed to discover himself to them as wise and good, as well as powerful; for thus he has given them greater evidences, through the whole earth, of his art, wisdom, design, and bounty, than they can possibly have for the reason, and counsel, and good-will of their fellow creatures, with whom they converse with full persuasion of this in their common affairs.

As to the operations of the Deity by general laws, there is a further reason from a sense still superior to these already considered, even that of virtue, or the beauty of action, which is the foundation of our greatest happiness. For were there no general laws fixed in the course of nature, there could be no prudence or design in men, no rational expectation of effects from causes, no schemes of action projected, nor any regular execution. If then according to the frame of our nature, our greatest happiness must depend upon our actions, as it may perhaps be made appear it does, "the universe must be governed, not by particular wills, but by general laws, upon which we can found our expectations, and project our schemes of action."

DAVID HUME

(1711-1776)

At the age of twenty-six Hume had virtually completed his great *Treatise of Human Nature,* which was presented to the public two years later. This work was greeted with a silence that was painful to Hume, who was confessedly eager for literary fame. Even when in the course of years he had become moderately renowned as an essayist and historian, his earlier (and more profound) philosophical works wanted readers. (The first serious notice of the *Treatise* was to come, after decades, in the "refutations" published by Scottish realists beginning with Reid.) Hume might have said with the astronomer Kepler, "I can afford to wait a hundred years for a reader, seeing that God Almighty had to wait five thousand years before finding such an observer as myself." Through most of his life he could not begin to support himself with his pen, and, having also failed to secure academic appointments at Edinburgh and Glasgow, he subsisted on a small inheritance combined with services to various persons as librarian, tutor, and secretary.

Compared with Hume's writings on the understanding, passions, and morals, the essay on the standard of taste was a minor work. Yet, like the *Dialogues Concerning Natural Religion* (still later in composition), it rounds out Hume's philosophy: without either of these works one could not say that Hume's examination of the grounds for human conviction had truly universal scope.

The early pages of the essay are as good a statement as has ever been made of the one problem in aesthetics that a conscientious critic will inevitably face: "By what method, if any, can disputes concerning the merits of works of art be resolved?" Hume's answer might be described as a kind of semi-objectivism. He believes that there are "rules of composition" followed more or less wittingly by artists; and these are the same as the "general principles of approbation or blame" that are available to critics. But these principles or rules are founded upon observation of what, in the long run, has been found pleasing by a consensus of normal and well-qualified judges. What *should* give pleasure is therefore not independent of what in fact *does* please—but neither is the one identical with the other. Everything turns upon Hume's (or our own) ability to give independent criteria for "normality" or for the "qualifications" of the judge. For suppose that, following Hume, we should require a critic to have training and practice, delicacy of taste, impartiality, and so forth. And suppose we should then meet a critic who prefers Ogilby to Milton. Can we disqualify his judgment on the ground, say, of "prejudice," if our only basis for imputing prejudice to this man is the fact that he prefers Ogilby to Milton? (Can Hume, in short, be acquitted of a charge of circularity in his reasoning?) But suppose, on the other hand, that the enthusiast for Ogilby was one whose judgment of poetry was chronically influenced by a detestation of puritans and regicides (of whom, according to Dr. Johnson, Milton was one). How, and in what way, would *that* bear upon the acceptability of his judgment in the particular case of John Milton?

One may also be inclined to ask (as one asks later on with the selection from Lewis) whether, granted that certain principles can be drawn from works that are supported by a consensus of good judges, each of these judges has drawn his principles from observation of a consensus of good judges. Has every critic, from the first person who ever praised Homer, judged each work by the standard of what is pleasing to everyone, that is, by standards of universal and normal human nature?

Our second selection is drawn from the chapter on the association of ideas in his *Enquiry Concerning Human Understanding*. After the first edition, the section on association was inexplicably shortened to include only the first three of the paragraphs that appear here.

DAVID HUME

Of the Standard of Taste

(First published: 1757.)

The great variety of taste, as well as of opinion, which prevails in the world, is too obvious not to have fallen under everyone's observation. Men of the most confined knowledge are able to remark a difference of taste in the narrow circle of their acquaintance, even where the persons have been educated under the same government, and have early imbibed the same prejudices. But those who can enlarge their view to contemplate distant nations and remote ages are still more surprised at the great inconsistence and contrariety. We are apt to call *barbarous* whatever departs widely from our own taste and apprehension, but soon find the epithet of reproach retorted on us. And the highest arrogance and self-conceit is at last startled, on observing an equal assurance on all sides, and scruples, amidst such a contest of sentiment, to pronounce positively in its own favour.

As this variety of taste is obvious to the most careless enquirer; so will it be found, on examination, to be still greater in reality than in appearance. The sentiments of men often differ with regard to beauty and deformity of all kinds, even while their general discourse is the same. There are certain terms in every language which import blame, and others praise; and all men who use the same tongue must agree in their application of them. Every voice is united in applauding elegance, propriety, simplicity, spirit in writing; and in blaming fustian, affectation, coldness, and a false brilliancy; but when critics come to particulars, this seeming unanimity vanishes; and it is found that they had affixed a very different meaning to their expressions. In all matters of opinion and science, the case is opposite; the difference among men is there oftener found to lie in generals than in particulars, and to be less in reality than in appearance. An explanation of the terms commonly ends the controversy; and the disputants are surprised to find that they had been quarrelling, while at bottom they agreed in their judgment.

Those who found morality on sentiment, more than on reason, are inclined to comprehend ethics under the former observations, and to maintain that, in all questions which regard conduct and manners, the difference among men is really greater than at first sight it appears. It is indeed obvious that writers of all nations and all ages concur in applauding justice, humanity, magnanimity, prudence, veracity; and in blaming the opposite qualities. Even poets and other authors, whose compositions are chiefly calculated to please the imagination, are yet found, from Homer down to Fénelon, to inculcate the same moral precepts, and to bestow their applause and blame on the same virtues and vices. This great unanimity is usually ascribed to the influence of plain reason, which, in all these cases, maintains similar sentiments in all men, and prevents those controversies to which the abstract sciences are so much exposed. So far as the unanimity is real, this account may be admitted as satisfactory; but we must also allow that some part of the seeming harmony in morals may be accounted for from the very nature of language. The word *virtue,* with its equivalent in every tongue, implies praise; as that of *vice* does blame. And no one, without the most obvious and grossest impropriety, could affix reproach to a term which in general acceptation is understood in a good sense; or

bestow applause where the idiom requires disapprobation. Homer's general precepts, where he delivers any such, will never be controverted; but it is obvious that, when he draws particular pictures of manners, and represents heroism in Achilles and prudence in Ulysses, he intermixes a much greater degree of ferocity in the former, and of cunning and fraud in the latter, than Fénelon would admit of. The sage Ulysses in the Greek poet seems to delight in lies and fictions, and often employs them without any necessity or even advantage. But his more scrupulous son, in the French epic writer, exposes himself to the most imminent perils, rather than depart from the most exact line of truth and veracity.

The admirers and followers of the Alcoran insist on the excellent moral precepts interspersed throughout that wild and absurd performance. But it is to be supposed that the Arabic words, which correspond to the English equity, justice, temperance, meekness, charity, were such as, from the constant use of that tongue, must always be taken in a good sense; and it would have argued the greatest ignorance, not of morals, but of language, to have mentioned them with any epithets besides those of applause and approbation. But would we know whether the pretended prophet had really attained a just sentiment of morals? Let us attend to his narration; and we shall soon find that he bestows praise on such instances of treachery, inhumanity, cruelty, revenge, bigotry as are utterly incompatible with civilized society. No steady rule of right seems there to be attended to; and every action is blamed or praised, so far only as it is beneficial or hurtful to the true believers.

The merit of delivering true general precepts in ethics is indeed very small. Whoever recommends any moral virtues really does no more than is implied in the terms themselves. That people who invented the word *charity,* and used it in a good sense, inculcated more clearly and much more efficaciously the precept, *be charitable,* than any pretended legislator or prophet who should insert such a maxim in his writings. Of all expressions, those which, together with their other meanings, imply a degree either of blame or approbation are the least liable to be perverted or mistaken.

It is natural for us to seek a *standard of taste*; a rule, by which the various sentiments of men may be reconciled; at least, a decision, afforded, confirming one sentiment, and condemning another.

There is a species of philosophy which cuts off all hopes of success in such an attempt, and represents the impossibility of ever attaining any standard of taste. The difference, it is said, is very wide between judgment and sentiment. All sentiment is right, because sentiment has a reference to nothing beyond itself, and is always real, wherever a man is conscious of it. But all determinations of the understanding are not right, because they have a reference to something beyond themselves, to wit, real matter of fact, and are not always conformable to that standard. Among a thousand different opinions which different men may entertain of the same subject, there is one, and but one, that is just and true; and the only difficulty is to fix and ascertain it. On the contrary, a thousand different sentiments, excited by the same object, are all right, because no sentiment represents what is really in the object. It only marks a certain conformity or relation between the object and the organs or faculties of the mind; and if that conformity did not really exist, the sentiment could never possibly have being. Beauty is no quality in things themselves. It exists merely in the mind which contemplates them; and each mind perceives a different beauty. One person may even perceive deformity, where another is sensible of beauty; and every individual ought to acquiesce in his own sentiment, without pretending to regulate those of others. To seek the real beauty, or real deformity, is as fruitless an enquiry as to pretend to ascertain the real sweet or the real bitter. According to the disposition of the organs, the same object may be both sweet and bitter; and the proverb has justly determined it to be fruitless to dispute concerning tastes. It is very natural, and even quite necessary, to extend this axiom to mental, as well as bodily taste; and thus common sense, which is so often at variance with philosophy, especially with the sceptical kind, is found, in one instance at least, to agree in pronouncing the same decision.

But though this axiom, by passing into a proverb, seems to have attained the sanction of common sense, there is certainly a species of common sense which opposes it, at least serves to modify and restrain it. Whoever would assert an equality of genius and elegance between Ogilby and Milton, or Bunyan and Addison, would be thought to defend no less an extravagance than if he had maintained a mole-hill to be as high as Teneriffe, or a pond as extensive as the ocean. Though there may be found persons who give the preference to the former authors, no one pays attention to such a taste; and we pronounce without scruple the sentiment of these pretended critics to be absurd and ridiculous. The principle of the natural equality of tastes is then totally forgot, and while we admit it on some occasions, where the objects seem near an equality, it appears an extravagant paradox, or rather a palpable absurdity, where objects so disproportioned are compared together.

It is evident that none of the rules of composition are fixed by reasonings a priori, or can be esteemed abstract conclusions of the understanding, from comparing those habitudes and relations of ideas which are eternal and immutable. Their foundation is the same with that of all the practical sciences, experience; nor are they anything but general observations, concerning what has been universally found to please in all countries and in all ages. Many of the beauties of poetry and even of eloquence are founded on falsehood and fiction, on hyperboles, metaphors, and an abuse or perversion of terms from their natural meaning. To check the sallies of the imagination, and to reduce every expression to geometrical truth and exactness, would be the most contrary to the laws of criticism, because it would produce a work, which, by universal experience, has been found the most insipid and disagreeable. But though poetry can never submit to exact truth, it must be confined by rules of art, discovered to the author either by genius or observation. If some negligent or irregular writers have pleased, they have not pleased by their transgressions of rule or order, but in spite of these transgressions. They have possessed other beauties, which were conformable to just criticism; and the force of these beauties has been able to overpower censure, and give the mind a satisfaction superior to the disgust arising from the blemishes. Ariosto pleases; but not by his monstrous and improbable fictions, by his bizarre mixture of the serious and comic styles, by the want of coherence in his stories, or by the continual interruptions of his narration. He charms by the force and clearness of his expression, by the readiness and variety of his inventions, and by his natural pictures of the passions, especially those of the gay and amorous kind. And however his faults may diminish our satisfaction, they are not able entirely to destroy it. Did our pleasure really arise from those parts of his poem which we denominate faults, this would be no objection to criticism in general. It would only be an objection to those particular rules of criticism which would establish such circumstances to be faults, and would represent them as universally blameable. If they are found to please, they cannot be faults; let the pleasure which they produce be ever so unexpected and unaccountable.

But though all the general rules of art are founded only on experience and on the observation of the common sentiments of human nature, we must not imagine that, on every occasion, the feelings of men will be conformable to these rules. Those finer emotions of the mind are of a very tender and delicate nature, and require the concurrence of many favorable circumstances to make them play with facility and exactness, according to their general and established principles. The least exterior hindrance to such small springs, or the least internal disorder, disturbs their motion, and confounds the operation of the whole machine. When we would make an experiment of this nature, and would try the force of any beauty or deformity, we must choose with care a proper time and place, and bring the fancy to a suitable situation and disposition. A perfect serenity of mind, a recollection of thought, a due attention to the object; if any of these circumstances be wanting, our experiment will be fallacious, and we shall be unable to judge of the catholic and universal beauty. The relation which nature has placed between the form and the sentiment will at least be more obscure; and it will require greater accuracy to trace and discern it. We shall be able to ascertain its influence not so much from the operation of each particular beauty, as from the durable admiration which attends those works that have survived all the caprices of mode and fashion, all the mistakes of ignorance and envy.

The same Homer, who pleased at Athens and Rome two thousand years ago, is still admired at Paris and at London. All the changes of climate, government, religion, and language have not been able to obscure his glory. Authority or prejudice may give a temporary vogue to a bad poet or orator; but his reputation will never be durable or general. When his compositions are examined by posterity or by foreigners, the enchantment is dissipated, and his faults appear in their true colors. On the contrary, a real genius, the longer his works endure, and the more wide they are spread, the more sincere is the admiration which he meets with. Envy and jealousy have too much place in a narrow circle; and even familiar acquaintance with his person may diminish the applause due to his performances. But when these obstructions are removed, the beauties, which are naturally fitted to excite agreeable sentiments, immediately display their energy; and while the world endures, they maintain their authority over the minds of men.

It appears then that, amidst all the variety and caprice of taste, there are certain general principles of approbation or blame, whose influence a careful eye may trace in all operations of the mind. Some particular forms or qualities, from the original structure of the internal fabric, are calculated to please, and others to displease; and if they fail of their effect in any particular instance, it is from some apparent defect or imperfection in the organ. A man in a fever would not insist on his palate as able to decide concerning flavours; nor would one, affected with the jaundice, pretend to give a verdict with regard to colours. In each creature, there is a sound and a defective state; and the former alone can be supposed to afford us a true standard of taste and sentiment. If, in the sound state of the organ, there be an entire or a considerable uniformity of sentiment among men, we may thence derive an idea of the perfect beauty; in like manner as the appearance of objects in day-light, to the eye of a man in health, is denominated their true and real colour, even while colour is allowed to be merely a phantasm of the senses.

Many and frequent are the defects in the internal organs, which prevent or weaken the influence of those general principles on which depends our sentiment of beauty or deformity. Though some objects, by the structure of the mind, be naturally calculated to give pleasure, it is not to be expected that in every individual the pleasure will be equally felt. Particular incidents and situations occur, which either throw a false light on the objects, or hinder the true from conveying to the imagination the proper sentiment and perception.

One obvious cause why many feel not the proper sentiment of beauty is the want of that *delicacy* of imagination, which is requisite to convey a sensibility of those finer emotions. This delicacy everyone pretends to; everyone talks of it; and would reduce every kind of taste or sentiment to its standard. But as our intention in this essay is to mingle some light of the understanding with the feelings of sentiment, it will be proper to give a more accurate definition of delicacy than has hitherto been attempted. And not to draw our philosophy from too profound a source, we shall have recourse to a noted story in *Don Quixote*.

"It is with good reason," says Sancho to the squire with the great nose, "that I pretend to have a judgment in wine: This is a quality hereditary in our family. Two of my kinsmen were once called to give their opinion of a hogshead, which was supposed to be excellent, being old and of a good vintage. One of them tastes it; considers it; and after mature reflection pronounces the wine to be good, were it not for a small taste of leather which he perceived in it. The other, after using the same precautions, gives also his verdict in favour of the wine; but with the reserve of a taste of iron, which he could easily distinguish. You cannot imagine how much they were both ridiculed for their judgment. But who laughed in the end? On emptying the hogshead, there was found at the bottom, an old key with a leathern thong tied to it."

The great resemblance between mental and bodily taste will easily teach us to apply this story. Though it be certain that beauty and deformity, more than sweet and bitter, are not qualities in objects, but belong entirely to the sentiment, internal or external, it must be allowed that there are certain qualities in objects which are fitted by nature to produce those particular feelings. Now as these qualities may be found in a small degree, or may be mixed and confounded with each other, it often happens that the taste is not affected with such minute qualities, or is not able to distinguish all the particular flavours, amidst the disorder in which they are presented. Where the organs are so fine, as to allow nothing to escape them, and at the same time so exact as to perceive every ingredient in the composition, this we call delicacy of taste, whether we employ these terms in the literal or metaphorical sense. Here then the general rules of beauty are of use; being drawn from established models, and from the observation of what pleases or displeases, when presented singly and in a high degree. And if the same qualities, in a continued composition and in a smaller degree, affect not the organs with a sensible delight or uneasiness, we exclude the person from all pretensions to this delicacy. To produce these general rules or avowed patterns of composition is like finding the key with the leathern thong, which justified the verdict of Sancho's kinsmen, and confounded those pretended judges who had condemned them. Though the hogshead had never been emptied, the taste of the one was still equally delicate, and that of the other equally dull and languid, but it would have been more difficult to have proved the superiority of the former, to the conviction of every bystander. In like manner, though the beauties of writing had never been methodized, or reduced to general principles; though no excellent models had ever been acknowledged; the different degrees of taste would still have subsisted, and the judgment of one man been preferable to that of another; but it would not have been so easy to silence the bad critic, who might always insist upon his particular sentiment, and refuse to submit to his antagonist. But when we show him an avowed principle of art; when we illustrate this principle by examples, whose operation, from his own particular taste, he acknowledges to be conformable to the principle; when we prove that the same principle may be applied to the present case, where he did

not perceive or feel its influence, he must conclude, upon the whole, that the fault lies in himself, and that he wants the delicacy which is requisite to make him sensible of every beauty and every blemish, in any composition or discourse.

It is acknowledged to be the perfection of every sense or faculty to perceive with exactness its most minute objects, and allow nothing to escape its notice and observation. The smaller the objects are which become sensible to the eye, the finer is that organ, and the more elaborate its make and composition. A good palate is not tried by strong flavours, but by a mixture of small ingredients, where we are still sensible of each part, notwithstanding its minuteness and its confusion with the rest. In like manner, a quick and acute perception of beauty and deformity must be the perfection of our mental taste; nor can a man be satisfied with himself while he suspects that any excellence or blemish in a discourse has passed him unobserved. In this case, the perfection of the man and the perfection of the sense or feeling are found to be united. A very delicate palate, on many occasions, may be a great inconvenience both to a man himself and to his friends. But a delicate taste of wit or beauty must always be a desirable quality, because it is the source of all the finest and most innocent enjoyments of which human nature is susceptible. In this decision the sentiments of all mankind are agreed. Wherever you can ascertain a delicacy of taste, it is sure to meet with approbation; and the best way of ascertaining it is to appeal to those models and principles which have been established by the uniform consent and experience of nations and ages.

But though there be naturally a wide difference in point of delicacy between one person and another, nothing tends further to increase and improve this talent than *practice* in a particular art, and the frequent survey or contemplation of a particular species of beauty. When objects of any kind are first presented to the eye or imagination, the sentiment which attends them is obscure and confused; and the mind is, in a great measure, incapable of pronouncing concerning their merits or defects. The taste cannot perceive the several excellences of the performance, much less distinguish the particular character of each excellency, and ascertain its quality and degree. If it pronounce the whole in general to be beautiful or deformed, it is the utmost that can be expected; and even this judgment, a person, so unpracticed, will be apt to deliver with great hesitation and reserve. But allow him to acquire experience in those objects, his feeling becomes more exact and nice. He not only perceives the beauties and defects of each part, but marks the distinguishing species of each quality, and assigns it suitable praise or blame. A clear and distinct sentiment attends him through the whole survey of the object; and he discerns that very degree and kind of approbation or displeasure, which each part is naturally fitted to produce. The mist dissipates, which seemed formerly to hang over the object; the organ acquires greater perfection in its operations; and can pronounce, without danger of mistake, concerning the merits of every performance. In a word, the same address and dexterity which practice gives to the execution of any work is also acquired by the same means, in the judging of it.

So advantageous is practice to the discernment of beauty that, before we can give judgment on any work of importance, it will even be requisite that that very individual performance be more than once perused by us, and be surveyed in different lights with attention and deliberation. There is a flutter or hurry of thought which attends the first perusal of any piece, and which confounds the genuine sentiment of beauty. The relation of the parts is not discerned; the true characters of style are little distinguished; the several perfections and defects seem wrapped up in a species of confusion, and present themselves indistinctly to the imagination. Not to mention that there is a species of beauty, which, as it is florid and superficial, pleases at first; but being found incompatible with a just expression either of reason or passion, soon palls upon the taste, and is then rejected with disdain, at least rated at a much lower value.

It is impossible to continue in the practice of contemplating any order of beauty, without being frequently obliged to form *comparisons* between the several species and degrees of excellence, and estimating their proportion to each other. A man who has had no opportunity of comparing the different kinds of beauty is indeed totally unqualified to pronounce an opinion with regard to any object presented to him. By comparison alone we fix the epithets of praise or blame, and learn how to assign the due degree of each. The coarsest daubing contains a certain lustre of colors and exactness of imitation, which are so far beauties, and would affect the mind of a peasant or Indian with the highest admiration. The most vulgar ballads are not entirely destitute of harmony or nature; and none but a person familiarized to superior beauties would pronounce their numbers harsh, or narration uninteresting. A great inferiority of beauty gives pain to a person conversant in the highest excellence of the kind, and is for that reason pronounced a deformity, as the most finished object with which we are acquainted is naturally supposed to have reached the pinnacle of perfection, and to be entitled to the highest applause. One accustomed to see, and examine, and weigh the several performances, admired in different ages and nations, can only rate the merits of a work exhibited to his view, and assign its proper rank among the productions of genius.

But to enable a critic the more fully to execute this undertaking, he must preserve his mind free from all *prejudice,* and allow nothing to enter into his consideration but the very object which is submitted to his examination. We may observe that every work of art, in order to produce its due effect on the mind, must be surveyed in a certain point of view, and cannot be relished by persons whose situation, real or imaginary, is not conformable to that which is required by the performance. An orator addresses himself to a particular audience, and must have a regard to their particular genius, interests, opinions, passions, and prejudices; otherwise he hopes in vain to govern their resolutions, and inflame their affections. Should they even have entertained some prepossessions against him, however unreasonable, he must not overlook this disadvantage; but, before he enters upon the subject, must endeavour to conciliate their affection, and acquire their good graces. A critic of a different age or nation who should peruse this discourse must have all these circumstances in his eye, and must place himself in the same situation as the audience in order to form a true judgment of the oration. In like manner, when any work is addressed to the public, though I should have a friendship or enmity with the author, I must depart from this situation; and considering myself as a man in general, forget, if possible, my individual being and my peculiar circumstances. A person influenced by prejudice complies not with this condition, but obstinately maintains his natural position, without placing himself in that point of view which the performance supposes. If the work be addressed to persons of a different age or nation, he makes no allowance for their peculiar views and prejudices; but, full of the manners of his own age and country, rashly condemns what seemed admirable in the eyes of those for whom alone the discourse was calculated. If the work be executed for the public, he never sufficiently enlarges his comprehension, or forgets his interest as a friend or enemy, as a rival or commentator. By this means, his sentiments are perverted; nor have the same beauties and blemishes the same influence upon him, as if he had im-

posed a proper violence on his imagination, and had forgotten himself for a moment. So far his taste evidently departs from the true standard, and of consequence loses all credit and authority.

It is well known that in all questions submitted to the understanding, prejudice is destructive of sound judgment, and perverts all operations of the intellectual faculties; it is no less contrary to good taste; nor has it less influence to corrupt our sentiment of beauty. It belongs to *good sense* to check its influence in both cases; and in this respect, as well as in many others, reason, if not an essential part of taste, is at least requisite to the operations of this latter faculty. In all the nobler productions of genius, there is a mutual relation and correspondence of parts; nor can either the beauties or blemishes be perceived by him whose thought is not capacious enough to comprehend all those parts, and compare them with each other in order to perceive the consistence and uniformity of the whole. Every work of art has also a certain end or purpose for which it is calculated; and is to be deemed more or less perfect, as it is more or less fitted to attain this end. The object of eloquence is to persuade, of history to instruct, of poetry to please by means of the passions and the imagination. These ends we must carry constantly in our view, when we peruse any performance; and we must be able to judge how far the means employed are adapted to their respective purposes. Besides, every kind of composition, even the most poetical, is nothing but a chain of propositions and reasonings; not always, indeed, the justest and most exact, but still plausible and specious, however disguised by the colouring of the imagination. The persons introduced in tragedy and epic poetry must be represented as reasoning, and thinking, and concluding, and acting, suitably to their character and circumstances; and without judgment, as well as taste and invention, a poet can never hope to succeed in so delicate an undertaking.

Not to mention that the same excellence of faculties which contributes to the improvement of reason, the same clearness of conception, the same exactness of distinction, the same vivacity of apprehension, are essential to the operations of true taste, and are its infallible concomitants. It seldom, or never, happens that a man of sense, who has experience in any art, cannot judge of its beauty; and it is no less rare to meet a man who has a just taste without a sound understanding.

Thus, though the principles of taste be universal, and, nearly, if not entirely the same in all men; yet few are qualified to give judgment on any work of art, or establish their own sentiment as the standard of beauty. The organs of internal sensation are seldom so perfect as to allow the general principles their full play, and produce a feeling correspondent to those principles. They either labour under some defect, or are vitiated by some disorder; and by that means excite a sentiment which may be pronounced erroneous. When the critic has no delicacy, he judges without any distinction, and is only affected by the grosser and more palpable qualities of the object; the finer touches pass unnoticed and disregarded. Where he is not aided by practice, his verdict is attended with confusion and hesitation. Where no comparison has been employed, the most frivolous beauties, such as rather merit the name of defects, are the object of his admiration. Where he lies under the influence of prejudice, all his natural sentiments are perverted. Where good sense is wanting, he is not qualified to discern the beauties of design and reasoning, which are the highest and most excellent. Under some or other of these imperfections, the generality of men labour; and hence a true judge in the finer arts is observed, even during the most polished ages, to be so rare a character. Strong sense, united to delicate sentiment, improved by practice, perfected by comparison, and cleared of all prejudice, can alone entitle critics to this valuable character; and the joint verdict of such, wherever they are to be found, is the true standard of taste and beauty.

But where are such critics to found? By what marks are they to be known? How distinguish them from pretenders? These questions are embarrassing, and seem to throw us back into the same uncertainty from which, during the course of this essay, we have endeavoured to extricate ourselves.

But if we consider the matter aright, these are questions of fact, not of sentiment. Whether any particular person be endowed with good sense and a delicate imagination, free from prejudice, may often be the subject of dispute, and be liable to great discussion and enquiry; but that such a character is valuable and estimable will be agreed on by all mankind. Where these doubts occur, men can do no more than in other disputable questions which are submitted to the understanding: They must produce the best arguments that their invention suggests to them; they must acknowledge a true and decisive standard to exist somewhere, to wit, real existence and matter of fact; and they must have indulgence to such as differ from them in their appeals to this standard. It is sufficient for our present purpose if we have proved that the taste of all individuals is not upon an equal footing, and that some men in general, however difficult to be particularly pitched upon, will be acknowledged by universal sentiment to have a preference above others.

But in reality the difficulty of finding, even in particulars, the standard of taste is not so great as it is represented. Though in speculation we may readily avow a certain criterion in science and deny it in sentiment, the matter is found in practice to be much more hard to ascertain in the former case than in the latter. Theories of abstract philosophy, systems of profound theology, have prevailed during one age. In a successive period, these have been universally exploded; their absurdity has been detected;

other theories and systems have supplied their place, which again gave place to their successors; and nothing has been experienced more liable to the revolutions of chance and fashion than these pretended decisions of science. The case is not the same with the beauties of eloquence and poetry. Just expressions of passion and nature are sure, after a little time, to gain public applause, which they maintain forever. Aristotle, and Plato, and Epicurus, and Descartes may successively yield to each other; but Terence and Virgil maintain a universal, undisputed empire over the minds of men. The abstract philosophy of Cicero has lost its credit; the vehemence of his oratory is still the object of our admiration.

Though men of delicate taste be rare, they are easily to be distinguished in society, by the soundness of their understanding and the superiority of their faculties above the rest of mankind. The ascendant which they acquire gives a prevalence to that lively approbation with which they receive any productions of genius, and renders it generally predominant. Many men, when left to themselves, have but a faint and dubious perception of beauty, who yet are capable of relishing any fine stroke which is pointed out to them. Every convert to the admiration of the real poet or orator is the cause of some new conversion. And though prejudices may prevail for a time, they never unite in celebrating any rival to the true genius, but yield at last to the force of nature and just sentiment. Thus, though a civilized nation may easily be mistaken in the choice of their admired philosopher, they never have been found long to err in their affection for a favorite epic or tragic author.

But notwithstanding all our endeavours to fix a standard of taste, and reconcile the discordant apprehensions of men, there still remain two sources of variation which are not sufficient indeed to confound all the boundaries of beauty and deformity, but

will often serve to produce a difference in the degrees of our approbation or blame. The one is the different humours of particular men; the other, the particular manners and opinions of our age and country. The general principles of taste are uniform in human nature. Where men vary in their judgments, some defect or perversion in the faculties may commonly be remarked, proceeding either from prejudice, from want of practice, or want of delicacy; and there is just reason for approving one taste, and condemning another. But where there is such a diversity in the internal frame or external situation as is entirely blameless on both sides, and leaves no room to give one the preference above the other; in that case a certain degree of diversity in judgment is unavoidable, and we seek in vain for a standard by which we can reconcile the contrary sentiments.

A young man whose passions are warm will be more sensibly touched with amorous and tender images than a man more advanced in years who takes pleasure in wise, philosophical reflections concerning the conduct of life and moderation of the passions. At twenty, Ovid may be the favourite author; Horace at forty; and perhaps Tacitus at fifty. Vainly would we, in such cases, endeavour to enter into the sentiments of others, and divest ourselves of those propensities which are natural to us. We choose our favourite author as we do our friend, from a conformity of humour and disposition. Mirth or passion, sentiment or reflection; whichever of these most predominates in our temper, it gives us a peculiar sympathy with the writer who resembles us.

One person is more pleased with the sublime; another with the tender; a third with raillery. One has a strong sensibility to blemishes, and is extremely studious of correctness; another has a more lively feeling of beauties, and pardons twenty absurdities and defects for one elevated or pathetic stroke. The ear of this man is entirely turned toward conciseness and energy; that man is delighted with a copious, rich, and harmonious expression. Simplicity is affected by one; ornament by another. Comedy, tragedy, satire, odes have each its partisans, who prefer that particular species of writing to all others. It is plainly an error in a critic to confine his approbations to one species or style of writing, and condemn all the rest. But it is almost impossible not to feel a predilection for that which suits our particular turn and disposition. Such preferences are innocent and unavoidable, and can never reasonably be the object of dispute, because there is no standard by which they can be decided.

For a like reason, we are more pleased, in the course of our reading, with pictures and characters that resemble objects which are found in our own age or country than with those which describe a different set of customs. It is not without some effort that we reconcile ourselves to the simplicity of ancient manners, and behold princesses carrying water from the spring, and kings and heroes dressing their own victuals. We may allow in general that the representation of such manners is no fault in the author, nor deformity in the piece; but we are not so sensibly touched with them. For this reason, comedy is not easily transferred from one age or nation to another. A Frenchman or Englishman is not pleased with the *Andria* of Terence, or *Clizia* of Machiavel, where the fine lady, upon whom all the play turns, never once appears to the spectators, but is always kept behind the scenes, suitably to the reserved humour of the ancient Greeks and modern Italians. A man of learning and reflection can make allowance for these peculiarities of manners; but a common audience can never divest themselves so far of their usual ideas and sentiments as to relish pictures which in no wise resemble them.

But here there occurs a reflection which may, perhaps, be useful in examining the celebrated controversy concerning ancient and modern learning; where we often find the one side excusing any seeming absurdity in the ancients from the manners of the age, and the other refusing to admit this excuse or, at least, admitting it only as an apology for the author, not for the performance. In my opinion, the proper boundaries in this subject have seldom been fixed between the contending parties. Where any innocent peculiarities of manners are represented, such as those above mentioned, they ought certainly to be admitted; and a man who is shocked with them gives an evident proof of false delicacy and refinement. The poet's *monument more durable than brass,* must fall to the ground like common brick or clay, were men to make no allowance for the continual revolutions of manners and customs, and would admit of nothing but what was suitable to the prevailing fashion. Must we throw aside the pictures of our ancestors because of their ruffs and farthingales? But where the ideas of morality and decency alter from one age to another, and where vicious manners are described without being marked with the proper characters of blame and disapprobation, this must be allowed to disfigure the poem, and to be a real deformity. I cannot, nor is it proper I should, enter into such sentiments; and however I may excuse the poet, on account of the manners of his age, I never can relish the composition. The want of humanity and of decency, so conspicuous in the characters drawn by several of the ancient poets, even sometimes by Homer and the Greek tragedians, diminishes considerably the merit of their noble performances, and gives modern authors an advantage over them. We are not interested in the fortunes and sentiments of such rough heroes; we are displeased to find the limits of vice and virtue so much confounded. And whatever indulgence we may give to the writer on account of his prejudices, we cannot prevail on ourselves to enter into his sentiments, or bear an affection to characters which we plainly discover to be blameable.

The case is not the same with moral principles as with speculative opinions of any kind. These are in continual flux and revolution. The son embraces a different system from the father. Nay, there scarcely is any man who can boast of great constancy and uniformity in this particular. Whatever speculative errors may be found in the polite writings of any age or country, they detract but little from the value of those compositions. There needs but a certain turn of thought or imagination to make us enter into all the opinions which then prevailed, and relish the sentiments or conclusions derived from them. But a very violent effort is requisite to change our judgment of manners, and excite sentiments of approbation or blame, love or hatred, different from those to which the mind from long custom has been familiarized. And where a man is confident of the rectitude of that moral standard by which he judges, he is justly jealous of it, and will not pervert the sentiments of his heart for a moment, in complaisance to any writer whatsoever.

Of all speculative errors, those which regard religion are the most excusable in compositions of genius; nor is it ever permitted to judge of the civility or wisdom of any people, or even of single persons, by the grossness or refinement of their theological principles. The same good sense that directs men in the ordinary occurrences of life is not hearkened to in religious matters, which are supposed to be placed altogether above the cognizance of human reason. On this account, all the absurdities of the pagan system of theology must be overlooked by every critic who would pretend to form a just notion of ancient poetry; and our posterity, in their turn, must have the same indulgence to their forefathers. No religious principles can ever be imputed as a fault to any poet, while they remain merely principles, and take not such strong possession of his heart as to lay him under the imputation of *bigotry* or *superstition*. Where that

happens, they confound the sentiments of morality, and alter the natural boundaries of vice and virtue. They are therefore eternal blemishes, according to the principle above mentioned; nor are the prejudices and false opinions of the age sufficient to justify them.

It is essential to the Roman Catholic religion to inspire a violent hatred of every other worship, and to represent all pagans, mahometans, and heretics as the objects of divine wrath and vengeance. Such sentiments, though they are in reality very blameable, are considered as virtues by the zealots of that communion, and are represented in their tragedies and epic poems as a kind of divine heroism. This bigotry has disfigured two very fine tragedies of the French theatre, *Polyeucte* and *Athalie,* where an intemperate zeal for particular modes of worship is set off with all the pomp imaginable, and forms the predominant character of the heroes. "What is this," says the sublime Joad to Josabet, finding her in discourse with Mathan, the priest of Baal, "Does the daughter of David speak to this traitor? Are you not afraid lest the earth should open and pour forth flames to devour you both? Or lest these holy walls should fall and crush you together? What is his purpose? Why comes that enemy of God hither to poison the air which we breathe with his horrid presence?" Such sentiments are received with great applause in the theatre of Paris; but in London the spectators would be full as much pleased to hear Achilles tell Agamemnon that he was a dog in his forehead, and a deer in his heart, or Jupiter threaten Juno with a sound drubbing if she will not be quiet.

Religious principles are also a blemish in any polite composition, when they rise up to superstition, and intrude themselves into every sentiment, however remote from any connection with religion. It is no excuse for the poet that the customs of his country had burdened life with so many religious ceremonies and observances that no part of it was exempt from that yoke. It must forever be ridiculous in Petrarch to compare his mistress Laura to Jesus Christ. Nor is it less ridiculous in that agreeable libertine, Boccace, very seriously to give thanks to God Almighty and the ladies for their assistance in defending him against his enemies.

DAVID HUME

An Enquiry Concerning Human Understanding

(First published: 1748.)

Of the Association of Ideas

It is evident that there is a principle of connection between the different thoughts or ideas of the mind, and that, in their appearance to the memory or imagination, they introduce each other with a certain degree of method and regularity. In our more serious thinking or discourse this is so observable that any particular thought which breaks in upon the regular tract or chain of ideas is immediately remarked and rejected. And even in our wildest and most wandering reveries, nay, in our very dreams, we shall find, if we reflect, that the imagination ran not altogether at adventures, but that there was still a connection upheld among the different ideas which succeeded each other. Were the loosest and freest conversation to be transcribed, there would immediately be observed something which connected it in all its transitions. Or where this is wanting, the person who broke the thread of discourse might still inform you that there had secretly revolved in his mind a succession of thought which had gradually led him from the subject of conversation. Among different languages, even when we cannot suspect the least connection or communication, it is found that the words expressive of ideas the most compounded do yet nearly correspond to each other—a certain proof that the simple ideas comprehended in the compound ones were bound together by some universal principle which had an equal influence on all mankind.

Though it be too obvious to escape observation that different ideas are connected together, I do not find that any philosopher has attempted to enumerate or class all the principles of association—a subject, however, that seems worthy of curiosity. To me there appear to be only three principles of connection among ideas, namely, *resemblance, contiguity* in time or place, and *cause* or *effect*.

That these principles serve to connect ideas will not, I believe, be much doubted. A picture naturally leads our thoughts to the original.[1] The mention of one apartment in a building naturally introduces an inquiry or discourse concerning the others;[2] and if we think of a wound, we can scarcely forbear reflecting on the pain which follows it.[3] But that this enumeration is complete, and that there are no other principles of association except these, may be difficult to prove to the satisfaction of the reader or even to a man's own satisfaction. All we can do, in such cases, is to run over several instances and examine carefully the principle which binds the different thoughts to each other, never stopping till we render the principle as general as possible.[4] The more instances we examine and the more care we employ, the more assurance shall we acquire that the enumeration which we form from the whole is complete and entire.

Instead of entering into a detail of this kind, which would lead us into many useless subtilities, we shall consider some of the effects of this connection upon the passions

---

[1] Resemblance.
[2] Contiguity.
[3] Cause and effect.
[4] For instance, *contrast* or *contrariety* is also a connection among ideas, but it may perhaps be considered as a mixture of *causation* and *resemblance*. Where two objects are contrary, the one destroys the other; that is, the cause of its annihilation, and the idea of the annihilation of an object, implies the idea of its former existence.

and imagination; where we may open up a field of speculation more entertaining, and perhaps more instructive, than the other.

As man is a reasonable being and is continually in pursuit of happiness, which he hopes to find in the gratification of some passion or affection, he seldom acts or speaks or thinks without a purpose and intention. He has still some object in view; and however improper the means may sometimes be which he chooses for the attainment of his end, he never loses view of an end, nor will he so much as throw away his thoughts or reflections where he hopes not to reap any satisfaction from them.

In all compositions of genius, therefore, it is requisite that the writer have some plan or object; and though he may be hurried from this plan by the vehemence of thought, as in an ode, or drop it carelessly, as in an epistle or essay, there must appear some aim or intention in his first setting out, if not in the composition of the whole work. A production without a design would resemble more the ravings of a madman than the sober efforts of genius and learning.

As this rule admits of no exception, it follows that in narrative compositions the events or actions which the writer relates must be connected together by some bond or tie: They must be related to each other in the imagination, and form a kind of *unity* which may bring them under one plan or view, and which may be the object or end of the writer in his first undertaking.

This connecting principle among the several events which form the subject of a poem or history may be very different according to the different designs of the poet or historian. Ovid has formed his plan upon the connecting principle of resemblance. Every fabulous transformation produced by the miraculous power of the gods falls within the compass of his work. There needs but this one circumstance, in any event, to bring it under his original plan or intention.

An annalist or historian who should undertake to write the history of Europe during any century would be influenced by the connection of contiguity in time or place. All events which happen in that portion of space and period of time are comprehended in his design, though in other respects different and unconnected. They have still a species of unity amidst all their diversity.

But the most usual species of connection among the different events which enter into any narrative composition is that of cause and effect; while the historian traces the series of actions according to their natural order, remounts to their secret springs and principles, and delineates their most remote consequences. He chooses for his subject a certain portion of that great chain of events which compose the history of mankind: each link in this chain he endeavours to touch in his narration; sometimes unavoidable ignorance renders all his attempts fruitless; sometimes he supplies by conjecture what is wanting in knowledge; and always he is sensible that the more unbroken the chain is which he presents to his readers, the more perfect is his production. He sees that the knowledge of causes is not only the most satisfactory, this relation or connection being the strongest of all others, but also the most instructive; since it is by this knowledge alone we are enabled to control events and govern futurity.

Here, therefore, we may attain some notion of that *unity* of *action* about which all critics after Aristotle have talked so much, perhaps to little purpose, while they directed not their taste or sentiment by the accuracy of philosophy. It appears that in all productions, as well as in the epic and tragic, there is a certain unity required, and that on no occasion our thoughts can be allowed to run at adventures if we would produce a work that will give any lasting entertainment to mankind. It appears, also, that even a biographer who should write the life of Achilles would connect the events by showing their mutual dependence and relation, as much as a poet who should make the anger of that hero the subject of his

narration.[5] Not only in any limited portion of life a man's actions have a dependence on each other, but also during the whole period of his duration from the cradle to the grave; nor is it possible to strike off one link, however minute, in this regular chain without affecting the whole series of events which follow. The unity of action, therefore, which is to be found in biography or history differs from that of epic poetry, not in kind, but in degree. In epic poetry, the connection among the events is more close and sensible; the narration is not carried on through such a length of time; and the actors hasten to some remarkable period which satisfies the curiosity of the reader. This conduct of the epic poet depends on that particular situation of the imagination and of the passions which is supposed in that production. The imagination both of writer and reader is more enlivened, and the passions more inflamed than in history, biography, or any species of narration that confine themselves to strict truth and reality. Let us consider the effect of these two circumstances of an enlivened imagination and inflamed passions which belong to poetry, especially the epic kind, above any other species of composition; and let us see for what reason they require a stricter and closer unity in the fable.

First, all poetry, being a species of painting, approaches us nearer to the objects than other species of narration, throws a stronger light upon them, and delineates more distinctly those minute circumstances which, though to the historian they seem superfluous, serve mightily to enliven the imagery and gratify the fancy. If it be not necessary, as in the *Iliad,* to inform us each time the hero buckles his shoes and ties his garters, it will be requisite, perhaps, to enter into a greater detail than in the *Henriade,* where the events are run over with such rapidity that we scarce have leisure to become acquainted with the scene or action.

---

5 Contrary to Aristotle (cf. *Poetics* 1450a).

Were a poet, therefore, to comprehend in his subject any great compass of time or series of events, and trace up the death of Hector to its remote causes in the rape of Helen or the judgment of Paris, he must draw out his poem to an immeasurable length in order to fill this large canvas with just painting and imagery. The reader's imagination, inflamed with such a series of poetical descriptions, and his passions, agitated by a continual sympathy with the actors, must flag long before the period of narration and must sink into lassitude and disgust from the repeated violence of the same movements.

Secondly, that an epic poet must not trace the causes to any great distance will further appear if we consider another reason, which is drawn from a property of the passions still more remarkable and singular. It is evident that in a just composition all the affections excited by the different events described and represented add mutual force to each other; and that, while the heroes are all engaged in one common scene, and each action is strongly connected with the whole, the concern is continually awake, and the passions make an easy transition from one object to another. The strong connection of the events, as it facilitates the passage of the thought or imagination from one to another, facilitates also the transfusion of the passions and preserves the affection still in the same channel and direction. Our sympathy and concern for Eve prepare the way for a like sympathy with Adam: the affection is preserved almost entire in the transition, and the mind seizes immediately the new object as strongly related to that which formerly engaged its attention. But were the poet to make a total digression from his subject and introduce a new actor no way connected with the personages, the imagination, feeling a breach in the transition, would enter coldly into the new scene; would kindle by slow degrees; and in returning to the main subject of the poem would pass, as it were, upon foreign ground

and have its concern to excite anew in order to take party with the principal actors. The same inconvenience follows in a lesser degree where the poet traces his events to too great a distance and binds together actions which, though not altogether disjoined, have not so strong a connection as is requisite to forward the transition of the passions.

Hence arises the artifice of oblique narration employed in the *Odyssey* and *Æneid*— where the hero is introduced, at first, near the period of his designs, and afterwards shows us, as it were in perspective, the more distant events and causes. By this means, the reader's curiosity is immediately excited; the events follow with rapidity, and in a very close connection; and the concern is preserved alive, and continually increases by means of the near relation of the objects, from the beginning to the end of the narration.

The same rule takes place in dramatic poetry; nor is it ever permitted in a regular composition to introduce an actor who has no connection, or but a small one, with the principal personages of the fable. The spectator's concern must not be diverted by any scenes disjoined and separated from the rest. This breaks the course of the passions, and prevents that communication of the several emotions by which one scene adds force to another, and transfuses the pity and terror which it excites upon each succeeding scene until the whole produces that rapidity of movement which is peculiar to the theater. How must it extinguish this warmth of affection to be entertained on a sudden with a new action and new personages no way related to the former; to find so sensible a breach or vacuity in the course of the passions, by means of this breach in the connection of ideas; and instead of carrying the sympathy of one scene into the following, to be obliged every moment to excite a new concern, and take party in a new scene of action?

But though this rule of unity of action be common to dramatic and epic poetry, we may still observe a difference betwixt them which may, perhaps, deserve our attention. In both these species of composition it is requisite the action be one and simple, in order to preserve the concern or sympathy entire and undiverted: but in epic or narrative poetry, this rule is also established upon another foundation, viz., the necessity that is incumbent on every writer to form some plan or design before he enter on any discourse or narration, and to comprehend his subject in some general aspect or united view which may be the constant object of his attention. As the author is entirely lost in dramatic compositions, and the spectator supposes himself to be really present at the actions represented, this reason has no place with regard to the stage; but any dialogue or conversation may be introduced which, without improbability, might have passed in that determinate portion of space represented by the theatre. Hence, in all our English comedies, even those of Congreve, the unity of action is never strictly observed; but the poet thinks it sufficient if his personages be any way related to each other by blood, or by living in the same family; and he afterwards introduces them in particular scenes, where they display their humours and characters without much forwarding the main action. The double plots of Terence are licenses of the same kind, but in a lesser degree. And though this conduct be not perfectly regular, it is not wholly unsuitable to the nature of comedy, where the movements and passions are not raised to such a height as in tragedy; at the same time that the fiction or representation palliates, in some degree, such licenses. In a narrative poem, the first proposition or design confines the author to one subject; and any digressions of this nature would, at first view, be rejected as absurd and monstrous. Neither Boccace, La Fontaine, nor any author of that kind, though pleasantry be their chief object, have ever indulged them.

To return to the comparison of history and epic poetry, we may conclude from the foregoing reasonings that as a certain unity is requisite in all productions, it cannot be wanting to history more than to any other; that in history the connection among the several events which unites them into one body is the relation of cause and effect, the same which takes place in epic poetry; and that, in the latter composition, this connection is only required to be closer and more sensible on account of the lively imagination and strong passions which must be touched by the poet in his narration. The Peloponnesian war is a proper subject for history, the siege of Athens for an epic poem, and the death of Alcibiades for a tragedy.

As the difference, therefore, betwixt history and epic poetry consists only in the degrees of connection which bind together those several events of which their subject is composed, it will be difficult, if not impossible, by words to determine exactly the bounds which separate them from each other. That is a matter of taste more than of reasoning; and perhaps this unity may often be discovered in a subject where, at first view, and from an abstract consideration, we should least expect to find it.

It is evident that Homer, in the course of his narration, exceeds the first proposition of his subject; and that the anger of Achilles, which caused the death of Hector, is not the same with that which produced so many ills to the Greeks. But the strong connection betwixt these two movements, the quick transition from one to the other, the contrast betwixt the effects of concord and discord amongst the princes, and the natural curiosity we have to see Achilles in action after so long repose—all these causes carry on the reader, and produce a sufficient unity in the subject.

It may be objected to Milton that he has traced up his causes to too great a distance, and that the rebellion of the angels produces the fall of man by a train of events which is both very long and very casual. Not to mention that the creation of the world, which he has related at length, is no more the cause of that catastrophe than of the battle of Pharsalia, or any other event that has ever happened. But if we consider on the other hand, that all these events, the rebellion of the angels, the creation of the world, and the fall of man, *resemble* each other in being miraculous, and out of the common course of nature; that they are supposed to be *contiguous* in time; and that, being detached from all other events, and being the only original facts which revelation discovers, they strike the eye at once, and naturally recall each other to the thought or imagination—if we consider all these circumstances, I say, we shall find that these parts of the action have a sufficient unity to make them be comprehended in one fable or narration. To which we may add that the rebellion of the angels and the fall of man have a peculiar resemblance, as being counterparts to each other, and presenting to the reader the same moral of obedience to our Creator.

These loose hints I have thrown together in order to excite the curiosity of philosophers, and beget a suspicion at least if not a full persuasion that this subject is very copious, and that many operations of the human mind depend on the connection or association of ideas which is here explained. Particularly, the sympathy betwixt the passions and imagination will, perhaps, appear remarkable; while we observe that the affections, excited by one object, pass easily to another connected with it, but transfuse themselves with difficulty, or not at all, along different objects which have no manner of connection together. By introducing into any composition personages and actions foreign to each other, an injudicious author loses that communication of emotions by which alone he can interest the heart and raise the passions to their proper height and period. The full explication of this principle and all its consequences would lead us into reasonings too profound and too copious for these essays. It is sufficient for us, at present, to have established this conclusion, that the three connecting principles of all ideas are the relations of *resemblance, contiguity,* and *causation.*

DENIS DIDEROT

(1713-1784)

Diderot says that in the *Greater Hippias* Plato told us "more about what it [beauty] is not, than what it is." A number of our authors—Plotinus, for example, and Diderot himself—are sometimes more effective as critics of views that they cannot accept than as sponsors of positive ideas. The conception of beauty as something to be defined in terms of "the perception of relations," if not original with Diderot, was still something momentous; it led to arguments, which neither Kant nor Fechner nor Santayana nor Roger Fry seems to have been able to settle, about the place of sensation and of the "lower" senses in aesthetic experience, or the line of demarcation between sensation and perception. Does it succeed, where other proposals fail, in deciding "what beauty is"? The criticism of the main thesis in Diderot is an exercise worthy of our best faculties.

Diderot, a cutler's son, was trained by Jesuits at the College of Louis-le-Grand in Paris, but later passed through phases of modified belief, unbelief, and disbelief. For many years he managed to live, amidst difficulties, as a free-lance writer. From about the year 1745 and for twenty years thereafter he was the instigating and sustaining figure behind the famous project of the *Encyclopedia*. The article on beauty was one of many, ranging over diverse fields of thought, that he contributed to that work. It is agreed by historians that in point of curiosity, energy, and versatility he has had few equals, even in the Italian Renaissance or among philosophers of the seventeenth century. He was a philosopher, novelist, dramatist, critic of the fine arts, something of a musician, and a mathematician. It might be said that his aesthetics is to be found, not spelled out in any single work, but spread over volumes of his criticism of literature and painting. But precisely in view of the dramatic or dialectical form that his thinking so often takes, it is interesting to consider the example, which follows, of a methodical treatment of the subject.

DENIS DIDEROT

The Beautiful

(Translated by Karl Aschenbrenner)

(First published: 1752.)

§ A BRIEF REVIEW OF AESTHETIC
DOCTRINES FROM PLATO TO
HUTCHESON

Before beginning the difficult task of inquiring into the origin of the beautiful, I
shall remark at the outset, in accord with
all the authors who have written about it,
that it is the fate of those things of which
men speak most to be quite commonly the
ones least known, and that the nature of the
beautiful, among many others, is one of
these. Everyone is concerned about beauty.
It is admired in the works of nature and
demanded in works of art. It is constantly
affirmed or denied of things. But if one
asks of those who have sure and refined
taste what its origin is, its nature, its
precise concept and true idea, its exact
definition, if one asks whether it is something absolute or relative, whether there is
an eternal, immutable beauty, the rule and
model for lesser beauty, or whether it is in
any better case than the whims of fashion,
then one immediately finds a divergence of
opinions, some confessing ignorance, others
falling into skepticism. Why is it that all
men agree that there is such a thing as
beauty, and that so many of them so surely
know it when confronted by it, and yet so
few know what it is?

In order to achieve, if possible, a solution
to these difficulties, we shall begin by exam-

ining various ideas by authors who have written most about beauty. We shall then propound our own ideas on this subject, and finally offer some general observations on the human understanding and its operations as they relate to the matter in question.

Plato wrote two dialogues on beauty, the *Phaedrus* and the *Greater Hippias*. In the latter he tells us more about what it is not, than what it is. In the other he speaks less of beauty than of natural love for it. In the *Greater Hippias* the problem is little more than that of pricking the vanity of a sophist, and in the *Phaedrus,* of passing a few pleasant moments with a friend in a charming place.

St. Augustine wrote a treatise on beauty, but the work is lost and there remain only a few ideas of his on this important subject, scattered through his writings. We learn that that precise interconnection between parts within a whole which renders them *one,* is, in his view, the unique character of beauty. If, he says, I ask an architect why, after erecting a row of arches on one of the wings of a building, he also adds one on the other, he will doubtless reply that it is in just this way that the members of the building will unite in a fitting symmetry. But why does this symmetry seem necessary? Because it pleases. But who are you that you undertake to judge that which will or will not please men? And how do you know that symmetry pleases? I know, because things so arranged have propriety, rightness and grace, or, in a word, because it is beautiful. Very well, but tell me, is it beautiful because it pleases or does it please because it is beautiful? Undoubtedly it pleases because it is beautiful. This too I believe, but I must still ask, why is it beautiful? If my question disturbs you, because the masters of your art hardly carry matters to such lengths, you will at least agree readily that resemblance, equality, and the agreement of the parts of your building reduce to a kind of unity which is satisfying

to reason. That is what I should say. Yes, but beware! There is no true unity in bodies, for bodies consist of innumerable parts, each of which again consists of an infinity of others.

Where then do you perceive this unity which inspires you in making your plans, and which in your art is taken as an inviolable law? Whence is this unity which your building must imitate in order to be beautiful but which nothing on earth can imitate perfectly because nothing on earth can be perfectly one? And what now follows from this? Must we not conclude that above our minds there is a certain original unity, sovereign, eternal, and perfect, which is the fundamental rule of beauty and which you seek in the practice of your art? From this St. Augustine concludes, in another work, that unity is, as it were, the form and essence of beauty of every kind. *Omnis porro pulchritudinis forma, unitas est.*[1]

Wolff says, in his *Psychologia,* that there are things which please us and things which do not and that this constitutes the difference between the beautiful and the ugly. That which pleases us is called beautiful, that which displeases ugly.

He adds that beauty consists in perfection in such a way that a thing which is clothed with this perfection is for that reason adapted to produce pleasure in us.

He also distinguishes two kinds of beauty, the real and the apparent. Real beauty arises from a real perfection, apparent from an apparent perfection.

It is obvious that St. Augustine went much further in his analysis of beauty than this Leibnizian philosopher, who assumes at the outset that a thing is beautiful because it is beautiful, as Plato and Aristotle so well observed. It is true that he then introduces perfection into the ideas of beauty, but what is perfection? Is the perfect a more intelligible idea than the beautiful?

All those who pride themselves on not

---

[1] ["The form of all beauty is unity."—TR. NOTE.]

speaking simply from habit and without reflection, says Crousaz, will wish to look within themselves and attend to what they experience, how they think, and what they feel when they say, "That is beautiful"; they will perceive that by this term they express a certain relation of the object to their feelings of pleasure or sentiments of approval, and will agree that to say, that is beautiful, is to say, I apprehend something which I approve of or which gives me pleasure.

Obviously Crousaz' definition is not of the nature of beauty but only of the effect one experiences in the presence of it. It has the same defect as Wolff's. This Crousaz seems to have been aware of, and for the rest he contents himself with determining the characteristics of beauty. These he reduces to five: variety, unity, regularity, order, and proportion.

From this it follows that either St. Augustine's definition is incomplete or that of Crousaz is redundant. If the idea of unity does not include the ideas of variety, regularity, order, and proportion, and if these qualities are essential to beauty, St. Augustine ought not to have omitted them. If the idea of unity does include them, Crousaz need not have added them.

Crousaz does not define what he means by variety. He seems to mean by unity, the relation of all parts to a single end. Regularity lies in the parts having a comparable relation to one another. Order is a certain progression of parts which must be observed in going from part to part. He defines proportion as unity in which variety, regularity and order are mingled in each part.

I am not attacking this definition of beauty because of the vague ideas it contains. I shall confine myself to saying that it is too narrow, that it is applicable only to architecture or at most to whole structures in other genres, to a piece of eloquence, a drama, and the like, but not to a word, a thought, a fragment of an object.

Francis Hutcheson, the esteemed professor of moral philosophy in the University of Glasgow, has created a unique system which can be summed up by saying that it is no more proper to ask, what is the beautiful, than to ask, what is the visible. We mean by "visible" that which is suitable to be perceived by the eye. Hutcheson understands by "beautiful" that which is made to be grasped by the internal sense of beauty. His internal sense of beauty is a faculty by which we distinguish beautiful things just as the sense of vision is a faculty by which we receive the ideas of colors and figures. This author and his followers put forth every effort to demonstrate this sixth sense. And this is how they proceed:

1. Our minds, they say, are passive in pleasure or displeasure. Objects do not affect us exactly as we might wish them to. Some produce in the mind an involuntary impression of pleasure. Others just as involuntarily displease us. The whole power of our wills is confined to seeking the one and fleeing the other. It is by the very constitution of our nature, of our particular being, that we find the one agreeable and the others disagreeable.

2. There is scarcely any object which can affect our mind without being more or less an inevitable cause of pleasure or displeasure. A form, a work of architecture or painting, a musical composition, an action, a sentiment, a character, a word, a discourse, all these things please or displease us in some manner. We feel that the pleasure or displeasure is inevitably aroused by the mind's contemplating such an idea in all its circumstances. And this impression arises even though there may be nothing of what we commonly call sensible perception in such ideas; and in those which do come from the senses the pleasure or displeasure which accompanies them arises from the order or disorder, from the presence or absence of symmetry, from the lifelikeness or the strangeness of what is represented, and not from simple ideas of color, sound, or filled space, taken severally.

3. This being granted, I call by the name *internal sense,* says Mr. Hutcheson, the capacity of the mind of being pleased or displeased by certain forms or ideas whenever it attends to them, and in order to distinguish the internal senses from the corporeal faculties known by this name, I call *internal sense of beauty* the faculty which discerns beauty in regularity, order, and harmony, and *internal sense of the good* that which gives approval to the inclinations, actions, and characters of reasonable and virtuous agents.

4. The capacity of the mind of being pleased or displeased by certain forms or by certain ideas when it attends to them can be observed in all except the most dull of men. Hence without further investigation of just what beauty is, we may affirm that there is in all men a natural sense which is adapted to this object, that they agree in finding beauty in figures as commonly as they experience pain when too intense heat is brought close to them, or finding pleasure in eating when they are urged by appetite, even though there may be a great diversity of taste among them.

5. As soon as we are born our external senses begin to act and to convey to us perceptions of sensible objects, and this no doubt convinces us that they are natural. But the objects of what I call the internal senses or of the senses of the beautiful and the good are not presented to us as soon as these. Some time passes before children reflect, or at least give evidence of reflecting, upon proportions, resemblances and symmetries, and upon inclinations and characters. Only somewhat later do they know things which arouse taste or inner aversion. This is what leads to the opinion that these faculties, which Hutcheson calls the internal senses of the beautiful and the good, develop entirely from instruction and education. But whatever one's notion of virtue or of beauty, a virtuous or beautiful object is the occasion of approbation and pleasure as naturally as food is the object of appetite.

Does it matter whether the former are presented early or late? If our senses developed only gradually and one after the other, would we have any fewer senses or faculties? And would we be wise to suppose that there is actually neither color nor figure in visible objects because we should need time and instruction to perceive them and because there are scarcely two persons who would perceive them in the same manner?

6. Perceptions which arise in the mind in the presence of external objects and from the impressions they make on our organs are called sensations. When two perceptions differ entirely from one another and have nothing in common but the generic designation "sensation," the faculties through which we receive these different sensations are called different senses. Sight and hearing, for example, designate different faculties one of which gives us ideas of color, the other of sound. Regardless of the difference of sounds among one another, and of colors, all sounds are referred to one sense, all colors to another. Evidently each sense has its own organ. Now if we apply the foregoing observation to the good and the beautiful, we see that the same is true of them.

7. Protagonists of the "internal sense" mean by "beautiful" the idea which certain objects produce in the mind, and by the "internal sense of the beautiful" our faculty for receiving this idea. They hold that animals have faculties similar to our external senses, and sometimes they are of a degree superior to our own. But none of them shows any sign of what we here understand by the term "internal sense." Moreover, they say, a being can experience exactly the same external sensations as ourselves without discerning resemblances and relations between their objects. It can even be aware of these without feeling very much pleasure in them. Besides, individual ideas of figure, form, and the like, are something distinct from pleasure. Pleasure may turn

up where proportions are neither known nor sought for. It may be absent in spite of our attending to order and proportion. How then shall we designate this faculty which is active in us without our knowing why? Internal sense is the reply.

8. This designation is based on the connection between the faculty designated and the other faculties. This connection consists mainly in the difference between the pleasure which we experience through the internal sense and our knowledge of principles. The knowledge of principles can make the pleasure increase or diminish, but it is neither identical with it nor is it its cause. This sense has certain inevitable pleasures; for the beauty or ugliness of an object is always the same for us no matter what effort we make to judge otherwise. A disagreeable object does not appear more beautiful because it is useful, and a beautiful object does not appear more ugly because it is noisome. Suppose the whole world should tempt us with some reward to find ugliness beautiful and beauty ugly, and reinforce this with grim threats; no change could hereby be produced in our perceptions and in the judgment of the internal sense. Though the tongue might praise or blame at command, the internal sense would remain uncorrupted.

9. Hence it appears to the defenders of this system that certain objects are immediately and of themselves the occasions of the pleasure which beauty gives, that we have a special sense for discerning it, and that it is unique and has nothing in common with interest. Indeed, are there not hundreds of occasions when we sacrifice utility to beauty? Is not this disinterested preference often confirmed in even the most trivial situations? A sober workman will indulge in the pleasure of making a masterpiece which will ruin him rather than seek the profit of making a bad work which will make him rich.

10. If one does not add to the consideration of utility a certain feeling, a subtle

effect from a faculty different from the understanding or the will, one judges a house only by its usefulness, a garden by its fertility, a garment by its comfortableness. So narrow an evaluation of things does not exist even among children and savages. But leave nature free to assert itself and the internal sense will hold sway. Perhaps it will be deceived in its object, but the feeling of pleasure will be no less real. A puritanical philosophy inimical to luxury, will break statues in pieces, overturn obelisks, transform palaces into cabins and gardens into thickets, but it will feel no less the real beauty of such objects. The internal sense will rebel against it and force it to make a virtue of its audacity.

Thus we see how Hutcheson and his followers strive to establish the necessity of an internal sense of the beautiful. But they succeed only in showing that there is something obscure and recondite in the pleasure which the beautiful stirs in us, that this pleasure appears to be independent of any knowledge of relations and of perceptual content, that it is entirely distinct from the quest for utility, and that it has partisans who cannot be shaken either by threats or rewards.

For the rest, such philosophers distinguish between an absolute and a relative beauty in corporeal things. They do not mean by "absolutely beautiful" a quality intrinsic to the object rendering it beautiful by itself without any relation to the mind which sees or judges of it. The term "beautiful," similarly to other names of sensible ideas, properly designates a perception of a mind, on this view, just as the cold, warm, sweet, and bitter are sensations of the mind although there is doubtless nothing which resembles these sensations in the objects which cause them, contrary to popular opinion, which supposes otherwise. It is inconceivable, they say, how objects could be called beautiful if there were no mind endowed with a sense of beauty to attend to them. Hence, by "absolute beauty" they mean that which one apprehends in certain objects without comparing them to any external thing of which they are the image and semblance. Such, they say, is the beauty which we perceive in the works of nature, in certain artificial forms, and in figures, solids, and surfaces. By "relative beauty" they understand that which one perceives in objects usually considered to be imitations or images of certain others. Hence their division has its basis much more in the different sources of the pleasure which the beautiful causes in us than in objects, for it is certain that absolute beauty has, so to speak, a relative beauty, and relative beauty an absolute.

We have shown the necessity, they say, of a unique sense which, through the presence of pleasure, evinces the presence of the beautiful. Let us now see what must be the qualities of an object in order to move this sense. One must not forget, they say, that this concerns these qualities only in relation to man, for there are certainly a good many objects which make on him the impression of beauty, but which displease other animals. These have organs and senses of a constitution different from our own and if they were to judge of the beautiful, their ideas of it would refer to altogether different forms. The bear finds his den comfortable, but neither beautiful nor ugly. Perhaps if he had the internal sense of the beautiful, he would think of it as a delightful haunt. Notice in passing that a very unhappy being would be one who had the internal sense of the beautiful and discovered the beautiful only in objects noxious to him. Providence arranges for this in relation to ourselves. Quite commonly a truly beautiful thing is also good.

In order to discover that which universally produces ideas of the beautiful in men, the followers of Hutcheson study the simplest things, such as figures, and find that among them those which we call beautiful produce an impression of unity in variety. They assert that an equilateral triangle

is less beautiful than a square, a pentagon than a hexagon, and so also other figures in the same order, because objects of equal uniformity are the more beautiful the more varied they are; and they are the more varied the greater the number of comparable sides they have. Of course, they say, in increasing very greatly the number of sides one loses sight of the relations which these have to one another and with the radius; hence the beauty of such figures does not always increase in proportion to the number of sides. They mention this objection but do not trouble to answer it. They remark only that the lack of parallelism between the sides of heptagons and other odd-numbered polygons diminishes their beauty. They always, however, maintain that, other things being equal, a regular figure of twenty sides surpasses in beauty a figure of only twelve sides, of twelve one of only eight, of eight a square. The same reasoning holds for solids as well as for surfaces. Amongst the regular solids those having the greatest number of surfaces are said by them to be the most beautiful, their beauty diminishing down to the regular pyramid.

But if among objects equally uniform the most varied are the most beautiful, then conversely, in their view, among objects equally varied the most beautiful are the most uniform. Hence the equilaterial triangle, or even the isosceles, is more beautiful than the scalene, the square more beautiful than the rhombus or diamond. The same holds of regular solid bodies and in general for all those which have a certain uniformity, such as cylinders, prisms, obelisks, and one must agree with them that such bodies are certainly more pleasing to sight than are crude figures in which neither uniformity, symmetry, nor unity is perceptible.

In order to provide explanatory principles which relate uniformity and variety to one another, they compare circles and spheres with ellipses and eccentric spheroids and maintain that the perfect uniformity of the first of these is balanced by the variety of the second and that their beauty is approximately equal.

They hold that the beautiful in the works of nature has the same foundation. No matter what you consider, they say, be it the forms of heavenly bodies, their revolutions and phases, or, descending from the heavens, the plants which cover the earth, the colors that tint the flowers, the structure of animals, their several species, their motions, the proportions of their parts, the subtle adjustment between their mechanism and their state of well-being, or, taking flight in space, birds and meteors, or again, descending into the waters, varieties of fish compared with one another—everywhere you will encounter unity amid variety. Everywhere you will see these qualities nicely balanced in things of equal beauty, and an explanatory principle compounded unequally of these two in things of unequal beauty. In short, to resort to the language of the geometers, you will find in the bowels of the earth, in the depths of the sea, in the summit of the heavens, in nature everywhere and in every part, uniformity in variety, and beauty always in a principle made up of these two.

Next they expound the beauty of arts which cannot be treated as actually representational, that is, architecture, the mechanical arts and natural harmony. They bend every effort to submit these to their law of uniformity in variety. If their demonstration errs, it is not for lack of examples. They go from the most splendid palace to the humblest cottage, from the most exquisite works to mere trifles, showing how lack of uniformity leads to caprice and lack of variety to insipidity.

There is, however, a class of things very different from the foregoing which the followers of Hutcheson find a source of embarrassment because beauty is found in them and yet the rule of uniformity in variety is not applicable to them. These are the demonstrations of abstract and universal truths. If a theorem contains an infinity of particular truths which are but consequences of it, the theorem is properly only a corollary of an axiom from which proceed an infinite number of other theorems. And yet, one says, "There's a beautiful theorem," and not, "There's a beautiful axiom."

We shall later on give a solution of this difficulty based on other principles. We consider next *relative beauty,* the beautiful which one perceives in an object considered as an imitation of an original as this is treated from the standpoint of Hutcheson and his followers.

This part of his system has nothing unique about it. According to him, and indeed to everyone else, such beauty consists in nothing but conformity between a model and a copy.

It follows that for relative beauty it is not necessary that there be any beauty in the original. Forests, mountains, cliffs, disorder, the wrinkles of old age, the pallor of death, the effects of disease, are all pleasing in painting. They are pleasurable also in poetry. That which Aristotle calls a moral character is not necessarily that of a virtuous man. What is called a *fabula bene morata*[2] is nothing but an epic or dramatic poem in which actions, sentiments and speech are consistent with the characters, whether good or bad.

But undeniably a painting of an object which has a certain absolute beauty ordinarily pleases us no more than a painting of an object which lacks such beauty. Perhaps the only exception to this rule occurs when the accord of the painting with the state of the observer outweighs the lack of absolute beauty in the model, and the painting becomes that much more interesting. Such interest arises from imperfection and is the reason why we want the hero

2 [Horace, *Ars Poetica,* 319–320: *morata recte fabula,* a tale in which the characters are accurately drawn.—TR. NOTE.]

of an epic or dramatic poem to be not without some (moral) shortcoming.

Most of the other beauties of poetry and eloquence follow the law of relative beauty. Conformity with truth renders comparisons, metaphors, and allegories beautiful even when there is no absolute beauty in the objects represented.

Hutcheson lays stress upon our relish for comparisons. Its origin, he says, is this: Passions nearly always produce the same motions in animals as they do in us. Inanimate natural objects are often found in positions that resemble the postures of the human body, and sometimes even of the soul. Little more than this, says the author, is necessary for us to see the lion as the symbol of fury, the tiger of cruelty, the oak, whose crest rises proudly into the sky, the emblem of boldness, the motions of a stormy sea, and the depiction of its tumult, a symbol of wrath, and the stem of a poppy, its bloom drooping under a few drops of rain, the image of lassitude.

Such is the system of Hutcheson, which doubtless seems more unusual than true. But we cannot urge too strongly the reading of his work, especially in the original. It contains a great many subtle observations on the way to attain perfection in the practice of the fine arts. . . .

I know that there is no objection which I have raised against the system I have attacked to which there may not be rejoinders, but I think these would be more subtle than substantial.

It follows from the foregoing that Plato, being less concerned to teach the truth to his followers than to disabuse his fellow citizens of the claims of the Sophists, offers us in every line of his work examples of beauty, and shows us indeed what it is not, but tells us nothing at all about what it is;

That St. Augustine has reduced all beauty to unity or to the exact relation of parts to one another, and to the exact relation of the parts of a part considered as a whole, and so on *ad infinitum*; this appears rather to define the essence of the perfect than of the beautiful;

That Wolff has confused the beautiful with the pleasure it produces, and with perfection, and yet there are things which please without being beautiful, others which are beautiful without pleasing; that all things are capable of the highest perfection and that there are things which are not susceptible in the least of beauty, for example, all the objects of smell and taste considered in relation to these senses;

That Crousaz overburdens his definition of the beautiful, not perceiving that the more he multiplies the characteristics of the beautiful the more he particularizes them; that in setting out to treat the beautiful in general he begins by giving a concept of it which is applicable only to certain particular varieties of beautiful things;

That Hutcheson, who undertakes first to explain the origin of the pleasure we experience in the presence of the beautiful, and, second, to discover the qualities which a thing must have in order to produce in us this particular pleasure and therefore appear beautiful to us, has much less proved the existence of a sixth sense than made evident the difficulty of explaining without this stratagem the source of the pleasure which the beautiful gives us; that his principle of uniformity in variety is not universal; that he makes an application of it to the figures of geometry which is more subtle than true, and that the principle does not apply to another kind of beauty, namely, of the demonstration of abstract and universal truths. . . .

§ THE THEORY OF AESTHETIC RELATIONS (RAPPORTS)

We are born with the faculty of feeling and thinking. The first effort of the faculty of thinking is to examine perceptions, to unite, compare, and combine them, to perceive among them relations of fitness and unfitness, and so forth. We are born with needs which compel us to have recourse to various measures, among which we often choose by the effect we expect from them, by the results they have produced, by whatever there be in them of good or evil, of what is prompt, efficient, complete or incomplete, and so on. Most such expedients are tools or machines or some other device of this sort. But every machine involves a combination and arrangement of parts toward a single end. Here then are our needs, and the readiest exercise of our faculties, tending as soon as we are born to give us the ideas of order, arrangement, symmetry, of mechanism, proportion, and unity. All these ideas come to us from the senses and are factitious. We pass from the notion of a multitude of artificial and natural beings which are ordered, proportioned, combined, and symmetrically arranged, to the abstract and negative notion of disproportion, disorder, and chaos.

These notions, like all the others, arise from experience and have come to us through the senses. We should have no notion of God if we had not had them. They preceded in us by a long time the idea of his existence. They are as positive, distinct, clear, and real as the ideas of length, size, depth, quantity, and number. Since they have their origin in our needs and in the exercise of our faculties, if there should be somewhere on earth a people in whose language there was no name for such ideas, they would nonetheless exist in their minds to a greater or lesser extent, be more or less developed, founded on a fair number of experiences, and applied to a considerable number of existent things. For this is all the difference there can be between one people and another, or between one man and another among the same people. And whatever high-flown expressions may be used to designate the abstract notions of order, proportion, relation, and harmony, whether one calls them, as one wishes, the eternal, original, sovereign, inherent rules of the beautiful, they have nevertheless

passed from the senses to the understanding, just like the most commonplace notions, and are only abstractions of our minds.

But scarcely have the exercise of our intellectual faculties and the necessity of providing for our needs by inventions, machines, and the like sketched out in our understandings the notions of order, relation, proportion, connection, arrangement, symmetry, than we find ourselves surrounded by things in which these notions are, so to speak, repeated to infinity. We can take hardly a step in the universe without some artifact displaying them. They enter our minds at every instant, from every quarter. Everything that happens in us or exists outside us, everything that remains of ages gone by, all that industry or thought or the discovery of our contemporaries has produced before our eyes constantly impresses on us the notions of order, relation, arrangement, symmetry, fitness, unfitness, and the like. And there is no notion, except perhaps that of existence, which might have become more familiar to men than the one we are considering.

If then there is nothing in the notion of the beautiful, whether absolute or relative, general or particular, but the notions of order, relation, proportion, arrangement, symmetry, fitness and unfitness, and if these notions derive from no other source than those of existence, number, length, width, depth, and an infinity of others about which there is no question, one can, I think, use the former as a definition of the beautiful without being accused of merely putting one term in place of another, or of turning in a vicious circle.

"Beautiful" is a term that we apply to an infinite number of instances. But whatever the differences among these may be, either we make a false application of the term "beautiful," or these instances have a single quality of which the term "beautiful" is the sign.

This quality cannot be among those which constitute their specific difference, for then there would either be only a single beautiful thing or at most only a single beautiful species of thing.

But among the qualities common to all the things that we call beautiful, which should we choose as that of which the term "beautiful" is the sign? It can be no other, I think, than that which makes all of them beautiful, that whose frequency or rarity, if it is capable of these, makes them more beautiful or less, that whose absence makes them cease to be beautiful, that which cannot alter its nature without altering the beautiful in kind, that whose negation renders the most beautiful things disagreeable and ugly. In a word, it is that through which beauty begins, increases, varies to infinity, declines and disappears. Now only the notion of relations (*rapports*) is capable of such effects.

I call all that outside myself beautiful which contains in itself that which can reveal to my understanding the idea of relation, and I call all that beautiful as related to myself which can reveal this idea.

When I say "all," I except however the qualities of smell and taste. Although these qualities might reveal to us the idea of relations, we do not call those objects in which they reside beautiful when we think of them only in respect to these qualities. We speak of fine food or a delightful aroma but not of beautiful food or a beautiful aroma. And when we speak of a beautiful turbot, or a beautiful rose, we are thinking of other qualities in the turbot or rose than those related to the senses of smell or taste.

When I say "all that which contains in itself that which can reveal to my understanding the idea of relatedness or that which reveals this idea," it is necessary to distinguish carefully between the forms in the objects and the notions I have of them. My understanding does not put anything into things nor does it deprive them of anything. Whether I think of the facade of the Louvre or not, all the parts which constitute

it have nonetheless such and such a form and arrangement among themselves. Whether there are any human beings or not, it would be nonetheless beautiful, but only for possible beings constituted of mind and body like ourselves. For all others it could be neither beautiful nor ugly, nor be simply ugly. From this it follows that although there is no such thing as the absolutely beautiful, there are two kinds of beauty in relation to us, real beauty and beauty perceived.

When I say "all that which reveals in us the idea of relatedness," I do not mean that in order to call something beautiful it is necessary to grasp exactly what kind of relation is present therein. I do not demand that he who looks at a work of architecture should be in a state of awareness of that which even the architect is unaware of, that this part has to another the relation of one number to another, or that he who listens to a concert should know more than sometimes even the musician knows, that one sound is in the relation two to four, or four to five, to another. It is sufficient if he perceives and feels that the members of this architectural work, and the tones of this piece of music, are related either among themselves or to other objects. It is the indeterminacy of these relations, the ease with which they are grasped and the pleasure that accompanies their perception which have led us to imagine that the beautiful is more an affair of feeling than of reason. I make bold to say that whenever a principle is known to us from tenderest childhood and we by habit make a quick and easy application of it to objects outside us, we think we judge of it by feeling. But whenever we are forced to admit our mistake on all those occasions when the complexity of the relations and the unfamiliarity of the object suspend application of the principle, then our pleasure will wait to make itself felt until the understanding has decreed that the object is beautiful. Moreover, the judgment in such cases is nearly always of relative beauty, not of real beauty.

Whether one considers relations of customs and thus moral beauty, or works of literature and literary beauty, or pieces of music and musical beauty, or works of nature and natural beauty, or the mechanical works of men and artificial beauty, or representations of works of art or of nature and thus the beauty of imitation, in each object and under whatever aspect you consider the relations in a single object, the beautiful will assume different names.

But any single object whatever can be considered either solely by itself or in relation to others. When I say of a flower or of a fish that it is beautiful, what do I mean? If I consider the flower or the fish by itself, I mean nothing other than that I perceive a certain order, arrangement, or symmetry (for all these words merely designate different ways of thinking of relations themselves) between the parts of which it is composed. In this sense every flower, every fish is beautiful. But what kind of beauty? It is what I call *real beauty*.

If I consider the flower and the fish relatively to other flowers and other fish and call them beautiful, this means that among things of this type, among these flowers or among these fish, certain ideas of relations and certain relations in particular are very clearly evident to me. And I hasten to point out that since not all these relations are of the same nature, some contribute more than others to beauty. But I can affirm that under this new way of looking at objects there is a beautiful and an ugly. Of what kind are they then? We may describe them as *relative*.

If in place of taking a flower or a fish one generalizes and takes a plant or an animal, or particularizes and takes a rose or a turbot, one will always draw the same distinction, between relative beauty and real beauty.

From this we see that there are numerous relative beauties, that a tulip may be beautiful or ugly among tulips, or among flowers, or among plants, or among the products of nature.

Admittedly one must have seen many roses or turbots to declare that certain ones among them are beautiful or ugly among roses and turbots, many plants or fish to declare that the rose and the turbot are beautiful or ugly among plants and fish, and must have extensive acquaintance with nature to declare that they are beautiful or ugly among the products of nature.

What then does one mean when one says to an artist that he ought to imitate beautiful nature? Either one doesn't understand one's own command or one is saying to him, if you have to paint a flower and it is indifferent which one, paint the most beautiful among flowers; if you are to paint a plant and your subject does not demand that it be an oak or elm, withered, broken and bare, paint the most beautiful among plants; if you are to paint just a natural object, no matter which, paint the most beautiful.

From this it follows:

1. That the principle of the imitation of beautiful nature demands the most thoroughgoing and extensive study of nature's products in every kind;

2. That if one had the most perfect knowledge of nature and of the natural limits in the production of each kind, the number of occasions on which the most beautiful would be used in the arts of imitation would stand in relation to the occasions on which the less beautiful was to be preferred as the ratio of one to infinity;

3. That although there is in fact a maximum of beauty in each work of nature considered by itself, or, to use an example, that although the most beautiful rose which nature produces has neither the height nor the spread of an oak, yet there is neither beauty nor ugliness in the products of nature considered in relation to the use one may make of them in the arts of imitation.

Depending upon the nature of a thing,

upon whether it prompts in us the perception of a great number of relations, and upon the nature of the relations so perceived, it will be called pleasing, beautiful, more beautiful, very beautiful, or ugly; or, inferior, small, great, elevated, sublime, extravagant, comical or pleasant. We should be writing a work of grand scope rather than a dictionary article to enter into all these details. It is sufficient to set forth the principles, and we shall leave to the reader the derivation of consequences and applications. But we can assure him that whether he takes his examples from nature or borrows them from painting, morals, architecture, or music, he will always find that he may give the name "real beauty" to whatever contains within it something exhibiting the idea of relatedness, and the name "relative beauty" to whatever exhibits relations to other things we see fit to compare with it.

I shall confine myself to adducing an example from literature: Everyone knows the sublime words of the tragedy *Horace: Qu'il mourût*.[3] Suppose I ask of anyone who does not know Corneille's play and who has no idea of the answer of the aged Horatius what he makes of the line, *qu'il mourût*. Clearly, the person addressed, not knowing at all what this *qu'il mourût* may be, nor able to guess whether it is a complete phrase or a fragment, and scarcely even perceiving any grammatical relation among the three terms, will reply that to him it is neither beautiful nor ugly. But if I tell him that it is the response of a man who is asked what one should do in combat, he begins to perceive in the speaker a kind of courage which does not let him believe that it is always better to live than to die. Now the *qu'il mourût* begins to be of interest. If I add that upon the struggle depends a country's honor, that the combatant is the son of the speaker, that the young man is facing three enemies who have already taken the life of two of his brothers, that the older man is

speaking to his daughter, that he is a Roman—then, the reply *qu'il mourût,* which at first was neither beautiful nor ugly, is enriched in just the degree in which I develop its relations to the circumstances. It ends by being sublime.

Change the situation and the relationships, and move the scene of the *qu'il mourût* from a French to an Italian stage and from the mouth of the aged Horatius to that of Scapin, and it will become burlesque.

Change the situation still more and suppose that Scapin is in the service of a severe, miserly and peevish master and that they are attacked on a highway by three or four brigands. Scapin flees. The master defends himself, but outnumbered by his assailants he too has to flee. And now Scapin has just learned that his master has escaped from danger. "How's that," says Scapin, his hopes dashed, "did he run away? Ah! what a poltroon!" "But," runs the reply, "alone against three! What would you have him do?" *Qu'il mourût,* he replies. Now the *qu'il mourût* will be amusing. Thus it is certain that beauty begins, grows, varies, declines, and disappears in dependence upon relations, as we have already said above.

But I shall be asked what I mean by relations. Is it not to alter the meaning of words to give the name "beautiful" to what has never borne it before? In our language the idea of the beautiful has apparently always been joined with that of greatness. This is but to define "beautiful" by locating its specific difference in a quality which belongs to innumerable other beings which have neither greatness nor sublimity. Crousaz has undoubtedly erred when he qualifies his definition of "beautiful" with so many specific characteristics that it is found to be restricted to a very small number of things. But is it not to fall into the contrary error to construe it so broadly that it appears to embrace everything not even excepting a heap of shapeless stones tossed by chance to the edge of a quarry? All objects, it must be added, are capable of

---

3 ["Let him die."—TR. NOTE.]

relations among one another, among their parts, and with other things. There is none of them which cannot be arranged, ordered, and symmetrized. Perfection is a quality that can belong to everything, but the same does not apply to beauty, which belongs only to a small number of objects.

This, I think, is not the only but it is the strongest objection which can be raised against my view, and I shall try to reply to it.

Relation, in general, is an operation of the understanding which considers a thing or a quality in respect to the way in which it presupposes the existence of another thing or quality. For example, when I say that Peter is a good father I consider in him a quality which presupposes the existence of another person, his son, and similarly for other relations, whatever they may be. From this it follows that although relation exists only in the understanding, in reference to perception it has nonetheless its basis in things. I shall therefore say that a thing contains in itself real relations whenever it is endowed with qualities which a being constituted of mind and body like myself could not conceive of without supposing the existence of other beings or other qualities whether in the thing itself or outside it. I shall distinguish their relations into the real and the perceived. But there is a third sort of relations, the intellectual and the fictional. These the human understanding seems to put into things. A sculptor glances at a block of marble. His imagination, quicker than his chisel, removes the superfluous matter and discerns a figure in it. But actually this figure is imaginary and fictional. In a portion of space terminating in imaginary lines he could make in a formless block of marble that which he has just executed in his imagination. A philosopher glances at a heap of stones casually strewn. In thought he ignores all the irregular aspects of this heap and proceeds to make of it a sphere, a cube, a regular figure. What does this signify? That, although the

hand of the artist can impress a design only upon resistant surfaces, he can bear the image in thought beyond the body. Or rather, not just beyond the body, but into space, into the void. The image, whether transported by thought through the air, or extracted from the most shapeless bodies by the imagination, can be either beautiful or ugly, but not the ideal canvas on which it is painted, or the formless body from which it is to be evoked.

Hence when I say that a thing is beautiful because of the relations discerned in it, I do not speak of intellectual or fictional relations which the imagination imparts into them but of real relations which are actually there and which our imagination discovers there with the aid of sense.

Our reply then is that whatever these relations may be it is they which constitute beauty, not in the narrow sense in which the pleasing is opposed to the beautiful but in a sense, I dare say, more philosophical and more in conformity with the beautiful in general and with the nature of languages and of things.

Should anyone have the patience to gather together all the things to which we give the name "beautiful," he would soon find in this mass a vast number where one pays no attention to largeness or smallness. The latter count for nothing whenever the thing is isolated, or whenever an individual member of a numerous class is considered by itself. When the first clock or the first watch was declared to be beautiful, did one draw attention to anything more than its mechanism or to the internal relation of its parts? And when today one says that the watch is beautiful, does one attend to anything but its use and mechanism? Hence if the general definition of "beautiful" must fit all those things to which the term is applied, the idea of greatness must be excluded from it. I am thus led to remove the notion of greatness from that of the beautiful, for it seems to me ordinarily to be attached to it. In mathematics we mean by a "beautiful problem" a problem difficult to solve, by a "beautiful solution" a simple and easy solution to a difficult and complex problem. The ideas of the great, sublime, and elevated are inappropriate on those occasions where one cannot help using the term "beautiful." If in this way one reviews all the things which are called beautiful one of them will lack greatness, another utility, a third symmetry, some even the explicit semblance of order and symmetry, for example in a painting of a storm or tempest or chaotic scene. In the end we shall be compelled to agree that the only quality common to all these things is the notion of relations.

But if one asks that the general idea of the beautiful conform to all the things designated by the term does one speak only of his own language or of all languages generally? Should the definition conform only to what is called beautiful in French or also to what is called beautiful in Hebrew, Syriac, Arabian, Chaldean, Greek, Latin, English, Italian, and all the other languages that have existed, do exist, or ever will exist? And to prove that the notion of relations is the only one which remains after imposing so extensive a rule of exclusion, will the philosopher have to take account of them all? Will it not be enough to have examined the usage of the term "beautiful" in all languages and to have found it applied in one place to one sort of thing, in another not at all to the same sort of thing, and yet to find that whatever the idiom one employs, it always presupposes the perception of relations? The English say, "a fine flavor, a fine woman." Where would an English philosopher be if, having to discuss the nature of the beautiful, he were obliged to take note of this singularity of his language. It is the people who have invented languages, it is up to the philosopher to discover the origin of things. And it would be quite surprising if the principles underlying the one did not often contradict the usages of the other. But the principle of the perception of relations, applied to the nature of the beautiful, is not at the same disadvantage. It is, moreover, so general that it would be difficult for any thing to escape it.

Among all peoples everywhere on earth, and at all times, there has been a word for color in general, and there have been other names for specific colors and their shades. What would a philosopher do who was required to explain what is a *beautiful color* except to indicate the origin of the application of the term "beautiful" to a color in general and then the reasons that have been offered for preferring one shade to another? Thus it is the perception of relations which has given rise to the invention of the term "beautiful." According to the way in which these relations and the minds of men have varied there have arisen the terms "pretty," "beautiful," "pleasing," "great," "sublime," "exquisite," and innumerable others which are as much of physical as of moral origin. Such are the nuances of the beautiful. In respect to such ideas I offer the following:

When one demands that this general concept of the beautiful should conform to all the beautiful things, does one speak only of those which bear this designation here and now, or of those which have been called beautiful since the origin of the world, or five thousand years ago and three thousand miles away, and which will be so called in ages to come? Should it apply to those things which we thought beautiful in childhood, in maturity, in old age, to things admired by civilized people and those which fascinate savages? Shall the truth of the definition be local, particular, momentary? Or shall it be extended to all things, all times, all persons, all places? If one chooses the latter alternative, one will be much less satisfied with my principle and there will be scarcely any other way of reconciling the judgments of the child and the adult. The child requires only a trace of symmetry and of verisimilitude to be entertained and to have his interest aroused. The adult needs places and works of great size to be thrilled. As to the judgments of the savage and the civilized man, the one will be enchanted by an ear-drop of glass, a brass ring, a bracelet of base metal; the other will pay attention only to the most perfect productions. Then too, primitive man lavishes terms such as "beautiful" or "magnificent" on huts, cottages, and barns. Modern man limits the terms to the most advanced efforts of man's talents.

Locate beauty in the perception of relations and you have the history of man's advancement, from the origin of the world to the present day. Choose as the differential characteristic of beauty in general any other quality you please and your concept will at once be limited to a point in space and time.

Thus the perception of relations is the foundation of beauty and it is the perception of relations which is designated in various languages by different names, each indicating a different type of beauty.

But in our language and in nearly all others the term "beautiful" is often used in contrast to "pleasing." Under this interpretation, the question of the beautiful seems to be only a matter of grammar and the whole problem appears to be no more than that of specifying precisely the ideas attaching to the term.

§ DIVERSITY OF AESTHETIC
  JUDGMENTS

After having tried to expound the origin of the beautiful, there remains only to inquire into the different opinions which men have about beauty. This inquiry will confer a certain certitude upon our principles, for we shall demonstrate that all these differences arise from the diversity of the relations perceived or imposed upon objects both in the products of nature and those of the arts.

1. The beauty which arises from the perception of a single relation is ordinarily less than that which arises from the perception of several such relations. The sight of a beautiful face or of a beautiful prospect involves more than a single color, a starry sky than a blue expanse, a country scene than open prairie, a building than a plot of ground, a piece of music than a single tone. Yet it is unnecessary to multiply the number of relations; beauty does not follow this *progressus ad infinitum*. We confine ourselves to the relations which a sensitive spirit can grasp clearly and easily. But what is a sensitive spirit? Where is the dividing line in works of art such that on one side for lack of relations they are too unified and on the other they may be charged with an excess of relations? This is the *first* source of diversity in aesthetic judgments. Here conflict begins. Everyone agrees that there is but one beauty which is the result of perceived relations. But according as there is more or less knowledge, experience, practice in judging, contemplativeness, vision, natural scope of mind, the object is said to be poor or rich, confused or complete, mean or meaningful.

But in how many compositions must the artist make use of more relations than the mass of men can grasp, and then there will be scarcely any more than the practitioners of his own art, and hence those little disposed to render him justice, who will know the merit of his work. What then becomes of the beautiful? Either it is presented to an ignorant and insensitive public or to a few jealous rivals who hold their tongues. This is often the fate of an important piece of music. D'Alembert has said in his *Discours préliminaire* to the *Dictionnaire encyclopédique,* which very much merits being cited in the present context, that now that there is an art of teaching music there ought also to be one of listening to it. Let me add that since poetry and painting have become arts it serves no purpose to turn them into arts of reading and seeing. A certain superficial uniformity will always prevail about certain works which is indeed less harmful to the artist than a difference of opinion, but it is also always more distressing.

2. Countless types of relations can be distinguished. Some strengthen, some weaken, and some temper one another. What a difference in one's opinion about the beauty of an object if one grasps all of them, or but a few! This is a second source of diversity of judgment. Relations are either indeterminate or determinate. Whenever it is not the immediate and specific purpose of a science or art to determine them, we confine ourselves to the former in conferring the name "beautiful." But if such determination *is* the immediate and specific purpose of a science or art, we require not only the relations but their values. That is why we speak of a beautiful theorem but not of a beautiful axiom, although undeniably an axiom expressing a relation has also a real beauty. When in mathematics we say that the whole is greater than any of its parts we certainly assert an infinity of propositions about the quantity so divided. But we specify nothing about the precise amount by which the whole exceeds its parts. It is about as if we were to say that the cylinder is greater than the inscribed sphere, and the sphere than the inscribed cone. But the immediate and proper task of mathematics is to determine by how much one of these volumes is greater or less than the other. He who demonstrates that they are always to one another as the numbers 3, 2, 1 has expounded a fine theorem. Beauty, which consists in relations, will on this occasion in principle consist of the number of relations and the degree of difficulty there is in grasping them. The theorem which asserts that every line dropped from the apex of an isosceles triangle to the midpoint of the base divides the angle into two equal angles does not appear remarkable. But there is beauty in the fact that the asymptotes of a curve approach one another endlessly without intersecting, and that the spaces formed by a portion of the axis, a part of the curve, the asymptote, and the prolongation of the ordinate stand to another as one number to another. One circumstance not indifferent to beauty on this and many other occasions, is an operation combining both the relations and surprise that always occur when the theorem whose truth has just been demonstrated was taken at first for a false proposition.

3. There are relations which we judge to be more or less essential, for example, the size of a thing in relation to that of a man, a woman, or a child. We say that a child is beautiful, although it is small. It is absolutely necessary that a handsome man be tall. We are much less inclined to demand this in a woman. It is much more possible for a short woman to be beautiful than for a short man. I think we consider things not only in themselves, but also relative to the places they occupy in nature, in the grand whole of things. And according as this whole is more or less known to us the scale which we form to ourselves of the sizes of things is more or less exact. But we never know precisely when it is correct. This is a third source of diversity of judgment in the arts of imitation. The great minds have preferred their scale to be rather too great than too small. But none of them has exactly the same scale nor perhaps even one that conforms to nature.

4. Interest, passions, ignorance, prejudices, usages, manners, climates, customs, governments, religions, historical events, all these interfere with the things around us, and either help or hinder the awakening in us of ideas about them. They destroy the inherently natural relations in things and supplant them with what is capricious and fortuitous. This is a fourth source of diversity of judgment.

5. We relate everything to our own talents and our own knowledge. We all more or less play the role of the critic of Apelles; given only the shoe we infer the leg, or knowing only the leg, we deduce the shoe. But we do not confine our rash-

ness or our ostentatiousness about small matters to judgments about works of art. Even those of nature are not exempt. The most beautiful among the tulips in a garden for a flower-fancier will be one in which he discerns the size, color, and foliage of a rare variety. But the painter occupied with effects of light, tint, and shading, and with form relevant to his art will ignore the fruits which florists admire and use as his model a flower that may even be despised by the connoisseur. Difference in talent and in knowledge is the fifth source of diversity in judgments.

6. The mind has the power of combining ideas which it receives separately, of comparing objects through the ideas it has of them, of observing their relations to one another, of separating and uniting its ideas at will, of considering separately each of the simple ideas which may be found united in the sensation it has received of them. The last of these operations is called *abstraction*. The ideas of material substances are composed of various simple ideas which together make an impression when material substances are presented to our senses. Substances can be defined only by specifying these sensible ideas in detail. Such definitions can produce a perfectly clear idea of a substance in one who has never immediately perceived them, provided that he has on other occasions received separately through his senses all the simple ideas which enter into the composition of the complex idea of the substance defined. But if he lacks the notion of any one of the simple ideas of which the substance is composed and lacks the sense necessary to perceive it, or if this sense is irremediably impaired, there is no definition which can produce in him the idea of which he has not already had a sensible perception. This is a sixth source of diversity in the judgments which men pronounce about beauty of a given description. How many are the false notions they have, and how many the half-notions of one and the same object!

7. But they are by no means bound to agree any better on intellectual matters. These are always represented by signs, and scarcely any signs are so precisely defined that their meaning may not be broader or narrower for one man than for another. Logic and metaphysics would be well-nigh perfect if the dictionary of the language were so. But as yet it is still something to be desired. Since words are the colors used by poetry and oratory, what agreement can one expect in the judgments of a picture so long as one does not know the truth even about colors and their shades? This is a seventh source of diversity of judgment.

8. Whatever be the thing we are judging, our preferences and rejections, originating in tutelage or education, in prejudice or in a certain artificial sytem of ideas, are all based on our opinion that these objects have a certain perfection or imperfection in their qualities, for the perception of which we have senses or appropriate faculties. This is the eighth source of diversity.

9. We may be certain that the simple ideas which one and the same object produces in different persons are as different as the pleasure or displeasure that is taken in them. This is true also of feelings. And it is no more remarkable that several persons should differ among themselves at the same time about simple ideas, than that the same person should be of two opinions at different times. Our senses are in a state of continual flux. One day we see nothing, another day we hear poorly, and from one day to the next we see, feel, and hear differently. This is the ninth source of difference in the judgment, in several persons at the same time, and the same person at different times.

10. Disagreeable ideas often attach themselves accidentally to the most beautiful objects. If one loves Spanish wine, one need only take it with a bit of emetic to detest it; we are not free to experience or not experience nausea under those conditions; Spanish wine is always good, but our

state is not always the same in relation to it. Likewise, this hall is ever splendid, but here my friend lost his life. This theatre has not ceased to be beautiful, since they have taken to jeering me; but I can no longer look at it without my ears echoing the catcalls. In this hall I see only my dying friend and do not sense its beauty. A tenth source of diversity in judgment which we are powerless to dispel from the idea in question. *Post equitem sedet atra cura.*[4]

11. When it is a question of complex objects having both natural and artificial forms, as in architecture, gardens, garments, and the like, taste is based upon another association of ideas, in part rational, in part capricious: the gait, cry, form, or color of some hideous object, the opinion of one's country, the ways of one's compatriots, all these affect our judgments. Do such causes tend to make us regard brilliant and lively colors as marks of vanity or of some other evil disposition of heart or mind? Are certain forms common among peasants or people whose occupation or business or character we loathe or despise? Such contributory ideas will return in spite of us along with the colors and the forms and we shall pronounce judgment against these colors and forms although there is nothing disagreeable in them in and of themselves. The eleventh source of diversity.

12. On the beauty of what object in nature then will men be in perfect accord? The structure of plants, the mechanism of animal bodies, the Universe? But they who are most struck by the relation, order, symmetry, and connection which prevail throughout this great whole, ignoring the end which the Creator intended in forming it, must they not declare it to be the perfection of beauty because of the ideas they have of the Deity? Do they not regard it as a masterpiece largely because the Creator lacked no degree of power or will to

make it so? But often we have no such right to infer the perfection of the work, merely from the name of its creator, and yet we do not cease admiring it. This picture is Raphael's: that is enough. A twelfth source, if not of diversity, at least of error in judgment.

Concerning the beauty of purely imaginary beings, the sphinx, siren, faun, minotaur, the ideal man, and the like, there is much less conflict of opinion, nor is this surprising. Such imaginary beings are truly formed in accord with the relations which are observed in real beings. But the model to which they conform, scattered among all the productions of nature, is actually everywhere and nowhere.

Despite all these causes of the diversity of our judgments, there is no reason to infer that real beauty, the beauty which consists in the perception of relations, is an illusion. There can be infinite variation in the application of this principle, and its incidental modification may precipitate disputes and literary conflicts. Yet the principle remains nonetheless constant. Scarcely two men in the whole world will perceive exactly the same relations in one and the same object, and their judgment of its beauty will be correspondingly varied. But no one is altogether imperceptive of relations in one or another kind of subject unless he be a complete dullard. If he is insensitive only to certain kinds, this decreases in him his want of perfection in natural endowment. And we should still be far removed from skepticism because of the general state of the rest of our species.

The beautiful is not always produced by an intelligent cause. Motion often exhibits a vast number of surprising relations both in things considered by themselves and among several things compared with one another. Natural history collections offer many examples of them. In that case, relations are the results of fortuitous combinations, at least in relation to ourselves. Nature in its free play imitates the productions

---

4 [Horace, *Odes,* III, i, 40: "Behind the splendid knight sits black care."—TR. NOTE.]

of art on a hundred occasions. I shall not go so far as to say that the philosopher who was shipwrecked on the shores of an unknown island was right when he exclaimed at the sight of certain geometrical figures, "Courage, my friends, here are the footsteps of men." And yet, we may ask how many relations a thing must be observed to have for us to be completely certain that it is the work of an artist, in what circumstance a single defect of symmetry proves more than a whole given quantity of relations, how the time of occurrence of fortuitous causes stands to the relations observed in the effects produced, and whether, excepting the works of the Almighty, there are instances where the number of relations can never equal the number of throws of the dice.

THOMAS REID

(1710-1796)

Though Reid was slightly older than David Hume, his principal works appeared after Hume's and were intended, often explicitly, as replies or refutations of Hume's skepticism and subjectivism. With Dugald Steward he is the founder of the Scottish school of common-sense realism, which exerted a marked influence on philosophical ideas in the United States in the nineteenth century. Reid succeeded Adam Smith as professor at Glasgow.

Members of the British school in aesthetics, especially those of the Scottish wing, were very numerous and influential in Europe toward the end of the eighteenth century. Among these, Reid is undoubtedly the most capable and influential philosopher, and indeed in his reaction away from Hume he is often compared to Kant. The present essay is Chapter 4 of Essay VIII of the *Essays on the Intellectual Powers of Man,* which appeared in 1785, five years before Kant's third Critique. What reminds one of Kant is Reid's insistence that aesthetic judgments have a prima facie claim to objectivity. As is often noted, Reid's rejection of Locke's "way of ideas" and his view that common sense and a just understanding of language must condemn subjectivism as paradoxical anticipate numerous moves on the part of present-day "analytical philosophers." Philosophers, he tells us, should be cautious in opposing the instincts and linguistic habits of mankind. But we may well wish to inquire whether his conclusion that "it is in the moral and intellectual perfections of mind, and in its active powers, that beauty originally dwells" is consistent with this caution.

Among the valuable ideas to be encountered in Reid's essay is his distinction between original and derivative beauty. This of course is another way of introducing the idea of association, which we encounter again in Francis Jeffrey.

THOMAS REID

On the Intellectual Powers of Man

(First published: 1785.)

Of Beauty

Beauty is found in things, so various, and so very different in nature, that it is difficult to say wherein it consists, or what there can be common to all the objects in which it is found.

Of the objects of sense, we find beauty in colour, in sound, in form, in motion. There are beauties of speech, and beauties of thought; beauties in the arts, and in the sciences; beauties in actions, in affections, and in characters.

In things so different, and so unlike, is there any quality, the same in all, which we may call by the name of beauty? What can it be that is common to the thought of a mind, and the form of a piece of matter, to an abstract theorem, and a stroke of wit?

I am indeed unable to conceive any quality in all the different things that are called beautiful, that is the same in them all. There seems to be no identity, nor even similarity, between the beauty of a theorem and the beauty of a piece of music, though both may be beautiful. The kinds of beauty seem to be as various as the objects to which it is ascribed.

But why should things so different be called by the same name? This cannot be without a reason. If there be nothing common in the things themselves, they must have some common relation to us, or to something else, which leads us to give them the same name.

All the objects we call beautiful agree in two things, which seem to concur in our sense of beauty. First, when they are perceived, or even imagined, they produce a certain agreeable emotion or feeling in the mind; and secondly, this agreeable emotion is accompanied with an opinion or belief of their having some perfection or excellence belonging to them.

Whether the pleasure we feel in contemplating beautiful objects may have any necessary connection with the belief of their excellence, or whether that pleasure be conjoined with this belief, by the good pleasure only of our Maker, I will not determine. The reader may see Dr. Price's sentiments upon this subject, which merit consideration, in the second chapter of his *Review of the Principal Questions in Morals.*

Though we may be able to conceive these two ingredients of our sense of beauty disjoined, this affords no evidence that they have no necessary connection. It has indeed been maintained, that whatever we can conceive, is possible: but I endeavoured, in treating of conception, to show, that this opinion, though very common, is a mistake. There may be, and probably are, many necessary connections of things in nature, which we are too dim-sighted to discover.

The emotion produced by beautiful objects is gay and pleasant. It sweetens and humanizes the temper, is friendly to every benevolent affection, and tends to allay sullen and angry passions. It enlivens the mind, and disposes it to other agreeable emotions, such as those of love, hope, and joy. It gives a value to the object, abstracted from its utility.

In things that may be possessed as property, beauty greatly enhances the price. A beautiful dog or horse, a beautiful coach or house, a beautiful picture or prospect, is valued by its owner and by others, not only for its utility, but for its beauty.

If the beautiful object be a person, his company and conversation are, on that account, the more agreeable, and we are disposed to love and esteem him. Even in a perfect stranger, it is a powerful recommendation, and disposes us to favour and think well of him, if of our own sex, and still more if of the other.

"There is nothing" says Mr. Addison, "that makes its way more directly to the soul than beauty, which immediately diffuses a secret satisfaction and complacence through the imagination, and gives a finishing to anything that is great and uncommon. The very first discovery of it strikes the mind with an inward joy, and spreads a cheerfulness and delight through all its faculties."

As we ascribe beauty, not only to persons, but to inanimate things, we give the name of love or liking to the emotion, which beauty, in both these kinds of objects, produces. It is evident, however, that liking to a person is a very different affection of mind from liking to an inanimate thing. The first always implies benevolence; but what is inanimate cannot be the object of benevolence. The two affections, however different, have a resemblance in some respects; and, on account of that resemblance, have the same name: and perhaps beauty, in these two different kinds of objects, though it has one name, may be as different in its nature as the emotions which it produces in us.

Besides the agreeable emotion which beautiful objects produce in the mind of the spectator, they produce also an opinion or judgment of some perfection or excellence in the object. This I take to be a second ingredient in our sense of beauty, though it seems not to be admitted by modern philosophers.

The ingenious Dr. Hutcheson, who perceived some of the defects of Mr. Locke's system, and made very important improvements upon it, seems to have been carried away by it, in his notion of beauty. In his *Inquiry Concerning Beauty,* Section 1,

"Let it be observed," says he, "that, in the following papers, the word *beauty* is taken for the idea raised in us, and the sense of beauty, for our power of receiving that idea." And again: "Only let it be observed, that, by absolute or original beauty, is not understood any quality supposed to be in the object which should, of itself, be beautiful, without relation to any mind which perceives it: for beauty, like other names of sensible ideas, properly denotes the perception of some mind; so cold, hot, sweet, bitter, denote the sensations in our minds, to which perhaps there is no resemblance in the objects which excite these ideas in us; however, we generally imagine otherwise. Were there no mind, with a sense of beauty, to contemplate objects, I see not how they could be called beautiful."

There is no doubt an analogy between the external senses of touch and taste, and the internal sense of beauty. This analogy led Dr. Hutcheson, and other modern philosophers, to apply to beauty what Descartes and Locke had taught concerning the secondary qualities, perceived by the external senses.

Mr. Locke's doctrine concerning the secondary qualities of body, is not so much an error in judgment, as an abuse of words. He distinguished very properly between the sensations we have of heat and cold, and that quality or structure in the body which is adapted by nature to produce those sensations in us. He observed very justly, that there can be no similitude between one of these and the other. They have the relation of an effect to its cause, but no similitude. This was a very just and proper correction of the doctrine of the Peripatetics, who taught that all our sensations are the very form and image of the quality in the object by which they are produced.

What remained to be determined was, whether the words heat and cold, in common language, signify the sensations we feel, or the qualities of the object which are the cause of these sensations. Mr. Locke made heat and cold to signify only the sensations we feel, and not the qualities which are the cause of them. And in this, I apprehend, lay his mistake. For it is evident, from the use of language, that hot and cold, sweet and bitter, are attributes of external objects, and not of the person who perceives them. Hence it appears a monstrous paradox to say, there is no heat in the fire, no sweetness in sugar: but when explained according to Mr. Locke's meaning, it is only, like most other paradoxes, an abuse of words.

The sense of beauty may be analyzed in a manner very similar to the sense of sweetness. It is an agreeable feeling of emotion, accompanied with an opinion or judgment of some excellence in the object, which is fitted by nature to produce that feeling.

The feeling is, no doubt, in the mind, and so also is the judgment we form of the object: but this judgment, like all others, must be true or false. If it be a true judgment, there is some real excellence in the object. And the use of all languages shows that the name of beauty belongs to this excellence of the object, and not to the feelings of the spectator.

To say that there is in reality no beauty in those objects in which all men perceive beauty, is to attribute to man fallacious senses. But we have no ground to think so disrespectfully of the Author of our being; the faculties he has given us are not fallacious; nor is that beauty, which he has so liberally diffused over all the works of his hands, a mere fancy in us, but a real excellence in his works, which express the perfection of their Divine Author.

We have reason to believe, not only that the beauties we see in nature are real, and not fanciful, but that there are thousands which our faculties are too dull to perceive. We see many beauties, both of human and divine art, which the brute animals are incapable of perceiving; and superior beings may excel us as far in their discernment of true beauty as we excel the brutes.

The man who is skilled in painting or statuary, sees more of the beauty of a fine picture or statue, than a common spectator. The same thing holds in all the fine arts. The most perfect works of art have a beauty that strikes even the rude and ignorant; but they see only a small part of that beauty which is seen in such works by those who understand them perfectly and can produce them.

This may be applied with no less justice to the works of nature. They have a beauty that strikes even the ignorant and inattentive. But the more we discover of their structure, of their mutual relations, and of the laws by which they are governed, the greater beauty, and the more delightful marks of art, wisdom, and goodness we discern.

Thus the expert anatomist sees numberless beautiful contrivances in the structure of the human body which are unknown to the ignorant.

Although the vulgar eye sees much beauty in the face of the heavens, and in the various motions and changes of the heavenly bodies, the expert astronomer, who knows their order and distances, their periods, the orbits they describe in the vast regions of space, and the simple and beautiful laws by which their motions are governed, and all the appearances of their stations, progressions, and retrogradations, their eclipses, occultations, and transits are produced, sees a beauty, order, and harmony reign through the whole planetary system, which delights the mind. The eclipses of the sun and moon, and the blazing tails of comets, which strike terror into barbarous nations, furnish the most pleasing entertainment to his eye, and a feast to his understanding.

In every part of nature's works, there are numberless beauties, which, on account of our ignorance, we are unable to perceive. Superior beings may see more than we; but he only who made them, and, upon a review, pronounced them all to be very good, can see all their beauty.

Our determinations with regard to the beauty of objects, may, I think, be distinguished into two kinds; the first we may call instinctive, the other rational.

Some objects strike us at once, and appear beautiful at first sight, without any reflection, without our being able to say why we call them beautiful, or being able to specify any perfection which justifies our judgment. Something of this kind there seems to be in brute animals; and in children before the use of reason; nor does it end with infancy, but continues through life.

In the plumage of birds, and of butterflies, in the colours and form of flowers, of shells, and of many other objects, we perceive a beauty that delights; but cannot say what it is in the object that should produce that emotion.

The beauty of the object may in such cases be called an occult quality. We know well how it affects our senses; but what it is in itself we know not. But this, as well as other occult qualities, is a proper subject of philosophical disquisition; and, by a careful examination of the objects to which nature has given this amiable quality, we may perhaps discover some real excellence in the object, or at least, some valuable purpose that is served by the effect which it produces upon us.

This instinctive sense of beauty, in different species of animals, may differ as much as the external sense of taste, and in each species be adapted to its manner of life. By this perhaps the various tribes are led to associate with their kind, to dwell among certain objects rather than others, and to construct their habitation in a particular manner.

There seem likewise to be varieties in the sense of beauty in the individuals of the same species, by which they are directed in the choice of a mate, and in the love and care of their offspring.

"We see," says Mr. Addison, "that every different species of sensible creatures has its different notions of beauty, and that each of them is most affected with the beauties of its own kind. This is nowhere more remarkable than in birds of the same shape and proportion, where we often see the mate determined in his courtship by the single grain or tincture of a feather, and never discovering any charms but in the colour of its own species.". . .

In the human kind, there are varieties in the taste of beauty, of which we can no more assign a reason than of the variety of their features, though it is easy to perceive that very important ends are answered by both. These varieties are most observable in the judgments we form of the features of the other sex; and in this the intention of nature is most apparent.

As far as our determinations of the comparative beauty of objects are instinctive, they are no subject of reasoning or of criticism; they are purely the gift of nature, and we have no standard by which they may be measured.

But there are judgments of beauty that may be called rational, being grounded on some agreeable quality of the object which is distinctly conceived, and may be specified.

This distinction between a rational judgment of beauty and that which is instinctive, may be illustrated by an instance.

In a heap of pebbles, one that is remarkable for brilliancy of colour and regularity of figure will be picked out of the heap by a child. He perceives a beauty in it, puts a value upon it, and is fond of the property of it. For this preference, no reason can be given, but that children are, by their constitution, fond of brilliant colours, and of regular figures.

Suppose again that an expert mechanic views a well constructed machine. He sees all its parts to be made of the fittest materials, and of the most proper form; nothing superfluous, nothing deficient; every part adapted to its use, and the whole fitted in the most perfect manner to the end for which it is intended. He pronounces it to be a beautiful machine. He views it with the same agreeable emotion as the child viewed the pebble; but he can give a reason for his judgment, and point out the particular perfections of the object on which it is grounded.

Although the instinctive and the rational sense of beauty may be perfectly distinguished in speculation, yet, in passing judgment upon particular objects, they are often so mixed and confounded, that it is difficult to assign to each its own province. Nay, it may often happen, that a judgment of the beauty of an object, which was at first merely instinctive, shall afterward become rational, when we discover some latent perfection of which that beauty in the object is a sign.

As the sense of beauty may be distinguished into instinctive and rational; so I think beauty itself may be distinguished into original and derived.

As some objects shine by their own light, and many more by light that is borrowed and reflected; so I conceive the luster of beauty in some objects is inherent and original, and in many others, is borrowed and reflected.

There is nothing more common in the sentiments of all mankind, and in the language of all nations, than what may be called a communication of attributes; that is, transferring an attribute, from the subject to which it properly belongs, to some related or resembling subject.

The various objects which nature presents to our view, even those that are most different in kind, have innumerable similitudes, relations, and analogies, which we contemplate with pleasure, and which lead us naturally to borrow words and attributes from one object to express what belongs to another. The greatest part of every language under heaven is made up of words borrowed from one thing, and applied to something supposed to have some relation or analogy to their first signification.

The attributes of body we ascribe to

mind, and the attributes of mind to material objects. To inanimate things we ascribe life, and even intellectual and moral qualities. And although the qualities that are thus made common belong to one of the subjects in the proper sense, and to the other metaphorically, these different senses are often so mixed in our imagination, as to produce the same sentiment with regard to both.

It is therefore natural, and agreeable to the strain of human sentiments and of human language, that in many cases the beauty which originally and properly is in the thing signified, should be transferred to the sign; that which is in the cause, to the effect; that which is in the end, to the means; and that which is in the agent, to the instrument.

If...the distinction between the grandeur which we ascribe to qualities of mind, and that which we ascribe to material objects be well founded, this distinction of the beauty of objects will easily be admitted as perfectly analogous to it. I shall therefore only illustrate it by an example.

There is nothing in the exterior of a man more lovely and more attractive than perfect good breeding. But what is this good breeding? It consists of all the external signs of due respect to our superiors, condescension to our inferiors, politeness to all with whom we converse or have to do, joined in the fair sex with that delicacy of outward behaviour which becomes them. And how comes it to have such charms in the eyes of all mankind? For this reason only, as I apprehend, that it is a natural sign of that temper, and those affections and sentiments with regard to others, and with regard to ourselves, which are in themselves truly amiable and beautiful.

This is the original, of which good breeding is the picture; and it is the beauty of the original that is reflected to our sense by the picture. The beauty of good breeding, therefore, is not originally in the external behaviour in which it consists, but is derived from the qualities of mind which it expresses. And though there may be good breeding without the amiable qualities of mind, its beauty is still derived from what it naturally expresses.

Having explained these distinctions of our sense of beauty into instinctive and rational, and of beauty itself into original and derived, I would now proceed to give a general view of those qualities in objects, to which we may justly and rationally ascribe beauty, whether original or derived.

But here some embarrassment arises from the vague meaning of the word *beauty*, which I had occasion before to observe.

Sometimes it is extended, so as to include every thing that pleases a good taste, and so comprehends grandeur and novelty, as well as what in a more restricted sense is called beauty. At other times, it is even by good writers confined to the objects of sight, when they are either seen, or remembered, or imagined. Yet it is admitted by all men, that there are beauties in music; that there is beauty as well as sublimity in composition, both in verse and in prose; that there is beauty in characters, in affections, and in actions. These are not objects of sight; and a man may be a good judge of beauty of various kinds, who has not the faculty of sight.

To give a determinate meaning to a word so variously extended and restricted, I know no better way than what is suggested by the common division of the objects of taste into novelty, grandeur, and beauty. Novelty, it is plain, is no quality of the new object, but merely a relation which it has to the knowledge of the person to whom it is new. Therefore, if this general division be just, every quality in an object that pleases a good taste, must, in one degree or another, have either grandeur or beauty. It may still be difficult to fix the precise limit between grandeur and beauty; but they must together comprehend everything fitted by its nature to please a good taste, that is, every real perfection and excellence in the objects we contemplate.

In a poem, in a picture, in a piece of music, it is real excellence that pleases a good taste. In a person, every perfection of the mind, moral or intellectual, and every perfection of the body, gives pleasure to the spectator as well as to the owner, when there is no envy nor malignity to destroy that pleasure.

It is therefore in the scale of perfection and real excellence that we must look for what is either grand or beautiful in objects. What is the proper object of admiration is grand, and what is the proper object of love and esteem is beautiful.

This, I think, is the only notion of beauty that corresponds with the division of the objects of taste which has been generally received by philosophers. And this connection of beauty with real perfection was a capital doctrine of the Socratic school. It is often ascribed to Socrates in the dialogues of Plato and of Xenophon.

We may therefore take a view, first, of those qualities of mind to which we may justly and rationally ascribe beauty, and then of the beauty we perceive in the objects of sense. We shall find, if I mistake not, that, in the first, original beauty is to be found, and that the beauties of the second class are derived from some relation they bear to mind, as the signs or expressions of some amiable mental quality, or as the effects of design, art, and wise contrivance.

As grandeur naturally produces admiration, beauty naturally produces love. We may therefore justly ascribe beauty to those qualities which are the natural objects of love and kind affection.

Of this kind chiefly are some of the moral virtues, which in a peculiar manner constitute a lovely character. Innocence, gentleness, condescension, humanity, natural affection, public spirit, and the whole train of the soft and gentle virtues. These qualities are amiable from their very nature, and on account of their intrinsic worth.

There are other virtues that raise admiration, and are therefore grand; such as magnanimity, fortitude, self-command, superiority to pain and labour, superiority to pleasure, and to the smiles of fortune, as well as to her frowns.

These awful virtues constitute what is most grand in the human character; the gentle virtues, what is most beautiful and lovely. As they are virtues, they draw the approbation of our moral faculty; as they are becoming and amiable, they affect our sense of beauty.

Next to the amiable moral virtues, there are many intellectual talents which have an intrinsic value, and draw our love and esteem to those who possess them. Such are, knowledge, good sense, wit, humour, cheerfulness, good taste, excellence in any of the fine arts, in eloquence, in dramatic action; and we may add, excellence in every art of peace or war that is useful in society.

There are likewise talents which we refer to the body, which have an original beauty and comeliness; such as health, strength, and agility, the usual attendants of youth; skill in bodily exercises, and skill in the mechanic arts. These are real perfections of the man, as they increase his power and render the body a fit instrument for the mind.

I apprehend, therefore, that it is in the moral and intellectual perfections of mind, and in its active powers, that beauty originally dwells; and that from this as the fountain, all the beauty which we perceive in the visible world is derived.

This, I think, was the opinion of the ancient philosophers before named; and it has been adopted by Lord Shaftesbury and Dr. Akenside among the moderns.

Mind, mind alone! bear witness earth and
 heav'n,
The living fountains in itself contains
Of beauteous and sublime. Here hand in
 hand
Sit paramount the graces. Here enthron'd,
Celestial Venus, with divinest airs,
Invites the soul to never fading joy.

But neither mind, nor any of its qualities or powers, is an immediate object of perception to man. We are, indeed, immediately conscious of the operations of our own mind; and every degree of perfection in them gives the purest pleasure, with a proportional degree of self-esteem, so flattering to self-love, that the great difficulty is to keep it within just bounds, so that we may not think of ourselves above what we ought to think.

Other minds we perceive only through the medium of material objects, on which their signatures are impressed. It is through this medium that we perceive life, activity, wisdom, and every moral and intellectual quality in other beings. The signs of those qualities are immediately perceived by the senses; by them the qualities themselves are reflected to our understanding; and we are very apt to attribute to the sign, the beauty or the grandeur, which is properly and originally in the things signified.

The invisible Creator, the fountain of all perfection, has stamped upon all his works signatures of his divine wisdom, power and benignity, which are visible to all men. The works of men in science, in the arts of taste, and in the mechanical arts, bear the signatures of those qualities of mind which were employed in their production. Their external behaviour and conduct in life expresses the good or bad qualities of their mind.

In every species of animals, we perceive by visible signs their instincts, their appetites, their affections, their sagacity. Even in the inanimate world there are many things analogous to the qualities of mind; so that there is hardly anything belonging to mind which may not be represented by images taken from the objects of sense; and on the other hand, every object of sense is beautified, by borrowing attire from the attributes of mind.

Thus the beauties of mind, though invisible in themselves, are perceived in the objects of sense, on which their image is impressed.

If we consider, on the other hand, the qualities in sensible objects to which we ascribe beauty, I apprehend we shall find in all of them some relation to mind, and the greatest in those that are most beautiful.

When we consider inanimate matter abstractly, as a substance endowed with the qualities of extension, solidity, divisibility, and mobility, there seems to be nothing in these qualities that affects our sense of beauty. But when we contemplate the globe which we inhabit, as fitted by its form, by its motions, and by its furniture, for the habitation and support of an infinity of various orders of living creatures, from the lowest reptile up to man, we have a glorious spectacle indeed! with which the grandest and the most beautiful structures of human art can bear no comparison.

The only perfection of dead matter is its being, by its various forms and qualities, so admirably fitted for the purposes of animal life, and chiefly that of man. It furnishes the materials of every art that tends to the support or embellishment of human life. By the Supreme Artist, it is organized in the various tribes of the vegetable kingdom, and endowed with a kind of life; a work which human art cannot imitate, nor human understanding comprehend.

In the bodies and various organs of the animal tribes, there is a composition of matter still more wonderful and more mysterious, though we see it to be admirably adapted to the purposes and manner of life of every species. But in every form, unorganized, vegetable, or animal, it derives its beauty from the purposes to which it is subservient, or from the signs of wisdom, or of other mental qualities which it exhibits.

The qualities of inanimate matter, in which we perceive beauty, are sound, colour, form, and motion; the first an object of hearing, the other three of sight; which we may consider in order.

In a single note, sounded by a very fine

voice, there is a beauty which we do not perceive in the same note, sounded by a bad voice or an imperfect instrument. I need not attempt to enumerate the perfections in a single note, which give beauty to it. Some of them have names in the science of music, and there perhaps are others which have no names. But I think it will be allowed that every quality which gives beauty to a single note, is a sign of some perfection, either in the organ, whether it be the human voice or an instrument, or in the execution. The beauty of the sound is both the sign and the effect of this perfection; and the perfection of the cause is the only reason we can assign for the beauty of the effect.

In a composition of sounds, or a piece of music, the beauty is either in the harmony, the melody, or the expression. The beauty of expression must be derived, either from the beauty of the thing expressed, or from the art and skill employed in expressing it properly.

In harmony, the very names of concord and discord are metaphorical, and suppose some analogy between the relations of sound, to which they are figuratively applied, and the relations of minds and affections, which they originally and properly signify.

As far as I can judge by my ear, when two or more persons of a good voice and ear, converse together in amity and friendship, the tones of their different voices are concordant, but become discordant when they give vent to angry passions; so that, without hearing what is said, one may know by the tones of the different voices, whether they quarrel or converse amicably. This, indeed, is not so easily perceived in those who have been taught, by good breeding, to suppress angry tones of voice, even when they are angry, as in the lowest rank, who express their angry passions without any restraint.

When discord arises occasionally in conversation, but soon terminates in perfect amity, we receive more pleasure than from perfect unanimity. In like manner, in the harmony of music, discordant sounds are occasionally introduced, but it is always in order to give a relish to the most perfect concord that follows.

Whether these analogies, between the harmony of a piece of music, and harmony in the intercourse of minds, be merely fanciful, or have any real foundation in fact, I submit to those who have a nicer ear and have applied it to observations of this kind. If they have any just foundation, as they seem to me to have, they serve to account for the metaphorical application of the names of concord and discord to the relations of sounds; to account for the pleasure we have from harmony in music; and to show, that the beauty of harmony is derived from the relation it has to agreeable affections of mind.

With regard to melody, I leave it to the adepts in the science of music, to determine whether music, composed according to the established rules of harmony and melody, can be altogether void of expression; and whether music that has no expression can have any beauty. To me it seems that every strain in melody that is agreeable, is an imitation of the tones of the human voice in the expression of some sentiment or passion, or an imitation of some other object in nature; and that music, as well as poetry, is an imitative art.

The sense of beauty in the colours, and in the motions of inanimate objects, is, I believe, in some cases instinctive. We see, that children and savages are pleased with brilliant colours and sprightly motions. In persons of an improved and rational taste, there are many sources from which colours and motions may derive their beauty. They, as well as the forms of objects, admit of regularity and variety. The motions produced by machinery, indicate the perfection or imperfection of the mechanism, and may be better or worse adapted to their end, and from that derive their beauty or deformity.

The colours of natural objects are commonly signs of some good or bad quality in the object; or they may suggest to the imagination something agreeable or disagreeable.

In dress and furniture, fashion has a considerable influence on the preference we give to one colour above another.

A number of clouds of different and ever changing hue, seen on the ground of a serene azure sky at the going down of the sun, present to the eye of every man a glorious spectacle. It is hard to say whether we should call it grand or beautiful. It is both in a high degree. Clouds towering above clouds, variously tinged, according as they approach nearer to the direct rays of the sun, enlarge our conceptions of the regions above us. They give us a view of the furniture of those regions, which, in an unclouded air, seem to be a perfect void; but are now seen to contain the stores of wind and rain, bound up for the present, but to be poured down upon the earth in due season. Even the simple rustic does not look upon this beautiful sky merely as a show to please the eye, but as a happy omen of fine weather to come.

The proper arrangement of colour, and of light and shade, is one of the chief beauties of painting; but this beauty is greatest, when that arrangement gives the most distinct, the most natural, and the most agreeable image of that which the painter intended to represent.

If we consider, in the last place, the beauty of form or figure in inanimate objects, this, according to Dr. Hutcheson, results from regularity, mixed with variety. Here it ought to be observed that regularity, in all cases, expresses design and art: for nothing regular was ever the work of chance; and where regularity is joined with variety, it expresses design more strongly. Besides, it has been justly observed, that regular figures are more easily and more perfectly comprehended by the mind, than the irregular, of which we can never form an adequate conception.

Although straight lines and plain surfaces have a beauty from their regularity, they admit of no variety, and therefore are beauties of the lowest order. Curved lines and surfaces admit of infinite variety, joined with every degree of regularity; and therefore, in many cases, excel in beauty those that are straight.

But the beauty arising from regularity and variety, must always yield to that which arises from the fitness of the form for the end intended. In everything made for an end, the form must be adapted to that end; and everything in the form that suits the end, is a beauty; everything that unfits it for its end, is a deformity.

The forms of a pillar, of a sword, and of a balance, are very different. Each may have great beauty; but that beauty is derived from the fitness of the form, and of the matter for the purpose intended.

Were we to consider the form of the earth itself, and the various furniture it contains, of the inanimate kind; its distribution into land and sea, mountains and valleys, rivers and springs of water, the variety of soils that cover its surface, and of mineral and metallic substances laid up within it, the air that surrounds it, the vicissitudes of day and night, and of the seasons; the beauty of all these, which indeed is superlative, consists in this, that they bear the most lively and striking impression of the wisdom and goodness of their Author, in contriving them so admirably for the use of man, and of their other inhabitants.

The beauties of the vegetable kingdom are far superior to those of inanimate matter, in any form which human art can give it. Hence, in all ages, men have been fond to adorn their persons and their habitations with the vegetable productions of nature.

The beauties of the field, of the forest, and of the flower garden, strike a child long before he can reason. He is delighted with what he sees; but he knows not why. This is instinct, but it is not confined to child-hood; it continues through all the stages of life. It leads the florist, the botanist, the philosopher, to examine and compare the objects which nature, by this powerful instinct, recommends to his attention. By degrees, he becomes a critic in beauties of this kind, and can give a reason why he prefers one to another. In every species, he sees the greatest beauty in the plants or flowers that are most perfect in their kind, which have neither suffered from unkindly soil, nor inclement weather; which have not been robbed of their nourishment by other plants, nor hurt by any accident. When he examines the internal structure of those productions of nature, and traces them from their embryo state in the seed to their maturity, he sees a thousand beautiful con-trivances of nature, which feast his under-standing more than their external form de-lighted his eye.

Thus, every beauty in the vegetable crea-tion, of which he has formed any rational judgment, expresses some perfection in the object, or some wise contrivance in its Author.

In the animal kingdom, we perceive still greater beauties than in the vegetable. Here we observe life, and sense, and activity, various instincts and affections, and, in many cases, great sagacity. These are attributes of mind, and have an original beauty.

As we allow to brute animals a thinking principle or mind, though far inferior to that which is in man; and as, in many of their intellectual and active powers, they very much resemble the human species, their actions, their motions, and even their looks, derive a beauty from the powers of thought which they express.

There is a wonderful variety in their manner of life; and we find the powers they possess, their outward form, and their in-ward structure, exactly adapted to it. In every species, the more perfectly any indi-vidual is fitted for its end and manner of life, the greater is its beauty.

In a racehorse, everything that expresses agility, ardour, and emulation, gives beauty to the animal. In a pointer, acuteness of scent, eagerness on the game, and tractable-ness, are the beauties of the species. A sheep derives its beauty from the fineness and quantity of its fleece; and in the wild animals, every beauty is a sign of their per-fection in their kind.

It is an observation of the celebrated Linnaeus, that, in the vegetable kingdom, the poisonous plants have commonly a lurid and disagreeable appearance to the eye, of which he gives many instances. I apprehend the observation may be extended to the animal kingdom, in which we commonly see something shocking to the eye in the noxi-ous and poisonous animals.

The beauties which anatomists and phys-iologists describe in the internal structure of the various tribes of animals; in the organs of sense, of nutrition, and of motion, are expressive of wise design and contriv-ance, in fitting them for the various kinds of life, for which they are intended.

Thus, I think, it appears that the beauty which we perceive in the inferior animals is expressive, either of such perfections as their several natures may receive, or ex-pressive of wise design in him who made them, and that their beauty is derived from the perfections which it expresses.

But of all the objects of sense, the most striking and attractive beauty is perceived in the human species, and particularly in the fair sex.

Milton represents Satan himself, in surveying the furniture of this globe, as struck with the beauty of the first happy pair.

> Two of far nobler shape, erect and tall,
> Godlike erect! with native honour clad
> In naked majesty, seem'd lords of all.
> And worthy seem'd; for in their looks
>   divine,
> The image of their glorious Maker, shone
> Truth, wisdom, sanctitude severe, and
>   pure;
> Severe, but in true filial freedom plac'd,

Whence true authority in man, though
  both
Not equal, as their sex not equal seem'd,
For contemplation he, and valour form'd,
For softness she, and sweet attractive
  grace.

In this well known passage of Milton, we see that this great poet derives the beauty of the first pair in Paradise from those expressions of moral and intellectual qualities which appeared in their outward form and demeanour.

The most minute and systematical account of beauty in the human species, and particularly in the fair sex, I have met with, is in *Crito; or a Dialogue on Beauty,* said to be written by the author of *Polymetis,* and republished by Dodsley in his collection of fugitive pieces.[1]

I shall borrow from that author some observations, which, I think, tend to show that the beauty of the human body is derived from the signs it exhibits of some perfection of the mind or person.

All that can be called beauty in the human species may be reduced to these four heads; colour, form, expression, and grace. The two former may be called the body, the two latter the soul of beauty.

The beauty of colour is not owing solely to the natural liveliness of flesh colour and red, nor to the much greater charms they receive from being properly blended together; but is also owing, in some degree, to the idea they carry with them of good health, without which all beauty grows languid and less engaging, and with which it always recovers an additional strength and lustre. This is supported by the authority of Cicero: *Venustas et pulchritudo corporis secerni non potest a valetudine.*[2]

Here I observe, that as the colour of the body is very different in different climates, every nation preferring the colour of its climate; and as among us one man prefers a fair beauty, another a brunette, without being able to give any reason for his preference; this diversity of taste has no standard in the common principles of human nature, but must arise from something that is different in different nations, and in different individuals of the same nation.

I observed before, that fashion, habit, associations, and perhaps some peculiarity of constitution, may have great influence upon this internal sense, as well as upon the external. Setting aside the judgments arising from such causes, there seems to remain nothing that, according to the common judgment of mankind, can be called beauty in the colour of the species, but what expresses perfect health and liveliness, and in the fair sex, softness and delicacy; and nothing that can be called deformity but what indicates disease and decline. And if this be so, it follows, that the beauty of colour is derived from the perfections which it expresses. This, however, of all the ingredients of beauty is the least.

The next in order is form, or proportion of parts. The most beautiful form, as the author thinks, is that which indicates delicacy and softness in the fair sex, and in the male either strength or agility. The beauty of form, therefore, lies all in expression.

The third ingredient, which has more power than either colour or form, he calls expression, and observes, that it is only the expression of the tender and kind passions that gives beauty; that all the cruel and unkind ones add to deformity; and that, on this account, good nature may very justly be said to be the best feature, even in the finest fact. Modesty, sensibility, and sweetness, blended together, so as either to enliven or to correct each other, give almost as much attraction as the passions are capable of adding to a very pretty face.

---

1 [Joseph Spence (1699–1768), writing under the name Sir Harry Beaumont, is the author of *Crito* (1725). Robert Dodsley (1703–1764) issued *Fugitive Pieces on Various Subjects* (1761).—ED. NOTE.]

2 ["Physical grace and beauty cannot be separated from health."—ED. NOTE.]

It is owing, says the author, to the great force of pleasingness which attends all the kinder passions, that lovers not only seem, but really are, more beautiful to each other than they are to the rest of the world; because, when they are together, the most pleasing passions are more frequently exerted in each of their faces than they are in either before the rest of the world. "There is then," as a French author very well expresses it, "a soul upon their countenances, which does not appear when they are absent from one another, or even in company that lays a restraint upon their features."

There is a great difference in the same face, according as the person is in a better or a worse humour, or more or less lively. The best complexion, the finest features, and the exactest shape, without anything of the mind expressed in the face, is insipid and unmoving. The finest eyes in the world, with an excess of malice or rage in them, will grow shocking. The passions can give beauty without the assistance of colour or form, and take it away where these have united most strongly to give it; and therefore this part of beauty is greatly superior to the other two.

The last and noblest part of beauty is grace, which the author thinks undefinable.

Nothing causes love so generally and irresistibly as grace. Therefore, in the mythology of the Greeks and Romans, the graces were the constant attendants of Venus the goddess of love. Grace is like the cestus of the same goddess, which was supposed to comprehend everything that was winning and engaging, and to create love by a secret and inexplicable force, like that of some magical charm.

There are two kinds of grace, the majestic and the familiar; the first more commanding, the last more delightful and engaging. The Grecian painters and sculptors used to express the former most strongly in the looks and attitudes of their Minervas, and the latter in those of Venus. This distinction is marked in the description of the personages of virtue and pleasure in the ancient fable of the choice of Hercules.

> Graceful, but each with different grace
> they move,
> This striking sacred awe, that softer
> winning love.

In the persons of Adam and Eve in Paradise, Milton has made the same distinction.

> For contemplation he, and valour form'd,
> For softness she, and sweet attractive
> grace.

Though grace be so difficult to be defined, there are two things that hold universally with relation to it. First, there is no grace without motion; some genteel or pleasing motion, either of the whole body or of some limb, or at least some feature. Hence, in the face, grace appears only on those features that are moveable, and change with the various emotions and sentiments of the mind, such as the eyes and eyebrows, the mouth and parts adjacent. When Venus appeared to her son Aeneas in disguise, and, after some conversation with him, retired, it was by the grace of her motion in retiring that he discovered her to be truly a goddess (*Aeneid* I, 524 ff.).

A second observation is, that there can be no grace with impropriety, or that nothing can be graceful that is not adapted to the character and situation of the person.

From these observations, which appear to me to be just, we may, I think, conclude, that grace, as far as it is visible, consists of those motions, either of the whole body, or of a part or feature, which express the most perfect propriety of conduct and sentiment in an amiable character.

Those motions must be different in different characters; they must vary with every variation of emotion and sentiment; they may express either dignity or respect, confidence or reserve, love or just resentment, esteem or indignation, zeal or indifference. Every passion, sentiment, or emotion, that in its nature and degree is just and proper, and corresponds perfectly with the character of the person, and with the occasion, is what we may call the soul of grace. The body or visible part consists of those motions and features which give the true and unaffected expression of the soul.

Thus, I think, all the ingredients of human beauty, as they are enumerated and described by this ingenious author, terminate in expression: They either express some perfection of the body, as a part of the man, and an instrument of the mind, or some amiable quality or attribute of the mind itself.

It cannot indeed be denied, that the expression of a fine countenance may be unnaturally disjoined from the amiable qualities which it naturally expresses: but we presume the contrary, till we have a clear evidence; and even then, we pay homage to the expression, as we do to the throne when it happens to be unworthily filled.

Whether what I have offered, to show that all the beauty of the objects of sense is borrowed, and derived from the beauties of mind which it expresses or suggests to the imagination, be well founded or not; I hope this terrestrial Venus will not be deemed less worthy of the homage which has always been paid to her, by being conceived more nearly allied to the celestial, than she has commonly been represented.

To make an end of this subject, taste seems to be progressive as man is. Children, when refreshed by sleep, and at ease from pain and hunger, are disposed to attend to the objects about them; they are pleased with brilliant colours, gaudy ornaments, regular forms, cheerful countenances, noisy mirth, and glee. Such is the taste of childhood, which we must conclude to be given for wise purposes. A great part of the happiness of that period of life is derived from it; and therefore it ought to be indulged. It leads them to attend to objects which they may afterward find worthy of their attention. It puts them upon exerting their infant faculties of body and mind, which,

by such exertions, are daily strengthened and improved.

As they advance in years and in understanding, other beauties attract their attention, which, by their novelty or superiority, throw a shade upon those they formerly admired. They delight in feats of agility, strength, and art; they love those that excel in them, and strive to equal them. In the tales and fables they hear, they begin to discern beauties of mind. Some characters and actions appear lovely, others give disgust. The intellectual and moral powers begin to open, and, if cherished by favourable circumstances, advance gradually in strength, till they arrive at that degree of perfection, to which human nature, in its present state, is limited.

In our progress from infancy to maturity, our faculties open in a regular order appointed by nature; the meanest first; those of more dignity in succession, until the moral and rational powers finish the man. Every faculty furnishes new notions, brings new beauties into view, and enlarges the province of taste; so that we may say, there is a taste of childhood, a taste of youth, and a manly taste. Each is beautiful in its season; but not so much so, when carried beyond its season. Not that the man ought to dislike the things that please the child or the youth, but to put less value upon them, compared with other beauties, with which he ought to be acquainted.

Our moral and rational powers justly claim dominion over the whole man. Even taste is not exempted from their authority; it must be subject to that authority in every case wherein we pretend to reason or dispute about matters of taste; it is the voice of reason that our love or our admiration ought to be proportioned to the merit of the object. When it is not grounded on real worth, it must be the effect of constitution, or of some habit or casual association. A fond mother may see a beauty in her darling child, or a fond author in his work, to which the rest of the world are blind.

In such cases, the affection is pre-engaged, and, as it were, bribes the judgment, to make the object worthy of that affection. For the mind cannot be easy in putting a value upon an object beyond what it conceives to be due. When affection is not carried away by some natural or acquired bias, it naturally is, and ought to be led by the judgment.

IMMANUEL KANT

(1724-1804)

The immense scope of Kant's mind and achievement makes him one of the supreme names in the history of modern thought. He spent a lifetime in, or near, Königsberg in East Prussia, now Kaliningrad in the Soviet Union. His writings and teaching in the university treated many different scientific, cultural, and philosophical subjects. His greatest works, *The Critique of Pure Reason* (1781), *The Critique of Practical Reason* (1788), and *The Critique of Judgment* (1790) began to appear only as the author approached the age of sixty.

It is difficult to offer even a glance at Kant's achievement in a few sentences. His three great works, which are intimately connected, seek to examine critically the foundations of science, conduct, and art, respectively. If the third Critique did not accomplish as profound a reorientation of ideas in its field as the other two did in theirs, it is partly because the subject matter of aesthetics was not sufficiently organized and agreed upon before Kant's time even to undergo a revolution. It is nevertheless a landmark in the philosophy of art. It not only recapitulates but also rethinks the ideas of the preceding century in Britain as well as on the continent, and it has exercised an influence over nearly everyone who has spoken on the subject since its time.

The abridgment in this book of the last Critique is intended to free the work as far as possible from its involvement with the other Critiques. First, we have eliminated the long introduction, in which Kant argues the relation of this Critique to the others, and then the second half of the Critique, which is devoted to the question of teleology, or purpose in the universe. Finally, an abridgment of the last part of the remaining portion is effected, since it contains much repetition of the preceding argument. There remains the analytic of the beautiful and of the sublime as the two principal and supplementary ingredients of man's artistic striving, and an extended discussion of art and the artist. But it is impossible, and unnecessary, to excise all the references in this Critique to the rest of Kant's philosophy; that is, the abridgment should not be regarded as exactly "cut at the joints." Part of the very heart of aesthetics has always been just this relation of art to the rest of life, and a complete understanding of the Critique calls for study of the whole of Kant's Critical Philosophy—no trifling task.

What is perhaps most astonishing about the third Critique (referring now only to the first portion, on aesthetic judgment) is that a person such as Kant was known to be should have attempted to write about art at all. That Kant had little opportunity to acquaint himself with great works of visual art is well known. He had probably little ear for music. But like all men who had gone through the universities, he was acquainted with a good part of classical poetry and literature. Much of what he knew of the arts, it must be conceded, he learned indirectly from critics and others who wrote *about* art. But he was a voluminous reader with great retentive powers, and he consulted and evaluated the best that had been said on this and most other subjects. He knew the characteristics of artistic appreciation well enough to see what great issues about aesthetic judgment it raised, and once he saw what these were he could also begin to comprehend the problems of artistic creation.[1]

The division into the analytic of the beautiful and of the sublime was part of the current coin of aesthetic thought in the eighteenth century. Kant could have taken it over from Burke, whom he studied, if from no one else. One may also wish to refer to a much more readable, if less profound, essay of Kant's called *Reflections on the Feeling of the Sublime and Beautiful,* which appeared in 1764.

What is the distinction between these two ideas, and what is its significance? Are there in fact two modes of aesthetic feeling and doing? Are they both art, or is art both of them? Both at once, or now one and then the other? If there are two such modes, why not three or a dozen? We can consider but a few of these questions.

First of all, if "beautiful" means, in general, aesthetic or artistic success as against failure, then the word is not used in the sense of Kant's and Burke's distinction. They do not think of it as the *summum genus* of aesthetic value. It is rather a specific or regional aesthetic mode or virtue or value. Beauty is one mode among others. So in the ancient world a literary aesthetician such as Demetrius of Phalerum classified poetry into four kinds: plain, stately, polished, and powerful. If this or an analogous distinction could be thought to hold for all art, we should be proceeding, in principle, as Kant does.

One of the oldest theories of art and beauty defined beauty as perfection of form. Further specification of this definition was afforded by such a formula as unity-in-variety, and this satisfied whatever need was felt, apart from other explanatory factors such as "imitation," for a theoretical summation of beauty. In this view, beauty is, we might say, the "formful"—that which succeeds by virtue of its form—and it is contrasted with what does not have form—the formless, a thing dark, terrifying, ugly, and evil, contrary to the rules of good taste, and a positive disvalue.

So matters might have remained, with the further task of aesthetics simply to perfect the analysis of the idea of perfection of form. Though this might not have

---

1 See Reinhold Bernhard Jachmann, *Immanuel Kant Geschildert in Briefen an einen Freund* (Halle: Hugo Peter, 1902), especially the tenth letter. Jachmann was Kant's pupil and amanuensis from 1784 to 1794.

been an easy task, it would have been a neat and straightforward one. But the entire scheme was altogether too neat, and the devising of the concept of the sublime, a massive and menacing companion to the concept of the beautiful, constitutes recognition of this fact. Much more, it was found, is aesthetically important than the trimly beautiful, beauty which is finite and controlled. Thus arises the notion of what might be called the "beauty of the formless," and this is the sublime. A semblance of tidiness is still preserved in the theory, for the beautiful and the sublime equally divide and exhaust the field. What is aesthetically satisfying is either finite or infinite, has form or is formless. Aesthetic excellence is no longer identified with beauty, and beauty with form.

To see beauty regarded as finite order and control accords with our notions of the orderliness and decorousness of mid-eighteenth-century art and life. The other side of the matter, the sublime, is obviously a recognition of those more elemental forces of irrationality that were to burst forth in German and other romanticisms. Another interpretation is that the sublime is essentially a baroque notion to express the mysterious and infinite.

But we must not misinterpret the place of the formless in the sublime and the pained feelings that it seems to generate. Burke regarded the sublime as exemplified in our terror of the horrible. In Kant, however, terror remains terror and is not by itself sublime. The sublime is, in fact, a state of mind that cannot be felt in a terrorized state. On the contrary, we must be secure or capable of ignoring danger so that we may rise above it, conscious of our moral and supersensible destiny. The excruciating dissonance is resolved in a chord of triumph and transfiguration. In this light, Kant leads us to see that there is a kinship between the sublime and reason, which in the earlier Critiques reaches toward transcendent moral ideas such as God, freedom, and immortality. The beautiful, on the other hand, devoted to the more sensuous glories of this world, is akin to the understanding and to science.

This excerpt, translated by Bishop Bernard, was later reissued in an American reprint with various changes. Some of them are minor improvements; a few others are more substantive changes, sometimes unwarranted. The editors have checked the translation against the original and have made use of the work of previous scholars of the Critique.

IMMANUEL KANT

The Critique of Aesthetic Judgment

(Translated by J. H. Bernard)

From Critique of Judgment, *J. H. Bernard, trans. London: Macmillan & Co., Ltd., 1892; and New York: Hafner Publishing Company, Inc., 1951. Reprinted by permission of Macmillan & Co., Ltd., St. Martin's Press, Inc., and Hafner Publishing Company, Inc. (First published: 1790.)*

I. *Analytic of the Beautiful*

First Moment
Of the Judgment of Taste,[1] According to Quality

§ 1. THE JUDGMENT OF TASTE IS AESTHETICAL

In order to distinguish whether anything is beautiful or not, we refer the representation, not by the understanding to the object for cognition, but by the imagination (perhaps in conjunction with the understanding) to the subject and its feeling of pleasure or pain. The judgment of taste is therefore not a judgment of cognition, and is consequently not logical but aesthetical, by which we understand that whose determining ground can be *no other than subjective*. Every reference of representations, even that of sensations, may be objective (and then it signifies the real of an empirical

---

1 The definition of "taste" which is laid down here is that it is the faculty of judging of the beautiful. But the analysis of judgments of taste must show what is required in order to call an object beautiful. The moments to which this judgment has regard in its reflection I have sought in accordance with the guidance of the logical functions of judgment (for in a judgment of taste a reference to the understanding is always involved). I have considered the moment of quality first because the aesthetical judgment upon the beautiful first pays attention to it.

representation), save only the reference to the feeling of pleasure and pain, by which nothing in the object is signified, but through which there is a feeling in the subject as it is affected by the representation.

To apprehend a regular, purposive building by means of one's cognitive faculty (whether in a clear or a confused way of representation) is something quite different from being conscious of this representation as connected with the sensation of satisfaction. Here the representation is altogether referred to the subject and to its feeling of life, under the name of the feeling of pleasure or pain. This establishes a quite separate faculty of distinction and of judgment, adding nothing to cognition, but only comparing the given representation in the subject with the whole faculty of representations, of which the mind is conscious in the feeling of its state. Given representations in a judgment can be empirical (consequently, aesthetical); but the judgment which is formed by means of them is logical, provided they are referred in the judgment to the object. Conversely, if the given representations are rational, but are referred in a judgment simply to the subject (to its feeling), the judgment is so far always aesthetical.

§ 2. THE SATISFACTION WHICH DETERMINES THE JUDGMENT OF TASTE IS DISINTERESTED

The satisfaction which we combine with the representation of the existence of an object is called "interest." Such satisfaction always has reference to the faculty of desire, either as its determining ground or as necessarily connected with its determining ground. Now when the question is if a thing is beautiful, we do not want to know whether anything depends or can depend on the existence of the thing, either for myself or for anyone else, but how we judge it by mere observation (intuition or reflection). If anyone asks me if I find that palace beautiful which I see before me, I may answer: I do not like things of that kind which are made merely to be stared at. Or I can answer like that Iroquois Sachem, who was pleased in Paris by nothing more than by the cook shops. Or again, after the manner of Rousseau, I may rebuke the vanity of the great who waste the sweat of the people on such superfluous things. In fine, I could easily convince myself that if I found myself on an uninhabited island without the hope of ever again coming among men, and could conjure up just such a splendid building by my mere wish, I should not even give myself the trouble if I had a sufficiently comfortable hut. This may all be admitted and approved, but we are not now talking of this. We wish only to know if this mere representation of the object is accompanied in me with satisfaction, however indifferent I may be as regards the existence of the object of this representation. We easily see that, in saying it is *beautiful* and in showing that I have taste, I am concerned, not with that in which I depend on the existence of the object, but with that which I make out of this representation in myself. Everyone must admit that a judgment about beauty, in which the least interest mingles, is very partial and is not a pure judgment of taste. We must not be in the least prejudiced in favor of the existence of the things, but be quite indifferent in this respect, in order to play the judge in things of taste.

We cannot, however, better elucidate this proposition, which is of capital importance, than by contrasting the pure disinterested[2]

---

[2] A judgment upon an object of satisfaction may be quite *disinterested,* but yet very *interesting,* i.e. not based upon an interest, but bringing an interest with it; of this kind are all pure moral judgments. Judgments of taste, however, do not in themselves establish any interest. Only in society is it *interesting* to have taste; the reason of this will be shown in the sequel.

satisfaction in judgments of taste with that which is bound up with an interest, especially if we can at the same time be certain that there are no other kinds of interest than those which are now to be specified.

§ 3. THE SATISFACTION IN THE PLEASANT IS BOUND UP WITH INTEREST

That which pleases the senses in sensation is "pleasant." Here the opportunity presents itself of censuring a very common confusion of the double sense which the word "sensation" can have, and of calling attention to it. All satisfaction (it is said or thought) is itself sensation (of a pleasure). Consequently everything that pleases is pleasant because it pleases (and according to its different degrees or its relations to other pleasant sensations it is *agreeable, lovely, delightful, enjoyable,* etc.) But if this be admitted, then impressions of sense which determine the inclination, fundamental propositions of reason which determine the will, mere reflective forms of intuition which determine the judgment, are quite the same as regards the effect upon the feeling of pleasure. For this would be pleasantness in the sensation of one's state; and since in the end all the operations of our faculties must issue in the practical and unite in it as their goal, we could suppose no other way of estimating things and their worth than that which consists in the gratification that they promise. It is of no consequence at all how this is attained, and since then the choice of means alone could make a difference, men could indeed blame one another for stupidity and indiscretion, but never for baseness and wickedness. For thus they all, each according to his own way of seeing things, seek one goal, that is, gratification.

If a determination of the feeling of pleasure or pain is called sensation, this expression signifies something quite different from what I mean when I call the representation of a thing (by sense, as a receptivity belonging to the cognitive faculty) sensation. For in the latter case the representation is referred to the object, in the former simply to the subject, and is available for no cognition whatever, not even for that by which the subject *cognizes* itself.

In the above elucidation we understand by the word "sensation" an objective representation of sense; and, in order to avoid misinterpretation, we shall call that which must always remain merely subjective and can constitute absolutely no representation of an object by the ordinary term "feeling." The green color of the meadows belongs to *objective* sensation, as a perception of an object of sense; the pleasantness of this belongs to *subjective* sensation by which no object is represented, i.e. to feeling, by which the object is considered as an object of satisfaction (which does not furnish a cognition of it).

Now that a judgment about an object by which I describe it as pleasant expresses an interest in it, is plain from the fact that by sensation it excites a desire for objects of that kind; consequently the satisfaction presupposes, not the mere judgment about it, but the relation of its existence to my state, so far as this is affected by such an object. Hence we do not merely say of the pleasant, *it pleases,* but, *it gratifies.* I give to it no mere assent, but inclination is aroused by it; and in the case of what is pleasant in the most lively fashion there is no judgment at all upon the character of the object, for those who always lay themselves out only for enjoyment (for that is the word describing intense gratification) would fain dispense with all judgment.

§ 4. THE SATISFACTION IN THE GOOD IS BOUND UP WITH INTEREST

Whatever by means of reason pleases

through the mere concept is *good*. That which pleases only as a means we call *good for something* (the useful), but that which pleases for itself is *good in itself*. In both there is always involved the concept of a purpose, and consequently the relation of reason to the (at least possible) volition, and thus a satisfaction in the *presence* of an object or an action, i.e. some kind of interest.

In order to find anything good, I must always know what sort of a thing the object ought to be, i.e. I must have a concept of it. But there is no need of this to find a thing beautiful. Flowers, free delineations, outlines intertwined with one another without design and called [conventional] foliage, have no meaning, depend on no definite concept, and yet they please. The satisfaction in the beautiful must depend on the reflection upon an object, leading to any concept (however indefinite), and it is thus distinguished from the pleasant, which rests entirely upon sensation.

It is true, the pleasant seems in many cases to be the same as the good. Thus people are accustomed to say that all gratification (especially if it lasts) is good in itself, which is very much the same as to say that lasting pleasure and the good are the same. But we can soon see that this is merely a confusion of words, for the concepts which properly belong to these expressions can in no way be interchanged. The pleasant, which, as such, represents the object simply in relation to sense, must first be brought by the concept of a purpose under principles of reason, in order to call it good, as an object of the will. But that there is a quite different relation to satisfaction in calling that which gratifies at the same time *good* may be seen from the fact that, in the case of the good, the question always is whether it is mediately or immediately good (useful or good in itself); but on the contrary in the case of the pleasant, there can be no question about this at all, for the word always signifies something

which pleases immediately. (The same is applicable to what I call beautiful.)

Even in common speech men distinguish the pleasant from the good. Of a dish which stimulates the taste by spices and other condiments we say unhesitatingly that it is pleasant, though it is at the same time admitted not to be good; for though it immediately *delights* the senses, yet mediately, i.e. considered by reason, which looks to the after results, it displeases. Even in the judging of health we may notice this distinction. It is immediately pleasant to everyone possessing it (at least negatively, i.e. as the absence of all bodily pains). But in order to say that it is good, it must be considered by reason with reference to purposes, viz. that it is a state which makes us fit for all our business. Finally, in respect of happiness, everyone believes himself entitled to describe the greatest sum of the pleasantnesses of life (as regards both their number and their duration) as a true, even as the highest, good. However, reason is opposed to this. Pleasantness is enjoyment. And if we were concerned with this alone, it would be foolish to be scrupulous as regards the means which procure it for us, or [to care] whether it is obtained passively by the bounty of nature or by our own activity and work. But reason can never be persuaded that the existence of a man who merely lives for *enjoyment* (however busy he may be in this point of view) has a worth in itself, even if he at the same time is conducive as a means to the best enjoyment of others and shares in all their gratifications by sympathy. Only what he does, without reference to enjoyment, in full freedom and independently of what nature can procure for him passively, gives an absolute worth to his presence [in the world] as the existence of a person; and happiness, with the whole abundance of its pleasures, is far from being an unconditioned good.[3]

---

[3] An obligation to enjoyment is a manifest absurdity. Thus the obligation to all actions which have merely enjoyment for their aim can only be

However, notwithstanding all this difference between the pleasant and the good, they both agree in this that they are always bound up with an interest in their object: This is true not only of the pleasant (§ 3), and the mediate good (the useful) which is pleasing as a means toward pleasantness somewhere, but also of that which is good absolutely and in every aspect, viz. moral good, which brings with it the highest interest. For the good is the object of will (i.e. of a faculty of desire determined by reason). But to wish for something and to have a satisfaction in its existence, i.e. to take an interest in it, are identical.

§ 5. COMPARISON OF THE THREE SPECIFICALLY DIFFERENT KINDS OF SATISFACTION

The pleasant and the good have both a reference to the faculty of desire, and they bring with them, the former a satisfaction pathologically conditioned (by impulses, *stimuli*), the latter a pure practical satisfaction which is determined not merely by the representation of the object but also by the represented connection of the subject with the existence of the object. It is not merely the object that pleases, but also its existence. On the other hand, the judgment of taste is merely *contemplative*; i.e. it is a judgment which, indifferent as regards the existence of an object, compares its character with the feeling of pleasure and pain. But this contemplation itself is not directed to concepts; for the judgment of taste is not a cognitive judgment (either theoretical or practical), and thus is not *based* on concepts, nor has it concepts as its *purpose*.

The pleasant, the beautiful, and the good designate then three different relations of representations to the feeling of pleasure and pain, in reference to which we distinguish from one another objects or methods

of representing them. And the expressions corresponding to each, by which we mark our complacency in them, are not the same. That which *gratifies* a man is called *pleasant*; that which merely *pleases* him is *beautiful*; that which is *esteemed* or *approved* by him, i.e. that to which he accords an objective worth, is *good*. Pleasantness concerns irrational animals also, but beauty only concerns men, i.e. animal, but still rational, beings—not merely *qua* rational (e.g. spirits), but *qua* animal also—and the good concerns every rational being in general. This is a proposition which can only be completely established and explained in the sequel. We may say that, of all these three kinds of satisfaction, that of taste in the beautiful is alone a disinterested and *free* satisfaction; for no interest, either of sense or of reason, here forces our assent. Hence we may say of satisfaction that it is related in the three aforesaid cases to *inclination,* to *favor,* or to *respect.* Now *favor* is the only free satisfaction. An object of inclination and one that is proposed to our desire by a law of reason leave us no freedom in forming for ourselves anywhere an object of pleasure. All interest presupposes or generates a want, and, as the determining ground of assent, it leaves the judgment about the object no longer free.

As regards the interest of inclination in the case of the pleasant, everyone says that hunger is the best sauce, and everything that is eatable is relished by people with a healthy appetite; and thus a satisfaction of this sort shows no choice directed by taste. It is only when the want is appeased that we can distinguish which of many men has or has not taste. In the same way there may be manners (conduct) without virtue, politeness without good will, decorum without modesty, etc. For where the moral law speaks there is no longer, objectively, a free choice as regards what is to be done; and to display taste in its fulfillment (or in judging of another's fulfillment of it) is something quite different from manifesting the

---

a pretended one, however spiritually it may be conceived (or decked out), even if it is a mystical, or so-called heavenly, enjoyment.

moral attitude of thought. For this involves a command and generates a want, while moral taste only plays with the objects of satisfaction, without attaching itself to one of them.

Explanation of the beautiful resulting from the First Moment: Taste is the faculty of judging of an object or a method of representing it by an *entirely disinterested* satisfaction or dissatisfaction. The object of such satisfaction is called *beautiful*.

Second Moment
Of the Judgment of Taste, According to Quantity

§ 6. THE BEAUTIFUL IS THAT WHICH APART FROM CONCEPTS IS REPRESENTED AS THE OBJECT OF A UNIVERSAL SATISFACTION

This explanation of the beautiful can be derived from the preceding explanation of it as the object of an entirely disinterested satisfaction. For the fact of which everyone is conscious, that the satisfaction is for him quite disinterested, implies in his judgment a ground of satisfaction for all men. For since it does not rest on any inclination of the subject (nor upon any other premeditated interest), but since the person who judges feels himself quite *free* as regards the satisfaction which he attaches to the object, he cannot find the ground of this satisfaction in any private conditions connected with his own subject, and hence it must be regarded as grounded on what he can presuppose in every other person. Consequently he must believe that he has reason for attributing a similar satisfaction to everyone. He will therefore speak of the beautiful as if beauty were a characteristic of the object and the judgment logical (constituting a cognition of the object by means of concepts of it), although it is only aesthetical and involves merely a reference of

the representation of the object to the subject. For it has this similarity to a logical judgment that we can presuppose its validity for all men. But this universality cannot arise from concepts; for from concepts there is no transition to the feeling of pleasure or pain (except in pure practical laws, which bring an interest with them such as is not bound up with the pure judgment of taste). Consequently the judgment of taste, accompanied with the consciousness of separation from all interest, must claim validity for every man, without this universality depending on objects. That is, there must be bound up with it a title to subjective universality.

§ 7. COMPARISON OF THE BEAUTIFUL WITH THE PLEASANT AND THE GOOD BY MEANS OF THE ABOVE CHARACTERISTIC

As regards the pleasant, everyone is content that his judgment, which he bases upon private feeling and by which he says of an object that it pleases him, should be limited merely to his own person. Thus he is quite contented that if he says, "Canary wine is pleasant," another man may correct his expression and remind him that he ought to say, "It is pleasant *to me*." And this is the case not only as regards the taste of the tongue, the palate, and the throat, but for whatever is pleasant to anyone's eyes and ears. To one, violet color is soft and lovely; to another, it is washed out and dead. One man likes the tone of wind instruments, another that of strings. To strive here with the design of reproving as incorrect another man's judgment which is different from our own, as if the judgments were logically opposed, would be folly. As regards the pleasant, therefore, the fundamental proposition is valid: *everyone has his own taste* (the taste of sense).

The case is quite different with the beautiful. It would (on the contrary) be laughable if a man who imagined anything to his own taste thought to justify himself by saying: "This object (the house we see, the coat that person wears, the concert we hear, the poem submitted to our judgment) is beautiful *for me*." For he must not call it *beautiful* if it pleases only himself. Many things may have for him charm and pleasantness—no one troubles himself at that— but if he gives out anything as beautiful, he supposes in others the same satisfaction; he judges not merely for himself, but for everyone, and speaks of beauty as if it were a property of things. Hence he says "the *thing* is beautiful"; and he does not count on the agreement of others with this his judgment of satisfaction, because he has found this agreement several times before, but he *demands* it of them. He blames them if they judge otherwise and he denies them taste, which he nevertheless requires from them. Here, then, we cannot say that each man has his own particular taste. For this would be as much as to say that there is no taste whatever, i.e. no aesthetical judgment which can make a rightful claim upon everyone's assent.

At the same time we find as regards the pleasant that there is an agreement among men in their judgments upon it in regard to which we deny taste to some and attribute it to others, by this not meaning one of our organic senses, but a faculty of judging in respect of the pleasant generally. Thus we say of a man who knows how to entertain his guests with pleasures (of enjoyment for all the senses), so that they are all pleased, "he has taste." But here the universality is only taken comparatively; and there emerge rules which are only *general* (like all empirical ones), and not *universal*, which latter the judgment of taste upon the beautiful undertakes or lays claim to. It is a judgment in reference to sociability, so far as this rests on empirical rules. In respect of the good it is true that judgments make rightful claim to validity for everyone; but the good is represented only *by means of a concept* as the object of a universal satisfaction, which is the case neither with the pleasant nor with the beautiful.

§ 8. THE UNIVERSALITY OF THE SATISFACTION IS REPRESENTED IN A JUDGMENT OF TASTE ONLY AS SUBJECTIVE

This particular determination of the universality of an aesthetical judgment, which is to be met with in a judgment of taste, is noteworthy, not indeed for the logician, but for the transcendental philosopher. It requires no small trouble to discover its origin, but we thus detect a property of our cognitive faculty which without this analysis would remain unknown.

First, we must be fully convinced of the fact that in a judgment of taste (about the beautiful) the satisfaction in the object is imputed to *everyone,* without being based on a concept (for then it would be the good). Further, this claim to universal validity so essentially belongs to a judgment by which we describe anything as *beautiful* that, if this were not thought in it, it would never come into our thoughts to use the expression at all, but everything which pleases without a concept would be counted as pleasant. In respect of the latter, everyone has his own opinion; and no one assumes in another agreement with his judgment of taste, which is always the case in a judgment of taste about beauty. I may call the first the taste of sense, the second the taste of reflection, so far as the first lays down mere private judgments and the second judgments supposed to be generally valid (public), but in both cases aesthetical (not practical) judgments about an object merely in respect of the relation of its representation to the feeling of pleasure and pain. Now here is something strange. As regards the taste of sense, not only does experience show that its judgment (of pleasure or pain connected with anything) is not valid universally, but everyone is content not to impute agreement with it to others (although actually there is often found a very extended concurrence in these judgments). On the other hand, the taste of reflection has its claim to the universal validity of its judgments (about the beautiful) rejected often enough, as experience teaches, although it may find it possible (as it actually does) to represent judgments which can demand this universal agreement. In fact it imputes this to everyone for each of its judgments of taste, without the persons that judge disputing as to the possibility of such a claim, although in particular cases they cannot agree as to the correct application of this faculty.

Here we must, in the first place, remark that a universality which does not rest on concepts of objects (not even on empirical ones) is not logical but aesthetical; i.e. it involves no objective quantity of the judgment, but only that which is subjective. For this I use the expression *general validity,* which signifies the validity of the reference of a representation, not to the cognitive faculty, but to the feeling of pleasure and pain for every subject. (We can avail ourselves also of the same expression for the logical quantity of the judgment, if only we prefix "objective" to "universal validity," to distinguish it from that which is merely subjective and aesthetical.)

A judgment with *objective universal validity* is also always valid subjectively; i.e. if the judgment holds for everything contained under a given concept, it holds also for everyone who represents an object by means of this concept. But from a *subjective universal validity,* i.e. aesthetical and resting on no concept, we cannot infer that which is logical because that kind of judgment does not extend to the object. But, therefore, the aesthetical universality which is ascribed to a judgment must be of a particular kind, because it does not unite the predicate of beauty with the concept of the object, considered in its whole logical sphere, and yet extends it to the whole sphere of judging persons.

In respect of logical quantity, all judgments of taste are *singular* judgments. For because I must refer the object immediately to my feeling of pleasure and pain, and that not by means of concepts, they cannot have the quantity of objective generally valid judgments. Nevertheless, if the singular representation of the object of the judgment of taste, in accordance with the conditions determining the latter, were transformed by comparison into a concept, a logically universal judgment could result therefrom. E.g. I describe by a judgment of taste the rose that I see as beautiful. But the judgment which results from the comparison of several singular judgments, "Roses in general are beautiful," is no longer described simply as aesthetical, but as a logical judgment based on an aesthetical one. Again the judgment, "The rose is pleasant" (to smell) is, although aesthetical and singular, not a judgment of taste but of sense. It is distinguished from the former by the fact that the judgment of taste carries with it an *aesthetic quantity* of universality, i.e. of validity for everyone, which cannot be found in a judgment about the pleasant. It is only judgments about the good which, although they also determine satisfaction in an object, have logical and not merely aesthetical universality, for they are valid of the object as cognitive of it, and thus are valid for everyone.

If we judge objects merely according to concepts, then all representation of beauty is lost. Thus there can be no rule according to which anyone is to be forced to recognize anything as beautiful. We cannot press upon others by the aid of any reasons or fundamental propositions our judgment that a coat, a house, or a flower is beautiful. People wish to submit the object to their own eyes, as if the satisfaction in it depended on sensation; and yet, if we then call the object beautiful, we believe that we speak with a universal voice, and we claim the assent of everyone, although on the contrary all private sensation can only decide for the observer himself and his satisfaction.

We may see now that in the judgment of taste nothing is postulated but such a *universal voice,* in respect of the satisfaction without the intervention of concepts, and thus the *possibility* of an aesthetical judgment that can, at the same time, be regarded as valid for everyone. The judgment of taste itself does not *postulate* the agreement of everyone (for that can only be done by a logically universal judgment because it can adduce reasons); it only *imputes* this agreement to everyone, as a case of the rule in respect of which it expects, not confirmation by concepts, but assent from others. The universal voice is, therefore, only an idea (we do not yet inquire upon what it rests). It may be uncertain whether or not the man who believes that he is laying down a judgment of taste is, as a matter of fact, judging in conformity with that idea; but that he refers his judgment thereto, and consequently that it is intended to be a judgment of taste, he announces by the expression "beauty." He can be quite certain of this for himself by the mere consciousness of the separating off everything belonging to the pleasant and the good from the satisfaction which is left; and this is all for which he promises himself the agreement of everyone—a claim which would be justifiable under these conditions, provided only he did not often make mistakes, and thus lay down an erroneous judgment of taste.

§ 9. INVESTIGATION OF THE QUESTION WHETHER IN THE JUDGMENT OF TASTE THE FEELING OF PLEASURE PRECEDES OR FOLLOWS THE JUDGING OF THE OBJECT

The solution of this question is the key to the critique of taste, and so is worthy of all attention.

If the pleasure in the given object precedes, and it is only its universal communicability that is to be acknowledged in the judgment of taste about the representation of the object, there would be a contradiction. For such pleasure would be nothing different from the mere pleasantness in the sensation, and so in accordance with its nature could have only private validity, because it is immediately dependent on the representation through which the object *is given.*

Hence it is the universal capability of communication of the mental state in the given representation which, as the subjective condition of the judgment of taste, must be fundamental and must have the pleasure in the object as its consequent. But nothing can be universally communicated except cognition and representation, so far as it belongs to cognition. For it is only thus that this latter can be objective, and only through this has it a universal point of reference, with which the representative power of everyone is compelled to harmonize. If the determining ground of our judgment as to this universal communicability of the representation is to be merely subjective, i.e. is conceived independently of any concept of the object, it can be nothing else than the state of mind, which is to be met with in the relation of our representative powers to each other, so far as they refer a given representation to *cognition in general.*

The cognitive powers, which are involved by this representation, are here in free play, because no definite concept limits them to a particular rule of cognition. Hence the state of mind in this representation must be a feeling of the free play of the representative powers in a given representation with reference to a cognition in general. Now a representation by which an object is given that is to become a cognition in general requires *imagination* for the gathering together the manifold of intuition, and *understanding* for the unity of the concept uniting the representations. This state of *free play* of the cognitive faculties in a representation by which an object is given must be universally communicable, because cognition, as the determination of the object with which given representations (in whatever subject) are to agree, is the only kind of representation which is valid for everyone.

The subjective universal communicability of the mode of representation in a judgment of taste, since it is to be possible without presupposing a definite concept, can refer to nothing else than the state of mind in the free play of the imagination and the understanding (so far as they agree with each other, as is requisite for *cognition in general*). We are conscious that this subjective relation, suitable for cognition in general, must be valid for everyone, and thus must be universally communicable, just as if it were a definite cognition, resting always on that relation as its subjective condition.

This merely subjective (aesthetical) judging of the object, or of the representation by which it is given, precedes the pleasure in the same and is the ground of this pleasure in the harmony of the cognitive faculties; but on that universality of the subjective conditions for judging of objects is alone based the universal subjective validity of the satisfaction bound up by us with the representation of the object that we call beautiful. . . .

Explanation of the beautiful resulting from the Second Moment: The *beautiful* is that which pleases universally without a concept.

Third Moment
Of Judgments of Taste, According to the Relation of the Purposes which are Brought into Consideration in Them

§ 10. OF PURPOSIVENESS IN GENERAL

If we wish to explain what a purpose is according to its transcendental determinations (without presupposing anything empirical like the feeling of pleasure), [we say

that] the purpose is the object of a concept, in so far as the concept is regarded as the cause of the object(the real ground of its possibility); and the causality of a *concept* in respect of its *object* is its purposiveness (*forma finalis*). Where then not merely the cognition of an object but the object itself (its form and existence) is thought as an effect only possible by means of the concept of this latter, there we think a purpose. The representation of the effect is here the determining ground of its cause and precedes it. The consciousness of the causality of a representation, for *maintaining* the subject in the same state, may here generally denote what we call pleasure; while on the other hand pain is that representation which contains the ground of the determination of the state of representations into their opposite of *restraining* or removing them.

The faculty of desire, so far as it is determinable to act only through concepts, i.e. in conformity with the representation of a purpose, would be the will. But an object, or a state of mind, or even an action is called purposive, although its possibility does not necessarily presuppose the representation of a purpose, merely because its possibility can be explained and conceived by us only so far as we assume for its ground a causality according to purposes, i.e. in accordance with a will which has regulated it according to the representation of a certain rule. There can be, then, purposiveness without purpose, so far as we do not place the causes of this form in a will, but yet can only make the explanation of its possibility intelligible to ourselves by deriving it from a will.[4] Again, we are not always forced to regard what we observe

---

4 [What Kant intends here is not a "purposeless purpose." The terms in the original are *Zweck* (purpose), and *Zweckmässigkeit,* (translated as "purposiveness"), and the adjective *zweckgemäss.* By the latter he intends the notion of a thing's having traits which are *compatible with* its being interpreted as exhibiting a purpose that it does not literally have.—ED. NOTE.]

(in respect of its possibility) from the point of view of reason. Thus we can at least observe a purposiveness according to form, without basing it on a purpose (as the material of the *nexus finalis*), and remark it in objects, although only by reflection. . . .

§ 13. THE PURE JUDGMENT OF TASTE IS INDEPENDENT OF CHARM AND EMOTION

Every interest spoils the judgment of taste and takes from its impartiality, especially if the purposiveness is not, as with the interest of reason, placed before the feeling of pleasure but grounded on it. This last always happens in an aesthetical judgment upon anything, so far as it gratifies or grieves us. Hence judgments so affected can lay no claim at all to a universally valid satisfaction, or at least so much the less claim, in proportion as there are sensations of this sort among the determining grounds of taste. That taste is always barbaric which needs a mixture of *charms* and *emotions* in order that there may be satisfaction, and still more so if it make these the measure of its assent.

Nevertheless charms are often not only taken account of in the case of beauty (which properly speaking ought merely to be concerned with form) as contributory to the aesthetical universal satisfaction, but they are passed off as in themselves beauties; and thus the matter of satisfaction is substituted for the form. This misconception, however, which like so many others, has something true at its basis, may be removed by a careful determination of these concepts.

A judgment of taste on which charm and emotion have no influence (although they may be bound up with the satisfaction in the beautiful)—which therefore has as its determining ground merely the purposiveness of the form—is a *pure judgment of taste.*

§ 14. ELUCIDATION BY MEANS OF EXAMPLES

Aesthetical judgments can be divided just like theoretical (logical) judgments into empirical and pure. The first assert pleasantness or unpleasantness; the second assert the beauty of an object or of the manner of representing it. The former are judgments of sense (material aesthetical judgments); the latter as formal, are alone strictly judgments of taste.

A judgment of taste is therefore pure only so far as no merely empirical satisfaction is mingled with its determining ground. But this always happens if charm or emotion have any share in the judgment by which anything is to be described as beautiful.

Now here many objections present themselves, which fallaciously put forward charm not merely as a necessary ingredient of beauty, but as alone sufficient [to justify] a thing's being called beautiful. A mere color, e.g. the green of a grass plot, a mere tone (as distinguished from sound and noise), like that of a violin, are by most people described as beautiful in themselves, although both seem to have at their basis merely the matter of representations, viz. simply sensation, and therefore only deserve to be called pleasant. But we must at the same time remark that the sensations of colors and of tone have a right to be regarded as beautiful only so far as they are *pure*. This is a determination which concerns their form and is the only [element] of these representations which admits with certainty of universal communicability; for we cannot assume that the quality of sensations is the same in all subjects, and we can hardly say that the pleasantness of one color or the tone of one musical instrument is judged preferable to that of another in the same way by everyone.

If we assume with Euler that colors are

isochronous vibrations (*pulsus*) of the ether, as sounds are of the air in a state of disturbance, and—what is the most important—that the mind not only perceives by sense the effect of these in exciting the organ, but also perceives by reflection the regular play of impressions and thus the form of the combination of different representations)—which I do not at all doubt[5]— then colors and tone cannot be reckoned as mere sensations, but as the formal determination of the unity of a manifold of sensations, and thus as beauties.

But "pure" in a simple mode of sensation means that its uniformity is troubled and interrupted by no foreign sensation, and it belongs merely to the form; because here we can abstract from the quality of that mode of sensation (abstract from the colors and tone, if any, which it represents). Hence all simple colors, so far as they are pure, are regarded as beautiful; composite colors have not this advantage because, as they are not simple, we have no standard for judging whether they should be called pure or not.

But as regards the beauty attributed to the object on account of its form, to suppose it to be capable of augmentation through the charm of the object is a common error and one very prejudicial to genuine, uncorrupted, well-founded taste. We can doubtless add these charms to beauty, in order to interest the mind by the representation of the object, apart from the bare satisfaction [received], and thus they may serve as a recommendation of taste and its cultivation, especially when it is yet crude and unexercised. But they actually do injury to the judgment of taste if they draw attention to themselves as the grounds for judging of beauty. So far are they from adding to beauty that they must only be admitted by indulgence as aliens, and pro-

vided always that they do not disturb the beautiful form in cases when taste is yet weak and unexercised.

In painting, sculpture, and in all the formative arts—in architecture and horticulture, so far as they are fine arts—the *delineation* is the essential thing; and here it is not what gratifies in sensation but what pleases by means of its form that is fundamental for taste. The colors which light up the sketch belong to the charm; they may indeed enliven the object for sensation, but they cannot make it worthy of contemplation and beautiful. In most cases they are rather limited by the requirements of the beautiful form, and even where charm is permissible it is ennobled solely by this.

Every form of the objects of sense (both of external sense and also mediately of internal) is either *figure* or *play*. In the latter case it is either play of figures (in space, viz. pantomime and dancing) or the mere play of sensations (in time). The *charm* of colors or of the pleasant tones of an instrument may be added, but the *delineation* in the first case and the composition in the second constitute the proper object of the pure judgment of taste. To say that the purity of colors and of tones, or their variety and contrast, seem to add to beauty does not mean that they supply a homogeneous addition to our satisfaction in the form because they are pleasant in themselves; but they do so because they make the form more exactly, definitely, and completely, intuitible, and besides, by their charm excite the representation, while they awaken and fix our attention on the object itself.

Even what we call "ornaments" (*parerga*), i.e. those things which do not belong to the complete representation of the object internally as elements, but only externally as complements, and which augment the satisfaction of taste, do so only by their form; as, for example, the frames of pictures or the draperies of statues or the colonnades of palaces. But if the ornament does

---

5 [Reading *nicht* for *sehr* with Windelband. See Prussian Academy edition and the Philosophische Bibliothek edition of the *Kritik der Urteilskraft* (ed. Karl Vorländer).—ED. NOTE.]

not itself consist in beautiful form, and if it is used as a golden frame is used, merely to recommend the painting by its *charm,* it is then called *finery* and injures genuine beauty.

Emotion, that is, a sensation in which pleasantness is produced by means of a momentary checking and a consequent more powerful outflow of the vital force, does not belong at all to beauty. But sublimity with which the feeling of emotion is bound up requires a different standard of judgment from that which is at the foundation of taste; and thus a pure judgment of taste has for its determining ground neither charm nor emotion—in a word, no sensation as the material of the aesthetical judgment.

§ 15. THE JUDGMENT OF TASTE IS QUITE INDEPENDENT OF THE CONCEPT OF PERFECTION

Objective purposiveness can only be cognized by means of the reference of the manifold to a definite purpose, and therefore only through a concept. From this alone it is plain that the beautiful, the judging of which has at its basis a merely formal purposiveness, i.e. a purposiveness without purpose, is quite independent of the concept of the good, because the latter presupposes an objective purposiveness, i.e. the reference of the object to a definite purpose.

Objective purposiveness is either external, i.e. the *utility,* or internal, i.e. the *perfection* of the object. That the satisfaction in an object, on account of which we call it beautiful, cannot rest on the representation of its utility is sufficiently obvious from the two preceding sections; because in that case it would not be an immediate satisfaction in the object, which is the essential condition of a judgment about beauty. But objective internal purposiveness, i.e. perfection, comes nearer to the predicate of beauty; and it has been regarded by celebrated philosophers[6]

as the same as beauty, with the proviso, *if it is thought in a confused way.* It is of the greatest importance in a critique of taste to decide whether beauty can thus actually be resolved into the concept of perfection.

To judge of objective purposiveness we always need, not only the concept of a purpose, but (if that purposiveness is not to be external utility but internal) the concept of an internal purpose which shall contain the ground of the internal possibility of the object. Now as a purpose in general is that whose *concept* can be regarded as the ground of the possibility of the object itself; so, in order to represent objective purposiveness in a thing, the concept of *what sort of thing it is to be* must come first. The agreement of the manifold in it with this concept (which furnishes the rule for combining the manifold) is the *qualitative perfection* of the thing. Quite different from this is *quantitative* perfection, the completeness of a thing after its kind, which is a mere concept of magnitude (of totality).[7] In this *what the thing ought to be* is conceived as already determined, and it is only asked if it has *all* its requisites. The formal [element] in the representation of a thing, i.e. the agreement of the manifold with a unity (it being undetermined what this ought to be), gives to cognition no objective purposiveness whatever. For since abstraction is made of this unity as *purpose* (what the thing ought to

---

6 [Kant probably refers here to Baumgarten (1714–1762), who was the first writer to give the name of aesthetics to the philosophy of taste. He defined beauty as "perfection apprehended through the senses." Kant is said to have used as a textbook at lectures a work by Georg Friedrich Meier, a pupil of Baumgarten's, on this subject (*Anfangsgründe aller Schönen Künste und Wissenschaften,* 1748, 1750).—TR. NOTE.]

7 [Cf. Preface to the *Metaphysical Elements of Ethics,* p. v: "The word perfection is liable to many misconceptions. It is sometimes understood as a concept belonging to Transcendental Philosophy; viz. the concept of the *totality* of the manifold, which, taken together, constitutes a Thing; sometimes, again, it is understood as belonging to Teleology, so that it signifies the agreement of the characteristics of a thing with a *purpose.* Perfection in the former sense might be called *quantitative* (material), in the latter *qualitative* (formal), perfection."—TR. NOTE.]

be), nothing remains but the subjective purposiveness of the representations in the mind of the intuiting subject. And this, although it furnishes a certain purposiveness of the representative state of the subject, and so a facility of apprehending a given form by the imagination, yet furnishes no perfection of an object, since the object is not here conceived by means of the concept of a purpose. For example, if in a forest I come across a plot of sward around which trees stand in a circle and do not then represent to myself a purpose, viz. that it is intended to serve for country dances, not the least concept of perfection is furnished by the mere form. But to represent to oneself a formal *objective* purposiveness without purpose, i.e. the mere form of a *perfection* (without any matter and without the *concept* of that with which it is accordant, even if it were merely the idea of conformity to law in general), is a veritable contradiction.

Now the judgment of taste is an aesthetical judgment, i.e. such as rests on subjective grounds, the determining ground of which cannot be a concept, and consequently cannot be the concept of a definite purpose. Therefore by means of beauty, regarded as a formal subjective purposiveness, there is in no way thought a perfection of the object, as a purposiveness alleged to be formal but which is yet objective. And thus to distinguish between the concepts of the beautiful and the good as if they were only different in logical form, the first being a confused, the second a clear concept of perfection, but identical in content and origin, is quite fallacious. For then there would be no *specific* difference between them, but a judgment of taste would be as much a cognitive judgment as the judgment by which a thing is described as good; just as when the ordinary man says that fraud is unjust he bases his judgment on confused grounds, while the philosopher bases it on clear grounds, but both on identical principles of reason. I have already, however,

said that an aesthetical judgment is unique of its kind and gives absolutely no cognition (not even a confused cognition) of the object; this is only supplied by a logical judgment. On the contrary, it simply refers the representation, by which an object is given, to the subject, and brings to our notice no characteristic of the object, but only the purposive form in the determination of the representative powers which are occupying themselves therewith. The judgment is called aesthetical just because its determining ground is not a concept, but the feeling (of internal sense) of that harmony in the play of the mental powers, so far as it can be felt in sensation. On the other hand, if we wish to call confused concepts and the objective judgment based on them aesthetical, we will have an understanding judging sensibly or a sense representing its objects by means of concepts, both of which are contradictory. The faculty of concepts, be they confused or clear, is the understanding; and although understanding has to do with the judgment of taste as an aesthetical judgment (as it has with all judgments), yet it has to do with it, not as a faculty by which an object is cognized, but as the faculty which determines the judgment and its representation (without any concept) in accordance with its relation to the subject and the subject's internal feeling, in so far as this judgment may be possible in accordance with a universal rule.

§ 16. THE JUDGMENT OF TASTE, BY WHICH AN OBJECT IS DECLARED TO BE BEAUTIFUL UNDER THE CONDITION OF A DEFINITE CONCEPT, IS NOT PURE

There are two kinds of beauty: free beauty (*pulchritudo vaga*), or merely dependent beauty (*pulchritudo adhaerens*). The first presupposes no concept of what the object ought to be; the second does presuppose such a concept and the perfection of the object in accordance therewith. The first is called the (self-subsistent) beauty of this or that thing; the second, as dependent upon a concept (conditioned beauty), is ascribed to objects which come under the concept of a particular purpose.

Flowers are free natural beauties. Hardly anyone but a botanist knows what sort of a thing a flower ought to be; and even he, though recognizing in the flower the reproductive organ of the plant, pays no regard to this natural purpose if he is passing judgment on the flower by taste. There is, then, at the basis of this judgment no perfection of any kind, no internal purposiveness, to which the collection of the manifold is referred. Many birds (such as the parrot, the humming bird, the bird of paradise) and many sea shells are beauties in themselves, which do not belong to any object determined in respect of its purpose by concepts, but please freely and in themselves. So also delineations *à la grecque,* foliage for borders or wall papers, mean nothing in themselves; they represent nothing—no object under a definite concept— and are free beauties. We can refer to the same class what are called in music phantasies (i.e. pieces without any theme), and in fact all music without words.

In the judging of a free beauty (according to the mere form), the judgment of taste is pure. There is presupposed no concept of any purpose which the manifold of the given object is to serve, and which therefore is to be represented in it. By such a concept the freedom of the imagination which disports itself in the contemplation of the figure would be only limited.

But human beauty (i.e. of a man, a woman, or a child), the beauty of a horse, or a building (be it church, palace, arsenal, or summer house), presupposes a concept of the purpose which determines what the thing is to be, and consequently a concept of its perfection; it is therefore adherent beauty. Now as the combination of the pleasant (in sensation) with beauty, which properly is only concerned with form, is a hindrance to the purity of the judgment of taste, so also is its purity injured by the combination with beauty of the good (viz. that manifold which is good for the thing itself in accordance with its purpose).

We could add much to a building which would immediately please the eye if only it were not to be a church. We could adorn a figure with all kinds of spirals and light but regular lines, as the New Zealanders do with their tattooing, if only it were not the figure of a human being. And again this could have much finer features and a more pleasing and gentle cast of countenance provided it were not intended to represent a man, much less a warrior.

Now the satisfaction in the manifold of a thing in reference to the internal purpose which determines its possibility is a satisfaction grounded on a concept; but the satisfaction in beauty is such as presupposes no concept, but is immediately bound up with the representation through which the object is given (not through which it is thought). If now the judgment of taste in respect of the beauty of a thing is made dependent on the purpose in its manifold, like a judgment of reason, and thus limited, it is no longer a free and pure judgment of taste.

It is true that taste gains by this combination of aesthetical with intellectual satisfaction, inasmuch as it becomes fixed; and though it is not universal, yet in respect to certain purposively determined objects it becomes possible to prescribe rules for it. These, however, are not rules of taste, but merely rules for the unification of taste with reason, i.e. of the beautiful with the good, by which the former becomes available as an instrument of design in respect of the latter. Thus the tone of mind which is self-maintaining and of subjective universal validity is subordinated to the way of thinking which can be maintained only by painful resolve, but is of objective universal validity. Properly speaking, however, perfection gains nothing by beauty, or beauty by perfection;

but when we compare the representation by which an object is given to us with the object (as regards what it ought to be) by means of a concept, we cannot avoid considering along with it the sensation in the subject. And thus when both states of mind are in harmony our *whole faculty* of representative power gains.

A judgment of taste, then, in respect of an object with a definite internal purpose, can only be pure if either the person judging has no concept of this purpose or else abstracts from it in his judgment. Such a person, although forming an accurate judgment of taste in judging of the object as free beauty, would yet by another who considers the beauty in it only as a dependent attribute (who looks to the purpose of the object) be blamed and accused of false taste, although both are right in their own way—the one in reference to what he has before his eyes, the other in reference to what he has in his thought. By means of this distinction we can settle many disputes about beauty between judges of taste, by showing that the one is speaking of free, the other of dependent, beauty—that the first is making a pure, the second an applied, judgment of taste.

§ 17. OF THE IDEAL OF BEAUTY

There can be no objective rule of taste which shall determine by means of concepts what is beautiful. For every judgment from this source is aesthetical; i.e. the feeling of the subject, and not a concept of the object, is its determining ground. To seek for a principle of taste which shall furnish, by means of definite concepts, a universal criterion of the beautiful is fruitless trouble, because what is sought it impossible and self-contradictory. The universal communicability of sensation (satisfaction or dissatisfaction) without the aid of a concept—the agreement, as far as is possible, of all times and peoples as regards this feeling in the representation of certain objects—this

is the empirical criterion, although weak and hardly sufficing for probability, of the derivation of a taste, thus confirmed by examples, from the deep-lying general grounds of agreement in judging of the forms under which objects are given.

Hence we consider some products of taste as *exemplary*. Not that taste can be acquired by imitating others, for it must be an original faculty. He who imitates a model shows no doubt, in so far as he attains to it, skill; but only shows taste in so far as he can judge of this model itself.[8] It follows from hence that the highest model, the archetype of taste, is a mere idea, which everyone must produce in himself and according to which he must judge every object of taste, every example of judgment by taste, and even the taste of everyone. *Idea* properly means a rational concept, and *ideal* the representation of an individual being, regarded as adequate to an idea.[9] Hence that archetype of taste, which certainly rests on the indeterminate idea that reason has of a maximum, but which cannot be represented by concepts but only in an individual presentation, is better called the ideal of the beautiful. Although we are not in possession of this, we yet strive to produce it in ourselves. But it can only be an ideal of the imagination, because it rests on a presentation and not on concepts, and the imagination is the faculty of presentation. How do we arrive at such an ideal of beauty? *A priori,* or empirically? Moreover,

[8] Models of taste as regards the arts of speech must be composed in a dead and learned language. The first in order that they may not suffer that change which inevitably comes over living languages, in which noble expressions become flat, common ones antiquated, and newly created ones have only a short currency. The second because learned languages have a grammar which is subject to no wanton change of fashion, but the rules of which are preserved unchanged.
[9] [This distinction between an *idea* and an *ideal,* as also the further contrast between ideals of the reason and ideals of the imagination, had already been given by Kant in the *Critique of Pure Reason,* "Dialectic," Book II, Chapter 3, Section 1.—TR. NOTE.]

what species of the beautiful is susceptible of an ideal?

First, it is well to remark that the beauty for which an ideal is to be sought cannot be *free* beauty, but is *fixed* by a concept of objective purposiveness; and thus it cannot appertain to the object of a quite pure judgment of taste, but to that of a judgment of taste which is in part intellectual. That is, in whatever grounds of judgment an ideal is to be found, an idea of reason in accordance with definite concepts must lie at its basis, which determines *a priori* the purpose on which the internal possibility of the object rests. An ideal of beautiful flowers, of a beautiful piece of furniture, of a beautiful view, is inconceivable. But neither can an ideal be represented of a beauty dependent on definite purposes, e.g. of a beautiful dwelling house, a beautiful tree, a beautiful garden, etc.; presumably because their purpose is not sufficiently determined and fixed by the concept, and thus the purposiveness is nearly as free as in the case of *vague* beauty. The only being which has the purpose of its existence in itself is *man,* who can determine his purposes by reason; or, where he must receive them from external perception, yet can compare them with essential and universal purposes and can judge this their accordance aesthetically. This *man* is, then, alone of all objects in the world, susceptible of an ideal of *beauty,* as it is only *humanity* in his person, as an intelligence, that is susceptible of the ideal of *perfection.*

But there are here two elements. *First,* there is the aesthetical *normal idea,* which is an individual intuition (of the imagination), representing the standard of our judgment [upon man] as a thing belonging to a particular animal species. *Secondly,* there is the *rational idea* which makes the purposes of humanity, so far as they cannot be sensibly represented, the principle for judging of a figure through which, as their phenomenal effect, those purposes are revealed. The

normal idea of the figure of an animal of a particular race must take its elements from experience. But the greatest purposiveness in the construction of the figure that would be available for the universal standard of aesthetical judgment upon each individual of this species—the image which is as it were designedly at the basis of nature's technique, to which only the whole race and not any isolated individual is adequate—this lies merely in the idea of the judging [subject]. And this, with its proportions as an aesthetical idea, can be completely presented *in concreto* in a model. In order to make intelligible in some measure (for who can extract her whole secret from nature?) how this comes to pass, we shall attempt a psychological explanation.

We must remark that, in a way quite incomprehensible by us, the imagination cannot only recall on occasion the signs for concepts long past, but can also reproduce the image of the figure of the object out of an unspeakable number of objects of different kinds or even of the same kind. Further, if the mind is concerned with comparisons, the imagination can, in all probability, actually, though unconsciously, let one image glide into another; and thus, by the concurrence of several of the same kind, come by an average, which serves as the common measure of all. Everyone has seen a thousand full-grown men. Now if you wish to judge of their normal size, estimating it by means of comparison, the imagination (as I think) allows a great number of images (perhaps the whole thousand) to fall on one another. If I am allowed to apply here the analogy of optical presentation, it is in the space where most of them are combined and inside the contour, where the place is illuminated with the most vivid colors, that the *average size* is cognizable, which, both in height and breadth, is equally far removed from the extreme bounds of the greatest and smallest stature. And this is the stature of a beautiful man. (We could arrive at the same thing mechanically by adding together all thousand magnitudes, heights, breadths, and thicknesses, and dividing the sum by a thousand. But the imagination does this by means of a dynamical effect, which arises from the various impressions of such figures on the organ of internal sense.) If now, in a similar way, for this average man we seek the average head, for this head the average nose, etc., such figure is at the basis of the normal idea in the country where the comparison is instituted. Thus necessarily under these empirical conditions a Negro must have a different normal idea of the beauty of the [human figure] from a white man, a Chinese a different normal idea from a European, etc. And the same is the case with the model of a beautiful horse or dog (of a certain breed). This *normal idea* is not derived from proportions gotten from experience [and regarded] *as definite rules,* but in accordance with it rules for judging become in the first instance possible. It is the image for the whole race, which floats among all the variously different intuitions of individuals, which nature takes as archetype in her productions of the same species, but which appears not to be fully reached in any individual case. It is by no means the whole *archetype of beauty* in the race, but only the form constituting the indispensable condition of all beauty, and thus merely *correctness* in the [mental] presentation of the race. It is, like the celebrated *Doryphorus* of Polycletus, the *rule* (Myron's "Cow"[10] might also be used thus for its kind). It can therefore contain nothing specifically characteristic, for otherwise it would not be the *normal idea* for the race. Its presentation pleases, not by its beauty, but merely because it contradicts no condi-

tion, under which alone a thing of this kind can be beautiful. The presentation is merely correct.[11]

We must yet distinguish the *normal idea* of the beautiful from the *ideal,* which latter, on grounds already alleged, we can only except in the *human* figure. In this the ideal consists in the expression of the *moral,* without which the object would not please universally and thus positively (not merely negatively in an accurate presentation). The visible expression of moral ideas that rule men inwardly can indeed only be gotten from experience; but to make its connection with all [that] our reason unites with the morally good in the idea of the highest purposiveness—goodness of heart, purity, strength, peace, etc.—visible as it were in bodily manifestation (as the effect of that which is internal) requires a union of pure ideas of reason with great imaginative power even in him who wishes to judge of it, still more in him who wishes to present it. The correctness of such an ideal of beauty is shown by its permitting no sensible charm to mingle with the satisfaction in the object, and yet allowing us to take a great interest therein. This shows that a judgment in accordance with such a standard can never be purely aesthetical, and that a judgment in accordance with an ideal of beauty is not a mere judgment of taste.

---

10 [Polycletus of Argos flourished about 430 B.C. His statue of the "Spearbearer" (*Doryphorus*), afterward became known as the "Canon," because in it the artist was supposed to have embodied a perfect representation of the ideal of the human figure. The "Cow" was a celebrated statue executed by Myron, a Greek sculptor, contemporary with Polycletus.—TR. NOTE.]

---

11 It will be found that a perfectly regular countenance, such as a painter might wish to have for a model, ordinarily tells us nothing because it contains nothing characteristic, and therefore rather expresses the idea of the race than the specific [traits] of a person. The exaggeration of a characteristic of this kind, i.e. such as does violence to the normal idea (the purposiveness of the race), is called *caricature.* Experience also shows that these quite regular countenances commonly indicate internally only a mediocre man, presumably (if it may be assumed that external nature expresses the proportions of internal) because, if no mental disposition exceeds that proportion which is requisite in order to constitute a man free from faults, nothing can be expected of what is called *genius,* in which nature seems to depart from the ordinary relations of the mental powers on behalf of some special one.

Explanation of the beautiful derived from this Third Moment: Beauty is the form of the *purposiveness* of an object, so far as this is perceived in it *without any representation of a purpose.*[12]

Fourth Moment
Of the Judgment of Taste, According to the Modality of the Satisfaction in the Object

§ 18. WHAT THE MODALITY IN A JUDGMENT OF TASTE IS

I can say of every representation that it is at least *possible* that (as a cognition) it should be bound up with a pleasure. Of a representation that I call *pleasant* I say that it *actually* excites pleasure in me. But the *beautiful* we think as having a *necessary* reference to satisfaction. Now this necessity is of a peculiar kind. It is not a theoretical objective necessity, in which case it would be cognized *a priori* that everyone *will feel* this satisfaction in the object called beautiful by me. It is not a practical necessity, in which case, by concepts of a pure rational will serving as a rule for freely acting beings, the satisfaction is the necessary result of an objective law and only indicates that we absolutely (without any further design) ought to act in a certain way. But the necessity which is thought in an aesthetical judgment can only be called exemplary, i.e.

---

12 It might be objected to this explanation that there are things in which we see a purposive form without cognizing any purpose in them, like the stone implements often gotten from old sepulchral tumuli with a hole in them, as if for a handle. These, although they plainly indicate by their shape a purposiveness of which we do not know the purpose, are nevertheless not described as beautiful. But if we regard a thing as a work of art, that is enough to make us admit that its shape has reference to some design and definite purpose. And hence there is no immediate satisfaction in the contemplation of it. On the other hand a flower, e.g. a tulip, is regarded as beautiful, because in perceiving it we find a certain purposiveness which, in our judgment, is referred to no purpose at all.

a necessity of the assent of *all* to a judgment which is regarded as the example of a universal rule that we cannot state. Since an aesthetical judgment is not an objective cognitive judgment, this necessity cannot be derived from definite concepts and is therefore not apodictic. Still less can it be inferred from the universality of experience (of a complete agreement of judgments as to the beauty of a certain object). For not only would experience hardly furnish sufficiently numerous vouchers for this, but also, on empirical judgments, we can base no concept of the necessity of these judgments.

§ 19. THE SUBJECTIVE NECESSITY, WHICH WE ASCRIBE TO THE JUDGMENT OF TASTE, IS CONDITIONED

The judgment of taste requires the agreement of everyone, and he who describes anything as beautiful claims that everyone *ought* to give his approval to the object in question and also describe it as beautiful. The *ought* in the aesthetical judgment is therefore pronounced in accordance with all the data which are required for judging, and yet is only conditioned. We ask for the agreement of everyone else, because we have for it a ground that is common to all; and we could count on this agreement, provided we were always sure that the case was correctly subsumed under that ground as rule of assent.

§ 20. THE CONDITION OF NECESSITY WHICH A JUDGMENT OF TASTE ASSERTS IS THE IDEA OF A COMMON SENSE

If judgments of taste (like cognitive judgments) had a definite objective principle, then the person who lays them down in accordance with this latter would claim an unconditioned necessity for his judgment. If they were devoid of all principle, like those of the mere taste of sense, we would not allow them in thought any necessity whatever. Hence they must have a subjective principle which determines what pleases or displeases only by feeling and not by concepts, but yet with universal validity. But such a principle could only be regarded as a *common sense*, which is essentially different from common understanding which people sometimes call common sense (*sensus communis*); for the latter does not judge by feeling but always by concepts, although ordinarily only as by obscurely represented principles.

Hence it is only under the presupposition that there is a common sense (by which we do not understand an external sense, but the effect resulting from the free play of our cognitive powers)—it is only under this presupposition, I say, that the judgment of taste can be laid down.

§ 21. HAVE WE GROUND FOR PRESUPPOSING A COMMON SENSE?

Cognitions and judgments must, along with the conviction that accompanies them, admit of universal communicability; for otherwise there would be no harmony between them and the object, and they would be collectively a mere subjective play of the representative powers, exactly as skepticism would have it. But if cognitions are to admit of communicability, so must also the state of mind—i.e. the accordance of the cognitive powers with a cognition generally and that proportion of them which is suitable for a representation (by which an object is given to us) in order that a cognition may be made out of it—admit of universal communicability. For without this as the subjective condition of cognition, cognition as an effect could not arise. This actually always takes place when a given object by means of sense excites the imagination to collect the manifold, and the imagination in its turn excites the understanding to bring about a unity of this collective process in concepts. But this accordance of the cognitive powers has a different proportion according to the variety of the objects which are given. However, it must be such that this internal relation, by which one mental faculty is excited by another, shall be generally the most beneficial for both faculties in respect of cognition (of given objects); and this accordance can only be determined by feeling (not according to concepts). Since now accordance itself must admit of universal communicability, and consequently also our feeling of it (in a given representation), and since the universal communicability of a feeling presupposes a common sense, we have grounds for assuming this latter. And this common sense is assumed without relying on psychological observations, but simply as the necessary condition of the universal communicability of our knowledge, which is presupposed in every logic and in every principle of knowledge that is not skeptical.

§ 22. THE NECESSITY OF THE UNIVERSAL AGREEMENT THAT IS THOUGHT IN A JUDGMENT OF TASTE IS A SUBJECTIVE NECESSITY, WHICH IS REPRESENTED AS OBJECTIVE UNDER THE PRESUPPOSITION OF A COMMON SENSE

In all judgments by which we describe anything as beautiful, we allow no one to be of another opinion, without, however, grounding our judgment on concepts, but only on our feeling, which we therefore place at its basis, not as a private, but as a communal feeling. Now this common sense cannot be grounded on experience, for it aims at justifying judgments which contain an *ought*. It does not say that everyone *will* agree with my judgment, but that he *ought*. And so common sense, as an example of whose judgment I here put forward my judgment of taste and on account of which I attribute to the latter an *exemplary* validity, is a mere ideal norm, under the supposition of which I have a right to make into a rule for everyone a judgment that accords therewith, as well as the satisfaction in an object expressed in such judgment. For the principle which concerns the agreement of different judging persons, although only subjective, is yet assumed as subjectively universal (an idea necessary for everyone), and thus can claim universal assent (as if it were objective) provided we are sure that we have correctly subsumed [the particulars] under it.

This indeterminate norm of a common sense is actually presupposed by us, as is shown by our claim to lay down judgments of taste. Whether there is in fact such a common sense, as a constitutive principle of the possibility of experience, or whether a yet higher principle of reason makes it only a regulative principle for producing in us a common sense for higher purposes; whether, therefore, taste is an original and natural faculty or only the idea of an artificial one yet to be acquired, so that a judgment of taste with its assumption of a universal assent in fact is only a requirement of reason for producing such harmony of sentiment; whether the ought, i.e. the objective necessity of the confluence of the feeling of any one man with that of every other, only signifies the possibility of arriving at this accord, and the judgment of taste only affords an example of the application of this principle—these questions we have neither the wish nor the power to investigate as yet; we have now only to resolve the faculty of taste into its elements in order to unite them at last in the idea of a common sense.

Explanation of the beautiful resulting from the Fourth Moment: The *beautiful* is that which without any concept is cognized as the object of a *necessary* satisfaction. . . .

II. *Analytic of the Sublime*

§ 23. TRANSITION FROM THE FACULTY WHICH JUDGES OF THE BEAUTIFUL TO THAT WHICH JUDGES OF THE SUBLIME

The beautiful and the sublime agree in this that both please in themselves. Further, neither presupposes a judgment of sense nor a judgment logically determined, but a judgment of reflection. Consequently the satisfaction [belonging to them] does not depend on a sensation, as in the case of the pleasant, nor on a definite concept, as in the case of the good; but it is nevertheless referred to concepts, although indeterminate ones. And so the satisfaction is connected with the mere presentation [of the object] or with the faculty of presentation, so that in the case of a given intuition this faculty or the imagination is considered as in agreement with the *faculty of concepts* of understanding or reason, regarded as promoting these latter. Hence both kinds of judgments are *singular,* and yet announce themselves as universally valid for every subject; although they lay claim merely to the feeling of pleasure, and not to any cognition of the object.

But there are also remarkable differences between the two. The beautiful in nature is connected with the form of the object, which consists in having [definite] boundaries. The sublime, on the other hand, is to be found in a formless object, so far as in it or by occasion of it *boundlessness* is represented, and yet its totality is also present to thought. Thus the beautiful seems to be regarded as the presentation of an indefinite concept of understanding, the sublime as that of a like concept of reason. Therefore the satisfaction in the one case is bound up with the representation of *quality,* in the other with that of *quantity.* And the latter satisfaction is quite different in kind from the former, for this, the beautiful, directly brings with it a feeling of the furtherance of life, and thus is compatible with charms and with the play of the imagination. But the other, the feeling of the sublime, is a pleasure that arises only indirectly; viz. it is produced by the feeling of a momentary checking of the vital powers and a consequent stronger outflow of them, so that it seems to be regarded as emotion—not play, but earnest in the exercise of the imagination. Hence it is incompatible with charm; and as the mind is not merely attracted by the object but is ever being alternately repelled, the satisfaction in the sublime does not so much involve a positive pleasure as admiration or respect, which rather deserves to be called negative pleasure.

But the inner and most important distinction between the sublime and beautiful is, certainly, as follows. (Here, as we are entitled to do, we only bring under consideration in the first instance the sublime in natural objects, for the sublime of art is always limited by the conditions of agreement with nature.) Natural beauty (which is independent) brings with it a purposiveness in its form by which the object seems to be, as it were, preadapted to our judgment, and thus constitutes in itself an object of satisfaction. On the other hand, that which excites in us, without any reasoning about it, but in the mere apprehension of it, the feeling of the sublime may appear, as regards its form, to violate purpose in respect of the judgment, to be unsuited to our presentative faculty, and as it were to do violence to the imagination; and yet it is judged to be only the more sublime.

Now we may see from this that, in general, we express ourselves incorrectly if we call any *object of nature* sublime, although we can quite correctly call many objects of nature beautiful. For how can that be marked by an expression of approval which is apprehended in itself as being a violation of purpose? All that we can say is that the object is fit for the presentation of a sub-

limity which can be found in the mind, for no sensible form can contain the sublime properly so-called. This concerns only ideas of the reason which, although no adequate presentation is possible for them, by this very inadequateness, which admits of sensible presentation, are aroused and summoned into the mind. Thus the wide ocean, disturbed by the storm, cannot be called sublime. Its aspect is horrible; and the mind must be already filled with manifold ideas if it is to be determined by such an intuition to a feeling itself sublime, as it is incited to abandon sensibility and to busy itself with ideas that involve higher purposiveness.

Independent natural beauty discovers to us a technique of nature which represents it as a system in accordance with laws, the principle of which we do not find in the whole of our faculty of understanding. That principle is the principle of purposiveness, in respect of the use of our judgment in regard to phenomena, [which requires] that these must not be judged as merely belonging to nature in its purposeless mechanism, but also as belonging to something analogous to art. It therefore actually extends, not indeed our cognition of natural objects, but our concept of nature, [which is now not regarded] as mere mechanism but as art. This leads to profound investigations as to the possibility of such a form. But in what we are accustomed to call sublime there is nothing at all that leads to particular objective principles and forms of nature corresponding to them; so far from it that, for the most part, nature excites the ideas of the sublime in its chaos or in its widest and most irregular disorder and desolation, provided size and might are perceived. Hence, we see that the concept of the sublime is not nearly so important or rich in consequences as the concept of the beautiful; and that, in general, it displays nothing purposive in nature itself, but only in that possible use of our intuitions of it by which there is produced in us a feeling of a purposiveness quite independent of nature. We must seek a ground external to ourselves for the beautiful of nature, but seek it for the sublime merely in ourselves and in our attitude of thought, which introduces sublimity into the representation of nature. This is a very needful preliminary remark, which quite separates the ideas of the sublime from that of a purposiveness of *nature* and makes the theory of the sublime a mere appendix to the aesthetical judging of that purposiveness, because by means of it no particular form is represented in nature, but there is only developed a purposive use which the imagination makes of its representation.

§ 24. OF THE DIVISIONS OF AN INVESTIGATION INTO THE FEELING OF THE SUBLIME

As regards the division of the moments of the aesthetical judging of objects in reference to the feeling of the sublime, the Analytic can proceed according to the same principle as was adopted in the analysis of judgments of taste. For as an act of the aesthetical reflective judgment, the satisfaction in the sublime must be represented just as in the case of the beautiful—according to *quantity* as universally valid, according to *quality* as devoid of *interest,* according to *relation* as subjective purposiveness, and according to *modality* as necessary. And so the method here will not diverge from that of the preceding section, unless indeed we count it a difference that in the case where the aesthetical judgment is concerned with the form of the object we began with the investigation of its quality, but here, in view of the formlessness which may belong to what we call sublime, we will begin with quantity, as the first moment of the aesthetical judgment as to the sublime. The reason for this may be seen from the preceding paragraph.

But the analysis of the sublime involves a division not needed in the case of the beautiful, viz. a division into the *mathematically* and the *dynamically sublime.*

For the feeling of the sublime brings with it as its characteristic feature a *movement* of the mind bound up with the judging of the object, while in the case of the beautiful taste presupposes and maintains the mind in *restful* contemplation. Now this movement ought to be judged as subjectively purposive (because the sublime pleases us), and thus it is referred through the imagination either to the *faculty of cognition* or *of desire*. In either reference the purposiveness of the given representation ought to be judged only in respect of this *faculty* (without purpose or interest), but in the first case it is ascribed to the object as a *mathematical* determination of the imagination, in the second as *dynamical*. And hence we have this twofold way of representing the sublime.

Of the Mathematically Sublime

§ 25. EXPLANATION OF THE TERM "SUBLIME"

We call that *sublime* which is *absolutely great*. But to be great and to be of a certain greatness are quite different concepts (*magnitudo* and *quantitas*). In like manner to say simply (*simpliciter*) that anything is *great* is quite different from saying that it is *absolutely great* (*absolute, non comparative magnum*). The latter is *what is great beyond all comparison*. What now is meant by the expression that anything is great or small or of medium size? It is not a pure concept of understanding that is thus signified; still less is it an intuition of sense; and just as little is it a concept of reason, because it brings with it no principle of cognition. It must therefore be a concept of judgment or derived from one, and a subjective purposiveness of the representation in reference to the judgment must lie at its basis. That anything is a magnitude (*quantum*) may be cognized from the thing itself, without any comparison of it with other things, viz. if there is a multiplicity of the homogeneous constituting one thing. But to cognize *how great* it is always requires some other magnitude as a measure. But because the judging of magnitude depends, not merely on multiplicity (number), but also on the magnitude of the unit (the measure), and since, to judge of the magnitude of this latter again requires another as measure with which it may be compared, we see that the determination of the magnitude of phenomena can supply no absolute concept whatever of magnitude, but only a comparative one.

If now I say simply that anything is great, it appears that I have no comparison in view, at least none with an objective measure, because it is thus not determined at all how great the object is. But although the standard of comparison is merely subjective, yet the judgment nonetheless claims universal assent; "this man is beautiful" and "he is tall" are judgments, not limited merely to the judging subject, but, like theoretical judgments, demanding the assent of everyone.

In a judgment by which anything is designated simply as great, it is not merely meant that the object has a magnitude, but that this magnitude is superior to that of many other objects of the same kind, without, however, any exact determination of this superiority. Thus there is always at the basis of our judgment a standard which we assume as the same for everyone; this, however, is not available for any logical (mathematically definite) judging of magnitude, but only for aesthetical judging of the same, because it is a merely subjective standard lying at the basis of the reflective judgment upon magnitude. It may be empirical, as e.g. the average size of the men known to us, of animals of a certain kind, trees, houses, etc. Or it may be a standard given *a priori* which, through the defects of the judging subject, is limited by the subjective conditions of presentation *in concreto,* as e.g. in the practical sphere, the greatness of a certain virtue or of the public liberty and justice in a country, or, in the theoretical sphere, the greatness of the accuracy or the inaccuracy of an observation or measurement that has been made, etc.

Here it is remarkable that, although we have no interest whatever in an object— i.e. its existence is indifferent to us—yet its mere size, even if it is considered as formless, may bring a satisfaction with it that is universally communicable and that consequently involves the consciousness of a subjective purposiveness in the use of our cognitive faculty. This is not indeed a satisfaction in the object (because it may be formless), as in the case of the beautiful, in which the reflective judgment finds itself purposively determined in reference to cognition in general, but [a satisfaction] in the extension of the imagination by itself.

If (under the above limitation) we say simply of an object "it is great," this is no mathematically definite judgment, but a mere judgment of reflection upon the representation of it, which is subjectively purposive for a certain use of our cognitive powers in the estimation of magnitude; and we always then bind up with the representation a kind of respect, as also a kind of contempt, for what we simply call "small." Further, the judging of things as great or small extends to everything, even to all their characteristics; thus we describe beauty as great or small. The reason of this is to be sought in the fact that whatever we present in intuition according to the precept of the judgment (and thus represent aesthetically) is always a phenomenon, and thus a quantum.

But if we call anything, not only great, but absolutely great in every point of view (great beyond all comparison), i.e. sublime, we soon see that it is not permissible to seek for an adequate standard of this outside itself, but merely in itself. It is a magnitude which is like itself alone. It follows hence that the sublime is not to be sought in the things of nature, but only in our ideas. . . .

The foregoing explanation can be thus expressed: *the sublime is that in comparison with which everything else is small.* Here we easily see that nothing can be given in nature, however great it is judged by us to be, which could not, if considered in another relation, be reduced to the infinitely small; and conversely there is nothing so small which does not admit of extension by our imagination to the greatness of a world if compared with still smaller standards. Telescopes have furnished us with abundant material for making the first remark, microscopes for the second. Nothing, therefore, which can be an object of the senses is, considered on this basis, to be called sublime. But because there is in our imagination a striving toward infinite progress and in our reason a claim for absolute totality, regarded as a real idea, therefore this very inadequateness for that idea in our faculty for estimating the magnitude of things of sense excites in us the feeling of a supersensible faculty. And it is not the object of sense, but the use which the judgment naturally makes of certain objects on behalf of this latter feeling that is absolutely great, and in comparison every other use is small. Consequently it is the state of mind produced by a certain representation with which the reflective judgment is occupied, and not the object, that is to be called sublime.

We can therefore append to the preceding formulas explaining the sublime this other: *the sublime is that, the mere ability to think which shows a faculty of the mind surpassing every standard of sense.*

§ 26. OF THAT ESTIMATION OF THE MAGNITUDE OF NATURAL THINGS WHICH IS REQUISITE FOR THE IDEA OF THE SUBLIME

The estimation of magnitude by means of concepts of number (or their signs in algebra) is mathematical, but that in mere intuition (by the measurement of the eye) is aesthetical. Now we can come by definite concepts of *how great* a thing is only by numbers, of which the unit is the measure (at all events by series of numbers progressing to infinity), and so far all logical estimation of magnitude is mathematical. But since the magnitude of the measure must then be assumed known, and this again is only to be estimated mathematically by means of numbers—the unit of which must be another [smaller] measure—we can never have a first or fundamental measure, and therefore can never have a definite concept of a given magnitude. So the estimation of the magnitude of the fundamental measure must consist in this, that we can immediately apprehend it in intuition and use it by the imagination for the presentation of concepts of number. That is, all estimation of the magnitude of the objects of nature is in the end aesthetical (i.e. subjectively and not objectively determined).

Now for the mathematical estimation of magnitude there is, indeed, no maximum (for the power of numbers extends to infinity); but for its aesthetical estimation there is always a maximum, and of this I say that that, if it is judged as the absolute measure than which no greater is possible subjectively (for the judging subject), it brings with it the idea of the sublime and produces that emotion which no mathematical estimation of its magnitude by means of numbers can bring about (except so far as that aesthetical fundamental measure remains vividly in the imagination). For the former only presents relative magnitude by means of comparison with others of the same kind, but the latter presents magnitude absolutely, so far as the mind can grasp it in an intuition.

In receiving a quantum into the imagination by intuition, in order to be able to use it for a measure or as a unit for the estimation of magnitude by means of numbers, there are two operations of the imagination involved: *apprehension* (*apprehensio*) and *comprehension* (*comprehensio aesthetica*). As to apprehension there is no difficulty, for it can go on *ad infinitum,* but comprehension becomes harder the further apprehension advances, and soon attains to its maximum, viz. the greatest possible aesthetical fundamental measure for the estimation of magnitude. For when apprehension has gone so far that the partial representations of sensuous intuition at first apprehended begin to vanish in the imagination, while this ever proceeds to the apprehension of others, then it loses as much on the one side as it gains on the other; and in comprehension there is a maximum beyond which it cannot go.

Hence can be explained what Savary[13] remarks, in his account of Egypt, viz. that we must keep from going very near the Pyramids just as much as we keep from going too far from them, in order to get the full emotional effect from their size. For if we are too far away, the parts to be apprehended (the stones lying one over the other) are only obscurely represented, and the representation of them produces no effect upon the aesthetical judgment of the subject. But if we are very near, the eye requires some time to complete the apprehension of the tiers from the bottom up to the apex, and then the first tiers are always partly forgotten before the imagination has taken in the last, and so the comprehension of them is never complete. The same thing may sufficiently explain the bewilderment or, as it were, perplexity which it is said seizes the spectator on his first entrance into St. Peter's at Rome. For there is here a feeling of the inadequacy of his imagination for presenting the ideas of a whole, wherein the imagination reaches its maximum, and, in striving to surpass it, sinks back into itself, by which, however, a kind of emotional satisfaction is produced.

I do not wish to speak as yet of the ground of this satisfaction, which is bound up with a representation from which we should least of all expect it, viz. a representation which makes us remark its inadequacy and consequently its subjective want of purposiveness for the judgment in the estimation of magnitude. I only remark that if the aesthetical judgment is *pure* (i.e. *mingled with no teleological judgment* or judgment of reason) and is to be given as a completely suitable example of the critique of the *aesthetical* judgment, we must not exhibit the sublime in products of art (e.g. buildings, pillars, etc.) where human purpose determines the form as well as the size, nor yet in things of nature *the concepts of which bring with them a definite purpose* (e.g. animals with a known natural destination), but in rude nature (and in this only in so far as it does not bring with it any charm or emotion produced by actual danger) merely as containing magnitude. For in this kind of representation nature contains nothing monstrous (either magnificent or horrible); the magnitude that is apprehended may be increased as much as you wish, provided it can be comprehended in a whole by the imagination. An object is *monstrous* if, by its size, it destroys the purpose which constitutes the concept of it. But the mere presentation of a concept is called *colossal,* which is almost too great for any presentation (bordering on the relatively monstrous), because the purpose of the presentation of a concept is made harder [to realize] by the intuition of the object being almost too great for our faculty of apprehension. A pure judgment upon the sublime must, however, have no purpose of the object as its determining ground if it is to be aesthetical and not mixed up with any judgment of understanding or reason.

Because everything which is to give disinterested pleasure to the merely reflective judgment must bring with the representation of it, subjective and, as subjective, universally valid purposiveness—although no purposiveness of the *form* of the object lies (as in the case of the beautiful) at the ground of the judgment—the question arises,

---

13 [M. Savary, *Lettres sur l'Egypte* (Amsterdam, 1787).—TR. NOTE.]

What is this subjective purposiveness? And how does it come to be prescribed as the norm by which a ground for universally valid satisfaction is supplied in the mere estimation of magnitude, even in that which is forced up to the point where our faculty of imagination is inadequate for the presentation of the concept of magnitude?

In the process of combination requisite for the estimation of magnitude, the imagination proceeds of itself to infinity without anything hindering it; but the understanding guides it by means of concepts of number, for which it must furnish the schema. And in this procedure, as belonging to the logical estimation of magnitude, there is indeed something objectively purposive— in accordance with the concept of a purpose (as all measurement is)—but nothing purposive and pleasing for the aesthetical judgment. There is also in this designed purposiveness nothing which would force us to push the magnitude of the measure, and consequently the *comprehension* of the manifold in an intuition, to the bounds of the faculty of imagination, or as far as ever this can reach in its presentations. For in the estimation of magnitude by the understanding (arithmetic) we only go to a certain point, whether we push the comprehension of the units up to the number 10 (as in the decimal scale) or only up to 4 (as in the quaternary scale); the further production of magnitude proceeds by combination, or, if the quantum is given in intuition, by apprehension, but merely by way of progression (not of comprehension) in accordance with an assumed principle of progression. In this mathematical estimation of magnitude the understanding is equally served and contented, whether the imagination chooses for unit a magnitude that we can take in in a glance, e.g. a foot or rod, or a German mile or even the earth's diameter—of which the apprehension is indeed possible, but not the comprehension in an intuition of the imagination (not possible by *comprehensio aesthetica,* although

quite possible by *comprehensio logica* in a concept of number). In both cases the logical estimation of magnitude goes on without hindrance to infinity.

But now the mind listens to the voice of reason which, for every given magnitude— even for those that can never be entirely apprehended, although (in sensible representation) they are judged as entirely given —requires totality. Reason consequently desires comprehension in *one* intuition. and so the [joint] *presentation* of all these members of a progressively increasing series. It does not even exempt the infinite (space and past time) from this requirement; it rather renders it unavoidable to think the infinite (in the judgment of common reason) as *entirely given* (according to its totality).

But the infinite is absolutely (not merely comparatively) great. Compared with it everything else (of the same kind of magnitudes) is small. And what is most important is that to be able only to think it as *a whole* indicates a faculty of mind which surpasses every standard of sense. For [to represent it sensibly] would require a comprehension having for unit a standard bearing a definite relation, expressible in numbers, to the infinite, which is impossible. Nevertheless, *the bare capability of thinking* this infinite without contradiction requires in the human mind a faculty itself supersensible. For it is only by means of this faculty and its idea of a noumenon—which admits of no intuition, but which yet serves as the substrate for the intuition of the world, as a mere phenomenon—that the infinite of the world of sense, in the pure intellectual estimation of magnitude, can be *completely* comprehended under one *concept,* although in the mathematical estimation of magnitude by means of *concepts of number* it can never be completely thought. The faculty of being able to think the infinite of supersensible intuition as given (in its intelligible substrate) surpasses every standard of sensibility and is great beyond all comparison even with the faculty of mathematical estimation, not, of course, in a theoretical point of view and on behalf of the cognitive faculty, but as an extension of the mind which feels itself able in another (practical) point of view to go beyond the limits of sensibility.

Nature is therefore sublime in those of its phenomena whose intuition brings with it the idea of its infinity. This last can only come by the inadequacy of the greatest effort of our imagination to estimate the magnitude of an object. But now, in mathematical estimation of magnitude, the imagination is equal to providing a sufficient measure for every object, because the numerical concepts of the understanding, by means of progression, can make any measure adequate to any given magnitude. Therefore it must be the *aesthetical* estimation of magnitude in which the effort toward comprehension surpasses the power of the imagination. Here it is felt that we can comprehend in a whole of intuition the progressive apprehension, and at the same time we perceive the inadequacy of this faculty, unbounded in its progress, for grasping and using any fundamental measure available for the estimation of magnitude with the easiest application of the understanding. Now the proper unchangeable fundamental measure of nature is its absolute whole, which, regarding nature as a phenomenon, would be infinity comprehended. But since this fundamental measure is a self-contradictory concept (on account of the impossibility of the absolute totality of an endless progress), that magnitude of a natural object on which the imagination fruitlessly spends its whole faculty of comprehension must carry our concept of nature to a supersensible substrate (which lies at its basis and also at the basis of our faculty of thought). As this, however, is great beyond all standards of sense, it makes us judge as *sublime,* not so much the object, as our own state of mind in the estimation of it.

Therefore, just as the aesthetical judg-

ment in judging the beautiful refers the imagination in its free play to the *understanding,* in order to harmonize it with the *concepts* of the latter in general (without any determination of them), so does the same faculty, when judging a thing as sublime, refer itself to the *reason,* in order that it may subjectively be in accordance with its *ideas* (no matter what they are)—i.e. that it may produce a state of mind conformable to them and compatible with that brought about by the influence of definite (practical) ideas upon feeling.

We hence see also that true sublimity must be sought only in the mind of the [subject] judging, not in the natural object the judgment upon which occasions this state. Who would call sublime, e.g., shapeless mountain masses piled in wild disorder upon one another with their pyramids of ice, or the gloomy, raging sea? But the mind feels itself raised in its own judgment if, while contemplating them without any reference to their form, and abandoning itself to the imagination and to the reason—which, although placed in combination with the imagination without any definite purpose, merely extends it—it yet finds the whole power of the imagination inadequate to its ideas.

Examples of the mathematically sublime of nature in mere intuition are all the cases in which we are given, not so much a larger numerical concept, as a large unit for the measure of the imagination (for shortening the numerical series). A tree, [the height of] which we estimate with reference to the height of a man, at all events gives a standard for a mountain; and if this were a mile high, it would serve as unit for the number expressive of the earth's diameter, so that the latter might be made intuitible. The earth's diameter [would supply a unit] for the known planetary system; this again for the Milky Way; and the immeasurable number of Milky Way systems called nebulae, which presumably constitute a system of the same kind among themselves, lets us expect no bounds here. Now the sublime in the aesthetical judging of an immeasurable whole like this lies, not so much in the greatness of the number [of units], as in the fact that in our progress we ever arrive at yet greater units. To this the systematic division of the universe contributes, which represents every magnitude in nature as small in its turn, and represents our imagination with its entire freedom from bounds, and with it nature, as a mere nothing in comparison with the ideas of reason if it is sought to furnish a presentation which shall be adequate to them.

§ 27. OF THE QUALITY OF THE SATIS-FACTION IN OUR JUDGMENTS UPON THE SUBLIME

The feeling of our incapacity to attain to an idea *which is a law for us* is *respect*. Now the idea of the comprehension of every phenomenon that can be given us in the intuition of a whole is an idea prescribed to us by a law of reason, which recognizes no other measure, definite, valid for everyone, and invariable, than the absolute whole. But our imagination, even in its greatest efforts, in respect of that comprehension which we expect from it of a given object in a whole of intuition (and thus with reference to the presentation of the idea of reason) exhibits its own limits and inadequacy, although at the same time it shows that its destination is to make itself adequate to this idea regarded as a law. Therefore the feeling of the sublime in nature is respect for our own destination, which, by a certain subreption,[14] we attribute to an object of nature (conversion of respect for the idea of humanity in our own subject into respect for the object). This makes intuitively evident the superiority of the rational determi-

nation of our cognitive faculties to the greatest faculty of our sensibility.

The feeling of the sublime is therefore a feeling of pain arising from the want of accordance between the aesthetical estimation of magnitude formed by the imagination and the estimation of the same formed by reason. There is at the same time a pleasure thus excited, arising from the correspondence with rational ideas of this very judgment of the inadequacy of our greatest faculty of sense, in so far as it is a law for us to strive after these ideas. In fact it is for us a law (of reason) and belongs to our destination to estimate as small, in comparison with ideas of reason, everything which nature, regarded as an object of sense, contains that is great for us; and that which arouses in us the feeling of this supersensible destination agrees with that law. Now the greatest effort of the imagination in the presentation of the unit for the estimation of magnitude indicates a reference to something. *absolutely great,* and consequently a reference to the law of reason, which bids us take this alone as our highest measure of magnitude. Therefore the inner perception of the inadequacy of all sensible standards for rational estimation of magnitude indicates a correspondence with rational laws; it involves a pain, which arouses in us the feeling of our supersensible destination, according to which it is purposive and therefore pleasurable to find every standard of sensibility inadequate to the ideas of understanding.

The mind feels itself *moved* in the representation of the sublime in nature, while in aesthetical judgments about the beautiful it is in *restful* contemplation. This movement may (especially in its beginnings) be compared to a vibration, i.e. to a quickly alternating attraction toward, and repulsion from, the same object. The transcendent (toward which the imagination is impelled in its apprehension of intuition) is for the imagination like an abyss in which it fears to lose itself; but for the rational idea of

---

14 [A ready clue to the meaning of this rather barbarous term is its etymological kinship with "surreptitious." It is approximately the noun form of that adjective.—ED. NOTE.]

the supersensible it is not transcendent, but in conformity with law to bring about such an effort of the imagination, and consequently here there is the same amount of attraction as there was of repulsion for the mere sensibility. But the judgment itself always remains in this case only aesthetical, because, without having any determinate concept of the object at its basis, it merely represents the subjective play of the mental powers (imagination and reason) as harmonious through their very contrast. For just as imagination and *understanding,* in judging of the beautiful, generate a subjective purposiveness of the mental powers by means of their harmony, so in this case imagination and *reason* do so by means of their conflict. That is, they bring about a feeling that we possess pure self-subsistent reason, or a faculty for the estimation of magnitude, whose superiority can be made intuitively evident only by the inadequacy of that faculty [imagination] which is itself unbounded in the presentation of magnitudes (of sensible objects).

The measurement of a space (regarded as apprehension) is at the same time a description of it, and thus an objective movement in the act of imagination and a progress. On the other hand, the comprehension of the manifold in the unity—not of thought but of intuition—and consequently the comprehension of the successively apprehended [elements] in one glance is a regress which annihilates the condition of time in this progress of the imagination and makes *coexistence* intuitible. It is therefore (since the time series is a condition of the internal sense and of an intuition) a subjective movement of the imagination, by which it does violence to the internal sense; this must be the more noticeable, the greater the quantum is which the imagination comprehends in one intuition. The effort, therefore, to receive in one single intuition a measure for magnitude that requires a considerable time to apprehend is a kind of representation which, subjectively con-

sidered, is contrary to purpose; but objectively, as requisite for the estimation of magnitude, it is purposive. Thus that very violence which is done to the subject through the imagination is judged as purposive *in reference to the whole determination* of the mind.

The *quality* of the feeling of the sublime is that it is a feeling of pain in reference to the faculty by which we judge aesthetically of an object, which pain, however, is represented at the same time as purposive. This is possible through the fact that the very incapacity in question discovers the consciousness of an unlimited faculty of the same subject, and that the mind can only judge of the latter aesthetically by means of the former.

In the logical estimation of magnitude, the impossibility of ever arriving at absolute totality, by means of the progress of the measurement of things of the sensible world in time and space, was cognized as objective, i.e. as an impossibility of *thinking* the infinite as entirely given, and not as merely subjective or that there was only an incapacity to *grasp* it. For there we have not to do with the degree of comprehension in an intuition, regarded as a measure, but everything depends on a concept of number. But in aesthetical estimation of magnitude, the concept of number must disappear or be changed, and the comprehension of the imagination in reference to the unit of measure (thus avoiding the concepts of a law of the successive production of concepts of magnitude) is alone purposive for it. If now a magnitude almost reaches the limit of our faculty of comprehension in an intuition, and yet the imagination is invited by means of numerical magnitudes (in respect of which we are conscious that our faculty is unbounded) to aesthetical comprehension in a greater unit, then we mentally feel ourselves confined aesthetically within bounds. But nevertheless the pain in regard to the necessary extension of the imagination for accordance with that which is unbounded in our faculty of reason, viz. the idea of the absolute whole, and consequently the very unpurposiveness of the faculty of imagination for rational ideas and the arousing of them, are represented as purposive. Thus it is that the aesthetical judgment itself is subjectively purposive for the reason as the source of ideas, i.e. as the source of an intellectual comprehension for which all aesthetical comprehension is small, and there accompanies the reception of an object as sublime a pleasure, which is only possible through the medium of a pain.

Of the Dynamically Sublime in Nature

§ 28. OF NATURE REGARDED AS MIGHT

Might is that which is superior to great hindrances. It is called *dominion* if it is superior to the resistance of that which itself possesses might. Nature, considered in an aesthetical judgment as might that has no dominion over us, is *dynamically sublime*.

If nature is to be judged by us as dynamically sublime, it must be represented as exciting fear (although it is not true conversely that every object which excites fear is regarded in our aesthetical judgment as sublime). For in aesthetical judgments (without the aid of concepts) superiority to hindrances can only be judged according to the greatness of the resistance. Now that which we are driven to resist is an evil and, if we do not find our faculties a match for it, is an object of fear. Hence nature can be regarded by the aesthetical judgment as might, and consequently as dynamically sublime, only so far as it is considered an object of fear.

But we can regard an object as *fearful* without being afraid *of* it, viz. if we judge of it in such a way that we merely *think* a case in which we would wish to resist it and yet in which all resistance would be altogether vain. Thus the virtuous man fears God without being afraid of Him, because to wish to resist Him and His commandments he thinks is a case that need cause *him* no concern. But in every such case that he thinks as not intrinsically impossible, he cognizes Him as fearful.

He who fears can form no judgment about the sublime in nature, just as he who is seduced by inclination and appetite can form no judgment about the beautiful. The former flies from the sight of an object which inspires him with awe, and it is impossible to find satisfaction in a terror that is seriously felt. Hence the pleasurableness arising from the cessation of an uneasiness is *a state of joy*. But this, because of the deliverance from a danger, is a state of joy when conjoined with the resolve that we shall never again be exposed to the danger; we cannot willingly look back upon our sensations of danger, much less seek the occasion for them again.

Bold, overhanging, and as it were threatening rocks; clouds piled up in the sky, moving with lightning flashes and thunder peals; volcanoes in all their violence of destruction; hurricanes with their track of devastation; the boundless ocean in a state of tumult; the lofty waterfall of a mighty river, and the like—these exhibit our faculty of resistance as insignificantly small in comparison with their might. But the sight of them is the more attractive, the more fearful it is, provided only that we are in security; and we willingly call these objects sublime, because they raise the energies of the soul above their accustomed height and discover in us a faculty of resistance of a quite different kind, which gives us courage to measure ourselves against the apparent almightiness of nature.

Now, in the immensity of nature and in the inadequacy of our faculties to take in a standard proportionate to the aesthetical estimation of the magnitude of its *realm*, we find our own limitation, although at the same time in our rational faculty we find a different, nonsensuous standard, which has that infinity itself under it as a unity, in comparison with which everything in nature is small, and thus in our mind we find a superiority to nature even in its immensity. And so also the irresistibility of its might, while making us recognize our own physical impotence, considered as beings of nature, discloses to us a faculty of judging independently of and a superiority over nature, on which is based a kind of self-preservation entirely different from that which can be attacked and brought into danger by external nature. Thus humanity in our person remains unhumiliated, though the individual might have to submit to this dominion. In this way nature is not judged to be sublime in our aesthetical judgments in so far as it excites fear, but because it calls up that power in us (which is not nature) of regarding as small the things about which we are solicitous (goods, health, and life), and of regarding its might (to which we are no doubt subjected in respect of these things) as nevertheless without any dominion over us and our personality to which we must bow where our highest fundamental propositions, and their assertion or abandonment, are concerned. Therefore nature is here called sublime merely because it elevates the imagination to a presentation of those cases in which the mind can make felt the proper sublimity of its destination, in comparison with nature itself.

This estimation of ourselves loses nothing through the fact that we must regard ourselves as safe in order to feel this inspiriting satisfaction and that hence, as there is no seriousness in the danger, there might be also (as might seem to be the case) just as little seriousness in the sublimity of our spiritual faculty. For the satisfaction here concerns only the *destination* of our faculty which discloses itself in such a case, so far as the tendency to this destination lies in our nature, while its development and exercise remain incumbent and obligatory. And in this there is truth, however conscious the man may be of his present actual powerlessness, when he turns his reflection to it.

No doubt this principle seems to be too farfetched and too subtly reasoned, and consequently seems to go beyond the scope of an aesthetical judgment; but observation of men proves the opposite and shows that it may lie at the root of the most ordinary judgments, although we are not always conscious of it. For what is that which is, even to the savage, an object of the greatest admiration? It is a man who shrinks from nothing, who fears nothing, and therefore does not yield to danger, but rather goes to face it vigorously and in complete deliberation. Even in the most highly civilized state this peculiar veneration for the soldier remains, though only under the condition that he exhibit all the virtues of peace, gentleness, compassion, and even a becoming care for his own person; because even by these it is recognized that his mind is unsubdued by danger. Hence whatever disputes there may be about the superiority of the respect which is to be accorded them, in the comparison of a statesman and a general, the aesthetical judgment decides for the latter. War itself, if it is carried on with order and with a sacred respect for the rights of citizens, has something sublime in it, and makes the disposition of the people who carry it on thus only the more sublime, the more numerous are the dangers to which they are exposed and in respect of which they behave with courage. On the other hand, a long peace generally brings about a predominant commercial spirit and, along with it, low selfishness, cowardice, and effeminacy, and debases the disposition of the people.

It appears to conflict with this solution of the concept of the sublime, so far as sublimity is ascribed to might, that we are accustomed to represent God as presenting Himself in His wrath and yet in His sublimity, in the tempest, the storm, the earthquake, etc.; and that it would be foolish and criminal to imagine a superiority of our minds over these works of His and, as it seems, even over the designs of such might.

Hence it would appear that no feeling of the sublimity of our own nature, but rather subjection, abasement, and a feeling of complete powerlessness, is a fitting state of mind in the presence of such an object; and this is generally bound up with the idea of it during natural phenomena of this kind. In religion in general, prostration, adoration with bent head, with contrite, anxious demeanor and voice, seems to be the only fitting behavior in presence of the Godhead, and hence most peoples have adopted and still observe it. But this state of mind is far from being necessarily bound up with the idea of the *sublimity* of a religion and its object. The man who is actually afraid, because he finds reasons for fear in himself, while conscious by his culpable disposition of offending against a might whose will is irresistible and at the same time just, is not in the frame of mind for admiring the divine greatness. For this a mood of calm contemplation and a quite free judgment are needed. Only if he is conscious of an upright disposition pleasing to God do those operations of might serve to awaken in him the idea of the sublimity of this Being, for then he recognizes in himself a sublimity of disposition conformable to His will; and thus he is raised above the fear of such operations of nature, which he no longer regards as outbursts of His wrath. Even humility, in the shape of a stern judgment upon his own faults—which otherwise, with a consciousness of good intentions, could be easily palliated from the frailty of human nature— is a sublime state of mind, consisting in a voluntary subjection of himself to the pain of remorse, in order that the causes of this may be gradually removed. In this way religion is essentially distinguished from superstition. The latter establishes in the mind, not reverence for the sublime, but fear and apprehension of the all-powerful Being to whose will the terrified man sees himself subject, without according Him any high esteem. From this nothing can arise but a seeking of favor and flattery, instead of a religion which consists in a good life.[15]

Sublimity, therefore, does not reside in anything of nature, but only in our mind, in so far as we can become conscious that we are superior to nature within, and therefore also to nature without us (so far as it influences us). Everything that excites this feeling in us, e.g. the *might* of nature which calls forth our forces, is called then (although improperly) sublime. Only by supposing this idea in ourselves and in reference to it are we capable of attaining to the idea of the sublimity of that Being which produces respect in us, not merely by the might that it displays in nature, but rather by means of the faculty which resides in us of judging it fearlessly and of regarding our destination as sublime in respect of it.

§ 29. OF THE MODALITY OF THE JUDGMENT UPON THE SUBLIME IN NATURE

There are numberless beautiful things in nature about which we can assume and even expect, without being widely mistaken, the harmony of everyone's judgment with our own. But in respect of our judgment upon the sublime in nature, we cannot promise ourselves so easily the accordance of others. For a far greater culture, as well of the aesthetical judgment as of the cognitive faculties which lie at its basis, seems requisite in order to be able to pass judgment on this peculiarity of natural objects.

That the mind be attuned to feel the sublime postulates a susceptibility of the mind for ideas. For in the very inadequacy of nature to these latter, and thus only by presupposing them and by straining the imagination to use nature as a schema for

---

[15] [In the *Philosophical Theory of Religion*, Part 1, Kant, as here, divides "all religions into two classes—*favor-seeking* religion (mere worship) and *moral* religion, that is, the religion *of a good life*"; and he concludes that "amongst all the public religions that have ever existed the Christian alone is moral."—TR. NOTE.]

them, is to be found that which is terrible to sensibility and yet is attractive. [It is attractive] because reason exerts a dominion over sensibility in order to extend it in conformity with its proper realm (the practical) and to make it look out into the infinite, which is for it an abyss. In fact, without development of moral ideas, that which we, prepared by culture, call sublime presents itself to the uneducated man merely as terrible. In the indications of the dominion of nature in destruction, and in the great scale of its might, in comparison with which his own is a vanishing quantity, he will only see the misery, danger, and distress which surround the man who is exposed to it. So the good, and indeed intelligent, Savoyard peasant (as M. de Saussure[16] relates) unhesitatingly called all lovers of snow-mountains fools. And who knows whether he would have been so completely wrong if Saussure had undertaken the danger to which he exposed himself merely, as most travelers do, from amateur curiosity, or that he might be able to give a pathetic account of them? But his design was the instruction of men, and this excellent man gave the readers of his travels soul-stirring sensations such as he himself had, into the bargain.

But although the judgment upon the sublime in nature needs culture (more than the judgment upon the beautiful), it is not therefore primarily produced by culture and introduced in a merely conventional way into society. Rather has it its root in human nature, even in that which, alike with common understanding, we can impute to and expect of everyone, viz. in the tendency to the feeling for (practical) ideas, i.e. to what is moral.

Hereon is based the necessity of that agreement of the judgment of others about the sublime with our own which we include in the latter. For just as we charge with

want of *taste* the man who is indifferent when passing judgment upon an object of nature that we regard as beautiful, so we say of him who remains unmoved in the presence of that which we judge to be sublime: he has no *feeling*. But we claim both from every man, and we presuppose them in him if he has any culture at all—only with the difference that we expect the former directly of everyone because in it the judgment refers the imagination merely to the understanding, the faculty of concepts; but the latter because in it the imagination is related to the reason, the faculty of ideas, only under a subjective presupposition (which, however, we believe we are authorized in imputing to everyone), viz. the presupposition of the moral feeling in man. Thus it is that we ascribe necessity to this aesthetical judgment also.

In this modality of aesthetical judgments, viz. in the necessity claimed for them, lies an important moment of the critique of judgment. For it enables us to recognize in them an *a priori* principle, and raises them out of empirical psychology, in which otherwise they would remain buried among the feelings of gratification and grief (only with the unmeaning addition of being called *finer* feelings). Thus it enables us too to place the judgment among those faculties that have *a priori* principles at their basis, and so to bring it into transcendental philosophy. . . .

III. Art and the Artist

§ 43. OF ART IN GENERAL

1. *Art* is distinguished from *nature* as doing (*facere*) is distinguished from acting or working generally (*agere*), and as the product or result of the former is distinguished as work (*opus*) from the working (*effectus*) of the latter.

By right we ought only to describe as art, production through freedom, i.e. through a will that places reason at the basis of its actions. For although we like to call the

---

16 [H. B. de Saussure, *Voyages dans les Alpes.* Volume I was published at Neuchâtel, in 1779; Volume II at Geneva, in 1786.—TR. NOTE.]

product of bees (regularly built cells of wax) a work of art, this is only by way of analogy; as soon as we feel that this work of theirs is based on no proper rational deliberation, we say that it is a product of nature (of instinct), and as art only ascribe it to their Creator.

If, as sometimes happens, in searching through a bog we come upon a bit of shaped wood, we do not say, this is a product of nature, but of art. Its producing cause has conceived a purpose to which the wood owes its form. Elsewhere too we should see art in everything which is made, so that a representation of it in its cause must have preceded its actual existence (as even in the case of the bees), though without the effect of it even being capable of being *thought*. But if we call anything absolutely a work of art, in order to distinguish it from a natural effect, we always understand by that a work of man.

2. Art regarded as human skill differs from *science* (as *can* from *know*) as a practical faculty does from a theoretical, as technique does from theory (as mensuration from geometry). And so what we *can* do, as soon as we merely *know* what ought to be done and therefore are sufficiently cognizant of the desired effect, is not called art. Only that which a man, even if he knows it completely, may not therefore have the skill to accomplish belongs to art. Camper[17] describes very exactly how the best shoes must be made, but he certainly could not make one.[18]

3. Art also differs from *handicraft;* the first is called "free," the other may be called "mercenary." We regard the first as if it could only prove purposive as play, i.e. as occupation that is pleasant in itself. But the second is regarded as if it could only be compulsorily imposed upon one as work, i.e. as occupation which is unpleasant (a trouble) in itself and which is only attractive on account of its effect (e.g. the wage). Whether or not in the grade of the professions we ought to count watchmakers as artists, but smiths only as handicraftsmen, would require another point of view from which to judge than that which we are here taking up, viz. [we should have to consider] the proportion of talents which must be assumed requisite in these several occupations. Whether or not, again, under the so-called seven free arts, some may be included which ought to be classed as sciences and many that are akin rather to handicraft I shall not here discuss. But it is not inexpedient to recall that, in all free arts, there is yet requisite something compulsory or, as it is called, mechanism, without which the spirit, which must be free in art and which alone inspires the work, would have no body and would evaporate altogether; e.g. in poetry there must be an accuracy and wealth of language, and also prosody and measure. [It is not inexpedient, I say, to recall this], for many modern educators believe that the best way to produce a free art is to remove it from all constraint, and thus to change it from work into mere play.

§ 44. OF FINE ART

There is no science of the beautiful, but only a critique of it; and there is no such thing as beautiful science, but only beautiful art.[19] For as regards the first point, if it

---

[17] [Peter Camper (1722–1789), a celebrated naturalist and comparative anatomist, for some years professor at Groningen.—TR. NOTE.]

[18] In my country the common man, if you propose to him such a problem as that of Columbus with his egg, says, "That is not art, it is only science." That is, if we *know* how, we can *do* it; and he says the same of all the pretended arts of jugglers. On the other hand, he will not refuse to apply the term "art" to the performance of a rope dancer.

[19] [The expressions "beautiful science" (*schöne Wissenschaft*) and "beautiful art" (*schöne Kunst*), both of them awkward and unidiomatic in English, must of course be retained occasionally in the translation to convey the argument. The latter of these expressions is properly rendered by "fine art." The former denotes especially what are called the humanities, considered as a division of knowledge coordinate with the natural sciences.—ED. NOTE.]

could be decided scientifically, i.e. by proofs, whether a thing was to be regarded as beautiful or not, the judgment upon beauty would belong to science and would not be a judgment of taste. And as far as the second point is concerned, a science which should be beautiful as such is a nonentity. For if in such a science we were to ask for grounds and proofs, we would be put off with tasteful phrases (*bon mots*). The source of the common expression, *beautiful science,* is without doubt nothing else than this, as it has been rightly remarked, that for fine art in its entire completeness much science is requisite, e.g. a knowledge of ancient languages, a learned familiarity with classical authors, history, a knowledge of antiquities, etc. And hence these historical sciences, because they form the necessary preparation and basis for fine art, and also partly because under them is included the knowledge of the products of fine art (rhetoric and poetry), have come to be called beautiful sciences by a transposition of words.

If art which is adequate to the *cognition* of a possible object performs the actions requisite therefore merely in order to make it actual, it is *mechanical* art; but if it has for its immediate design the feeling of pleasure, it is called *aesthetical* art. This is again either *pleasant* or *beautiful*. It is the first if its purpose is that the pleasure should accompany the representations [of the object] regarded as mere *sensations;* it is the second if they are regarded as *modes of cognition.*

Pleasant arts are those that are directed merely to enjoyment. Of this class are all those charming arts that can gratify a company at table, e.g. the art of telling stories in an entertaining way, of starting the company in frank and lively conversation, of raising them by jest and laugh to a certain pitch of merriment;[20] when, as people say,

there may be a great deal of gossip at the feast, but no one will be answerable for what he says, because they are only concerned with momentary entertainment, and not with any permanent material for reflection or subsequent discussion. (Among these are also to be reckoned the way of arranging the table for enjoyment and, at great feasts, the management of the music. This latter is a wonderful thing. It is meant to dispose to gaiety the minds of the guests, regarded solely as a pleasant noise, without anyone paying the least attention to its composition; and it favors the free conversation of each with his neighbor.) Again, to this class belong all games which bring with them no further interest than that of making the time pass imperceptibly.

On the other hand, fine art is a mode of representation which is purposive for itself and which, although devoid of [definite] purpose, yet furthers the culture of the mental powers in reference to social communication.

The universal communicability of pleasure carries with it in its very concept that the pleasure is not one of enjoyment, from mere sensation, but must be derived from reflection; and thus aesthetical art, as the art of beauty, has for standard the reflective judgment and not sensation.

§ 45. FINE ART IS ART IN SO FAR AS IT SEEMS LIKE NATURE

In a product of fine art, we must become conscious that it is art and not nature; but yet the purposiveness in its form must seem to be as free from all constraint of arbitrary rules as if it were a product of mere nature. On this feeling of freedom in the play of our cognitive faculties, which must at the same time be purposive, rests that pleasure which alone is universally communicable,

---

20 [Kant was accustomed to say that the talk at a dinner table should always pass through these three stages: narrative, discussion, and jest; and

punctilious in this, as in all else, he is said to have directed the conversation at his own table accordingly (William Wallace, *Kant,* Edinburgh: William Blackwood & Sons, Ltd., 1882, p. 39).—TR. NOTE.]

without being based on concepts. Nature is beautiful because it looks like art, and art can only be called beautiful if we are conscious of it as art while yet it looks like nature.

For whether we are dealing with natural or with artificial beauty, we can say generally: *That is beautiful which pleases in the mere act of judging it* (not in the sensation of it or by means of a concept). Now art has always a definite design of producing something. But if this something were bare sensation (something merely subjective), which is to be accompanied with pleasure, the product would please in the act of judgment only by mediation of sensible feeling. And again, if the design were directed toward the production of a definite object, then, if this were attained by art, the object would only please by means of concepts. But in both cases the art would not please *in the mere act of judging,* i.e. it would not please as beautiful but as mechanical.

Hence the purposiveness in the product of fine art, although it is designed, must not seem to be designed, i.e. fine art must *look* like nature, although we are conscious of it as art. But a product of art appears like nature when, although its agreement with the rules, according to which alone the product can become what it ought to be, is *punctiliously* observed, yet this is not *painfully* apparent; [the form of the schools does not obtrude itself]—it shows no trace of the rule having been before the eyes of the artist and having fettered his mental powers.

§ 46. FINE ART IS THE ART OF GENIUS

Genius is the talent (or natural gift) which gives the rule to art. Since talent, as the innate productive faculty of the artist, belongs itself to nature, we may express the matter thus: Genius is the innate mental disposition (*ingenium*) through which nature gives the rule to art.

Whatever may be thought of this definition, whether it is merely arbitrary or whether it is adequate to the concept that we are accustomed to combine with the word *genius* (which is to be examined in the following paragraphs), we can prove already beforehand that, according to the signification of the word here adopted, the fine arts must necessarily be considered as arts of *genius*.

For every art presupposes rules by means of which in the first instance a product, if it is to be called artistic, is represented as possible. But the concept of fine art does not permit the judgment upon the beauty of a product to be derived from any rule which has a *concept* as its determining ground, and therefore has at its basis a concept of the way in which the product is possible. Therefore fine art cannot itself devise the rule according to which it can bring about its product. But since at the same time a product can never be called art without some precedent rule, nature in the subject must (by the harmony of its faculties) give the rule to art; i.e. fine art is only possible as a product of genius.

We thus see (1) that genius is a *talent* for producing that for which no definite rule can be given; it is not a mere aptitude for what can be learned by a rule. Hence *originality* must be its first property. (2) But since it also can produce original nonsense, its products must be models, i.e. *exemplary,* and they consequently ought not to spring from imitation, but must serve as a standard or rule of judgment for others. (3) It cannot describe or indicate scientifically how it brings about its products, but it gives the rule just as nature does. Hence the author of a product for which he is indebted to his genius does not know himself how he has come by his ideas; and he has not the power to devise the like at pleasure or in accordance with a plan, and to communicate it to others in precepts that will enable them to produce similar products. (Hence it is probable that the word "genius" is derived from *genius,* that peculiar guiding and guardian spirit given to a man at his birth, from whose suggestion these original ideas proceed.)[21] (4) Nature, by the medium of genius, does not prescribe rules to science but to art, and to it only in so far as it is to be fine art.

§ 47. ELUCIDATION AND CONFIRMATION OF THE ABOVE EXPLANATION OF GENIUS

Everyone is agreed that genius is entirely opposed to the *spirit of imitation.* Now since learning is nothing but imitation, it follows that the greatest ability and teachableness (capacity) regarded *qua* teachableness cannot avail for genius. Even if a man thinks or composes for himself and does not merely take in what others have taught, even if he discovers many things in art and science, this is not the right ground for calling such a (perhaps great) *head* a genius (as opposed to him who, because he can only learn and imitate, is called a *shallowpate*). For even these things could be learned; they lie in the natural path of him who investigates and reflects according to rules, and they do not differ specifically from what can be acquired by industry through imitation. Thus we can readily learn all that Newton has set forth in his immortal work on the *Principles of Natural Philosophy,* however great a head was required to discover it, but we cannot learn to write spirited poetry, however express may be the precepts of the art and however excellent its models. The reason is that Newton could make all his steps, from the first elements of geometry to his own great and profound discoveries, intuitively plain and definite as regards consequence, not only to himself but to everyone else. But a Homer or a Wieland cannot show how his

ideas, so rich in fancy and yet so full of thought, come together in his head, simply because he does not know and therefore cannot teach others. In science, then, the greatest discoverer only differs in degree from his laborious imitator and pupil, but he differs specifically from him whom nature has gifted for fine art. And in this there is no depreciation of those great men to whom the human race owes so much gratitude, as compared with nature's favorites in respect of the talent for fine art. For in the fact that the former talent is directed to the ever advancing greater perfection of knowledge and every advantage depending on it, and at the same time to the imparting this same knowledge to others—in this it has a great superiority over [the talent of] those who deserve the honor of being called geniuses. For art stands still at a certain point; a boundary is set to it beyond which it cannot go, which presumably has been reached long ago and cannot be extended further. Again, artistic skill cannot be communicated; it is imparted to every artist immediately by the hand of nature; and so it dies with him, until nature endows another in the same way, so that he only needs an example in order to put in operation in a similar fashion the talent of which he is conscious.

If now it is a natural gift which must prescribe its rule to art (as fine art), of what kind is this rule? It cannot be reduced to a formula and serve as a precept, for then the judgment upon the beautiful would be determinable according to concepts; but the rule must be abstracted from the fact, i.e. from the product, on which others may try their own talent by using it as a model, not to be *copied* but to be *emulated.* How this is possible is hard to explain. The ideas of the artist excite like ideas in his pupils if nature has endowed them with a like proportion of their mental powers. Hence models of fine art are the only means of handing down these ideas to posterity. This

---

21 [I.e. the German word *Genie* is derived from the Latin *Genius,* a tutelary deity or spirit.—ED. NOTE.]

cannot be done by mere descriptions, especially not in the case of the arts of speech; and in this latter classical models are only to be had in the old dead languages, now preserved only as "the learned languages."

Although mechanical and fine art are very different, the first being a mere art of industry and learning and the second of genius, yet there is no fine art in which there is not a mechanical element that can be comprehended by rules and followed accordingly, and in which therefore there must be something *scholastic* as an essential condition. For [in every art] some purpose must be conceived; otherwise we could not ascribe the product to art at all; it would be a mere product of chance. But in order to accomplish a purpose, definite rules from which we cannot dispense ourselves are requisite. Now since the originality of the talent constitutes an essential (though not the only) element in the character of genius, shallow heads believe that they cannot better show themselves to be full-blown geniuses than by throwing off the constraint of all rules; they believe, in effect, that one could make a braver show on the back of a wild horse than on the back of a trained animal. Genius can only furnish rich *material* for products of fine art; its execution and its *form* require talent cultivated in the schools, in order to make such a use of this material as will stand examination by the judgment. But it is quite ridiculous for a man to speak and decide like a genius in things which require the most careful investigation by reason. One does not know whether to laugh more at the impostor who spreads such a mist round him that we cannot clearly use our judgment, and so use our imagination the more, or at the public which naïvely imagines that his inability to cognize clearly and to comprehend the masterpiece before him arises from new truths crowding in on him in such abundance that details (duly weighed definitions and accurate examination of fundamental propositions) seem but clumsy work.

§ 48. OF THE RELATION OF GENIUS TO TASTE

For *judging* of beautiful objects as such, *taste* is requisite; but for fine art, i.e. for the *production* of such objects, *genius* is requisite.

If we consider genius as the talent for fine art (which the special meaning of the word implies) and in this point of view analyze it into the faculties which must concur to constitute such a talent, it is necessary in the first instance to determine exactly the difference between natural beauty, the judging of which requires only taste, and artificial beauty, the possibility of which (to which reference must be made in judging such an object) requires genius.

A natural beauty is a *beautiful thing;* artificial beauty is a *beautiful representation* of a thing.

In order to judge of a natural beauty as such, I need not have beforehand a concept of what sort of thing the object is to be; i.e. I need not know its material purposiveness (the purpose), but its mere form pleases by itself in the act of judging it without any knowledge of the purpose. But if the object is given as a product of art and as such is to be declared beautiful, then, because art always supposes a purpose in the cause (and its causality), there must be at bottom in the first instance a concept of what the thing is to be. And as the agreement of the manifold in a thing with its inner destination, its purpose, constitutes the perfection of the thing, it follows that in judging of artificial beauty the perfection of the thing must be taken into account; but in judging of natural beauty (as such) there is no question at all about this. It is true that in judging of objects of nature, especially objects endowed with life, e.g. a man or a horse, their objective purposiveness also is commonly taken into consideration in judging of their beauty; but then the judgment is no longer purely aesthetical, i.e. a mere judgment of taste. Nature is no longer judged inasmuch as it appears like art, but in so far as it *is* actual (although superhuman) art; and the teleological judgment serves as the basis and condition of the aesthetical, as a condition to which the latter must have respect. In such a case, e.g. if it is said "That is a beautiful woman," we think nothing else than this; nature represents in her figure the purposes in view in the shape of a woman's figure. For we must look beyond the mere form to a concept, if the object is to be thought in such a way by means of a logically conditioned aesthetical judgment.

Fine art shows its superiority in this, that it depicts as beautiful things which may be in nature ugly or displeasing. The Furies, diseases, the devastations of war, etc., may, even regarded as calamitous,[22] be described as very beautiful, as they are represented in a picture. There is only one kind of ugliness which cannot be represented in accordance with nature without destroying all aesthetical satisfaction, and consequently artificial beauty, viz. that which excites *disgust*. For in this singular sensation, which rests on mere imagination, the object is represented as it were obtruding itself for our enjoyment, while we strive against it with all our might. And the artistic representation of the object is no longer distinguished from the nature of the object itself in our sensation, and thus it is impossible that it can be regarded as beautiful. The art of sculpture again, because in its products art is almost

interchangeable with nature, excludes from its creations the immediate representation of ugly objects; e.g. it represents death by a beautiful genius, the warlike spirit by Mars, and permits [all such things] to be represented only by an allegory or attribute that has a pleasing effect, and thus only indirectly by the aid of the interpretation of reason, and not for the mere aesthetical judgment.

So much for the beautiful representation of an object, which is properly only the form of the presentation of a concept, by means of which this latter is communicated universally. But to give this form to the product of fine art, mere taste is requisite. By taste the artist estimates his work after he has exercised and corrected it by manifold examples from art or nature, and after many, often toilsome, attempts to content himself he finds that form which satisfies him. Hence this form is not, as it were, a thing of inspiration or the result of a free swing of the mental powers, but of a slow and even painful process of improvement, by which he seeks to render it adequate to his thought, without detriment to the freedom of the play of his powers.

But taste is merely a judging and not a productive faculty, and what is appropriate to it is therefore not a work of fine art. It can only be a product belonging to useful and mechanical art or even to science, produced according to definite rules that can be learned and must be exactly followed. But the pleasing form that is given to it is only the vehicle of communication and a mode, as it were, of presenting it, in respect of which we remain free to a certain extent, although it is combined with a definite purpose. Thus we desire that table appointments, a moral treatise, even a sermon, should have in themselves this form of fine art, without it seeming to be *sought;* but we do not therefore call these things works of fine art. Under the latter class are reckoned a poem, a piece of music, a picture

---

22 [Cf. Aristotle, *Poetics,* IV, 1448[b]: "It is natural for all to delight in works of imitation... Though the objects themselves may be painful to see, we delight to view the most realistic representations of them in art, the forms for example of the lowest animals and of dead bodies." Cf. also Aristotle, *Rhetoric,* I, 11. 1371[b], and Edmund Burke, *On the Sublime and Beautiful,* Part I, § 16. Boileau, *L'Art poétique,* Chant 3, makes a similar observation: "There is no snake or odious monster which may not be pleasing to the eyes if it is skillfully represented. With a subtle brush, graceful art can make a winsome thing of the most horrific subject."—ED. NOTE.]

gallery, etc.; and in some works of this kind asserted to be works of fine art we find genius without taste, while in others we find taste without genius.

§ 49. OF THE FACULTIES OF THE MIND THAT CONSTITUTE GENIUS

We say of certain products of which we expect that they should at least in part appear as fine art, they are without *spirit*,[23] although we find nothing to blame in them on the score of taste. A poem may be very neat and elegant, but without spirit. A history may be exact and well arranged, but without spirit. A festal discourse may be solid and at the same time elaborate, but without spirit. Conversation is often not devoid of entertainment, but it is without spirit; even of a woman we say that she is pretty, an agreeable talker, and courteous, but without spirit. What then do we mean by spirit?

Spirit, in an aesthetical sense, is the name given to the animating principle of the mind. But that by means of which this principle animates the soul, the material which it applies to that [purpose], is what puts the mental powers purposively into swing, i.e. into such a play as maintains itself and strengthens the mental powers in their exercise.

Now I maintain that this principle is no other than the faculty of presenting *aesthetical ideas*. And by an aesthetical idea I understand that representation of the imagination which occasions much thought, without however any definite thought, i.e. any *concept*, being capable of being adequate to it; it consequently cannot be completely compassed and made intelligible by language. We easily see that it is the counterpart (pendant) of a *rational idea,* which

conversely is a concept to which no *intuition* (or representation of the imagination) can be adequate.[24]

The imagination (as a productive faculty of cognition) is very powerful in creating another nature, as it were, out of the material that actual nature gives it. We entertain ourselves with it when experience becomes too commonplace, and by it we remold experience, always indeed in accordance with analogical laws, but yet also in accordance with principles which occupy a higher place in reason (laws, too, which are just as natural to us as those by which understanding comprehends empirical nature). Thus we feel our freedom from the law of association (which attaches to the empirical employment of imagination), so that the material supplied to us by nature in accordance with this law can be worked up into something different which surpasses nature.

Such representations of the imagination we may call *ideas,* partly because they at least strive after something which lies beyond the bounds of experience and so seek to approximate to a presentation of concepts of reason (intellectual ideas), thus giving to the latter the appearance of objective reality, but especially because no concept can be fully adequate to them as internal intuitions. The poet ventures to realize to sense, rational ideas of invisible beings, the kingdom of the blessed, hell, eternity, creation, etc.; or even if he deals with things of which there are examples in experience—e.g. death, envy and all vices, also love, fame, and the like—he tries, by means of imagination, which emulates the play of reason in its quest after a maximum, to go beyond the limits of experience and to present them to sense with a complete-

---

[23] [In English we would rather say "without soul," but I (Bernard) prefer to translate *Geist* consistently by "spirit," to avoid the confusion of it with *Seele.*—TR. NOTE.]

[24] [In the *Critique of Pure Reason* (Transcendental Dialectic, Section 1, The Ideas in General), A321, B369 ff., Kant explains at length his use of the word "idea." That use is neither Plato's nor Locke's.—ED. NOTE.]

ness of which there is no example in nature. This is properly speaking the art of the poet, in which the faculty of aesthetical ideas can manifest itself in its entire strength. But this faculty, considered in itself, is properly only a talent (of the imagination).

If now we place under a concept a representation of the imagination belonging to its presentation, but which occasions solely by itself more thought than can ever be comprehended in a definite concept and which consequently aesthetically enlarges the concept itself in an unbounded fashion, the imagination is here creative, and it brings the faculty of intellectual ideas (the reason) into movement; i.e. a movement occasioned by a representation, toward more thought (though belonging, no doubt, to the concept of the object) than can be grasped in the representation or made clear.

Those forms which do not constitute the presentation of a given concept itself but only, as approximate representations of the imagination, express the consequences bound up with it and its relationship to other concepts, are called (aesthetical) *attributes* of an object whose concept as a rational idea cannot be adequately presented. Thus Jupiter's eagle with the lighting in its claws is an attribute of the mighty king of heaven, as the peacock is of his magnificent queen. They do not, like *logical attributes,* represent what lies in our concepts of the sublimity and majesty of creation, but something different, which gives occasion to the imagination to spread itself over a number of kindred representations that arouse more thought than can be expressed in a concept determined by words. They furnish an *aesthetical idea,* which for that rational idea takes the place of logical presentation; and thus, as their proper office, they enliven the mind by opening out to it the prospect into an illimitable field of kindred representations. But fine art does this not only in the case of painting or sculpture (in which the term "attribute" is commonly employed);

poetry and rhetoric also get the spirit that animates their works simply from the aesthetical attributes of the object, which accompany the logical and stimulate the imagination, so that it thinks more by their aid, although in an undeveloped way, than could be comprehended in a concept and therefore in a definite form of words. For the sake of brevity, I must limit myself to a few examples only.

When the great King in one of his poems expresses himself as follows:

> Oui, finissons sans trouble et mourons sans regrets,
> En laissant l'univers comblé de nos bienfaits.
> Ainsi l'astre du jour au bout de sa carrière,
> Répand sur l'horizon une douce lumière;
> Et les derniers rayons qu'il darde dans les airs,
> Sont les derniers soupirs qu'il donne à l'univers;[25]

he quickens his rational idea of a cosmopolitan disposition at the end of life by an attribute which the imagination (in remembering all the pleasures of a beautiful summer day that are recalled at its close by a serene evening) associates with that representation, and which excites a number of sensations and secondary representations for which no expression is found. On the other hand, an intellectual concept may serve conversely as an attribute for a representation of sense, and so can quicken this latter by means of the idea of the supersensible, but only by the aesthetical [element], that subjectively attaches to the concept of the latter, being here employed. Thus, for example, a certain poet says, in his description of a beautiful morning:

---

25 [See Prussian Academy Edition of Kant, V, 529. The verses by Frederick the Great, are in *Oeuvres de Frédéric le Grand,* X, 203. Freely rendered: "Ah, let us die calmly and without regret, leaving behind us the world enriched by our good deeds. So does the sun at day's end spread a gentle light across the heavens, its last rays a sigh for the world it leaves."—ED. NOTE.]

Die Sonne quoll hervor,
Wie Ruh' aus Tugend quillt.[26]

The consciousness of virtue, if we subsitute it in our thoughts for a virtuous man, diffuses in the mind a multitude of sublime and restful feelings, and a boundless prospect of a joyful future, to which no expression that is measured by a definite concept completely attains.[27]

In a word, the aesthetical idea is a representation of the imagination associated with a given concept, which is bound up with such a multiplicity of partial representations in its free employment that for it no expression marking a definite concept can be found; and such a representation, therefore, adds to a concept much ineffable thought, the feeling of which quickens the cognitive faculties, and with language, which is the mere letter, binds up spirit also.

The mental powers, therefore, whose union (in a certain relation) constitutes genius are imagination and understanding. In the employment of the imagination for cognition, it submits to the constraint of the understanding and is subject to the limitation of being conformable to the concept of the latter. On the contrary, in an aesthetical point of view it is free to furnish unsought, over and above that agreement with a concept, abundance of undeveloped material for the understanding, to which the understanding paid no regard in its concept but which it applies, though not objectively for cogni-

tion, yet subjectively to quicken the cognitive powers and therefore also indirectly to cognitions. Thus genius properly consists in the happy relation [between these faculties], which no science can teach and no industry can learn, by which ideas are found for a given concept; and, on the other hand, we thus find for these ideas the expression by means of which the subjective state of mind brought about by them, as an accompaniment of the concept, can be communicated to others. The latter talent is, properly speaking, what is called spirit; for to express the ineffable element in the state of mind implied by a certain representation and to make it universally communicable—whether the expression be in speech or painting or statuary—this requires a faculty of seizing the quickly passing play of imagination and of unifying it in a concept (which is even on that account original and discloses a new rule that could not have been inferred from any preceding principles or examples) that can be communicated without any constraint of rules.

If, after this analysis, we look back to the explanation given above of what is called *genius,* we find: first, that it is a talent for art, not for science, in which clearly known rules must go beforehand and determine the procedure. Secondly, as an artistic talent it presupposes a definite concept of the product as the purpose, and therefore understanding; but it also presupposes a representation (although an indeterminate one) of the material, i.e. of the intuition, for the presentment of this concept, and, therefore a relation between the imagination and the understanding. Thirdly, it shows itself, not so much in the accomplishment of the proposed purpose in a presentment of a definite *concept,* as in the enunciation or expression of aesthetical *ideas* which contain abundant material for that very design; and consequently it represents the imagination as free from all guid-

---

26 [J. P. L. Withof, *Akademische Gedichte* Leipzig, 1782, I, p. 70. "The sun arose, as calm from virtue rises."—ED. NOTE.]

27 Perhaps nothing more sublime was ever said and no sublimer thought ever expressed than the famous inscription on the Temple of Isis (Mother Nature): "I am all that is and that was and that shall be, and no mortal hath lifted my veil." Segner availed himself of this idea in a suggestive vignette prefixed to his *Natural Philosophy,* in order to inspire beforehand the pupil whom he was about to lead into that temple with a holy awe, which should dispose his mind to serious attention. [J. A. de Segner (1704–1777) was Professor of Natural Philosophy at Göttingen and the author of several scientific works of repute.—TR. NOTE.]

ance of rules and yet as purposive in reference to the presentment of the given concept. Finally, in the fourth place, the unsought undesigned subjective purposiveness in the free accordance of the imagination with the legality of the understanding presupposes such a proportion and disposition of these faculties as no following of rules, whether of science or of mechanical imitation, can bring about, but which only the nature of the subject can produce.

In accordance with these suppositions, genius is the exemplary originality of the natural gifts of a subject in the *free* employment of his cognitive faculties. In this way the product of a genius (as regards what is to be ascribed to genius and not to possible learning or schooling) is an example, not to be imitated (for then that which in it is genius and constitutes the spirit of the work would be lost), but to be followed by another genius, whom it awakens to a feeling of his own originality and whom it stirs so to exercise his art in freedom from the constraint of rules, that thereby a new rule is gained for art; and thus his talent shows itself to be exemplary. But because a genius is a favorite of nature and must be regarded by us as a rare phenomenon, his example produces for other good heads a school, i.e. a methodical system of teaching according to rules, so far as these can be derived from the peculiarities of the products of his spirit. For such persons fine art is so far imitation, to which nature through the medium of a genius supplied the rule.

But this imitation becomes a mere *aping* if the scholar *copies* everything down to the deformities, which the genius must have let pass only because he could not well remove them without weakening his idea. This mental characteristic is meritorious only in the case of a genius. A certain *audacity* in expression—and in general many a departure from common rules—becomes him well, but it is in no way worthy of imitation; it always remains a fault in itself which we must seek to remove, though the genius

is, as it were, privileged to commit it, because the inimitable rush of his spirit would suffer from overanxious carefulness. *Mannerism* is another kind of aping, viz. of mere *peculiarity* (originality) in general, by which a man separates himself as far as possible from imitators, without however possessing the talent to be at the same time *exemplary*. There are indeed in general two ways (*modi*) in which such a man may put together his notions of expressing himself; the one is called a *manner* (*modus aestheticus*), the other a *method* (*modus logicus*). They differ in this that the former has no other standard than the *feeling* of unity in the presentment, but the latter follows definite *principles;* hence the former alone avails for fine art. But an artistic product is said to show *mannerism* only when the exposition of the artist's idea is *founded* on its very singularity and is not made appropriate to the idea itself. The ostentatious (*précieux*), contorted, and affected [manner adopted] to differentiate oneself from ordinary persons (though devoid of spirit) is like the behavior of a man of whom we say that he hears himself talk, or who stands and moves about as if he were on a stage in order to be stared at; this always betrays a bungler.

§ 50. OF THE COMBINATION OF TASTE WITH GENIUS IN THE PRODUCTS OF FINE ART

To ask whether it is more important for the things of fine art that genius or taste should be displayed is the same as to ask whether in it more depends on imagination or on judgment. Now since in respect of the first an art is rather said to be *full of spirit,* but only deserves to be called a *fine* art on account of the second, this latter is at least, as its indispensable condition (*conditio sine qua non*), the most important thing to which one has to look in the judging of art as fine art. Abundance and originality of ideas are less necessary to beauty than the accordance of the imagination in its freedom with the conformity to law of the understanding. For all the abundance of the former produces in lawless freedom nothing but nonsense; on the other hand, the judgment is the faculty by which it is adjusted to the understanding.

Taste, like the judgment in general, is the discipline (or training) of genius; it clips its wings, it makes it cultured and polished; but, at the same time, it gives guidance as to where and how far it may extend itself if it is to remain purposive. And while it brings clearness and order into the multitude of the thoughts [of genius], it makes the ideas susceptible of being permanently and, at the same time, universally assented to, and capable of being followed by others, and of an ever progressive culture. If, then, in the conflict of these two properties in a product something must be sacrificed, it should be rather on the side of genius; and the judgment, which in the things of fine art gives its decision from its own proper principles, will rather sacrifice the freedom and wealth of the imagination than permit anything prejudicial to the understanding.

For fine art, therefore, *imagination, understanding, spirit,* and *taste* are requisite.[28]

§ 51. OF THE DIVISION OF THE FINE ARTS

We may describe beauty in general (whether natural or artificial) as the expression of aesthetical ideas; only that in fine art this idea must be occasioned by a concept of the object, while in beautiful nature the mere reflection upon a given intuition, without any concept of what the object is to be, is sufficient for the awakening and communicating of the idea of which that object is regarded as the expression.

If, then, we wish to make a division of the fine arts, we cannot choose a more convenient principle, at least tentatively, than the analogy of art with the mode of expression of which men avail themselves in speech, in order to communicate to one another as perfectly as possible not merely their concepts but also their sensations.[29] This is done by *word, deportment,* and *tone* (articulation, gesticulation, and modulation). It is only by the combination of these three kinds of expression that communication between the speaker [and his hearers] can be complete. For thus thought, intuition, and sensation are transmitted to others simultaneously and conjointly.

There are, therefore, only three kinds of fine arts: the arts of *speech,* the *formative* arts, and the art of the *play of sensations* (as external sensible impressions). We may also arrange a division by dichotomy: thus fine art may be divided into the art of expression of thoughts and of intuitions, and these further subdivided in accordance with their form or their matter (sensation). But this would appear to be too abstract, and not so accordant with ordinary concepts.

1. The *arts of speech* are *rhetoric* and *poetry. Rhetoric* is the art of carrying on a serious business of the understanding as if it were a free play of the imagination; *poetry,* the art of conducting a free play of the imagination as if it were a serious business of the understanding.

The *orator,* then, promises a serious business, and in order to entertain his audience conducts it as if it were a mere *play* with

---

28 The three former faculties are *united* in the first instance by means of the fourth. Hume gives us to understand in his *History of England* that although the English are inferior in their productions to no people in the world as regards the evidences they display of the three former properties, *separately* considered, yet they must be put after their neighbors the French as regards that which unites these properties. [In his *Observations on the Beautiful and Sublime,* § 4, Kant remarks that the English have the keener sense of the *sublime,* the French of the *beautiful.*—TR. NOTE.]

29 The reader is not to judge this scheme for a possible division of the fine arts as a deliberate theory. It is only one of various attempts which we may and ought to devise.

ideas. The *poet* merely promises an entertaining play with ideas, and yet it has the same effect upon the understanding as if he had only intended to carry on its business. The combination and harmony of both cognitive faculties, sensibility and understanding, which cannot dispense with each other but which yet cannot well be united without constraint and mutual prejudice, must appear to be undesigned and so to be brought about by themselves; otherwise it is not *fine* art. Hence, all that is studied and anxious must be avoided in it, for fine art must be free art in a double sense. It is not a work like a mercenary employment, the greatness of which can be judged according to a definite standard, which can be demanded or paid for; and again, though the mind is here occupied; it feels itself thus contented and aroused without looking to any other purpose (independently of reward).

The orator therefore gives something which he does not promise, viz. an entertaining play of the imagination; but he also fails to supply what he did promise, which is indeed his announced business, viz. the purposive occupation of the understanding. On the other hand, the poet promises little and announces a mere play with ideas; but he supplies something which is worth occupying ourselves with, because he provides in this play food for the understanding and, by the aid of imagination, gives life to his concepts. Thus the orator on the whole gives less, the poet more, than he promises.

2. The *formative arts*, or those by which expression is found for ideas in *sensible intuition* (not by representations of mere imagination that are aroused by words), are either arts of *sensible truth* or of *sensible illusion*. The former is called *plastic,* the latter *painting*. Both express ideas by figures in space: the former makes figures cognizable by two senses, sight and touch (although not by the latter as far as beauty is concerned); the latter only by one, the first

of these. The aesthetical idea (the archetype or original image) is fundamental for both in the imagination, but the figure which expresses this (the ectype or copy) is either given in its bodily extension (as the object itself exists) or as it paints itself on the eye (according to its appearance when projected on a flat surface). In the first case the condition given to reflection may be either the reference to an actual purpose or only the semblance of it.

To *plastic,* the first kind of beautiful formative art, belong *sculpture* and *architecture*. The first presents corporeally concepts of things, *as they might have existed in nature* (though as fine art it has regard to aesthetical purposiveness). The second is the art of presenting concepts of things that are possible *only through art* and whose form has for its determining ground, not nature, but an arbitrary purpose, with the view of presenting them with aesthetical purposiveness. In the latter the chief point is a certain *use* of the artistic object, by which condition the aesthetical ideas are limited. In the former the main design is the mere *expression* of aesthetical ideas. Thus statues of men, gods, animals, etc., are of the first kind; but temples, splendid buildings for public assemblies, even dwelling houses, triumphal arches, columns, mausoleums, and the like, erected in honorable remembrance, belong to architecture. Indeed all house furniture (upholsterer's work and such like things which are for use) may be reckoned under this art, because the suitability of a product for a certain use is the essential thing in an *architectural work*. On the other hand, a mere *piece of sculpture,* which is simply made for show and which is to please in itself, is as a corporeal presentation a mere imitation of nature, though with a reference to aesthetical ideas; in it *sensible truth* is not to be carried so far that the product ceases to look like art and a product of deliberate effort.

Painting, as the second kind of formative art, which presents a *sensible illusion* artificially combined with ideas, I would divide into the art of the beautiful *depiction of nature* and that of the beautiful *arrangement of its products*. The first is *painting proper*, the second is the art of *landscape gardening*. The first gives only the illusory appearance of corporeal extension; the second gives this in accordance with truth, but only the appearance of utility and availableness for other purposes than the mere play of the imagination in the contemplation of its forms.[30] This latter is nothing else than the ornamentation of the soil with a variety of those things (grasses, flowers, shrubs, trees, even ponds, hillocks, and dells) which nature presents to an observer, only arranged differently and in conformity with certain ideas. But, again, the beautiful arrangement of corporeal things is only apparent to the eye, like painting; the sense of touch cannot supply any intuitive presentation of such a form. Under painting in the wide sense I would reckon the decoration of rooms by the aid of tapestry, bric-a-brac, and all beautiful furniture which is merely available to be *looked* at; and the same may be said of the art of tasteful dressing (with rings, snuffboxes, etc.). For a bed of various flowers, a room filled with various ornaments (including under this head even ladies' finery), make at a fête a kind of picture which, like pictures

---

[30] That landscape gardening may be regarded as a species of the art of painting, although it presents its forms corporeally, seems strange. But since it actually takes its forms from nature (trees, shrubs, grasses, and flowers from forest and field—at least in the first instance) and so far is not an art like plastic, and since it also has no concept of the object and its purpose (as in architecture) conditioning its arrangements, but involves merely the free play of the imagination in contemplation, it so far agrees with mere aesthetical painting which has no definite theme (which arranges sky, land, and water so as to entertain us by means of light and shade only). In general the reader is only to judge of this as an attempt to combine the beautiful arts under one principle, viz. that of the expression of aesthetical ideas (according to the analogy of speech), and not to regard it as a definitive analysis of them.

properly so called (that are not intended to *teach* either history or natural science), has in view merely the entertainment of the imagination in free play with ideas and the occupation of the aesthetical judgment without any definite purpose. The detailed work in all this decoration may be quite distinct in the different cases and may require very different artists, but the judgment of taste upon whatever is beautiful in these various arts is always determined in the same way, viz. it only judges the forms (without any reference to a purpose) as they present themselves to the eye, either singly or in combination, according to the effect they produce upon the imagination. But that formative art may be compared (by analogy) with deportment in speech is justified by the fact that the spirit of the artist supplies by these figures a bodily expression to his thought and its mode, and makes the thing itself, as it were, speak in mimic language. This is a very common play of our fancy, which attributes to lifeless things a spirit suitable to their form by which they speak to us.

3. The art of the beautiful play of sensations (externally produced), which admits at the same time of universal communication, can be concerned with nothing else than the proportion of the different degrees of the disposition (tension) of the sense to which the sensation belongs, i.e. with its tone. In this far-reaching signification of the word it may be divided into the artistic play of the sensations of hearing and sight, i.e. into *music* and the *art of color*. It is noteworthy that these two senses, beside their susceptibility for impressions so far as these are needed to gain concepts of external objects, are also capable of a peculiar sensation bound up therewith of which we cannot strictly decide whether it is based on sense or reflection. This susceptibility may sometimes be wanting, although in other respects the sense, as regards its use for the cognition of objects, is not at all deficient but is peculiarly fine. That is, we

cannot say with certainty whether colors or tones (sounds) are merely pleasant sensations or whether they form in themselves a beautiful play of sensations, and as such bring with them in aesthetical judgment a satisfaction in the form [of the object]. If we think of the velocity of the vibrations of light or in the second case of the air, which probably far surpasses all our faculty of judging immediately in perception the time interval between them, we must believe that it is only the *effect* of these vibrations upon the elastic parts of our body that is felt, but that the *time interval* between them is not remarked or brought into judgment; and thus that only pleasantness, and not beauty of composition, is bound up with colors and tones. But on the other hand, first, we think of the mathematical [element] which enables us to pronounce on the proportion between these oscillations in music and thus to judge of them; and by analogy with which we easily may judge of the distinctions between colors. Secondly, we recall instances (although they are rare) of men who, with the best sight in the world, cannot distinguish colors and, with the sharpest hearing, cannot distinguish tones; while for those who can do this the perception of an altered quality (not merely of the degree of sensation) in the different intensities in the scale of colors and tones is definite; and further, the very number of these is fixed by *intelligible* differences. Thus we may be compelled to see that both kinds of sensations are to be regarded, not as mere sensible impressions, but as the effects of a judgment passed upon the form in the play of divers sensations. The difference in our definition, according as we adopt the one or the other opinion in judging of the grounds of music, would be just this: either, as we have done, we must explain it as the beautiful play of sensations (of hearing), or else as a play of *pleasant* sensations. According to the former mode of explanation, music is represented altogether as a fine art; according to the latter, as a *pleasant* art (at least in part).

§ 52. OF THE COMBINATION OF THE FINE ARTS IN ONE AND THE SAME PRODUCT

Rhetoric may be combined with a pictorial presentation of its subjects and objects in a *theatrical piece*; poetry may be combined with music in a *song,* and this again with pictorial (theatrical) presentation in an *opera*; the play of sensations in music may be combined with the play of figures in the *dance,* and so on. Even the presentation of the sublime, so far as it belongs to fine art, may combine with beauty in a *tragedy in verse,* in a *didactic poem,* in an *oratorio*; and in these combinations fine art is yet more artistic. Whether it is also more beautiful may in some of these cases be doubted (since so many different kinds of satisfaction cross one another). Yet in all fine art the essential thing is the form, which is purposive as regards our observation and judgment, where the pleasure is at the same time cultivation and disposes the spirit to ideas, and consequently makes it susceptible of still more of such pleasure and entertainment. The essential element is not the matter of sensation (charm or emotion), which has only to do with enjoyment; this leaves behind nothing in the idea, and it makes the spirit dull, the object gradually distasteful, and the mind, on account of its consciousness of a disposition that conflicts with purpose in the judgment of reason, discontented with itself and peevish.

If the fine arts are not brought into more or less close combination with moral ideas, which alone bring with them a self-sufficing satisfaction, this latter fate must ultimately be theirs. They then serve only as a distraction, of which we are the more in need the more we avail ourselves of them to disperse the discontent of the mind with itself, so that we thus render ourselves ever more useless and ever more discontented. The beauties of nature are generally of most benefit in this point of view, if we are early accustomed to observe, appreciate, and admire them.

§ 53. COMPARISON OF THE RESPECTIVE AESTHETICAL WORTH OF THE FINE ARTS

Of all the arts *poetry* (which owes its origin almost entirely to genius and will least be guided by precept or example) maintains the first rank. It expands the mind by setting the imagination at liberty and by offering, within the limits of a given concept, amid the unbounded variety of possible forms accordant therewith, that which unites the presentment of this concept with a wealth of thought to which no verbal expression is completely adequate, and so rising aesthetically to ideas. It strengthens the mind by making it feel its faculty—free, spontaneous, and independent of natural determination—of considering and judging nature as a phenomenon in accordance with aspects which it does not present in experience either for sense or understanding, and therefore of using it on behalf of, and as a sort of schema for, the supersensible. It plays with illusion, which it produces at pleasure, but without deceiving by it; for it declares its exercise to be mere play, which however can be purposively used by the understanding. Rhetoric, in so far as this means the art of persuasion, i.e. of deceiving by a beautiful show (*ars oratoria*), and not mere elegance of speech (eloquence and style), is a dialectic which borrows from poetry only so much as is needful to win minds to the side of the orator before they have formed a judgment and to deprive them of their freedom; it cannot therefore be recommended either for the law courts or for the pulpit. For if we are dealing with civil law, with the rights of individual persons, or with lasting instruction and determination of people's minds to an accurate knowledge and a conscientious observance of their duty, it is unworthy of so important a business to allow a trace of any luxuriance of wit and imagination to appear, and still less any trace of the art of winning people over and of captivating them for the advantage of any chance person. For although this art may sometimes be directed to legitimate and praiseworthy designs, it becomes objectionable when in this way maxims and dispositions are spoiled in a subjective point of view, though the action may objectively be lawful. It is not enough to do what is right; we should practice it solely on the ground that it is right. Again, the mere concept of this species of matters of human concern, when clear and combined with a lively presentation of it in examples, without any offense against the rules of euphony of speech or propriety of expression, has by itself for ideas of reason (which collectively constitute eloquence) sufficient influence upon human minds; so that it is not needful to add the machinery of persuasion, which, since it can be used equally well to beautify or to hide vice and error, cannot quite lull the secret suspicion that one is being artfully overreached. In poetry everything proceeds with honesty and candor. It declares itself to be a mere entertaining play of the imagination, which wishes to proceed as regards form in harmony with the laws of the understanding; and it does not desire to steal upon and ensnare the understanding by the aid of sensible presentation.[31]

---

[31] I must admit that a beautiful poem has always given me a pure gratification, while the reading of the best discourse, whether of a Roman orator or of a modern parliamentary speaker or of a preacher, has always been mingled with an unpleasant feeling of disapprobation of a treacherous art which means to move men in important matters like machines to a judgment that must lose all weight for them on quiet reflection. Readiness and accuracy in speaking (which taken together constitute rhetoric) belong to fine art, but the art of

After poetry, *if we are to deal with charm and with moving people's spirits,* I would place that art which comes nearest to the art of speech and can very naturally be united with it, viz. *the art of tone.* For although it speaks by means of mere sensations without concepts, and so does not, like poetry, leave anything over for reflection, it yet moves the mind in a greater variety of ways and more intensely, although only transitorily. It is, however, rather enjoyment than cultivation (the further play of thought that is excited by its means is merely the effect of a rather mechanical association), and in the judgment of reason it has less worth than any other of the fine arts. Hence, like all enjoyment, it desires constant change and does not bear frequent repetition without producing weariness. Its charm, which admits of universal communication, appears to rest on this that every expression of speech has in its context a tone appropriate to the sense. This tone indicates more or less an affection of the speaker and produces it also in the hearer, which affection excites in its turn in the hearer the idea that is expressed in speech by the tone in question. Thus as modulation is, as it were, a universal language of sensations intelligible to every man, the art of tone employs it by itself alone in its full force, viz. as a language of the affections, and thus communicates universally according to the laws of association the aesthetical ideas naturally combined therewith. Now these aesthetical

ideas are not concepts or determinate thoughts. Hence the form of the composition of these sensations (harmony and melody) only serves instead of the form of language, by means of their proportionate accordance, to express the aesthetical idea of a connected whole of an unspeakable wealth of thought, corresponding to a certain theme which produces the dominating affection in the piece. This can be brought mathematically under certain rules, because it rests in the case of tones on the relation between the number of vibrations of the air in the same time, so far as these tones are combined simultaneously or successively. To this mathematical form, although not represented by determinate concepts, alone attaches the satisfaction that unites the mere reflection upon such a number of concomitant or consecutive sensations with this their play, as a condition of its beauty valid for every man. It is this alone which permits taste to claim in advance a rightful authority over everyone's judgment.

But in the charm and moving of the spirit produced by music, mathematics has certainly not the slightest share. It is only the indispensable condition (*conditio sine qua non*) of that proportion of the impressions in their combination and in their alternation by which it becomes possible to gather them together and prevent them from destroying each other, and to harmonize them so as to produce a continual movement and animation of the mind, by means of affections consonant therewith, and thus a delightful personal enjoyment.

If, on the other hand, we estimate the worth of the fine arts by the culture they supply to the mind and take as a standard the expansion of the faculties which must concur in the judgment for cognition, music will have the lowest place among them (as it has perhaps the highest among those arts which are valued for their pleasantness), because it merely plays with sensations. The formative arts are far ahead of it in this point of view, for in putting the imagina-

---

the orator (*ars oratoria*), the art of availing oneself of the weaknesses of men for one's own designs (whether these be well meant or even actually good does not matter), is worthy of no *respect*. Again, this art only reached its highest point, both at Athens and at Rome, at a time when the state was hastening to its ruin and true patriotic sentiment had disappeared. The man who, along with a clear insight into things, has in his power a wealth of pure speech, and who with a fruitful imagination capable of presenting his ideas unites a lively sympathy with what is truly good, is the *vir bonus dicendi peritus,* the orator without art but of great impressiveness, as Cicero has it, though he may not always remain true to this ideal.

tion in a free play, which is also accordant with the understanding, they at the same time carry on a serious business. This they do by producing a product that serves for concepts as a permanent self-commendatory vehicle for promoting their union with sensibility and thus, as it were, the urbanity of the higher cognitive powers. These two species of art take quite different courses; the first proceeds from sensations to indeterminate ideas, the second from determinate ideas to sensations. The latter produce *permanent*, the former only *transitory* impressions. The imagination can recall the one and entertain itself pleasantly therewith; but the other either vanish entirely, or, if they are recalled involuntarily by the imagination, they are rather wearisome than pleasant. Besides, there attaches to music a certain want of urbanity from the fact that, chiefly from the character of its instruments, it extends its influence further than is desired (in the vicinity), and so, as it were, obtrudes itself and does violence to the freedom of others who are not of the musical company. The arts which appeal to the eyes do not do this, for we need only turn our eyes away if we wish to avoid being impressed. The case of music is almost like that of the delight derived from a smell that diffuses itself widely. The man who pulls his perfumed handkerchief out of his pocket attracts the attention of all around him, even against their will, and he forces them, if they are to breathe at all, to enjoy the scent; hence this habit has gone out of fashion.[32]

Among the formative arts I would give the palm to painting, partly because as the art of delineation it lies at the root of all the other formative arts, and partly because it can penetrate much further into the region of ideas and can extend the field of intuition in conformity with them further than the others can.

§ 54. REMARK

As we have often shown, there is an essential difference between *what satisfies simply in the act of judging it* and that which *gratifies* (pleases in sensation). We cannot ascribe the latter [kind of satisfaction] to everyone, as we can the former. Gratification (the causes of which may even be situate in ideas) appears always to consist in a feeling of the furtherance of the whole life of the man, and consequently also of his bodily wellbeing, i.e. his health, so that Epicurus, who maintained that all gratification was at bottom bodily sensation, may perhaps not have been wrong, but only misunderstood himself, when he reckoned intellectual and even practical satisfaction under gratification. If we have this distinction in view, we can explain how a gratification may dissatisfy the man who sensibly feels it (e.g. the joy of a needy but well-meaning man at becoming the heir of an affectionate but penurious father); or how a deep grief may satisfy the person experiencing it (the sorrow of a widow at the death of her husband); or how a gratification can in addition satisfy (as in the sciences that we pursue); or how a grief (e.g. hatred, envy, revenge) can moreover dissatisfy. The satisfaction or dissatisfaction here depends on reason and is the same as *approbation* or *disapprobation*; but gratification and grief can only rest on the feel-

---

[32] Those who recommend the singing of spiritual songs at family prayers do not consider that they inflict a great hardship upon the public by such *noisy* (and therefore in general pharisaical) devotions, for they force the neighbors either to sing with them or to abandon their meditations. [Kant suffered himself from such annoyances, which may account for the asperity of this note. At one period he was disturbed by the devotional exercises of the prisoners in the adjoining jail. In a letter to the burgomaster "he suggested the advantage of closing the windows during these hymn-singings, and added that the warders of the prison might probably be directed to accept less sonorous and neighbor-annoying chants as evidence of the penitent spirit of their captives" (Wallace, *Kant, op. cit.*, p. 42).—TR. NOTE.]

ing or prospect of a possible (on whatever grounds) *well-being* or *its opposite*.

All changing free play of sensations (that have no design at their basis) gratifies, because it furthers the feeling of health. In the judgment of reason, we may or may not have any satisfaction in its object or even in this gratification; and this latter may rise to the height of an affection, although we take no interest in the object, at least none that is proportionate to the degree of the gratification. We may subdivide this free play of sensations into the *play of fortune* [games of chance], he *play of tone* [music], and the *play of thought* [wit]. The first requires an *interest,* whether of vanity or of selfishness, which however is not nearly so great as the interest that attaches to the way in which we are striving to procure it. The second requires merely the change of *sensations,* all of which have a relation to affection, though they have not the degree of affection, and excite aesthetical ideas. The third springs merely from the change of representations in the judgment; by it, indeed, no thought that brings an interest with it is produced, but yet the mind is animated thereby.

How much gratification games must afford, without any necessity of placing at their basis an interested design, all our evening parties show, for hardly any of them can be carried on without a game. But the affections of hope, fear, joy, wrath, scorn, are put in play by them, alternating every moment; and they are so vivid that, by them, as by a kind of internal motion, all the vital processes of the body seem to be promoted, as is shown by the mental vivacity excited by them, although nothing is gained or learned thereby. But as the beautiful does not enter into games of chance, we will here set it aside. On the other hand, music and that which excites laughter are two different kinds of play with aesthetical ideas, or of representations of the understanding through which ultimately nothing is thought, which can give lively gratification merely by their changes. Thus

we recognize pretty clearly that the animation in both cases is merely bodily, although it is excited by ideas of the mind, and that the feeling of health produced by a motion of the intestines corresponding to the play in question makes up that whole gratification of a gay party which is regarded as so refined and so spiritual. It is not the judging the harmony in tones or sallies of wit, which serves only in combination with their beauty as a necessary vehicle, but the furtherance of the vital bodily processes, the affection that moves the intestines and the diaphragm—in a word, the feeling of health (which without such inducements one does not feel) that makes up the gratification felt by us, so that we can thus reach the body through the soul and use the latter as the physician of the former.

In music, this play proceeds from bodily sensations to aesthetical ideas (the objects of our affections), and then from these back again to the body with redoubled force. In the case of jokes (the art of which, just like music, should rather be reckoned as pleasant than beautiful), the play begins with the thoughts which together occupy the body, so far as they admit of sensible expression; and as the understanding stops suddenly short at this presentment, in which it does not find what it expected, we feel the effect of this slackening in the body by the oscillation of the organs, which promotes the restoration of equilibrium and has a favorable influence upon health.

In everything that is to excite a lively convulsive laugh there must be something absurd (in which the understanding, therefore, can find no satisfaction). *Laughter is an affection arising from the sudden transformation of a tense expectation into nothing.* This transformation, which is certainly not enjoyable to the understanding, yet indirectly gives it very active enjoyment for a moment. Therefore its cause must consist in the influence of the representation upon the body and the reflex effect of this upon the mind; not, indeed, through the representation being objectively an object of gratification[33] (for how could a delusive expectation gratify?), but simply through it as a mere play of representations bringing about an equilibrium of the vital powers in the body.

Suppose this story to be told: An Indian at the table of an Englishman in Surat, when he saw a bottle of ale opened and all the beer turned into froth and overflowing, testified his great astonishment with many exclamations. When the Englishman asked him, "What is there in this to astonish you so much?" he answered, "I am not at all astonished that it should flow out, but I do wonder how you ever got it in." At this story we laugh, and it gives us hearty pleasure, not because we deem ourselves cleverer than this ignorant man or because of anything in it that we note as satisfactory to the understanding, but because our expectation was strained [for a time] and then was suddenly dissipated into nothing. Again: The heir of a rich relative wished to arrange for an imposing funeral, but he lamented that he could not properly succeed, "for (said he) the more money I give my mourners to look sad, the more cheerful they look!"[34] When we hear this story we laugh loud, and the reason is that an expectation is suddenly transformed into nothing. We must note well that it does not transform itself into the positive opposite of an expected object—for then there would still be something, which might even be a cause of grief—but it must be transformed into nothing. For if a man arouses great expectations in us when telling a story, and at the end we see its falsehood immediately, it displeases us, e.g. the story of the people whose hair in consequence of great grief turned gray in one night. But if a wag, to repair the effect of this story, describes very

circumstantially the grief of the merchant returning from India to Europe with all his wealth in merchandise who was forced to throw it overboard in a heavy storm, and who grieved thereat so much that his *wig* turned gray the same night, we laugh and it gives us gratification. For we treat our own mistake in the case of an object otherwise indifferent to us, or rather the idea which we are following out, as we treat a ball which we knock to and fro for a time, though our only serious intention is to seize it and hold it fast. It is not the mere dismissal of a liar or a simpleton that arouses our gratification; for the latter story told with assumed seriousness would set a whole company in a roar of laughter, while the former would ordinarily not be regarded as worth attending to.

It is remarkable that, in all such cases, the jest must contain something that is capable of deceiving for a moment. Hence, when the illusion is dissipated, the mind turns back to try it once again, and thus through a rapidly alternating tension and relaxation it is jerked back and put into a state of oscillation. This, because the strain on the cord as it were is suddenly (and not gradually) relaxed, must occasion a mental movement, and an inner bodily movement harmonizing therewith, which continues involuntarily and fatigues, even while cheering us (the effects of a motion conducive to health).

For if we admit that with all our thoughts is harmonically combined a movement in the organs of the body, we will easily comprehend how to this sudden transposition of the mind, now to one, now to another standpoint in order to contemplate its object, may correspond an alternating tension and relaxation of the elastic portions of our intestines, which communicates itself to the diaphragm (like that which ticklish people feel). In connection with this the lungs expel the air at rapidly succeeding intervals, and thus bring about a movement beneficial to health, which alone, and not what precedes it in the mind, is the proper

---

33 [The first edition adds: "as in the case of a man who gets the news of a great commercial success."—TR. NOTE.]

34 [The jest may have been taken from Steele's play, "The Funeral, or Grief *à la mode,*" where it occurs verbatim. This play was published in 1802.—TR. NOTE.]

cause of the gratification in a thought that at bottom represents nothing. Voltaire said that heaven had given us two things to counterbalance the many miseries of life— *hope* and *sleep*.[35] He could have added *laughter,* if the means of exciting it in reasonable men were only as easily attainable and the requisite wit or originality of humor were not so rare, as the talent is common of imagining things which *break one's head,* as mystic dreamers do, or which *break one's neck,* as your genius does, or which *break one's heart,* as sentimental romance writers (and even moralists of the same kidney) do.

We may therefore, as it seems to me, readily concede to Epicurus that all gratification, even that which is occasioned through concepts excited by aesthetical ideas, is *animal,* i.e. bodily sensation, without the least prejudice to the *spiritual* feeling of respect for moral ideas, which is not gratification at all but an esteem for self (for humanity in us), that raises us above the need of gratification, and even without the slightest prejudice to the less noble [satisfactions] of *taste.*

We find a combination of these two last in *naïveté,* which is the breaking out of the sincerity originally natural to humanity in opposition to that art of dissimulation which has become a second nature. We laugh at the simplicity that does not understand how to dissemble, and yet we are delighted with the simplicity of the nature which thwarts that art. We look for the commonplace manner of artificial utterance devised with foresight to make a fair show, and behold! it is the unspoiled innocent nature which we do not expect to find and which he who displays it did not think of disclosing. That the fair but false show which generally has so much influence upon our judgment is here suddenly transformed into nothing, so that, as it were, the rogue in us is laid bare, produces a movement of the mind in two opposite directions, which gives a wholesome shock to the body. But

---

35 [*Henriade,* Chant 7.—TR. NOTE.]

the fact that something infinitely better than all assumed manner, viz. purity of disposition (or at least the tendency thereto), is not quite extinguished yet in human nature, blends seriousness and high esteem with this play of the judgment. But because it is only a transitory phenomenon and the veil of dissimulation is soon drawn over it again, there is mingled therewith a compassion which is an emotion of tenderness; this, as play, readily admits of combination with a good-hearted laugh and ordinarily is actually so combined, and withal is wont to compensate him who supplies its material for the embarrassment which results from not yet being wise after the manner of men. An art that is to be *naïve* is thus a contradiction, but the representation of naïveté in a fictitious personage is quite possible and is a beautiful though a rare art. Naïveté must not be confounded with openhearted simplicity, which does not artificially spoil nature solely because it does not understand the art of social intercourse.

The *humorous* manner again may be classified as that which, as exhilarating us, is near akin to the gratification that proceeds from laughter, and belongs to the originality of spirit but not to the talent of beautiful art. *Humor,* in the good sense, means the talent of being able voluntarily to put oneself into a certain mental disposition, in which everything is judged quite differently from the ordinary method (reversed, in fact), and yet in accordance with certain rational principles in such a frame of mind. He who is involuntarily subject to such mutations is called a man of humors [*launisch*]; but he who can assume them voluntarily and purposively (on behalf of a lively presentment brought about by the aid of a contrast that excites a laugh), he and his exposition are called humorous [*launig*]. This manner, however, belongs rather to pleasant than to beautiful art, because the object of the latter must always show proper worth in itself, and hence requires a certain seriousness in the presentation, as taste does in the act of judging.

ADAM SMITH

(1723-1790)

Adam Smith, a classical figure in the history of economic theory, is chiefly known as the author of the *Wealth of Nations,* which first appeared in 1776. Moral philosophers know him also as the author of the *Theory of the Moral Sentiments* (1759). Indeed the work on economics that brought him fame was conceived systematically as but a component part of moral theory.

Adam Smith was a student at Glasgow under Francis Hutcheson, and at seventeen he went to Balliol College, Oxford. Returning to Scotland, he formed a warm friendship with David Hume that lasted until Hume's death in 1776. Smith was a professor at the University of Glasgow from 1751 to 1763 and was elected lord rector in 1787. He also resided at Toulouse and Paris, where he made the acquaintance of the most distinguished French philosophers of the day, including d'Alembert, Helvétius, and Marmontel. From 1766 to 1776 he was occupied in the writing of the *Wealth of Nations.* Thereafter, until his death, he lived mostly in Edinburgh, the center of a circle of many friends.

The following brief essay differs from most of the other readings in this collection in that it addresses itself not to questions about what art essentially is or what the most satisfactory definition of beauty is, but to a descriptive analysis of a certain concept that is usually indispensable to discourse about the arts, that is, imitation. Smith does not say that art is imitation, nor even that the visual arts are imitative. He begins by asking whether imitation, the deliberate production of resemblance, does indeed please, and, if so, why it does. Painting and sculpture are reviewed in reference to this question, and certain interesting differences between the two media are underlined. In painting, he thinks, the artist can and does imitate nearly anything, but in sculpture, where mean and trifling subjects are out of place, the artist ought not imitate indiscriminately. The second section raises the much more difficult cases of arts such as poetry, dance, and music. We are constrained to move from the rather simple idea of imitation to the richer and more modern notion of expression. When we come finally to instrumental music, we have an art that is really at an opposite pole from imitation. It has no reference to anything outside itself. Its meaning, says Adam Smith, is "complete in itself."

Even in earlier periods no one could hold to a purely imitative theory of art without a dozen qualifications. But Adam Smith's fragmentary essay on the subject has the merit of showing how to do justice to the peculiarities of each of the several arts. It is not clear whether he intended to develop his ideas into a more comprehensive scheme. Evidently he had a genuine feeling for all of the arts, and this enthusiasm gives the essay a certain authority.

ADAM SMITH

Of the Nature of That Imitation Which Takes Place in What Are Called the Imitative Arts

(First published: 1795.)

§ IMITATION IN PAINTING AND
SCULPTURE

The most perfect imitation of an object
of any kind must in all cases, it is evident,
be another object of the same kind, made
as exactly as possible after the same model.
What, for example, would be the most perfect imitation of the carpet which now lies
before me?—Another carpet, certainly,
wrought as exactly as possible after the
same pattern. But, whatever might be the
merit or beauty of this second carpet, it
would not be supposed to derive any from
the circumstance of its having been made
in imitation of the first. This circumstance
of its being not an original, but a copy,
would even be considered as some diminution of that merit; a greater or smaller, in
proportion as the object was of a nature to
lay claim to a greater or smaller degree of
admiration. It would not much diminish
the merit of a common carpet, because in
such trifling objects, which at best can lay
claim to so little beauty or merit of any
kind, we do not always think it worth while
to affect originality: it would diminish a
good deal that of a carpet of very exquisite
workmanship. In objects of still greater importance, this exact, or, as it would be
called, this servile imitation, would be considered as the most unpardonable blemish.
To build another St. Peter's or St. Paul's
church, of exactly the same dimensions,

proportions, and ornaments with the present buildings at Rome or London, would be supposed to argue such a miserable barrenness of genius and invention in the architect as would disgrace the most expensive magnificence.

The exact resemblance of the correspondent parts of the same object is frequently considered as a beauty, and the want of it as a deformity; as in the correspondent members of the human body, in the opposite wings of the same building, in the opposite trees of the same alley, in the correspondent compartments of the same piece of carpet-work, or of the same flower-garden, in the chairs or tables which stand in the correspondent parts of the same room, etc. But in objects of the same kind, which in other respects are regarded as altogether separate and unconnected, this exact resemblance is seldom considered as a beauty, nor the want of it as a deformity. A man, and in the same manner a horse, is handsome or ugly, each of them, on account of his own intrinsic beauty or deformity, without any regard to their resembling or not resembling, the one, another man, or the other, another horse. A set of coach-horses, indeed, is supposed to be handsomer when they are all exactly matched; but each horse is, in this case, considered not as a separated and unconnected object, or as a whole by himself, but as a part of another whole, to the other parts of which he ought to bear a certain correspondence: separated from the set, he derives neither beauty from his resemblance, nor deformity from his unlikeness to the other horses which compose it.

Even in the correspondent parts of the same object, we frequently require no more than a resemblance in the general outline. If the inferior members of those correspondent parts are too minute to be seen distinctly, without a separate and distinct examination of each part by itself, as a separate and unconnected object, we should sometimes even be displeased if the re-semblance was carried beyond this general outline. In the correspondent parts of a room we frequently hang pictures of the same size; those pictures, however, resemble one another in nothing but the frame, or, perhaps, in the general character of the subject; if the one is a landscape, the other is a landscape too; if the one represents a religious or a bacchanalian subject, its companion represents another of the same kind. Nobody ever thought of repeating the same picture in each correspondent frame. The frame, and the general character of two or three pictures, is as much as the eye can comprehend at one view, or from one station. Each picture, in order to be seen distinctly, and understood thoroughly, must be viewed from a particular station, and examined by itself as a separate and unconnected object. In a hall or portico, adorned with statues, the niches, or perhaps the pedestals, may exactly resemble one another, but the statues are always different. Even the masks which are sometimes carried upon the different key-stones of the same arcade, or of the correspondent doors and windows of the same front, though they may all resemble one another in the general outline, yet each of them has always its own peculiar features, and a grimace of its own. There are some Gothic buildings in which the correspondent windows resemble one another only in the general outline, and not in the smaller ornaments and subdivisions. These are different in each, and the architect had considered them as too minute to be seen distinctly, without a particular and separate examination of each window by itself, as a separate and unconnected object. A variety of this sort, however, I think, is not agreeable. In objects which are susceptible only of a certain inferior order of beauty, such as the frames of pictures, the niches or the pedestals of statues, etc., there seems frequently to be affectation in the study of variety, of which the merit is scarcely ever sufficient to compensate the want of that perspicuity and distinctness, of that easiness to be comprehended and remembered, which is the natural effect of exact uniformity. In a portico of the Corinthian or Ionic order, each column resembles every other, not only in the general outline, but in all the minutest ornaments; though some of them, in order to be seen distinctly, may require a separate and distinct examination in each column, and in the entablature of each intercolumnation. In the inlaid tables, which, according to the present fashion, are sometimes fixed in the correspondent parts of the same room, the pictures only are different in each. All the other more frivolous and fanciful ornaments are commonly, so far at least as I have observed the fashion, the same in them all. Those ornaments, however, in order to be seen distinctly, require a distinct examination of each table.

The extraordinary resemblance of two natural objects, of twins, for example, is regarded as a curious circumstance; which, though it does not increase, yet does not diminish the beauty of either, considered as a separate and unconnected object. But the exact resemblance of two productions of art, seems to be always considered as some diminution of the merit of at least one of them; as it seems to prove, that one of them, at least, is a copy either of the other, or of some other original. One may say, even of the copy of a picture, that it derives its merit, not so much from its resemblance to the original, as from its resemblance to the object which the original was meant to resemble. The owner of the copy, so far from setting any high value upon its resemblance to the original, is often anxious to destroy any value or merit which it might derive from this circumstance. He is often anxious to persuade both himself and other people that it is not a copy, but an original, of which what passes for the original is only a copy. But, whatever merit a copy may derive from its resemblance to the original, an original can derive none from the resemblance of its copy.

But though a production of art seldom derives any merit from its resemblance to another object of the same kind, it frequently derives a great deal from its resemblance to an object of a different kind, whether that object be a production of art or of nature. A painted cloth, the work of some laborious Dutch artist, so curiously shaded and coloured as to represent the pile and softness of a woollen one, might derive some merit from its resemblance even to the sorry carpet which now lies before me. The copy might, and probably would, in this case, be of much greater value than the original. But if this carpet was represented as spread, either upon a floor or upon a table, and projecting from the background of the picture, with exact observation of perspective, and of light and shade, the merit of the imitation would be still even greater.

In Painting, a plain surface of one kind is made to resemble, not only a plain surface of another, but all the three dimensions of a solid substance. In Statuary and Sculpture, a solid substance of one kind, is made to resemble a solid substance of another. The disparity between the object imitating, and the object imitated, is much greater in the one art than in the other; and the pleasure arising from the imitation seems greater in proportion as this disparity is greater.

In Painting, the imitation frequently pleases, though the original object be indifferent, or even offensive. In Statuary and Sculpture it is otherwise. The imitation seldom pleases, unless the original object be in a very high degree either great, or beautiful, or interesting. A butcher's-stall, or a kitchen-dresser, with the objects which they commonly present, are not certainly the happiest subjects, even for Painting. They have, however, been represented with so much care and success by some Dutch masters, that it is impossible to view the pictures without some degree of pleasure. They would be most absurd subjects for Statuary or Sculpture, which are, however, capable of representing them. The picture of a very ugly or deformed man, such as Æsop, or Scarron, might not make a disagreeable piece of furniture. The statue certainly would. Even a vulgar ordinary man or woman, engaged in a vulgar ordinary action, like what we see with so much pleasure in the pictures of Rembrandt, would be too mean a subject for Statuary. Jupiter, Hercules, and Apollo, Venus and Diana, the Nymphs and the Graces, Bacchus, Mercury, Antinous, and Meleager, the miserable death of Laocoön, the melancholy fate of the children of Niobe, the Wrestlers, the fighting, the dying gladiator, the figures of gods and goddesses, of heroes and heroines, the most perfect forms of the human body, placed either in the noblest attitudes, or in the most interesting situations which the human imagination is capable of conceiving, are the proper, and therefore have always been the favorite, subjects of Statuary: that art cannot, without degrading itself, stoop to represent any thing that is offensive, or mean, or even indifferent. Painting is not so disdainful; and, though capable of representing the noblest objects, it can, without forfeiting its title to please, submit to imitate those of a much more humble nature. The merit of the imitation alone, and without any merit in the imitated object, is capable of supporting the dignity of Painting: it cannot support that of Statuary. There would seem, therefore, to be more merit in the one species of imitation than in the other.

In Statuary, scarcely any drapery is agreeable. The best of the ancient statues were either altogether naked or almost naked; and those of which any considerable part of the body is covered, are represented as clothed in wet linen—a species of clothing which most certainly never was agreeable to the fashion of any country. This drapery too is drawn so tight, as to express beneath its narrow foldings the exact form and outline of any limb, and almost of every muscle of the body. The clothing which thus approached the nearest to no clothing at all, had, it seems, in the judgment of the great artists of antiquity, been that which was most suitable to Statuary. A great painter of the Roman school, who had formed his manner almost entirely upon the study of the ancient statues, imitated at first their drapery in his pictures; but he soon found that in Painting it had the air of meanness and poverty, as if the persons who wore it could scarce afford clothes enough to cover them; and that larger folds, and a looser and more flowing drapery, were more suitable to the nature of his art. In Painting, the imitation of so very inferior an object as a suit of clothes is capable of pleasing; and, in order to give this object all the magnificence of which it is capable, it is necessary that the folds should be large, loose, and flowing. It is not necessary in Painting that the exact form and outline of every limb, and almost of every muscle of the body, should be expressed beneath the folds of the drapery; it is sufficient if these are so disposed as to indicate in general the situation and attitude of the principal limbs. Painting, by the mere force and merit of its imitation, can venture, without the hazard of displeasing, to substitute, upon many occasions, the inferior in the room of the superior object, by making the one, in this manner, cover and entirely conceal a great part of the other. Statuary can seldom venture to do this, but with the utmost reserve and caution; and the same drapery, which is noble and magnificent in the one art, appears clumsy and awkward in the other. Some modern artists, however, have attempted to introduce into Statuary the drapery which is peculiar to Painting. It may not, perhaps, upon every occasion, be quite so ridiculous as the marble periwigs in Westminster Abbey: but if it does not always appear clumsy and awkward, it is at best always insipid and uninteresting.

It is not the want of colouring which hinders many things from pleasing in Statuary which please in Painting; it is the want of that degree of disparity between the imitating and the imitated object, which is necessary, in order to render interesting the imitation of an object which is itself not interesting. Colouring, when added to Statuary, so far from increasing, destroys almost entirely the pleasure which we receive from the imitation; because it takes away the great source of that pleasure, the disparity between the imitating and the imitated object. That one solid and coloured object should exactly resemble another solid and coloured object, seems to be a matter of no great wonder or admiration. A painted statue, though it may resemble a human figure much more exactly than any statue which is not painted, is generally acknowledged to be a disagreeable and even an offensive object; and so far are we from being pleased with this superior likeness, that we are never satisfied with it; and, after viewing it again and again, we always find that it is not equal to what we are disposed to imagine it might have been: though it should seem to want scarce any thing but the life, we could not pardon it for thus wanting what it is altogether impossible it should have. The works of Mrs. Wright, a self-taught artist of great merit, are perhaps more perfect in this way than any thing I have ever seen. They do admirably well to be seen now and then as a show; but the best of them we shall find, if brought home to our own house, and placed in a situation where it was to come often into view, would make, instead of an ornamental, a most offensive piece of household furniture. Painted statues, accordingly, are universally reprobated, and we scarce ever meet with them. To colour the eyes of statues is not altogether so uncommon: even this, however, is disapproved by all good judges. "I cannot bear it," (a gentleman used to say, of great knowledge and judgment in this art), "I cannot bear it; I always want them to speak to me."

Artificial fruits and flowers sometimes imitate so exactly the natural objects which they represent, that they frequently deceive us. We soon grow weary of them, however; and, though they seem to want nothing but the freshness and the flavour of natural fruits and flowers, we cannot pardon them, in the same manner, for thus wanting what it is altogether impossible they should have. But we do not grow weary of a good flower and fruit painting. We do not grow weary of the foliage of the Corinthian capital, or of the flowers which sometimes ornament the frieze of that order. Such imitations, however, never deceive us; their resemblance to the original objects is always much inferior to that of artificial fruits and flowers. Such as it is, however, we are contented with it; and, where there is such disparity between the imitating and the imitated objects, we find that it is as great as it can be, or as we expect that it should be. Paint that foliage and those flowers with the natural colours, and, instead of pleasing more, they will please much less. The resemblance, however, will be much greater; but the disparity between the imitating and the imitated objects will be so much less, that even this superior resemblance will not satisfy us. Where the disparity is so very great, on the contrary, we are often contented with the most imperfect resemblance; with the very imperfect resemblance, for example, both as to the figure and the colour, of fruits and flowers in shell-work.

It may be observed, however, that, though in Sculpture the imitation of flowers and foliage pleases as an ornament of architecture, as a part of the dress which is to set off the beauty of a different and a more important object, it would not please alone, or as a separate and unconnected object, in the same manner as a fruit and flower painting pleases. Flowers and foliage, how elegant and beautiful soever, are not sufficiently interesting; they have not dignity enough, if I may say so, to be proper subjects for a piece of Sculpture, which is to please alone, and not to appear as the ornamental appendage of some other object.

In Tapestry and Needle-work, in the same manner as in Painting, a plain surface is sometimes made to represent all the three dimensions of a solid substance. But both the shuttle of the weaver, and the needle of the embroiderer, are instruments of imitation so much inferior to the pencil of the painter, that we are not surprised to find a proportionable inferiority in their productions. We have all more or less experience that they usually are much inferior: and, in appreciating a piece of Tapestry or Needlework, we never compare the imitation of either with that of a good picture, for it never could stand that comparison, but with that of other pieces of Tapestry or Needlework. We take into consideration, not only the disparity between the imitating and the imitated object, but the awkwardness of the instruments of imitation; and if it is as well as any thing that can be expected from these, if it is better than the greater part of what actually comes from them, we are often not only contented but highly pleased.

A good painter will often execute in a few days a subject which would employ the best tapestry-weaver for many years; though, in proportion to his time, therefore, the latter is always much worse paid than the former, yet his work in the end comes commonly much dearer to market. The great expense of good Tapestry, the circumstance which confines it to the palaces of princes and of great lords, gives it, in the eyes of the greater part of the people, an air of riches and magnificence, which contributes still further to compensate the imperfection of its imitation. In arts which address themselves, not to the prudent and the wise, but to the rich and the great, to the proud and the vain, we ought not to wonder if the appearances of great expense, of being what few people can purchase, of being one of the surest characteristics of great fortune, should often stand in the place of exquisite beauty, and contribute equally to recommend their productions. As the idea of expense seems often to embellish, so that of cheapness seems as frequently to tarnish the lustre even of very agreeable objects. The difference between real and false jewels is what even the experienced eye of a jeweller can sometimes with difficulty distinguish. Let an unknown lady, however, come into a public assembly, with a head-dress which appears to be very richly adorned with diamonds, and let a jeweller only whisper in our ear that they are false stones, not only the lady will immediately sink in our imagination from the rank of a princess to that of a very ordinary woman, but the head-dress, from being an object of the most splendid magnificence, will at once become an impertinent piece of tawdry and tinsel finery.

It was some years ago the fashion to ornament a garden with yew and holly trees, clipped into the artificial shapes of pyramids, and columns, and vases, and obelisks. It is now the fashion to ridicule this taste as unnatural. The figure of a pyramid or obelisk, however, is not more unnatural to a yew-tree than to a block of porphyry or marble. When the yew-tree is presented to the eye in this artificial shape, the gardener does not mean that it should be understood to have grown in that shape: he means, first, to give it the same beauty of regular figure, which pleases so much in porphyry and marble; and, secondly, to imitate in a growing tree the ornaments of those precious materials: he means to make an object of one kind resembling another object of a very different kind; and to the original beauty of figure to join the relative beauty of imitation: but the disparity between the imitating and the imitated object is the foundation of the beauty of imitation. It is because the one object does not naturally resemble the other, that we are so much pleased with it, when by art it is made to do so. The shears of the gardener, it may be said, indeed, are very clumsy instruments of Sculpture. They are so, no doubt, when employed to imitate the figures of men, or even of animals. But in the simple and regular forms of pyramids, vases, and obelisks, even the shears of the gardener do well enough. Some allowance, too, is naturally made for the necessary imperfection of the instrument, in the same manner as in Tapestry and Needle-work. In short, the next time you have an opportunity of surveying those out-of-fashion ornaments, endeavour only to let yourself alone, and to restrain for a few minutes the foolish passion for playing the critic, and you will be sensible that they are not without some degree of beauty; that they give the air of neatness and correct culture at least to the whole garden; and that they are not unlike what the "retired leisure, that" (as Milton says) "in trim gardens takes his pleasure," might be amused with. What then, it may be said, has brought them into such universal disrepute among us? In a pyramid or obelisk of marble, we know that the materials are expensive, and that the labour which wrought them into that shape must have been still more so. In a pyramid or obelisk of yew, we know that the materials could cost very little, and the labour still less. The former are ennobled by their expense; the latter degraded by their cheapness. In the cabbage-garden of a tallow-chandler we may sometimes perhaps have seen as many columns and vases and other ornaments in yew, as there are in marble and porphyry at Versailles: it is this vulgarity which has disgraced them. The rich and the great, the proud and the vain will not admit into their gardens an ornament which the meanest of the people can have as well as they. The taste for these ornaments came originally from France; where, notwithstanding that inconstancy of fashion with which we sometimes reproach the natives of that country, it still continues in good repute. In France, the condition of the inferior ranks of people is seldom so happy as it frequently is in England; and you will there seldom find even pyramids and obelisks of yew in the garden of a tallow-chandler. Such ornaments, not having in that country been degraded by their vulgarity, have not yet been excluded from the gardens of princes and lords.

The works of the great masters in Statuary and Painting, it is to be observed, never produce their effect by deception. They never are, and it never is intended that they should be, mistaken for the real objects which they represent. Painted Statuary may sometimes deceive an inattentive eye: proper Statuary never does. The little pieces of perspective in Painting, which it is intended should please by deception, represent always some very simple, as well as insignificant, objects: a roll of paper, for example, or the steps of a staircase, in the dark corner of some passage or gallery. They are generally the works too of some very inferior artists. After being seen once, and producing the little surprise which it is meant they should excite, together with the mirth which commonly accompanies it, they never please more, but appear to be ever after insipid and tiresome.

The proper pleasure which we derive from those two imitative arts, so far from being the effect of deception, is altogether incompatible with it. That pleasure is founded altogether upon our wonder at seeing an object of one kind represent so well an object of a very different kind, and upon our admiration of the art which surmounts so happily that disparity which Nature had established between them. The nobler works of Statuary and Painting appear to us a sort of wonderful phenomena, differing in this respect from the wonderful phenomena of Nature, that they carry, as it were, their own explication along with them, and demonstrate, even to the eye, the way and manner in which they are produced. The eye, even of an unskilful spectator, immediately discerns, in some measure, how it is that a certain modification of figure in

Statuary, and of brighter and darker colours in Painting, can represent, with so much truth and vivacity, the actions, passions, and behaviour of men, as well as a great variety of other objects. The pleasing wonder of ignorance is accompanied with the still more pleasing satisfaction of science. We wonder and are amazed at the effect; and we are pleased ourselves, and happy to find that we can comprehend, in some measure, how that wonderful effect is produced upon us.

A good looking-glass represents the objects which are set before it with much more truth and vivacity than either Statuary or Painting. But, though the science of optics may explain to the understanding, the looking-glass itself does not at all demonstrate to the eye how this effect is brought about. It may excite the wonder of ignorance; and in a clown, who had never beheld a looking-glass before, I have seen that wonder rise almost to rapture and extasy; but it cannot give the satisfaction of science. In all looking-glasses the effects are produced by the same means, applied exactly in the same manner. In every different statue and picture the effects are produced, though by similar, yet not by the same means; and those means too are applied in a different manner in each. Every good statue and picture is a fresh wonder, which at the same time carries, in some measure, its own explication along with it. After a little use and experience, all looking-glasses cease to be wonders altogether; and even the ignorant become so familiar with them, as not to think that their effects require any explication. A looking-glass, besides, can represent only present objects; and, when the wonder is once fairly over, we choose, in all cases, rather to contemplate the substance than to gaze at the shadow. One's own face becomes then the most agreeable object which a looking-glass can represent to us, and the only object which we do not soon grow weary with looking at; it is the only present object of which we can see

only the shadow: whether handsome or ugly, whether old or young, it is the face of a friend always, of which the features correspond exactly with whatever sentiment, emotion, or passion we may happen at that moment to feel.

In Statuary, the means by which the wonderful effect is brought about appear more simple and obvious than in Painting; where the disparity between the imitating and the imitated object being much greater, the art which can conquer that greater disparity appears evidently, and almost to the eye, to be founded upon a much deeper science, or upon principles much more abstruse and profound. Even in the meanest subjects we can often trace with pleasure the ingenious means by which Painting surmounts this disparity. But we cannot do this in Statuary, because the disparity not being so great, the means do not appear so ingenious. And it is upon this account, that in Painting we are often delighted with the representation of many things, which in Statuary would appear insipid, and not worth the looking at.

It ought to be observed, however, that though in Statuary the art of imitation appears, in many respects, inferior to what it is in Painting, yet, in a room ornamented with both statues and pictures of nearly equal merit, we shall generally find that the statues draw off our eye from the pictures. There is generally but one or little more than one, point of view from which a picture can be seen with advantage, and it always presents to the eye precisely the same object. There are many different points of view from which a statue may be seen with equal advantage, and from each it presents a different object. There is more variety in the pleasure which we receive from a good statue, than in that which we receive from a good picture; and one statue may frequently be the subject of many good pictures or drawings, all different from one another. The shadowy relief and projection of a picture, besides, is much flattened, and seems almost to vanish away altogether, when brought into comparison with the real and solid body which stands by it. How nearly soever these two arts may seem to be akin, they accord so very ill with one another, that their different productions ought, perhaps, scarce ever to be seen together.

§ IMITATION IN POETRY AND MUSIC

After the pleasures which arise from the gratification of the bodily appetites, there seem to be none more natural to man than Music and Dancing. In the progress of art and improvement they are, perhaps, the first and earliest pleasures of his own invention; for those which arise from the gratification of the bodily appetites cannot be said to be his own invention. No nation has yet been discovered so uncivilized as to be altogether without them. It seems even to be amongst the most barbarous nations that the use and practice of them is both most frequent and most universal, as among the negroes of Africa and the savage tribes of America. In civilized nations, the inferior ranks of people have very little leisure, and the superior ranks have many other amusements; neither the one nor the other, therefore, can spend much of their time in Music and Dancing. Among savage nations, the great body of the people have frequently great intervals of leisure, and they have scarce any other amusement; they naturally, therefore, spend a great part of their time in almost the only one they have.

What the ancients called Rhythmus, what we call Time or Measure, is the connecting principle of those two arts; Music consisting in a succession of a certain sort of sounds, and Dancing in a succession of a certain sort of steps, gestures, and motions, regulated according to time or measure, and thereby formed into a sort of whole or system; which in the one art is called a song or tune, and in the other a dance; the time or measure of the dance corresponding always exactly with that of the song or tune which accompanies and directs it.[1]

The human voice, as it is always the best, so it would naturally be the first and earliest of all musical instruments: in singing, or in its first attempts towards singing, it would naturally employ sounds as similar as possible to those which it had been accustomed to; that is, it would employ words of some kind or other, pronouncing them only in time and measure, and generally with a more melodious tone than had been usual in common conversation. Those words, however, might not, and probably would not, for a long time have any meaning, but might resemble the syllables which we make use of in *sol-faing,* or the *derry-down-down* of our common ballads; and serve only to assist the voice in forming sounds proper to be modulated into melody, and to be lengthened or shortened according to the time and measure of the tune. This rude form of vocal Music, as it is by far the most simple and obvious, so it naturally would be the first and earliest.

In the succession of ages it could not fail to occur, that in room of those unmeaning or musical words, if I may call them so, might be substituted words which expressed some sense or meaning, and of which the pronunciation might coincide as exactly with the time and measure of the tune, as that of the musical words had done before. Hence the origin of Verse or Poetry. The Verse would for a long time be rude and imperfect. When the meaning words fell short of the measure required, they would frequently be eked out with the unmeaning ones, as is sometimes done in our common ballads. When the public ear came to be so refined as to reject, in all serious Poetry, the unmeaning words altogether, there would still be a liberty assumed of altering

---

[1] The Author's Observations on the Affinity between Music, Dancing, and Poetry, are annexed to the end of Part Three of this Essay.

and corrupting, upon many occasions, the pronunciation of the meaning ones, for the sake of accommodating them to the measure. The syllables which composed them would, for this purpose, sometimes be improperly lengthened, and sometimes improperly shortened; and though no unmeaning words were made use of, yet an unmeaning syllable would sometimes be stuck to the beginning, to the end, or into the middle of a word. All these expedients we find frequently employed in the verses even of Chaucer, the father of the English Poetry. Many ages might pass away before verse was commonly composed with such correctness, that the usual and proper pronunciation of the words alone, and without any other artifice, subjected the voice to the observation of a time and measure, of the same kind with the time and measure of the science of Music.

The Verse would naturally express some sense which suited the grave or gay, the joyous or melancholy humour of the tune which it was sung to; being as it were blended and united with that tune, it would seem to give sense and meaning to what otherwise might not appear to have any, or at least any which could be clearly understood, without the accompaniment of such an explication.

A pantomime dance may frequently answer the same purpose, and, by representing some adventure in love or war, may seem to give sense and meaning to a Music, which might not otherwise appear to have any. It is more natural to mimic, by gestures and motions, the adventures of common life, than to express them in Verse or Poetry. The thought itself is more obvious, and the execution is much more easy. If this mimicry was accompanied by Music, it would of its own accord, and almost without any intention of doing so, accommodate, in some measure, its different steps and movements to the time and measure of the tune; especially if the same person both sung the tune and performed the mimicry, as is said

to be frequently the case among the savage nations of Africa and America. Pantomime Dancing might in this manner serve to give a distinct sense and meaning to Music many ages before the invention, or at least before the common use of Poetry. We hear little, accordingly, of the Poetry of the savage nations who inhabit Africa and America, but a great deal of their pantomime dances.

Poetry, however, is capable of expressing many things fully and distinctly, which Dancing either cannot represent at all, or can represent but obscurely and imperfectly; such as the reasonings and judgments of the understanding; the ideas, fancies, and suspicions of the imagination; the sentiments, emotions, and passions of the heart. In the power of expressing a meaning with clearness and distinctness, Dancing is superior to Music, and Poetry to Dancing.

Of those three Sister Arts, which originally, perhaps, went always together, and which at all times go frequently together, there are two which can subsist alone, and separate from their natural companions, and one which cannot. In the distinct observation of what the ancients called Rhythmus, of what we call Time and Measure, consists the essence both of Dancing and of Poetry or Verse; or the characteristical quality which distinguishes the former from all other motion and action, and the latter from all other discourse. But, concerning the proportion between those intervals and divisions of duration which constitute what is called time and measure, the ear, it would seem, can judge with much more precision than the eye; and Poetry, in the same manner as Music, addresses itself to the ear, whereas Dancing addresses itself to the eye. In Dancing, the rhythmus, the proper proportion, the time and measure of its motions, cannot distinctly be perceived, unless they are marked by the more distinct time and measure of Music. It is otherwise in Poetry; no accompaniment is necessary to mark the measure of good Verse. Music and Poetry, therefore, can each of them subsist alone;

Dancing always requires the accompaniment of Music.

It is Instrumental Music which can best subsist apart, and separate from both Poetry and Dancing. Vocal Music, though it may, and frequently does, consist of notes which have no distinct sense or meaning, yet naturally calls for the support of Poetry. But, "Music, married to immortal Verse," as Milton says, or even to words of any kind which have a distinct sense or meaning, is necessarily and essentially imitative. Whatever be the meaning of those words, though, like many of the songs of ancient Greece, as well as some of those of more modern times, they may express merely some maxims of prudence and morality, or may contain merely the simple narrative of some important event, yet even in such didactic and historical songs there will still be limitation; there will still be a thing of one kind, which by art is made to resemble a thing of a very different kind; there will still be Music imitating discourse; there will still be Rhythmus and Melody, shaped and fashioned into the form either of a good moral counsel, or of an amusing and interesting story.

In this first species of imitation, which being essential to, is therefore inseparable from, all such Vocal Music, there may be, and there commonly is, added a second. The words may, and commonly do, express the situation of some particular person, and all the sentiments and passions which he feels from that situation. It is a joyous companion who gives vent to the gaiety and mirth with which wine, festivity, and good company inspire him. It is a lover who complains, or hopes, or fears, or despairs. It is a generous man who expresses either his gratitude for the favours, or his indignation at the injuries, which may have been done to him. It is a warrior who prepares himself to confront danger, and who provokes or desires his enemy. It is a person in prosperity who humbly returns thanks for the goodness, or one in affliction who with contrition implores the mercy and forgiveness of that invisible Power to whom he looks up as the Director of all the events of human life. The situation may comprehend, not only one, but two, three, or more persons; it may excite in them all either similar or opposite sentiments; what is a subject of sorrow to one, being an occasion of joy and triumph to another; and they may all express, sometimes separately and sometimes together, the particular way in which each of them is affected, as in a duo, trio, or a chorus.

All this it may, and it frequently has been said is unnatural; nothing being more so, than to sing when we are anxious to persuade, or in earnest to express any very serious purpose. But it should be remembered, that to make a thing of one kind resemble another thing of a very different kind, is the very circumstance which, in all the Imitative Arts, constitutes the merits of imitation; and that to shape, and as it were to bend, the measure and the melody of Music, so as to imitate the tone and the language of counsel and conversation, the accent and the style of emotion and passion, is to make a thing of one kind resemble another thing of a very different kind.

The tone and the movements of Music, though naturally very different from those of conversation and passion, may, however, be so managed as to seem to resemble them. On account of the great disparity between the imitating and the imitated object, the mind in this, as in the other cases, cannot only be contented, but delighted, and even charmed and transported, with such an imperfect resemblance as can be had. Such imitative Music, therefore, when sung to words which explain and determine its meaning, may frequently appear to be a very perfect imitation. It is upon this account, that even the incomplete Music of a recitative seems to express sometimes all the sedateness and composure of serious but calm discourse, and sometimes all the exquisite sensibility of the most interesting passion. The more complete Music of an air is still superior, and, in the imitation of the more animated passions, has one great advantage over every sort of discourse, whether Prose or Poetry, which is not sung to Music. In a person who is either much depressed by grief or enlivened by joy, who is strongly affected either with love or hatred, with gratitude or resentment, with admiration or contempt, there is commonly one thought or idea which dwells upon his mind, which continually haunts him, which, when he has chased it away, immediately returns upon him, and which in company makes him absent and inattentive. He can think but of one object, and he cannot repeat to them that object so frequently as it recurs upon him. He takes refuge in solitude, where he can with freedom either indulge the ecstasy or give way to the agony of the agreeable or disagreeable passion which agitates him; and where he can repeat to himself, which he does sometimes mentally, and sometimes even aloud, and almost always in the same words, the particular thought which either delights or distresses him. Neither Prose nor Poetry can venture to imitate those almost endless repetitions of passion. They may describe them as I do now, but they dare not imitate them; they would become most insufferably tiresome if they did. The Music of a passionate air, not only may, but frequently does, imitate them; and it never makes its way so directly or so irresistibly to the heart as when it does so. It is upon this account that the words of an air, especially of a passionate one, though they are seldom very long, yet are scarce ever sung straight on to the end, like those of a recitative; but are almost always broken into parts, which are transposed and repeated again and again, according to the fancy or judgment of the composer. It is by means of such repetitions only, that Music can exert those peculiar powers of imitation which distinguish it, and in which it excels all the other Imitative Arts. Poetry and Eloquence, it has accordingly been often observed, produce their effect always by a connected variety and succession of different thoughts and ideas: but Music frequently produces its effects by a repetition of the same idea; and the same sense expressed in the same, or nearly the same, combination of sounds, though at first perhaps it may make scarce any impression upon us, yet, by being repeated again and again, it comes at last gradually, and by little and little, to move, to agitate, and to transport us.

To these powers of imitating, Music naturally, or rather necessarily, joins the happiest choice in the objects of its imitation. The sentiments and passions which Music can best imitate are those which unite and bind men together in society; the social, the decent, the virtuous, the interesting and affecting, the amiable and agreeable, the awful and respectable, the noble, elevating, and commanding passions. Grief and distress are interesting and affecting; humanity and compassion, joy and admiration, are amiable and agreeable; devotion is awful and respectable; the generous contempt of danger, the honourable indignation at injustice, are noble, elevating, and commanding. But it is these and such like passions which Music is fittest for imitating, and which it in fact most frequently imitates. They are, if I may say so, all Musical Passions; their natural tones are all clear, distinct, and almost melodious; and they naturally express themselves in a language which is distinguished by pauses at regular, and almost equal, intervals; and which, upon that account, can more easily be adapted to the regular returns of the correspondent periods of a tune. The passions, on the contrary, which drive men from one another, the unsocial, the hateful, the indecent, the vicious passions, cannot easily be imitated by Music. The voice of furious anger, for example, is harsh and discordant; its periods are all irregular, sometimes very long and sometimes very short, and distinguished by no regular pauses. The obscure and almost inarticulate grumblings of black malice and envy, the screaming outcries of dastardly fear, the hideous growlings of brutal and implacable revenge, are all equally discordant. It is with difficulty that Music can imitate any of those passions, and the Music which does imitate them is not the most agreeable. A whole entertainment may consist, without any impropriety, of the imitation of the social and amiable passions. It would be a strange entertainment which consisted altogether in the imitation of the odious and the vicious. A single song expresses almost always some social, agreeable, or interesting passion. In an opera the unsocial and disagreeable are sometimes introduced, but it is rarely, and as discords are introduced into harmony, to set off by their contrast the superior beauty of the opposite passions. What Plato said of Virtue, that it was of all beauties the brightest, may with some sort of truth be said of the proper and natural objects of musical imitation. They are either the sentiments and passions, in the exercise of which consist both the glory and the happiness of human life, or they are those from which it derives its most delicious pleasures, and most enlivening joys; or, at the worst and the lowest, they are those by which it calls upon our indulgence and compassionate assistance to its unavoidable weaknesses, distresses, and misfortunes.

To the merit of its imitation and to that of its happy choice in the objects which it imitates, the great merits of Statuary and Painting, Music joins another peculiar and exquisite merit of its own. Statuary and Painting cannot be said to add any new beauties of their own to the beauties of Nature which they imitate; they may assemble a greater number of those beauties, and group them in a more agreeable manner than they are commonly, or perhaps ever, to be found in Nature. It may perhaps be true, what the artists are so very fond of telling us, that no woman ever equalled,

in all the parts of her body, the beauty of the Venus of Medicis, nor any man that of the Apollo of Belvedere. But they must allow, surely, that there is no particular beauty in any part or feature of those two famous statues, which is not at least equalled, if not much excelled, by what is to be found in many living subjects. But Music, by arranging, and as it were bending to its own time and measure, whatever sentiments and passions it expresses, not only assembles and groups, as well as Statuary and Painting, the different beauties of Nature which it imitates, but it clothes them, besides, with a new and an exquisite beauty of its own; it clothes them with melody and harmony, which, like a transparent mantle, far from concealing any beauty, serve only to give a brighter colour, a more enlivening lustre and a more engaging grace to every beauty which they infold.

To these two different sorts of imitation, —to that general one, by which Music is made to resemble discourse, and to that particular one, by which it is made to express the sentiments and feelings with which a particular situation inspires a particular person,—there is frequently joined a third. The person who sings may join to this double imitation of the singer the additional imitation of the actor; and express, not only by the modulation and cadence of his voice, but by his countenance, by his attitudes, by his gestures, and by his motions, the sentiments and feelings of the person whose situation is painted in the song. Even in private company, though a song may sometimes perhaps be said to be well sung, it can never be said to be well performed, unless the singer does something of this kind; and there is no comparison between the effect of what is sung coldly from a music-book at the end of a harpsichord, and of what is not only sung, but acted with proper freedom, animation, and boldness. An opera actor does no more than this; and an imitation which is so pleasing, and which appears even so natural, in private society, ought not to appear forced, unnatural, or disagreeable upon the stage.

In a good opera actor, not only the modulations and pauses of his voice, but every motion and gesture, every variation, either in the air of his head, or in the attitude of his body, correspond to the time and measure of Music: they correspond to the expression of the sentiment or passion which the Music imitates, and that expression necessarily corresponds to this time and measure. Music is as it were the soul which animates him, which informs every feature of his countenance, and even directs every movement of his eyes. Like the musical expression of a song, his action adds to the natural grace of the sentiment or action which it imitates, a new and peculiar grace of its own; the exquisite and engaging grace of those gestures and motions, of those airs and attitudes which are directed by the movement, by the time and measure of Music; this grace heightens and enlivens that expression. Nothing can be more deeply affecting than the interesting scenes of the serious opera, when to good Poetry and good Music, to the Poetry of Metastasio and the Music of Pergolese, is added the execution of a good actor. In the serious opera, indeed, the action is too often sacrificed to the Music; the castrati, who perform the principal parts, being always the most insipid and miserable actors. The sprightly airs of the comic opera are, in the same manner, in the highest degree enlivening and diverting. Though they do not make us laugh so loud as we sometimes do at the scenes of the common comedy, they make us smile more frequently; and the agreeable gaiety, the temperate joy, if I may call it so, with which they inspire us, is not only an elegant, but a most delicious pleasure. The deep distress and the great passions of tragedy are capable of producing some effect, though it should be but indifferently acted. It is not so with the lighter misfortunes and less affecting situations of comedy: unless it is

at least tolerably acted, it is altogether insupportable. But the castrati are scarce ever tolerable actors; they are accordingly seldom admitted to play in the comic opera; which, being upon that account commonly better performed than the serious, appears to many people the better entertainment of the two.

The imitative powers of Instrumental are much inferior to those of Vocal Music; its melodious but unmeaning and inarticulated sounds cannot, like the articulations of the human voice, relate distinctly the circumstances of any particular story, or describe the different situations which those circumstances produced; or even express clearly, and so as to be understood by every hearer, the various sentiments and passions which the parties concerned felt from these situations: even its imitation of other sounds, the objects which it can certainly best imitate, is commonly so indistinct, that alone, and without any explication, it might not readily suggest to what was the imitated object. The rocking of a cradle is supposed to be imitated in that concerto of Corelli, which is said to have been composed for the Nativity: but unless we were told beforehand, it might not readily occur to us what it meant to imitate, or whether it meant to imitate any thing at all; and this imitation (which, though perhaps as successful as any other, is by no means the distinguished beauty of that admired composition) might only appear to us a singular and odd passage in Music. The ringing of bells and the singing of the lark and nightingale are imitated in the symphony of Instrumental Music which Mr. Handel has composed for the "Allegro" and "Penseroso" of Milton: these are not only sounds but musical sounds, and may therefore be supposed to be more within the compass of the powers of musical imitation. It is accordingly universally acknowledged, that in these imitations this great master has been remarkably successful; and yet, unless the verses of

Milton explained the meaning of the music, it might not even in this case readily occur to us what it meant to imitate, or whether it meant to imitate any thing at all. With the explication of the words, indeed, the imitation appears, what it certainly is, a very fine one; but without that explication it might perhaps appear only a singular passage, which had less connection either with what went before or with what came after it, than any other in the Music.

Instrumental Music is said sometimes to imitate motion; but in reality it only either imitates the particular sounds which accompany certain motions, or it produces sounds of which the time and measure bear some correspondence to the variations, to the pauses and interruptions, to the successive accelerations and retardations of the motion which it means to imitate: it is in this way that it sometimes attempts to express the march and array of an army, the confusion and hurry of a battle, etc. In all these cases, however, its imitation is so very indistinct, that without the accompaniment of some other art, to explain and interpret its meaning, it would be almost always unintelligible; and we could scarce ever know with certainty, either what it meant to imitate, or whether it meant to imitate any thing at all.

In the imitative arts, though it is by no means necessary that the imitating should so exactly resemble the imitated object, that the one should sometimes be mistaken for the other, it is, however, necessary that they should resemble at least so far, that the one should always readily suggest the other. It would be a strange picture which required an inscription at the foot to tell us, not only what particular person it meant to represent, but whether it meant to represent a man or a horse, or whether it meant to be a picture at all, and to represent any thing. The imitations of Instrumental Music may, in some respects, be said to resemble such pictures. There is, however, this very

essential difference between them, that the picture would not be much mended by the inscription; whereas, by what may be considered as very little more than such an inscription, Instrumental Music, though it cannot always even then, perhaps, be said properly to imitate, may, however, produce all the effects of the finest and most perfect imitation. In order to explain how this is brought about, it will not be necessary to descend into any great depth of philosophical speculation.

That train of thoughts and ideas which is continually passing through the mind does not always move on with the same pace, if I may say so, or with the same order and connection. When we are gay and cheerful, its motion is brisker and more lively, our thoughts succeed one another more rapidly, and those which immediately follow one another seem frequently either to have but little connection, or to be connected rather by their opposition than by their mutual resemblance. As in this wanton and playful disposition of mind we hate to dwell long upon the same thought, so we do not much care to pursue resembling thoughts; and the variety of contrast is more agreeable to us than the sameness of resemblance. It is quite otherwise when we are melancholy and desponding; we then frequently find ourselves haunted, as it were, by some thought which we would gladly chase away, but which constantly pursues us, and which admits no followers, attendants, or companions, but such as are of its own kindred and complexion. A slow succession of resembling or closely connected thoughts is the characteristic of this disposition of mind; a quick succession of thoughts, frequently contrasted and in general very slightly connected, is the characteristic of the other. What may be called the natural state of the mind, the state in which we are neither elated nor dejected, the state of sedateness, tranquillity, and composure, holds a sort of middle place between those two opposite extremes; our thoughts may succeed one another more slowly, and with a more distinct connection, than in the one; but more quickly and with a greater variety, than in the other.

Acute sounds are naturally gay, sprightly, and enlivening; grave sounds solemn, awful, and melancholy. There seems too to be some natural connection between acuteness in tune and quickness in time or succession, as well as between gravity and slowness: an acute sound seems to fly off more quickly than a grave one: the treble is more cheerful than the bass; its notes likewise commonly succeed one another more rapidly. But Instrumental Music, by a proper arrangement, by a quicker or slower succession of acute and grave, of resembling and contrasted sounds, can not only accommodate itself to the gay, the sedate, or the melancholy mood; but if the mind is so far vacant as not to be disturbed by any disorderly passion, it can, at least for the moment, and to a certain degree, produce every possible modification of each of those moods or dispositions. We all readily distinguish the cheerful, the gay, and the sprightly Music, from the melancholy, the plaintive, and the affecting; and both these from what holds a sort of middle place between them, the sedate, the tranquil, and the composing. And we are all sensible that, in the natural and ordinary state of the mind, Music can, by a sort of incantation, sooth and charm us into some degree of that particular mood or disposition which accords with its own character and temper. In a concert of Instrumental Music the attention is engaged, with pleasure and delight, to listen to a combination of the most agreeable and melodious sounds, which follow one another, sometimes with a quicker, and sometimes with a slower succession; and in which those that immediately follow one another sometimes exactly or nearly resemble, and sometimes contrast with one another in tune, in time, and in order of arrangement. The mind being thus successively occupied by a train of objects, of which the nature, succession, and connection correspond, sometimes to the gay, sometimes to the tranquil, and sometimes to the melancholy mood or disposition, it is itself successively led into each of those moods or dispositions; and is thus brought into a sort of harmony or concord with the Music which so agreeably engages its attention.

It is not, however, by imitation properly, that Instrumental Music produces this effect: Instrumental Music does not imitate, as Vocal Music, as Painting, or as Dancing would imitate, a gay, a sedate, or a melancholy person; it does not tell us, as any of those other arts could tell us, a pleasant, a serious, or a melancholy story. It is not, as in Vocal Music, in Painting, or in Dancing, by sympathy with the gaiety, the sedateness, or the melancholy and distress of some other person, that Instrumental Music soothes us into each of these dispositions: it becomes itself a gay, a sedate, or a melancholy object; and the mind naturally assumes the mood or disposition which at the time corresponds to the object which engages its attention. Whatever we feel from Instrumental Music is an original, and not a sympathetic feeling: it is our own gaiety, sedateness, or melancholy; not the reflected disposition of another person.

When we follow the winding alleys of some happily situated and well laid out garden, we are presented with a succession of landscapes, which are sometimes gay, sometimes gloomy, and sometimes calm and serene; if the mind is in its natural state, it suits itself to the objects which successively present themselves, and varies in some degree its mood and present humour with every variation of the scene. It would be improper, however, to say that those scenes imitated the gay, the calm, or the melancholy mood of the mind; they may produce in their turn each of those moods, but they cannot imitate any of them. Instrumental Music, in the same manner, though it can excite all those different dispositions, cannot imitate any of them. There are no two things in nature more perfectly disparate than sound and sentiment; and it is impossible by any human power to fashion the one into any thing that bears any real resemblance to the other.

This power of exciting and varying the different moods and dispositions of the mind, which Instrumental Music really possesses to a very considerable degree, has been the principal source of its reputation for those great imitative powers which have been ascribed to it. "Painting," says an author, more capable of feeling strongly than of analysing accurately, Mr. Rousseau of Geneva, "Painting, which presents its imitations, not to the imagination, but to the senses, and to only one of the senses, can represent nothing besides the objects of sight. Music, one might imagine, should be equally confined to those of hearing. It imitates, however, every thing, even those objects which are perceivable by sight only. By a delusion that seems almost inconceivable, it can, as it were, put the eye into the ear; and the greatest wonder, of an art which acts only by motion and succession, is, that it can imitate rest and repose. Night, Sleep, Solitude, and Silence are all within the compass of musical imitation. Though all Nature should be asleep, the person who contemplates it is awake; and the art of the musician consists in substituting, in the room of an image of what is not the object of hearing, that of the movements which its presence would excite in the mind of the spectator."—That is, of the effects which it would produce upon his mood and disposition. "The musician" (continues the same author) "will sometimes, not only agitate the waves of the sea, blow up the flames of a conflagration, make the rain fall, the rivulets flow and swell the torrents, but he will paint the horrors of a hideous desert, darken the walls of a subterraneous dungeon, calm the tempest, restore serenity and tranquillity to the air and the sky, and shed from the orchestra a new freshness over the groves and the fields. He will not directly represent any of these objects, but he will excite in the mind the same movements which it would feel from seeing them."

Upon this very eloquent description of Mr. Rousseau I must observe, that without the accompaniment of the scenery and action of the opera, without the assistance either of the scene-painter or of the poet, or of both, the Instrumental Music of the orchestra could produce none of the effects which are here ascribed to it; and we could never know, we could never even guess, which of the gay, melancholy, or tranquil objects above mentioned it meant to represent to us; or whether it meant to represent any of them, and not merely to entertain us with a concert of gay, melancholy, or tranquil Music; or, as the ancients called them, of the Diastaltic, of the Systaltic, or of the Middle Music. With that accompaniment, indeed, though it cannot always even then, perhaps, be said properly to imitate, yet by supporting the imitation of some other art, it may produce all the same effects upon us as if itself had imitated in the finest and most perfect manner. Whatever be the object or situation which the scene-painter represents upon the theatre, the music of the orchestra, by disposing the mind to the same sort of mood and temper which it would feel from the presence of that object, or from sympathy with the person who was placed in that situation, can greatly enhance the effect of that imitation: it can accommodate itself to every diversity of scene. The melancholy of the man who, upon some great occasion, only finds himself alone in the darkness, the silence and solitude of the night, is very different from that of one who, upon a like occasion, finds himself in the midst of some dreary and inhospitable desert; and even in this situation his feelings would not be the same as if he was shut up in a subterraneous dungeon. The different degrees of precision with which the music of the orchestra can accommodate itself to each of those diversities, must depend upon the taste, the sensibility, the fancy and imagination of the composer: it may sometimes, perhaps, contribute to this precision, that it should imitate, as well as it can, the sounds which either naturally accompany, or which might be supposed to accompany, the particular objects represented. The symphony in the French opera of *Alcyone,* which imitated the violence of the winds and the dashing of the waves, in the tempest which was to drown Coix, is much commended by contemporary writers. That in the opera of *Isse,* which imitated that murmuring in the leaves of the oaks of Dodona, which might be supposed to precede the miraculous pronunciation of the oracle: and that in the opera of *Amadis,* of which the dismal accents imitated the sounds which might be supposed to accompany the opening of the tomb of Ardan, before the apparition of the ghost of that warrior, are still more celebrated. Instrumental Music, however, without violating too much its own melody and harmony, can imitate but imperfectly the sounds of natural objects, of which the greater part have neither melody nor harmony. Great reserve, great discretion, and a very nice discernment are requisite, in order to introduce with propriety such imperfect imitations, either into Poetry or Music; when repeated too often, when continued too long, they appear to be what they really are, mere tricks, in which a very inferior artist, if he will only give himself the trouble to attend to them, can easily equal the greatest. I have seen a Latin translation of Mr. Pope's "Ode on St. Cecilia's Day," which in this respect very much excelled the original. Such imitations are still easier in Music. Both in the one art and in the other, the difficulty is not in making them as well as they are capable of being made, but in knowing when and how far to make them at all: but to be able to accommodate the temper and character of the music to every peculiarity of the scene and situation with such exact precision, that the one shall produce the very same effect upon the mind as

the other, is not one of those tricks in which an inferior artist can easily equal the greatest; it is an art which requires all the judgment, knowledge, and invention of the most consummate master. It is upon this art, and not upon its imperfect imitation, either of real or imaginary sounds, that the great effects of Instrumental Music depend; such imitations ought perhaps to be admitted only so far as they may sometimes contribute to ascertain the meaning, and thereby to enhance the effects of this art.

By endeavouring to extend the effects of scenery beyond what the nature of the thing will admit of, it has been much abused; and in the common, as well as in the musical drama, many imitations have been attempted, which, after the first and second time we have seen them, necessarily appear ridiculous: such are, the Thunder rumbling from the Mustard-bowl, and the Snow of Paper and thick Hail of Pease, so finely exposed by Mr. Pope. Such imitations resemble those of painted Statuary; they may surprise at first, but they disgust ever after, and appear evidently such simple and easy tricks as are fit only for the amusement of children and their nurses at a puppet-show. The thunder of either theatre ought certainly never to be louder than that which the orchestra is capable of producing; and their most dreadful tempests ought never to exceed what the scene painter is capable of representing. In such imitations there may be an art which merits some degree of esteem and admiration. In the other there can be none which merits any.

This abuse of scenery has both subsisted much longer, and been carried to a much greater degree of extravagance, in the musical than in the common drama. In France it has been long banished from the latter; but it still continues, not only to be tolerated, but to be admired and applauded in the former. In the French operas, not only thunder and lightning, storms and tempests, are commonly represented in the ridiculous manner above mentioned, but all the marvellous, all the supernatural of Epic Poetry, all the metamorphoses of Mythology, all the wonders of Witchcraft and Magic, every thing that is most unfit to be represented upon the stage, are every day exhibited with the most complete approbation and applause of that ingenious nation. The music of the orchestra producing upon the audience nearly the same effect which a better and more artful imitation would produce, hinders them from feeling, at least in its full force, the ridicule of those childish and awkward imitations which necessarily abound in that extravagant scenery. And in reality such imitations, though no doubt ridiculous every where, yet certainly appear somewhat less so in the musical than they would in the common drama. The Italian opera, before it was reformed by Apostolo, Zeno, and Metastasio, was in this respect equally extravagant, and was upon that account the subject of the agreeable raillery of Mr. Addison in several different papers of the *Spectator*. Even since that reformation it still continues to be a rule, that the scene should change at least with every act; and the unity of place never was a more sacred law in the common drama, than the violation of it has become in the musical: the latter seems in reality to require both a more picturesque and a more varied scenery, than is at all necessary for the former. In an opera, as the music supports the effect of the scenery, so the scenery often serves to determine the character, and to explain the meaning of the Music; it ought to vary therefore as that character varies. The pleasure of an opera, besides, is in its nature more a sensual pleasure, than that of a common comedy or tragedy; the latter produce their effect principally by means of the imagination: in the closet, accordingly, their effect is not much inferior to what it is upon the stage. But the effect of an opera is seldom very great in the closet; it addresses itself more to the external senses, and as it soothes the ear by its melody and harmony, so we feel that it ought to dazzle the eye with the splendour of its scenery.

In an opera the Instrumental Music of the orchestra supports the imitation both of the poet and of the actor, as well as of the scene-painter. The overture disposes the mind to that mood which fits it for the opening of the piece. The Music between the acts keeps up the impression which the foregoing had made, and prepares us for that which the following is to make. When the orchestra interrupts, as it frequently does, either the recitative or the air, it is in order either to enforce the effect of what had gone before, or to put the mind in the mood which fits it for hearing what is to come after. Both in the recitatives and in the airs it accompanies and directs the voice, and often brings it back to the proper tone and modulation, when it is upon the point of wandering away from them; and the correctness of the best Vocal Music is owing in a great measure to the guidance of Instrumental; though in all these cases it supports the imitation of another art, yet in all of them it may be said rather to diminish than to increase the resemblance between the imitating and the imitated object. Nothing can be more unlike to what really passes in the world, than that persons engaged in the most interesting situations, both of public and private life, in sorrow, in disappointment, in distress, in despair, should, in all that they say and do, be constantly accompanied with a fine concert of Instrumental Music. Were we to reflect upon it, such accompaniment must in all cases diminish the probability of the action, and render the representation still less like nature than it otherwise would be. It is not by imitation, therefore, that Instrumental Music supports and enforces the imitations of the other arts; but it is by producing upon the mind, in consequences of other powers, the same sort of effect which the most exact imitation of nature, which the most perfect observation of probability, could produce. To produce this effect is, in such entertainments, the sole end and purpose of that imitation and observation. If it can be equally well produced by other means, this end and purpose may be equally well answered.

But if Instrumental Music can seldom be said to be properly imitative, even when it is employed to support the imitation of some other art, it is commonly still less so when it is employed alone. Why should it embarrass its melody and harmony, or constrain its time and measure, by attempting an imitation which, without the accompaniment of some other art to explain and interpret its meaning, nobody is likely to understand? In the most approved Instrumental Music, accordingly, in the overtures of Handel and the concertos of Corelli, there is little or no imitation, and where there is any, it is the source of but a very small part of the merit of those compositions. Without any imitation, Instrumental Music can produce very considerable effects; though its powers over the heart and affections are, no doubt, much inferior to those of vocal Music, it has, however, considerable powers: by the sweetness of its sounds it awakens agreeably, and calls upon the attention; by their connection and affinity it naturally detains that attention, which follows easily a series of agreeable sounds, which have all a certain relation both to a common, fundamental, or leading note, called the key note; and to a certain succession or combination of notes, called the song or composition. By means of this relation each foregoing sound seems to introduce, and as it were prepare the mind for the following: by its rhythmus, by its time and measure, it disposes that succession of sounds into a certain arrangement, which renders the whole more easy to be comprehended and remembered. Time and measure are to Instrumental Music what order and method are to discourse; they break it into proper parts and divisions, by which we are enabled both to remember better what is gone before, and frequently to foresee somewhat of what is to come after; we frequent-

ly foresee the return of a period which we know must correspond to another which we remember to have gone before; and, according to the saying of an ancient philosopher and musician, the enjoyment of Music arises partly from memory and partly from foresight. When the measure, after having been continued so long as to satisfy us, changes to another, that variety, which thus disappoints, becomes more agreeable to us than the uniformity which would have gratified our expectation: but without this order and method we could remember very little of what had gone before, and we could foresee still less of what was to come after; and the whole enjoyment of Music would be equal to little more than the effect of the particular sounds which rung in our ears at every particular instant. By means of this order and method it is, during the progress of the entertainment, equal to the effect of all that we remember, and of all that we foresee; and at the conclusion of the entertainment, to the combined and accumulated effect of all the different parts of which the whole was composed.

A well-composed concerto of Instrumental Music, by the number and variety of the instruments, by the variety of the parts which are performed by them, and the perfect concord or correspondence of all these different parts; by the exact harmony or coincidence of all the different sounds which are heard at the same time, and by that happy variety of measure which regulates the succession of those which are heard at different times, presents an object so agreeable, so great, so various, and so interesting, that alone, and without suggesting any other object, either by imitation or otherwise, it can occupy, and as it were fill up, completely the whole capacity of the mind, so as to leave no part of its attention vacant for thinking of any thing else. In the contemplation of that immense variety of agreeable and melodious sounds, arranged and digested, both in their coincidence and in their succession, into so complete and regular a system, the mind in reality enjoys not only a very great sensual, but a very high intellectual pleasure, not unlike that which it derives from the contemplation of a great system in any other science. A full concerto of such Instrumental Music, not only does not require, but it does not admit of any accompaniment. A song or a dance, by demanding an attention which we have not to spare, would disturb, instead of heightening, the effect of the Music; they may often very properly succeed, but they cannot accompany it. That music seldom means to tell any particular story, or to imitate any particular event, or in general to suggest any particular object, distinct from that combination of sounds of which itself is composed. Its meaning, therefore, may be said to be complete in itself, and to require no interpreters to explain it. What is called the subject of such Music is merely, as has already been said, a certain leading combination of notes, to which it frequently returns, and to which all its digressions and variations bear a certain affinity. It is altogether different from what is called the subject of a poem or a picture, which is always something which is not either in the poem or in the picture, or something distinct from that combination, either of words on the one hand or of colours on the other, of which they are respectively composed. The subject of a composition of Instrumental Music is part of that composition: the subject of a poem or picture is part of neither.

The effect of Instrumental Music upon the mind has been called its expression. In the feeling it is frequently not unlike the effect of what is called the expression of Painting, and is sometimes equally interesting. But the effect of the expression of Painting arises always from the thought of something which, though distinctly and clearly suggested by the drawing and colouring of the picture, is altogether different from that drawing and colouring. It arises sometimes from sympathy with, sometimes from antipathy and aversion to, the sentiments, emotions, and passions which the countenance, the action, the air and attitude of the persons represented suggest. The melody and harmony of Instrumental Music, on the contrary, do not distinctly and clearly suggest any thing that is different from that melody and harmony. Whatever effect it produces is the immediate effect of that melody and harmony, and not of something else which is signified and suggested by them: they in fact signify and suggest nothing. It may be proper to say that the complete art of Painting, the complete merit of a picture, is composed of three distinct arts or merits; that of drawing, that of colouring, and that of expression. But to say, as Mr. Addison does, that the complete art of a musician, the complete merit of a piece of Music, is composed or made up of three distinct arts or merits, that of melody, that of harmony, and that of expression, is to say, that it is made up of melody and harmony, and of the immediate and necessary effect of melody and harmony: the division is by no means logical; expression in Painting is not the necessary effect either of good drawing or of good colouring, or of both together; a picture may be both finely drawn and finely coloured, and yet have very little expression: but that effect upon the mind which is called expression in Music, is the immediate and necessary effect of good melody. In the power of producing this effect consists the essential characteristic which distinguishes such melody from what is bad or indifferent. Harmony may enforce the effect of good melody, but without good melody the most skilful harmony can produce no effect which deserves the name of expression; it can do little more than fatigue and confound the ear. A painter may possess, in a very eminent degree, the talents of drawing and colouring, and yet possess that of expression in a very inferior degree. Such a painter, too, may have great merit. In the judgment of Du Piles, even the celebrated Titian was a painter of this kind. But to say that a musician possessed the talents of melody and harmony in a very eminent degree, and that of expression in a very inferior one, would be to say, that in his works the cause was not followed by its necessary and proportionable effect. A musician may be a very skilful harmonist, and yet be defective in the talents of melody, air, and expression; his songs may be dull and without effect. Such a musician too may have a certain degree of merit, not unlike that of a man of great learning, who wants fancy, taste, and invention.

Instrumental Music, therefore, though it may, no doubt, be considered in some respects as an imitative art, is certainly less so than any other which merits that appellation; it can imitate but a few objects, and even these so imperfectly, that without the accompaniment of some other art, its imitation is scarce ever intelligible: imitation is by no means essential to it, and the principal effect it is capable of producing arises from powers altogether different from those of imitation.

§ IMITATION IN THE DANCE

The imitative powers of Dancing are much superior to those of Instrumental Music, and are at least equal, perhaps superior, to those of any other art. Like Instrumental Music, however, it is not necessarily or essentially imitative, and it can produce very agreeable effects, without imitating any thing. In the greater part of our common dances there is little or no imitation, and they consist almost entirely of a succession of such steps, gestures, and motions, regulated by the time and measure of Music, as either display extraordinary grace or require extaordinary agility. Even some of our dances, which are said to have been originally imitative, have, in the way in in which we practise them, almost ceased to be so. The minuet, in which the woman, after passing and repassing the man several times, first gives him up one hand, then the

other, and then both hands, is said to have been originally a Moorish dance, which emblematically represented the passion of love. Many of my readers may have frequently danced this dance, and, in the opinion of all who saw them, with great grace and propriety, though neither they nor the spectators once thought of the allegorical meaning which it originally intended to express.

A certain measured, cadenced step, commonly called a dancing step, which keeps time with, and as it were beats the measure of, the Music which accompanies and directs it, is the essential characteristic which distinguishes a dance from every other sort of motion. When the dancer, moving with a step of this kind, and observing this time and measure, imitates either the ordinary or the more important actions of human life, he shapes and fashions, as it were, a thing of one kind, into the resemblance of another thing of a very different kind: his art conquers the disparity which Nature has placed between the imitating and the imitated object, and has upon that account some degree of that sort of merit which belongs to all the imitative arts. This disparity, indeed, is not so great as in some other of those arts, nor consequently the merit of the imitation which conquers it. Nobody would compare the merit of a good imitative dancer to that of a good painter or statuary. The dancer, however, may have a very considerable degree of merit, and his imitation perhaps may sometimes be capable of giving us as much pleasure as that of either of the other two artists. All the subjects, either of Statuary or of History Painting, are within the compass of his imitative powers; and in representing them, his art has even some advantage over both the other two. Statuary and History Painting can represent but a single instant of the action which they mean to imitate: the causes which prepared, the consequences which followed, the situation of that single instant are altogether beyond the compass of their imitation. A pantomime dance can represent distinctly those causes and consequences; it is not confined to the situation of a single instant; but, like Epic Poetry, it can represent all the events of a long story, and exhibit a long train and succession of connected and interesting situations. It is capable therefore of affecting us much more than either Statuary or Painting. The ancient Romans used to shed tears at the representations of their pantomimes, as we do at that of the most interesting tragedies; an effect which is altogether beyond the powers of Statuary or Painting.

The ancient Greeks appear to have been a nation of dancers, and both their common and their stage dances seem to have been all imitative. The stage dances of the ancient Romans appear to have been equally so. Among that grave people it was reckoned indecent to dance in private societies; and they could therefore have no common dances; and among both nations imitation seems to have been considered as essential to dancing.

It is quite otherwise in modern times: though we have pantomime dances upon the stage, yet the greater part even of our stage dances are not pantomime, and cannot well be said to imitate any thing. The greater part of our common dances either never were pantomime, or, with a very few exceptions, have almost all ceased to be so.

This remarkable difference of character between the ancient and the modern dances seems to be the natural effect of a correspondent difference in that of the music, which has accompanied and directed both the one and the other.

In modern times we almost always dance to instrumental music, which being itself not imitative, the greater part of the dances which it directs, and as it were inspires, have ceased to be so. In ancient times, on the contrary, they seem to have danced almost always to vocal music; which being necessarily and essentially imitative, their dances became so too. The ancients seem to have had little or nothing of what is properly called instrumental music, or of music composed not to be sung by the voice, but to be played upon instruments, and both their wind and stringed instruments seem to have served only as an accompaniment and direction to the voice.

In the country it frequently happens, that a company of young people take a fancy to dance, though they have neither fiddler nor piper to dance to. A lady undertakes to sing while the rest of the company dance: in most cases she sings the notes only, without the words, and then the voice being little more than a musical instrument, the dance is performed in the usual way, without any imitation. But if she sings the words, and if in those words there happens to be somewhat more than ordinary spirit and humour, immediately all the company, especially all the best dancers, and all those who dance most at their ease, become more or less pantomimes, and by their gestures and motions express, as well as they can, the meaning and story of the song. This would be still more the case, if the same person both danced and sung; a practice very common among the ancients: it requires good lungs and a vigorous constitution; but with these advantages and long practice, the very highest dances may be performed in this manner. I have seen a Negro dance to his own song, the war-dance of his own country, with such vehemence of action and expression, that the whole company, gentlemen as well as ladies, got up upon chairs and tables, to be as much as possible out of the way of his fury. In the Greek language there are two verbs which both signify to dance; each of which has its proper derivatives, signifying a dance and a dancer. In the greater part of Greek authors, these two sets of words, like all others which are nearly synonymous, are frequently confounded, and used promiscuously. According to the best critics, however, in strict propriety, one of these verbs signifies to dance and sing at the same time, or to dance to one's own music. The other to dance without singing, or to dance to the music of other people. There is said too to be a correspondent difference in the signification of their respective derivatives. In the choruses of the ancient Greek tragedies, consisting sometimes of more than fifty persons, some piped and some sung, but all danced, and danced to their own music.

§ OF THE AFFINITY BETWEEN MUSIC, DANCING, AND POETRY[2]

In the second part of the preceding Essay I have mentioned the connection between the two arts of Music and Dancing, formed by the Rhythmus, as the ancients termed it, or, as we call it, the tune or measure that equally regulates both.

It is not, however, every sort of step, gesture, or motion, of which the correspondence with the tune or measure of Music will constitute a Dance. It must be a step, gesture, or motion of a particular sort. In a good opera-actor, not only the modulations and pauses of his voice, but every motion and gesture, every variation, either in the air of his head or in the attitude of his body, correspond to the time and measure of Music. The best opera-actor, however, is not, according to the language of any country in Europe, understood to dance, yet in the performance of his part, he makes use of what is called the stage step; but even this step is not understood to be a dancing step.

Though the eye of the most ordinary spectator readily distinguishes between what is called a dancing step and any other step, gesture, or motion, yet it may not perhaps be very easy to express what it is which constitutes this distinction. To ascertain

exactly the precise limits at which the one species begins, and the other ends, or to give an accurate definition of this very frivolous matter, might perhaps require more thought and attention than the very small importance of the subject may seem to deserve. Were I, however, to attempt to do this, I should observe, that though in performing any ordinary action—in walking, for example—from the one end of the room to the other, a person may show both grace and agility, yet if he betrays the least intention of showing either, he is sure of offending more or less, and we never fail to accuse him of some degree of vanity and affectation. In the performance of any such ordinary action, every person wishes to appear to be solely occupied about the proper purpose of the action: if he means to show either grace or agility, he is careful to conceal that meaning, and he is very seldom successful in doing so: he offends, however, just in proportion as he betrays it, and he almost always betrays it. In Dancing, on the contrary, every person professes, and avows, as it were, the intention of displaying some degree either of grace or of agility, or of both. The display of one, or other, or both of these qualities, is in reality the proper purpose of the action; and there can never be any disagreeable vanity or affectation in following out the proper purpose of any action. When we say of any particular person, that he gives himself many affected airs and graces in Dancing, we mean either that he gives himself airs and graces which are unsuitable to the nature of the Dance, or that he executes awkwardly, perhaps exaggerates too much (the most common fault in Dancing), the airs and graces which are suitable to it. Every Dance is in reality a succession of airs and graces of some kind or other, and of airs and graces which, if I may say so, profess themselves to be such. The steps, gestures, and motions which, as it were, avow the intention of exhibiting a succession of such airs and graces, are the steps, the gestures, and the motions which

---

2 The following Observations were found among Mr. Smith's Manuscripts, without any intimation whether they were intended as part of this, or of a different Essay. As they appeared too valuable to be suppressed, the Editors have annexed them to this Essay.

are peculiar to Dancing, and when these are performed to the time and the measure of Music, they constitute what is properly called a Dance.

But though every sort of step, gesture, or motion, even though performed to the time and measure of Music, will not alone make a Dance, yet almost any sort of sound, provided it is repeated with a distinct rhythmus, or according to a distinct time and measure, though without any variation as to gravity or acuteness, will make a sort of Music, no doubt indeed, an imperfect one. Drums, cymbals, and, so far as I have observed, all other instruments of percussion, have only one note; this note, however, when repeated with a certain rhythmus, or according to a certain time and measure, and sometimes, in order to mark more distinctly that time and measure, with some little variation as to loudness and lowness, though without any as to acuteness and gravity, does certainly make a sort of Music, which is frequently far from being disagreeable, and which even sometimes produces considerable effects. The simple note of such instruments, it is true, is generally a very clear, or what is called a melodious, sound. It does not however seem indispensably necessary that it should be so. The sound of the muffled drum, when it beats the dead march, is far from being either clear or melodious, and yet it certainly produces a species of Music which is sometimes affecting. Even in the performance of the most humble of all artists, of the man who drums upon the table with his fingers, we may sometimes distinguish the measure, and perhaps a little of the humour, of some favourite song; and we must allow that even he makes some sort of Music. Without a proper step and motion, the observation of tune alone will not make a Dance; time alone, without tune, will make some sort of Music.

That exact observation of tune, or of the proper intervals of gravity and acuteness, which constitutes the great beauty of all perfect Music, constitutes likewise its great difficulty. The time, or measure of a song are simple matters, which even a coarse and unpractised ear is capable of distinguishing and comprehending: but to distinguish and comprehend all the variations of the tune, and to conceive with precision the exact proportion of every note, is what the finest and most cultivated ear is frequently no more than capable of performing. In the singing of the common people we may generally remark a distinct enough observation of time, but a very imperfect one of tune. To discover and to distinguish with precision the proper intervals of tune, must have been a work of long experience and much observation. In the theoretical treatises upon Music, what the authors have to say upon time is commonly discussed in a single chapter of no great length or difficulty. The theory of tune fills commonly all the rest of the volume, and has long ago become both an extensive and an abstruse science, which is often but imperfectly comprehended, even by intelligent artists. In the first rude efforts of uncivilized nations towards singing, the niceties of tune could be but little attended to: I have, upon this account, been frequently disposed to doubt of the great antiquity of those national songs, which it is pretended have been delivered down from age to age by a sort of oral tradition, without having been ever noted or distinctly recorded for many successive generations. The measure, the humour of the song, might perhaps have been delivered down in this manner, but it seems scarcely possible that the precise notes of the tune should have been so preserved. The method of singing some of what we reckon our old Scotch songs, has undergone great alterations within the compass of my memory, and it may have undergone still greater before.

The distinction between the sounds or tones of singing and those of speaking seems to be of the same kind with that between the steps, gestures, and motions of

Dancing, and those of any other ordinary action; though in speaking, a person may show a very agreeable tone of voice, yet if he seems to intend to show it, if he appears to listen to the sound of his own voice, and as it were to tune it into a pleasing modulation, he never fails to offend, as guilty of a most disagreeable affectation. In speaking, as in every other ordinary action, we expect and require that the speaker should attend only to the proper purpose of the action, the clear and distinct expression of what he has to say. In singing, on the contrary, every person professes the intention to please by the tone and cadence of his voice; and he not only appears to be guilty of no disagreeable affectation in doing so, but we expect and require that he should do so. To please by the choice and arrangement of agreeable sounds is the proper purpose of all Music, vocal as well as instrumental; and we always expect and require, that every person should attend to the proper purpose of whatever action he is performing. A person may appear to sing, as well as to dance, affectedly; he may endeavour to please by sounds and tones which are unsuitable to the nature of the song, or he may dwell too much on those which are suitable to it, or in some other way he may show an overweening conceit of his own abilities, beyond what seems to be warranted by his performance. The disagreeable affectation appears to consist always, not in attempting to please by a proper, but by some improper modulation of the voice. It was early discovered that the vibrations of chords or strings, which either in their lengths, or in their densities, or in their degrees of tension, bear a certain propor-

tion to one another, produce sounds which correspond exactly, or, as the musicians say, are the unisons of those sounds or tones of the human voice which the ear approves of in singing. This discovery has enabled musicians to speak with distinctness and precision concerning the musical sounds or tones of the human voice; they can always precisely ascertain what are the particular sounds or tones which they mean, by ascertaining what are the proportions of the strings of which the vibrations produce the unisons of those sounds or tones. What are called the intervals; that is, the differences, in point of gravity and acuteness, between the sounds or tones of a singing voice, are much greater and more distinct than those of the speaking voice. Though the former, therefore, can be measured and appreciated by the proportions of chords of strings, the latter cannot. The nicest instruments cannot express the extreme minuteness of these intervals. The heptamerede of Mr. Sauveur could express an interval so small as the seventh part of what is called a comma, the smallest interval that is admitted in modern Music. Yet even this instrument, we are informed by Mr. Duclos, could not express the minuteness of the intervals in the pronunciation of the Chinese language; of all the languages in the world, that of which the pronunciation is said to approach the nearest to singing, or in which the intervals are said to be the greatest.

As the sounds or tones of the singing voice, therefore, can be ascertained or appropriated, while those of the speaking voice cannot; the former are capable of being noted or recorded, while the latter are not.

SAMUEL TAYLOR
COLERIDGE

(1772-1834)

Son of a clergyman and grammar-school master, Coleridge was his father's tenth child. In 1782, in view of his precocious brilliance, he was sent as a "charity-boy" to Christ's Hospital, where he met and became a friend of Charles Lamb. From 1791 to 1794 he was more or less at Cambridge University, but did not take a degree. For some years after that Coleridge tried his hand at journalism and preaching, but he was not successful enough in these vocations to support himself and his family. In the end he was to subsist largely on annuities provided by sympathetic friends and admirers. The pains of the rheumatism and neuralgia that he had contracted while still in school led him, starting in 1796, to try laudanum as an anodyne; and the habit of taking opiates, which became fixed about 1803, stayed with him (despite interruptions) for the rest of his life.

The milestones of his career as a poet and of his friendships with Southey, Words-worth, and Hazlitt need not be mentioned here. Of greater pertinence is the fact that as early as 1787 he had made a study of a book entitled *Plotinus Concerning the Beautiful*. In 1798 he made an eight-month trip to Germany with the Wordsworths for the purpose of studying the Kantian philosophy, and in 1802 he settled down once more to a serious study of Kant. In Germany he became acquainted with currents of aesthetic speculation other than the strictly Kantian,and, indeed, he has been accused of having borrowed rather too liberally from a set of lectures delivered by one of the German philosophers.

According to the *Dictionary of National Biography*, Coleridge is the only Englishman who "takes first rank as a poet, critic, and philosopher." He himself would probably not have drawn a line between the criticism of art and aesthetics. His literary criticism is shot through with philosophical preoccupations. Perhaps only Nietzsche gives us an example of a mind that moves as naturally as Coleridge's from concrete interests to theory and speculation and back again. In some of the passages reprinted here, nevertheless, aesthetic theory is more predominant than critical appreciation. The "Fragment of an Essay on Taste," for example, reflects a knowledge both of eighteenth-century critical theory and of contemporary German aesthetics. Nearly all of the selections are unabridged and are in the form in which Coleridge left them.

SAMUEL TAYLOR COLERIDGE

Selections

Definition of Poetry

Poetry is not the proper antithesis to prose, but to science. Poetry is opposed to science, and prose to metre. The proper and immediate object of science is the acquirement, or communication, of truth; the proper and immediate object of poetry is the communication of immediate pleasure. This definition is useful; but as it would include novels and other works of fiction, which yet we do not call poems, there must be some additional character by which poetry is not only divided from opposites, but likewise distinguished from disparate, though similar, modes of composition. Now how is this to be effected? In animated prose, the beauties of nature, and the passions and accidents of human nature, are often expressed in that natural language which the contemplation of them would suggest to a pure and benevolent mind; yet still neither we nor the writers call such a work a poem, though no work could deserve that name which did not include all this, together with something else. What is this? It is that pleasurable emotion, that peculiar state and degree of excitement, which arises in the poet himself in the act of composition;—and in order to understand this, we must combine a more than ordinary sympathy with the objects, emo-

From Lectures on Shakspeare. *New York: Everyman's Library, E. P. Dutton & Co., Inc., 1956. Reprinted by permission of E. P. Dutton & Co., Inc. (First published: 1810–1818.)*

tions, or incidents contemplated by the poet, consequent on a more than common sensibility, with a more than ordinary activity of the mind in respect of the fancy and the imagination. Hence is produced a more vivid reflection of the truths of nature and of the human heart, united with a constant activity modifying and correcting these truths by that sort of pleasurable emotion, which the exertion of all our faculties gives in a certain degree; but which can only be felt in perfection under the full play of those powers of mind, which are spontaneous rather than voluntary, and in which the effort required bears no proportion to the activity enjoyed. This is the state which permits the production of a highly pleasurable whole, of which each part shall also communicate for itself a distinct and conscious pleasure; and hence arises the definition, which I trust is now intelligible, that poetry, or rather a poem, is a species of composition, opposed to science, as having intellectual pleasure for its object, and as attaining its end by the use of language natural to us in a state of excitement,—but distinguished from other species of composition, not excluded by the former criterion, by permitting a pleasure from the whole consistent with a consciousness of pleasure from the component parts; —and the perfection of which is, to communicate from each part the greatest immediate pleasure compatible with the largest sum of pleasure on the whole. This, of course, will vary with the different modes of poetry;—and that splendour of particular lines, which would be worthy of admiration in an impassioned elegy, or a short indignant satire, would be a blemish and proof of vile taste in a tragedy or an epic poem.

It is remarkable, by the way, that Milton in three incidental words has implied all which for the purposes of more distinct apprehension, which at first must be slow-paced in order to be distinct, I have endeavoured to develope in a precise and strictly adequate definition. Speaking of

poetry, he says, as in a parenthesis, "which is simple, sensuous, passionate." How awful is the power of words!—fearful often in their consequences when merely felt, not understood; but most awful when both felt and understood!—Had these three words only been properly understood by, and present in the minds of, general readers, not only almost a library of false poetry would have been either precluded or still-born, but, what is of more consequence, works truly excellent and capable of enlarging the understanding, warming and purifying the heart, and placing in the centre of the whole being the germs of noble and manlike actions, would have been the common diet of the intellect instead. For the first condition, simplicity,— while, on the one hand, it distinguishes poetry from the arduous processes of science, labouring towards an end not yet arrived at, and supposes a smooth and finished road, on which the reader is to walk onward easily, with streams murmuring by his side, and trees and flowers and human dwellings to make his journey as delightful as the object of it is desirable, instead of having to toil with the pioneers and painfully make the road on which others are to travel,—precludes, on the other hand, every affectation and morbid peculiarity;—the second condition, sensuousness, insures that framework of objectivity, that definiteness and articulation of imagery, and that modification of the images themselves, without which poetry becomes flattened into mere didactics of practice, or evaporated into a hazy, unthoughtful day-dreaming; and the third condition, passion, provides that neither thought nor imagery shall be simply objective, but that the *passio vera* of humanity shall warm and animate both.

To return, however, to the previous definition, this most general and distinctive character of a poem originates in the poetic genius itself; and though it comprises whatever can with any propriety be called a poem (unless that word be a mere lazy synonym for a composition in metre), it yet becomes a just, and not merely discriminative, but full and adequate, definition of poetry in its highest and most peculiar sense, only so far as the distinction still results from the poetic genius, which sustains and modifies the emotions, thoughts, and vivid representations of the poem by the energy without effort of the poet's own mind,—by the spontaneous activity of his imagination and fancy, and by whatever else with these reveals itself in the balancing and reconciling of opposite or discordant qualities, sameness with difference, a sense of novelty and freshness with old or customary objects, a more than usual state of emotion with more than usual order, self-possession and judgment with enthusiasm and vehement feeling, — and which, while it blends and harmonizes the natural and the artificial, still subordinates art to nature, the manner to the matter, and our admiration of the poet to our sympathy with the images, passions, characters, and incidents of the poem:—

> Doubtless, this could not be, but that she turns
> Bodies to *spirit* by sublimation strange,
> As fire converts to fire the things it burns—
> As we our food into our nature change!
>
> From their gross matter she abstracts *their* forms,
> And draws a kind of quintessence from things,
> Which to her proper nature she transforms
> To bear them light on her celestial wings!
>
> *Thus* doth she, when from *individual states*
> She doth abstract the universal kinds,
> *Which then reclothed in divers names and fates*
> *Steal access thro' our senses to our minds.*[1]

---

[1] [This paragraph closely resembles one in Chapter XIV of Coleridge's *Biographia Literaria*. The stanzas quoted are from a long poem on the immortality of the soul by Sir John Davies (1569–

Second Lecture on Shakspeare and Milton

Readers may be divided into four classes:

1. Sponges, who absorb all they read, and return it nearly in the same state, only a little dirtied.

2. Sand-glasses, who retain nothing, and are content to get through a book for the sake of getting through the time.

3. Strain-bags, who retain merely the dregs of what they read.

4. Mogul diamonds, equally rare and valuable, who profit by what they read, and enable others to profit by it also.

I adverted in my last lecture to the prevailing laxity in the use of terms: this is the principal complaint to which the moderns are exposed; but it is a grievous one, inasmuch as it inevitably tends to the misapplication of words, and to the corruption of language. I mentioned the word "taste," but the remark applies not merely to substantives and adjectives, to things and their epithets, but to verbs: thus, how frequently is the verb "indorsed" strained from its true signification, as given by Milton in the expression—"And elephants indorsed with towers." Again "virtue" has been equally perverted: originally it signified merely strength; it then became strength of mind and valour, and it has now been changed to the class term for moral excellence in all its various species. I only introduce these as instances by the way, and nothing could be easier than to multiply them.

At the same time, while I recommend precision both of thought and expression, I am far from advocating a pedantic niceness in the choice of language: such a course would only render conversation stiff and stilted. Dr. Johnson used to say that in the

---

1626). The italics represent certain alterations that Coleridge made in order to adapt the verses to the idea of the creative power of poetry rather than of the soul, which is the thought of the original.— ED. NOTE.]

most unrestrained discourse he always sought for the properest word,—that which best and most exactly conveyed his meaning: to a certain point he was right, but because he carried it too far, he was often laborious where he ought to have been light, and formal where he ought to have been familiar. Men ought to endeavour to distinguish subtilely, that they may be able afterwards to assimilate truly.

I have often heard the question put whether Pope is a great poet, and it has been warmly debated on both sides, some positively maintaining the affirmative, and others dogmatically insisting upon the negative; but it never occurred to either party to make the necessary preliminary inquiry —What is meant by the words "poet" and "poetry?" Poetry is not merely invention: if it were, *Gulliver's Travels* would be poetry; and before you can arrive at a decision of the question, as to Pope's claim, it is absolutely necessary to ascertain what people intend by the words they use. Harmonious versification no more makes poetry than mere invention makes a poet; and to both these requisites there is much besides to be added. In morals, politics, and philosophy no useful discussion can be entered upon, unless we begin by explaining and understanding the terms we employ. It is therefore requisite that I should state to you what I mean by the word "poetry," before I commence any consideration of the comparative merits of those who are popularly called "poets."

Words are used in two ways:—

1. In a sense that comprises everything called by that name. For instance, the words "poetry" and "sense" are employed in this manner, when we say that such a line is bad poetry or bad sense, when in truth it is neither poetry nor sense. If it be bad poetry, it is not poetry; if it be bad sense, it is not sense. The same of "metre": bad meter is not metre.

2. In a philosophic sense, which must include a definition of what is essential to the thing. Nobody means mere metre by

poetry; so, mere rhyme is not poetry. Something more is required, and what is that something? It is not wit, because we may have wit where we never dream of poetry. Is it the just observation of human life? Is it a peculiar and a felicitous selection of words? This, indeed, would come nearer to the taste of the present age, when sound is preferred to sense; but I am happy to think that this taste is not likely to last long.

The Greeks and Romans, in the best period of their literature, knew nothing of any such taste. High-flown epithets and violent metaphors, conveyed in inflated language, is not poetry. Simplicity is indispensable, and in Catullus it is often impossible that more simple language could be used; there is scarcely a word or a line, which a lamenting mother in a cottage might not have employed. That I may be clearly understood, I will venture to give the following definition of poetry.

It is an art (or whatever better term our language may afford) representing, in words, external nature and human thoughts and affections, both relatively to human affections, by the production of as much immediate pleasure in parts, as is compatible with the largest sum of pleasure in the whole.

Or, to vary the words, in order to make the abstract idea more intelligible:—

It is the art of communicating whatever we wish to communicate, so as both to express and produce excitement, but for the purpose of immediate pleasure; and each part is fitted to afford as much pleasure, as is compatible with the largest sum in the whole.

You will naturally ask my reasons for this definition of poetry, and they are these:—

"It is a representation of nature"; but that is not enough: the anatomist and the topographer give representations of nature; therefore I add:

"And of the human thoughts and affections." Here the metaphysician interferes:

here our best novelists interfere likewise,—excepting that the latter describe with more minuteness, accuracy, and truth, than is consistent with poetry. Consequently I subjoin:

"It must be relative to the human affections." Here my chief point of difference is with the novel-writer, the historian, and all those who describe not only nature, and the human affections, but relatively to the human affections: therefore I must add:

"And it must be done for the purpose of immediate pleasure." In poetry the general good is to be accomplished through the pleasure, and if the poet do not do that, he ceases to be a poet to him to whom he gives it not. Still, it is not enough, because we may point out many prose writers to whom the whole of the definition hitherto furnished would apply. I add, therefore, that it is not only for the purpose of immediate pleasure, but—

"The work must be so constructed as to produce in each part that highest quantity of pleasure, or a high quantity of pleasure." There metre introduces its claim, where the feeling calls for it. Our language gives to expression a certain measure, and will, in a strong state of passion, admit of scansion from the very mouth. The very assumption that we are reading the work of a poet supposes that he is in a continuous state of excitement; and thereby arises a language in prose unnatural, but in poetry natural.

There is one error which ought to be peculiarly guarded against, which young poets are apt to fall into, and which old poets commit, from being no poets, but desirous of the end which true poets seek to attain. No: I revoke the words; they are not desirous of that of which their little minds can have no just conception. They have no desire of fame—that glorious immortality of true greatness—

> That lives and spreads aloft by those
>   pure eyes,
> And perfect witness of all judging Jove;
>   MILTON's "Lycidas"

but they struggle for reputation, that echo of an echo, in whose very etymon its signification is contained. Into this error the author of "The Botanic Garden" has fallen, through the whole of which work, I will venture to assert, there are not twenty images described as a man would describe them in a state of excitement. The poem is written with all the tawdry industry of a milliner anxious to dress up a doll in silks and satins. Dr. Darwin laboured to make his style fine and gaudy, by accumulating and applying all the sonorous and handsome-looking words in our language. This is not poetry, and I subjoin to my definition—

That a true poem must give "as much pleasure in each part as is compatible with the greatest sum of pleasure in the whole." We must not look to parts merely, but to the whole, and to the effect of that whole. In reading Milton, for instance, scarcely a line can be pointed out which, critically examined, could be called in itself good: the poet would not have attempted to produce merely what is in general understood by a good line; he sought to produce glorious paragraphs and systems of harmony, or, as he himself expresses it,

> Many a winding bout
> Of linked sweetness long drawn out.
>   MILTON's "L'Allegro"

Such, therefore, as I have now defined it, I shall consider the sense of the word "Poetry": pleasurable excitement is its origin and object; pleasure is the magic circle out of which the poet must not dare to tread. Part of my definition, you will be aware, would apply equally to the arts of painting and music, as to poetry; but to the last are added words and metre, so that my definition is strictly and logically applicable to poetry, and to poetry only, which produces delight, the parent of so many virtues. When I was in Italy, a friend of mine, who pursued painting almost with the enthusiasm of madness, believing it superior to every other art, heard the definition I have given, acknowledged its correctness, and admitted the pre-eminence of poetry.

Shakspeare's Judgment Equal to His Genius

Shakspeare appears, from his *Venus and Adonis* and *Rape of Lucrece* alone, apart from all his great works, to have possessed all the conditions of the true poet. Let me now proceed to destroy, as far as may be in my power, the popular notion that he was a great dramatist by mere instinct, that he grew immortal in his own despite, and sank below men of second or third-rate power, when he attempted aught beside the drama—even as bees construct their cells and manufacture their honey to admirable perfection; but would in vain attempt to build a nest. Now this mode of reconciling a compelled sense of inferiority with a feeling of pride, began in a few pedants, who having read that Sophocles was the great model of tragedy, and Aristotle the infallible dictator of its rules, and finding that the *Lear, Hamlet, Othello* and other master-pieces were neither in imitation of Sophocles, nor in obedience to Aristotle,—and not having (with one or two exceptions) the courage to affirm, that the delight which their country received from generation to generation, in defiance of the alterations of circumstances and habits, was wholly groundless,—took upon them, as a happy medium and refuge, to talk of Shakspeare as a sort of beautiful *lusus naturæ*, a delightful monster,—wild, indeed, and without taste or judgment, but like the inspired idiots so much venerated in the East, uttering, amid the strangest follies, the sublimest truths. In nine places out of ten in which I find his awful name mentioned, it is with some epithet of "wild," "irregular," "pure child of nature," etc. If all this be true, we must submit to it; though to a thinking mind it cannot but be painful to find any excellence, merely human, thrown out of all human analogy, and thereby leaving us neither rules for imitation, nor motives to imitate;—but if false, it is a dangerous falsehood;—for it affords a refuge to secret self-conceit,—enables a vain man at once to escape his reader's indignation by general swoln panegyrics, and merely by his *ipse dixit* to treat, as contemptible, what he has not intellect enough to comprehend, or soul to feel, without assigning any reason, or referring his opinion to any demonstrative principle;—thus leaving Shakspeare as a sort of grand Lama, adored indeed, and his very excrements prized as relics, but with no authority or real influence. I grieve that every late voluminous edition of his works would enable me to substantiate the present charge with a variety of facts one tenth of which would of themselves exhaust the time allotted to me. Every critic, who has or has not made a collection of black letter books—in itself a useful and respectable amusement,—puts on the seven-league boots of self-opinion, and strides at once from an illustrator into a supreme judge, and blind and deaf, fills his three-ounce phial at the waters of Niagara; and determines positively the greatness of the cataract to be neither more nor less than his three-ounce phial has been able to receive.

I think this a very serious subject. It is my earnest desire—my passionate endeavour,—to enforce at various times and by various arguments and instances the close and reciprocal connexion of just taste with pure morality. Without that acquaintance with the heart of man, or that docility and childlike gladness to be made acquainted with it, which those only can have, who dare look at their own hearts—and that with a steadiness which religion only has the power of reconciling with sincere humility;—without this, and the modesty produced by it, I am deeply convinced that no man, however wide his erudition, however patient his antiquarian researches, can possibly understand, or be worthy of understanding, the writings of Shakspeare.

Assuredly that criticism of Shakspeare

will alone be genial which is reverential. The Englishman, who without reverence, a proud and affectionate reverence, can utter the name of William Shakspeare, stands disqualified for the office of critic. He wants one at least of the very senses, the language of which he is to employ, and will discourse, at best, but as a blind man, while the whole harmonious creation of light and shade with all its subtle interchange of deepening and dissolving colours rises in silence to the silent *fiat* of the uprising Apollo. However inferior in ability I may be to some who have followed me, I own I am proud that I was the first in time who publicly demonstrated to the full extent of the position, that the supposed irregularity and extravagances of Shakspeare were the mere dreams of a pedantry that arraigned the eagle because it had not the dimensions of the swan. In all the successive courses of lectures delivered by me, since my first attempt at the Royal Institution, it has been, and it still remains, my object, to prove that in all points from the most important to the most minute, the judgment of Shakspeare is commensurate with his genius,—nay, that his genius reveals itself in his judgment, as in its most exalted form. And the more gladly do I recur to this subject from the clear conviction, that to judge aright, and with distinct consciousness of the grounds of our judgment, concerning the works of Shakspeare, implies the power and the means of judging rightly of all other works of intellect, those of abstract science alone excepted.

It is a painful truth that not only individuals, but even whole nations, are ofttimes so enslaved to the habits of their education and immediate circumstances, as not to judge disinterestedly even on those subjects, the very pleasure arising from which consists in its disinterestedness, namely, on subjects of taste and polite literature. Instead of deciding concerning their own modes and customs by any rule of reason, nothing appears rational, becoming, or beautiful to them, but what coincides with the peculiarities of their education. In this narrow circle, individuals may attain to exquisite discrimination, as the French critics have done in their own literature; but a true critic can no more be such without placing himself on some central point, from which he may command the whole, that is, some general rule, which, founded in reason, or the faculties common to all men, must therefore apply to each,—than an astronomer can explain the movements of the solar system without taking his stand in the sun. And let me remark, that this will not tend to produce despotism, but, on the contrary, true tolerance, in the critic. He will, indeed, require, as the spirit and substance of a work, something true in human nature itself, and independent of all circumstances; but in the mode of applying it, he will estimate genius and judgment according to the felicity with which the imperishable soul of intellect shall have adapted itself to the age, the place, and the existing manners. The error he will expose, lies in reversing this, and holding up the mere circumstances as perpetual to the utter neglect of the power which can alone animate them. For art cannot exist without, or apart from, nature; and what has man of his own to give to his fellow man, but his own thoughts and feelings, and his observations, so far as they are modified by his own thoughts or feelings?

Let me, then, once more submit this question to minds emancipated alike from national, or party, or sectarian prejudice:— Are the plays of Shakspeare works of rude uncultivated genius, in which the splendour of the parts compensates, if aught can compensate, for the barbarous shapelessness and irregularity of the whole?—Or is the form equally admirable with the matter, and the judgment of the great poet, not less deserving wonder than his genius?—Or, again, to repeat the question in other words:—Is Shakspeare a great dramatic poet on account only of those beauties and excellences which he possesses in common with the ancients, but with diminished claims to our love and honour to the full extent of his differences from them?—Or are these very differences additional proofs of poetic wisdom, at once results and symbols of living power as contrasted with lifeless mechanism—of free and rival originality as contra-distinguished from servile imitation, or, more accurately, a blind copying of effects, instead of a true imitation, of the essential principles?—Imagine not that I am about to oppose genius to rules. No! the comparative value of these rules is the very cause to be tried. The spirit of poetry, like all other living powers, must of necessity circumscribe itself by rules, were it only to unite power with beauty. It must embody in order to reveal itself; but a living body is of necessity an organized one; and what is organization but the connection of parts in and for a whole, so that each part is at once end and means? —This is no discovery of criticism;—it is a necessity of the human mind; and all nations have felt and obeyed it, in the invention of metre, and measured sounds, as the vehicle and *involucrum* of poetry—itself a fellow-growth from the same life,—even as the bark is to the tree!

No work of true genius dares want its appropriate form, neither indeed is there any danger of this. As it must not, so genius cannot, be lawless; for it is even this that constitutes it genius—the power of acting creatively under laws of its own origination. How then comes it that not only single *Zoili,* but whole nations have combined in unhesitating condemnation of our great dramatist, as a sort of African nature, rich in beautiful monsters—as a wild heath where islands of fertility look the greener from the surrounding waste, where the loveliest plants now shine out among unsightly weeds, and now are choked by their parasitic growth, so intertwined that we cannot disentangle the weed without snapping the flower?—In this statement I have

had no reference to the vulgar abuse of Voltaire,[2] save as far as his charges are coincident with the decisions of Shakspeare's own commentators and (so they would tell you) almost idolatrous admirers. The true ground of the mistake lies in the confounding mechanical regularity with organic form. The form is mechanic, when on any given material we impress a predetermined form, not necessarily arising out of the properties of the material;—as when to a mass of wet clay we give whatever shape we wish it to retain when hardened. The organic form, on the other hand, is innate; it shapes, as it develops, itself from

---

[2] [What Coleridge had in mind was no doubt passages such as the following from Voltaire's essay on "Ancient and Modern Tragedy":

The Roman philosophers had no faith in ghosts in the time of the emperors, and yet young Pompey raises one in the *Pharsalia.* The English have certainly no more belief in spirits than the Romans had, and yet they see every day with pleasure, in the tragedy of *Hamlet,* the ghost of a king, who appears nearly the same as the apparition of Ninus did at Paris. I am at the same time far from justifying the tragedy of *Hamlet* in every respect; it is a gross and barbarous piece, and would never be borne by the lowest of the rabble in France or Italy. Hamlet runs mad in the second act, and his mistress in the third; the prince kills the father of his mistress and fancies he is killing a rat; and the heroine of the play throws herself into the river. They dig her grave on the stage, and the grave-diggers, holding the dead men's skulls in their hands, talk nonsense worthy of them. Hamlet answers their abominable stuff by some whimsies not less disgusting; during this time one of the actors makes the conquest of Poland. Hamlet, his mother, and father-in-law, drink together on the stage: they sing at table, quarrel, beat and kill one another: one would think the whole piece was the product of the imagination of a drunken savage: and yet, among all these gross irregularities, which make the English theatre even at this day so absurd and barbarous, we find in *Hamlet,* which is still more strange and unaccountable, some sublime strokes worthy of the greatest genius. It seems as if nature took pleasure to unite in the head of Shakespeare all that we can imagine great and forcible, together with all that the grossest dullness could produce of everything that is most low and detestable.

Translation from *The Works of Voltaire,* Vol. XXXVII, pp. 136–137 (London: E. R. DuMont, 1901).—ED. NOTE.]

within, and the fulness of its developement is one and the same with the perfection of its outward form. Such as the life is, such is the form. Nature, the prime genial artist, inexhaustible in diverse powers, is equally inexhaustible in forms;—each exterior is the physiognomy of the being within,—its true image reflected and thrown out from the concave mirror;—and even such is the appropriate excellence of her chosen poet, of our own Shakspeare,—himself a nature humanized, a genial understanding directing self-consciously a power and an implicit wisdom deeper even than our consciousness.

I greatly dislike beauties and selections in general; but as proof positive of his unrivalled excellence, I should like to try Shakspeare by this criterion. Make out your amplest catalogue of all the human faculties, as reason or the moral law, the will, the feeling of the coincidence of the two (a feeling *sui generis et demonstratio demonstrationum*) called the conscience, the understanding or prudence, wit, fancy, imagination, judgment,—and then of the objects on which these are to be employed, as the beauties, the terrors, and the seeming caprices of nature, the realities and the capabilities, that is, the actual and the ideal, of the human mind, conceived as an individual or as a social being, as in innocence or in guilt, in a play-paradise, or in a war-field of temptation;—and then compare with Shakspeare under each of these heads all or any of the writers in prose and verse that have ever lived! Who, that is competent to judge, doubts the result?—And ask your own hearts,—ask your own common sense —to conceive the possibility of this man being—I say not, the drunken savage of that wretched sciolist, whom Frenchmen, to their shame, have honoured before their elder and better worthies,—but the anomalous, the wild, the irregular, genius of our daily criticism! What! are we to have miracles in sport?—Or, I speak reverently, does God choose idiots by whom to convey divine truths to man?

Progress of the Drama

We call, for we see and feel, the swan and the dove both transcendently beautiful. As absurd as it would be to institute a comparison between their separate claims to beauty from any abstract rule common to both, without reference to the life and being of the animals themselves,—or as if, having first seen the dove, we abstracted its outlines, gave them a false generalization, called them the principles or ideal of bird-beauty, and then proceeded to criticise the swan or the eagle;—not less absurd is it to pass judgment on the works of a poet on the mere ground that they have been called by the same class-name with the works of other poets in other times and circumstances, or on any ground, indeed, save that of their inappropriateness to their own end and being, their want of significance, as symbols or physiognomy.

O! few have there been among critics, who have followed with the eye of the imagination the imperishable yet ever wandering spirit of poetry through its various metempsychoses, and consequent metamorphoses;— or who have rejoiced in the light of clear perception at beholding with each new birth, with each rare *avatar*, the human race frame to itself a new body, by assimilating materials of nourishment out of its new circumstances, and work for itself new organs of power appropriate to the new sphere of its motion and activity!

I have before spoken of the Romance, or the language formed out of the decayed Roman and the Northern tongues; and comparing it with the Latin, we find it less perfect in simplicity and relation—the privileges of a language formed by the mere attraction of homogeneous parts;—but yet more rich, more expressive and various, as one formed by more obscure affinities out of a chaos of apparently heterogeneous atoms. As more than a metaphor,—as an analogy of this, I have named the true genuine modern poetry the romantic; and the works of Shakspeare are romantic poetry revealing itself in the drama. If the tragedies of Sophocles are in the strict sense of the word tragedies, and the comedies of Aristophanes comedies, we must emancipate ourselves from a false association arising from misapplied names, and find a new word for the plays of Shakspeare. For they are, in the ancient sense, neither tragedies nor comedies, nor both in one,—but a different *genus,* diverse in kind, and not merely different in degree. They may be called romantic dramas, or dramatic romances.

A deviation from the simple forms and unities of the ancient stage is an essential principle, and, of course, an appropriate excellence, of the romantic drama. For these unities were to a great extent the natural form of that which in its elements was homogeneous, and the representation of which was addressed pre-eminently to the outward senses;—and though the fable, the language and the characters appealed to the reason rather than to the mere understanding, inasmuch as they supposed an ideal state rather than referred to an existing reality, —yet it was a reason which was obliged to accommodate itself to the senses, and so far became a sort of more elevated understanding. On the other hand, the romantic poetry—the Shakspearian drama —appealed to the imagination rather than to the senses, and to the reason as contemplating our inward nature, and the workings of the passions in their most retired recesses. But the reason, as reason, is independent of time and space; it has nothing to do with them: and hence the certainties of reason have been called eternal truths. As for example —the endless properties of the circle:—what connection have they with this or that age, with this or that country?—The reason is aloof from time and space; the imagination is an arbitrary controller over both;—and if only the poet have such power of exciting our internal emotions as to make us present

to the scene in imagination chiefly, he acquires the right and privilege of using time and space as they exist in imagination, and obedient only to the laws by which the imagination itself acts. These laws it will be my object and aim to point out as the examples occur, which illustrate them. But here let me remark what can never be too often reflected on by all who would intelligently study the works either of the Athenian dramatists, or of Shakspeare, that the very essence of the former consists in the sternest separation of the diverse in kind and the disparate in the degree, whilst the latter delights in interlacing, by a rainbow-like transfusion of hues, the one with the other.

And here it will be necessary to say a few words on the stage and on stage-illusion.

A theatre, in the widest sense of the word, is the general term for all places of amusement through the ear or eye, in which men assemble in order to be amused by some entertainment presented to all at the same time and in common. Thus, an old Puritan divine says:—"Those who attend public worship and sermons only to amuse themselves, make a theatre of the church, and turn God's house into the devil's. *Theatra ædes diabololatricæ."* The most important and dignified species of this *genus* is, doubtless, the stage, (*res theatralis histrionica*), which, in addition to the generic definition above given, may be characterized in its idea, or according to what it does, or ought to, aim at, as a combination of several or of all the fine arts in an harmonious whole, having a distinct end of its own, to which the peculiar end of each of the component arts, taken separately, is made subordinate and subservient,—that, namely, of imitating reality—whether external things, actions, or passions—under a semblance of reality. Thus, Claude imitates a landscape at sunset, but only as a picture; while a forest-scene is not presented to the spectators as a picture, but as a forest; and though, in the full sense of the word, we are no more deceived by the one than by the other, yet are our feelings very differently affected; and the pleasure derived from the one is not composed of the same elements as that afforded by the other, even on the supposition that the *quantum* of both were equal. In the former, a picture, it is a condition of all genuine delight that we should not be deceived; in the latter, stage-scenery, (inasmuch as its principal end is not in or for itself, as is the case in a picture, but to be an assistance and means to an end out of itself) its very purpose is to produce as much illusion as its nature permits. These, and all other stage presentations, are to produce a sort of temporary half-faith, which the spectator encourages in himself and supports by a voluntary contribution on his own part, because he knows that it is at all times in his power to see the thing as it really is. I have often observed that little children are actually deceived by stage-scenery, never by pictures; though even these produce an effect on their impressible minds, which they do not on the minds of adults. The child, if strongly impressed, does not indeed positively think the picture to be the reality; but yet he does not think the contrary. As Sir George Beaumont was shewing me a very fine engraving from Rubens, representing a storm at sea without any vessel or boat introduced, my little boy, then about five years old, came dancing and singing into the room, and all at once (if I may so say) *tumbled* in upon the print. He instantly started, stood silent and motionless, with the strongest expression, first of wonder and then of grief in his eyes and countenance, and at length said, "And where is the ship? But that is sunk, and the men are all drowned!" still keeping his eyes fixed on the print. Now what pictures are to little children, stage illusion is to men, provided they retain any part of the child's sensibility; except, that in the latter instance, the suspension of the act of compari-

son, which permits this sort of negative belief, is somewhat more assisted by the will, than in that of a child respecting a picture.

The true stage-illusion in this and in all other things consists—not in the mind's judging it to be a forest, but, in its remission of the judgment that it is not a forest. And this subject of stage-illusion is so important, and so many practical errors and false criticisms may arise, and indeed have arisen, either from reasoning on it as actual delusion, (the strange notion, on which the French critics built up their theory, and on which the French poets justify the construction of their tragedies), or from denying it altogether, (which seems the end of Dr. Johnson's reasoning, and which, as extremes meet, would lead to the very same consequences, by excluding whatever would not be judged probable by us in our coolest state of feeling, with all our faculties in even balance), that these few remarks will, I hope, he pardoned, if they should serve either to explain or to illustrate the point. For not only are we never absolutely deluded—or any thing like it, but the attempt to cause the highest delusion possible to beings in their senses sitting in a theatre, is a gross fault, incident only to low minds, which, feeling that they cannot affect the heart or head permanently, endeavour to call forth the momentary affections. There ought never to be more pain than is compatible with co-existing pleasure, and to be amply repaid by thought.

Shakspeare found the infant stage demanding an intermixture of ludicrous character as imperiously as that of Greece did the chorus, and high language accordant. And there are many advantages in this;— a greater assimilation to nature, a greater scope of power, more truths, and more feelings;—the effects of contrast, as in Lear and the Fool; and especially this, that the true language of passion becomes sufficiently elevated by your having previously heard, in the same piece, the lighter conversation of men under no strong emotion. The very nakedness of the stage, too, was advantageous,—for the drama thence became something between recitation and a re-presentation; and the absence or paucity of scenes allowed a freedom from the laws of unity of place and unity of time, the observance of which must either confine the drama to as few subjects as may be counted on the fingers, or involve gross improbabilities, far more striking than the violation would have caused. Thence, also, was precluded the danger of a false ideal,—of aiming at more than what is possible on the whole. What play of the ancients, with reference to their ideal, does not hold out more glaring absurdities than any in Shakspeare? On the Greek plan a man could more easily be a poet than a dramatist; upon our plan more easily a dramatist than a poet.

The Drama Generally and Public Taste

In my last address I defined poetry to be the art, or whatever better term our language may afford, of representing external nature and human thoughts, both relatively to human affections, so as to cause the production of as great immediate pleasure in each part, as is compatible with the largest possible sum of pleasure on the whole. Now this definition applies equally to painting and music as to poetry; and in truth the term poetry is. alike applicable to all three. The vehicle alone constitutes the difference; and the term "poetry" is rightly applied by eminence to measured words, only because the sphere of their action is far wider, the power of giving permanence to them much more certain, and incomparably greater the facility, by which men, not defective by nature or disease, may be enabled to derive habitual pleasure and instruction from them. . . .

On Poesy or Art

Man communicates by articulation of sounds, and paramountly by the memory in the ear; nature by the impression of bounds and surfaces on the eye, and through the eye it gives significance and appropriation, and thus the conditions of memory, or the capability of being remembered, to sounds, smells, etc. Now, Art, used collectively for painting, sculpture, architecture and music, is the mediatress between, and reconciler of, nature and man. It is, therefore, the power of humanizing nature, of infusing the thoughts and passions of man into every thing which is the object of his contemplation; colour, form, motion and sound are the elements which it combines, and it stamps them into unity in the mould of a moral idea.

The primary art is writing;—primary, if we regard the purpose abstracted from the different modes of realizing it, those steps of progression of which the instances are still visible in the lower degrees of civilization. First, there is mere gesticulation; then rosaries or *wampum;* then picture-language; then hieroglyphics, and finally alphabetic letters. These all consist of a translation of man into nature, of a substitution of the visible for the audible.

The so-called music of savage tribes as little deserves the name of art for the understanding as the ear warrants it for music. Its lowest state is a mere expression of passion by sounds which the passion itself necessitates;—the highest amounts to no more than a voluntary reproduction of these sounds in the absence of the occasioning causes, so as to give the pleasure of contrast, —for example, by the various outcries of battle in the song of security and triumph. Poetry also is purely human; for all its materials are from the mind, and all its products are for the mind. But it is the apotheosis of the former state, in which by excitement of the associative power passion itself imitates order, and the order resulting produces a pleasurable passion, and thus it elevates the mind by making its feelings the object of its reflexion. So likewise, whilst it recalls the sights and sounds that had accompanied the occasions of the original passions, poetry impregnates them with an interest not their own by means of the passions, and yet tempers the passion by the calming power which all distinct images exert on the human soul. In this way poetry is the preparation for art, inasmuch as it avails itself of the forms of nature to recall, to express, and to modify the thoughts and feelings of the mind. Still, however, poetry can only act through the intervention of articulate speech, which is so peculiarly human, that in all languages it constitutes the ordinary phrase by which man and nature are contradistinguished. It is the original force of the word "brute"; and even "mute," and "dumb" do not convey the absence of sound, but the absence of articulated sounds.

As soon as the human mind is intelligibly addressed by an outward image exclusively of articulate speech, so soon does art commence. But please to observe that I have laid particular stress on the words "human mind," meaning to exclude thereby all results common to man and all other sentient creatures, and consequently confining myself to the effect produced by the congruity of the animal impression with the reflective powers of the mind; so that not the thing presented, but that which is represented by the thing shall be the source of the pleasure. In this sense nature itself is to a religious observer the art of God; and for the same cause art itself might he defined as of a middle quality between a thought and a thing; or, as I said before, the union and reconciliation of that which is nature with that which is exclusively human. It is the figured language of thought, and is distinguished from nature by the unity of all the parts in one thought or idea. Hence nature itself would give us the impression

of a work of art if we could see the thought which is present at once in the whole and in every part; and a work of art will be just in proportion as it adequately conveys the thought, and rich in proportion to the variety of parts which it holds in unity.

If, therefore, the term "mute" be taken as opposed not to sound but to articulate speech, the old definition of painting will in fact be the true and best definition of the Fine Arts in general, that is, *muta poesis,* mute poesy, and so of course poesy. And, as all languages perfect themselves by a gradual process of desynonymizing words originally equivalent, I have cherished the wish to use the word "poesy" as the generic or common term, and to distinguish that species of poesy which is not *muta poesis* by its usual name "poetry"; while of all the other species which collectively form the Fine Arts, there would remain this as the common definition,—that they all, like poetry, are to express intellectual purposes, thoughts, conceptions, and sentiments which have their origin in the human mind, not, however, as poetry does, by means of articulate speech, but as nature or the divine art does, by form, colour, magnitude, proportion, or by sound, that is, silently or musically.

Well! it may be said—but who has ever thought otherwise! We all know that art is the imitatress of nature. And, doubtless, the truths which I hope to convey, would be barren truisms, if all men meant the same by the words "imitate" and "nature." But it would be flattering mankind at large, to presume that such is the fact. First, to imitate. The impression on the wax is not an imitation, but a copy, of the seal; the seal itself is an imitation. But, further, in order to form a philosophic conception, we must seek for the kind, as the heat in ice, invisible light, etc. whilst, for practical purposes, we must have reference to the degree. It is sufficient that philosophically we understand that in all imitation two elements must coexist, and not only coexist, but must be perceived as coexisting. These two constituent elements are likeness and unlikeness, or sameness and difference. And in all genuine creations of art there must be a union of these disparates. The artist may take his point of view where he pleases, provided that the desired effect be perceptibly produced,—that there be likeness in the difference, difference in the likeness, and a reconcilement of both in one. If there be likeness to nature without any check of difference, the result is disgusting, and the more complete the delusion, the more loathsome the effect. Why are such simulations of nature, as wax-work figures of men and women, so disagreeable? Because, not finding the motion and the life which we expected, we are shocked as by a falsehood, every circumstance of detail, which before induced us to be interested, making the distance from truth more palpable. You set out with a supposed reality and are disappointed and disgusted with the deception; whilst, in respect to a work of genuine imitation, you begin with an acknowledged total difference, and then every touch of nature gives you the pleasure of an approximation to truth. The fundamental principle of all this is undoubtedly the horror of falsehood and the love of truth inherent in the human breast. The Greek tragic dance rested on these principles, and I can deeply sympathize in imagination with the Greeks in this favourite part of their theatrical exhibitions, when I call to mind the pleasure I felt in beholding the combat of the Horatii and Curiatii most exquisitely danced in Italy to the music of Cimarosa.

Secondly, as to nature. We must imitate nature! yes, but what in nature,—all and everything? No, the beautiful in nature. And what then is the beautiful? What is beauty? It is, in the abstract, the unity of the manifold, the coalescence of the diverse; in the concrete, it is the union of the shapely (*formosum*) with the vital. In the dead organic it depends on regularity of form, the first and lowest species of which is the triangle with all its modifications, as in crystals, architecture, etc., in the living organic it is not mere regularity of form, which would produce a sense of formality; neither is it subservient to any thing beside itself. It may be present in a disagreeable object, in which the proportion of the parts constitutes a whole; it does not arise from association, as the agreeable does, but sometimes lies in the rupture of association; it is not different to different individuals and nations, as has been said, nor is it connected with the ideas of the good, or the fit, or the useful. The sense of beauty is intuitive, and beauty itself is all that inspires pleasure without, and aloof from, and even contrarily to, interest.

If the artist copies the mere nature, the *natura naturata,* what idle rivalry! If he proceeds only from a given form, which is supposed to answer to the notion of beauty, what an emptiness, what an unreality there always is in his productions, as in Cipriani's pictures! Believe me, you must master the essence, the *natura naturans,* which presupposes a bond between nature in the higher sense and the soul of man.

The wisdom in nature is distinguished from that in man, by the co-instantaneity of the plan and the execution; the thought and the product are one, or are given at once; but there is no reflex act, and hence there is no moral responsibility. In man there is reflexion, freedom, and choice; he is, therefore, the head of the visible creation. In the objects of nature are presented, as in a mirror, all the possible elements, steps, and processes of intellect antecedent to consciousness, and therefore to the full development of the intelligential act; and man's mind is the very focus of all the rays of intellect which are scattered throughout the images of nature. Now so to place these images, totalized, and fitted to the limits of the human mind, as to elicit from, and to superinduce upon, the forms themselves the moral reflexions to which they approximate, to make the external internal, the internal external, to make nature thought, and thought nature,—this is the mystery of genius in the Fine Arts. Dare I add that the genius must act on the feeling, that body is but a striving to become mind, that it is mind in its essence!

In every work of art there is a reconcilement of the external with the internal; the conscious is so impressed on the unconscious as to appear in it; as compare mere letters inscribed on a tomb with figures themselves constituting the tomb. He who combines the two is the man of genius; and for that reason he must partake of both. Hence there is in genius itself an unconscious activity; nay, that is the genius in the man of genius. And this is the true exposition of the rule that the artist must first eloign himself from nature in order to return to her with full effect. Why this? Because if he were to begin by mere painful copying, he would produce masks only, not forms breathing life. He must out of his own mind create forms according to the severe laws of the intellect, in order to generate in himself that co-ordination of freedom and law, that involution of obedience in the prescript, and of the prescript in the impulse to obey, which assimilates him to nature, and enables him to understand her. He merely absents himself for a season from her, that his own spirit, which has the same ground with nature, may learn her unspoken language in its main radicals, before he approaches to her endless compositions of them. Yes, not to acquire cold notions—lifeless technical rules—but living and life-producing ideas, which shall contain their own evidence, the certainty that they are essentially one with the germinal causes in nature—his consciousness being the focus and mirror of both,—for this does the artist for a time abandon the external real in order to return to it with a complete sympathy with its internal and actual. For of all we see, hear, feel and touch the substance is and must be in ourselves; and therefore there is no alternative in reason between the dreary (and thank heaven! almost impossible) belief that every thing around us is but a phantom, or that the life which is in us is in them likewise; and that to know is to resemble, when we speak of objects out of ourselves, even as within ourselves to learn is, according to Plato, only to recollect;—the only effective answer to which, that I have been fortunate enough to meet with, is that which Pope has consecrated for future use in the line—

> And coxcombs vanquish Berkeley with a grin!

The artist must imitate that which is within the thing, that which is active through form and figure, and discourses to us by symbols —the *Naturgeist,* or spirit of nature, as we unconsciously imitate those whom we love; for so only can he hope to produce any work truly natural in the object and truly human in the effect. The idea which puts the form together cannot itself be the form. It is above form, and is its essence, the universal in the individual, or the individuality itself, —the glance and the exponent of the indwelling power.

Each thing that lives has its moment of self-exposition, and so has each period of each thing, if we remove the disturbing forces of accident. To do this is the business of ideal art, whether in images of childhood, youth, or age, in man or in woman. Hence a good portrait is the abstract of the personal; it is not the likeness for actual comparison, but for recollection. This explains why the likeness of a very good portrait is not always recognized because some persons never abstract, and amongst these are especially to be numbered the near relations and friends of the subject, in consequence of the constant pressure and check exercised on their minds by the actual presence of the original. And each thing that only appears to live has also its possible position of relation to life, as nature herself testifies, who, where she cannot be, prophesies her being in the crystallized metal, or the inhaling plant.

The charm, the indispensable requisite, of sculpture is unity of effect. But painting rests in a material remoter from nature, and its compass is therefore greater. Light and shade give external, as well as internal, being even with all its accidents, whilst sculpture is confined to the latter. And here I may observe that the subjects chosen for works of art, whether in sculpture or painting, should be such as really are capable of being expressed and conveyed within the limits of those arts. Moreover they ought to be such as will affect the spectator by their truth, their beauty, or their sublimity, and therefore they may be addressed to the judgment, the senses, or the reason. The peculiarity of the impression which they may make, may be derived either from colour and form, or from proportion and fitness, or from the excitement of the moral feelings; or all these may be combined. Such works as do combine these sources of effect must have the preference in dignity.

Imitation of the antique may be too exclusive, and may produce an injurious effect on modern sculpture;—first, generally, because such an imitation cannot fail to have a tendency to keep the attention fixed on externals rather than on the thought within; —secondly, because, accordingly, it leads the artist to rest satisfied with that which is always imperfect, namely, bodily form, and circumscribes his views of mental expression to the ideas of power and grandeur only;—thirdly, because it induces an effort to combine together two incongruous things, that is to say, modern feelings in antique forms;—fourthly, because it speaks in a language, as it were, learned and dead, the tones of which, being unfamiliar, leave the common spectator cold and unimpressed;— and lastly, because it necessarily causes a neglect of thoughts, emotions and images of profounder interest and more exalted dignity, as motherly, sisterly, and brotherly love, piety, devotion, the divine become human,—the Virgin, the Apostle, the Christ. The artist's principle in the statue of a great

man should be the illustration of departed merit; and I cannot but think that a skilful adoption of modern habiliments would, in many instances, give a variety and force of effect which a bigoted adherence to Greek or Roman costume precludes. It is, I believe, from artists finding Greek models unfit for several important modern purposes, that we see so many allegorical figures on monuments and elsewhere. Painting was, as it were, a new art, and being unshackled by old models it chose its own subjects, and took an eagle's flight. And a new field seems opened for modern sculpture in the symbolical expression of the ends of life, as in Guy's monument, Chantrey's children in Worcester Cathedral, etc.

Architecture exhibits the greatest extent of the difference from nature which may exist in works of art. It involves all the powers of design, and is sculpture and painting inclusively. It shews the greatness of man, and should at the same time teach him humility.

Music is the most entirely human of the fine arts, and has the fewest *analoga* in nature. Its first delightfulness is simple accordance with the ear; but it is an associated thing, and recalls the deep emotions of the past with an intellectual sense of proportion. Every human feeling is greater and larger than the exciting cause,—a proof, I think, that man is designed for a higher state of existence, and this is deeply implied in music, in which there is always something more and beyond the immediate expression.

With regard to works in all the branches of the fine arts, I may remark that the pleasure arising from novelty must of course be allowed its due place and weight. This pleasure consists in the identity of two opposite elements, that is to say—sameness and variety. If in the midst of the variety there be not some fixed object for the attention, the unceasing succession of the variety will prevent the mind from observing the difference of the individual objects; and the only thing remaining will be the succession, which will then produce precisely the same effect as sameness. This we experience when we let the trees or hedges pass before the fixed eye during a rapid movement in a carriage, or on the other hand, when we suffer a file of soldiers or ranks of men in procession to go on before us without resting the eye on any in particular. In order to derive pleasure from the occupation of the mind, the principle of unity must always be present, so that in the midst of the multeity the centripetal force be never suspended, nor the sense be fatigued by the predominance of the centrifugal force. This unity in multeity I have elsewhere stated as the principle of beauty. It is equally the source of pleasure in variety, and in fact a higher term including both. What is the seclusive or distinguishing term between them!

Remember that there is a difference between form as proceeding, and shape as superinduced;—the latter is either the death or the imprisonment of the thing;—the former is its self-witnessing and self-effected sphere of agency. Art would or should be the abridgment of nature. Now the fulness of nature is without character, as water is purest when without taste, smell, or colour; but this is the highest, the apex only,—it is not the whole. The object of art is to give the whole *ad hominem;* hence each step of nature hath its ideal and hence the possibility of a climax up to the perfect form of a harmonized chaos.

To the idea of life victory or strife is necessary; as virtue consists not simply in the absence of vices, but in the overcoming of them. So it is in beauty. The sight of what is subordinated and conquered heightens the strength and the pleasure; and this should be exhibited by the artist either inclusively in his figure, or else out of it and beside it to act by way of supplement and contrast. And with a view to this, remark the seeming identity of body and mind in infants, and thence the loveliness of the former; the commencing separation in boyhood, and the struggle of equilibrium in youth: thence onward the body is first simply indifferent; then demanding the translucency of the mind not to be worse than indifferent; and finally all that presents the body as body becoming almost of an excremental nature.

Fragment of an Essay on Taste

The same arguments that decide the question, whether taste has any fixed principles, may probably lead to a determination of what those principles are. First then, what is taste in its metaphorical sense, or, which will be the easiest mode of arriving at the same solution, what is there in the primary sense of the word, which may give to its metaphorical meaning an import different from that of sight or hearing, on the one hand, and of touch or smell on the other? And this question seems the more natural, because in correct language we confine beauty, the main subject of taste, to objects of sight and combinations of sounds, and never, except sportively or by abuse of words, speak of a beautiful flavour, or a beautiful scent.

Now the analysis of our senses in the commonest books of anthropology has drawn our attention to the distinction between the perfectly organic, and the mixed senses;—the first presenting objects, as distinct from the perception;—the last as blending the perception with the sense of the object. Our eyes and ears—(I am not now considering what is or is not the case really, but only that of which we are regularly conscious as appearance,) our eyes most often appear to us perfect organs of the sentient principle, and wholly in action, and our hearing so much more so than the three other senses, and in all the ordinary exertions of that sense, perhaps, equally so with the sight, that all languages place them in one class, and express their different modifications by nearly the same metaphors. The three remaining senses appear in part passive, and combine with the perception of the outward object a distinct sense of our own life. Taste, therefore, as opposed to vision and sound, will teach us to expect in its metaphorical use a certain reference of any given object to our own being, and not merely a distinct notion of the object as in itself, or in its independent properties. From the sense of touch, on the other hand, it is distinguishable by adding to this reference to our vital being some degree of enjoyment, or the contrary,—some perceptible impulse from pleasure or pain to complacency or dislike. The sense of smell, indeed, might perhaps have furnished a metaphor of the same import with that of taste; but the latter was naturally chosen by the majority of civilized nations on account of the greater frequency, importance, and dignity of its employment or exertion in human nature.

By taste, therefore, as applied to the fine arts, we must be supposed to mean an intellectual perception of any object blended with a distinct reference to our own sensibility of pain or pleasure, or, *vice versa*, a sense of enjoyment or dislike co-instantaneously combined with, and appearing to proceed from, some intellectual perception of the object;—intellectual perception, I say; for otherwise it would be a definition of taste in its primary rather than in its metaphorical sense. Briefly, taste is a metaphor taken from one of our mixed senses, and applied to objects of the more purely organic senses, and of our moral sense, when we would imply the co-existence of immediate personal dislike or complacency. In this definition of taste, therefore, is involved the definition of fine arts, namely, as being such the chief and discriminative purpose of which it is to gratify the taste,—that is, not merely to connect, but to combine and unite, a sense of immediate pleasure in ourselves, with the perception of external arrangement.

The great question, therefore, whether taste in any one of the fine arts has any fixed principle or ideal, will find its solution in the ascertainment of two facts:—first whether in every determination of the taste concerning any work of the fine arts, the individual does not, with or even against the approbation of his general judgment, involuntarily claim that all other minds ought to think and feel the same; whether the common expressions, "I dare say I may be wrong, but that is my particular taste";—are uttered as an offering of courtesy, as a sacrifice to the undoubted fact of our individual fallibility, or are spoken with perfect sincerity, not only of the reason but of the whole feeling, with the same entireness of mind and heart, with which we concede a right to every person to differ from another in his preference of bodily tastes and flavours. If we should find ourselves compelled to deny this, and to admit that, notwithstanding the consciousness of our liability to error, and in spite of all those many individual experiences which may have strengthened the consciousness, each man does at the moment so far legislate for all men, as to believe of necessity that he is either right or wrong, and that if it be right for him, it is universally right,—we must then proceed to ascertain: — secondly, whether the source of these phenomena is at all to be found in those parts of our nature, in which each intellect is representative of all,—and whether wholly, or partially. No person of common reflection demands even in feeling, that what tastes pleasant to him ought to produce the same effect on all living beings; but every man does and must expect and demand the universal acquiescence of all intelligent beings in every conviction of his understanding.

Fragment of an Essay on Beauty

The only necessary, but this the absolutely necessary, pre-requisite to a full insight into the grounds of the beauty in the objects of sight, is—the directing of the attention to the action of those thoughts in our own mind which are not consciously distinguished. Every man may understand this, if he will but recall the state of his feelings in endeavouring to recollect a name, which he is quite sure that he remembers, though he cannot force it back into consciousness. This region of unconscious thoughts, oftentimes the more working the more indistinct they are, may, in reference to this subject, be conceived as forming an ascending scale from the most universal associations of motion with the functions and passions of life,—as when on passing out of a crowded city into the fields on a day in June, we describe the grass and king-cups as nodding their heads and dancing in the breeze,—up to the half perceived, yet not fixable, resemblance of a form to some particular object of a diverse class, which resemblance we need only increase but a little, to destroy, or at least injure, its beauty-enhancing effect, and to make it a fantastic intrusion of the accidental and the arbitrary, and consequently a disturbance of the beautiful. This might be abundantly exemplified and illustrated from the paintings of Salvator Rosa.

I am now using the term beauty in its most comprehensive sense, as including expression and artistic interest,—that is, I consider not only the living balance, but likewise all the accompaniments that even by disturbing are necessary to the renewal and continuance of the balance. And in this sense I proceed to show, that the beautiful in the object may be referred to two elements,—lines and colours; the first belonging to the shapely (*forma, formalis, formosus*), and in this, to the law, and the reason; and the second, to the lively, the free, the spontaneous, and the self-justifying. As to lines, the rectilineal are in themselves the lifeless, the determined *ab extra,* but still in immediate union with the cycloidal, which are expressive of function. The curve line is a modification of the force from without by the force from within, or the

spontaneous. These are not arbitrary symbols, but the language of nature, universal and intuitive, by virtue of the law by which man is impelled to explain visible motions by imaginary causative powers analogous to his own acts, as the Dryads, Hamadryads, Naiads, etc.

The better way of applying these principles will be by a brief and rapid sketch of the history of the fine arts,—in which it will be found, that the beautiful in nature has been appropriated to the works of man, just in proportion as the state of the mind in the artists themselves approached to the subjective beauty. Determine what predominance in the minds of the men is preventive of the living balance of excited faculties, and you will discover the exact counterpart in the outward products. Egypt is an illustration of this. Shapeliness is intellect without freedom; but colours are significant. The introduction of the arch is not less an epoch in the fine than in the useful arts.

Order is beautiful arrangement without any purpose *ad extra;*—therefore there is a beauty of order, or order may be contemplated exclusively as beauty.

The form given in every empirical intuition,—the stuff, that is, the quality of the stuff, determines the agreeable: but when a thing excites us to receive it in such and such a mould, so that its exact correspondence to that mould is what occupies the mind,—this is taste or the sense of beauty. Whether dishes full of painted wood or exquisite viands were laid out on a table in the same arrangement, would be indifferent to the taste, as in ladies patterns; but surely the one is far more agreeable than the other. Hence observe the disinterestedness of all taste; and hence also a sensual perfection with intellect is occasionally possible without moral feeling. So it may be in music and painting, but not in poetry. How far it is a real preference of the refined to the gross pleasures, is another question, upon the supposition that pleasure, in some form or other, is that alone which determines men to the objects of the former;—whether experience does not show that if the latter were equally in our power, occasioned no more trouble to enjoy, and caused no more exhaustion of the power of enjoying them by the enjoyment itself, we should in real practice prefer the grosser pleasure. It is not, therefore, any excellence in the quality of the refined pleasures themselves, but the advantages and facilities in the means of enjoying them, that give them the pre-eminence.

This is, of course, on the supposition of the absence of all moral feeling. Suppose its presence, and then there will accrue an excellence even to the quality of the pleasures themselves; not only, however, of the refined, but also of the grosser kinds,—inasmuch as a larger sweep of thoughts will be associated with each enjoyment, and with each thought will be associated a number of sensations; and so, consequently, each pleasure will become more the pleasure of the whole being. This is one of the earthly rewards of our being what we ought to be, but which would be annihilated, if we attempted to be it for the sake of this increased enjoyment. Indeed it is a contradiction to suppose it. Yet this is the common *argumentum in circulo,* in which the eudaemonists flee and pursue.

FRANCIS JEFFREY

(1773-1850)

Francis Jeffrey is remembered principally as a journalist and critic, but he is also known as a lawyer and judge. He was born at Edinburgh and studied at Glasgow and Oxford. He was a student at Glasgow when Adam Smith was the lord rector, and he himself received this honor in 1820 and again in 1822. Though trained in the law, he devoted many years of his maturity, from 1802 to 1829, to literary criticism as the editor of the *Edinburgh Review,* to which he contributed some two hundred articles. Since the *Edinburgh Review* was anything but narrowly literary, Jeffrey, as an ardent Whig, commented on all the stirring events of his day. His criticism of the Romantic poets often decried their obscurity, mysticism, and lack of form. A famous review of Wordsworth's "Excursion" begins, "This will never do." In 1829 he was elected to the high honor of Dean of the Faculty of Advocates. Thereafter he served in Parliament, and in 1834 he returned to Scotland with the title of Lord Jeffrey, to serve as a judge until 1850.

The following essay, written in 1816 as a critical survey of Archibald Alison's *Essays on the Nature and Principles of Taste,* which first appeared in 1790, draws its principal ideas from that source. The essay appeared first in the *Review* and then, its opening page slightly altered, in the eighth edition of the *Encyclopaedia Britannica.* Like Alison, Jeffrey argues that beauty is not an inherent property of objects but "the result of accidental relations in which they may stand to our experience of pleasures or emotions." It "does not depend upon any particular configuration, parts, proportions, or colours, in external things, nor upon the unity, coherence, or simplicity of intellectual creations; but merely upon the associations which, in the case of every individual may enable these inherent, and otherwise indifferent qualities, to suggest or recall to the mind emotions of a pleasurable or interesting description." The great diversity of objects we call beautiful have "nothing in common but this accidental power of reminding us of other emotions."

The associationist theory, which Jeffrey defends against all contrary views, is persuasive, and it enjoyed an enormous vogue. Beauty and other aesthetic predicates can be traced, or "reduced," to other qualities and circumstances whose appeal or pleasurableness is presumably easy to understand. The beautiful, sublime, and picturesque are "substantially identical," and association is the explanatory key for all of them.

Associationism is the natural origin of many later ideas, including, for example, Freud's idea of sublimation. The theoretical issue is fairly clear: Should one follow Jeffrey, or should one follow Kant in thinking that beauty is neither any ordinary form of pleasantness or agreeableness nor reducible to it, and that the sublime is no ordinary pang or pain? In other words, one's acceptance of associationism depends on one's feelings about the autonomy or heteronomy of aesthetic value.

FRANCIS JEFFREY

Essay on Beauty

(First published: 1816.)

§ THE PROBLEM OF DEFINING BEAUTY

There are few parts of our nature which have given more trouble to philosophers, or appeared more simple to the unreflecting, than the perceptions we have of Beauty, and the circumstances under which these are presented to us. If we ask one of the latter (and larger) class, what beauty is? we shall most probably be answered, that it is what makes things pleasant to look at; and if we remind him that many other things are called and perceived to be beautiful, besides objects of sight, and ask how, or by what faculty he supposes that we distinguish such objects, we must generally be satisfied with hearing that it has pleased God to make us capable of such a perception. The science of mind may not appear to be much advanced by these responses; and yet, if it could be made out, as some have alleged, that our perception of beauty was a simple sensation, like our perception of colour; and that taste was an original and distinct sense, like that of seeing or hearing; this would be truly the only definition that could be given, either of the sense or of its object—and all that we could do in investigating the nature of the latter, would be to digest and enumerate the circumstances under which it was found to present itself to its appropriate organ. All that we can say of colour, if we consider it very strictly, is, that it is that property in objects

277

by which they are recommended to the faculty of sight; and the faculty of sight can scarcely be defined in any other way than as that by which we are enabled to discover the existence of colour. When we attempt to proceed farther, and say that green is the colour of grass, and red of roses or blood, it is plain that we do not in any respect explain the nature of those colours, but only give instances of their occurrence; and that one who had never seen them could learn nothing whatever from these pretended definitions. Complex ideas, on the other hand, and compound emotions, may be always defined, and explained to a certain extent by enumerating the parts of which they are made up, or resolving them into the elements of which they are composed: and we thus acquire, a substantial knowledge of their nature, and a practical power in their regulation or production.

It becomes of importance, therefore, in the very outset of this inquiry, to consider whether our sense of beauty be really a simple sensation, like some of those we have enumerated, or a compound or derivative feeling, the sources or elements of which may be investigated and ascertained. If it be the former, we have then only to refer it to the peculiar sense or faculty of which it is the object, and to determine, by repeated observation, under what circumstances it occurs; but if it be the latter, we have to proceed, by a joint process of observation and reflection, to ascertain what are the primary feelings to which it may be referred; and by what peculiar modification of them it is produced and distinguished. We are not quite prepared, as yet, to exhaust the whole of this important discussion, to which we shall be obliged to return in the sequel of our inquiry; but it is necessary, in order to explain and to set forth, in their natural order, the difficulties with which the subject is surrounded, to state here, in a very few words, one or two of the most obvious and, as we think, decisive objections against the notion of beauty being a simple sensation, or the object of a separate and peculiar faculty.

§ BEAUTY A REAL PROPERTY OF OBJECTS?

The first, and perhaps the most considerable, is the want of agreement as to the presence and existence of beauty in particular objects, among men whose organization is perfect, and who are plainly possessed of the faculty, whatever it may be, by which beauty is discerned. Now, no such thing happens, we imagine, or can be conceived to imagine, in the case of any other simple sensation, or the exercise of any other distinct faculty. Where one man sees light, all men who have eyes, see light also: all men allow grass to be green; and sugar to be sweet; and ice to be cold; and the unavoidable inference from any apparent disagreement in such matters necessarily is, that the party is insane, or entirely destitute of the sense or organ concerned in the perception. With regard to beauty, however, it is obvious, at first sight, that the case is quite different; one man sees it perpetually, where to another it is quite invisible, or even where its reverse seems to be conspicuous; nor is this owing to the insensibility of either of the parties, for the same contrariety exists where both are keenly alive to the influences of the beauty they respectively discern. A Chinese or African lover would probably see nothing at all attractive in a belle of London or Paris, and undoubtedly, an *elegans formarum* spectator, from either of these cities, would discover nothing but deformity in the Venus of the Hottentots. A little distance in time produces the same effects as distance in place; the gardens, the furniture, the dress, which appeared beautiful in the eyes of our grandfathers, are odious and ridiculous in ours. Nay, the difference of rank, education, or employments give rise to the same diversity of sensation. The little shopkeeper sees a beauty in his roadside box, and in the staring tile roof, wooden lions, and clipped boxwood, which strike horror into the soul of the student of the picturesque; while he is transported in surveying the fragments of ancient sculpture, which are nothing but ugly masses of mouldering stone in the judgment of the admirer of neatness. It is needless, however, to multiply instances, since the fact admits of no contradiction, but how can we believe that beauty is the object of a peculiar sense or faculty, when persons undoubtedly possessed of the faculty, and even in an eminent degree, can discover nothing of it in objects where it is distinctly felt and perceived by others with the same use of the faculty?

This one consideration, we confess, appears to us conclusive against the supposition of beauty being a real property of objects, addressing itself to the power of taste as a separate sense or faculty, and seems to point irresistibly to the conclusion that our sense of it is the result of more elementary feelings, into which it may be analyzed or resolved. A second objection, however, if possible of still greater force, is suggested, by considering the prodigious and almost infinite variety of things to which this property of beauty is ascribed, and the impossibility of imagining any one inherent quality which can belong to them all, and yet, at the same time, possess so much unity as to be the peculiar object of a separate sense or faculty. All simple qualities that are perceived in one object, are immediately recognized to be the same, when they are again perceived in another; and the objects in which they are thus perceived, are at once felt so far to resemble each other, and to partake of the same nature. Thus, snow is seen to be white, and chalk is seen to be white; but this is no sooner seen, than the two substances, however unlike in other respects, are felt at once to have this quality in common, and to resemble each other in all that relates to the quality of colour, and the sense of seeing. Now, is this felt, or could it be in-

telligibly asserted with regard to the quality of beauty? Take even a limited and specific sort of beauty: for instance, the beauty of form: the form of a fine tree is beautiful, and the form of a fine woman, and the form of a column, and a vase, and a chandelier. Yet how can it be said that the form of a woman has anything in common with that of a tree or a temple? or to which of the senses by which forms are distinguished, does it appear they have any resemblance or affinity? The matter, however, becomes still more inextricable when we recollect that beauty does not belong merely to forms or colours, but to sounds, and perhaps to the objects of other senses; nay, that in all languages and in all nations, it is not supposed to reside exclusively in material objects, but to belong also to sentiments and ideas, and intellectual and moral existences. Not only is a tree beautiful, as well as a palace or a waterfall; but a poem is beautiful, and a theorem in mathematics, and a contrivance in mechanics. But if things intellectual and totally segregated from matter may thus possess beauty, how can it possibly be a quality of material objects, or what sense or faculty can that be, whose proper office it is to intimate to us the existence of some property which is common to a flower and a demonstration, a valley and an eloquent discourse?

§ BEAUTY AND AGREEABLENESS

The only answer which occurs to this, is plainly enough a bad one; but the statement of it, and of its insufficiency, will serve better, perhaps, than any thing else, to develope the actual difficulties of the subject and the true state of the question with regard to them. It may be said, then, in answer to the questions we have suggested above, that all these objects, however various and dissimilar, agree at least in being agreeable, and that this agreeableness, which is the only quality they possess in common, may probably be the beauty which is ascribed to them all. Now to those who are accustomed to such discussions, it would be quite enough to reply, that though the agreeableness of such objects depend plainly enough upon their beauty, it by no means follows, but quite the contrary, that their beauty depends upon their agreeableness; the latter being the more comprehensive or generic term under which beauty must rank as one of the species. Its nature, therefore, is no more explained, nor is less absurdity substantially committed, by saying that things are beautiful, because they are agreeable, than if we were to give the same explanation of the sweetness of sugar; for no one, we suppose, will dispute, that though it be very true that sugar is agreeable because it is sweet, it would be manifestly preposterous to say that it was sweet because it was agreeable. For the benefit, however, of those who wish or require to be more regularly initiated in these mysteries, we beg leave to add a few observations.

In the first place, then, it seems evident, that agreeableness, in general, cannot be the same with beauty, because there are very many things in the highest degree agreeable, that can in no sense be called beautiful. Moderate heat, and savoury food, and rest, and exercise, are agreeable to the body; but none of these can be called beautiful; and many objects of a higher class, the love and esteem of others; and fame and a good conscience, and health, and riches, and wisdom, are all eminently agreeable, but not at all beautiful, according to my intelligible use of the word. It is quite absurd to say that beauty consists in agreeableness, without specifying in consequence of what it is agreeable,—or to hold that anything whatever is taught as to its nature, by merely classing it among our pleasurable emotions.

In the second place, however, we may remark, that among all the objects that are agreeable, whether they are also beautiful or not, scarcely any two are agreeable on

account of the same qualities, or even suggest their agreeableness to the same faculty or organ. Most certainly there is no resemblance or affinity whatever between the qualities which make a peach agreeable to the palate, and a beautiful statue to the eye; which soothe us in an easy chair by the fire, or delight us in the philosophical discovery. The truth is, that agreeableness is not properly a quality of any object whatever, but the effect or result of certain qualities, the nature of which we can generally define pretty exactly, or of which we know at least that they manifest themselves to some one particular sense or faculty, and no other; and consequently it would be just as obviously ridiculous to suppose a faculty or organ, whose office it was to perceive agreeableness, as to suppose that agreeableness was a distinct quality that could thus be perceived.

The class of agreeable, thanks to the bounty of Providence, is exceedingly large. Certain things are agreeable to the palate, and others to the smell and the touch. Some again are agreeable to our faculty of imagination, or to our understanding, or to our moral feelings; and none of all these we call beautiful; but there are others which we do call beautiful; and those we say are agreeable to our faculty of taste. But when we come to ask what is the faculty of taste, and what are the qualities which recommend them to that faculty? we find ourselves just where we were at the beginning of the discussion, and embarrassed with all the difficulties arising from the prodigious diversity of objects which seem to possess the qualities.

We know pretty well what is the faculty of seeing or hearing; or, at least, we know that what is agreeable to one of those faculties, has no effect whatever on the other. We know that bright colours afford no delight to the ear, nor sweet tones to the eye; and are therefore perfectly assured that the qualities which make the visible objects agreeable, cannot be the same with those which give pleasure to the ear; but it is by the eye and by the ear that all material beauty is perceived; and yet the beauty which discloses itself to these two separate senses, and plainly depends upon qualities which have no sort of affinity, is supposed to be one distinct quality, and to be perceived by a peculiar sense or faculty! The perplexity becomes still greater when we think of the beauty of poems or theorems, and endeavour to imagine what qualities they can possess in common with the agreeable modifications of light or of sound.

It is in these considerations that the difficulty of the subject consists. The faculty of taste, plainly, is not a faculty like any of the external senses—the range of whose objects is limited and precise, as well as the qualities by which they are gratified or offended,—and beauty, accordingly, is discovered in an infinite variety of objects, among which it seems at first sight impossible to discover any other bond or connection. Yet, boundless as their diversity may appear, it is plain that they must resemble each other in something, and in something more definite and definable than merely in being agreeable;—since they are all classed together, in every tongue and nation, under the common appellation of beautiful, and are felt indeed to produce emotions in the mind that have some sort of kindred or affinity. The words beauty and beautiful, in short, must mean something; and are universally felt to mean something much more definite than agreeableness or gratification in general; and while it is by no means easy to describe or define what that something is, the force and clearness of our perception of it is demonstrated by the readiness with which we determine, in any particular instance, whether the object of a given pleasurable emotion is or is not properly described as beauty.

§ BEAUTY DEPENDS UPON ASSOCIATION

What we have already said, we confess, appears to us conclusive against the idea of this beauty being any fixed or inherent property of the objects to which it is ascribed, or itself the object of any separate and independent faculty; and we will no longer conceal from the reader what we take to be the true solution of the difficulty. In our opinion, then, our sense of beauty depends entirely on our previous experience of similar pleasures or emotions, and consists in the suggestion of agreeable or interesting sensations with which we had formerly been made familiar by the direct and intelligible agency of our common sensibilities; and that vast variety of objects, to which we give the common name of beautiful, become entitled to that appellation, merely because they all possess the power of recalling or reflecting those sensations of which they have been the accompaniments, or with which they have been associated in our imagination by any other more casual bond of connection. According to this view of the matter, therefore, beauty is not an inherent property or quality of objects at all, but the result of the accidental relations in which they may stand to our experience of pleasures or emotions, and does not depend upon any particular configuration of parts, proportions, or colours, in external things, nor upon the unity, coherence, or simplicity of intellectual creations; but merely upon the associations which, in the case of every individual may enable these inherent, and otherwise indifferent qualities, to suggest or recall to the mind emotions of a pleasurable or interesting description. It follows, therefore, that no object is beautiful in itself, or could appear so, antecedent to our experience of direct pleasures or emotions; and that as an infinite variety of objects may thus reflect interesting ideas, so all of them may acquire the title of beautiful, although utterly diverse and disparate in their nature, and possessing nothing in common but this accidental power of reminding us of other emotions.

This theory, which, we believe, is now very generally adopted, though under many needless qualifications, shall be farther developed and illustrated in the sequel; but at present we shall only remark, that it serves at least to solve the great problem involved in the discussion, by rendering it easily conceivable how objects which have no inherent resemblance, nor, indeed, any one quality in common, should yet be united in one common relation, and consequently acquire one common epithet. Just as all the things that belonged to a beloved individual may serve to remind us of him, and thus to awake a kindred class of emotions, though just as unlike each other as any of the objects that are classed under the general name of beautiful. His poetry, or his slippers,—his acts of bounty, or his saddle-horse,—may lead to the same chain of interesting remembrances, and thus agree in possessing a power of excitement, for the sources of which we should look in vain through all the variety of their physical or metaphysical qualities.

By the help of the same consideration, we get rid of all the mystery of a peculiar sense or faculty, imagined for the express purpose of perceiving beauty; and discover that the power of taste is nothing more than the habit of tracing those associations, by which almost all objects may be connected with interesting emotions. It is easy to understand that the recollection, that any sense of delight or emotion must produce a certain agreeable sensation, and that the objects which introduce these recollections should not appear altogether indifferent to us: nor is it very difficult to imagine, that recollections thus suggested by some real and present existence, should present themselves under a different aspect, and move the mind somewhat from those which arise spontaneously in the ordinary course of our

reflections, and not thus grow out of a direct and peculiar impression....

§ THE ASSOCIATION THEORY: BEAUTY DERIVATIVE NOT ORIGINAL

...The...beauty which we impute to outward objects, is nothing more than the reflection of our own inward emotions, and is made up entirely of certain portions of love, pity, and affection, which have been connected with these objects, and still as it were belong to them, and move us anew whenever they are presented to our observation. Before proceeding to bring any proof of the truth of this proposition, there are two things that it may be proper to explain a little more distinctly. First, what are the primary affections, by the suggestion of which the sense of beauty is produced? and secondly, what is the nature of the connexion by which we suppose that the objects we call beautiful are enabled to suggest these affections?

With regard to the first of these points, it fortunately is not necessary either to enter into any tedious details, or to have recourse to any nice distinctions. All sensations that are not absolutely indifferent, and are at the same time, either agreeable, when experienced by ourselves, or attractive when contemplated in others, may form the foundation of the emotions of sublimity or beauty. The love of sensation seems to be the ruling appetite of human nature; and many sensations, in which the painful seem to bear no little share, are consequently sought for with avidity, and recollected with interest, even in our own persons. In the persons of others, emotions still more painful are contemplated with eagerness and delight; and therefore we must not be surprised to find that many of the pleasing sensations of beauty or sublimity resolve themselves ultimately into recollections of feelings that may appear to have a very opposite character. The sum of the whole is, that every feeling which it is agreeable to experience, to recall, or to witness, may become the source of beauty in external objects, when it is so connected with them as that their appearance reminds us of that feeling. Now, in real life, and from daily experience and observation, we know that it is agreeable in the first place, to recollect our pleasurable sensations, or to be enabled to form a lively conception of the pleasures of other men, or even of sentient beings of any description. We know likewise, from the same sure authority, that there is a certain delight in the remembrance of our past or the conception of our future emotions, even though attended with great pain, provided they be not forced too rudely on the mind, and be softened by the accompaniment of any milder feeling. And finally we know, in the same manner, that the spectacle or conception of the emotions of others, even when in a high degree painful, is extremely interesting and attractive, and draws us away, not only from the consideration of indifferent objects, but even from the pursuit of light or frivolous enjoyments. All these are plain and familiar facts, of the experience of which, however they may be explained, no one can entertain the slightest doubt, and into which, therefore, we shall have made no inconsiderable progress, if we can resolve the more mysterious fact, of the emotions we receive from the contemplation of sublimity or beauty.

Our proposition then is, that these emotions are not original emotions, nor produced directly by any qualities in the objects which excite them; but are reflections, or images, of the more radical and familiar emotions to which we have already alluded; and are occasioned, not by any inherent virtue in the objects before us, but by the accidents, if we may so express ourselves, by which these may have been enabled to suggest or recall to us our own past sensations or sympathies. We might almost venture indeed, to lay it down as an axiom, that except in the plain and palpable case of bodily pain or pleasure, we can never be interested in anything but the fortunes of sentient beings; and that everything partaking of the nature of mental emotion must have for its object the feelings, past, present, or possible, of something capable of sensation. Independent therefore, of all evidence, and without the help of any explanation, we should have been apt to conclude, that the emotions of beauty and sublimity must have for their objects the sufferings or enjoyments of sentient beings; and to reject, as intrinsically absurd and incredible, the supposition, that material objects, which obviously do neither hurt nor delight the body, should yet excite, by their mere physical qualities, the very powerful emotions which are sometimes excited by the spectacle of beauty.

§ HOW THE ASSOCIATION IS PRODUCED: BY NATURAL SIGNS AND UNIVERSAL CONCOMITANTS

Of the feelings, by their connexion with which external objects become beautiful, we do not think it necessary to speak more minutely; and, therefore, it only remains, under this preliminary view of the subject, to explain the nature of that connexion by which we conceive this effect to be produced. Here, also, there is but little need for minuteness, or fullness of enumeration. Almost every tie by which two objects can be bound together in the imagination in such a manner as that the presentment of the one shall recall the memory of the other; or, in other words, almost every possible relation which can subsist between such objects, may serve to connect the things we call sublime or beautiful, with feelings that are interesting or delightful. It may be useful, however, to class these bonds of association between mind and matter in a rude and general way.

It appears to us, then, that objects are sublime or beautiful, first, when they are the natural signs, and perpetual concomitants of pleasurable sensations, or, at any rate, of some lively feeling or emotion in ourselves or in some other sentient beings; or, secondly, when they are the arbitrary or accidental concomitants of such feelings; or, thirdly, when they bear some analogy or fanciful resemblance to things with which these emotions are necessarily connected. In endeavouring to illustrate the nature of these several relations, we shall be led to lay before our readers some proofs that appear to us satisfactory of the truth of the general theory.

The most obvious, and the strongest association that can be established between inward feelings and external objects is, where the object is necessarily and universally connected with the feeling by the law of nature, so that it is always presented to the senses when the feeling is impressed upon the mind, as the sight or the sound of laughter, with the feeling of gaiety; of weeping with distress; of the sound of thunder, with ideas of danger and power. Let us dwell for a moment on the last instance. Nothing, perhaps, in the whole range of nature, is more strikingly and universally sublime than the sound we have just mentioned; yet it seems obvious that the sense of sublimity is produced, not by any quality that is perceived by the ear, but altogether by the impression of power and of danger that is necessarily made upon the mind, whenever that sound is heard. That it is not produced by any peculiarity in the sound itself, is certain, from the mistakes that are frequently made with regard to it. The noise of a cart rolling over the stones, is often mistaken for thunder; and as long as the mistake lasts, this very vulgar and insignificant noise is actually felt to be prodigiously sublime. It is so felt, however, it is perfectly plain, merely because it is associated with ideas of prodigious power and undefined danger; and the sublimity is destroyed, the moment the association is dissolved, though the sound itself, and its effect on the organ, continue exactly the same. This, therefore, is an instance in which sublimity is distinctly proved to consist, not in any physical quality of the object to which it is ascribed, but in its necessary connexion with that vast and uncontrolled power which is the natural object of awe and veneration.

We may now take an example a little less plain and elementary. The most beautiful object in nature, perhaps, is the countenance of a young and beautiful woman; and we are apt at first to imagine that, independent of all associations, the forms and colours which it displays are, in themselves, lovely and engaging, and would appear charming to all beholders, with whatever other qualities or impressions they might happen to be connected. A very little reflection, however, will probably be sufficient to convince us of the fallacy of this impression; and to satisfy us, that what we admire is not a combination of forms and colours, which could never excite any mental emotion, but a collection of signs and tokens of certain mental feelings and affections, which are universally recognised as the proper objects of love and sympathy. Laying aside the emotions arising from difference of sex, and supposing female beauty to be contemplated by the pure and unenvying eye of a female, it seems quite obvious, that, among its ingredients, we should trace the signs of two different sets of qualities that are neither of them the object of sight, but of a higher faculty; in the first place, of youth and health; and in the second place, of innocence, gaiety, sensibility, intelligence, delicacy, or vivacity. Now, without enlarging upon the natural effect of the suggestions, we shall just suppose that the appearances, which must be admitted at all events to be actually significant of the qualities we have enumerated, had been by the law of nature attached to the very opposite qualities; that the smooth forehead, the firm cheek, and the full lip, which are now so distinctly expressive to us of the gay and vigorous periods of youth, and the clear and blooming complexion, which indicates health and activity, had been in fact the forms and colours by which old age and sickness were characterized, and that, instead of being found united to those sources and seasons of enjoyment, they had been the badges by which nature pointed out that state of suffering and decay which is now signified to us by the livid and emaciated face of sickness, or the wrinkled front, the quivering lip, and hollow cheek of age; if this were the familiar law of our nature, can it be doubted that we should look upon these appearances, not with rapture, but with aversion, and consider it as absolutely ludicrous or disgusting, to speak of the beauty of what was interpreted by every one as the lamented sign of pain and decrepitude? Mr. Knight himself, though a firm believer in the intrinsic beauty of colours, is so much of this opinion, that he thinks it entirely owing to those associations that we prefer the tame smoothness, and comparatively poor colours of a youthful face, to the richly fretted and variegated countenance of a pimpled drunkard.

Such we conceive, would be the inevitable effect of dissolving the subsisting connexion between the animating ideas of hope and enjoyment, and those visible appearances which are now significant of those emotions, and derive their whole beauty from that signification; but the effect would be still stronger if we could suppose the moral expression of those appearances to be reversed in the same manner. If the smile, which now enchants us, as the expression of innocence and affection, were the sign attached by nature to guilt and malignity; if the blush which expresses delicacy and the glance that speaks intelligence, vivacity, and softness, had always been found united with brutal passion or idiot moodiness; is it not certain, that the whole of their beauty would be extinguished, and that our emotions from the sight of them would be the reverse of what they now are?

That the beauty of a living and sentient creature should depend, in a great degree, upon qualities peculiar to such a creature, rather than upon the mere physical attributes which it may possess in common with the inert matter around it, cannot indeed appear a very improbable supposition to any one; but it may be more difficult for some persons to understand how the beauty of mere dead matter should be derived from the feelings and sympathies of sentient beings. It is absolutely necessary, therefore, that we should give an instance or two of this derivation.

It is easy enough to understand how the sight of a picture or statue should affect nearly in the same way as the sight of the original; nor is it much more difficult to conceive, how the sight of a cottage should give us something of the same feeling as the sight of a peasant's family; and the aspect of a town raise many of the same ideas as the appearance of a multitude of persons. We may begin, therefore, with an example a little more complicated; take, for instance, the case of a common English landscape—green meadows with fat cattle—canals or navigable rivers—well fenced, well cultivated fields—neat, clean, scattered cottages—humble antique church with churchyard elms, and crossing hedge-rows—all seen under bright skies, and in good weather;—there is much beauty, as every one will acknowledge, in such a scene. But in what does the beauty consist? Not certainly in the mere mixture of colours and forms; for colours more pleasing and lines more graceful (according to any theory of grace that may be preferred), might be spread upon a board, or a painter's pallet, without engaging the eye to a second glance, or raising the least emotion in the mind; but in the picture of human happiness that is presented to our imaginations and affections, in the visible and unequivocal signs of comfort, and cheerful and peaceful enjoyment, and of that secure and successful industry that ensures it continuance, and of the piety by which it is exalted, and of the simplicity by which it is contrasted with the guilt and fever of a city life; in the images of health and temperance and plenty which it exhibits to every eye, and in the glimpses which it affords to warmer imaginations of the primitive or fabulous times, when man was uncorrupted by luxury and ambition, and of those humble retreats in which we still delight to imagine that love and philosophy may find an unpolluted asylum. At all events, however, it is human feeling that excites our sympathy, and forms the object of our emotions. It is man, and man alone, that we see in the beauties of the earth which he inhabits; or, if a more sensitive and extended sympathy connect us with the lower families of animated nature, and make us rejoice with the lambs that bleat on the uplands, or the cattle that ruminate in the valley, or even with the living plants that drink the bright sun and the balmy air, it is still the idea of enjoyment of feelings that animate the existence of sentient beings, that calls forth all our emotions, and is the parent of all the beauty with which we proceed to invest the inanimate creation around us.

Instead of this quiet and tame English landscape, let us now take a Welsh or a Highland scene, and see whether its beauties will admit of being explained on the same principle. Here we shall have lofty mountains, and rocky and lonely recesses,—tufted woods hung over precipices,—lakes intersected with castled promontories,—ample solitudes of unploughed and untrodden valleys,—nameless and gigantic ruins,—and mountain echoes repeating the scream of the eagle and the roar of the cataract. This, too, is beautiful; and to those who can interpret the language it speaks, far more beautiful than the prosperous scene with which we have contrasted it. Yet, lonely as it is, it is to the recollection of man and of human feelings that its beauty also is owing. The mere forms and colours that compose its visible appearance, are no more capable of

exciting any emotion in the mind, than the forms and colours of a Turkey carpet. It is sympathy with the present or the past, or the imaginary inhabitants of such a region, that alone gives it either interest or beauty; and the delight of those who behold it, will always be found to be in exact proportion to the force of their imaginations, and the warmth of their social affections. The leading impressions here, are those of romantic seclusion and primeval simplicity; lovers sequestered in these blissful solitudes, "from towns and toils remote," and rustic poets and philosophers communing with nature, at a distance from the low pursuits and selfish malignity of ordinary mortals; then is the sublime impression of the mighty power which piled the massive cliffs upon each other, and rent the mountains asunder, and scattered their giant fragments at their base; and all the images connected with the monuments of ancient magnificence and extinguished hostility, the feuds, and the combats, and the triumphs of its wild and primitive inhabitants, contrasted with the stillness and desolation of the scenes where they lie interred; and the romantic ideas attached to their ancient traditions, and the peculiarities of their present life, their wild and enthusiastic poetry, their gloomy superstitions, their attachment to their chiefs, the dangers and the hardships and enjoyments of their lonely huntings and fishings, their pastoral shieling on the mountains in summer, and the tales and the sports that amuse the little groups that are frozen into their vast and trackless valleys in the winter. Add to all this, the traces of vast and obscure antiquity that are impressed on the language and the habits of the people, and on the cliffs, and caves, and gulfy torrents of the land; and the solemn and touching reflection, perpetually recurring, of the weakness and insignificance of perishable man, whose generations thus pass away into oblivion, with all their toils and ambition, while nature holds on her unvarying course, and pours out her streams, and renews her forests, with undecaying activity, regardless of the fate of her proud and perishable sovereign.

We have said enough, we believe, to let our readers understand what we mean by external objects being the natural signs or concomitants of human sympathies or emotions. Yet we cannot refrain from adding one other illustration, and asking on what other principle we can account for the beauty of spring? Winter has shades as deep, and colours as brilliant; and the great forms of nature are substantially the same through all the revolutions of the year.

We shall seek in vain, therefore, for the sources of that "vernal delight and joy" which subject all finer spirits to an annual intoxication, and strike home the sense of beauty even to hearts that seem proof against it under all other aspects. And it is not among the dead, but among the living, that this beauty originates. It is the renovation of life and of joy to all animated beings, that constitutes this great jubilee of nature; the young of animals bursting into existence; the simple and universal pleasures which are diffused by the mere temperature of the air, and the profusion of sustenance; the pairing of birds; the cheerful resumption of rustic toils; the great alleviation of all the miseries of poverty and sickness; our sympathy with the young life; and the promise and the hazards of the vegetable creation; the solemn, yet cheering, impression of the constancy of nature to her great periods of renovation; and the hopes that dart spontaneously forward with the new circle of exertions and enjoyments that is opened up by her hand and her example. Such are some of the conceptions that are forced upon us by the appearances of returning spring; and that seem to account for the emotions of delight with which these appearances are hailed by every mind endowed with any degree of sensibility, somewhat better than the bright-

ness of the colours, or the agreeableness of the smells that are then presented to our senses.

They are kindred conceptions that constitute the beauty of childhood. The forms and colours that are peculiar to that age, are not necessarily or absolutely beautiful in themselves; for, in a grown person, the same forms and colours would be either ludicrous or disgusting. It is their indestructible connection with the engaging ideas of innocence, of careless gaiety, of suspecting confidence; made still more tender and attractive by the recollection of helplessness, and blameless and happy ignorance of the anxious affection that watches over all their ways; and the hopes and fears that seek to pierce futurity, for those who have neither fears nor cares nor anxieties for themselves.

§ BY ACCIDENTAL CONCOMITANTS

These few illustrations will probably be sufficient to give our readers a general conception of the character and grounds of that theory of beauty which we think affords the only true or consistent account of its nature. They are all examples, it will be observed, of the *first* and most important connection which we think may be established between external objects and the sentiments or emotions of the mind; or cases in which the visible phenomena are the natural and universal accompaniments of the emotion, in some degree, in the breast of every beholder. If the tenor of these illustrations has been such as to make any impression in favour of the general theory, we conceive that it must be very greatly confirmed by the slightest consideration of the *second* class of cases, or those in which the external object is not the natural and necessary, but only the occasional or accidental concomitant of the emotion which it recalls. In the former instances, some conception of beauty seems to be inseparable from the appearance of the objects; and being impressed, in some degree, upon all persons to whom they are presented, there is evidently room for insinuating that it is an independent and intrinsic quality of their nature; and does not arise from association with anything else. In the instances, however, in which we are now to allude, this perception of beauty is not universal, but entirely dependent upon the opportunities which each individual has had to associate ideas of emotion with the object to which it is a ascribed; the same thing appearing beautiful to those who have been exposed to the influence of such associations, and indifferent to those who have not. Such instances, therefore, really afford [an] *experimentum crucis* to the truth of the theory in question; nor is it easy to conceive any more complete evidence, both that there is no such thing as absolute or intrinsic beauty, and that it depends altogether on those associations with which it is thus found to come and to disappear.

The accidental or arbitrary relations that may thus be established between natural sympathies or emotions and external objects, may be either such as occur to whole classes of men, or are confined to particular individuals. Among the former, those that apply to different nations or races of men, are the most important and remarkable; and constitute the basis of those peculiarities by which national tastes are distinguished. Take again, for example, the instance of female beauty, and think what different and inconsistent standards would be fixed for it in the different regions of the world; in Africa, in Asia, and in Europe, in Tartary and in Greece, in Lapland, Patagonia, and Circassia. If there was anything absolutely or intrinsically beautiful in any of the forms thus distinguished, it is inconceivable that men should differ so outrageously in their conceptions of it. If beauty was a real and independent quality, it seems impossible that it should be distinctly and clearly felt by one set of persons, where another set, altogether as sensitive, could see nothing but its opposite. And if it were actually and in-

separably attached to certain forms, colors, or proportions, it must appear utterly inexplicable that it should be felt and perceived in the most opposite forms and proportion, in objects of the same description. On the other hand, if all beauty consist in reminding us of certain natural sympathies and objects of emotion, it is easy to perceive how the most different forms should be felt to be equally beautiful. If female beauty, for instance, consist in the visible signs and expressions of youth and health, and of gentleness, vivacity, and kindness, then it will necessarily happen, that the forms, and colours, and proportions, which nature may have connected with those qualities, in the different climates or regions of the world, will all appear equally beautiful to those who have been accustomed to recognise them as the signs of such qualities; while they will be respectively indifferent to those who have not learned to interpret them in this sense, and displeasing to those whom experience has led to consider them as the signs of opposite qualities. The case is the same, though perhaps to a smaller degree, as to the peculiarity of national taste in other particulars.

The style of dress and architecture in every nation, if not adopted from mere want of skill, or penury of materials, always appears beautiful to the natives, and somewhat monstrous and absurd to foreigners. And the general character and aspect of their landscape, in like manner, if not associated with substantial evils and inconveniences, always appears more beautiful and enchanting than the scenery of any other region. The fact is still more striking, perhaps, in the case of music; in the effects of those national airs with which even the most uncultivated imaginations have connected so many interesting recollections; and in the delight with which all persons of sensibility catch the strains of their native melodies in strange or in distant lands. It is owing chiefly to the same sort of arbitrary and national association, that white is thought a gay color in Europe, where it is used at weddings, and a dismal color in China, where it is used for mourning; that we think yew trees gloomy, because they are planted in church-yards, and large masses of powdered horsehair majestic, because we see them on the heads of judges and bishops.

Next to these curious instances of arbitrary or limited associations that are exemplified in the diversities of national taste, are those that are produced by the differences of instruction or education. If external objects were sublime or beautiful in themselves, it is plain, that they would appear equally so to those who were acquainted with their origin, and to those to whom it was unknown. Yet it is not easy, perhaps, to calculate the degree to which our notions of beauty and sublimity are now influenced, over all Europe, by the study of classical literature; or the number of impressions of this sort which the well-educated receive, from objects that are utterly indifferent to uninstructed persons of the same natural sensibility. We gladly avail ourselves, upon this subject, of the beautiful expressions of Mr. Alison.

"The delight which most men of education receive from the consideration of antiquity, and the beauty that they discover in every object which is connected with ancient times, is in a great measure to be ascribed to the same cause. The antiquarian, in his cabinet, surrounded with the relics of former ages, seems to himself to be removed to periods that are long since past, indulges in the imagination of living in a world, which, by a very natural kind of prejudice, we are always willing to believe was both wiser and better than the present. All that is venerable or laudable in the history of these times, present themselves to his memory. The gallantry, the heroism, the patriotism of antiquity, rise again before his view, softened by the obscurity in which they are involved, and rendered more seducing to the imagination by that obscurity itself,

which, while it mingles a sentiment of regret amid his pursuits, serves at the same time to stimulate his fancy to fill up, by its own creation, those long intervals of time of which history has preserved no record. The relics he contemplates, seem to approach him still nearer to the ages of his regard. The dress, the furniture, the arms of the times, are so many assistances to his imagination, in guiding or directing its exercise; and offering him a thousand sources or imagery, provide him with an almost inexhaustible field in which his memory and his fancy may expatiate. There are few men who have not felt somewhat, at least, of the delight of such an employment. There is no man in the least acquainted with the history of antiquity, who does not love to let his imagination loose on the prospect of its remains, and to whom they are not in some measure sacred, from the innumerable images which they bring. Even the peasant, whose knowledge of former times extends but to a few generations, has yet in his village some monument of the deeds or virtues of his forefathers and cherishes with a fond veneration, the memorial of those good old times to which his imagination returns with delight, and of which he loves to recount the simple tales that tradition has brought him.

"And what is it that constitutes that emotion of sublime delight, which every man of common sensibility feels upon the first prospect of Rome. It is not the scene of destruction which is before him; it is not the Tiber, diminished in his imagination to a paltry stream, flowing amid the ruins of that magnificence which it once adorned; it is not the triumph of superstition over the wreck of human features, and its monuments erected upon the very spot where the first honours of humanity have been gained. It is ancient Rome which fills imagination. It is the country of Cæsar, and Cicero, and Virgil, which is before him. It is the mistress of the world which he sees, and who seems to him to rise again from her tomb, to give laws to the universe. All that the labours of his youth, or the studies of his maturer age have required, with regard to the history of this great people, open at once before his imagination, and present him with a field of high and solemn imagination, which can never be exhausted. Take from him these associations, conceal from him that it is Rome that he sees, and how different would be his emotion!"[1]

The influence of the same studies may be traced, indeed, through almost all our impressions of beauty, and especially in the feelings which we receive from the contemplation of rural scenery; where the images and recollections which have been associated with such objects, in the enchanting strains of the poets, are perpetually recalled by their appearance, and give an interest and a beauty to the prospect of which the uninstructed cannot have the slightest conception. Upon this subject, also, Mr. Alison has expressed himself with his usual warmth and elegance. After observing that in childhood the beauties of nature have scarcely any existence for those who have as yet but little general sympathy with mankind, he proceeds to state, that they are usually first recommended to notice by the poets, to whom we are introduced in the course of education; and who, in a manner, create them for us by the associations which they enable us to form with their visible appearance.

"How different, from this period, become the sentiments with which the scenery of nature is contemplated by those who have any imagination. The beautiful forms of ancient mythology, with which the fancy of poets peopled every element, are now ready to appear to their minds upon the prospect of every scene. The descriptions of ancient authors, so long admired, and so deserving of admiration, occur to them at

every moment, and with them all those enthusiastic ideas of ancient genius and glory, which the study of so many years of youth so naturally leads them to form. Or if the study of modern poetry has succeeded to that of the ancient, a thousand other beautiful associations are acquired, which, instead of destroying, serve easily to unite with the former, and to afford a new source of delight. The awful forms of Gothic superstition, the wild and romantic imagery, which the turbulence of the middle ages, the crusades, and the institution of chivalry, have spread over every country of Europe, arise to the imagination in every scene; accompanied with all those pleasing recollections of prowess, and adventure, and courteous manners, which distinguish those memorable times. With such images in their minds, it is not common nature that appears to surround them. It is nature embellished and made sacred by the memory of Theocritus and Virgil, Milton and Tasso; their genius seems still to linger among the scenes which inspired it, and to irradiate every object where it dwells; and the creation of their fancy seem the fit inhabitants of that nature, which their descriptions have clothed with beauty."[2]

It is needless, for the purpose of mere illustration, to pursue this subject of arbitrary or accidental association through all the divisions of which it is susceptible; and, indeed, the task would be endless, since there is scarcely any class in society which could not be shown to have peculiar associations of interest and emotion with objects which are not so connected in the minds of any other class. The young and the old, the rich and the poor, the artist and the man of science, the inhabitants of the city and the inhabitants of the country, the man of business and the man of pleasure, the domestic and the dissipated,—nay, even the followers of almost every different study or profession, have perceptions of beauty, be-

---

[1] [Archibald Alison, *Essays on the Nature and Principles of Taste* (New York: Harper & Brothers, Publishers, 1846), pp. 39–41.—ED. NOTE.]

[2] [*Ibid.*, pp. 54–55.—ED. NOTE.]

cause they have associations with external objects that are peculiar to themselves, and have no existence for any other persons. But though the detail of such instances could not fail to show, in the clearest and most convincing manner, how directly the notion of beauty is derived from some more radical and familiar emotion, and how many and various are the channels by which such emotions are transmitted, enough, perhaps, has been said to put our readers in possession of the principles and bearings of an argument which we must not think of exhausting. . . .

§ CONSEQUENCES OF THIS VIEW: BEAUTY AND SUBLIMITY

Having now explained, as fully as we think necessary, the grounds of that opinion as to the nature of beauty which appears to be most conformable to the truth, we have only to add a word or two as to the necessary consequences of its adoption upon several other controversies of a kindred description.

In the first place, then, we conceive that it establishes the substantial identity of the sublime, the beautiful, and the picturesque; and, consequently, puts an end to all controversy that is not purely verbal as to the difference of those several qualities. Every material object that interests without actually hurting or gratifying our bodily feelings, must do so, according to this theory, in one and the same manner,—that is, by suggesting or recalling some emotion or affection of ourselves, or some other sentient being, and presenting, to our imagination at least, some natural object of love, pity, admiration, or awe. The interest of material objects, therefore, is always the same, and arises, in every case, not from any physical qualities they may possess, but from their association with some idea of emotion. But, though material objects have but one means of exciting emotion, the emotions they do excite are infinite.

They are mirrors that may reflect all shades and all colours; and, in point of fact, do seldom reflect the same hues twice. No two interesting objects, perhaps, whether known by the name of beautiful, sublime, or picturesque, ever produced exactly the same emotion in the beholder; and no one object, it is most probable, ever moved any two persons to the very same conceptions. As they may be associated with all the feelings and affections of which the human mind is susceptible, so they may suggest those feelings in all their variety, and, in fact, do daily excite all sorts of emotions—running through every gradation, from extreme gaiety and elevation, to the borders of horrors and disgust.

Now, it is certainly true, that all the variety of emotions raised in this way, on the single basis of association, may be classed, in a rude way, under the denominations of sublime, beautiful, and picturesque, according as they partake of awe, tenderness, or admiration; and we have no other objection to this nomenclature, except its extreme imperfection, and the delusions to which we know that it has given occasion. If objects that interest by their association with ideas of power, and danger, and terror, are to be distinguished by the peculiar name of sublime, why should there not be a separate name also for objects that interest by associations of mirth and gaiety, another for those that please by suggestions of softness and melancholy, another for such as are connected with impressions of comfort and tranquility, and another, for those that are related to pity, and admiration, and love, and regret, and all the other distinct emotions and affections of our nature? These are not in reality less distinguishable from each other, than from the emotions of awe and veneration that confer the title of sublime on their representatives; and while all the former are confounded under the comprehensive appellation of beauty, this partial attempt at distinction is only apt to mislead us into an erroneous opinion of our accuracy, and to make us believe, both that there is a greater conformity among the things that pass under the same name and a greater difference between those that pass under different names, than is really the case. We have seen already, that the radical error of almost all preceding inquiries, has lain in supposing that everything that passed under the name of beautiful must have some real and inherent quality in common with everything else that obtained that name. And it is scarcely necessary for us to observe, that it has been almost as general an opinion, that sublimity was not only something radically different from beauty, but actually opposite to it; whereas the fact is, that it is far more nearly related to some sorts of beauty, than many sorts of beauty are to each other; and that both are founded exactly upon the same principle of suggesting some past or possible emotion of some sentient being.

Upon this important point, we are happy to find our opinions confirmed by the authority of Mr. Stewart, who, in his essay on the beautiful, has observed, not only that there appears to him to be no inconsistency or impropriety in such expressions as the sublime beauties of nature, or of the Sacred Scriptures; but has added, in express terms, that "to oppose the beautiful to the sublime, or to the picturesque, strikes him as something analogous to a contrast between the beautiful and the comic—the beautiful and the tragic —the beautiful and the pathetic—or the beautiful and the romantic."

§ THE STANDARD OF TASTE

The only other advantage which we shall specify as likely to result from the general adoption of the theory we have been endeavouring to illustrate, is, that it seems calculated to put an end to all these perplexing and vexations questions about the standard of taste, which have given occasion to so much impertinent and so much

elaborate discussion. If things are not beautiful in themselves, but only as they serve to suggest interesting conceptions to the mind, then every thing which does in point of fact suggest such a conception to any individual, is beautiful to that individual; and it is not only quite true that there is no room for disputing about tastes, but that all tastes are equally just and correct, in so far as each individual speaks only of his own emotions. When a man calls a thing beautiful, however, he may indeed mean to make two very different assertions; he may mean that it gives him pleasure, by suggesting to him some interesting emotion; and, in this sense, there can be no doubt that, if he merely speak the truth, the thing is beautiful; and that it pleases him precisely in the same way that all other things please those to whom they appear beautiful. But if he mean farther to say that the thing possesses some quality which should make it appear beautiful to every other person, and that it is owing to some prejudice or defect in them if it appear otherwise, then he is as unreasonable and absurd as he would think those who should attempt to convince him that he felt no emotion of beauty.

All tastes, then, are equally just and true, in so far as concerns the individual whose taste is in question; and what a man feels distinctly to be beautiful is beautiful to him, whatever other people may think of it. All this follows clearly from the theory now in question; but it does not follow from it that all tastes are equally good or desirable, or that there is any difficulty in describing that which is really the best and the most to be envied. The only use of the faculty of taste is to afford an innocent delight, and to aid the cultivation of a finer morality; and that man certainly will have the most delight from this faculty, who has the most numerous and the most powerful perceptions of beauty. But, if beauty consist in the reflection of our affections and sympathies, it is plain that he will always see the most beauty whose affections are warmest and most exercised, whose imagination is most powerful, and who has most accustomed himself to attend to the objects by which he is surrounded. In so far as mere feeling and enjoyment are concerned, therefore, it seems evident that the best taste must be that which belongs to the best affections, the most active fancy, and the most attentive habits of observation. It will follow pretty exactly, too, that all men's perceptions of beauty will be nearly in proportion to the degree of their sensibility and social sympathies; and that those who have no affections towards sentient beings will be just as insensible to beauty in external objects, as he, who cannot hear the sounds of his friend's voice, must be deaf to its echo.

In so far as the sense of beauty is regarded as a mere source of enjoyment, this seems to be the only distinction that deserves to be attended to; and the only cultivation that taste should ever receive, with a view to the gratification of the individual, should be through the indirect channel of cultivating the affections and powers of observation. If we aspire, however, to be creators, as well as observers of beauty, and place any part of our happiness in ministering to the gratification of others, as artists, or poets, or authors of any sort, then, indeed, a new distinction of taste, and a far more laborious system of cultivation will be necessary. A man who pursues only his own delight, will be as much charmed with objects that suggest powerful emotions, in consequence of personal and accidental associations, as with those that introduce similar emotions by means of associations that are universal and indestructable. To him, all objects of the former class are really as beautiful as those of the latter; and for his own gratification, the creation of that sort of beauty is just as important an occupation. But if he conceive the ambition of creating beauties for the admiration of others, he must be cautious to employ only such objects as are the natural signs, or the inseparable concomitants of emotions, of which the greater part of mankind are susceptible; and his taste will then deserve to be called bad and false, if he obtrude upon the public, as beautiful, objects that are not likely to be associated in common minds with any interesting impressions.

For a man himself, then, there is no taste that is either bad or false; and the only difference worthy of being attended to, is that between a great deal and a very little. Some who have cold affections, sluggish imaginations, and no habits of observation, can with difficulty discern beauty in anything; while others, who are full of kindness and sensibility, and who have been accustomed to attend to all the objects around them, feel it almost in everything. It is no matter what other people may think of the objects of their admiration; nor ought it to be any concern of theirs that the public would be astonished or offended, if they were called upon to join in that admiration. So long as no such call is made, this anticipated discrepancy of feeling need give them no uneasiness; and the suspicion of it should produce no contempt in any other persons. It is a strange aberration indeed of vanity that makes us despise persons for being happy, for having sources of enjoyment in which we cannot share; and yet this is the true account of the ridicule, which is so generally poured upon individuals who seek only to enjoy their peculiar tastes unmolested. For, if there be any truth in the theory we have been expounding, no taste is bad for any other reason than because it is peculiar, as the objects in which it delights must actually serve to suggest to the individual those common emotions and universal affections upon which the sense of beauty is everywhere founded. The misfortune is, however, that we are apt to consider all persons who make known their peculiar relishes, and especially all who create any objects for their gratification, as in some measure dictating to the public, and setting up an idol for general adoration; and hence this intolerant interference with almost all peculiar perceptions of beauty, and the unsparing derision that pursues all deviations from acknowledged standards. This intolerance, we admit, is often provoked by something of a spirit of proselytism and arrogance in those who mistake their own casual associations for natural or universal relations; and the consequence is, that mortified vanity dries up the fountain of their peculiar enjoyment, and disenchants, by a new association of general contempt or ridicule, the scenes that had been consecrated by some innocent but accidental emotion.

As all men must have some peculiar associations, all men must have some peculiar notions of beauty, and, of course, to a certain extent, a taste that the public would be entitled to consider as false or vitiated. For those who make no demands on public admiration, however, it is hard to be obliged to sacrifice this source of enjoyment; and, even for those who labour for applause, the wisest course, perhaps, if it were only practicable, would be, to have two tastes; one to enjoy, and one to work by; one founded upon universal associations, according to which they finished those performances for which they challenged universal praise, and another guided by all casual and individual associations, through which they looked fondly upon nature, and upon the objects of their secret admiration.

GEORG WILHELM FRIEDRICH HEGEL

(1770-1831)

The milestones in Hegel's outwardly uneventful life were his successive appointments to professorships at Jena, Heidelberg, and, in 1816, Berlin, and the appearance of his principal works: *The Phenomenology of the Spirit* (1807), *The Science of Logic* (1812–1816), *Encyclopaedia of the Philosophical Sciences* (1817–1821), and *The Philosophy of Law* (1821). *The Philosophy of Fine Art* was one of the books that were put together after his death from his unpublished literary works, his lecture notes, and the notes of some of his students.

Hegel's system of aesthetics, according to some of his critics, is one of those whose function has been to round out a system of philosophy. Hegel no doubt intended his aesthetic to serve this purpose. But as the reader of the following selection will readily concede, it would be unfair to regard the aesthetic of Hegel as a mere appendage to his system of absolute idealism. It is obvious that he examines the concepts and doctrines, as well as the "data," of the philosophy of art with an unprejudiced eye and with no attempt to deform them so that they will fit neatly into his own philosophy. At the same time, the features of his complete philosophy manifest themselves almost everywhere—whether pertinently or gratuitously the reader may decide for himself. As a sort of bonus awarded to the persevering reader, Hegel introduces here and there a thumbnail sketch of his whole system, which has usually the merit of being more readily comprehensible than the longer statements to be found in other volumes.

Although the fifth chapter of the introduction is specifically entitled "Division of the Subject," the entire introduction is devoted to the organization of the field of aesthetics, the separation of its various provinces, the arbitrament of conflicting claims, and the like. In the course of this work, Hegel is led to make more or less profound and accurate observations on taste, feeling, sublimation and catharsis, nature and art, sense perception and thought, imitation and expression, genius and technique. The introduction, in other words, does not merely lead into, but actually contains, a good part of the substance of the work. It is unfortunate that the substantive portions should be separated by pages of connective tissue that hold little interest for the student of aesthetics. We have, however, thought it better to ask the reader to wade through these relatively barren passages than to offer him a series of fertile ones with no idea of their place in the exposition.

GEORG WILHELM
FRIEDRICH HEGEL

The Philosophy of Fine Art

(Translated by Bernard Bosanquet)

CHAPTER ONE:
THE RANGE OF AESTHETIC
DEFINED AND SOME OBJECTIONS
AGAINST THE PHILOSOPHY
OF ART REFUTED

From Introduction to Hegel's Philosophy of Fine Art, *Bernard Bosanquet, trans. London: Routledge & Kegan Paul, Ltd., 1905. Reprinted by permission of Routledge & Kegan Paul, Ltd. (First published: 1835.)*

The present course of lectures deals with "Aesthetic." Their subject is the wide *realm of the beautiful,* and, more particularly, their province is *Art*—we may restrict it, indeed, to *Fine Art.*

The name "Aesthetic" in its natural sense is not quite appropriate to this subject. "Aesthetic" means more precisely the science of sensation or feeling. Thus understood, it arose as a new science, or rather as something that was to become a branch of philosophy for the first time,[1] in the school of Wolff, at the epoch when works of art were being considered in Germany in the light of the feelings which they were supposed to evoke—feelings of pleasure, admiration, fear, pity, etc. The name was so inappropriate, or, strictly speaking, so superficial, that for this reason it was attempted to form other names, e.g., "Kallistic." But this name, again, is unsatisfactory, for the science to be designated does

---

[1] [In Baumgarten's *Aesthetica*, 1750. See Lotze's *Aesthetik in Deutschland*, p. 4, and Scherer's *History of German Literature,* English translation, Vol. II, p. 25.—TR. NOTE.]

not treat of beauty in general, but merely of *artistic* beauty. We shall, therefore, permit the name Aesthetic to stand, because it is nothing but a name, and so is indifferent to us, and, moreover, has up to a certain point passed into common language. As a name, therefore, it may be retained. The proper expression, however, for our science is the "Philosophy of Art," or, more definitely, the "Philosophy of Fine Art."

§ AESTHETIC CONFINED TO BEAUTY OF ART

By the above expression we at once exclude the *beauty of Nature*. Such a limitation of our subject may appear to be an arbitrary demarcation resting on the principle that every science has the prerogative of marking out its boundaries at pleasure. But this is not the sense in which we are to understand the limitation of Aesthetic to *the beauty of art*. It is true that in common life we are in the habit of speaking of beautiful colour, a beautiful sky, a beautiful river, and moreover, of beautiful flowers, beautiful animals, and, above all, of beautiful human beings. We will not just now enter into the controversy how far such objects can justly have the attribute of beauty ascribed to them, or how far, speaking generally, natural beauty ought to be recognized as existing besides artistic beauty. We may, however, begin at once by asserting that artistic beauty stands *higher* than nature. For the beauty of art is the beauty that is born—born again, that is—of the mind;[2] and by as much as the mind and its products are higher than nature and its appearances, by so much the beauty of art is higher than the beauty of nature. Indeed, if we look at it *formally*—i.e., only considering in what way it exists, not what there is in it,—even a silly fancy such as may pass through a man's head is *higher*

than any product of nature; for such a fancy must at least be characterized by intellectual being and by freedom.[3] In respect of its content, on the other hand, the sun, for instance, appears to us to be an absolutely necessary factor in the universe, while a blundering notion passes away as accidental and transient; but yet, in its own being, a natural existence such as the sun is indifferent,[4] is not free or self-conscious, while if we consider it in its necessary connection with other things we are not regarding it by itself or for its own sake, and, therefore, not as beautiful.

To say, as we have said in general terms, that mind and its artistic beauty stand *higher* than natural beauty, is no doubt to determine almost nothing. For "higher" is an utterly indefinite expression, which designates the beauty of nature and that of art as if merely standing side by side in the space of the imagination, and states the difference between them as purely quantitative, and, therefore, purely external. But the mind and its artistic beauty, in being "higher" as compared with nature, have a distinction which is not simply relative. Mind, and mind only, is capable of truth, and comprehends in itself all that is, so that whatever is beautiful can only be really and truly beautiful as partaking in this higher element and as created thereby. In this sense the beauty of nature reveals itself as but a reflection of the beauty which belongs to the mind, as an imperfect, incomplete mode of being, as a mode whose really substantial element is contained in the mind itself.

Moreover, we shall find the restriction to fine art very natural, for, however much has been and is said—though less by the

---

[2] [*Aus dem Geiste*—allusion to "born of water and of the Spirit."—TR. NOTE.]

[3] [Not in the sense of fancying what you please, but in the technical sense of having separate existence; detached, so to speak, from the general background of things, not a mere concurrence of other elements.—TR. NOTE.]

[4] [Has no power of distinguishing itself from other things.—TR. NOTE.]

ancients than by ourselves— of the beauties of nature, yet no one has taken it into his head to emphasize the point of view of the *beauty* of natural objects, and to attempt to make a science, a systematic account of these beauties. The aspect of *Utility*, indeed, has been accentuated, and a science, e.g., of natural things useful against diseases, a *materia medica*, has been compiled, consisting in a description of minerals, chemical products, plants, and animals that are of use for curative purposes. But the realm of nature has not been arrayed and estimated under the aspect of beauty. In dealing with natural beauty we find ourselves too open to vagueness, and too destitute of a *criterion;* for which reason such a review would have little interest. ...

CHAPTER THREE.
THE CONCEPTION OF ARTISTIC BEAUTY

Part I: The Work of Art as Made and as Sensuous

After the above prefatory remarks, we approach closer to our subject, the philosophy of artistic beauty. Inasmuch as we are undertaking to treat it scientifically we must begin with its *Conception*. Not till we have established this conception can we map out the division, and with it the plan of the entirety of the science; for a division, if it is not, as is the case with unphilosophical inquiries, taken in hand in a purely external manner, must find its principle in the conception of the object itself.

In presence of such a demand we are at once met by the question, "Whence do we get this conception?" If we begin with the given conception of artistic beauty itself, that is enough to make it a *pre-supposition* and mere assumption; now, mere assump-

tions are not admitted by the philosophical method, but whatever it allows to pass must have its truth demonstrated, i.e., displayed as necessary.

We will devote a few words to coming to an understanding upon this difficulty, which concerns the introduction to every philosophical branch of study when taken in hand by itself.

The object of every science presents *prima facie* two aspects: in the first place, that such an object *is;* in the second place, *what* it is.

In ordinary science little difficulty attaches to the first of these points. It might even, at first sight, look ridiculous, if the requirement were presented that in astronomy and physics it should be demonstrated that there was a sun, heavenly bodies, magnetic phenomena, etc. In these sciences, which have to do with what is given to sense, the objects are taken from external experience, and instead of demonstrating them *(beweisen),* it is thought sufficient to show them *(weisen).* Yet even within the non-philosophical sciences, doubts may arise about the existence of their objects, as, e.g., in psychology, the science of mind, it may be doubted if there *is* a soul, a mind, i.e., something subjective, separate, and independent, distinct from what is material; or in theology, whether a God *is.* If, moreover, the objects are of subjective kind, i.e., are given only in the mind, and not as external sensuous objects, we are confronted by our conviction that there is nothing in the mind but what its own activity has produced. This brings up the accidental question whether men have produced this inner idea or perception in their minds or not, and even if the former is actually the case, whether they have not made the idea in question vanish again, or at any rate degraded it to a merely *subjective idea,* whose content has no natural and independent being. So, for instance, the beautiful has often been regarded as not naturally and independently necessary in our ideas, but as a mere subjective pleasure or accidental sense. Our external intuitions, observations, and perceptions are often deceptive and erroneous, but still more is this the case with the inner ideas, even if they have in themselves the greatest vividness, and are forcible enough to transport us irresistibly into passion.

This doubt whether an object of inward ideas and inward perception as such is or is not, as also the accidental question whether the subjective consciousness has produced it in itself, and whether the act or mode in which it brought it before itself was in its turn adequate to the object in its essential and independent nature—all this is just what aroused in men the higher scientific need, which demands that, even if we have an idea that an object is, or that there is such an object, the object must yet be displayed or demonstrated in terms of its necessity.

This proof, if it is developed in a really scientific way, must also satisfy the further question *What* an object is. But to expound this relation would carry us too far in this place, and we can only make the following remarks on the point.

If we are to display the necessity of our object, the beautiful in art, we should have to prove that art or beauty was a result of antecedents such as, when considered in their true conception, to lead us on with scientific necessity to the idea of fine art. But in as far as we begin with *art,* and propose to treat of the essence of *its* idea and of the realization of that idea, not of antecedents which go before it *as demanded by* its idea, so far art, as a peculiar scientific object, has, for us, a pre-supposition which lies beyond our consideration, and which, being a different content, belongs in scientific treatment to a different branch of philosophical study. For it is nothing short of the whole of philosophy that is the knowledge of the universe as in itself *one single* organic totality which develops itself out of its own conception, and which, return-

ing into itself so as to form a whole in virtue of the necessity in which it is placed towards itself, binds itself together with itself into *one single* world of truth. In the coronal of this scientific necessity, each individual part is just as much a circle that returns into itself, as it has, at the same time, a necessary connection with other parts. This connection is a backward out of which it derives itself, as well as a forward, to which in its own nature it impels itself on and on, in as far as it is fertile by creating fresh matter out of itself, and issuing it into the further range of scientific knowledge. Therefore, it is not our present aim to demonstrate the idea of beauty from which we set out, that is, to derive it according to its necessity from the pre-suppositions which are its antecedents in science. This task belongs to an encyclopaedic development of philosophy as a whole and of its particular branches. For us, the idea of beauty and of art is a pre-supposition given in the system of philosophy. But as we cannot in this place discuss this system, and the connection of art with it, we have not yet the idea of the beautiful before us *in a scientific form;* what we have at command are merely the elements and aspects of it, as they are or have at former periods been presented, in the diverse ideas of the beautiful and of art in the mere common consciousness. Having started from this point, we shall subsequently pass to the more profound consideration of the views in question, in order thereby to gain the advantage of, in the first place, obtaining a general idea of our object, and further, by a brief criticism effecting a preliminary acquaintance with its higher principles, with which we shall have to do in the sequel. By this mode of treatment our final introduction will act, so to speak, as the overture to the account of the subject itself, and will serve the purpose of a general collection and direction of our thoughts towards the proper object-matter of our discussion.

What we know, to begin with, as a current idea of the work of art, comes under the three following general predicates:—

1. We suppose the work of art to be no natural product, but brought to pass by means of human activity.

2. To be essentially made *for* man, and, indeed, to be more or less borrowed from the sensuous and addressed to man's sense.

3. To contain an *end*.

Work of Art as Product of Human Activity

As regards the first point, that a work of art is taken to be a product of human activity, this view has given rise to:

§ CONSCIOUS PRODUCTION BY RULE

the view that this activity, being the *conscious* production of an external object, can also be *known,* and *expounded,* and learnt, and prosecuted by others. For, what one can do, it might seem, another can do,[5] or imitate,[6] as soon as he is acquainted with the mode of procedure; so that, supposing universal familiarity with the rules of artistic production, it would only be a matter of any one's will and pleasure to carry out the process in a uniform way, and so to produce works of art. It is thus that the above-mentioned rule-providing theories and their precepts, calculated for practical observance, have arisen. But that which can be executed according to such instruction, can only be something formally regular and mechanical. For only what is mechanical is of such an external kind that no more than a purely empty exercise of will and dexterity is required to receive it among our ideas and put it in act; such an exercise not needing to be supplemented by anything concrete, or anything that goes beyond the precepts conveyed in general rules. This is most vividly displayed when precepts of the kind in question do not limit themselves to what is purely external and mechanical, but extend to the meaning-laden spiritual activity of true art. In this region the rules contain nothing but indefinite generalities; e.g., "The theme ought to be interesting, and each individual ought to be made to speak according to his rank, age, sex, and position." But if rules are meant to be adequate on this subject, their precepts ought to have been drawn up with such determinateness that they could be carried out just as they are expressed, without further and original activity of mind. Being abstract, however, in their content, such rules reveal themselves, in respect of their pretension of being adequate to fill the consciousness of the artist, as wholly inadequate, inasmuch as artistic production is not formal activity in accordance with given determinations. For it is bound as spiritual activity to work by drawing on its own resources, and to bring before the mind's eye a quite other and richer content and ampler individual creations than any abstract formulae can dictate. Such rules may furnish guidance in case of need, if they contain anything really definite, and therefore of practical utility; but their directions can only apply to purely external circumstances.

§ ARTISTIC INSPIRATION

The tendency which we have just indicated has therefore been abandoned, and, in place of it, the opposite principle has been pursued to no less lengths. For the work of art came to be regarded no longer as the product of an *activity general* in mankind, but as the work of a mind endowed with wholly peculiar gifts. This mind, it is thought, has then nothing to do but *simply* to give free play to its particular gift, as though it were a specific force of nature, and is to be entirely released from

----

5 [*Machen.*—TR. NOTE.]
6 [*Nach-machen.*—TR. NOTE.]

attention to laws of universal validity, as also from the interference of reflection in its instinctively creative operation. And, indeed, it is to be guarded therefrom, inasmuch as its productions could only be infected and tainted by such a consciousness. In this aspect the work of art was pronounced to be the product of *talent* and *genius,* and stress was laid on the natural element which talent and genius contain. The view was partly right. Talent is specific, and genius universal capability, with which a man has not the power to endow himself simply by his own self-conscious activity. . . .

In this place we have only to mention the aspect of falsity in the view before us, in that all consciousness respecting the man's own activity was held, in the case of artistic production, not merely superfluous, but even injurious. Production on the part of talent and genius then appears, in general terms, as a *state,* and, in particular, as a state of *inspiration.* To such a state, it is said, genius is in part excited by a given object, and in part it has the power of its own free will to place itself therein, in which process, moreover, the good service of the champagne bottle is not forgotten. This notion became prominent in Germany in the so-called *epoch of genius,* which was introduced by the early poetical productions of Goethe, and subsequently sustained by those of Schiller.[7] In their earliest works these poets began everything anew, in scorn of all the rules which had then been fabricated, transgressed these rules of set purpose, and, while doing so, distanced all rivals by a long interval. I will not enter more closely into the confusions which have prevailed respecting the conception of inspiration and genius, and which prevail even at the present day respecting the omnipotence of inspiration as such. We need only lay down as essential the view that, though

the artist's talent and genius contains a natural element, yet it is essentially in need of cultivation by thought, and of reflection on the mode in which it produces, as well as of practice and skill in producing. A main feature of such production is unquestionably external workmanship, inasmuch as the work of art has a purely technical side, which extends into the region of handicraft; most especially in architecture and sculpture, less so in painting and music, least of all in poetry. Skill in this comes not by inspiration, but solely by reflection, industry, and practice; and such skill is indispensable to the artist, in order that he may master his external material, and not be thwarted by its stubbornness.

Moreover, the higher an artist ranks, the more profoundly ought he to represent the depths of heart and mind; and these are not known without learning them, but are only to be fathomed by the direction of a man's own mind to the inner and outer world. So here, too, *study* is the means whereby the artist brings this content into his consciousness, and wins the matter and burden of his conceptions.

In this respect one art may need the consciousness and cognition of such matter more than others. Music, for instance, which concerns itself only with the undefined movement of the inward spiritual nature, and deals with musical sounds as, so to speak, feeling without thought, needs little or no spiritual content to be present in consciousness. It is for this reason that musical talent generally announces itself in very early youth, while the head is still empty and the heart has been but little moved, and is capable of attaining to a very considerable height in early years, before mind and life have experience of themselves. And again, as a matter of fact we often enough see very great expertness in musical composition, as also in execution, subsist along with remarkable barrenness of mind and character. The reverse is the case with poetry. In poetry all depends on the

---

[7] [See Appendix to English translation of Scherer, Vol. II, p. 347. Goethe's *Götz von Berlichingen* appeared in 1773; Schiller's *Die Räuber* in 1781.—TR. NOTE.]

representation—which must be full of matter and thought—of man, of his profounder interests, and of the powers that move him; and therefore mind and heart themselves must be richly and profoundly educated by life, experience, and reflection, before genius can bring to pass anything mature, substantial, and self-complete. Goethe's and Schiller's first productions are of an immaturity, and even of a rudeness and barbarism, that are absolutely terrifying. This phenomenon, that the greater part of those attempts display a predominant mass of thoroughly prosaic and in part of frigid and commonplace elements, furnishes the chief objection to the common opinion, that inspiration is inseparable from youth and youthful fire. Those two men of genius, it may be said, were the first to give our nation works of true poetry, and yet it was only their mature manhood[8] that presented us with creations profound, substantial, and the outcome of genuine inspiration, while no less thoroughly perfect in form. Thus, too, it was not till his old age that Homer devised and uttered his immortal songs.

§ DIGNITY OF PRODUCTION BY MAN

A third view, which concerns the idea of the work of art as a product of human activity, refers to the position of such a work towards the external appearances of nature. It was an obvious opinion for the common consciousness to adopt on this head, that the work of art made by man ranked *below* the product of nature. The work of art has no feeling in itself, and is not through and through a living thing, but, regarded as an external object, is dead. But we are wont to prize the living more than the dead. We must admit, of course, that the work of art has not in itself movement and life. An animated being in nature is within and without an organization appropriately elaborated down to all its minutest parts, while the work of art attains the semblance of animation on its surface only, but within is common stone, or wood and canvas, or, as in the case of poetry, is idea, uttering itself in speech and letters. But this aspect, viz. its external existence, is not what makes a work into a production of fine art; it is a work of art only in as far as, being the offspring of mind, it continues to belong to the realm of mind, has received the baptism of the spiritual, and only represents that which has been moulded in harmony with mind. A human interest, the spiritual value which attaches to an incident, to an individual character, to an action in its plot and in its *dénouement,* is apprehended in the work of art, and exhibited more purely[9] and transparently than is possible on the soil of common unartistic reality. This gives the work of art a higher rank than anything produced by nature, which has not sustained this passage through the mind. So, for instance, by reason of the feeling and insight of which a landscape as depicted by an artist is a manifestation, such a work of mind assumes a higher rank than the mere natural landscape. For everything spiritual is better than anything natural. At any rate, no existence in nature is able, like art, to represent divine ideals.

Upon that which, in works of art, the mind borrows from its own inner life it is able, even on the side of external existence, to confer *permanence*; whereas the individual living thing of nature is transient, vanishing, and mutable in its aspect, while the work of art persists. Though, indeed, it is not mere permanence, but the accentuation of the character which animation by mind confers, that constitutes its genuine pre-eminence as compared with natural reality.

---

8 [The *Iphigenie* was completed in Goethe's thirty-eighth year, fourteen years later than *Götz*. The bulk of his great works are of the same date as the *Iphigenie,* or later. . . .Schiller's *Wallenstein* was completed after his thirty-fifth year.—TR. NOTE.]

9 [Free from irrelevancies.—TR. NOTE.]

Nevertheless, this higher rank assigned to the work of art is in turn disputed by another idea of the common consciousness. It is said that nature and its products are a work of God, created by his goodness and wisdom, whereas the work of art is *merely* a human production, made after man's devising by man's hands. In this antithesis between natural production as a divine creation and human activity as a merely finite creation, we at once come upon the misconception, that God does *not* work in man and through man, but limits the range of his activity to nature alone. This false opinion is to be entirely abandoned if we mean to penetrate the true conception of art. Indeed, in opposition to such an idea, we must adhere to the very reverse, believing that God is more honoured by what mind does or makes than by the productions or formations of nature. For not only is there a divinity in man, but in him it is operative under a form that is appropriate to the essence of God, in a mode quite other and higher than in nature. God is a Spirit, and it is only in man that the medium through which the divine element passes has the form of conscious spirit, that actively realizes itself. In nature the corresponding medium is the unconscious, sensible, and external, which is far below consciousness in value. In the products of art God is operative neither more nor less than in the phenomena of nature; but the divine element, as it makes itself known in the work of art, has attained, as being generated out of the mind, an adequate thoroughfare for its existence; while existence in the unconscious sensuousness of nature is not a mode of appearance adequate to the Divine Being.

§ MAN'S NEED TO PRODUCE WORKS
    OF ART

Granting, then, that the work of art is made by man as a creation of mind, we come to the last question, which will enable us to draw a deeper result from what has been said. What is man's need to produce works of art? On the one hand the production may be regarded as a mere toy of chance and of man's fancies, that might just as well be let alone as pursued. For, it may be said, there are other and better means for effecting that which is the aim of art, and man bears in him interests that are yet higher and of more import than art has power to satisfy. But, on the other hand, art appears to arise from the higher impulse and to satisfy the higher needs, at times, indeed, even the highest, the absolute need of man, being wedded to the religious interests of whole epochs and peoples, and to their most universal intuitions respecting the world. This inquiry concerning the not contingent but absolute need of art we cannot as yet answer completely, seeing that it is more concrete than any shape which could here be given to the answer.[10] We must, therefore, content ourselves for the present with merely establishing the following points.

The universal and absolute need out of which art, on its formal side,[11] arises has its source in the fact that man is a *thinking* consciousness, i.e., that he draws out of himself, and makes explicit *for himself*, that which he is, and, generally, whatever is. The things of nature are only *immediate and single,* but man as mind *reduplicates* himself, inasmuch as *prima facie* he *is* like the things of nature, but in the second place just as really is *for* himself, perceives himself, has ideas of himself, thinks himself, and only thus is active self-realizedness.[12] This consciousness of himself man obtains in a twofold way: *in the first place theoretically,* in as far as he has inwardly to bring himself into his own consciousness,

---

10 [That is, it requires a definite or determinate answer, depending on a number of ideas which cannot be explained in an introduction.—TR. NOTE.]

11 [That is, considered generally, apart from the wishes and, perhaps, selfish aims of individual artists.—TR. NOTE.]

12 [*Fürsichsein.*—TR. NOTE.]

with all that moves in the human breast, all that stirs and works therein, and, generally, to observe and form an idea of himself, to fix before himself what thought ascertains to be his real being, and, in what is summoned out of his inner self as in what is received from without, to recognize only himself. Secondly, man is realized for himself by *practical* activity, inasmuch as he has the impulse, in the medium which is directly given to him, and externally presented before him, to produce himself, and therein at the same time to recognize himself. This purpose he achieves by the modification of external things upon which he impresses the seal of his inner being, and then finds repeated in them his own characteristics. Man does this in order as a free subject to strip the outer world of its stubborn foreignness, and to enjoy in the shape and fashion of things a mere external reality of himself.[13] Even the child's first impulse involves this practical modification of external things. A boy throws stones into the river, and then stands admiring the circles that trace themselves on the water, as an effect in which he attains the sight of something that is his own doing. This need traverses the most manifold phenomena, up to the mode of self-production in the medium of external things as it is known to us in the work of art. And it is not only external things that man treats in this way, but himself no less, i.e., his own natural form, which he does not leave as he finds it, but alters of set purpose. This is the cause of all ornament and decoration, though it may be as barbarous, as tasteless, as utterly disfiguring or even destructive as crushing Chinese ladies' feet, or as slitting the ears and lips. It is only among cultivated men that change of the figure,[14] of behaviour, and of every kind and mode of

self-utterance emanates from spiritual education.[15]

The universal need for expression in art[16] lies, therefore, in man's rational impulse to exalt the inner and outer world into a spiritual consciousness for himself, as an object in which he recognizes his own self. He satisfies the need of this spiritual freedom when he makes all that exists explicit for himself *within,* and in a corresponding way realizes this his explicit self *without,* evoking thereby, in this reduplication of himself, what is in him into vision and into knowledge for his own mind and for that of others. This is the free rationality of man, in which, as all action and knowledge, so also art has its ground and necessary origin. The specific need of art, however, in contradistinction to other action, political or moral, to religious imagination and to scientific cognition, we shall consider later.

Work of Art as Addressed to Man's Sense

We have so far been considering that aspect of the work of art in which it is made by man. We have now to pass on to its second characteristic, that it is made for man's *sense,* and for this reason is more or less borrowed from the sensuous.

§ OBJECT OF ART—PLEASANT FEELING

This reflection has furnished occasion for the consideration to be advanced that fine art is intended to arouse feeling, and indeed more particularly the feeling which we find suits us—that is, pleasant feeling. Looking at the question thus, men have treated the investigation of fine art as an investigation of the feelings, and asked what feelings it must be held that art ought to

---

[13] [Reality derivative from his own reality.—TR. NOTE.]

[14] [He means, as in attitude, bearing, gentle movement, etc.—TR. NOTE.]

[15] [*Bildung.*—TR. NOTE.]

[16] [*Bedürfniss zur Kunst.*—TR. NOTE.]

evoke,—fear, for example, and compassion; and then, how these could be pleasant— how, for example, the contemplation of misfortune could produce satisfaction. This tendency of reflection is traceable particularly to Moses Mendelssohn's times, and many such discussions are to be found in his writings. Yet such an investigation did not lead men far, for feeling is the indefinite dull region of the mind; what is felt remains wrapped in the form of the most abstract individual subjectivity,[17] and therefore the distinctions of feeling are also quite abstract, and are not distinctions of the actual object-matter itself. For instance, fear, anxiety, alarm, terror, are no doubt of one and the same sort of feeling variously modified, but in part are mere quantitative heightenings, in part are forms which in themselves have nothing to do with their content itself, but are indifferent to it. In the case of fear, for instance, an existence is given in which the subject (i.e., a person) has an interest, but at the same time sees approaching the negative that threatens to annihilate this existence, and so finds immediately in himself, as a contradictory affection of his subjectivity, the two at once, this interest and that negative. Now, such fear considered in itself is not enough to condition any content, but is capable of receiving into itself the most diverse and opposite matters.[18] Feeling, as such, is a thoroughly empty form of subjective affection. No doubt this form may in some cases be manifold in itself, as is hope, grief, joy, or pleasure; and, again, may in such diversity comprehend varied contents, as there is a feeling of justice, moral feeling, sublime religious feeling, and so forth. But the fact that such content is forthcoming in different forms of feeling is not enough to bring to

light its essential and definite nature; they remain purely subjective affections of myself, in which the concrete matter vanishes, as though narrowed into a circle of the utmost abstraction.[19] Therefore, the inquiry into the feelings which art arouses, or ought to arouse, comes utterly to a standstill in the indefinite, and is a mode of study which precisely abstracts from the content proper and from its concrete essence and notion. For reflection upon feeling contents itself with the observation of the subjective affection in its isolation, instead of diving into and fathoming the matter in question itself, the work of art, and, while engaged with it, simply letting go the mere subjectivity and its states. In feeling it is just this vacant subjectivity that is—not merely retained, but—given the first place, and that is why men are so fond of having emotions. And, for the same reason such a study becomes tedious from its indefiniteness and vacancy, and repulsive from its attentiveness to little subjective peculiarities.

§ FEELING OF BEAUTY—TASTE

Now, as a work of art is not merely to do in general something of the nature of arousing emotion—for this is a purpose which it would have in common, without specific difference, with eloquence, historical composition, religious edification, and so forth— but is to do so only in as far as it is beautiful, reflection hit upon the idea, seeing that beauty was the object, of searching out a *peculiar feeling of beauty* to correspond to it, and of discovering a particular sense of beauty. In this search it soon appeared that such a sense is no blind instinct made rigidly definite by nature, and capable from the beginning in its own independent essence of discerning beauty. Hence it followed that education came to be demanded for this

---

17 [That is, you cannot describe it or picture it definitely, like a thing with attributes, although you feel it in yourself.—TR. NOTE.]

18 [That is, you may be afraid of anything; the fact that you are afraid does not in itself indicate what you are afraid of.—TR. NOTE.]

19 [My private feeling is compared to a small circle, in which morality, justice, etc., may *be,* but have not room to show their nature. Feeling allows of no definition.—TR. NOTE.]

sense, and the educated sense of beauty came to be called *taste,* which, although an educated appreciation and apprehension of the beautiful, was yet supposed to retain the nature of immediate feeling. We have already mentioned how abstract theories undertook to educate such a sense of taste, and how external and one-sided that sense remained. The criticism of the time when those views prevailed, was not only defective in *universal* principles, but also, in its particular references to individual works of art, was less directed to justifying a *definite* judgment—the power to make one not having at that time been acquired—than to advancing the general education of taste. For this reason such education in its turn came to a standstill in the indefinite, and merely endeavoured so to equip feeling as sense of beauty by help of reflection, that there might thenceforth be capacity to find out beauty whenever and wherever it should exist. Yet the depths of the matter remained a sealed book to mere taste, for these depths demand not only sensibility and abstract reflection, but the undivided reason and the mind in its solid vigour; while taste was only directed to the external surface about which the feelings play, and on which one-sided maxims may pass for valid. But, for this very reason, what is called good taste takes fright at all more profound effects of art, and is silent where the reality comes in question, and where externalities and trivialities vanish. For when great passions and the movements of a profound soul are unveiled, we are no longer concerned with the finer distinctions of taste and its pettifogging particularities. It feels that genius strides contemptuously over such ground as this, and, shrinking before its power, becomes uneasy, and knows not which way to turn.

§ ART SCHOLARSHIP

And thus, as we should expect, men have abandoned the tendency to consider works of art solely with an eye to the education of taste, and with the purpose of merely displaying taste. The connoisseur, or scholar of art, has replaced the art-judge, or man of taste. The positive side of art-scholarship, so far as it concerns a thorough acquaintance with the entire circumference[20] of the individual character in a given work of art, we have already pronounced to be essential to the study of art. For a work of art, owing to its nature as at once material and individual, is essentially originated by particular conditions of the most various kinds, to which belong especially the time and place of its production, then the peculiar individuality of the artist, and in particular the grade of technical development attained by his art. Attention to all these aspects is indispensable to distinct and thorough insight and cognition, and even to the enjoyment of a work of art; it is with them that connoisseurship, or art-scholarship, is chiefly occupied; and all that it can do for us in its own way is to be accepted with gratitude. Yet, though such scholarship is entitled to rank as something essential, still it ought not to be taken for the whole or supreme element in the relation which the mind adopts towards a work of art, and towards art in general. For art-scholarship (and this is its defective side) is capable of resting in an acquaintance with purely external aspects, such as technical or historical details, etc., and of guessing but little, or even knowing absolutely nothing, of the true and real nature of a work of art. It may even form a disparaging estimate of the value of more profound considerations in comparison with purely positive, technical, and historical information. Still, even so, art-scholarship, if only it is of a genuine kind, at least strives after definite grounds and information, and an intelligent judgment, with which is closely conjoined the more precise distinction of the different,

---

20 [*All* its positive aspects or relations, age, phase, artist's history, etc.—TR. NOTE.]

even if partly external, aspects in a work of art, and the estimation of their importance.

§ PROFOUNDER CONSEQUENCES OF THE SENSUOUS NATURE OF ART

After these remarks upon the modes of study which have arisen out of that aspect of a work of art in which, being a sensuous object, it is invested with a relation to man as a sensuous being, we will now consider this aspect in its more essential relations to art as such, and so partly as regards the work of art as object, partly with respect to the subjectivity of the artist, his genius, talent, and so on; but without entering into matter relative to these points that can only proceed from the knowledge of art in its universal idea. For we are not yet on genuinely scientific ground, but have only reached the province of external reflection.

Relations of the sensuous to the mind. The work of art then, of course, presents itself to sensuous apprehension. It is addressed to sensuous feeling, outer or inner, to sensuous perception and imagination, just as is the nature that surrounds us without, or our own sensitive nature within. Even a speech, for instance, may be addressed to sensuous imagination and feeling. Notwithstanding, the work of art is not only for the *sensuous* apprehension as sensuous object, but its position is of such a kind that as sensuous it is at the same time essentially addressed to the *mind,* that the mind is meant to be affected by it, and to find some sort of satisfaction in it.

This intention of the work of art explains how it is in no way meant to be a natural product and to possess natural life, whether a natural product is to be ranked higher or lower than a *mere* work of art, as it is often called in a depreciatory sense.

For the sensuous aspect of the work of art has a right to existence only in as far as it exists for man's mind, but not in as far as *qua* sensuous thing it has separate existence by itself.[21] If we examine more closely in what way the sensuous is presented to man, we find that what is sensuous may bear various relations to the mind.

The lowest mode of apprehension, and that least appropriate to the mind, is purely sensuous apprehension. It consists naturally in mere looking, listening, feeling, just as in seasons of mental fatigue it may often be entertaining to go about without thought, and just to hear and look around us. The mind, however, does not rest in the mere apprehension of external things by sight and hearing, it makes them objects for its own inner nature, which then is itself impelled in a correspondingly sensuous form to realize itself in the things, and relates itself to them as *desire*. In this appetitive relation to the outer world, the man stands as a sensuous particular over against the things as likewise particulars; he does not open his mind to them with general ideas as a thinking being, but has relations dictated by particular impulses and interests to the objects as themselves particulars, and preserves himself in them, inasmuch as he uses them, consumes them, and puts in act his self-satisfaction by sacrificing them to it. In this negative relation desire requires for itself not merely the superficial appearance of external things, but themselves in their concrete sensuous existence. Mere pictures of the wood that it wants to use, or of the animals that it wants to eat, would be of no service to desire. Just as little is it possible for desire to let the object subsist in its freedom. For its impulse urges it just precisely to destroy this independence and freedom of external things, and to show that they are only there to be destroyed and consumed. But, at the same time, the subject himself, as entangled in the particular limited and valueless interests of his desires,

---

21 [Its sensuous aspect has no independent warrant or justification, as that, for example, of an animal has in its own separate life. So it must simply be such as is enough to appeal to man's mind, e.g., mere surface painting.—TR. NOTE.]

is neither free in himself, for he does not determine himself out of the essential universality and rationality of his will, nor free in relation to the outer world, for his desire remains essentially determined by things, and related to them. This relation of desire is not that in which man stands to the work of art. He allows it to subsist as an object, free and independent, and enters into relation with it apart from desire, as with an object which only appeals to the theoretic side of the mind. For this reason the work of art, although it has sensuous existence, yet, in this point of view, does not require concrete sensuous existence and natural life; indeed, it even *ought* not to remain on such a level, seeing that it has to satisfy only the interests of mind, and is bound to exclude from itself all desire. Hence it is, indeed, that practical desire rates individual things in nature, organic and inorganic, which are serviceable to it, higher than works of art, which reveal themselves to be useless for its purpose, and enjoyable only for other modes of mind.

A second mode in which the externally present may be related to the mind is, in contrast with singular sensuous perception and desire, the purely theoretical relation to the *intelligence*. The theoretic contemplation of things has no interest in consuming them as particulars, in satisfying itself sensuously, and in preserving itself by their means, but rather in becoming acquainted with them in their universality, in finding their inner being and law, and in conceiving them in terms of their notion. Therefore the theoretical interest lets the single things be, and holds aloof from them as sensuous particulars, because this sensuous particularity is not what the contemplation exercised by the intelligence looks for. For the rational intelligence does not belong, as do the desires, to the individual subject[22] as such, but only to the individual as at the same time in his nature universal. In as far

as man has relation to things in respect of this universality, it is his universal reason which attempts to find himself in nature, and thereby to reproduce the inner essence of things, which sensuous existence, though having its ground therein, cannot immediately display. But again, this theoretic interest, the satisfaction of which is the work of science, is in the scientific form no more shared by art, than the latter makes common cause with the impulse of the purely practical desires. Science may, no doubt, start from the sensuous thing in its individuality, and may possess a sensuous idea of the way in which such an individual presents itself in its individual colour, shape, size, etc. Still, this isolated sensuous thing, as such, has no further relation to the mind, inasmuch as the intelligence aims at the universal, the law, the thought and notion of the object. Not only, therefore, does it abandon all intercourse with the thing as a given individual, but transforms it within the mind, making a concrete object of sense into an abstract matter of thought, and so into something quite other than the same object *qua* sensuous phenomenon. The artistic interest, as distinguished from science, does not act thus. Artistic contemplation accepts the work of art just as it displays itself *qua* external object, in immediate determinateness and sensuous individuality clothed in colour, figure, and sound, or as a single isolated perception, etc., and does not go so far beyond the immediate appearance of objectivity which is presented before it, as to aim, like science, at apprehending the notion of such an objective appearance as a universal notion.

Thus, the interest of art distinguishes itself from the practical interest of *desire* by the fact that it permits its object to subsist freely and in independence, while desire utilizes it in its own service by its destruction. On the other hand, artistic contemplation differs from theoretical consideration by the scientific intelligence, in cherishing interest for the object as an individual existence, and not setting to work to transmute it into its universal thought and notion.

It follows, then, from the above, that though the sensuous must be present in a work of art, yet it must only appear as surface and *semblance* of the sensuous. For, in the sensuous aspect of a work of art, the mind seeks neither the concrete framework of matter, that empirically thorough completeness and development of the organism which desire demands, nor the universal and merely ideal thought. What it requires is sensuous presence, which, while not ceasing to be sensuous, is to be liberated from the apparatus of its merely material nature. And thus the sensuous in works of art is exalted to the rank of a mere *semblance* in comparison with the immediate existence of things in nature, and the work of art occupies the mean between what is immediately sensuous and ideal thought. This semblance of the sensuous presents itself to the mind externally as the shape, the visible look, and the sonorous vibration of things— supposing that the mind leaves the objects uninterfered with (physically), but yet does not descend into their inner essence (by abstract thought), for if it did so, it would entirely destroy their external existence as separate individuals *for it*. For this reason the sensuous aspect of art only refers to the two *theoretical* senses of *sight* and *hearing,* while smell, taste, and feeling remain excluded from being sources of artistic enjoyment. For smell, taste, and feeling have to do with matter as such, and with its immediate sensuous qualities; smell with material volatilization in air, taste with the material dissolution of substance,[23] and feeling with warmth, coldness, smoothness, etc. On this account these senses cannot have to do with the objects of art, which are destined to maintain themselves in their actual independent existence, and admit of

no purely sensuous relation. The pleasant for these latter senses is not the beautiful in art. Thus art on its sensuous side purposely produces no more than a shadow-world of shapes, sounds, and imaginable ideas;[24] and it is absolutely out of the question to maintain that it is owing to simple powerlessness and to the limitations on his actions that man, when evoking worlds of art into existence, fails to present more than the mere surface of the sensuous, than mere *schemata*.[25] In art, these sensuous shapes and sounds present themselves, not simply for their own sake and for that of their immediate structure,[26] but with the purpose of affording in that shape satisfaction to higher spiritual interests, seeing that they are powerful to call forth a response and echo in the mind from all the depths of consciousness. It is thus that, in art, the sensuous is *spiritualized,* i.e., the *spiritual* appears in sensuous shape.

The sensuous element, how present in the artist. But for this very reason we have a product of art only in so far as it has found a passage through the mind, and has been generated by spiritually productive activity. This leads us to the other question which we have to answer—how, that is, the sensuous side, which is indispensable to art, is operative in the artist as a productive state of the subject or person. This, the method and fashion of production, contains in itself as a subjective activity just the same properties which we found objectively present in the work of art; it must be a spiritual activity which, nevertheless, at the same time has in itself the element of sensuousness and immediateness. It is neither, on the one hand, purely mechanical work, as mere unconscious skill in sensuous sleight of hand,[27] or a formal activity according to fixed rules learnt by rote; nor is it, on the

---

[23] [Nothing can be tasted which is not dissolved in a liquid.—TR. NOTE.]

[24] [*Anschauungen.*—TR. NOTE.]

[25] [Abstract forms, which are to reality as a diagram to a picture.—TR. NOTE.]

[26] [*Gestalt,* literally "figure."—TR. NOTE.]

[27] [*Handgriffen.*—TR. NOTE.]

other hand, a scientific productive process, which passes from sense to abstract ideas and thoughts, or exercises itself exclusively in the element of pure thinking; rather the spiritual and the sensuous side must in artistic production be as one. For instance, it would be possible in poetical creation to try to proceed by first apprehending the theme to be treated as a prosaic thought, and by then putting it into pictorial ideas, and into rhyme, and so forth; so that the pictorial element would simply be hung upon the abstract reflections as an ornament or decoration. Such a process could only produce bad poetry, for in it there would be operative as two *separate activities* that which in artistic production has its right place only as undivided unity. This genuine mode of production constitutes the activity of artistic *fancy*. It is the rational element which, *qua* spirit, only exists in as far as it actively extrudes itself into consciousness, but yet does not array before it what it bears within itself till it does so in sensuous form. This activity has, therefore, a spiritual import, which, however, it embodies in sensuous shape. Such a process may be compared with the habit even of a man with great experience of the world, or, again, with that of a man of *esprit*[28] or wit, who, although he has complete knowledge of the main stakes of life, of the substantive interests that hold men together, of what moves them, and of what is the power that they recognize, yet neither has himself apprehended this content in the form of general rules, nor is able to explain it to others in general reflections, but makes plain to himself and to others what occupies his consciousness always in particular cases, whether real or invented, in adequate instances, and the like. For in his ideas, everything shapes itself into concrete images, determinate in time and place, to which, therefore, names and other external circumstances of all kinds must not be wanting.

Yet such a kind of imagination rather rests on the recollection of states that he has gone through, and of experiences that have befallen him, than is creative in its own strength. His recollection preserves and reproduces the individuality and external fashion of occurrences that had such and such results with all their external circumstances, and prevents the universal from emerging in its own shape. But the productive fancy of the *artist* is the fancy of a great mind and heart, the apprehension and creation of ideas and of shapes, and, indeed, the exhibition of the profoundest and most universal human interests in the definite sensuous mould of pictorial representation. From this it follows at once, that in one aspect Fancy unquestionably rests on natural gifts—speaking generally, on talent—because its mode of production requires a sensuous medium. It is true that we speak in the same way of scientific "talent," but the sciences only presuppose the universal capacity of thought, which has not, like Fancy, a natural mode (as well as an intellectual one), but abstracts just precisely from all that is natural (or native) in an activity; and thus it would be more correct to say that there is no specifically scientific talent in the sense of a *mere* natural endowment. Now, Fancy *has* in it a mode of instinct-like productiveness, inasmuch as the essential plasticity and sensuousness of the work of art must be subjectively present in the artist as natural disposition and natural impulse, and, considering that it is unconscious operation, must belong to the natural element in man, as well as to the rational. Of course, natural capacity leaves room for other elements in talent and genius, for artistic production is just as much of a spiritual and self-conscious nature; we can but say that its spirituality must, somehow, have an element of natural, plastic, and formative tendency. For this reason, though nearly every one can reach a certain point in an art, yet, in order to go beyond this point, with which the art in the strict sense begins, it is impossible to dispense with native artistic talent of the highest order.

Considered as a natural endowment, moreover, such talent reveals itself for the most part in early youth, and is manifested in the impelling restlessness that busies itself, with vivacity and industry, in creating shapes in some particular sensuous medium, and in seizing on this species of utterance and communication as the only one, or as the chief and the most suitable one. And thus, too, a precocious technical facility, that up to a certain grade of attainment is without effort, is a sign of natural talent. A sculptor finds everything transmute itself into shapes, and he soon begins to take up the clay and model it. And, speaking generally, whatever men of such talents have in their imagination, whatever rouses and moves their inner nature, turns at once into shape, drawing, melody, or poem.

Thirdly, and to conclude: the *content* of art is also in some respects borrowed from the sensuous, from nature; or, in any case, even if the content is of a spiritual kind, it can only be seized and fixed by representing the spiritual fact, such as human relations, in the shape of phenomena with external reality....

Part II: The End of Art

The Interest or End of Art

The question then arises, what the interest or the *End* is which man proposes to himself when he reproduces such a content in the form of works of art. This was the third point of view which we set before us with reference to the work of art, and the closer discussion of which will finally make the transition to the actual and true conception of art.

If in this aspect we glance at the common consciousness, a current idea which may occur to us is—

§ IMITATION OF NATURE

The principle of the *imitation of nature*. According to this view the essential purpose of art consists in imitation, in the sense of a facility in copying natural forms as they exist in a way that corresponds precisely to them; and the success of such a representation, exactly corresponding to nature, is supposed to be what affords complete satisfaction.

This definition contains, *prima facie,* nothing beyond the purely formal[29] aim that whatever already exists in the external world, just *as* it is therein, is now to be made a second time by man as a copy of the former, as well as he can do it with the means at his command. But we may at once regard this repetition as—

A *superfluous* labour, seeing that the things which pictures, theatrical representations, etc., imitate and represent—animals, natural scenes, incidents in human life—are before us in other cases already, in our own gardens or our own houses, or in cases within our closer or more remote circle of acquaintance. And, looking more closely, we may regard this superfluous labour as a presumptuous sport which—

Comes far short of nature. For art is restricted in its means of representation; and can produce only *one-sided* deceptions, i.e., for instance, a semblance of reality addressed to one sense only; and, in fact, it invariably gives rise, if it rests in the formal purpose of *mere imitation,* to a mere parody[30] of life, instead of a genuine vitality. Just so the Turks, being Mohammedans, tolerate, as is well known, no pictures copied from men or the like; and when James Bruce, on his journey to Abyssinia, showed paintings of fish to a Turk, the man was amazed at first, but soon enough made answer: "If this fish shall rise up against

---

29 [General, abstract, as much applicable to one thing as to another.—TR. NOTE.]

30 [*Heuchelei*, literally "hypocrisy."—TR. NOTE.]

you on the last day, and say, 'You have created for me a body, but no living soul,' how will you defend yourself against such an accusation?" The prophet, moreover, it is recorded in the *Sunna* [orthodox Moslem tradition], said to the two women, Ommi Habiba and Ommi Selma, who told him of pictures in Ethiopian churches—"These pictures will accuse their authors on the day of judgment!"

There are, no doubt, as well, examples of completely deceptive imitation. Zeuxis' painted grapes have from antiquity downward been taken to be the triumph of this principle of the imitation of nature, because the story is that living doves pecked at them. We might add to this ancient example the modern one of Büttner's monkey, which bit in pieces a painted cockchafer in Rösel's "Diversions of the Insect World," and was pardoned by his master, in spite of his having thereby spoilt a beautiful copy of this valuable work, because of this proof of the excellence of the pictures. But when we reflect on these and similar instances, it must at once occur to us that, in place of commending works of art because they have *actually* deceived *even* pigeons and monkeys, we ought simply to censure the people who mean to exalt a work of art by predicating, as its highest and ultimate quality, so poor an effect as this. In general, we may sum up by saying that, as a matter of mere imitation, art cannot maintain a rivalry with nature, and, if it tries, must look like a worm trying to crawl after an elephant.

Considering the unvarying failure—comparative failure, at least—of imitation when contrasted with the original in nature, there remains as end nothing beyond our pleasure in the sleight of hand[31] which can produce something so like nature. And it is doubtless open to man to be pleased at producing over again what is already present in its own right, by his labour, skill, and industry.

But enjoyment and admiration, even of this kind, naturally grow frigid or chilled precisely in proportion to the resemblance of the copy to the natural type, or are even converted into tedium and repugnance. There are portraits which, as has been wittily said, are sickeningly like; and Kant adduces another instance relative to this pleasure in imitation as such, viz. that we soon grow tired of a man—and there are such men—who is able to mimic the nightingale's strain quite perfectly; and as soon as it is discovered that a man is producing the notes, we are at once weary of the song. We then recognize in it nothing but a conjuring trick, neither the free production of nature, nor a work of art; for we expect from the free productive capacity of human beings something quite other than such music as this, which only interests us when, as is the case with the nightingale's note, it gushes forth from the creature's own vitality without special purpose, and yet recalls the utterance of human feeling. In general, such delight at our skill in mimicking can be but limited, and it becomes man better to take delight in what he produces out of himself. In this sense the invention of any unimportant and technical product has the higher value, and man may be prouder of having invented the hammer, the nail, and so forth, than of achieving feats of mimicry. For this fervour of abstract[32] copying is to be evened with the feat of the man who had taught himself to throw lentils through a small opening without missing. He displayed this skill of his before Alexander, and Alexander presented him with a bushel of lentils as a reward for his frivolous and meaningless art.

Moreover, seeing that the principle of imitation is purely formal, to make it the end has the result that *objective beauty*

---

31 [*Kunststück.*—TR. NOTE.]

32 [That is, *mere* copying, devoting oneself to the one-sided purpose of making a thing over again, without putting any life or meaning into it.—TR. NOTE.]

itself disappears. For the question is in that case no longer *of what nature* that is which is to be copied, but only whether it is *correctly* copied. The object and content of the beautiful come then to be regarded as matter of entire indifference. That is to say, if we go outside the principle and speak of a difference of beauty and ugliness in considering beasts, men, landscapes, actions, or characters, this must nevertheless, in presence of the maxim in question,[33] be set down as a distinction that does not belong particularly to art, for which nothing is left but abstract imitation. In this case the above-mentioned lack of a criterion in dealing with the endless forms of nature reduces us, as regards the selection of objects and their distinction in beauty and ugliness, to subjective *taste* as an ultimate fact, which accepts no rule and admits of no discussion. And, in fact, if in selecting objects for representation we start from what *men* think beautiful or ugly, and therefore deserving artistic imitation—that is, from their taste,—then all circles of natural objects open to us, and not one of them will be likely to fail of a patron. Among men, for instance, it is the case that at any rate every bridegroom thinks his bride beautiful, and indeed, perhaps, he alone; though not, it may be, every husband his wife; and that subjective taste for such beauty has no fixed rule one may hold to be the good fortune of both parties. If we, moreover, look quite beyond individuals and their accidental taste, to the taste of nations, this again is full of extreme diversity and contrast. How often we hear it said that a European beauty would not please a Chinese or even a Hottentot, in as far as the Chinese has quite a different conception of beauty from the Negro, and the Negro in turn from the European, and so forth. Indeed, if we look at the works of art of those extra-European peoples—their

images of the gods, for instance—which their fancy has originated as venerable and sublime, they may appear to us as the most gruesome idols, and their music may sound to our ears as the most horrible noise; while they, on their side, will regard our sculptures, paintings, and musical productions as trivial or ugly.

But even if we abstract from an objective principle of art, and if beauty is to be based on subjective and individual taste, we shall still soon find on the side of art itself that the imitation of nature, which certainly appeared to be a universal principle and one guaranteed by high authority, is at any rate not to be accepted in this universal and merely abstract form. For if we look at the different arts it will at once be admitted that even if painting and sculpture represent objects which appear like those of nature, or the type of which is essentially borrowed from nature, yet works of architecture on the other hand—and architecture belongs to the fine arts—and the productions of poetry, in as far as they do not confine themselves to mere description, are by no means to be called imitations of nature. At least, if we desired to maintain the principle as valid in the case of these latter arts, we should have to make a long circuit by conditioning the proposition in various ways, and reducing the so-called truth[34] at any rate to probability. But if we admitted probability we should again be met by a great difficulty in determining what is probable and what is not; and still, moreover, one would neither consent nor find it possible to exclude from poetry all wholly arbitrary and completely original[35] imaginations.

The end of art must, therefore, lie in something different from the purely formal[36] imitation of what we find given, which in

---

[33] [Which says that the business of art is to imitate.—TR. NOTE.]

[34] [Of imitation.—TR. NOTE.]

[35] [*Phantastischen.* "Fantastic" means "odd" or "wild." Hegel only means "original," "creative."—TR. NOTE.]

[36] [Mechanical, without origination.—TR. NOTE.]

any case can bring to the birth only *tricks* and not *works* of art. It is, indeed, an element essential to the work of art to have natural shapes for its foundation; seeing that its representation is in the medium of external and therefore of natural phenomena. In painting, for instance, it is an important study to know how to copy with precision the colours in their relations to one another, the effects of light, reflections, etc., and, no less, the forms and figures of objects down to their subtlest characteristics.[37] It is in this respect chiefly that the principle of naturalism in general and of copying nature has recovered its influence in modern times. Its aim is to recall an art which has grown feeble and indistinct to the vigour and crispness of nature; or, again, to invoke against the purely arbitrary and artificial conventionalism, as unnatural as it was inartistic, into which art had strayed, the uniform, direct, and solidly coherent sequences of nature. But however true it is that there is something right in this endeavour from one point of view, yet still the naturalism at which it aims is not as such the substantive and primary concern that underlies fine art. And, therefore, although external appearance in the shape of natural reality constitutes an essential condition of art, yet, nevertheless, neither is the given natural world its *rule,* nor is the mere imitation of external appearance *as* external its *end.*

§ HUMANI NIHIL

The further question then arises—What *is* the true content of art, and with what aim is this content to be presented. On this subject our consciousness supplies us with the common opinion that it is the task and aim of art to bring in contact with our sense, our feeling, our inspiration, *all* that

finds a place in the mind of man. Art, it is thought, should realize in us that familiar saying, *Homo sum: humani nihil a me alienum puto.* [I am a man: nothing human do I deem alien to me.] Its aim is therefore placed in arousing and animating the slumbering emotions, inclinations, and passions; in filling the *heart,* in forcing the human being, whether cultured or uncultured, to feel the whole range of what man's soul in its inmost and secret corners has power to experience and to create, and all that is able to move and to stir the human breast in its depths and in its manifold aspects and possibilities; to present as a delight to emotion and to perception all that the mind possesses of real and lofty in its thought and in the Idea—all the splendour of the noble, the eternal, and the true; and no less to make intelligible misfortune and misery, wickedness and crime; to make men realize the inmost nature of all that is shocking and horrible, as also of all pleasure and delight; and, finally, to set imagination roving in idle toyings of fancy, and luxuriating in the seductive spells of sense-stimulating visions. This endlessly varied content, it is held, art is bound to embrace, partly in order to complete the natural experience in which our external existence consists, and partly with the general aim of provoking the passions of our nature, both in order that the experiences of life may not leave us unmoved, and because we desire to attain to a receptivity that welcomes all phenomena. Now, such a stimulus is not given in this sphere by actual experience itself, but can only come by the semblance thereof, by art, that is, deceptively substituting its creations for reality. The possibility of this deception by means of artistic semblance rests on the fact that all reality must, for man, traverse the medium of perception and ideas, and cannot otherwise penetrate the feelings and the will. In this process it is quite indifferent whether his attention is claimed by immediate external reality, or whether this effect

---

37 [*Nüancen.* Context seems to forbid referring it to colour. I suspect it of meaning "character of outline."—TR. NOTE.]

is produced by another means—that is, by images, symbols, and ideas, containing or representing *the content* of reality. Man can frame to himself ideas of things that are not actual as though they were actual. Hence it is all the same to our feelings whether external reality or only the semblance of it is the means of bringing in contact with us a situation, a relation, or the import of a life. Either mode suffices to awaken our response to its burden, in grief and in rejoicing, in pathos and in horror,[38] and in traversing the emotions and the passions of wrath, hatred, compassion, of anxiety, fear, love, reverence, and admiration, or of the desire of honour and of fame.

This awakening of all feelings in us, the dragging of the heart through the whole significance of life, the realization of all such inner movements by means of a presented exterior consisting merely in deception—all this was what, from the point of view which we have been considering, constituted the peculiar and pre-eminent power of art.

Now, as this mode of treatment credits art with the vocation of impressing on the heart and on the imagination good and bad alike, and of strengthening man to the noblest, as of enervating him to the most sensuous and selfish emotions, it follows that the task set before art is still purely formal, and so it would have no certain purpose, but would merely furnish the empty form for every possible kind of significance and content.

§ MITIGATION OF THE PASSIONS

It is a fact that art does include this formal side, in that it has power to present every possible subject-matter in artistic dress, before perception and feeling, just exactly as argumentative[39] reflection has the power of manipulating all possible objects and

modes of action, and of furnishing them with reasons and justifications. But when we admit so great a variety of content we are at once met by the remark that the manifold feelings and ideas, which art aims at provoking or reinforcing, intersect and contradict, and by mutual interference cancel one another. Indeed, in this aspect, in so far as art inspires men to directly opposite emotions, it only magnifies the contradiction of our feelings and passions, and either sets them staggering like Bacchantes, or passes into sophistry and scepticism, in the same way as argumentation.[40] This diversity of the material of art itself compels us, therefore, not to be content with so formal[41] an aim for it, seeing that rationality forces its way into this wild diversity, and demands to see the emergence of a higher and more universal purpose from these elements in spite of their self-contradiction, and to be assured of its being attained. Just in the same way the State and the social life of men are, of course, credited with the purpose that in them *all* human capacities and *all* individual powers are to be developed and to find utterance in *all* directions and with *all* tendencies. But in opposition to so formal a view there at once arises the question in what *unity* these manifold formations must be comprehended, and what *single end* they must have for their fundamental idea and ultimate purpose.

As such an end, reflection soon suggests the notion that art has the capacity and the function of mitigating the fierceness of the desires.

How art mitigates the passions. In respect to this first idea, we have only to ascertain in what feature peculiar to art it is that the capacity lies of eliminating brutality and taming and educating the

---

38 [*Erschüttern.*—TR. NOTE.]

39 [*Raisonnirende;* a term of disparagement in Hegel, applied to proofs, *pro* and *con,* which do not rest on a thorough conception of the funda-

mental nature of what is being discussed.—TR. NOTE.]

40 [*Raisonnement.*—TR. NOTE.]

41 ["Formal" means here as usual, empty, or general; i.e., not taking account of varieties in the matter to which it is applied.—TR. NOTE.]

impulses, desires, and passions. Brutality in general has its reason in a direct selfishness of the impulses, which go to work right away, and exclusively for the satisfaction of their concupiscence. Now, desire is most savage and imperious in proportion as, being isolated and narrow, it occupies the *whole man,* so that he does not retain the power of separating himself as a universal being from this determinateness, and becoming aware of himself as universal. Even if the man in such a case says, "The passion is stronger than I," it is true that the abstract I is then separated for consciousness from the particular passion; but still only in a formal way, inasmuch as this separation is only made in order to pronounce that, against the power of the passion, the I as such is of no account whatever. The savageness of passion consists, therefore, in the oneness of the I as universal with the limited content of its desires, so that the man has no will outside this particular passion. Now, such brutality and untamed violence of passion is softened through art, to begin with, by the mere fact that it brings before the man as an idea what in such a state he feels and does. And even if art restricts itself to merely setting up pictures of the passions before the mind's eye, or even if it were actually to flatter them, still this is by itself enough to have a softening power, inasmuch as the man is thereby at least *made aware,* of what, apart from such presentation, he simply *is.* For then the man observes his impulses and inclinations, and whereas before they bore him on without power of reflection, he now sees them outside himself, and begins already to be free from them, in so far as they form an object which he contrasts with himself. Hence it may frequently be the case with the artist that when attacked by grief he softens and weakens the intensity of his own feelings in its effect on his own mind by representing it in art. Tears, even, are enough to bring comfort; the man, who to begin with is utterly sunk and concentrated in grief, is able thus, at any rate, to utter in a direct fashion this his inner state. Still more of a relief, however, is the utterance of what is within in words, images, pictures, sounds, and shapes. For this reason it was a good old custom at deaths and funerals to appoint wailing women, in order to bring the grief before the mind in its utterance. Manifestations of sympathy, too, hold up the content of a man's misfortune to his view; when it is much talked about he is forced to reflect upon it, and is thereby relieved. And so it has always been held that to weep and to speak one's fill is a means to obtain freedom from the oppressive weight of care, or at least to find momentary relief for the heart. Hence the mitigation of the violence of passion has for its universal reason that man is released from his immediate sunkenness[42] in a feeling, and becomes conscious of it as of something external to him, towards which he must now enter into an *ideal* relation. Art, by means of its representations, while remaining within the sensuous sphere, delivers man at the same time from the power of sensuousness. Of course we may often hear those favourite phrases about man's duty being to remain in immediate oneness with nature, but such oneness in its abstraction is simply and solely coarseness and savagery; and art, in the very process of dissolving this oneness for man, is raising him with gentle hand above and away from mere sunkenness in nature. Man's mode of occupying himself with works of art is always purely contemplative,[43] and educates thereby, in the first place, no doubt, merely attention to the representations themselves, but then, going beyond this, it cultivates attention to their significance, the power of comparison with other contents, and receptivity for the general consideration of them, and for the points of view which it involves.

---

42 [*Befangensein.*—TR. NOTE.]

43 [*Theoretisch.* I have no doubt that it has here the meaning of θεωρεῖν without a trace of allusion to "theory." It is opposed to "destructive," or "appetitive."—TR. NOTE.]

How art purifies the passions. To the above there attaches itself in natural connection the second characteristic which has been ascribed to art as its essential purpose, viz. the *purification* of the passions, instruction and *moral* perfecting. For the characteristic that art was to bridle savageness and educate the passions remained quite abstract and general, so that a question must again arise about a *determinate* kind and an essential *end* of this education.

The doctrine of the purification of passion suffers indeed under the same defect as the above doctrine of the mitigation of the desires; yet, when more closely looked at, it at any rate arrives at the point of accentuating the fact that the representations of art may be held to lack a standard by which their worth or unworthiness could be measured. This standard simply means their effectiveness in separating pure from impure in the passions. It therefore requires a content that has capacity to exercise this purifying power, and, in as far as the production of such an effect is taken to constitute the substantive end of art, it must follow that the purifying content must be brought before consciousness in its *universality* and *essentiality*.

In this latter aspect the end of art has been pronounced to be that it should *teach.* Thus, on the one side, the peculiar character of art would consist in the movement of the emotions and in the satisfaction which lies in this movement, even in fear, compassion, in painful pathos and shock—that is to say, in the satisfying engagement of the emotions and passions, and to that extent in a complacency, entertainment, and delight in the objects of art, in their representation and effect; but, on the other side, this purpose (of art) is held to find its higher standard only in its instructiveness, in the *fabula docet*,[44] and thus in the useful influence which the work of art succeeds in exerting on the subject.[45] In this respect the Horatian saw,[46] *"Et prodesse volunt et delectare poetae"* ["Poets aim at utility and entertainment alike"], contains, concentrated in a few words, all that has subsequently been elaborated in infinite degrees, and diluted into the uttermost extreme of insipidity as a doctrine of art. As regards such instruction we have, then, to ask, whether it is meant to be directly or indirectly, explicitly or implicitly contained in the work of art.

If, speaking generally, we are concerned about a purpose which is universal and not contingent, it follows that this purpose, considering the essentially spiritual nature of art, cannot but be itself spiritual, and indeed, moreover, one which is not contingent,[47] but actual in its nature and for its own sake. Such a purpose in relation to teaching could only consist in bringing before consciousness, by help of the work of art, a really and explicitly significant spiritual content. From this point of view it is to be asserted that the higher art ranks itself, the more it is bound to admit into itself such a content as this, and that only in the essence of such a content can it find the standard which determines whether what is expressed is appropriate or inappropriate. Art was, in fact, the first *instructress* of peoples.

But the purpose of instruction may be treated as *purpose,* to such a degree that the universal nature of the represented content is doomed to be exhibited and expounded directly and obviously as abstract proposition, prosaic reflection, or general theorem, and not merely in an indirect way in the concrete form of a work of art. By such a severance the sensuous plastic form,

---

44 [The moral.—TR. NOTE.]

45 [Person, i.e., here, audience or spectator.—TR. NOTE.]

46 [*Kernspruch.*—TR. NOTE.]

47 ["Contingent" means, not so much "what may or may not exist," as the trivial, which makes no difference whether it exists or not.—TR. NOTE.]

which is just what makes the work of art a work of *art,* becomes a mere otiose accessory, a husk which is expressly pronounced to be mere husk, a semblance expressly pronounced to be mere semblance. But thereby the very nature of the work of art is distorted. For the work of art ought to bring a content before the mind's eye, not in its generality as such, but with this generality made absolutely individual, and sensuously particularized. If the work of art does not proceed from this principle, but sets in relief its generalized aspect with the purpose of abstract instruction, then the imaginative and sensuous aspect is only an external and superfluous adornment, and the work of art is a thing divided against itself,[48] in which form and content no longer appear as grown into one. In that case the sensuously individual and the spiritually general are become external to one another.

And further, if the purpose of art is limited to this *didactic* utility, then its other aspect, that of pleasure, entertainment, and delight, is pronounced to be in itself *unessential,* and ought to have its substance merely in the utility of the teaching on which it is attendant. But this amounts to pronouncing that art does not bear its vocation and purpose in itself, but that its conception is rooted in something else, to which it is a *means.* Art is, in this case, only one among the several means which prove useful and are applied for the purpose of instruction. This brings us to the boundary at which art is made no longer to be an end on its own merits, seeing that it is degraded into a mere toy of entertainment or a mere means of instruction.

This boundary becomes most sharply marked when a question is raised, in its turn, about a supreme end and aim for the sake of which the passions are to be purified and men are to be instructed. This aim has

often, in modern times, been declared to be *moral* improvement, and the aim of art has been placed in the function of preparing the inclinations and impulses for moral perfection, and of leading them to this goal. This idea combines purification with instruction, inasmuch as art is, by communicating an insight into genuine moral goodness—that is, by instruction,—at the same time to incite to purification, and in this way alone to bring about the improvement of mankind as its useful purpose and supreme goal.

Regarding art in reference to moral improvement, the same has *prima facie* to be said as about the didactic purpose. We may readily grant that art must not as a principle take for its aim the immoral and its furtherance. But it is one thing to take immorality for the express aim of representation, and another to abstain from taking morality. Every genuine work of art may have a good moral drawn from it, but, of course, in doing so much depends on interpretation and on him who draws the moral. Thus one may hear the most immoral representations defended by saying that we must know evil, or sin, in order to act morally; and, conversely, it has been said that the portrayal of Mary Magdalene, the beautiful sinner who afterwards repented, has seduced many into sin, because art makes it look so beautiful to repent, and you must sin before you can repent. But the doctrine of moral improvement, if consistently carried out, goes in general yet further. It would not be satisfied with the possibility of extracting a moral from a work of art by interpretation, but it would, on the contrary, display the moral instruction as the substantive purpose of the work of art, and, indeed, would actually admit to portrayal none but moral subjects, moral characters, actions, and incidents. For art has the choice among its subjects, in contradistinction to history or the sciences which have their matter fixed for them.

---

[48] [*In ihm selbst gebrochenes.* I do not suppose there is an allusion to the words I use.—TR. NOTE.]

In order that we may be able to form a thoroughly adequate estimate of the idea that the aim of art is moral from this point of view, we must inquire first of all for the definite standpoint of the morality on which this doctrine is based. If we look closely at the standpoint of morality as we have to understand it in the best sense at the present day, we soon find that its conception does not immediately coincide with what apart from it we are in the habit of calling in a general way virtue, respectability,[49] uprightness, etc. To be respectable and virtuous is not enough to make a man moral.[50] Morality involves *reflection* and the definite consciousness of that which duty prescribes, and acting out of such a prior consciousness. Duty itself is the law of the will, which man nevertheless lays down freely out of his own self, and then is supposed to determine himself to this duty for duty's and its fulfilment's sake, by doing good solely from the conviction which he has attained that it is the good. Now this law, the duty which is chosen for duty's sake to be the guide of action, out of free conviction and the inner conscience, and is then acted upon, is, taken by itself,[51] the abstract universal of the will, and is the direct antithesis of nature, the sensuous impulses, the self-seeking interests, the passions, and of all that is comprehensively entitled the feelings[52] and the heart. In this antagonism the one side is regarded as *negativing* the other; and, seeing that both are present as antagonists within the subject [person], he has, as determining himself out of himself, the choice of following the one or the other. But, according to the view under discussion, a *moral* aspect is acquired by such a decision, and by the act performed in accordance with it, only through the free conviction of duty on the one hand, and, on the other hand, through the conquest, not only of the particular or separate will, of the natural motives, inclinations, passions, etc., but also through that of the nobler emotions and the higher impulses. For the modern moralistic view starts from the fixed antithesis of the will in its spiritual universality to its sensuous natural particularity,[53] and consists not in the completed reconciliation of these contrasted sides, but in their conflict with one another, which involves the requirement that the impulses which conflict with duty ought to yield to it.

This antithesis does not merely display itself for our consciousness, in the limited region of moral action; but also emerges as a fundamental distinction and antagonism between that which is real essentially and in its own right,[54] and that which is external reality and existence. Formulated in the abstract, it is the contrast of the universal and particular, when the former is explicitly fixed over against the latter, just as the latter is over against the former; more concretely, it appears in nature as the opposition of the abstract law against the abundance of individual phenomena, each having its own character; in the mind, as the sensuous and spiritual in man, as the battle of the spirit against the flesh, of duty for duty's sake, the cold command, with the individual interest, the warm feelings, the sensuous inclinations and impulses, the individual disposition as such; as the hard conflict of inward freedom and of

---

49 [*Sittlichkeit,* almost equals "morality" in the English sense. It means the habit of virtue, without the reflective aspiration after goodness as an ideal.—TR. NOTE.]

50 [*Moralität,* almost equals "conscientiousness" or "scrupulosity." The above sentence is hardly true with the English word "moral."— TR. NOTE.]

51 [*Für sich,* is often used where there is no notion of development and seems very like *an sich.* —TR. NOTE.]

52 [*Gemüth.*—TR. NOTE.]

53 [As, e.g., if we suppose that an act done at the bidding of natural affection cannot also be a fulfilment of the command of duty. The "reconciliation" would be in supposing the natural affection, e.g., for parents, to operate as a moral motive, being transformed by a recognition of its sacred or spiritual character.—TR. NOTE.]

54 [*An und für sich.*—TR. NOTE.]

natural necessity; further, as the contradiction of the dead conception—empty in itself—compared with full concrete vitality, or of theory and subjective thought contrasted with objective existence and experience.

These are antitheses which have not been invented, either by the subtlety of reflection or by the pedantry of philosophy, but which have from all time and in manifold forms preoccupied and disquieted the human consciousness, although it was modern culture that elaborated them most distinctly, and forced them up to the point of most unbending contradiction. Intellectual culture and the modern play of understanding create in man this contrast, which makes him an amphibious animal, inasmuch as it sets him to live in two contradictory worlds at once; so that even consciousness wanders back and forward in this contradiction, and, shuttle-cocked from side to side, is unable to satisfy itself *as* itself on the one side as on the other. For, on the one side, we see man a prisoner in common reality and earthly temporality, oppressed by want and poverty, hard driven by nature, entangled in matter, in sensuous aims and their enjoyments; on the other side, he exalts himself to eternal ideas, to a realm of thought and freedom, imposes on himself as a *will* universal laws and attributions, strips the world of its living and flourishing reality and dissolves it into abstractions, inasmuch as the mind is put upon vindicating its rights and its dignity simply by denying the rights of nature and maltreating it, thereby retaliating the oppression and violence which itself has experienced from nature. Such a discrepancy in life and consciousness involves for modern culture and its understanding the demand that the contradiction should be resolved. Yet the understanding cannot release itself from the fixity of these antitheses. The solution, therefore, remains for consciousness a mere *ought,* and the present and reality only stir themselves in the unrest of a perpetual to and fro, which seeks a reconciliation without finding it. Then the question arises,, whether such a many-sided and fundamental opposition which never gets beyond a mere ought and a postulated solution, can be the genuine and complete[55] truth, and, in general, the supreme purpose. If the culture of the world[56] has fallen into such a contradiction, it becomes the task of philosophy to undo or cancel it, i.e., to show that neither the one alternative in its abstraction nor the other in similar one-sidedness possesses truth, but that they are essentially self-dissolving; that truth only lies in the conciliation and mediation of the two, and that this mediation is no mere postulate, but is in its nature and in reality accomplished and always self-accomplishing. This intuition agrees directly with the natural faith and will, which always has present to the mind's eye precisely this resolved antithesis, and in action makes it its purpose and achieves it. All that philosophy does is to furnish a reflective insight into the essence of the antithesis in as far as it shows that what constitutes truth is merely the resolution of this antithesis, and that not in the sense that the conflict and its aspects in any way *are not,* but in the sense that they *are, in reconciliation.*

§ ART HAS ITS OWN PURPOSE AS REVELATION OF TRUTH

Now, as an ultimate aim implied a higher standpoint in the case of moral improvement, we shall have to vindicate this higher standpoint for art no less than for morals. Thereby we at once lay aside the false position, which has already been remarked upon, that art has to serve as a means for moral ends, and to conduce to the moral end of the world, as such, by instruction and moral improvement, and thereby has its substantive aim, not in itself, but in

---

55 [*An und für sich Wahre.*—TR. NOTE.]
56 [*Allgemeine Bildung.*—TR. NOTE.]

something else. If, therefore, we now continue to speak of an aim or purpose, we
must, in the first instance, get rid of the
perverse idea, which, in asking "What is
the aim?" retains the accessory meaning of
the question, "What is the *use?*" The per-
verseness of this lies in the point that the
work of art would then be regarded as
aspiring to something else which is set before consciousness as the essential and as
what ought to be; so that then the work
of art would only have value as a useful
instrument in the realization of an end
having substantive importance *outside* the
sphere of art. Against this it is necessary
to maintain that art has the vocation of
revealing *the truth* in the form of sensuous
artistic shape, of representing the reconciled
antithesis just described, and, therefore, has
its purpose in itself, in this representation
and revelation. For other objects, such as
instruction, purification, improvement, pe-
cuniary gain, endeavour after fame and
honour, have nothing to do with the work
of art as such, and do not determine its
conception.

It is from this point of view, into which
reflective consideration of the matter re-
solves itself, that we have to apprehend the
idea of art in its inner necessity, as indeed
it was from this point of view, historically
speaking, that the true appreciation and
understanding of art took its origin. For
that antithesis, of which we spoke, made
itself felt, not only within general reflective culture, but no less in philosophy as
such, and it was not till philosophy discovered how to overcome this antithesis
absolutely, that it grasped its own conception and, just in as far as it did so, the
conception of nature and of art.

Hence this point of view, as it is the
re-awakening of philosophy in general, so
also is the re-awakening of the science of
art; and, indeed, it is this re-awakening to
which alone aesthetic as a science owes its
true origin, and art its higher estimation.

CHAPTER FIVE:
DIVISION OF THE SUBJECT

The Condition of Artistic Presentation Is the Correspondence of Matter and Plastic Form

After the above introductory remarks, it is
now time to pass to the study of our object-
matter. But we are still in the introduction,
and an introduction cannot do more than
lay down, for the sake of explanation, the
general sketch of the entire course which
will be followed by our subsequent scientific
considerations. As, however, we have spoken
of art as proceeding from the absolute Idea,
and have even assigned as its end the
sensuous representation of the absolute itself, we shall have to conduct this review
in a way to show, at least in general, how
the particular divisions of the subject
spring from the conception of artistic beauty as the representation of the absolute.
Therefore we must attempt to awaken a
very general idea of this conception itself.

It has already been said that the content
of art is the Idea, and that its form lies in
the plastic use of images accessible to sense.
These two sides art has to reconcile into a
full and united totality. The *first* attribution which this involves is the requirement
that the content, which is to be offered
to artistic representation, shall show itself
to be in its nature worthy of such representation. Otherwise we only obtain a bad
combination, whereby a content that will
not submit to plasticity and to external
presentation, is forced into that form, and
a matter which is in its nature prosaic is
expected to find an appropriate mode of
manifestation in the form antagonistic to
its nature.

The *second* requirement, which is deriva-
ble from this first, demands of the content

of art that it should not be anything abstract in itself. This does not mean that it must be concrete as the sensuous is concrete in contrast to everything spiritual and intellectual, these being taken as in themselves simple and abstract. For everything that has genuine truth in the mind as well as in nature is concrete in itself, and has, in spite of its universality, nevertheless, both subjectivity and particularity within it. If we say, e.g., of God that he is simply *One*, the supreme Being as such, we have only enunciated a lifeless abstraction of the irrational understanding. Such a God, as he himself is not apprehended in his concrete truth, can afford no material for art, least of all for plastic art. Hence the Jews and the Turks have not been able to represent their God, who does not even amount to such an abstraction of the understanding, in the positive way in which Christians have done so. For God in Christianity is conceived in his truth, and therefore, as in Himself thoroughly concrete, as a person, as a subject,[57] and more closely determined, as mind or spirit. What He is as spirit unfolds itself to the religious apprehension as the Trinity of Persons, which at the same time in relation with itself is *One*. Here is essentiality, universality, and particularity, together with their reconciled unity; and it is only such unity that constitutes the concrete. Now, as a content in order to possess truth at all must be of this

concrete nature, art demands the same concreteness, because a mere abstract universal has not in itself the vocation to advance to particularity and phenomenal manifestation and to unity with itself therein.

If a true and therefore concrete content is to have corresponding to it a sensuous form and modelling, this sensuous form must, in the third place, be no less emphatically something individual, wholly concrete in itself, and one. The character of concreteness as belonging to both elements of art, to the content as to the representation, is precisely the point in which both may coincide and correspond to one another; as, for instance, the natural shape of the human body is such a sensuous concrete as is capable of representing spirit, which is concrete in itself, and of displaying itself in conformity therewith. Therefore we ought to abandon the idea that it is a mere matter of accident that an actual phenomenon of the external world is chosen to furnish a shape thus conformable to truth. Art does not appropriate this form either because it simply finds it existing or because there is no other. The concrete content itself involves the element of external and actual, we may say indeed of sensible manifestation. But in compensation this sensuous concrete, in which a content essentially belonging to mind expresses itself, is in its own nature addressed to the inward being; its external element of shape, whereby the content is made perceptible and imaginable, has the aim of existing purely for the heart and mind. This is the only reason for which content and artistic shape are fashioned in conformity with each other. The *mere* sensuous concrete, external nature as such, has not this purpose for its exclusive ground of origin. The birds' variegated plumage shines unseen, and their song dies away unheard, the *Cereus*[58] which blossoms

---

[57] [It is natural for a reader to ask in *what* person or subject God is conceived to have reality. On this see below, p. 326. It appears certain to me that Hegel, when he writes thus, is referring to the self-consciousness of individual human beings, as constituting, and reflecting on, an ideal unity between them. This may seem to put a non-natural meaning on the term "person" or "subject," as if the common element of a number of intelligences could be a single person. It is obvious that the question hinges on the degree in which a unity that is not sensuous but ideal can be effective and actual. I can only say here, that the more we consider the nature of ideal unity, the higher we shall rate its capabilities.—TR. NOTE.]

[58] [*Fackeldistel,* "torch thistle," a plant of the genus *Cereus,* natural order *Cactaceae.*—TR. NOTE.]

only for a night withers without having been admired in the wilds of southern forests, and these forests, jungles of the most beautiful and luxuriant vegetation, with the most odorous and aromatic perfumes, perish and decay no less unenjoyed. The work of art has not such a naive self-centred being, but is essentially a question, an address to the responsive heart, an appeal to affections and to minds.

Although the artistic bestowal of sensuous form is in this respect not accidental, yet on the other hand it is not the highest mode of apprehending the spiritually concrete. Thought is a higher mode than representation by means of the sensuous concrete. Although in a relative sense abstract, yet it must be one-sided but concrete thinking, in order to be true and rational. Whether a given content has sensuous artistic representation for its adequate form, or in virtue of its nature essentially demands a higher and more spiritual embodiment, is a distinction that displays itself at once, if, for instance, we compare the Greek gods with God as conceived according to Christian ideas. The Greek god is not abstract but individual, and is closely akin to the natural human shape; the Christian God is equally a concrete personality, but in the mode of pure spiritual existence, and is to be known as mind[59] and in mind. His medium of existence is therefore essentially inward knowledge and not external natural form, by means of which He can only be represented imperfectly, and not in the whole depth of His idea.

But inasmuch as the task of art is to represent the idea to direct perception in sensuous shape, and not in the form of thought or of pure spirituality as such, and seeing that this work of representation has its value and dignity in the correspondence and the unity of the two sides, i.e., of the Idea and its plastic embodiment, it follows that the level and excellency of art in

attaining a realization adequate to its idea,[60] must depend upon the grade of inwardness and unity with which Idea and Shape display themselves as fused into one.

Thus the higher truth is spiritual being that has attained a shape adequate to the conception of spirit. This is what furnishes the principle of division for the science of art. For before the mind can attain the true notion of its absolute essence, it has to traverse a course of stages whose ground is in this idea itself; and to this evolution of the content with which it supplies itself, there corresponds an evolution, immediately connected therewith, of the plastic forms of art, under the shape of which the mind as artist presents to itself the consciousness of itself.

This evolution within the art-spirit has again in its own nature two sides. In the *first* place the development itself is a spiritual[61] and universal one, in so far as the graduated series of definite *conceptions of the world* as the definite but comprehensive consciousness of nature, man and God, gives itself artistic shape; and, in the *second* place, this *universal* development of art is obliged to provide itself with external existence and sensuous form, and the definite modes of the sensuous art-existence are themselves a totality of necessary distinctions in the realm of art—which are *the several arts*. It is true, indeed, that the necessary kinds of artistic representation are on the one hand *qua* spiritual of a very general nature, and not restricted to any one material;[62] while sensuous existence

---

59 [Or "as spirit and in spirit."—TR. NOTE.]

60 [The idea of art.—TR. NOTE.]

61 [The two evolutions are, speaking roughly, (i) that of the subject-matter; (ii) that of the particular mode of art: (i) e.g. you have Egyptian, Greek, Christian religion, etc., with the corresponding views and sentiments, each in its own relation to art; (ii) you have, as a cross division to the former, the several arts—sculpture, music, poetry, etc., each having its special ground and warrant.—TR. NOTE.]

62 [He is asking himself why sound or paint, etc., should correspond to one type of art as theoretically defined—this being intellectual, not

contains manifold varieties of matter. But as this latter, like the mind, has the Idea potentially for its inner soul, it follows from this that particular sensuous materials have a close affinity and secret accord with the spiritual distinctions and types of art presentation.

In its completeness, however, our science divides itself into three principal portions.

First, we obtain a *general part.* It has for its content and object the universal Idea of artistic beauty—this beauty being conceived as the Ideal—together with the nearer relation of the latter both to nature and to subjective artistic production.

Secondly, there develops itself out of the idea of artistic beauty a *particular* part, in as far as the essential differences which this idea contains in itself evolve themselves into a scale of *particular* plastic[63] forms.

In the *third* place there results a *final* part, which has for its subject the individualization of artistic beauty, that consists in the advance of art to the sensuous realization of its shapes and its self-completion as a system of the several arts[64] and their genera and species.

Part I: The Ideal

With respect to the first part, we must begin by recalling to mind, in order to make the sequel intelligible, that the Idea *qua* the beautiful in art is not the Idea as such, in the mode in which a metaphysical logic apprehends it as the absolute, but the Idea as developed into concrete form fit for

reality, and as having entered into immediate and adequate unity with this reality. For the *Idea as such,* although it is the essentially and actually true, is yet the truth only in its generality which has not yet taken objective shape; but the *Idea* as the *beautiful in art* is at once the Idea when specially determined as in its essence individual reality, and also an individual shape of reality essentially destined to embody and reveal the Idea. This amounts to enunciating the requirement that the Idea, and its plastic mould as concrete reality, are to be made completely adequate to one another. When reduced to such form the Idea, as a reality moulded in conformity with the conception of the Idea, is the *Ideal.* The problem of this conformity might, to begin with, be understood in the sense that any Idea would serve, so long as the actual shape, it did not matter what shape, represented this particular Idea and no other. But if so, the required truth of the Ideal is confounded with mere correctness, which consists in the expression of any meaning whatever in appropriate fashion so that its import may be readily recognized in the shape created. The Ideal is not to be thus understood. Any content whatever may attain to being represented quite adequately, judged by the standard of its own nature, but it does not therefore gain the right to claim the artistic beauty of the Ideal. Compared indeed with ideal beauty, even the presentation will in such a case appear defective. From this point of view we must remark to begin with, what cannot be proved till later, that the defects of a work of art are not to be regarded simply as always due, for instance, to individual unskilfulness. *Defectiveness of form* arises from *defectiveness of content.* So, for example, the Chinese, Indians, and Egyptians in their artistic shapes, their forms of deities, and their idols, never got beyond a formless phase, or one of a vicious and false definiteness of form, and were unable to attain genuine beauty; because their mythological

---

sensuous, at root—and answers that these media *qua* natural objects have, though more latent than in works of art, an import and purpose of their own, which reveals itself in their suitability to particular forms of art.—TR. NOTE.]

63 [*Gestaltungsformen.* I use "plastic" all through in a pregnant sense, as one speaks of plastic fancy, etc.; meaning ideally determinate, and fit for translating into pictures, poetry, etc. These "plastic forms" are the various modifications of the subject-matter of art. See note 61.—TR. NOTE.]

64 [See note 61.—TR. NOTE.]

ideas, the content and thought of their works of art, were as yet indeterminate in themselves, or of a vicious determinateness, and did not consist in the content that is absolute in itself. The more that works of art excel in true beauty of presentation, the more profound is the inner truth of their content and thought. And in dealing with this point, we have not to think merely perhaps of the greater or lesser skill with which the natural forms as given in external reality are apprehended and imitated. For in certain stages of art-consciousness and of representation, the distortion and disfigurement of natural structures is not unintentional technical inexpertness and want of skill, but intentional alteration, which emanates from the content that is in consciousness, and is required thereby. Thus, from this point of view, there is such a thing as imperfect art, which may be quite perfect, both technically and in other respects, *in its determinate* sphere, yet reveals itself to be defective when compared with the conception of art as such, and with the Ideal. Only in the highest art are the Idea and the representation genuinely adequate to one another, in the sense that the outward shape given to the Idea is in itself essentially and actually the true shape, because the content of the Idea, which that shape expresses is itself the true and real content. It is a corollary from this, as we indicated above, that the Idea must be defined in and through itself as concrete totality, and thereby possess in itself the principle and standard of its particularization and determination in external appearance. For example, the Christian imagination will be able to represent God only in human form and with man's intellectual expression, because it is herein that God Himself is completely known in Himself as mind. Determinateness is, as it were, the bridge to phenomenal existence. Where this determinateness is not totality derived from the Idea itself, where the Idea is not conceived

as self-determining and self-particularizing, the Idea remains abstract and has its determinateness, and therefore the principle that dictates its particular and exclusively appropriate mode of presentation, not in itself but external to it. Therefore, the Idea when still abstract has even its shape external, and not dictated by itself. The Idea, however, which is concrete in itself bears the principle of its mode of manifestation within itself, and is by that means the free process of giving shape to itself. Thus it is only the truly concrete Idea that can generate the true shape, and this correspondence of the two is the Ideal.

Part II: The Types of Art

Now because the Idea is in this fashion concrete unity, it follows that this unity can enter into the art-consciousness only by the expansion and reconciliation of the particularities of the Idea, and it is through this evolution that artistic beauty comes to possess a *totality of particular stages and forms*. Therefore, after we have studied the beauty of art in itself and on its own merits, we must see how beauty as a whole breaks up into its particular determinations. This gives, as our *second part, the doctrine of the types of art*. These forms find their genesis in the different modes of grasping the Idea as artistic content, whereby is conditioned a difference of the form in which it manifests itself. Hence the types of art are nothing but the different relations of content and shape, relations which emanate from the Idea itself, and furnish thereby the true basis of division for this sphere. For the principle of division must always be contained in *that* conception whose particularization and division is in question.

We have here to consider *three* relations of the Idea to its outward shaping.[65]

---

65 [*Gestaltung*. I do not think this means the process of shaping, but the shapes taken collectively.—TR. NOTE.]

§ SYMBOLIC ART

First, the Idea gives rise to the beginning of Art when, being itself still in its indistinctness and obscurity, or in vicious untrue determinateness, it is made the import of artistic creations. As indeterminate it does not yet possess in itself that individuality which the Ideal demands; its abstractness and one-sidedness leave its shape to be outwardly bizarre and defective. The first form of art is therefore rather a mere search after plastic portrayal than a capacity of genuine representation. The Idea has not yet found the true form even within itself, and therefore continues to be merely the struggle and aspiration thereafter. In general terms we may call this form the *Symbolic* form of art. In it the abstract Idea has its outward shape external to itself[66] in natural sensuous matter, with which the process of shaping begins, and from which, *qua* outward expression, it is inseparable.

Natural objects are thus primarily left unaltered, and yet at the same time invested with the substantial Idea as their significance, so that they receive the vocation of expressing it, and claim to be interpreted as though the Idea itself were present in them. At the root of this is the fact that natural objects have in them an aspect in which they are capable of representing a universal meaning. But as an adequate correspondence is not yet possible, this reference can only concern *an abstract attribute,* as when a lion is used to mean strength.

On the other hand, this abstractness of the relation brings to consciousness no less strongly the foreignness of the Idea to natural phenomena; and the Idea, having no other reality to express it, expatiates in all these shapes, seeks itself in them in all their unrest and disproportion, but nevertheless does not find them adequate to itself. Then it proceeds to exaggerate the natural shapes and the phenomena of reality into indefiniteness and disproportion, to intoxicate itself in them, to seethe and ferment in them, to do violence to them, to distort and explode them into unnatural shapes, and strives by the variety, hugeness, and splendour of the forms employed[67] to exalt the phenomenon to the level of the Idea. For the Idea is here still more or less indeterminate and non-plastic, but the natural objects are in their shape thoroughly determinate.

Hence, in view of the unsuitability of the two elements to each other, the relation of the Idea to objective reality becomes a *negative* one, for the former, as in its nature inward,[68] is unsatisfied with such an externality, and as being in its inner universal substance[69] persists in exaltation or *Sublimity* beyond and above all this inadequate abundance of shapes. In virtue of this sublimity the natural phenomena and the human shapes and incidents are accepted, and left as they were, though at the same time understood to be inadequate to their significance, which is exalted far above every earthly content.

These aspects may be pronounced in general terms to constitute the character of the primitive artistic pantheism of the East, which either charges even the meanest objects with the absolute import, or again

---

66 [That is, not in a separate ideal shape devoted to it. He means that man takes a stock or stone as representation or symbol of the divine, and as there is no real connection between divinity and the stone, it may either be left untouched and unshaped, or be hewn into any bizarre or arbitrary shape that comes to hand: see next paragraph.—TR. NOTE.]

67 [This description is probably directed, in the first place, to the Indian representation of deities, and would apply to those of many barbaric religions. But its truth may be very simply verified in daily observation of the first attempts, of the uneducated at plastic presentation of their ideas, where costliness, ingenuity, labour, or size take the place of beauty.—TR. NOTE.]

68 [*Sie als Inneres.*—TR. NOTE.]

69 [That is, an idea or purpose which gives these partial and defective representations all the meaning they have, although they are incapable of really expressing it.—TR. NOTE.]

coerces nature with violence into the expression of its view. By this means it becomes bizarre, grotesque, and tasteless, or turns the infinite but abstract freedom of the substantive Idea disdainfully against all phenomenal being as null and evanescent. By such means the import cannot be completely embodied in the expression, and in spite of all aspiration and endeavour the reciprocal inadequacy of shape and Idea remains insuperable. This may be taken as the first form of art—Symbolic art with its aspiration, its disquiet,[70] its mystery and its sublimity.

§ CLASSICAL ART

In the second form of art, which we propose to call *Classical,* the double defect of symbolic art is cancelled. The plastic shape of symbolic art is imperfect, because, in the first place, the Idea in it only enters into consciousness in *abstract* determinateness or indeterminateness, and, in the second place, this must always make the conformity of shape to import defective, and in its turn merely abstract. The classical form of art is the solution of this double difficulty; it is the free adequate embodiment of the Idea in the shape that, according to its conception, is peculiarly appropriate to the Idea itself. With it, therefore, the Idea is capable of entering into free and complete accord. Hence, the classical type of art is the first to afford the production and intuition of the completed Ideal, and to establish it as a realized fact.

The conformity, however, of notion and reality in classical art must not be taken in the purely *formal* sense of the agreement of a content with the external shape given to it, any more than this could be the case with the Ideal itself. Otherwise every copy from nature, and every type of countenance, every landscape, flower, or scene, etc.,

which forms the purport of any representation, would be at once made classical by the agreement which it displays between form and content. On the contrary, in classical art the peculiarity of the content consists in being itself concrete idea, and, as such, the concrete spiritual; for only the spiritual is the truly inner self. To suit such a content, then, we must search out that in Nature which on its own merits belongs to the essence and actuality of the mind. It must be the absolute notion[71] that *invented* the shape appropriate to concrete mind, so that the *subjective* notion—in this case the spirit of art—has merely *found* it, and brought it, as an existence possessing natural shape, into accord with free individual spirituality.[72] This shape, with which the Idea as spiritual—as individually determinate spirituality—invests itself when manifested as a temporal phenomenon, is *the human form.* Personification and anthropomorphism have often been decried as a degradation of the spiritual; but art, in as far as its end is to bring before perception the spiritual in sensuous form, must advance to such anthropomorphism, as it is only in its proper body that mind is adequately revealed to sense. The migration of souls is in this respect a false abstraction,[73] and physiology ought to have made it one of its axioms that life had necessarily in its evolution to attain to the human shape, as the sole sensuous phenomenon that is appropriate to mind. The human form is employed in the classical type of art not as mere sensuous existence, but exclusively as the existence and physical form corresponding to mind, and is therefore exempt from

---

70 [*Gährung,* literally *"fermentation."* — TR. NOTE.]

71 [*Der ursprüngliche Begriff,* literally "the original notion."—TR. NOTE.]

72 [That is, God or the Universe *invented* man to be the expression of mind; art *finds* him, and adapts his shape to the artistic embodiment of mind as concentrated in individual instances.—TR. NOTE.]

73 [Because it represents the soul as independent of an appropriate body—the human soul as capable of existing in a beast's body.—TR. NOTE.]

all the deficiencies of what is merely sensuous, and from the contingent finiteness of phenomenal existence. The outer shape must be thus purified in order to express in itself a content adequate to itself; and again, if the conformity of import and content is to be complete, the spiritual meaning which is the content must be of a particular kind. It must, that is to say, be qualified to express itself completely in the physical form of man, without projecting into another world beyond the scope of such an expression in sensuous and bodily terms. This condition has the effect that Mind is by it at once specified as a particular case of mind, as human mind, and not as simply absolute and eternal, inasmuch as mind in this latter sense is incapable of proclaiming and expressing itself otherwise than as intellectual being.[74]

Out of this latter point arises, in its turn, the defect which brings about the dissolution of classical art, and demands a transition into a third and higher form, viz. into the *romantic* form of art.

§ ROMANTIC ART

The romantic form of art destroys the completed union of the Idea and its reality, and recurs, though in a higher phase, to that difference and antagonism of two aspects which was left unvanquished by symbolic art. The classical type attained the highest excellence, of which the sensuous embodiment of art is capable; and if it is in any way defective, the defect is in art as a whole, i.e., in the limitation of its sphere. This limitation consists in the fact that art as such takes for its object Mind—the conception of which is *infinite* concrete universality—in the shape of *sensuous* concrete-

ness, and in the classical phase sets up the perfect amalgamation of spiritual and sensuous existence as a Conformity of the two. Now, as a matter of fact, in such an amalgamation Mind cannot be represented according to its true notion. For mind is the infinite subjectivity of the Idea, which, as absolute inwardness,[75] is not capable of finding free expansion in its true nature on condition of remaining transposed into a bodily medium as the existence appropriate to it.

As an escape from such a condition the romantic form of art in its turn dissolves the inseparable unity of the classical phase, because it has won a significance which goes beyond the classical form of art and its mode of expression.[76] This significance—if we may recall familiar ideas—coincides with what Christianity declares to be true of God as Spirit, in contradistinction to the Greek faith in gods which forms the essential and appropriate content for classical art. In Greek art the concrete import is potentially, but not explicitly, the unity of the human and divine nature; a unity which, just because it is purely *immediate*[77] and not *explicit,* is capable of adequate manifestation in an immediate and sensuous mode. The Greek god is the object of naive intuition and sensuous imagination. His shape is, therefore, the bodily shape of man. The circle of his power and of his being is individual and individually limited. In relation with the subject,[78] he is, therefore, an essence and a power with which the subject's inner being is merely in latent unity, not itself possessing this unity as inward sub-

---

74 [*Geistigkeit.* "The nature of thought, mind, or spirit." It cannot be here rendered by mind or spirit, because these words make us think of an isolated individual, *a* mind or soul, and neglect the common spiritual or intellectual nature, which is referred to by the author.—TR. NOTE.]

75 [It is the essence of mind or thought not to have its parts outside one another. The so-called terms of a judgment are a good instance of parts in thought which are inward to each other.—TR. NOTE.]

76 [Compare Browning's "Old Pictures in Florence."—TR. NOTE.]

77 [That is, in the form of feeling and imagination—not reflected upon.—TR. NOTE.]

78 [Subject, i.e., conscious individual person.—TR. NOTE.]

jective knowledge. Now the higher stage is the *knowledge* of this *latent* unity, which as latent is the import of the classical form of art, and capable of perfect representation in bodily shape. The elevation of the latent or potential into self-conscious knowledge produces an enormous difference. It is the infinite difference which, e.g., separates man as such from the animals. Man is animal, but even in his animal functions he is not confined within the latent and potential as the animal is, but becomes conscious of them, learns to know them, and raises them —as, for instance, the process of digestion —into self-conscious science. By this means Man breaks the boundary of merely potential and immediate consciousness, so that just for the reason that he knows himself to be animal, he ceases to be animal, and, as *mind,* attains to self-knowledge.

If in the above fashion the unity of the human and divine nature, which in the former phase was potential, is raised from an *immediate* to a *conscious* unity, it follows that the true medium for the reality of this content is no longer the sensuous immediate existence of the spiritual, the human bodily shape, but *self-conscious inward intelligence.*[79] Now, Christianity brings God before our intelligence *as spirit,* or mind—not as particularized individual spirit, but as absolute, in *spirit* and in truth. And for this reason Christianity retires from the sensuousness of imagination into intellectual inwardness, and makes this, not bodily shape, the medium and actual existence of its significance. So, too, the unity of the human and divine nature is a conscious unity, only to be realized by *spiritual* knowledge and in *spirit.* Thus the new content, won by this unity, is not inseparable from sensuous representation, as if that were adequate to it, but is freed from this immediate existence, which has to be posited[80] as negative, ab-

sorbed, and reflected into the spiritual unity. In this way, romantic art must be considered as art transcending itself, while remaining within the artistic sphere and in artistic form.

Therefore, in short, we may abide by the statement that in this third stage the object (of art) is *free,* concrete intellectual being, which has the function of revealing itself as spiritual existence for the inward[81] world of spirit. In conformity with such an object-matter, art cannot work for sensuous perception. It must address itself to the inward mind, which coalesces with its object simply and as though this were itself,[82] to the subjective inwardness, to the heart, the feeling, which, being spiritual, aspires to freedom within itself, and seeks and finds its reconciliation only in the spirit within. It is this *inner* world that forms the content of the romantic, and must therefore find its representation as such inward feeling, and in the show or presentation of such feeling. The world of inwardness celebrates its triumph over the outer world, and actually in the sphere of the outer and in its medium manifests this its victory, owing to which the sensuous appearance sinks into worthlessness.

But, on the other hand, this type of Art,[83] like every other, needs an external vehicle of expression. Now the spiritual has withdrawn into itself out of the external and its immediate oneness therewith. For this reason, the sensuous externality of concrete form is accepted and represented, as in symbolic art, as something transient and fugitive. And the same measure is dealt to the subjective finite mind and will, even including the peculiarity or caprice of the

---

79 [*Innerlichkeit,* literally "inwardness."— TR. NOTE.]

80 [Taken, considered as, or determined to be negative.—TR. NOTE.]

81 ["Inward," again, does not mean merely inside our heads, but having the character of spirit in that its parts are not external of one another. A judgment is thus "inward."—TR. NOTE.]

82 [That is, does not keep up a distinction between percipient and object, as between things in space. Goodness, nobleness, etc., are not felt to be other than or outside the mind.—TR. NOTE.]

83 [The romantic.—TR. NOTE.]

individual, of character, action, etc., or of incident and plot. The aspect of external existence is committed to contingency, and left at the mercy of freaks of imagination, whose caprice is no more likely to mirror what is given *as* it is given, than to throw the shapes of the outer world into chance medley, or distort them into grotesqueness. For this external element no longer has its notion and significance, as in classical art, in its own sphere, and in its own medium. It has come to find them in the feelings, the display of which is *in themselves* instead of being in the external and *its* form of reality, and which have the power to preserve or to regain their state of reconciliation with themselves, in every accident, in every unessential circumstance that takes independent shape, in all misfortune and grief, and even in crime.

Owing to this, the characteristics of symbolic art, in difference, discrepancy, and severance of Idea and plastic shape, are here reproduced, but with an essential difference. In the sphere of the romantic, the Idea, whose defectiveness in the case of the symbol produced the defect of external shape, has to reveal itself in the medium of spirit and feelings as perfected in itself. And it is because of this higher perfection that it withdraws itself from any adequate union with the external element, inasmuch as it can seek and achieve its true reality and revelation nowhere but in itself.

This we may take as in the abstract the character of the symbolic, classical, and romantic forms of art, which represent the three relations of the Idea to its embodiment in the sphere of art. They consist in the aspiration after, and the attainment and transcendence of the Ideal as the true Idea of beauty.

Part III: The Several Arts

The third part of our subject, in contradistinction to the two just described, presup-poses the conception of the Ideal, and the general types of art, inasmuch as it simply consists of their realization in particular sensuous media. Hence we have no longer to do with the inner development of artistic beauty in conformity with its general fundamental principles. What we have to study is how these principles pass into actual existence, how they distinguish themselves in their external aspect, and how they give actuality to every element contained in the idea of beauty, separately and by itself *as a work of art,* and not merely as a general type. Now, what art transfers into external existence are the differences[84] proper to the idea of beauty and immanent therein. Therefore, the general types of art must reveal themselves in this third part, as before, in the character of the fundamental principle that determines the arrangement and definition of the several arts; in other words, the species of art contain in themselves the same essential modifications as those with which we become acquainted as the general types of art. External objectivity, however, to which these forms are introduced through the medium of a sensuous and therefore particular material, affects these types in the way of making them separate into independent and so particular forms embodying their realization. For each type finds its definite character in some one definite external material, and its adequate actuality in the mode of portrayal which that prescribes. But, moreover these types of art, being for all their determinateness, its *universal* forms, break the bounds of *particular* realization by a determinate form of art, and achieve existence in other arts as well, although in subordinate fashion. Therefore, the particular arts belong each of them specifically to *one* of the general types of art, and constitute its adequate external actuality; and also they represent, each of them after its own mode of external

---

[84] [That is, species, modifications naturally arising out of a principle.—TR. NOTE.]

plasticity, the totality of the types of art.[85]

Then, speaking generally, we are dealing in this third principal division with the beautiful of art, as it unfolds itself in the several arts and in their creations into a *world* of actualized beauty. The content of this world is the beautiful, and the true beautiful, as we saw, is spiritual being in concrete shape, the Ideal; or, more closely looked at, the absolute mind, and the truth itself. This region, that of divine truth artistically represented to perception and to feeling, forms the centre of the whole world of art. It is the independent, free, and divine plasticity, which has thoroughly mastered the external elements of form and of medium, and wears them simply as a means to manifestation of itself. Still, as the beautiful unfolds itself in this region in the character of *objective* reality, and in so doing distinguishes within itself its individual aspects and elements, permitting them independent particularity, it follows that this centre erects its extremes, realized in their peculiar actuality, into its own antitheses. Thus one of these extremes comes to consist in an objectivity as yet devoid of mind, in the merely natural vesture of God. At this point the external element takes plastic shape as something that has its spiritual aim and content, not in itself, but in another.[86]

The other extreme is the divine as inward, as something known, as the variously particularized *subjective* existence of the Deity; it is the truth as operative and vital in sense, heart, and mind of individual subjects, not persisting in the mould of its external shapes, but as having returned into subjective, individual inwardness. In such a mode, the Divine is at the same time distinguished from its first manifestation as Deity, and passes thereby into the diversity of particulars which belongs to all subjective knowledge—emotion, perception, and feeling. In the analogous province of religion, with which art at its highest stage is immediately connected, we conceive this same difference as follows. *First,* we think of the earthly natural life in its finiteness as standing on one side; but, then, *secondly,* consciousness makes God its object, in which the distinction of objectivity and subjectivity is done away with. And at last, *thirdly,* we advance from God as such to the devotion of the community, that is, to God as living and present in the subjective consciousness. Just so these three chief modifications present themselves in the world of art in independent development.

§ ARCHITECTURE

The *first* of the particular arts with which, according to their fundamental principle, we have to begin, is architecture considered as a fine art.[87] Its task lies in so manipulating external inorganic nature that it becomes cognate to mind, as an artistic outer world. The material of architecture is matter itself in its immediate externality as a heavy mass subject to mechanical laws, and its forms do not depart from the forms of inorganic nature, but are merely set in order in conformity with relations of the abstract understanding, i.e., with relations of symmetry. In this material and in such forms, the ideal as concrete spirituality does not admit of being realized. Hence the reality which is represented in them remains contrasted with the Idea, as something external which it has not penetrated, or has penetrated only to establish an abstract relation. For these reasons, the fundamental

---

85 [Thus, e.g., Sculpture is the art which corresponds *par excellence* to the general type called Classical Art; but there is a Symbolic kind of sculpture, and I suppose a Romantic or modern kind of sculpture, although neither of these types are exactly fitted to the capabilities of Sculpture. —TR. NOTE.]

86 [Architecture as relative to the purposes of life and of religion. See p. 333.—TR. NOTE.]

87 [*Die schöne Architectur.*—TR. NOTE.]

type of the fine art of building is the *symbolical* form of art. It is architecture that pioneers the way for the adequate realization of the God, and in this its service bestows hard toil upon existing nature, in order to disentangle it from the jungle of finitude and the abortiveness of chance. By this means it levels a space for the God, gives form to his external surroundings, and builds him his temple as a fit place for concentration of spirit, and for its direction to the mind's absolute objects. It raises an enclosure round the assembly of those gathered together, as a defence against the threatening of the storm, against rain, the hurricane, and wild beasts, and reveals the will to assemble, although externally, yet in conformity with principles of art. With such import as this it has power to inspire its material and its forms more or less effectively, as the determinate character of the content on behalf of which it sets to work is more or less significant, more concrete or more abstract, more profound in sounding its own depths, or more dim and more superficial. So much, indeed, may architecture attempt in this respect as even to create an adequate artistic existence for such an import in its shapes and in its material. But in such a case it has already overstepped its own boundary, and is leaning to sculpture, the phase above it. For the limit of architecture lies precisely in this point, that it retains the spiritual as an inward existence over against the external forms of the art, and consequently must refer to what has soul only as to something other than its own creations.

§ SCULPTURE

Architecture, however, as we have seen, has purified the external world, and endowed it with symmetrical order and with affinity to mind; and the temple of the God, the house of his community, stands ready. Into this temple, then,

in the *second* place, the God enters in the lightning-flash of individuality, which strikes and permeates the inert mass, while the infinite[88] and no longer merely symmetrical form belonging to mind itself concentrates and gives shape to the corresponding bodily existence. This is the task of *Sculpture*. In as far as in this art the spiritual inward being which architecture can but indicate makes itself at home in the sensuous shape and its external matter, and in as far as these two sides are so adapted to one another that neither is predominant, sculpture must be assigned the *classical form of art* as its fundamental type. For this reason the sensuous element itself has here no expression which could not be that of the spiritual element, just as, conversely, sculpture can represent no spiritual content which does not admit throughout of being adequately presented to perception in bodily form. Sculpture should place the spirit before us in its bodily form and in immediate unity therewith at rest and in peace; and the form should be animated by the content of spiritual individuality. And so the external sensuous matter is here no longer manipulated, either in conformity with its mechanical quality alone, as a mass possessing weight, nor in shapes belonging to the inorganic world, nor as indifferent to colour, etc.; but it is wrought in ideal forms of the human figure, and, it must be remarked, in all three spatial dimensions.

In this last respect we must claim for sculpture, that it is in it that the inward and spiritual are first revealed in their eternal repose and essential self-completeness. To such repose and unity with

---

88 [In the sense "self-complete," "not primarily regarded as explained by anything outside," like a machine or an animal contrasted with a wheel or a limb, which latter are finite, because they demand explanation and supplementation from without, i.e., necessarily draw attention to their own limit.—TR. NOTE.]

itself there can correspond only that external shape which itself maintains its unity and repose. And this is fulfilled by shape in its abstract spatiality.[89] The spirit which sculpture represents is that which is solid in itself, not broken up in the play of trivialities and of passions; and hence its external form too is not abandoned to any manifold phases of appearance, but appears under this one aspect only, as the abstraction of space in the whole of its dimensions.

§ THE ROMANTIC ARTS:
PAINTING, MUSIC, POETRY

Now, after architecture has erected the temple, and the hand of sculpture has supplied it with the statue of the God, then, in the third place, this god present to sense is confronted in the spacious halls of his house by the *community*. The community is the spiritual reflection into itself of such sensuous existence, and is the animating subjectivity and inner life which brings about the result that the determining principle for the content of art, as well as for the medium which represents it in outward form, comes to be particularization [dispersion into various shapes, attributes, incidents, etc.] individualization, and the subjectivity which they require.[90] The solid unity which the God has in sculpture breaks up into the multitudinous inner lives of individuals, whose unity is not sensuous, but purely ideal.[91]

It is only in this stage that God Himself comes to be really and truly spirit—the spirit in His (God's) community; for He here begins to be a to-and-fro, an alternation between His unity within himself and his realization in the individual's knowledge and its separate being, as also in the common nature and union of the multitude. In the community, God is released from the abstractness of unexpanded self-identity, as well as from the simple absorption in a bodily medium, by which sculpture represents Him. And He is thus exalted into spiritual existence and into knowledge, into the reflected[92] appearance which essentially displays itself as inward and as subjectivity. Therefore the higher content is now the spiritual nature, and that in its absolute shape. But the dispersion of which we have spoken reveals this at the same time as particular spiritual being, and as individual character. Now, what manifests itself in this phase as the main thing is not the serene quiescence of the God in Himself, but appearance as such, being which is *for* another, self-manifestation. And hence, in the phase we have reached, all the most manifold subjectivity in its living movement and operation—as human passion, action, and incident, and, in general, the wide realm of human feeling, will, and its negation— is for its own sake the object of artistic representation. In conformity with this content, the sensuous element of art has at once to show itself as made particular in itself and as adapted to subjective inwardness. Media that fulfil this requirement we have in colour, in musical sound, and finally in sound as the mere indication of inward perceptions and ideas; and as modes of realizing the import in question by help of

---

89 [That is, shape taken simply as an object filling space.—TR. NOTE.]

90 [The terms used in the text explain themselves if we compare, e.g., a Teniers with a Greek statue, or again, say, a Turner with the same. "Subjectivity" means that the work of art appeals to our ordinary feelings, experiences, etc. Music and poetry are still stronger cases than painting, according to the theory. Poetry especially can deal with *everything*.—TR. NOTE.]

91 [The unity of the individuals forming a church or nation is not visible, but exists in common sentiments, purposes, etc., and in the recognition of their community.—TR. NOTE.]

---

92 [An expression constantly applied to consciousness, because it can look at itself. Cf.:—

"Tell me, good Brutus, can you see your face?"

"No, Cassius; for the eye sees not itself But by reflection, by some other things."
                    SHAKESPEARE—*Julius Caesar*
—TR. NOTE.]

these media we obtain painting, music, and poetry. In this region the sensuous medium displays itself as subdivided in its own being and universally set down as ideal.[93] Thus it has the highest degree of conformity with the content of art, which, as such, is spiritual, and the connection of intelligible import and sensuous medium develops into closer intimacy than was possible in the case of architecture and sculpture. The unity attained, however, is a more inward unity, the weight of which is thrown wholly on the subjective side, and which, in as far as form and content are compelled to particularize themselves and give themselves merely ideal existence, can only come to pass at the expense of the objective universality of the content and also of its amalgamation with the immediately sensuous element.[94]

The arts, then, of which form and content exalt themselves to ideality, abandon the character of symbolic architecture and the classical ideal of sculpture, and therefore borrow their type from the romantic form of art, whose mode of plasticity they are most adequately adapted to express. And they constitute a *totality* of arts, because the romantic type is the most concrete in itself.[95]

The articulation of this *third sphere* of the individual arts may be determined as follows. The first art in it, which comes next to sculpture, is *painting*. It employs as a medium for its content and for the plastic embodiment of that content visibility as such in as far as it is specialized in its own nature, i.e., as developed into colour. It is true that the material employed in architecture and sculpture is also visible and coloured; but it is not, as in painting, visibility as such, not the simple light which, differentiating itself in virtue of its contrast with darkness, and in combination with the latter, gives rise to colour.[96] This quality of visibility, made subjective in itself and treated as ideal, needs neither, like architecture, the abstractly mechanical attribute of mass as operative in the properties of heavy matter, nor, like sculpture, the complete sensuous attributes of space, even though concentrated into organic shapes. The visibility and the rendering visible which belong to painting have their differences in a more ideal form, in the several kinds of colour, and they liberate art from the sensuous completeness in space which attaches to material things, by restricting themselves to a plane surface.

On the other hand, the content also attains the most comprehensive specification. Whatever can find room in the human heart, as feeling, idea, and purpose; whatever it is capable of shaping into act—all this diversity of material is capable of entering into the varied content of painting. The whole realm of particular existence, from the highest embodiment of mind down to the most isolated object of nature, finds a place here.

---

93 [Posited or laid down to be ideal; almost equals "pronounced" or "made to be" in the sense of not being; e.g., musical sound is "ideal" as existing, *qua* work of art, in memory only, the moment in which it is actually heard being fugitive; a picture, in respect of the third dimension, which has to be read into it; and poetry is almost wholly ideal, i.e., uses hardly any sensuous element, but appeals almost entirely to what exists *in the mind*. "Subdivided," (*besondert*) like *particularisirt* above; because of the variety and diversity present in the mere material of colours, musical sounds, and ideas. —TR. NOTE.]

94 [Again, the subject of a Turner or Teniers is not objectively universal, in the simplest sense; not something that is actually and literally the same everywhere and for everyone. And both painting and music (immediately sensuous elements) are less completely amalgamated with the ideal, represent it less solidly and thoroughly than the statue, so far as the ideal is itself external or plastic.—TR. NOTE.]

95 [The greater affinity of Romantic art with

the movement and variety of the modern spirit displays itself not only in the greater flexibility of painting, music, or poetry, as compared with architecture and sculpture, but in the fact that the Romantic type contains these three arts at least, while the Symbolic and Classical types had only one art each.—TR. NOTE.]

96 [This is drawn from Goethe's doctrine of colour, which Hegel unfortunately adopted in opposition to Newton's theory.—TR. NOTE.]

For it is possible even for finite nature,[97] in its particular scenes and phenomena, to make its appearance in the realm of art, if only some allusion to an element of mind endows it with affinity to thought and feeling.

The *second* art in which the romantic type realizes itself is contrasted with painting, and is *music*. Its medium, though still sensuous, yet develops into still more thorough subjectivity and particularization. Music, too, treats the sensuous as ideal, and does so by negating,[98] and idealizing into the individual isolation of a single point, the indifferent externality[99] of space, whose complete semblance is accepted and imitated by painting. The single point, *qua* such a negativity (excluding space) is in itself a concrete and active process of positive negation[100] within the attributes of matter, in the shape of a motion and tremor of the material body within itself and in its relation to itself. Such an inchoate ideality of matter,[101] which appears no longer as under the form of space, but as temporal ideality,[102] is sound, the sensuous set down as negated, with its abstract visibility converted into audibility, inasmuch as sound, so to speak, liberates the ideal content

from its immersion in matter. This earliest inwardness of matter and inspiration of soul into it furnishes the medium for the mental inwardness—itself as yet indefinite—and for the soul[103] into which mind concentrates itself; and finds utterance in its tones for the heart with its whole gamut of feelings and passions. Thus music forms the centre of the romantic arts, just as sculpture represents the central point between architecture and the arts of romantic subjectivity. Thus, too, it forms the point of transition between abstract spatial sensuousness, such as painting employs, and the abstract spirituality of poetry. Music has within itself, like architecture, a relation of quantity conformable to the understanding, as the antithesis to emotion and inwardness; and has also as its basis a solid conformity to law on the part of the tones, of their conjunction, and of their succession.

As regards the *third* and most spiritual mode of representation of the romantic art-type, we must look for it in *poetry*. Its characteristic peculiarity lies in the power with which it subjects to the mind and to its ideas the sensuous element from which music and painting in their degree began to liberate art. For sound, the only external matter which poetry retains, is in it no longer the feeling of the sonorous itself, but is a *sign*, which by itself is void of import. And it is a sign of the idea which has become concrete in itself, and not merely of indefinite feeling and of its *nuances* and grades. This is how sound develops into the *Word*, as voice articulate in itself, whose import it is to indicate ideas and notions. The merely negative point up to which music had developed now makes its appearance as the completely concrete point, the point which is mind, the self-conscious individual, which, producing out of itself the

---

97 [He means landscape, principally—TR. NOTE.]

98 [*Aufheben,* used pregnantly by Hegel to mean *both* "cancel," "annul," *and* "preserve," "fix in mind," "idealize." The use of this word is a cardinal point of his dialectic. ... I know of no equivalent but "put by," provincial Scotch "put past." The negation of space is an attribute of music. The parts of a chord are no more in space than are the parts of a judgment. Hegel expresses this by saying that music idealizes space and concentrates it into a point.—TR. NOTE.]

99 [The parts of space, though external to each other, are not distinguished by qualitative peculiarities.—TR. NOTE.]

100 [*Aufheben.*—TR. NOTE.]

101 ["Ideality of matter": the distinctively material attribute of a sonorous body, its extension, only appears in its sound indirectly, or inferentially, by modifying the nature of the sound. It is, therefore, "idealized."—TR. NOTE.]

102 [Succession in time is a degree more "ideal" than co-existence in space, because it exists solely in the medium of memory.—TR. NOTE.]

103 [*Seele:* mind on its individual side, as a particular feeling subject. *Geist* is rather mind as the common nature of intelligence. Thus in feeling and self-feeling, mind is said to concentrate itself into a soul.—TR. NOTE.]

infinite space of its ideas, unites it with the temporal character of sound. Yet this sensuous element, which in music was still immediately one with inward feeling, is in poetry separated from the content of consciousness. In poetry the mind determines this content for its own sake, and apart from all else, into the shape of ideas, and though it employs sound to express them, yet treats it solely as a symbol without value or import. Thus considered, sound may just as well be reduced to a mere letter, for the audible, like the visible, is thus depressed into a mere indication of mind.[104] For this reason the proper medium of poetical representation is the poetical imagination and intellectual portrayal itself. And as this element is common to all types of art, it follows that poetry runs through them all and develops itself independently in each. Poetry is the universal art of the mind which has become free in its own nature, and which is not tied to find its realization in external sensuous matter, but expatiates exclusively in the inner space and inner time of the ideas and feelings. Yet just in this its highest phase art ends by transcending itself, inasmuch as it abandons the medium of a harmonious embodiment of mind in sensuous form, and passes from the poetry of imagination into the prose of thought.

---

[104] [Hegel seems to accept this view. Was he insensible to sound in poetry? Some very grotesque verses of his, preserved in his biography, go to show that his ear was not sensitive. Yet his critical estimate of poetry is usually just. Shakespeare and Sophocles were probably his favourites. And, as a matter of proportion, what he here says is true. It must be remembered that the beauty of sound in poetry is to a great extent indirect, being supplied by the passion or emotion which the ideas symbolized by the sounds arouse. The beauty of poetical sound in itself is very likely less than often supposed. It must have the capacity for receiving passionate expression; but that is not the same as the sensuous beauty of a note or a colour. If the words used in a noble poem were divested of all meaning, they would lose much, though not all, of the beauty of their sound.— TR. NOTE.]

Conclusion

Such we may take to be the articulated totality of the particular arts, viz. the external art of architecture, the objective art of sculpture, and the subjective art of painting, music and poetry. Many other classifications have been attempted, for a work of art presents so many aspects, that, as has often been the case, first one and then another is made the basis of classification. For instance, one might take the sensuous medium. Thus architecture is treated as crystallization; sculpture, as the organic modelling of the material in its sensuous and spatial totality; painting, as the coloured surface and line; while in music, space, as such, passes into the point of time possessed of content within itself, until finally the external medium is in poetry depressed into complete insignificance. Or, again, these differences have been considered with reference to their purely abstract attributes of space and time. Such abstract peculiarities of works of art may, like their material medium, be consistently explored in their characteristic traits; but they cannot be worked out as the ultimate and fundamental law, because any such aspect itself derives its origin from a higher principle, and must therefore be subordinate thereto.

This higher principle we have found in the types of art—symbolic, classical, and romantic—which are the universal stages or elements[105] of the Idea of beauty itself. For *symbolic art* attains its most adequate reality and most complete application in *architecture,* in which it holds sway in the full import of its notion, and is not yet degraded to be, as it were, the inorganic nature dealt with by another art. The *classical* type of art, on the other hand, finds

---

[105] ["Stages or elements." *Momente,* Hegel's technical phrase for the stages which form the essential parts or factors of any idea. They make their appearance successively, but the earlier are implied and retained in the later.—TR. NOTE.]

adequate realization in *sculpture,* while it treats architecture only as furnishing an enclosure in which it is to operate, and has not acquired the power of developing painting and music as absolute[106] forms for its content. The *romantic* type of art, finally, takes possession of *painting* and *music,* and in like manner of poetic representation, as substantive and unconditionally adequate modes of utterance. Poetry, however, is conformable to all types of the beautiful, and extends over them all, because the artistic

imagination is its proper medium, and imagination is essential to every product that belongs to the beautiful, whatever its type may be.

And, therefore, what the particular arts realize in individual works of art, are according to their abstract conception simply the universal types which constitute the self-unfolding Idea of beauty. It is as the external realization of this Idea that the wide Pantheon of art is being erected, whose architect and builder is the spirit of beauty as it awakens to self-knowledge, and to complete which the history of the world will need its evolution of ages.

---

106 [Adequate, and so of permanent value.— TR. NOTE.]

FRIEDRICH NIETZSCHE

(1844-1900)

Nietzsche was descended on both sides from long lines of Protestant pastors and perhaps would not have been displeased if his published writings had made them turn over in their graves. He studied at the Universities of Bonn and Leipzig, and before his student days were well over, was called to the University of Basel in Switzerland, where at the age of twenty-five he was appointed professor of classical philology. In the Franco-Prussian War, despite physical handicaps, he served as a medical aide in the ambulance and hospital branches of the German army. In 1868 he had met Richard Wagner, of whose music (notably, *Tristan*) he was at first passionately fond. He broke with him some time later, on both personal and ideological grounds. To Wagner this rupture was only an inexcusable defection from the ranks of his admirers; but to Nietzsche, who had both a great need for friendship and a stern and lofty concept of what it should be like, it was virtually a trauma, leaving an indelible imprint on his mind.

In 1879 Nietzsche gave up his professorship to become an independent writer, and thereafter he lived for the most part in Swiss and Italian hotels, suffering the pangs of loneliness and the torments of physical illnesses, which may have been in some degree psychologically aggravated. At the same time he wrote indefatigably, and it is by the books of this period that he is best known. By the year 1888 the signs of mental derangement were unmistakable, and he spent the remaining years of his life in a sanitarium.

In the works of Nietzsche, considered as a whole, the "Nietzschean" gospel—whose watchwords are "the superman," "the transvaluation of all values," "the will to power," and "the right of the stronger"—is much less prominent than one might suspect from their reputation. The overarching purpose is not—save now and then— to advance any one thesis but to understand the intellectual, moral, and aesthetic life of man in all its many forms and disguises. The collected volumes are a treasure-house of perceptions, with all the phenomena of history and civilized life as their themes—and these cannot well be disregarded, even by those who have little or no use for "Nietzscheanism" as a philosophy.

FRIEDRICH NIETZSCHE

The Birth of Tragedy

(Translated by Clifton Fadiman)

From The Philosophy of Nietzsche, *copyright 1927 and renewed 1954 by The Modern Library, Inc. Reprinted by permission of Random House, Inc. (First published: 1872.)*

Part I

We shall do a great deal for the science of esthetics, once we perceive not merely by logical inference, but with the immediate certainty of intuition, that the continuous development of art is bound up with the *Apollonian* and *Dionysian* duality: just as procreation depends on the duality of the sexes, involving perpetual strife with only periodically intervening reconciliations. The terms Dionysian and Apollonian we borrow from the Greeks, who disclose to the discerning mind the profound mysteries of their view of art, not, to be sure, in concepts, but in the impressively clear figures of their gods. Through Apollo and Dionysus, the two art-deities of the Greeks, we come to recognize that in the Greek world there existed a sharp opposition, in origin and aims, between the Apollonian art of sculpture, and the non-plastic, Dionysian, art of music. These two distinct tendencies run parallel to each other, for the most part openly at variance; and they continually incite each other to new and more powerful births, which perpetuate an antagonism, only superficially reconciled by the common term "Art"; till at last, by a metaphysical miracle of the Hellenic will, they appear coupled with each other, and through this coupling eventually generate the art-product, equally Dionysian and Apollonian, of Attic tragedy.

In order to grasp these two tendencies, let us first conceive of them as the separate art-worlds of *dreams* and *drunkenness*. These physiological phenomena present a contrast analogous to that existing between the Apollonian and the Dionysian. It was in dreams, says Lucretius, that the glorious divine figures first appeared to the souls of men; in dreams the great shaper beheld the splendid corporeal structure of superhuman beings; and the Hellenic poet, if questioned about the mysteries of poetic inspiration, would likewise have suggested dreams and he might have given an explanation like that of Hans Sachs in *Die Meistersinger:*

> Mein Freund, das grad' ist Dichters Werk,
> dass er sein Träumen deut' und merk'.
> Glaubt mir, des Menschen wahrster Wahn
> wird ihm im Traume aufgethan:
> all' Dichtkunst und Poëterei
> ist nichts als Wahrtraum-Deuterei.[1]

The beautiful appearance of the dream-worlds, in creating which every man is a perfect artist, is the prerequisite of all plastic art, and in fact, as we shall see, of an important part of poetry also. In our dreams we delight in the immediate apprehension of form; all forms speak to us; none are unimportant, none are superfluous. But, when this dream-reality is most intense, we also have, glimmering through it, the sensation of its appearance: at least this is my experience, as to whose frequency, aye, normality, I could adduce many proofs, in addition to the sayings of the poets. Indeed, the man of philosophic mind has a presentiment that underneath this reality in which we live and have our being, is concealed another and quite different reality, which, like the first, is an appearance; and Schopenhauer actually indicates as the criterion of philosophical ability the occa-

sional ability to view men and things as mere phantoms or dream-pictures. Thus the esthetically sensitive man stands in the same relation to the reality of dreams as the philosopher does to the reality of existence; he is a close and willing observer, for these pictures afford him an interpretation of life, and it is by these processes that he trains himself for life. And it is not only the agreeable and friendly pictures that he experiences in himself with such perfect understanding: but the serious, the troubled, the sad, the gloomy, the sudden restraints, the tricks of fate, the uneasy presentiments, in short, the whole Divine Comedy of life, and the Inferno, also pass before him, not like mere shadows on the wall—for in these scenes he lives and suffers—and yet not without that fleeting sensation of appearance. And perhaps many will, like myself, recall that amid the dangers and terrors of dream-life they would at times, cry out in self-encouragement, and not without success. "It is only a dream! I will dream on!" I have likewise heard of persons capable of continuing one and the same dream for three and even more successive nights: facts which indicate clearly that our innermost beings, our common subconscious experiences, express themselves in dreams because they must do so and because they take profound delight in so doing.

This joyful necessity of the dream-experience has been embodied by the Greeks in their Apollo: for Apollo, the god of all plastic energies, is at the same time the soothsaying god. He, who (as the etymology of the name indicates) is the "shining one," the deity of light, is also ruler over the fair appearance of the inner world of fantasy. The higher truth, the perfection of these states in contrast to the incompletely intelligible everyday world, this deep consciousness of nature, healing and helping in sleep and dreams, is at the same time the symbolical analogue of the soothsaying faculty and of the arts generally, which make life possible and worth living. But

---

1 ["My friend, this is exactly the poet's task, to mark his dreams and to attach meanings to them. Believe me, man's most profound illusions are revealed to him in dreams, and all versifying and poetizing is nothing but an interpretation of them." —TR. NOTE.]

we must also include in our picture of Apollo that delicate boundary, which the dream-picture must not overstep—lest it act pathologically (in which case appearance would impose upon us as pure reality). We must keep in mind that measured restraint, that freedom from the wilder emotions, that philosophical calm of the sculptor-god. His eye must be "sunlike," as befits his origin; even when his glance is angry and distempered, the sacredness of his beautiful appearance must still be there. And so, in one sense, we might apply to Apollo the words of Schopenhauer when he speaks of the man wrapped in the veil of Mâyâ[2]: "Just as in a stormy sea, unbounded in every direction, rising and falling with howling mountainous waves, a sailor sits in a boat and trusts in his frail barque: so in the midst of a world of sorrows the individual sits quietly, supported by and trusting in his *principium individuationis*." In fact, we might say of Apollo, that in him the unshaken faith in this *principium* and the calm repose of the man wrapped therein receive their sublimest expression; and we might consider Apollo himself as the glorious divine image of the *principium individuationis,* whose gestures and expression tell us of all the joy and wisdom of "appearance," together with its beauty.

In the same work Schopenhauer has depicted for us the terrible *awe* which seizes upon man, when he is suddenly unable to account for the cognitive forms of a phenomenon, when the principle of reason, in some one of its manifestations, seems to admit of an exception. If we add to this awe the blissful ecstasy which rises from the innermost depths of man, aye, of nature, at this very collapse of the *principium individuationis,* we shall gain an insight into the nature of the *Dionysian,* which is brought home to us most intimately per-

haps by the analogy of *drunkenness.* It is either under the influence of the narcotic draught, which we hear of in the songs of all primitive men and peoples, or with the potent coming of spring penetrating all nature with joy, that these Dionysian emotions awake, which, as they intensify, cause the subjective to vanish into complete self-forgetfulness. So also in the German Middle Ages singing and dancing crowds, ever increasing in number, were whirled from place to place under this same Dionysian impulse. In these dancers of St. John and St. Vitus, we rediscover the Bacchic choruses of the Greeks, with their early history in Asia Minor, as far back as Babylon and the orgiastic Sacæa. There are some, who, from obtuseness, or lack of experience, will deprecate such phenomena as "folk-diseases," with contempt or pity born of the consciousness of their own "healthy-mindedness." But, of course, such poor wretches cannot imagine how anemic and ghastly their so-called "healthy-mindedness" seems in contrast to the glowing life of the Dionysian revelers rushing past them.

Under the charm of the Dionysian not only is the union between man and man reaffirmed, but Nature which has become estranged, hostile, or subjugated, celebrates once more her reconciliation with her prodigal son, man. Freely earth proffers her gifts, and peacefully the beasts of prey approach from desert and mountain. The chariot of Dionysus is bedecked with flowers and garlands; panthers and tigers pass beneath his yoke. Transform Beethoven's "Hymn to Joy" into a painting; let your imagination conceive the multitudes bowing to the dust, awestruck—then you will be able to appreciate the Dionysian. Now the slave is free; now all the stubborn, hostile barriers, which necessity, caprice or "shameless fashion" have erected between man and man, are broken down. Now, with the gospel of universal harmony, each one feels himself not only united, reconciled, blended with his neighbor, but as one with

2 [Cf. *World as Will and Idea,* Vol. I, pp. 455 ff., 6th ed., Haldane and Kemp, trans.—TR. NOTE.]

him; he feels as if the veil of Mâyâ had been torn aside and were now merely fluttering in tatters before the mysterious Primordial Unity. In song and in dance man expresses himself as a member of a higher community; he has forgotten how to walk and speak; he is about to take a dancing flight into the air. His very gestures bespeak enchantment. Just as the animals now talk, just as the earth yields milk and honey, so from him emanate supernatural sounds. He feels himself a god, he himself now walks about enchanted, in ecstasy, like to the gods whom he saw walking about in his dreams. He is no longer an artist, he has become a work of art: in these paroxysms of intoxication the artistic power of all nature reveals itself to the highest gratification of the Primordial Unity. The noblest clay, the most costly marble, man, is here kneaded and cut, and to the sound of the chisel strokes of the Dionysian world-artist rings out the cry of the Eleusinian mysteries: "Do ye bow in the dust, O millions? Do you divine your creator, O world?"

Part II

Thus far we have considered the Apollonian and its antithesis, the Dionysian, as artistic energies which burst forth from nature herself, *without the mediation of the human artist;* energies in which nature's art-impulses are satisfied in the most immediate and direct way: first, on the one hand, in the pictorial world of dreams, whose completeness is not dependent upon the intellectual attitude or the artistic culture of any single being; and, on the other hand, as drunken reality, which likewise does not heed the single unit, but even seeks to destroy the individual and redeem him by a mystic feeling of Oneness. With reference to these immediate art-states of nature, every artist is an "imitator," that is to say, either an Apollonian artist in

dreams, or a Dionysian artist in ecstasies, or finally—as for example in Greek tragedy —at once artist in both dreams and ecstasies: so we may perhaps picture him sinking down in his Dionysian drunkenness and mystical self-abnegation, alone, and apart from the singing revelers, and we may imagine how now, through Apollonian dream-inspiration, his own state, i.e., his oneness with the primal nature of the universe is revealed to him in a *symbolical dream-picture.*

So much for these general premises and contrasts. Let us now approach the *Greeks* in order to learn how highly these *art-impulses of nature* were developed in them. Thus we shall be in a position to understand and appreciate more deeply that relation of the Greek artist to his archetypes, which, according to the Aristotelian expression, is "the imitation of nature." In spite of all the dream-literature and the numerous dream anecdotes of the Greeks, we can speak only conjecturally, though with reasonable assurance, of their *dreams.* If we consider the incredibly precise and unerring plastic power of their eyes, together with their vivid, frank delight in colors, we can hardly refrain (to the shame of all those born later) from assuming even for their dreams a certain logic of line and contour, colors and groups, a certain pictorial sequence reminding us of their finest bas-reliefs, whose perfection would certainly justify us, if a comparison were possible, in designating the dreaming Greeks as Homers and Homer as a dreaming Greek: in a deeper sense than that in which modern man, speaking of his dreams, ventures to compare himself with Shakespeare.

On the other hand, there is no conjecture as to the immense gap which separates the *Dionysian Greek* from the Dionysian barbarian. From all quarters of the Ancient World,—to say nothing here of the modern, —from Rome to Babylon, we can point to the existence of Dionysian festivals, types which bear, at best, the same relation to the Greek festivals as the bearded satyr, who borrowed his name and attributes from the goat, does to Dionysus himself. In nearly every case these festivals centered in extravagant sexual licentiousness, whose waves overwhelmed all family life and its venerable traditions; the most savage natural instincts were unleashed, including even that horrible mixture of sensuality and cruelty which has always seemed to me to be the genuine "witches' brew." For some time, however, it would appear that the Greeks were perfectly insulated and guarded against the feverish excitements of these festivals by the figure of Apollo himself rising here in full pride, who could not have held out the Gorgon's head to any power more dangerous than this grotesquely uncouth Dionysian. It is in Doric art that this majestically-rejecting attitude of Apollo is eternized. The opposition between Apollo and Dionysus became more hazardous and even impossible, when, from the deepest roots of the Hellenic nature, similar impulses finally burst forth and made a path for themselves: the Delphic god, by a seasonably effected reconciliation, now contented himself with taking the destructive weapons from the hands of his powerful antagonist. This reconciliation is the most important moment in the history of the Greek cult. Wherever we turn we note the revolutions resulting from this event. The two antagonists were reconciled; the boundary lines thenceforth to be observed by each were sharply defined, and there was to be a periodical exchange of gifts of esteem. At bottom, however, the chasm was not bridged over. But if we observe how, under the pressure of this treaty of peace, the Dionysian power revealed itself, we shall now recognize in the Dionysian orgies of the Greeks, as compared with the Babylonian Sacæa with their reversion of man to the tiger and the ape, the significance of festivals of world-redemption and days of transfiguration. It is with them that nature for the first time attains her artistic jubilee; it

is with them that the destruction of the *principium individuationis* for the first time becomes an artistic phenomenon. The horrible "witches' brew" of sensuality and cruelty becomes ineffective: only the curious blending and duality in the emotions of the Dionysian revelers remind us—as medicines remind us of deadly poisons—of the phenomenon that pain begets joy, that ecstasy may wring sounds of agony from us. At the very climax of joy there sounds a cry of horror or a yearning lamentation for an irretrievable loss. In these Greek festivals, nature seems to reveal a sentimental trait; it is as if she were heaving a sigh at her dismemberment into individuals. The song and pantomime of such dually-minded revelers was something new and unheard-of for the Homeric-Grecian world: and the Dionysian *music* in particular excited awe and terror. If music, as it would seem, had been known previously as an Apollonian art, it was so, strictly speaking, only as the wave-beat of rhythm, whose formative power was developed for the representation of Apollonian states. The music of Apollo was Doric architectonics in tones, but in tones that were merely suggestive, such as those of the cithara. The very element which forms the essence of Dionysian music (and hence of music in general) is carefully excluded as un-Apollonian: namely, the emotional power of the tone, the uniform flow of the melos, and the utterly incomparable world of harmony. In the Dionysian dithyramb man is incited to the greatest exaltation of all his symbolic faculties; something never before experienced struggles for utterance—the annihilation of the veil of Mâyâ, Oneness as the soul of the race, and of nature itself. The essence of nature is now to be expressed symbolically; we need a new world of symbols; for once the entire symbolism of the body is called into play, not the mere symbolism of the lips, face, and speech, but the whole pantomime of dancing, forcing every member into rhythmic movement. Thereupon the other symbolic powers suddenly press forward, particularly those of music, in rhythmics, dynamics, and harmony. To grasp this collective release of all the symbolic powers, man must have already attained that height of self-abnegation which wills to express itself symbolically through all these powers: and so the dithyrambic votary of Dionysus is understood only by his peers! With what astonishment must the Apollonian Greek have beheld him! With an astonishment that was all the greater the more it was mingled with the shuddering suspicion that all this was actually not so very alien to him after all, in fact, that it was only his Apollonian consciousness which, like a veil, hid this Dionysian world from his vision.

Part III

To understand this, it becomes necessary to level the artistic structure of the *Apollonian culture,* as it were, stone by stone, till the foundations on which it rests become visible. First of all we see the glorious *Olympian* figures of the gods, standing on the gables of this structure. Their deeds, pictured in brilliant reliefs, adorn its friezes. We must not be misled by the fact that Apollo stands side by side with the others as an individual deity, without any claim to priority of rank. For the same impulse which embodied itself in Apollo gave birth in general to this entire Olympian world, and so in this sense Apollo is its father. What terrific need was it that could produce such an illustrious company of Olympian beings?

He who approaches these Olympians with another religion in his heart, seeking among them for moral elevation, even for sanctity, for disincarnate spirituality, for charity and benevolence, will soon be forced to turn his back on them, discouraged and disappointed. For there is nothing here that suggests asceticism, spirituality, or duty. We

hear nothing but the accents of an exuberant, triumphant life, in which all things, whether good or bad, are deified. And so the spectator may stand quite bewildered before this fantastic superfluity of life, asking himself what magic potion these mad glad men could have imbibed to make life so enjoyable that, wherever they turned, their eyes beheld the smile of Helen, the ideal picture of their own existence, "floating in sweet sensuality." But to this spectator, who has his back already turned, we must perforce cry: "Go not away, but stay and hear what Greek folk-wisdom has to say of this very life, which with such inexplicable gayety unfolds itself before your eyes. There is an ancient story that King Midas hunted in the forest a long time for the wise *Silenus,* the companion of Dionysus, without capturing him. When Silenus at last fell into his hands, the king asked what was the best and most desirable of all things for man. Fixed and immovable, the demigod said not a word; till at last, urged by the king, he gave a shrill laugh and broke out into these words: 'Oh, wretched ephemeral race, children of chance and misery, why do ye compel me to tell you what it were most expedient for you not to hear? What is best of all is beyond your reach forever: not to be born, not to *be,* to be *nothing.* But the second best for you—is quickly to die.' "

How is the Olympian world of deities related to this folk-wisdom? Even as the rapturous vision of the tortured martyr to his suffering.

Now it is as if the Olympian magic mountain had opened before us and revealed its roots to us. The Greek knew and felt the terror and horror of existence. That he might endure this terror at all, he had to interpose between himself and life the radiant dream-birth of the Olympians. That overwhelming dismay in the face of the titanic powers of nature, the Moira enthroned inexorably over all knowledge, the vulture of the great lover of mankind,

Prometheus, the terrible fate of the wise Œdipus, the family curse of the Atridæ which drove Orestes to matricide: in short, that entire philosophy of the sylvan god, with its mythical exemplars, which caused the downfall of the melancholy Etruscans— all this was again and again overcome by the Greeks with the aid of the Olympian *middle world* of art; or at any rate it was veiled and withdrawn from sight. It was out of the direst necessity to live that the Greeks created these gods. Perhaps we may picture the process to ourselves somewhat as follows: out of the original Titan thearchy of terror the Olympian thearchy of joy gradually evolved through the Apollonian impulse towards beauty, just as roses bud from thorny bushes. How else could this people, so sensitive, so vehement in its desires, so singularly constituted for *suffering,* how could they have endured existence, if it had not been revealed to them in their gods, surrounded with a higher glory? The same impulse which calls art into being, as the complement and consummation of existence, seducing one to a continuation of life, was also the cause of the Olympian world which the Hellenic "will" made use of as a transfiguring mirror. Thus do the gods justify the life of man, in that they themselves live it—the only satisfactory Theodicy! Existence under the bright sunshine of such gods is regarded as desirable in itself, and the real *grief* of the Homeric men is caused by parting from it, especially by early parting: so that now, reversing the wisdom of Silenus, we might say of the Greeks that "to die early is worst of all for them, the next worst—some day to die at all." Once heard, it will ring out again; forget not the lament of the short-lived Achilles, mourning the leaflike change and vicissitude of the race of men and the decline of the heroic age. It is not unworthy of the greatest hero to long for a continuation of life, aye, even though he live as a slave. At the Apollonian stage of development, the "will" longs so vehemently for this existence, the Homeric man feels himself so completely at one with it, that lamentation itself becomes a song of praise.

Here we should note that this harmony which is contemplated with such longing by modern man, in fact, this oneness of man with nature (to express which Schiller introduced the technical term "naïve"), is by no means a simple condition, resulting naturally, and as if inevitably. It is not a condition which, like a terrestrial paradise, *must* necessarily be found at the gate of every culture. Only a romantic age could believe this, an age which conceived of the artist in terms of Rousseau's *Emile* and imagined that in Homer it had found such an artist Emile, reared in Nature's bosom. Wherever we meet with the "naïve" in art, we recognize the highest effect of the Apollonian culture, which in the first place has always to overthrow some Titanic empire and slay monsters, and which, through its potent dazzling representations and its pleasurable illusions, must have triumphed over a terrible depth of world-contemplation and a most keen sensitivity to suffering. But how seldom do we attain to the naïve— that complete absorption in the beauty of appearance! And hence how inexpressibly sublime is *Homer,* who, as individual being, bears the same relation to this Apollonian folk-culture as the individual dream-artist does to the dream-faculty of the people and of Nature in general. The Homeric "naïveté" can be understood only as the complete victory of the Apollonian illusion: an illusion similar to those which Nature so frequently employs to achieve her own ends. The true goal is veiled by a phantasm: and while we stretch out our hands for the latter, Nature attains the former by means of your illusion. In the Greeks the "will" wished to contemplate itself in the transfiguration of genius and the world of art; in order to glorify themselves, its creatures had to feel themselves worthy of glory; they had to behold themselves again in a higher sphere, without this perfect world of contemplation acting as a command or a reproach. Such is the sphere of beauty, in which they saw their mirrored images, the Olympians. With this mirroring of beauty the Hellenic will combated its artistically correlative talent for suffering and for the wisdom of suffering: and, as a monument of its victory, we have Homer, the naïve artist.

Part IV

Now the dream-analogy may throw some light on the problem of the naïve artist. Let us imagine the dreamer: in the midst of the illusion of the dream-world and without disturbing it, he calls out to himself: "It is a dream, I will dream on." What must we infer? That he experiences a deep inner joy in dream-contemplation; on the other hand, to be at all able to dream with this inner joy in contemplation, he must have completely lost sight of the waking reality and its ominous obtrusiveness. Guided by the dream-reading Apollo, we may interpret all these phenomena to ourselves somewhat in this way. Though it is certain that of the two halves of our existence, the waking and the dreaming states, the former appeals to us as infinitely preferable, important, excellent and worthy of being lived, indeed, as that which alone is lived: yet, in relation to that mysterious substratum of our nature of which we are the phenomena, I should, paradoxical as it may seem, maintain the very opposite estimate of the value of dream life. For the more clearly I perceive in Nature those omnipotent art impulses, and in them an ardent longing for release, for redemption through release, the more I feel myself impelled to the metaphysical assumption that the Truly-Existent and Primal Unity, eternally suffering and divided against itself, has need of the rapturous vision, the joyful appearance, for its continuous salvation: which appearance we, completely wrapped

up in it and composed of it, are compelled to apprehend as the True Non-Being,—i.e., as a perpetual becoming in time, space and causality,—in other words, as empiric reality. If, for the moment, we do not consider the question of our own "reality," if we conceive of our empirical existence, and that of the world in general, as a continuously manifested representation of the Primal Unity, we shall then have to look upon the dream as an *appearance of appearance,* hence as a still higher appeasement of the primordial desire for appearance. And that is why the innermost heart of Nature feels that ineffable joy in the naïve artist and the naïve work of art, which is likewise only "an appearance of appearance." In a symbolic painting, *Raphael,* himself one of these immortal "naïve" ones, has represented for us this devolution of appearance to appearance, the primitive process of the naïve artist and of Apollonian culture. In his "Transfiguration," the lower half of the picture, with the possessed boy, the despairing bearers, the bewildered, terrified disciples, shows us the reflection of suffering, primal and eternal, the sole basis of the world: the "appearance" here is the counter-appearance of eternal contradiction, the father of things. From this appearance now arises, like ambrosial vapor, a new visionary world of appearances, invisible to those wrapped in the first appearance—a radiant floating in purest bliss, a serene contemplation beaming from wide-open eyes. Here we have presented, in the most sublime artistic symbolism, that Apollonian world of beauty and its substratum, the terrible wisdom of Silenus; and intuitively we comprehend their necessary interdependence. Apollo, however, again appears to us as the apotheosis of the *principium individuationis,* in which alone is consummated the perpetually attained goal of the Primal Unity, its redemption through appearance. With his sublime gestures, he shows us how necessary is the entire world of suffering, that by means of it the individual may be impelled to realize the redeeming vision, and then, sunk in contemplation of it, sit quietly in his tossing barque, amid the waves.

If we at all conceive of it as imperative and mandatory, this apotheosis of individuation knows but one law—the individual, i.e., the delimiting of the boundaries of the individual, *measure* in the Hellenic sense. Apollo, as ethical deity, exacts measure of his disciples, and, that to this end, he requires self-knowledge. And so, side by side with the esthetic necessity for beauty, there occur the demands "know thyself" and "nothing overmuch"; consequently pride and excess are regarded as the truly inimical demons of the non-Apollonian sphere, hence as characteristics of the pre-Apollonian age—that of the Titans; and of the extra-Apollonian world—that of the barbarians. Because of his Titan-like love for man, Prometheus must be torn to pieces by vultures; because of his excessive wisdom, which could solve the riddle of the Sphinx, Œdipus must be plunged into a bewildering vortex of crime. Thus did the Delphic god interpret the Greek past.

Similarly the effects wrought by the *Dionysian* seemed "titan-like" and "barbaric" to the Apollonian Greek: while at the same time he could not conceal from himself that he too was inwardly related to these overthrown Titans and heroes. Indeed, he had to recognize even more than this: despite all its beauty and moderation, his entire existence rested on a hidden substratum of suffering and of knowledge, which was again revealed to him by the Dionysian. And lo! Apollo could not live without Dionysus! The "titanic" and the "barbaric" were in the last analysis as necessary as the Apollonian.

And now let us take this artistically limited world, based on appearance and moderation; let us imagine how into it there penetrated, in tones ever more bewitching and alluring, the ecstatic sound of the Dionysian festival; let us remember that in these strains all of Nature's excess in joy, sorrow, and knowledge become audible, even in piercing shrieks; and finally, let us ask ourselves what significance remains to the psalmodizing artist of Apollo, with his phantom harp-sound, once it is compared with this demonic folk-song! The muses of the arts of "appearance" paled before an art which, in its intoxication, spoke the truth. The wisdom of Silenus cried "Woe! woe!" to the serene Olympians. The individual, with all his restraint and proportion, succumbed to the self-oblivion of the Dionysian state, forgetting the precepts of Apollo. Excess revealed itself as truth. Contradiction, the bliss born of pain, spoke out from the very heart of Nature. And so, wherever the Dionysian prevailed, the Apollonian was checked and destroyed. But, on the other hand, it is equally certain that, wherever the first Dionysian onslaught was successfully withstood, the authority and majesty of the Delphic god exhibited itself as more rigid and menacing than ever. For to me the *Doric* state and Doric art are explicable only as a permanent citadel of the Apollonian. For an art so defiantly prim, and so encompassed with bulwarks, a training so warlike and rigorous, a political structure so cruel and relentless, could endure for any length of time only by incessant opposition to the titanic-barbaric nature of the Dionysian.

Up to this point we have simply enlarged upon the observation made at the beginning of this essay: that the Dionysian and the Apollonian, in new births ever following and mutually augmenting one another, controlled the Hellenic genius; that from out the age of "bronze," with its wars of the Titans and its rigorous folk-philosophy, the Homeric world developed under the sway of the Apollonian impulse to beauty; that this "naïve" splendor was again overwhelmed by the influx of the Dionysian; and that against this new power the Apollonian rose to the austere majesty of Doric art and the Doric view of the world. If, then, amid the strife of these two hostile principles, the older Hellenic history thus falls into four great periods of art, we are now impelled to inquire after the *final goal* of these developments and processes, lest perchance we should regard the last-attained period, the period of Doric art, as the climax and aim of these artistic impulses. And here the sublime and celebrated art of *Attic tragedy* and the dramatic dithyramb presents itself as the common goal of both these tendencies, whose mysterious union, after many and long precursory struggles, found glorious consummation in this child,—at once Antigone and Cassandra.

Part V

We now approach the real goal of our investigation, which is directed towards acquiring a knowledge of the Dionysian-Apollonian genius and its art-product, or at least an anticipatory understanding of its mysterious union. Here we shall first of all inquire after the first evidence in Greece of that new germ which subsequently developed into tragedy and the dramatic dithyramb. The ancients themselves give us a symbolic answer, when they place the faces of *Homer* and *Archilochus* as the forefathers and torchbearers of Greek poetry side by side on gems, sculptures, etc., with a sure feeling that consideration should be given only to these two thoroughly original compeers, from whom a stream of fire flows over the whole of later Greek history. Homer, the aged self-absorbed dreamer, the type of the Apollonian naïve artist, now beholds with astonishment the passionate genius of the war-like votary of the muses, Archilochus, passing through life with fury and violence; and modern esthetics, by way of interpretation, can only add that here the first "objective" artist confronts the first "subjective" artist. But this interpretation helps us but little, because we know the subjective artist only as the poor artist, and throughout the

entire range of art we demand specially and first of all the conquest of the Subjective, the release from the ego and the silencing of the individual will and desire; indeed, we find it impossible to believe in any truly artistic production, however insignificant, if it is without objectivity, without pure, detached contemplation. Hence our esthetic must first solve the problem of how the "lyrist" is possible as an artist—he who, according to the experience of all ages, is continually saying "I" and running through the entire chromatic scale of his passions and desires. Compared with Homer, this very Archilochus appalls us by his cries of hatred and scorn, by his drunken outbursts of desire. Therefore is not he, who has been called the first subjective artist, essentially the non-artist? But in this case, how explain the reverence which was shown to him—the poet—in very remarkable utterances by the Delphic oracle itself, the center of "objective" art?

Schiller has thrown some light on the poetic process by a psychological observation, inexplicable to himself, yet apparently valid. He admits that before the act of creation he did not perhaps have before him or within him any series of images accompanied by an ordered thought-relationship; but his condition was rather that of a *musical mood*. ("With me the perception has at first no clear and definite object; this is formed later. A certain musical mood of mind precedes, and only after this ensues the poetical idea.") Let us add to this the natural and most important phenomenon of all ancient lyric poetry, *the union,* indeed, the *identity,* of the *lyrist with the musician,*—compared with which our modern lyric poetry appears like the statue of a god without a head,—with this in mind we may now, on the basis of our metaphysics of esthetics set forth above, explain the lyrist to ourselves in this manner: In the first place, as Dionysian artist he has identified himself with the Primal Unity, its pain and contradiction. Assuming that music has been correctly termed a repetition and a recast of the world, we may say that he produces the copy of this Primal Unity as music. Now, however, under the Apollonian dream-inspiration, this music reveals itself to him again as a *symbolic dream-picture*. The inchoate, intangible reflection of the primordial pain in music, with its redemption in appearance, now produces a second mirroring as a specific symbol or example. The artist has already surrendered his subjectivity in the Dionysian process. The picture which now shows him his identity with the heart of the world, is a dream-scene, which embodies the primordial contradiction and primordial pain, together with the primordial joy, of appearance. The "I" of the lyrist therefore sounds from the depth of his being: its "subjectivity," in the sense of the modern esthetes, is pure imagination. When Archilochus, the first Greek lyrist, proclaims to the daughters of Lycambes both his mad love and his contempt, it is not his passion alone which dances before us in orgiastic frenzy; but we see Dionysus and the Mænads, we see the drunken reveler Archilochus sunk down in slumber—as Euripides depicts it in the *Bacchæ*, the sleep on the high mountain pasture, in the noonday sun. And now Apollo approaches and touches him with the laurel. Then the Dionyso-musical enchantment of the sleeper seems to emit picture sparks, lyrical poems, which in their highest form are called tragedies and dramatic dithyrambs.

The plastic artist, as also the epic poet, who is related to him, is sunk in the pure contemplation of images. The Dionysian musician is, without any images, himself pure primordial pain and its primordial reëchoing. The lyric genius is conscious of a world of pictures and symbols—growing out of his state of mystical self-abnegation and oneness. This state has a coloring, a causality and a velocity quite different from that of the world of the plastic artist and the epic poet. For the latter lives in these pictures, and only in them, with joyful satisfaction. He never grows tired of contemplating lovingly even their minutest

traits. Even the picture of the angry Achilles is only a picture to him, whose angry expression he enjoys with the dream-joy in appearance. Thus, by this mirror of appearance, he is protected against being united and blended with his figures. In direct contrast to this, the pictures of the *lyrist* are nothing but *his very* self and, as it were, only different projections of himself, by force of which he, as the moving center of this world, may say "I": only of course this self is not the same as that of the waking, empirically real man, but the only truly existent and eternal self resting at the basis of things, and with the help of whose images, the lyric genius can penetrate to this very basis.

Now let us suppose that among these images he also beholds *himself* as non-genius, i.e., his subject, the whole throng of subjective passions and agitations directed to a definite object which appears real to him. It may now seem as if the lyric genius and the allied non-genius were one, as if the former had of its own accord spoken that little word "I." But this identity is but superficial and it will no longer be able to lead us astray, as it certainly led astray those who designated the lyrist as the subjective poet. For, as a matter of fact, Archilochus, the passionately inflamed, loving and hating man, is but a vision of the genius, who by this time is no longer merely Archilochus, but a world-genius expressing his primordial pain symbolically in the likeness of the man Archilochus: while the subjectively willing and desiring man, Archilochus, can never at any time be a poet. It is by no means necessary, however, that the lyrist should see nothing but the phenomenon of the man Archilochus before him as a reflection of eternal being; and tragedy shows how far the visionary world of the lyrist may be removed from this phenomenon, which, of course, is intimately related to it.

Schopenhauer, who did not conceal from himself the difficulty the lyrist presents in the philosophical contemplation of art, thought he had found a solution, with which, however, I am not in entire accord. (Actually, it was in his profound metaphysics of music that he alone held in his hands the means whereby this difficulty might be definitely removed: as I believe I have removed it here in his spirit and to his honor). In contrast to our view, he describes the peculiar nature of song as follows[3]

> It is the subject of will, i.e., his own volition, which the consciousness of the singer feels; often as a released and satisfied desire (joy), but still oftener as a restricted desire (grief), always as an emotion, a passion, a moved frame of mind. Besides this, however, and along with it, by the sight of surrounding nature, the singer becomes conscious of himself as the subject of pure will-less knowing, whose unbroken, blissful peace now appears, in contrast to the stress of desire, which is always restricted and always needy. The feeling of this contrast, this alternation, is really what the lyric as a whole expresses and what principally constitutes the lyrical state of mind. In it pure knowing comes to us as it were to deliver us from desire and its strain; we follow, but only for an instant; desire, the remembrance of our own personal ends, tears us anew from peaceful contemplation; yet ever again the next beautiful surrounding in which the pure will-less knowledge presents itself to us, allures us away from desire. Therefore, in the lyric and the lyrical mood, desire (the personal interest of the ends) and pure perception of the surrounding presented are wonderfully mingled with each other; connections between them are sought for and imagined; the subjective disposition, the affection of the will, imparts its own hue to the perceived surrounding, and conversely, the surroundings communicate the reflex of their color to the will. The true lyric is the expression of the whole of this mingled and divided state of mind.

Who could fail to recognize in this description that lyric poetry is here character-

---

[3] [*World as Will and Idea,* Vol. I, p. 322, 6th ed., Haldane and Kemp, trans.—TR. NOTE.]

ized as an incompletely attained art, which arrives at its goal infrequently and only as it were by leaps? Indeed, it is described as a semi-art, whose essence is said to consist in this, that desire and pure contemplation, i.e., the unesthetic and the esthetic condition, are wonderfully mingled with each other. It follows that Schopenhauer still classifies the arts as subjective or objective, using the antithesis as if it were a criterion of value. But it is our contention, on the contrary, that this antithesis between the subjective and the objective is especially irrelevant in esthetics, since the subject, the desiring individual furthering his own egoistic ends, can be conceived of only as the antagonist, not as the origin of art. In so far as the subject is the artist, however, he has already been released from his individual will, and has become as it were the medium through which the one truly existent Subject celebrates his release in appearance. For, above all, to our humiliation *and* exaltation, one thing must be clear to us. The entire comedy of art is neither performed for our betterment or education nor are we the true authors of this art-world. On the contrary, we may assume that we are merely pictures and artistic projections for the true author, and that we have our highest dignity in our significance as works of art—for it is only as an *esthetic phenomenon* that existence and the world are eternally *justified*—while of course our consciousness of our own significance hardly differs from that which the soldiers painted on canvas have of the battle represented on it. Thus all our knowledge of art is basically quite illusory, because as knowing beings we are not one and identical with that Being who, as the sole author and spectator of this comedy of art, prepares a perpetual entertainment for himself. Only in so far as the genius in the act of artistic creation coalesces with this primordial artist of the world, does he catch sight of the eternal essence of art; for in this state he is, in a marvelous manner, like the weird picture of the fairy-tale which can turn its eyes at will and behold itself; he is now at once subject and object, at once poet, actor, and spectator.

Part VI

In connection with Archilochus, scholarly research has discovered that he introduced the *folk-song* into literature, and, on account of this, deserved, according to the general estimate of the Greeks, his unique position beside Homer. But what is the folk-song in contrast to the wholly Apollonian epos? What else but the *perpetuum vestigium* of a union of the Apollonian and the Dionysian? Its enormous diffusion among all peoples, further re-enforced by ever-new births, is testimony to the power of this artistic dual impulse of Nature: which leaves its vestiges in the folk-song just as the orgiastic movements of a people perpetuate themselves in its music. Indeed, it might also be historically demonstrable that every period rich in folk-songs has been most violently stirred by Dionysian currents, which we must always consider the substratum and prerequisite of the folk-song.

First of all, however, we must conceive the folk-song as the musical mirror of the world, as the original melody, now seeking for itself a parallel dream-phenomenon and expressing it in poetry. *Melody is therefore primary and universal,* and so may admit of several objectifications in several texts. Likewise, in the naïve estimation of the people, it is regarded as by far the more important and essential element. Melody generates the poem out of itself by a continuous process. *The strophic form of the folk-song* points to the same thing; a phenomenon which I had always beheld with astonishment, until at last I found this explanation. Any one who in accordance with this theory examines a collection of folk-songs, such as *Des Knaben Wunderhorn,* will find innumerable instances of the way the continuously generating melody scatters picture sparks all around, which in their variegation, their abrupt change, their mad precipitation, manifest a power quite unknown to the epic and its steady flow. From the standpoint of the epos, this unequal and irregular pictorial world of lyric poetry is definitely to be condemned: and it certainly has been thus condemned by the solemn epic rhapsodists of the Apollonian festivals in the age of Terpander.

Accordingly, we observe that in the poetry of the folk-song, language is strained to its utmost that it may *imitate music;* and hence with Archilochus begins a new world of poetry, which is basically opposed to the Homeric. And in saying this we have indicated the only possible relation between poetry and music, between word and tone: the word, the picture, the concept here seeks an expression analogous to music and now feels in itself the power of music. In this sense we may discriminate between two main currents in the history of the language of the Greek people, according to whether their language imitated the world of image and phenomenon, or the world of music. One need only reflect more deeply on the linguistic difference with regard to color, syntactical structure, and vocabulary in Homer and Pindar, in order to understand the significance of this contrast; indeed, it becomes palpably clear that in the period between Homer and Pindar there must have sounded out the *orgiastic flute tones of Olympus,* which, even in Aristotle's time, when music was infinitely more developed, transported people to drunken ecstasy, and which, in their primitive state of development, undoubtedly incited to imitation all the poetic means of expression of contemporaneous man. I here call attention to a familiar phenomenon of our own times, against which our esthetic raises many objections. We again and again have occasion to observe that a Beethoven symphony compels its individual auditors to use figurative speech in describing it, no matter how fantastically variegated and even contradictory may be the composition and make-up of the different pictorial world produced by a piece of music. To exercise its poor wit on such compositions, and to overlook a phenomenon which is certainly worth explaining, is quite in keeping with this esthetic. Indeed, even when the tone-poet expresses his composition in pictures, when for instance he designates a certain symphony as the "pastoral" symphony, or a passage in it as the "scene by the brook," or another as the "merry gathering of rustics," these too are only symbolical representations born of music—and not perhaps the imitated objects of music—representations which can teach us nothing whatsoever concerning the *Dionysian* content of music, and which indeed have no distinctive value of their own beside other pictorial expressions. We have now to transfer this process of a discharge of music in pictures to some fresh, youthful, linguistically creative people, in order to get a notion of how the strophic faculty of speech is stimulated by this new principle of the imitation of music.

If, therefore, we may regard lyric poetry as the fulguration of music in images and concepts, we should now ask: "In what form does music *appear* in the mirror of symbolism and conception?" *It appears as will,* taking the term in Schopenhauer's sense, i.e., as the antithesis of the esthetic, purely contemplative, and passive frame of mind. Here, however, we must make as sharp a distinction as possible between the concept of essence and the concept of phenomenon; for music, according to its essence, cannot possibly be will. To be will it would have to be wholly banished from the realm of art—for the will is the unesthetic-in-itself. Yet though *essentially* it is not will, *phenomenally* it *appears* as will. For in order to express the phenome-

non of music in images, the lyrist needs all the agitations of passion, from the whisper of mere inclination to the roar of madness. Impelled to speak of music in Apollonian symbols, he conceives of all nature, and himself therein, only as eternal Will, Desire, Longing. But in so far as he interprets music by means of images, he himself rests in the quiet calm of Apollonian contemplation, though everything around him which he beholds through the medium of music may be confused and violent. Indeed, when he beholds himself through this same medium, his own image appears to him as an unsatisfied feeling: his own willing, longing, moaning, rejoicing, are to him symbols by which he interprets music. This is the phenomenon of the lyrist: as Apollonian genius he interprets music through the image of the will, while he himself, completely released from the desire of the will, is the pure, undimmed eye of day.

Our whole discussion insists that lyric poetry is dependent on the spirit of music just as music itself in its absolute sovereignty does not need the picture and the concept, but merely *endures* them as accompaniments. The poems of the lyrist can express nothing which did not already lie hidden in the vast universality and absoluteness of the music which compelled him to figurative speech. Language can never adequately render the cosmic symbolism of music, because music stands in symbolic relation to the primordial contradiction and primordial pain in the heart of the Primal Unity, and therefore symbolizes a sphere which is beyond and before all phenomena. Rather are all phenomena, compared with it, merely symbols: hence *language,* as the organ and symbol of phenomena, can never, by any means, disclose the innermost heart of music; language, in its attempt to imitate it, can only be in superficial contact with music; while the deepest significance of the latter cannot with all the eloquence of lyric poetry be brought one step nearer to us.

CONRAD FIEDLER

(1841-1895)

Conrad Fiedler was born into a prosperous family in Saxony. At their urging he prepared himself at Heidelberg and elsewhere for a legal career, and he practiced law for a year. Thereafter he departed on a tour of Italy, the Near East, Greece, Egypt, Spain, France, and England. In Italy he found intellectually congenial companions in the young sculptor Adolf Hildebrand, the painter Anselm Feuerbach, and especially the painter Hans von Marées. Fiedler's subsequent career moved between the poles of Rome and Munich, two cities dear to the painters of the important late-nineteenth-century German school.

In Fiedler we have the rarity of a born art theorist, not just an artist *manqué*, or a philosopher rounding out a system. Fiedler's friendship with Marées was particularly remarkable in that the art philosopher participated in the development of an uncommonly talented painter on terms of professional intimacy and friendship, and the artist truly sought clarification of his aims by following a theoretician's lead. Both were utterly serious and devoted to their tasks. Not only did Fiedler dedicate his life and thoughts to the service of art (especially visual art), but he devoted large portions of his considerable fortune to support men such as Marées by purchasing their work.

Fiedler is plainly the source of much of Benedetto Croce's teaching on the relation between intuition and expression and on the ultimate cognitive character of art. This is clear from Fiedler's *Reality and Art, Aphorisms,* and the *Origin of Artistic Activity,* none of which has been translated into English. Fiedler thinks of art as the complement of science in the pursuit of *Erkenntnis,* or knowledge of the world. He regards the "aesthetic" side of art as trivial by comparison. The aesthetic side is but the stimulation of feelings of pleasure that, for the greater part, constitute the source of the mass appeal of art. And, says Fiedler, since works of art are not created by feelings, feelings do not suffice for the understanding of art. Neither is beauty everywhere and always the aim of the artist. The great northern artist, Dürer or Rembrandt, seeks something other than beauty. It is not the artist's duty to embrace the trivial aim of pleasing us. The sterner aspect of art looms great in Fiedler's interpretation and eventually covers the entire field that Kant divides into the beautiful and the sublime and Bosanquet into easy and difficult beauty.

What is especially refreshing in Fiedler is his concentration on creativity in art. His concern with this creativity caused him to ponder deeply the thought and activity of men such as Marées. Aesthetics has been oriented almost completely toward the spectator or observer, whose reactions and judgments have been painfully examined with all the apparatus of psychology and linguistic analysis. But art, Fiedler says, cannot be understood merely from its effects upon us. The essay included here would seem from its title to be devoted to the spectator's response, but its particular aim is not to show how the spectator judges but to teach him how to do so in terms of the primordial reality of this subject, the *artist's* response. In Fiedler what we call "aesthetics" is almost wholly "the philosophy of art."

CONRAD FIEDLER

On Judging Works of Visual Art

(Translated by Henry Schaefer-Simmern and Fulmer Mood)

From On Judging Works of Visual Art, *Henry Schaefer-Simmern and Fulmer Mood, trans. Berkeley, Cal.: University of California Press, 1949. Reprinted by permission of the University of California Press. (First published: 1876.)*

The understanding of art [is possible only in terms of art itself]. Only if we see the world before us in terms of the particular interest of the artist can we succeed in reaching an understanding of works of art that is founded solely on the innermost essence of artistic activity. In order to be able to grasp the artist's concern with the visible world it is well to remember that man's interest in appearances is divided into two principal types.[1] They start from perceptual experience but soon come into opposition to each other. It is to the independent and free development of perceptual experience that we must look for the peculiar power of artistic talent.

Man's ways of relating himself to the world by means of his sensibilities can be different in kind and degree. There are infinite gradations between dullness and indifference and the highest sensitivity. Many persons face objects with a sense of strangeness and are unable to establish any relationship with them; in their dependence upon their own inadequate sensibilities they are inaccessible to the power of visual phenomena, and rightly one regards this

---

[1] [Fiedler seeks to distinguish abstract, conceptual thought through the sciences from the intuitive grasp of the world through the arts. For the latter he uses several descriptions which are rendered as "visual conception" or "conceiving" in this translation.—ED. NOTE.]

unresponsiveness as a deficiency in the individual organization. Others, because their nature is richer and more highly refined, are more receptive to the visible world. And while the former, as it were, lack the organs by which they can grasp the qualities of things, the latter, at least now and then, are aware that they are being exposed to the influences of these qualities; they do not sink to the completely indifferent state, but neither do they rise above an occasional partial and limited sensitivity to things. Thus, one may feel beauty vividly, yet will always be touched by a single quality, whereas the complete object, whether beautiful or not, remains alien to him. It is the rare privilege of highly organized, sensitive persons that they can achieve immediate contact with nature. Their relation to an object does not arise from single effects; on the contrary, they grasp its very existence, and they feel the object as a whole even before they break up this general feeling into many separate sensations. For such persons as these there is a pleasure and a delight in the vital existence of things far above such differences as the beautiful and the ugly: it is a grasping not of single qualities but of all nature itself, which later on turns out to be the carrier of those many separate qualities. Such feelings for the single qualities of things, as well as that feeling for nature as a whole above and beyond the sensitive apprehension of its single qualities, can attain high degrees of intensity within persons at given moments. It rises to fervor and to ecstasy and forms the basis of passionate personal enthusiasms.

Sensation cannot be conceived apart from perception [i.e., the experience of the senses]. Yet it is questionable whether an increase in sensation also means an increase in perceptual comprehension. Sensation already occurs with perception that is little developed. The strength of sensation depends on the susceptibility of our feelings and not on the amount of our perceptual experiences. Indeed, if we watch ourselves closely we shall find that our sensation does not stimulate and further, but rather hinders, the growth of our visual conceptions. Our feeling is something else than our visual conceiving, and if the former dominates then the latter must step back. For example, in sensing the beauty of a particular object we may occupy ourselves with this sensation entirely, without proceeding a single step toward the perceptual mastering of the object. However, at that moment when interest based on visual conception takes hold of us again, we must be able to forget every sensation in order to further our perceptual grasp of the object for its own sake. Because many persons are all too quick to transform perceptual experience into feeling, their perceptual abilities remain on a low level of development.

It is a chief requirement of artistic talent that it shall possess an especially refined and sensitive susceptibility to certain qualities of things. In preëminent artists we may, indeed, occasionally meet with that profound relationship, mentioned earlier, of sensation and of a feeling for the totality of natural objects. But the presence of such refined feelings is not yet an indication of artistic talent. To possess such feelings is the main prerequisite for artistic as well as for every other mental productiveness; for he who does not seek to grasp nature with the power of his intuition will never succeed in subjugating her to his higher mental consciousness. But the artist becomes an artist by virtue of his ability to rise above his sensations. It is true that sensation accompanies him in all the phases of his artistic activity and keeps him continuously in a close relation to all things, that it nourishes in him the warmth of life by which he himself is connected with the world. Sensation continuously provides him with the material the transformation of which is the fulfillment of his mental existence. Yet, however heightened his sensations may be, he must always be able to master them with the clarity of his mind. And although the artist's creation is possible only on the basis of an extraordinarily intense feeling, nevertheless this artistic creation has been made possible by his still more extraordinary power of mind, which even in moments of the most intense sensory experience preserves unimpaired the calmness of objective interest and the energy of formative creation.

In abstract cognition we possess the means of subordinating appearances to certain demands of our thinking faculties, and thus of appropriating them for ourselves by transforming them into concepts. We exercise these faculties thousands of times without being aware of it. We consciously increase this ability when we are driven by our higher intellectual needs to comprehend the world. This is the process which leads us to the conceptual mastery of the world. Although the process is familiar to us, it is nevertheless a mysterious one, for by means of it a sudden inexplicable transition takes place from sensuous to nonsensuous, from visible to invisible, from perception to abstraction, from that which is seen to that which is a concept of the seen.

In times when science offers explanations of the world, and interest in those explanations not only possesses the most gifted minds but also penetrates all educated circles, we meet with the general opinion, first, that outward appearances of objects are unessential as compared to the inner meanings which scientific knowledge tries to draw out of them; and second, that science has already arrived at a complete understanding of the external appearance of objects and looks upon this knowledge as no more than a preliminary stage on the way to its own higher knowledge.

But how can we differentiate between essential and unessential when speaking of objects of nature? Such judgments are relative, changing with one's standpoint. And if only that seems essential upon which for the time being one is concentrating his contemplative gaze, one has no more than a subjective right to declare that other aspects of objects of nature are unessential.

As to the second point, it must be noted that scientific observation is by no means based upon complete perception. In scientific observation, perception can be of interest and value only so far as it makes possible the transition to abstract concepts, and this transition occurs on a comparatively low level. Already, in everyday life, man clings to perception only until the transition to abstract thinking becomes possible for him. He repeats this process innumerable times, and every perceptual experience vanishes as soon as, by means of his conceptual thinking, he draws out of perception that which all too often he believes to be its one and only essential content. Scientific observation would completely lose its way if outward appearances in themselves had value for it and if it stopped with them and did not advance to the creation of concepts. In remaining at the stage of perception one would soon face a rich profusion of experience which no concept could ever denote and encompass. Of all sciences, natural science is the most dependent upon the exact observation of the shapes and mutations of objects as well as the relationships between the parts and the whole. He who must with exactness observe objects with respect to their outward appearance, memorize them and make them his own in order to draw conclusions from his mental picture of them, would not admit that visual perception extends far beyond his own special purpose. But those persons who require for scientific purposes a rich perception of nature know that a tendency for abstract thinking makes the understanding of perception difficult. The more they advance in transforming perception into abstract concepts, the more incapable they become of remaining, even for a short while, at the stage of perception. And if they judge a work of art by the yardstick of their knowledge of nature and consider it to be a copy of nature, the meagerness of their perception of nature reveals itself at once in the insufficiency of their demands upon works of art. They believe that they are able to check upon the artist's knowledge of nature, transfer their way of looking at nature to the artistic imitation of nature, and see in it essentially nothing but a scientific illustration of conceptual abstraction. In effect, since a work of art would thereby be reduced to a mere instrument of evoking perceptions and of dissecting nature as a whole into isolated fragments and features in order to make more readily recognizable that which in the world of complicated appearances is difficult to grasp, they would thus ignore perception entirely in order to find the meaning of art.

Finally, even if one must admit that perceptual experience cannot be entirely transformed into abstract concepts, and that concepts derive from perception and therefore cannot be wholly given up, the scientific investigator will, nevertheless, always consider a perceptual activity inferior if it does not lead to clear concepts dominating perception. Although he may have grasped the world in his own way and thereby fulfilled the needs of his mind, he nevertheless errs if he believes that through abstract thinking alone all the intellectual capacities of human nature have been recognized and fulfilled. To remain at the stage of perception rather than to pass onward to the stage of abstraction does not mean remaining on a level which does not lead to the realm of cognition; on the contrary, it means to keep open other roads that also arrive at cognition. But if cognition attained by perceptual experience is different from cognition reached by abstract thinking, it can nevertheless be a true and final cognition.

Among different persons, we can notice even in their early youth different mental attitudes: some endeavor to draw concepts from their sensory experience and direct their attention to the inner causal connections between appearances, while others,

less concerned with these hidden connections, exercise their mental powers in the contemplation of the outward conditions of the visible world. Either way, it is a gift of observation that reveals itself quite early in distinguished men. But these different kinds of observation manifest different relations to the world. And as some persons, if really gifted, do not stop short with a desire for dry and barren knowledge, so others will be led beyond the desire to know the things transmitted to them by perception into an activity by which they begin to approach and to grasp the entire world of appearances.

However, the fallacy is widely diffused that by means of science man may be able to subjugate the world in accordance with the demands and faculties of abstract cognition so that he may hope to become capable of possessing the world mentally as it actually is. And although man admits that the solutions of the tasks assigned to science are infinitely remote, he still knows, even if these solutions can never be reached, that they lie at the end of the road on which he travels. But there is one thing that man is not always clear about: even should science reach its most distant aims and realize its boldest dreams, even should science grasp the entire essence of the world scientifically, we still would have to face riddles the very existence of which would be hidden from all science. The struggle for the conquest of nature, led by the scientist, results in his becoming the scientific conquerer of the world. This makes him vastly arrogant; yet he cannot prevent other persons from thinking that for them but little has been accomplished by the achievements of science, and they on their part may feel a peremptory desire to submit the world to an absolutely different process of mental appropriation.

As a rule, everyone will think that his way of making the world intelligible to himself is the most important way. Nature is very stingy in the procreation of individuals who, being endowed abundantly with all mental faculties, are able to express the multifarious content of the world. There are many who seek versatility by submitting many objects to one mode of contemplation; but there are few who can be versatile in submitting one object to many modes of contemplation.

Each time that sensation is awakened and abstract concepts appear, perception [i.e., pure sensory experience] vanishes. The quanta of perceptual experience that lead both to sensations and to concepts differ greatly, but even the largest quantum is small in contrast to the infinitude of perceptual experiences available to man. Only he who is able to hold onto his perceptual experiences in spite of both sensation and abstraction proves his artistic calling. It is rare, however, that perceptual experience attains independent development and impartial existence.

Man's sensitivity varies enormously with sex, natural gifts, age, and time; also, the quanta of concepts and abstract knowledge that he possesses vary widely. It is enough to remind oneself of simple, well-known facts in order to certify that in single individuals there is likewise a great variation in types and quanta of visual conceptions. And usually there is a low degree of development of the faculty of visual conceiving. Even if we were misled by assuming that persons equally gifted with the same keen senses and using them in identical surroundings would arrive at visual conceptions of the same quality, we should soon learn that the visual conception of each would be entirely different. The truth of this statement would be apparent the moment an argument should begin about the outward appearance of even a very simple object of daily use—an argument in which everyone would be forced to give an account of his memory image of that object. Rarely do visual conceptions mature to a stage of independent clarity. Knowledge of even a simple object is generally limited to the aspects common to the type, and rarely does such knowledge extend to the special peculiarities pertaining to that individualized object. Whenever we are long surrounded by particular objects, these become so impressed upon our memories that we notice immediately any slight change in their shapes, or their replacement by other objects, however small the differences in these may be. Yet we have only to change the conditions under which these objects were familiar to us in order to prove that the knowledge of which we seemed so certain is not certain, that that knowledge suffices only as long as the original conditions remain. Is it not sometimes difficult to recognize the identity of persons, even though one has always been intimate with them?

Of objects offered to his perceptions, man mostly acquires images that are composed of but a few of all the possible elements which objects actually present to his faculties of perception. This is not merely the fault of the reproductive memory, which is unable to keep a clear, complete image for a long time after the object is no longer present; rather it is the fault of the original act of perception itself, which was incomplete. Thus man carries on his visual perceptive experience in a very neglectful way. Generally he shows himself more inclined to extend his abstract knowing than his visual knowledge. Also, everyday life puts to the test much more frequently the extent and precision of a person's conceptual knowledge than the completeness of his visual conceptions. The total evaluation achieved by any one person is much more often founded upon his capacity for abstract knowing than upon his ability for concrete conceiving.

Education has the task of fitting the intellectual powers of man to the needs of life. Education almost exclusively furthers the capacity for forming concepts. If in education more attention than usual is at times given to perceptual experience, this additional attention is likely to be superfluous and may even be harmful if perception is given more room in the curriculum only as a means of attaining concepts. There is no need of special devices that will bring perception near to man. However strong and well trained man's thinking faculty may be, he will always find himself confronted with an infinite task if he has to master all the perceptual experiences which life inescapably presents to him. The more independent and self-reliant man's abstract thinking faculties are trained to become, the more powerful tools they will be in contrast to perceptual experience. The demand that more attention be paid to perception in man's education would only be justified if it were understood that, for man, perception is something of independent importance apart from all abstraction and that the capacity for concrete perceiving has as strong a claim to be developed by regular and conscious use as the capacity for abstract thinking has. It should be understood that man can attain the mental mastery of the world not only by the creation of concepts but also by the creation of visual conceptions.

Almost everywhere, however, the capacity of perceiving decays, becoming restricted to an almost unintentional casual use. Even persons who have but a very limited knowledge of the world, because their mental capacities are limited or because they must maintain themselves by manual occupations, nevertheless understand the meaning of the necessity that the human mind must grasp the world conceptually. They at least know the necessity that lies behind the questions which scientific research seeks to answer. Thus the infinite, before which man with his longing and striving for knowledge stands, will occasionally become clear to them. In contrast, those who restlessly enlarge their funds of abstract knowledge will only with difficulty grasp the fact that man with his mental capacities also stands face to face with an infinity in his percep-

tual experience and that the realm of the visible world can also be a field of investigation. For these it will be difficult to understand that even to the most eminent minds it is granted to take only some few steps toward the understanding of the visible world, and such efforts must appear immeasurable to those who endeavor to penetrate more and more into the comprehension of the visible.

Only he will be able to convince himself of the infinite possibilities for the visual comprehension of the world who has advanced to the free and independent use of his perceptive faculties.

As long as perception serves some purpose, it is limited, it is unfree. Whatever this purpose may be, perception remains a tool, and it becomes superfluous once the purpose is attained. If other mental activities should be recognized as justified only when employed for some definite explicit purpose, we would regard such an evaluation as a narrow-minded restriction. Man has ever felt an irresistible drive to make a free use of his powers, after once having found out that they are serviceable to the needs of life. Indeed, the products of the free use of mental capacities are honored as the highest of human achievements. That activity, however, which we should think the most natural one that man can engage in, namely, the grasping of the visible world, is a most complicated process. It is certain that man understands the necessity of educating himself to greater care in the observing of things and the memorizing of the acquired images. It is also certain that those purposes for which perception is a tool attain increased importance. Out of the drudgery of the daily needs of life, perception rises to the service of the noblest aspirations and becomes the tool of the highest efforts. But always, nevertheless, the aims of perception are predetermined and it terminates once the set goal is attained.

It is the essential characteristic of the artist's nature to be born with an ability in perceptual comprehension and to use that ability freely. To the artist, perceptual experience is from the beginning an impartial, free activity, which serves no purpose beyond itself and which ends in that purpose. Perceptual experiences alone can lead the artist to artistic configurations. To him the world is but a thing of appearances. He approaches it as a whole and endeavors to re-create it in a visual whole. The essence of the world which he tries to appropriate mentally and to subjugate to himself consists in the visible and tangible configuration of its objects. Thus we understand that to the artist perceptual experience can be endless, can have no aim or end fixed beyond itself. At the same time, also, we understand that to the artist perceptual experience must have immediate meaning, independent of any other purpose that can be produced by it.

The artist's relationship to the world, which to us remains incomprehensible as long as we as nonartists stand in our own relationship to the world, becomes intelligible to us once we consider the artist's relationship as a primary and peculiar connection between his powers of visual comprehension and the objects visually comprehended. And this relationship is based on a need which in turn is an attribute of man's spiritual nature. The origin and existence of art is based upon an immediate mastering of the visible world by a peculiar power of the human mind. Its significance consists solely in a particular form of activity by which man not only tries to bring the visible world into his consciousness, but even is forced to the attempt by his very nature. Thus the position in which the artist finds himself while confronting the world has not been chosen arbitrarily, but is determined by his own nature. The relation between himself and the objects is not a derived but an immediate one. The mental activity with which he opposes the world is not fortuitous, but necessary, and the product of

his mental activity will not be a subordinate and superfluous result, but a very high achievement, quite indispensable to the human mind if that mind does not want to cripple itself.

The artist's activity is often said to be a process of imitation. At the basis of this notion lie errors which beget new errors.

First, one can imitate an object only by making another which resembles it. But what agreement could exist between the copy and the object itself? The artist can take but very little from the quality of a model which makes it an object of nature. If he tries to imitate nature he will soon be compelled to combine in his copy some very different aspects of the natural object. He is on the way to encroaching upon nature's creative work—a childish, senseless enterprise, which often takes on the appearance of a certain ingenious boldness, usually based on absence of thought. Where efforts of this kind are concerned, the trivial objection is justified that art, so far as it is imitating nature, must remain far behind nature, and that imperfect imitation must appear as both useless and worthless since already we are amply supplied with originals.

Imitation which aims merely at copying outward appearances implies that one starts from the premise that there is in nature a substantial capital of minted and fixed forms at the disposal of the artist and that the copying of these forms is a purely mechanical activity. Hence arises the demand, on the one hand, that artistic imitation should serve higher purposes, that is, that it should be a means of expressing something independently existent, not in the realm of the visible but in the realm of the invisible; and on the other, that the artist in his imitations should represent nature purified, ennobled, perfected. Out of his own mastery he should make demands on the natural model; what nature offers should serve him as a basis for that which nature might be if he had been its creator.

Arrogance justifies itself and capriciousness becomes intellectual power. Man's unfettered imagination, inflated to vainglory, is taken to be artistic creative power. The artist is called upon to create another world beside and above the real one, a world freed from earthly conditions, a world in keeping with his own discretion. This realm of art opposes the realm of nature. It arrogates to itself a higher authority because it owes its existence to the human mind.

Artistic activity is neither slavish imitation nor arbitrary feeling; rather, it is free creative configuration. Anything that is copied must first of all have existed. But how should that nature which comes into being only through artistic representation have an existence outside of this production and prior to it? Even at the simplest, man must create his world in its visual forms; for we can say that nothing exists until it has entered into our discerning consciousness.

Who would dare to call science an imitation of nature? Yet one could do so with as much right as to call art an imitation. In science, however, one sees much more easily that it is simultaneously an investigation and a formulation, that it has no other meaning than to bring the world into a comprehensible and comprehended existence by means of man's mental nature. Scientific thinking is the natural, the necessary activity of man, as soon as he wakes up from a dull, animal-like state to a higher, clearer consciousness. Art as well as science is a kind of investigation, and science as well as art is a kind of mental configuration. Art as well as science necessarily appears at the moment when man is forced to create the world for his discerning consciousness.

The need of creating a scientifically comprehended world, and with it the possibility of producing such a world, arises only at a certain level of mental development. Likewise, art too becomes possible only at

that moment when the perceived world appears before man as something which can and should be lifted up to a rich and formed existence. It is the power of artistic phantasy that brings about this transformation. The phantasy of the artist is at bottom nothing else than the imaginative power which to a certain degree all of us need in order to get any grasp at all upon the world as a world of visible appearances.

But this power of ours is weak, and this world of ours remains poor and imperfect. Only where a powerful imagination with its indefatigable and sharp activity calls forth from the inexhaustible soil of the world elements after elements does man find himself suddenly confronted with a task immensely complicated, where before he has found his way without difficulty. It is phantasy that, looking far out round itself, summons together and conjures up on the narrowest ground the abundance of life which is withheld from dull minds. Through intuition one enters into a higher sphere of mental existence, thus perceiving the visible existence of things which in their endless profusion and their vacillating confusion man had taken for granted as simple and clear. Artistic activity begins when man finds himself face to face with the visible world as with something immensely enigmatical; when, driven by an inner necessity and applying the powers of his mind, he grapples with the twisted mass of the visible which presses in upon him and gives it creative form. In the creation of a work of art, man engages in a struggle with nature not for his physical but for his mental existence, because the gratification of his mental necessities also will fall to him solely as a reward for his strivings and his toil.

Thus it is that art has nothing to do with forms that are found ready-made prior to its activity and independent of it. Rather, the beginning and the end of artistic activity reside in the creation of forms which only thereby attain existence.

What art creates is no second world alongside the other world which has an existence without art; what art creates is the world, made by and for the artistic consciousness. And so it is that art does not deal with some materials which somehow have already become the mental possession of man; that which has already undergone some mental process is lost to art, because art itself is a process by which the mental possessions of man are immediately enriched. What excites artistic activity is that which is as yet untouched by the human mind. Art creates the form for that which does not yet in any way exist for the human mind and for which it contrives to create forms on behalf of the human mind. Art does not start from abstract thought in order to arrive at forms; rather, it climbs up from the formless to the formed, and in this process is found its entire mental meaning.

In the artist's mind a peculiar consciousness of the world is in process of development.

To some degree, everyone acquires that consciousness which, when developed to a higher level, becomes the artistic consciousness of the world. Every man harbors in his mind a world of forms and figures. His early consciousness is filled with the perceiving of visible objects. Before the capacities of forming concepts and of submitting the consequences of natural processes to the law of cause and effect have been developed in him, he stores his mind with the multifarious images of existing objects. He acquires and creates for himself the many-sided world, and the early substance of his mind is the consciousness of a visible, tangible world. Every child finds himself thus situated. To him the world is that which is visually apparent, so far as the world attains an existence through his mind. The child acquires a consciousness of the world and, even before he knows anything about it, before he can denote what it is by the expression "world,"

possesses the world. When other mental forces have grown in man and become active, and provide him with another consciousness, he very easily fails to appreciate that earlier consciousness by which he had been first awakened on entering life. He now believes that his early stage of existence was an unconscious one, like that of animals, when compared to the new consciousness of the world which he has attained. In mastering the world as a concept he believes that only thus does he possess it and that his early consciousness is doomed to decay. While he struggles to bring the world of concepts within himself to richer and clearer consciousness, the world of appearances remains for him scanty and obscure. He does not pass from a lower, unconscious stage to a higher, conscious one, but rather sacrifices the one for the sake of building up the other. He loses his world by acquiring it.

Had man's nature not been endowed with the artistic gift, an immense, an unending aspect of the world would have been lost to him, and would have remained lost. In the artist, a powerful impulse makes itself felt to increase, enlarge, display, and to develop toward a constantly growing clarity, that narrow, obscure consciousness with which he grasped the world at the first awakening of his mind. It is not the artist who has need of nature; nature much more has need of the artist. It is not that nature offers him something—which it offers as well to any other person; it is only that the artist knows how to use it differently. Moreover, through the activity of the artist, nature rather gains a richer and higher existence for him and for any other person who is able to follow him on his way. By comprehending and manifesting nature in a certain sense, the artist does not comprehend and manifest anything which could exist apart from his activity. His activity is much more an entirely creative one, and artistic production cannot in general be understood except as the creation of the world which takes place in the human consciousness and exclusively with respect to its visible appearance. An artistic consciousness comes into being in which solely the experience with appearances becomes important and leads to visual conception and in which everything steps back that is of other importance to man than the visual experience.

The mental life of the artist consists in constantly producing this artistic consciousness. This it is which is essentially artistic activity, the true artistic creation, of which the production of works of art is only an external result. Wherever men live, this activity appears. It is a necessary activity, not because men are in need of the effects produced as a consequence of it, but much more because man has been endowed with its power. Already, at a very low level of development, this faculty becomes active in very primitive individuals, be it ever so simple a manifestation. We can trace its existence back to where it does not yet manifest itself in a work of art. But it is not necessary for this activity to exist in a very high degree in order to outweigh the other sides of the mental nature and to imprint upon the individual the stamp of the predominantly artistic talent. From this point forward we discover an immense variety and gradation until we arrive at those rare appearances in which that power, risen to its highest degree, seems to be superhuman because it surpasses the common measure of human power.

The mental artistic activity of the artist has no result: the activity itself is the result. It expends itself every single moment in order to start afresh every following one. Only while his mind is active does man possess that to which he aspires. The clarity of consciousness toward which the individual advances at any given moment does not secure to him a lasting possession which he can enjoy at leisure. No; for each flash of consciousness vanishes at the moment at which it arises and so makes room

for a new one. Furthermore, the artist's mental activity is by no means constantly progressive and incessantly increasing. It reaches its culmination in a particular person at a single moment. His clouded consciousness of the world which is the substance of his mental existence rises, in happy moments, to clear mental images. But this momentary activity of the mind is the clear light that illuminates the world for him in a flash. In vain will he try to fix this flash. If he shall behold it again, he must re-create it himself. And just as this occurs in one person's life, so it occurs also in the life of mankind. Vainly do we flatter ourselves with the thought that the cognitive truth to which a single highly gifted person has penetrated is never lost to the world. With the individual, the individual's private cognition also passes away. No one possesses it who does not know how to re-create it anew. And often it happens that long years pass before nature produces individuals who can only just guess at the magnitude and the clarity of consciousness of their distant predecessors. Since Leonardo's time, who can boast of having seen, even from far away, the summits of this man's cognition of the world?

Artistic activity is endless. It is a continuous, incessant working of the mind to bring one's consciousness of the visible world to an ever richer development, to a configuration ever more complete. All the emotional forces serve this purpose, and all driving forces, passion, all enthusiasms, are of no avail to the artist if they are not harnessed in the service of this specific mental activity. Man allows form after form to emerge from the shapeless mass into his consciousness; yet, for all that, the mass still remains inexhaustible. It is not presumptuousness but shortsightedness to think that man's artistic activity could ever reach its ultimate, its highest aim. Only through artistic activity does man comprehend the visible world, and for as long as artistic activity has not disclosed them to his consciousness he does not know which regions are for him obscure and hidden. Whatever vantage points he has reached afford him views upon regions as yet unattained. And the more the artist extends his sway over the world, the more the limits of the visible world itself retreat before his eyes. The realm of appearance develops infinitely before him because it grows out of his ceaseless activity.

Artistic consciousness in its totality does not go beyond the limits of the individual; and it never finds a complete outward expression. A work of art is not the sum of the creative activity of the individual, but a fragmentary expression of something that cannot be totally expressed. The inner activity which the artist generates from the driving forces of his nature only now and then rises to expression as an artistic feat, and this feat does not represent the creative process in its entire course, but only a certain state. It affords views into the world of artistic consciousness by bringing from out of that world one formed work in a visible, communicable expression. This accomplishment does not exhaust, does not conclude this world, for just as infinite artistic activity precedes this feat, so can an infinite activity follow. "A good painter," says Dürer, "is inwardly full of figures, and if it were possible that he could live forever, he would have always something new from his inner stock of ideas, of which Plato writes, to pour forth through his works."

Although the mental activity of the artist can never fully express itself in the form of a work of art, it continuously strives toward expression and in a work of art it reaches for the moment its highest pitch. A work of art is the expression of artistic consciousness raised to a relative height. Artistic form is the immediate and sole expression of this consciousness. Not by roundabout ways does the artist arrive at the employment of the artistic form; he need not search for it in order to represent herein a content

which, born formless, is looking for a body in which it may find shelter. The artistic expression is much more immediate and necessary, and at the same time exclusive. A work of art is not an expression of something which can exist just as well without this expression. It is not an imitation of that figure as it lives within the artistic consciousness, since then the creation of a work of art would not be necessary for the artist; it is much more the artistic consciousness itself as it reaches its highest possible development in the single instance of one individual. The technical manipulation by which a work of art is contrived is a necessity for the artistic mind as soon as that mind feels the need of developing to the highest pitch that which dwells within it. Technical skill as such has no independent rights in the artistic process; it serves solely the mental process. Only when the mind is not able to govern the creative process does skill attain independent significance, importance, cultivation, and so becomes worthless artistically. From the very outset the mental processes of the artist must deal with nothing but that same substance which comes forth into visible appearance in the work of art itself. In a work of art the configurative activity finds its way to an externalized completion. The substance of such a work is nothing else than the creative configuration.

If we ask ourselves at what final, culminating point artistic endeavor should be fulfilled, we find that, as the human mind in general in its search for cognition cannot rest until convinced of the need of reaching such a culminating point, so the artist too is forced to cultivate his visual conception to the degree that that visual conception itself is absolutely necessary to him. Through the power of artistic imagination visual conception of the world grows ever richer in configurative forms. However, although we are compelled to admire this creative power that leads to breadth and variety, we must nevertheless acknowledge, if we are at all able to follow it so far, that the ability to bring each configuration to a complete artistic existence is the noblest artistic endeavor. Following along this path, the artist leaves behind him that which appearances had meant to him in various earlier stages of development. The more appearances are subjected to the powers of his artistic cognition, the more their qualities lose their power over him.

When the artist develops his visual conception to the point where "this way and no other" becomes a necessity for him, this process differs from that of the scientific investigator who regards a process of nature as a necessity. He who does not contemplate the world with the interest of the artist, if he at all feels the desire to take notice of the appearances of objects, attempts but to investigate the conditions of their origins. Only with difficulty, however, will he come to understand that there is a need of visually comprehending appearances as such, independently of a knowledge of their origins. To quote Goethe: "Thus a man, born and trained to the so-called exact sciences, will not easily conceive, at the height of his intelligence, that there could likewise exist a phantasy that is exact, without which art is essentially inconceivable." Very few persons feel any need of developing their visual conceptions to such a degree that these take on the character of necessity. However averse they may be to any unclearness and arbitrariness in their understanding of the internal relationships of the visible world, however strenuously they may strive to order this chaos of phenomena into a necessary whole, and however far they may have advanced in their endeavors, for them the visible world nevertheless remains a chaos in which the arbitrary rules. The artist, however, cannot acquiesce in such a state of affairs. Unconcerned with other things, he does not release his perceptual experiences until they are developed into a visual conception, clear in all its parts, something that has attained a complete, necessary existence. This is the highest stage to which his productive cognition can attain. Complete clearness and necessity have become one.

GEORGE SANTAYANA

(1863-1952)

Santayana was of Spanish birth and lineage, but, in consequence of his mother's first marriage, he was raised in Boston, and became a professor of philosophy at Harvard. At about the age of fifty he gave up teaching and thereafter, living abroad, devoted himself to writing. While he was still at Harvard, Santayana wrote *The Sense of Beauty* (1896) and the five-volume *Life of Reason: or The Phases of Human Progress* (1905–1906). His later philosophy is embodied in the brilliant *Scepticism and Animal Faith* (1923) and in the four volumes of *Realms of Being* (1927–1940). He produced much distinguished critical writing, including essays on Michelangelo and the Italian Platonists, Goethe, Shelley, Emerson, Whitman, Browning, and, above all, the brief, but memorable, *Three Philosophical Poets: Lucretius, Dante, and Goethe* (1910). Santayana remains one of the few very important philosophers of the first half of this century.

Santayana's writing, though it possesses a characteristically luminous style, is intense and compressed; there are few examples to assist the casual reader. By reading slowly and intensively, however, the reader should be able not only to comprehend what may at first seem an abstractly rhetorical style, but also to provide his own illustrations of Santayana's points.

The Sense of Beauty, although it contains many points that were original with Santayana, is primarily a summary of his reading in eighteenth-century English and nineteenth-century German aesthetics. Its usefulness is largely that it presents the tradition of modern aesthetics in lucid outline. Thus the second, third, and fourth chapters—on "The Materials of Beauty," "Form," and "Expression"—reflect the division of the cognitive powers into sensation, perception, and apperception (association of ideas), a division that was orthodox in philosophical psychology from Locke's time to that of James and Titchener.

In "The Nature of Beauty" Santayana proposes a *sub*jecti*vist* theory of value that reflects the influence of Hobbes, Spinoza, Hutcheson, and Hume; whereas his final definition—"Beauty is value, positive, intrinsic, and objectified"—betrays the influence of Kant in regard to *objectification*. After the reader has completed this selection, he will have encountered objectivist and subjectivist theories of aesthetic value, and he might at that point ask himself whether Santayana has been able to do justice to the merits of both theories and at the same time escape or resolve the difficulties in each.

GEORGE SANTAYANA

The Sense of Beauty

"The Nature of Beauty," from The Sense of Beauty. *New York: Charles Scribner's Sons, 1896. Reprinted by permission of Charles Scribner's Sons.*

The Nature of Beauty

§ THE PHILOSOPHY OF BEAUTY IS A
THEORY OF VALUES

It would be easy to find a definition of beauty that should give in a few words a telling paraphrase of the word. We know on excellent authority that beauty is truth, that it is the expression of the ideal, the symbol of divine perfection, and the sensible manifestation of the good. A litany of these titles of honour might easily be compiled, and repeated in praise of our divinity. Such phrases stimulate thought and give us a momentary pleasure, but they hardly bring any permanent enlightenment. A definition that should really define must be nothing less than the exposition of the origin, place, and elements of beauty as an object of human experience. We must learn from it, as far as possible, why, when, and how beauty appears, what conditions an object must fulfil to be beautiful, what elements of our nature make us sensible of beauty, and what the relation is between the constitution of the object and the excitement of our susceptibility. Nothing less will really define beauty or make us understand what aesthetic appreciation is. The definition of beauty in this sense will be the task of this whole book, a task that can be only very imperfectly accomplished within its limits.

371

The historical titles of our subject may give us a hint towards the beginning of such a definition. Many writers of the last century called the philosophy of beauty *Criticism,* and the word is still retained as the title for the reasoned appreciation of works of art. We could hardly speak, however, of delight in nature as criticism. A sunset is not criticised; it is felt and enjoyed. The word "criticism," used on such an occasion, would emphasize too much the element of deliberate judgment and of comparison with standards. Beauty, although often so described, is seldom so perceived, and all the greatest excellences of nature and art are so far from being approved of by a rule that they themselves furnish the standard and ideal by which critics measure inferior effects.

This age of science and of nomenclature has accordingly adopted a more learned word, *Aesthetics,* that is, the theory of perception or of susceptibility. If criticism is too narrow a word, pointing exclusively to our more artificial judgments, aesthetics seems to be too broad and to include within its sphere all pleasures and pains, if not all perceptions whatsoever. Kant used it, as we know, for his theory of time and space as forms of all perception; and it has at times been narrowed into an equivalent for the philosophy of art.

If we combine, however, the etymological meaning of criticism with that of aesthetics, we shall unite two essential qualities of the theory of beauty. Criticism implies judgment, and aesthetics perception. To get the common ground, that of perceptions which are critical, or judgments which are perceptions, we must widen our notion of deliberate criticism so as to include those judgments of value which are instinctive and immediate, that is, to include pleasures and pains; and at the same time we must narrow our notion of aesthetics so as to exclude all perceptions which are not appreciations, which do not find a value in their objects. We thus reach the sphere of critical or appreciative perception, which is, roughly speaking, what we mean to deal with. And retaining the word "aesthetics," which is now current, we may therefore say that aesthetics is concerned with the perception of values. The meaning and conditions of value are, then, what we must first consider.

Since the days of Descartes it has been a conception familiar to philosophers that every visible event in nature might be explained by previous visible events, and that all the motions, for instance, of the tongue in speech, or of the hand in painting, might have merely physical causes. If consciousness is thus accessory to life and not essential to it, the race of man might have existed upon the earth and acquired all the arts necessary for its subsistence without possessing a single sensation, idea, or emotion. Natural selection might have secured the survival of those automata which made useful reactions upon their environment. An instinct of self-preservation would have been developed, dangers would have been shunned without being feared, and injuries revenged without being felt.

In such a world there might have come to be the most perfect organization. There would have been what we should call the expression of the deepest interests and the apparent pursuit of conceived goods. For there would have been spontaneous and ingrained tendencies to avoid certain contingencies and to produce others; all the dumb show and evidence of thinking would have been patent to the observer. Yet there would surely have been no thinking, no expectation, and no conscious achievement in the whole process.

The onlooker might have feigned ends and objects of forethought, as we do in the case of the water that seeks its own level, or in that of the vacuum which nature abhors. But the particles of matter would have remained unconscious of their collocation, and all nature would have been insensible of their changing arrangement. We only, the possible spectators of that process, by virtue of our own interests and habits, could see any progress or culmination in it. We should see culmination where the result attained satisfied our practical or aesthetic demands, and progress wherever such a satisfaction was approached. But apart from ourselves, and our human bias, we can see in such a mechanical world no element of value whatever. In removing consciousness, we have removed the possibility of worth.

But it is not only in the absence of all consciousness that value would be removed from the world; by a less violent abstraction from the totality of human experience, we might conceive beings of a purely intellectual cast, minds in which the transformations of nature were mirrored without any emotion. Every event would then be noted, its relations would be observed, its recurrence might even be expected; but all this would happen without a shadow of desire, of pleasure, or of regret. No event would be repulsive, no situation terrible. We might, in a word, have a world of idea without a world of will. In this case, as completely as if consciousness were absent altogether, all value and excellence would be gone. So that for the existence of good in any form it is not merely consciousness but emotional consciousness that is needed. Observation will not do, appreciation is required.

§ PREFERENCE IS ULTIMATELY IRRATIONAL

We may therefore at once assert this axiom, important for all moral philosophy and fatal to certain stubborn incoherences of thought, that there is no value apart from some appreciation of it, and no good apart from some preference of it before its absence or its opposite. In appreciation, in preference, lies the root and essence of all excellence. Or, as Spinoza clearly expresses it, we desire nothing because it is good, but it is good only because we desire it.

It is true that in the absence of an instinctive reaction we can still apply these epithets by an appeal to usage. We may agree that an action is bad, or a building good, because we recognize in them a character which we have learned to designate by that adjective; but unless there is in us some trace of passionate reprobation or of sensible delight, there is no moral or aesthetic judgment. It is all a question of propriety of speech, and of the empty titles of things. The verbal and mechanical proposition, that passes for judgment of worth, is the great cloak of ineptitude in these matters. Insensibility is very quick in the conventional use of words. If we appealed more often to actual feeling, our judgments would be more diverse, but they would be more legitimate and instructive. Verbal judgments are often useful instruments of thought, but it is not by them that worth can ultimately be determined.

Values spring from the immediate and inexplicable reaction of vital impulse, and from the irrational part of our nature. The rational part is by its essence relative; it leads us from data to conclusions, or from parts to wholes; it never furnishes the data with which it works. If any preference or precept were declared to be ultimate and primitive, it would thereby be declared to be irrational, since mediation, inference, and synthesis are the essence of rationality. The ideal of rationality is itself as arbitrary, as much dependent on the needs of a finite organization, as any other ideal. Only as ultimately securing tranquillity of mind, which the philosopher instinctively pursues, has it for him any necessity. In spite of the verbal propriety of saying that reason demands rationality, what really demands rationality, what makes it a good and indispensable thing and gives it all its authority, is not its own nature, but our need of it both in safe and economical action and in the pleasures of comprehension.

It is evident that beauty is a species of value, and what we have said of value in general applies to this particular kind. A first approach to a definition of beauty has therefore been made by the exclusion of all intellectual judgments, all judgments of matter of fact or of relation. To substitute judgments of fact for judgments of value, is a sign of a pedantic and borrowed criticism. If we approach a work of art or nature scientifically, for the sake of its historical connexions or proper classification, we do not approach it aesthetically. The discovery of its date or of its author may be otherwise interesting; it only remotely affects our aesthetic appreciation by adding to the direct effect certain associations. If the direct effect were absent, and the object in itself uninteresting, the circumstances would be immaterial. Molière's *Misanthrope* says to the court poet who commends his sonnet as written in a quarter of an hour, *"Voyons, monsieur, le temps ne fait rien à l'affaire,"* and so we might say to the critic that sinks into the archaeologist, show us the work, and let the date alone.

In an opposite direction the same substitution of facts for values makes its appearance, whenever the reproduction of fact is made the sole standard of artistic excellence. Many half-trained observers condemn the work of some naïve or fanciful masters with a sneer, because, as they truly say, it is out of drawing. The implication is that to be correctly copied from a model is the prerequisite of all beauty. Correctness is, indeed, an element of effect and one which, in respect to familiar objects, is almost indispensable, because its absence would cause a disappointment and dissatisfaction incompatible with enjoyment. We learn to value truth more and more as our love and knowledge of nature increase. But fidelity is a merit only because it is in this way a factor in our pleasure. It stands on a level with all other ingredients of effect. When a man raises it to a solitary preeminence and becomes incapable of appreciating anything else, he betrays the decay of aesthetic capacity. The scientific habit in him inhibits the artistic.

That facts have a value of their own, at once complicates and explains this question. We are naturally pleased by every perception, and recognition and surprise are particularly acute sensations. When we see a striking truth in any imitation, we are therefore delighted, and this kind of pleasure is very legitimate, and enters into the best effects of all the representative arts. Truth and realism are therefore aesthetically good, but they are not all-sufficient, since the representation of everything is not equally pleasing and effective. The fact that resemblance is a source of satisfaction, justifies the critic in demanding it, while the aesthetic insufficiency of such veracity shows the different value of truth in science and in art. Science is the response to the demand for information, and in it we ask for the whole truth and nothing but the truth. Art is the response to the demand for entertainment, for the stimulation of our senses and imagination, and truth enters into it only as it subserves these ends.

Even the scientific value of truth is not, however, ultimate or absolute. It rests partly on practical, partly on aesthetic interests. As our ideas are gradually brought into conformity with the facts by the painful process of selection,—for intuition runs equally into truth and into error, and can settle nothing if not controlled by experience,—we gain vastly in our command over our environment. This is the fundamental value of natural science, and the fruit it is yielding in our day. We have no better vision of nature and life than some of our predecessors, but we have greater material resources. To know the truth about the composition and history of things is good for this reason. It is also good because of the enlarged horizon it gives us, because the spectacle of nature is a marvellous and fascinating one, full of a serious sadness and large peace, which gives us back our birthright as children of the planet and naturalizes us upon the earth. This is the poetic value of the scientific *Weltanschau-*

ung. From these two benefits, the practical and the imaginative, all the value of truth is derived.

Aesthetic and moral judgments are accordingly to be classed together in contrast to judgments intellectual; they are both judgments of value, while intellectual judgments are judgments of fact. If the latter have any value, it is only derivative, and our whole intellectual life has its only justification in its connexion with our pleasures and pains.

§ CONTRAST BETWEEN MORAL AND AESTHETIC VALUES

The relation between aesthetic and moral judgments, between the spheres of the beautiful and the good, is close, but the distinction between them is important. One factor of this distinction is that while aesthetic judgments are mainly positive, that is, perceptions of good, moral judgments are mainly and fundamentally negative, or perceptions of evil. Another factor of the distinction is that whereas, in the perception of beauty, our judgment is necessarily intrinsic and based on the character of the immediate experience, and never consciously on the idea of an eventual utility in the object, judgments about moral worth, on the contrary, are always based, when they are positive, upon the consciousness of benefits probably involved. Both these distinctions need some elucidation.

Hedonistic ethics have always had to struggle against the moral sense of mankind. Earnest minds, that feel the weight and dignity of life, rebel against the assertion that the aim of right conduct is enjoyment. Pleasure usually appears to them as a temptation, and they sometimes go so far as to make avoidance of it a virtue. The truth is that morality is not mainly concerned with the attainment of pleasure; it is rather concerned, in all its deeper and more authoritative maxims, with the prevention of suffering. There is something artificial in

the deliberate pursuit of pleasure; there is something absurd in the obligation to enjoy oneself. We feel no duty in that direction; we take to enjoyment naturally enough after the work of life is done, and the freedom and spontaneity of our pleasures is what is most essential to them.

The sad business of life is rather to escape certain dreadful evils to which our nature exposes us,—death, hunger, disease, weariness, isolation, and contempt. By the awful authority of these things, which stand like spectres behind every moral injunction, conscience in reality speaks, and a mind which they have duly impressed cannot but feel, by contrast, the hopeless triviality of the search for pleasure. It cannot but feel that a life abandoned to amusement and to changing impulses must run unawares into fatal dangers. The moment, however, that society emerges from the early pressure of the environment and is tolerably secure against primary evils, morality grows lax. The forms that life will farther assume are not to be imposed by moral authority, but are determined by the genius of the race, the opportunities of the moment, and the tastes and resources of individual minds. The reign of duty gives place to the reign of freedom, and the law and the covenant to the dispensation of grace.

The appreciation of beauty and its embodiment in the arts are activities which belong to our holiday life, when we are redeemed for the moment from the shadow of evil and the slavery to fear, and are following the bent of our nature where it chooses to lead us. The values, then, with which we here deal are positive; they were negative in the sphere of morality. The ugly is hardly an exception, because it is not the cause of any real pain. In itself it is rather a source of amusement. If its suggestions are vitally repulsive, its presence becomes a real evil towards which we assume a practical and moral attitude. And, correspondingly, the pleasant is never, as we have seen, the object of a truly moral injunction.

§ WORK AND PLAY

We have here, then, an important element of the distinction between aesthetic and moral values. It is the same that has been pointed to in the famous contrast between work and play. These terms may be used in different senses and their importance in moral classification differs with the meaning attached to them. We may call everything play which is useless activity, exercise that springs from the physiological impulse to discharge the energy which the exigencies of life have not called out. Work will then be all action that is necessary or useful for life. Evidently if work and play are thus objectively distinguished as useful and useless action, work is a eulogistic term and play a disparaging one. It would be better for us that all our energy should be turned to account, that none of it should be wasted in aimless motion. Play, in this sense, is a sign of imperfect adaptation. It is proper to childhood, when the body and mind are not yet fit to cope with the environment, but it is unseemly in manhood and pitiable in old age, because it marks an atrophy of human nature, and a failure to take hold of the opportunities of life.

Play is thus essentially frivolous. Some persons, understanding the term in this sense, have felt an aversion, which every liberal mind will share, to classing social pleasures, art, and religion under the head of play, and by that epithet condemning them, as a certain school seems to do, to gradual extinction as the race approaches maturity. But if all the useless ornaments of our life are to be cut off in the process of adaptation, evolution would impoverish instead of enriching our nature. Perhaps that is the tendency of evolution, and our barbarous ancestors amid their toils and wars, with their flaming passions and mythologies, lived better lives than are reserved to our well-adapted descendants.

We may be allowed to hope, however, that some imagination may survive parasitically even in the most serviceable brain. Whatever course history may take,—and we are not here concerned with prophecy,—the question of what is desirable is not affected. To condemn spontaneous and delightful occupations because they are useless for self-preservation shows an uncritical prizing of life irrespective of its content. For such a system the worthiest function of the universe should be to establish perpetual motion. Uselessness is a fatal accusation to bring against any act which is done for its presumed utility, but those which are done for their own sake are their own justification.

At the same time there is an undeniable propriety in calling all the liberal and imaginative activities of man play, because they are spontaneous, and not carried on under pressure of external necessity or danger. Their utility for self-preservation may be very indirect and accidental, but they are not worthless for that reason. On the contrary, we may measure the degree of happiness and civilization which any race has attained by the proportion of its energy which is devoted to free and generous pursuits, to the adornment of life and the culture of the imagination. For it is in the spontaneous play of his faculties that man finds himself and his happiness. Slavery is the most degrading condition of which he is capable, and he is as often a slave to the niggardness of the earth and the inclemency of heaven, as to a master or an institution. He is a slave when all his energy is spent in avoiding suffering and death, when all his action is imposed from without, and no breath or strength is left him for free enjoyment.

Work and play here take on a different meaning, and become equivalent to servitude and freedom. The change consists in the subjective point of view from which the distinction is now made. We no longer mean by work all that is done usefully, but only what is done unwillingly and by the spur of necessity. By play we are designating, no longer what is done fruitlessly, but whatever is done spontaneously and for its own sake, whether it have or not an ulterior utility. Play, in this sense, may be our most useful occupation. So far would a gradual adaptation to the environment be from making this play obsolete, that it would tend to abolish work, and to make play universal. For with the elimination of all the conflicts and errors of instinct, the race would do spontaneously whatever conduced to its welfare and we should live safely and prosperously without external stimulus or restraint.

§ ALL VALUES ARE IN ONE SENSE AESTHETIC

In this second and subjective sense, then, work is the disparaging term and play the eulogistic one. All who feel the dignity and importance of the things of the imagination, need not hesitate to adopt the classification which designates them as play. We point out thereby, not that they have no value, but that their value is intrinsic, that in them is one of the sources of all worth. Evidently all values must be ultimately intrinsic. The useful is good because of the excellence of its consequences; but these must somewhere cease to be merely useful in their turn, or only excellent as means; somewhere we must reach the good that is good in itself and for its own sake, else the whole process is futile, and the utility of our first object illusory. We here reach the second factor in our distinction, between aesthetic and moral values, which regards their immediacy.

If we attempt to remove from life all its evils, as the popular imagination has done at times, we shall find little but aesthetic pleasures remaining to constitute unalloyed happiness. The satisfaction of the passions and the appetites, in which we chiefly place earthly happiness, themselves take on an aesthetic tinge when we remove ideally the possibility of loss or variation. What could the Olympians honour in one another or

the seraphim worship in God except the embodiment of eternal attributes, of essences which, like beauty, make us happy only in contemplation? The glory of heaven could not be otherwise symbolized than by light and music. Even the knowledge of truth, which the most sober theologians made the essence of the beatific vision, is an aesthetic delight; for when the truth has no further practical utility, it becomes a landscape. The delight of it is imaginative and the value of it aesthetic.

This reduction of all values to immediate appreciations, to sensuous or vital activities, is so inevitable that it has struck even the minds most courageously rationalistic. Only for them, instead of leading to the liberation of aesthetic goods from practical entanglements and their establishment as the only pure and positive values in life, this analysis has led rather to the denial of all pure and positive goods altogether. Such thinkers naturally assume that moral values are intrinsic and supreme; and since these moral values would not arise but for the existence or imminence of physical evils, they embrace the paradox that without evil no good whatever is conceivable.

The harsh requirements of apologetics have no doubt helped them to this position, from which one breath of spring or the sight of one well-begotten creature should be enough to dislodge them. Their ethical temper and the fetters of their imagination forbid them to reconsider their original assumption and to conceive that morality is a means and not an end; that it is the price of human non-adaptation, and the consequence of the original sin of unfitness. It is the compression of human conduct within the narrow limits of the safe and possible. Remove danger, remove pain, remove the occasion of pity, and the need of morality is gone. To say "thou shalt not" would then be an impertinence.

But this elimination of precept would not be a cessation of life. The senses would still be open, the instincts would still operate, and lead all creatures to the haunts and occupations that befitted them. The variety of nature and the infinity of art, with the companionship of our fellows, would fill the leisure of that ideal existence. These are the elements of our positive happiness, the things which, amid a thousand vexations and vanities, make the clear profit of living.

§ AESTHETIC CONSECRATION OF
GENERAL PRINCIPLES

Not only are the various satisfactions which morals are meant to secure aesthetic in the last analysis, but when the conscience is formed, and right principles acquire an immediate authority, our attitude to these principles becomes aesthetic also. Honour, truthfulness, and cleanliness are obvious examples. When the absence of these virtues causes an instinctive disgust, as it does in well-bred people, the reaction is essentially aesthetic, because it is not based on reflection and benevolence, but on constitutional sensitiveness. This aesthetic sensitiveness is, however, properly enough called moral, because it is the effect of conscientious training and is more powerful for good in society than laborious virtue, because it is much more constant and catching. It is καλοκάγαθία, the aesthetic demand for the morally good, and perhaps the finest flower of human nature.

But this tendency of representative principles to become independent powers and acquire intrinsic value is sometimes mischievous. It is the foundation of the conflicts between sentiment and justice, between intuitive and utilitarian morals. Every human reform is the reassertion of the primary interests of man against the authority of general principles which have ceased to represent those interests fairly, but which still obtain the idolatrous veneration of mankind. Nor are chivalry and religion alone liable to fall into this moral superstition. It arises wherever an abstract

good is substituted for its concrete equivalent. The miser's fallacy is the typical case, and something very like it is the ethical principle of half our respectable population. To the exercise of certain useful habits men come to sacrifice the advantage which was the original basis and justification of those habits. Minute knowledge is pursued at the expense of largeness of mind, and riches at the expense of comfort and freedom.

This error is all the more specious when the derived aim has in itself some aesthetic charm, such as belongs to the Stoic idea of playing one's part in a vast drama of things, irrespective of any advantage thereby accruing to any one; somewhat as the miser's passion is rendered a little normal when his eye is fascinated not merely by the figures of a bank account, but by the glitter of the yellow gold. And the vanity of playing a tragic part and the glory of conscious self-sacrifice have the same immediate fascination. Many irrational maxims thus acquire a kind of nobility. An object is chosen as the highest good which has not only a certain representative value, but also an intrinsic one,—which is not merely a method for the realization of other values, but a value in its own realization.

Obedience to God is for the Christian, as conformity to the laws of nature or reason is for the Stoic, an attitude which has a certain emotional and passionate worth, apart from its original justification by maxims of utility. This emotional and passionate force is the essence of fanaticism, it makes imperatives categorical, and gives them absolute sway over the conscience in spite of their one-sidedness and their injustice to the manifold demands of human nature.

Obedience to God or reason can originally recommend itself to a man only as the surest and ultimately least painful way of balancing his aims and synthesizing his desires. So necessary is this sanction even to the most impetuous natures, that no martyr would go to the stake if he did not believe that the powers of nature, in the day of judgment, would be on his side. But the human mind is a turbulent commonwealth, and the laws that make for the greatest good cannot be established in it without some partial sacrifice, without the suppression of many particular impulses. Hence the voice of reason or the command of God, which makes for the maximum ultimate satisfaction, finds itself opposed by sundry scattered and refractory forces, which are henceforth denominated bad. The unreflective conscience, forgetting the vicarious source of its own excellence, then assumes a solemn and incomprehensible immediacy, as if its decrees were absolute and intrinsically authoritative, not of to-day or yesterday, and no one could tell whence they had arisen. Instinct can all the more easily produce this mystification when it calls forth an imaginative activity full of interest and eager passion. This effect is conspicuous in the absolutist conscience, both devotional and rationalistic, as also in the passion of love. For in all these a certain individuality, definiteness, and exclusiveness is given to the pursued object which is very favourable to zeal, and the heat of passion melts together the various processes of volition into the consciousness of one adorable influence.

However deceptive these complications may prove to men of action and eloquence, they ought not to impose on the critic of human nature. Evidently what value general goods do not derive from the particular satisfactions they stand for, they possess in themselves as ideas pleasing and powerful over the imagination. This intrinsic advantage of certain principles and methods is none the less real for being in a sense aesthetic. Only a sordid utilitarianism that subtracts the imagination from human nature, or at least slurs over its immense contribution to our happiness, could fail to give these principles the preference over others practically as good.

If it could be shown, for instance, that monarchy was as apt, in a given case, to secure the public well-being as some other form of government, monarchy should be preferred, and would undoubtedly be established, on account of its imaginative and dramatic superiority. But if, blinded by this somewhat ethereal advantage, a party sacrificed to it important public interests, the injustice would be manifest. In a doubtful case, a nation decides, not without painful conflicts, how much it will sacrifice to its sentimental needs. The important point is to remember that the representative or practical value of a principle is one thing, and its intrinsic or aesthetic value is another, and that the latter can be justly counted only as an item in its favour to be weighed against possible external disadvantages. Whenever this comparison and balancing of ultimate benefits of every kind is angrily dismissed in favour of some absolute principle, laid down in contempt of human misery and happiness, we have a personal and fantastic system of ethics, without practical sanctions. It is an evidence that the superstitious imagination has invaded the sober and practical domain of morals.

§ AESTHETIC AND PHYSICAL PLEASURE

We have now separated with some care intellectual and moral judgments from the sphere of our subject, and found that we are to deal only with perceptions of value, and with these only when they are positive and immediate. But even with these distinctions the most remarkable characteristic of the sense of beauty remains undefined. All pleasures are intrinsic and positive values, but all pleasures are not perceptions of beauty. Pleasure is indeed the essence of that perception, but there is evidently in this particular pleasure a complication which is not present in others and which is the basis of the distinction made by consciousness and language between it and the rest. It will be instructive to notice the degrees of this difference.

The bodily pleasures are those least resembling perceptions of beauty. By bodily pleasures we mean, of course, more than pleasures with a bodily seat; for that class would include them all, as well as all forms and elements of consciousness. Aesthetic pleasures have physical conditions, they depend on the activity of the eye and the ear, of the memory and the other ideational functions of the brain. But we do not connect those pleasures with their seats except in physiological studies; the ideas with which aesthetic pleasures are associated are not the ideas of their bodily causes. The pleasures we call physical, and regard as low, on the contrary, are those which call our attention to some part of our own body, and which make no object so conspicuous to us as the organ in which they arise.

There is here, then, a very marked distinction between physical and aesthetic pleasure; the organs of the latter must be transparent, they must not intercept our attention, but carry it directly to some external object. The greater dignity and range of aesthetic pleasure is thus made very intelligible. The soul is glad, as it were, to forget its connexion with the body and to fancy that it can travel over the world with the liberty with which it changes the objects of its thought. The mind passes from China to Peru without any conscious change in the local tensions of the body. This illusion of disembodiment is very exhilarating, while immersion in the flesh and confinement to some organ gives a tone of grossness and selfishness to our consciousness. The generally meaner associations of physical pleasures also help to explain their comparative crudity.

§ THE DIFFERENTIA OF AESTHETIC
PLEASURE NOT ITS
DISINTERESTEDNESS

The distinction between pleasure and the sense of beauty has sometimes been said to consist in the unselfishness of aesthetic satisfaction. In other pleasures, it is said, we gratify our senses and passions; in the contemplation of beauty we are raised above ourselves, the passions are silenced and we are happy in the recognition of a good that we do not seek to possess. The painter does not look at a spring of water with the eyes of a thirsty man, nor at a beautiful woman with those of a satyr. The difference lies, it is urged, in the impersonality of the enjoyment. But this distinction is one of intensity and delicacy, not of nature, and it seems satisfactory only to the least aesthetic minds.[1]

In the second place, the supposed disinterestedness of aesthetic delights is not very fundamental. Appreciation of a picture is not identical with the desire to buy it, but it is, or ought to be, closely related and preliminary to that desire. The beauties of nature and of the plastic arts are not consumed by being enjoyed; they retain all the efficacy to impress a second beholder. But this circumstance is accidental, and those aesthetic objects which depend upon change and are exhausted in time, as are all performances, are things the enjoyment of which is an object of rivalry and is coveted as much as any other pleasure. And even plastic beauties can often not be enjoyed

---

[1] Schopenhauer, indeed, who makes much of it, was a good critic, but his psychology suffered much from the pessimistic generalities of his system. It concerned him to show that the will was bad, and, as he felt beauty to be a good if not a holy thing, he hastened to convince himself that it came from the suppression of the will. But even in his system this suppression is only relative. The desire of individual objects, indeed, is absent in the perception of beauty, but there is still present that initial love of the general type and principles of things which is the first illusion of the absolute, and drives it on to the fatal experiment of creation. So that, apart from Schopenhauer's mythology, we have even in him the recognition that beauty gives satisfaction to some dim and underlying demand of our nature, just as particular objects give more special and momentary pleasures to our individualized wills. His psychology was, however, far too vague and general to undertake an analysis of those mysterious feelings.

except by a few, on account of the necessity of travel or other difficulties of access, and then this aesthetic enjoyment is as selfishly pursued as the rest.

The truth which the theory is trying to state seems rather to be that when we seek aesthetic pleasures we have no further pleasure in mind; that we do not mix up the satisfactions of vanity and proprietorship with the delight of contemplation. This is true, but it is true at bottom of all pursuits and enjoyments. Every real pleasure is in one sense disinterested. It is not sought with ulterior motives, and what fills the mind is no calculation, but the image of an object or event, suffused with emotion. A sophisticated consciousness may often take the idea of self as the touchstone of its inclinations; but this self, for the gratification and aggrandizement of which a man may live, is itself only a complex of aims and memories, which once had their direct objects, in which he had taken a spontaneous and unselfish interest. The gratifications which, merged together, make the selfishness are each of them ingenuous, and no more selfish than the most altruistic, impersonal emotion. The content of selfishness is a mass of unselfishness. There is no reference to the nominal essence called oneself either in one's appetites or in one's natural affections; yet a man absorbed in his meat and drink, in his houses and lands, in his children and dogs, is called selfish because these interests, although natural and instinctive in him, are not shared by others. The unselfish man is he whose nature has a more universal direction, whose interests are more widely diffused.

But as impersonal thoughts are such only in their object, not in their subject or agent, since all thoughts are the thoughts of somebody: so also unselfish interests have to be somebody's interests. If we were not interested in beauty, if it were of no concern to our happiness whether things were beautiful or ugly, we should manifest not the maxi-

mum, but the total absence of aesthetic faculty. The disinterestedness of this pleasure is, therefore, that of all primitive and intuitive satisfactions, which are in no way conditioned by a reference to an artificial general concept, like that of the self, all the potency of which must itself be derived from the independent energy of its component elements. I care about myself because "myself" is a name for the things I have at heart. To set up the verbal figment of personality and make it an object of concern apart from the interests which were its content and substance, turns the moralist into a pedant, and ethics into a superstition. The self which is the object of *amour propre* is an idol of the tribe, and needs to be disintegrated into the primitive objective interests that underlie it before the cultus of it can be justified by reason.

§ THE DIFFERENTIA OF AESTHETIC PLEASURE NOT ITS UNIVERSALITY

The supposed disinterestedness of our love of beauty passes into another characteristic of it often regarded as essential,—its universality. The pleasures of the senses have, it is said, no dogmatism in them; that anything gives me pleasure involves no assertion about its capacity to give pleasure to another. But when I judge a thing to be beautiful, my judgment means that the thing is beautiful in itself, or (what is the same thing more critically expressed) that it should seem so to everybody. The claim to universality is, according to this doctrine, the essence of the aesthetic; what makes the perception of beauty a judgment rather than a sensation. All aesthetic precepts would be impossible, and all criticism arbitrary and subjective, unless we admit a paradoxical universality in our judgment, the philosophical implications of which we may then go on to develope. But we are fortunately not required to enter the labyrinth into which this method leads; there is a much simpler and clearer way of studying such questions, which is to challenge and analyze the assertion before us and seek its basis in human nature. Before this is done, we should run the risk of expanding a natural misconception or inaccuracy of thought into an inveterate and pernicious prejudice by making it the centre of an elaborate construction.

That the claim of universality is such a natural inaccuracy will not be hard to show. There is notoriously no great agreement upon aesthetic matters; and such agreement as there is, is based upon similarity of origin, nature, and circumstance among men, a similarity which, where it exists, tends to bring about identity in all judgments and feelings. It is unmeaning to say that what is beautiful to one man *ought* to be beautiful to another. If their senses are the same, their associations and dispositions similar, then the same thing will certainly be beautiful to both. If their natures are different, the form which to one will be entrancing will be to another even invisible, because his classifications and discriminations in perception will be different, and he may see a hideous detached fragment or a shapeless aggregate of things, in what to another is a perfect whole—so entirely are the unities of objects unities of function and use. It is absurd to say that what is invisible to a given being *ought* to seem beautiful to him. Evidently this obligation of recognizing the same qualities is conditioned by the possession of the same faculties. But no two men have exactly the same faculties, nor can things have for any two exactly the same values.

What is loosely expressed by saying that any one ought to see this or that beauty is that he would see it if his disposition, training, or attention were what our ideal demands for him; and our ideal of what any one should be has complex but discoverable sources. We take, for instance, a certain pleasure in having our own judgments supported by those of others; we are intolerant, if not of the existence of a nature different

from our own, at least of its expression in words and judgments. We are confirmed or made happy in our doubtful opinions by seeing them accepted universally. We are unable to find the basis of our taste in our own experience and therefore refuse to look for it there. If we were sure of our ground, we should be willing to acquiesce in the naturally different feelings and ways of others, as a man who is conscious of speaking his language with the accent of the capital confesses its arbitrariness with gayety, and is pleased and interested in the variations of it he observes in provincials; but the provincial is always zealous to show that he has reason and ancient authority to justify his oddities. So people who have no sensations, and do not know why they judge, are always trying to show that they judge by universal reason.

Thus the frailty and superficiality of our own judgments cannot brook contradiction. We abhor another man's doubt when we cannot tell him why we ourselves believe. Our ideal of other men tends therefore to include the agreement of their judgments with our own; and although we might acknowledge the fatuity of this demand in regard to natures very different from the human, we may be unreasonable enough to require that all races should admire the same style of architecture, and all ages the same poets.

The great actual unity of human taste within the range of conventional history helps the pretension. But in principle it is untenable. Nothing has less to do with the real merit of a work of imagination than the capacity of all men to appreciate it; the true test is the degree and kind of satisfaction it can give to him who appreciates it most. The symphony would lose nothing if half mankind had always been deaf, as nine-tenths of them actually are to the intricacies of its harmonies; but it would have lost much if no Beethoven had existed. And more: incapacity to appreciate certain types of beauty may be the condition *sine qua non* for the appreciation of another kind; the greatest capacity both for enjoyment and creation is highly specialized and exclusive, and hence the greatest ages of art have often been strangely intolerant.

The invectives of one school against another, perverse as they are philosophically, are artistically often signs of health, because they indicate a vital appreciation of certain kinds of beauty, a love of them that has grown into a jealous passion. The architects that have pieced out the imperfections of ancient buildings with their own thoughts, like Charles V when he raised his massive palace beside the Alhambra, may be condemned from a certain point of view. They marred much by their interference; but they showed a splendid confidence in their own intuitions, a proud assertion of their own taste, which is the greatest evidence of aesthetic sincerity. On the contrary, our own gropings, eclecticism, and archaeology are the symptoms of impotence. If we were less learned and less just, we might be more efficient. If our appreciation were less general, it might be more real, and if we trained our imagination into exclusiveness, it might attain to character.

§ THE DIFFERENTIA OF AESTHETIC
  PLEASURE: ITS OBJECTIFICATION

There is, however, something more in the claim to universality in aesthetic judgments than the desire to generalize our own opinions. There is the expression of a curious but well-known psychological phenomenon, viz., the transformation of an element of sensation into the quality of a thing. If we say that other men should see the beauties we see, it is because we think those beauties *are in the object,* like its colour, proportion, or size. Our judgment appears to us merely the perception and discovery of an external existence, of the real excellence that is without. But this notion is radically absurd and contradictory. Beauty, as we have seen, is a value; it cannot be conceived as an in-dependent existence which affects our senses and which we consequently perceive. It exists in perception, and cannot exist otherwise. A beauty not perceived is a pleasure not felt, and a contradiction. But modern philosophy has taught us to say the same thing of every element of the perceived world; all are sensations; and their grouping into objects imagined to be permanent and external is the work of certain habits of our intelligence. We should be incapable of surveying or retaining the diffused experiences of life, unless we organized and classified them, and out of the chaos of impressions framed the world of conventional and recognizable objects.

How this is done is explained by the current theories of perception. External objects usually affect various senses at once, the impressions of which are thereby associated. Repeated experiences of one object are also associated on account of their similarity; hence a double tendency to merge and unify into a single percept, to which a name is attached, the group of those memories and reactions which in fact had one external thing for their cause. But this percept, once formed, is clearly different from those particular experiences out of which it grew. It is permanent, they are variable. They are but partial views and glimpses of it. The constituted notion therefore comes to be the reality, and the materials of it merely the appearance. The distinction between substance and quality, reality and appearance, matter and mind, has no other origin.

The objects thus conceived and distinguished from our ideas of them, are at first compacted of all the impressions, feelings, and memories, which offer themselves for association and fall within the vortex of the amalgamating imagination. Every sensation we get from a thing is originally treated as one of its qualities. Experiment, however, and the practical need of a simpler conception of the structure of objects lead us gradually to reduce the qualities of the object to a minimum, and to regard most perceptions as an effect of those few qualities upon us. These few primary qualities, like extension which we persist in treating as independently real and as the quality of a substance, are those which suffice to explain the order of our experiences. All the rest, like colour, are relegated to the subjective sphere, as merely effects upon our minds, and apparent or secondary qualities of the object.

But this distinction has only a practical justification. Convenience and economy of thought alone determine what combination of our sensations we shall continue to objectify and treat as the cause of the rest. The right and tendency to be objective is equal in all, since they are all prior to the artifice of thought by which we separate the concept from its materials, the thing from our experiences.

The qualities which we now conceive to belong to real objects are for the most part images of sight and touch. One of the first classes of effects to be treated as secondary were naturally pleasures and pains, since it could commonly conduce very little to intelligent and successful action to conceive our pleasures and pains as resident in objects. But emotions are essentially capable of objectification, as well as impressions of sense; and one may well believe that a primitive and inexperienced consciousness would rather people the world with ghosts of its own terrors and passions than with projections of those luminous and mathematical concepts which as yet it could hardly have formed.

This animistic and mythological habit of thought still holds its own at the confines of knowledge, where mechanical explanations are not found. In ourselves, where nearness makes observation difficult, in the intricate chaos of animal and human life, we still appeal to the efficacy of will and ideas, as also in the remote night of cosmic and religious problems. But in all the intermediate realm of vulgar day, where mechanical science has made progress, the inclusion of emotional or passionate elements in the concept of the reality would be now an extravagance. Here our idea of things is composed exclusively of perceptual elements, of the ideas of form and of motion.

The beauty of objects, however, forms an exception to this rule. Beauty is an emotional element, a pleasure of ours, which nevertheless we regard as a quality of things. But we are now prepared to understand the nature of this exception. It is the survival of a tendency originally universal to make every effect of a thing upon us a constituent of its conceived nature. The scientific idea of a thing is a great abstraction from the mass of perceptions and reactions which that thing produces; the aesthetic idea is less abstract, since it retains the emotional reaction, the pleasure of the perception, as an integral part of the conceived thing.

Nor is it hard to find the ground of this survival in the sense of beauty of an objectification of feeling elsewhere extinct. Most of the pleasures which objects cause are easily distinguished and separated from the perception of the object: the object has to be applied to a particular organ, like the palate, or swallowed like wine, or used and operated upon in some way before the pleasure arises. The cohesion is therefore slight between the pleasure and the other associated elements of sense; the pleasure is separated in time from the perception, or it is localized in a different organ, and consequently is at once recognized as an effect and not as a quality of the object. But when the process of perception itself is pleasant, as it may easily be, when the intellectual operation, by which the elements of sense are associated and projected, and the concept of the form and substance of the thing produced, is naturally delightful, then we have a pleasure intimately bound up in the thing, inseparable from its character and constitution, the seat of which in us is the same as the seat of the perception. We naturally fail, under these circumstances, to separate the pleasure from the other objectified feelings. It becomes, like them, a quality of the object, which we distinguish from pleasures not so incorporated in the perception of things, by giving it the name of beauty.

§ THE DEFINITION OF BEAUTY

We have now reached our definition of beauty, which, in the terms of our successive analysis and narrowing of the conception, is value positive, intrinsic, and objectified. Or, in less technical language, Beauty is pleasure regarded as the quality of a thing.

This definition is intended to sum up a variety of distinctions and identifications which should perhaps be here more explicitly set down. Beauty is a value, that is, it is not a perception of a matter of fact or of a relation: it is an emotion, an affection of our volitional and appreciative nature. An object cannot be beautiful if it can give pleasure to nobody: a beauty to which all men were forever indifferent is a contradiction in terms.

In the second place, this value is positive, it is the sense of the presence of something good, or (in the case of ugliness) of its absence. It is never the perception of a positive evil, it is never a negative value. That we are endowed with the sense of beauty is a pure gain which brings no evil with it. When the ugly ceases to be amusing or merely uninteresting and becomes disgusting, it becomes indeed a positive evil: but a moral and practical, not an aesthetic one. In aesthetics that saying is true—often so disingenuous in ethics—that evil is nothing but the absence of good: for even the tedium and vulgarity of an existence without beauty is not itself ugly so much as lamentable and degrading. The absence of aesthetic goods is a moral evil: the aesthetic evil is merely relative, and means less of

aesthetic good than was expected at the place and time. No form in itself gives pain, although some forms give pain by causing a shock of surprise even when they are really beautiful: as if a mother found a fine bull pup in her child's cradle, when her pain would not be aesthetic in its nature.

Further, this pleasure must not be in the consequence of the utility of the object or event, but in its immediate perception; in other words, beauty is an ultimate good, something that gives satisfaction to a natural function, to some fundamental need or capacity of our minds. Beauty is therefore a positive value that is intrinsic; it is a pleasure. These two circumstances sufficiently separate the sphere of aesthetics from that of ethics. Moral values are generally negative, and always remote. Morality has to do with the avoidance of evil and the pursuit of good: aesthetics only with enjoyment.

Finally, the pleasures of sense are distinguished from the perception of beauty, as sensation in general is distinguished from perception; by the objectification of the elements and their appearance as qualities rather of things than of consciousness. The passage from sensation to perception is gradual, and the path may be sometimes retraced: so it is with beauty and the pleasures of sensation. There is no sharp line between them, but it depends upon the degree of objectivity my feeling has attained at the moment whether I say "It pleases me," or "It is beautiful." If I am self-conscious and critical, I shall probably use one phrase; if I am impulsive and susceptible, the other. The more remote, interwoven, and inextricable the pleasure is, the more objective it will appear; and the union of two pleasures often makes one beauty. In Shakespeare's LIVth sonnet are these words:

O how much more doth beauty beauteous seem
By that sweet ornament which truth doth give!

The rose looks fair, but fairer we it deem
For that sweet odour which doth in it live.
The canker-blooms have full as deep a dye
As the perfumèd tincture of the roses,
Hang on such thorns, and play as
   wantonly
When summer's breath their maskèd
   buds discloses.
But, for their beauty only is their show,
They live unwooed and unrespected fade;
Die to themselves. Sweet roses do not so:
Of their sweet deaths are sweetest odours
   made.

One added ornament, we see, turns the deep dye, which was but show and mere sensation before, into an element of beauty and reality; and as truth is here the co-operation of perceptions, so beauty is the co-operation of pleasures. If colour, form, and motion are hardly beautiful without the sweetness of the odour, how much more necessary would they be for the sweetness itself to become a beauty! If we had the perfume in a flask, no one would think of calling it beautiful: it would give us too detached and controllable a sensation. There would be no object in which it could be easily incorporated. But let it float from the garden, and it will add another sensuous charm to objects simultaneously recognized, and help to make them beautiful. Thus beauty is constituted by the objectification of pleasure. It is pleasure objectified.

G. E. MOORE

(1873-1958)

The *Principia Ethica* of G. E. Moore, a large part of the sixth and final chapter of which (on "The Ideal") is presented here, was first published in 1903. Some of its leading points were later withdrawn or modified by the author; but the original text remains as good a statement as we have of this particular point of view. To the question asked by Diderot and so many others—"Is it [symmetry, for example] beautiful because it pleases, or does it please because it is beautiful?"—Moore answers—or does he not rather assume?—that the beauty of a thing is objective and independent of anyone's judgment, feelings, or consciousness. He is therefore aligned with Plato, Plotinus, and a number of modern writers who are often called intuitionists. (Richard Price, for example, expresses the intuitionist point of view in the first two chapters of *A Review of the Principal Questions in Morals,* written in 1758.) Moore is directly opposed to Hobbes, Spinoza, Hutcheson, and Santayana; his "objectivism" is stronger than that of Hume, Kant, or C. I. Lewis.

Moore's views on aesthetics are embedded in an ethical treatise with a particular doctrine. When he says here that the enjoyment of a beautiful thing is manifestly a greater good than the mere existence of that thing, he obviously takes it for granted that *beauty* is separate from, and exists prior to, the *enjoyment* of beauty. He further implies that we can judge and *know* a thing to be beautiful without consideration of its having to give pleasure. Also, judging a thing to be beautiful neither requires nor admits of any support by reasons or argument (though this point may not be perfectly clear in this particular selection). Judging something to be beautiful is not a conclusion from premises; it is an intellectual intuition. We are able somehow to "see," with the mind's eye, that an object of nature or of art is or is not beautiful.

Moore holds also that the propositions that "the existence of a *beautiful* thing is a *good*" and that "the enjoyment of beauty is a greater good still" can be "seen" to be true, directly and infallibly. For he holds that particular judgments of good and evil, as well as general judgments like those just cited, are self-evidently true or false.

Moore's version of intuitionist aesthetics is valuable because of the intricate chains of corollaries and assumptions that it brings to light. We are, as a result, able to evaluate the position as a whole, both Moore's and that of the nonnaturalism, as it is sometimes called, that he so well typifies.

G. E. MOORE

Principia Ethica

From Principia Ethica. *New York: Cambridge University Press, 1929. Reprinted by permission of the Cambridge University Press. (First published: 1903.)*

The Ideal

By far the most valuable things, which we know or can imagine, are certain states of consciousness, which may be roughly described as the pleasures of human intercourse and the enjoyment of beautiful objects. No one, probably, who has asked himself the question, has ever doubted that personal affection and the appreciation of what is beautiful in Art or Nature, are good in themselves; nor, if we consider strictly what things are worth having *purely for their own sakes,* does it appear probable that any one will think that anything else has *nearly* so great a value as the things which are included under these two heads. I have myself urged[1] . . . that the mere existence of what is beautiful does appear to have *some* intrinsic value; but I regard it as indubitable that Prof. Sidgwick was so far right, in the view there discussed, that such mere existence of what is beautiful has value, so small as to be negligible, in comparison with that which attaches to the *consciousness* of beauty. This simple truth may, indeed, be said to be universally recognised. What has *not* been recognised is that it is the ultimate and fundamental truth of Moral Philosophy. That it is only for the sake of these things—in order that

---

1 [In Chapter 3, Section 50.—ED. NOTE.]

389

as much of them as possible may at some time exist—that any one can be justified in performing any public or private duty; that they are the *raison d'être* of virtue; that it is they—these complex wholes *themselves,* and not any constituent or characteristic of them—that form the rational ultimate end of human action and the sole criterion of social progress: these appear to be truths which have been generally overlooked.

That they are truths—that personal affections and aesthetic enjoyments include *all* the greatest, and *by far* the greatest, goods we can imagine, will, I hope, appear more plainly in the course of that analysis of them, to which I shall now proceed. All the things, which I have meant to include under the above descriptions, are highly complex *organic unities;* and in discussing the consequences, which follow from this fact, and the elements of which they are composed, I may hope at the same time both to confirm and to define my position.

§I. THE GREATEST GOODS: AESTHETIC ENJOYMENTS

I propose to begin by examining what I have called aesthetic enjoyments, since the case of personal affections presents some additional complications. It is, I think, universally admitted that the proper appreciation of a beautiful object is a good thing in itself; and my question is: What are the main elements included in such an appreciation?

1. It is plain that in those instances of aesthetic appreciation, which we think most valuable, there is included, not merely a bare cognition of what is beautiful in the object, but also some kind of feeling or emotion. It is not sufficient that a man should merely see the beautiful qualities in a picture and know that they are beautiful, in order that we may give his state of mind the highest praise. We require that he should also appreciate the beauty of that

which he sees and which he knows to be beautiful—that he should feel and see *its beauty.* And by these expressions we certainly mean that he should have an appropriate emotion towards the beautiful qualities which he cognises. It is perhaps the case that all aesthetic emotions have some common quality; but it is certain that differences in the emotion seem to be appropriate to differences in the kind of beauty perceived: and by saying that different emotions are *appropriate* to different kinds of beauty, we mean that the whole which is formed by the consciousness of that kind of beauty *together with* the emotion appropriate to it, is better than if any other emotion had been felt in contemplating that particular beautiful object. Accordingly we have a large variety of different emotions, each of which is a necessary constituent in some state of consciousness which we judge to be good. All of these emotions are essential elements in great positive goods; they are *parts* of organic wholes, which have great intrinsic value. But it is important to observe that these wholes are organic, and that, hence, it does not follow that the emotion, *by itself,* would have any value whatsoever, nor yet that, if it were directed to a different object, the whole thus formed might not be positively bad. And, in fact, it seems to be the case that if we distinguish the emotional element, in any aesthetic appreciation, from the cognitive element, which accompanies it and is, in fact, commonly thought of as a part of the emotion; and if we consider what value this emotional element would have, *existing by itself,* we can hardly think that it has any great value, even if it has any at all. Whereas, if the same emotion be directed to a different object, if, for instance, it is felt towards an object that is positively ugly, the whole state of consciousness is certainly often positively bad in a high degree.

2. In the last paragraph I have pointed out the two facts, that the presence of some

emotion is necessary to give any very high value to a state of aesthetic appreciation, and that, on the other hand, this same emotion, in itself, may have little or no value: it follows that these emotions give to the wholes of which they form a part a value far greater than that which they themselves possess. The same is obviously true of the cognitive element which must be combined with these emotions in order to form these highly valuable wholes; and the present paragraph will attempt to define what is meant by this cognitive element, so far as to guard against a possible misunderstanding. When we talk of seeing a beautiful object, or, more generally, of the cognition or consciousness of a beautiful object, we may mean by these expressions something which forms no part of any valuable whole. There is an ambiguity in the use of the term "object," which has probably been responsible for as many enormous errors in philosophy and psychology as any other single cause. This ambiguity may easily be detected by considering the proposition, which, though a contradiction in terms, is obviously true: That when a man sees a beautiful picture, he may see nothing beautiful whatever. The ambiguity consists in the fact that, by the "object" of vision (or cognition), may be meant *either* the qualities actually seen *or* all the qualities possessed by the thing seen. Thus in our case: when it is said that the picture is beautiful, it is meant that it contains qualities which are beautiful; when it is said that the man sees the picture, it is meant that he sees a great number of the qualities contained in the picture; and when it is said that, nevertheless, he sees nothing beautiful, it is meant that he does *not* see those qualities of the picture which are beautiful. When, therefore, I speak of the cognition of a beautiful object, as an essential element in a valuable aesthetic appreciation, I must be understood to mean only the cognition of *the beautiful qualities* possessed by that object, and *not* the cognition

of other qualities of the object possessing them. And this distinction must itself be carefully distinguished from the other distinction expressed above by the distinct terms "seeing the beauty of a thing" and "seeing its beautiful qualities." By "seeing the beauty of a thing" we commonly mean the having an emotion towards its beautiful qualities; whereas in the "seeing of its beautiful qualities" we do not include any emotion. By the cognitive element, which is equally necessary with emotion to the existence of a valuable appreciation, I mean merely the actual cognition or consciousness of any or all of an object's *beautiful qualities*—that is to say any or all of those elements in the object which possess any positive beauty. That such a cognitive element is essential to a valuable whole may be easily seen, by asking: What value should we attribute to the proper emotion excited by hearing Beethoven's *Fifth Symphony,* if that emotion were entirely unaccompanied by any consciousness, either of the notes, or of the melodic and harmonic relations between them? And that the mere hearing of the *Symphony,* even accompanied by the appropriate emotion, is not sufficient, may be easily seen, if we consider what would be the state of a man, who should hear all the notes, but should *not* be aware of any of those melodic and harmonic relations, which are necessary to constitute the smallest beautiful elements in the *Symphony.*

3. Connected with the distinction just made between "object" in the sense of the qualities actually before the mind, and "object" in the sense of the whole thing which possesses the qualities actually before the mind, is another distinction of the utmost importance for a correct analysis of the constituents necessary to a valuable whole. It is commonly and rightly thought that to see beauty in a thing which has no beauty is in some way inferior to seeing beauty in that which really has it. But under this single description of "seeing

beauty in that which has no beauty," two very different facts, and facts of very different value, may be included. We may mean *either* the attribution to an object of really beautiful qualities which it does not possess *or* the feeling towards qualities, which the object does possess but which are in reality not beautiful, an emotion which is appropriate only to qualities really beautiful. Both these facts are of very frequent occurrence, and in most instances of emotion both no doubt occur together; but they are obviously quite distinct, and the distinction is of the utmost importance for a correct estimate of values. The former may be called an error of judgment, and the latter an error of taste; but it is important to observe that the "error of taste" commonly involves a false judgment *of value*; whereas the "error of judgment" is merely a false judgment *of fact*.

Now the case which I have called an error of taste, namely, where the actual qualities we admire (whether possessed by the "object" or not) are ugly, can in any case have no value, except such as may belong to the emotion *by itself*; and in most, if not in all, cases it is a considerable positive evil. In this sense, then, it is undoubtedly right to think that seeing beauty in a thing which has no beauty is inferior in value to seeing beauty where beauty really is. But the other case is much more difficult. In this case there is present all that I have hitherto mentioned as necessary to constitute a great positive good: there is a cognition of qualities really beautiful, together with an appropriate emotion towards these qualities. There can, therefore, be no doubt that we have here a great positive good. But there is present also something else; namely, a belief that these beautiful qualities exist, and that they exist in a certain relation to other things—namely, to some properties of the object to which we attribute these qualities: and further the object of this belief is false. And we may ask, with regard to the whole thus con-

stituted, whether the presence of the belief, and the fact that what is believed is false, make any difference to its value? We thus get three different cases of which it is very important to determine the relative values. Where both the cognition of beautiful qualities and the appropriate emotion are present we may *also* have either (1) a belief in the existence of these qualities, of which the object, i.e., that they exist, is true; or (2) a mere cognition, without belief, when it is (a) true, (b) false, that the object of the cognition, i.e., the beautiful qualities, exists; or (3) a belief in the existence of the beautiful qualities, when they do not exist. The importance of these cases arises from the fact that the second defines the pleasures of imagination, including a great part of the appreciation of those works of art which are *representative*; whereas the first contrasts with these the appreciation of what is beautiful in Nature, and the human affections. The third, on the other hand, is contrasted with both, in that it is chiefly exemplified in what is called misdirected affection; and it is possible also that the love of God, in the case of a believer, should fall under this head.

Now all these three cases, as I have said, have something in common, namely, that, in them all, we have a cognition of really beautiful qualities together with an appropriate emotion towards those qualities. I think, therefore, it cannot be doubted (nor is it commonly doubted) that all three include great positive goods; they are all things of which we feel convinced that they are worth having for their own sakes. And I think that the value of the second, in either of its two subdivisions, is precisely the same as the value of the element common to all three. In other words, in the case of purely imaginative appreciations we have merely the cognition of really beautiful qualities together with the appropriate emotion; and the question, whether the object cognised exists or not, seems here, where there is no belief either in its existence or in its non-existence, to make absolutely no difference to the value of the total state. But it seems to me that the two other cases do differ in intrinsic value both from this one and from one another, even though the object cognised and the appropriate emotion should be identical in all three cases. I think that the additional presence of a belief in the reality of the object makes the total state much better, if the belief is true; and worse, if the belief is false. In short, where there is belief, in the sense in which we *do* believe in the existence of Nature and horses, and do *not* believe in the existence of an ideal landscape and unicorns, the *truth* of what is believed does make a great difference to the value of the organic whole. If this be the case, we shall have vindicated the belief that *knowledge,* in the ordinary sense, as distinguished on the one hand from belief in what is false and on the other from the mere awareness of what is true, does contribute towards intrinsic value—that, at least in some cases, its presence as a part makes a whole more valuable than it could have been without.

Now I think there can be no doubt that we do judge that there is a difference of value, such as I have indicated, between the three cases in question. We do think that the emotional contemplation of a natural scene, supposing its qualities equally beautiful, is in some way a better state of things than that of a painted landscape: we think that the world would be improved if we could substitute for the best works of representative art *real* objects equally beautiful. And similarly we regard a misdirected affection or admiration, even where the error involved is a mere error of judgment and not an error of taste, as in some way unfortunate. And further, those, at least, who have a strong respect for truth, are inclined to think that a merely poetical contemplation of the Kingdom of Heaven *would be* superior to that of the religious believer, *if* it were the case that the King-

dom of Heaven does not and will not really exist. Most persons, on a sober, reflective judgment, would feel some hesitation even in preferring the felicity of a madman, convinced that the world was ideal, to the condition either of a poet imagining an ideal world, or of themselves enjoying and appreciating the lesser goods which do and will exist. But, in order to assure ourselves that these judgments are really judgments of intrinsic value upon the question before us, and to satisfy ourselves that they are correct, it is necessary clearly to distinguish our question from two others which have a very important bearing upon our total judgment of the cases in question.

In the first place (a) it is plain that, where we believe, the question whether what we believe is true or false, will generally have a most important bearing upon the value of our belief *as a means*. Where we believe, we are apt to act upon our belief, in a way in which we do not act upon our cognition of the events in a novel. The truth of what we believe is, therefore, very important as preventing the pains of disappointment and still more serious consequences. And it might be thought that a misdirected attachment was unfortunate solely for this reason: that it leads us to count upon results, which the real nature of its object is not of a kind to ensure. So too the Love of God, where, as usual, it includes the belief that he will annex to certain actions consequences, either in this life or the next, which the course of nature gives no reason to expect, may lead the believer to perform actions of which the actual consequences, supposing no such God to exist, may be much worse than he might otherwise have effected: and it might be thought that this was the sole reason (as it is a sufficient one) why we should hesitate to encourage the Love of God, in the absence of any proof that he exists. And similarly it may be thought that the only reason why beauty in Nature should be held superior to an equally beautiful landscape of imagination, is that its existence would ensure greater permanence and frequency in our emotional contemplation of that beauty. It is, indeed, certain that the chief importance of most *knowledge*—of the truth of most of the things which we believe—does, in this world, consist in its extrinsic advantages: it is immensely valuable *as a means*.

And secondly, (b) it may be the case that the existence of that which we contemplate is itself a great positive good, so that, for this reason alone, the state of things described by saying, that the object of our emotion really exists, would be intrinsically superior to that in which it did not. This reason for superiority is undoubtedly of great importance in the case of human affections, where the object of our admiration is the mental qualities of an admirable person; for that *two* such admirable persons should exist is greatly better than that there should be only one: and it would also discriminate the admiration of inanimate nature from that of its representations in art, in so far as we may allow a small intrinsic value to the existence of a beautiful object, apart from any contemplation of it. But it is to be noticed that this reason would not account for any difference in value between the cases where the truth was believed and that in which it was merely cognised, without either belief or disbelief. In other words, so far as this reason goes, the difference between the two subdivisions of our second class (that of imaginative contemplation) would be as great as between our first class and the second subdivision of our second. The superiority of the mere *cognition* of a beautiful object, when that object also happened to exist, over the same cognition when the object did not exist, would, on this count, be as great as that of the *knowledge* of a beautiful object over the mere imagination of it.

These two reasons for discriminating between the value of the three cases we are considering, must, I say, be carefully distinguished from that, of which I am now questioning the validity, if we are to obtain a correct answer concerning this latter. The question I am putting is this: Whether the *whole* constituted by the fact that there is an emotional contemplation of a beautiful object, which both is believed to be and is *real,* does not derive some of its value from the fact that the object *is* real? I am asking whether the value of this whole, *as a whole,* is not greater than that of those which differ from it, *either* by the absence of belief, with or without truth, *or,* belief being present, by the mere absence of truth? I am not asking *either* whether it is not superior to them as a means (which it certainly is), *nor* whether it may not contain a more valuable *part,* namely, the existence of the object in question. My question is solely whether the existence of its object does not constitute an addition to the value of the whole, quite distinct from the addition constituted by the fact that this whole does contain a valuable part.

If, now, we put this question, I cannot avoid thinking that it should receive an affirmative answer. We can put it clearly by the method of isolation; and the sole decision must rest with our reflective judgment upon it, as thus clearly put. We can guard against the bias produced by a consideration of value *as a means* by supposing the case of an illusion as complete and permanent as illusions in this world never can be. We can imagine the case of a single person, enjoying throughout eternity the contemplation of scenery as beautiful, and intercourse with persons as admirable, as can be imagined; while yet the whole of the objects of his cognition are absolutely unreal. I think we should definitely pronounce the existence of a universe, which consisted solely of such a person, to be *greatly* inferior in value to one in which the objects, in the existence of which he believes, did really exist just as he believes them to do; and that it would be thus inferior *not only* because it would lack the goods which consist in the existence of the objects in question, but *also* merely because his belief would be false. That it would be inferior *for this reason alone* follows if we admit, what also appears to me certain, that the case of a person, merely imagining, without believing, the beautiful objects in question, would, *although these objects really existed,* be yet inferior to that of the person who also believed in their existence. For here all the additional good, which consists in the existence of the objects, is present, and yet there still seems to be a great difference in value between this case and that in which their existence is believed. But I think that my conclusion may perhaps be exhibited in a more convincing light by the following considerations. (1) It does not seem to me that the small degree of value which we may allow to the existence of beautiful inanimate objects is nearly equal in amount to the difference which I feel that there is between the appreciation (accompanied by belief) of such objects, when they really exist, and the purely imaginative appreciation of them when they do not exist. This inequality is more difficult to verify where the object is an admirable person, since a *great* value must be allowed to his existence. But yet I think it is not paradoxical to maintain that the superiority of reciprocal affection, where both objects are worthy and both exist, over an unreciprocated affection, where both are worthy but one does not exist, does not lie solely in the fact that, in the former case, we have two good things instead of one, but also in the fact that each is such as the other believes him to be. (2) It seems to me that the important contribution to value made by true belief may be very plainly seen in the following case. Suppose that a worthy object of affection does really exist and is believed to do so, but that there enters into the case this error of fact, that the qualities loved, though exactly like, are yet not the *same* which really do exist. This state of things is easily imagined,

and I think we cannot avoid pronouncing that, *although* both persons here exist, it is yet not so satisfactory as where the very person loved and believed to exist is also the one which actually does exist.

If all this be so, we have, in this third section, added to our two former results the third result that a true belief in the reality of an object greatly increases the value of many valuable wholes. Just as in sections 1 and 2 it was maintained that aesthetic and affectionate emotions had little or no value apart from the cognition of appropriate objects, and that the cognition of these objects had little or no value apart from the appropriate emotion, so that the whole, in which both were combined, had a value greatly in excess of the sum of the values of its parts; so, according to this section, if there be added to these wholes a true belief in the reality of the object, the new whole thus formed has a value greatly in excess of the sum obtained by adding the value of the true belief, considered in itself, to that of our original wholes. This new case only differs from the former in this, that, whereas the true belief, by itself, has quite as little value as either of the two other constituents taken singly, yet they, taken together, seem to form a whole of very great value, whereas this is not the case with the two wholes which might be formed by adding the true belief to either of the others.

The importance of the result of this section seems to lie mainly in two of its consequences. (1) That it affords some justification for the immense intrinsic value, which seems to be commonly attributed to the mere *knowledge* of some truths, and which was expressly attributed to some kinds of knowledge by Plato and Aristotle. Perfect knowledge has indeed competed with perfect love for the position of Ideal. If the results of this section are correct, it appears that knowledge, though having little or no value by itself, is an absolutely essential constituent in the highest goods, and contributes immensely to their value. And it appears that this function may be performed not only by that case of knowledge, which we have chiefly considered, namely, knowledge of the reality of the beautiful object cognised, but also by knowledge of the numerical identity of this object with that which really exists, and by the knowledge that the existence of that object is truly good. Indeed all knowledge, which is directly concerned with the nature of the constituents of a beautiful object, would seem capable of adding greatly to the value of the contemplation of that object, although, by itself, such knowledge would have no value at all. And (2) The second important consequence, which follows from this section, is that the presence of true belief may, in spite of a great inferiority in the value of the emotion and the beauty of its object, constitute with them a whole equal or superior in value to wholes, in which the emotion and beauty are superior, but in which a true belief is wanting or a false belief present. In this way we may justify the attribution of equal or superior value to an appreciation of an inferior real object, as compared with the appreciation of a greatly superior object which is a mere creature of the imagination. Thus a just appreciation of nature and of real persons may maintain its equality with an equally just appreciation of the products of artistic imagination, in spite of much greater beauty in the latter. And similarly though God may be admitted to be a more perfect object than any actual human being, the love of God may yet be inferior to human love, *if* God does not exist.

4. In order to complete the discussion of this first class of goods—goods which have an essential reference to *beautiful* objects— it would be necessary to attempt a classification and comparative valuation of all the different forms of beauty, a task which properly belongs to the study called Aesthetics. I do not, however, propose to attempt any part of this task. It must only be understood that I intend to include among the essential constituents of the goods I have been discussing, every form and variety of beautiful object, if only it be truly beautiful; and, *if* this be understood, I think it may be seen that the consensus of opinion with regard to what is positively beautiful and what is positively ugly, and even with regard to great differences in degree of beauty, is quite sufficient to allow us a hope that we need not greatly err in our judgments of good and evil. In anything which is thought beautiful by any considerable number of persons, there is probably *some* beautiful quality; and differences of opinion seem to be far more often due to exclusive attention, on the part of different persons, to different qualities in the same object, than to the positive error of supposing a quality that is ugly to be really beautiful. When an object, which some think beautiful, is denied to be so by others, the truth is *usually* that it lacks some beautiful quality or is deformed by some ugly one, which engage the exclusive attention of the critics.

I may, however, state two general principles, closely connected with the results of this chapter, the recognition of which would seem to be of great importance for the investigation of what things are truly beautiful. The first of these is (1) a definition of beauty, of what is meant by saying that a thing is truly beautiful. The naturalistic fallacy has been quite as commonly committed with regard to beauty as with regard to good: its use has introduced as many errors into Aesthetics as into Ethics. It has been even more commonly supposed that the beautiful may be *defined* as that which produces certain effects upon our feelings; and the conclusion which follows from this —namely, that judgments of taste are merely *subjective*—that precisely the same thing may, according to circumstances, be *both* beautiful *and* not beautiful—has very frequently been drawn. The conclusions of this chapter suggest a definition of beauty, which may partially explain and entirely remove the difficulties which have led to this error. It appears probable that the beautiful should be *defined* as that of which the admiring contemplation is good in itself. That is to say: To assert that a thing is beautiful is to assert that the cognition of it is an essential element in one of the intrinsically valuable wholes we have been discussing; so that the question, whether it is *truly* beautiful or not, depends upon the *objective* question whether the whole in question is or is not truly good, and does not depend upon the question whether it would or would not excite particular feelings in particular persons. This definition has the double recommendation that it accounts both for the apparent connection between goodness and beauty and for the no less apparent difference between these two conceptions. It appears, at first sight, to be a strange coincidence, that there should be two *different* objective predicates of value, "good" and "beautiful," which are nevertheless so related to one another that whatever is beautiful is also good. But, if our definition be correct, the strangeness disappears; since it leaves only one *unanalysable* predicate of value, namely "good," while "beautiful," though not identical with, is to be defined by reference to this, being thus, at the same time, different from and necessarily connected with it. In short, on this view, to say that a thing is beautiful is to say, not indeed that it is *itself* good, but that it is a necessary element in something which is: to prove that a thing is truly beautiful is to prove that a whole, to which it bears a particular relation as a part, is truly good. And in this way we should explain the immense predominance, among objects commonly considered beautiful, of *material* objects—objects of the external senses; since these objects, though themselves having, as has been said, little or no intrinsic value, are yet essential constituents in the largest group of wholes which have intrinsic value. These wholes themselves may be, and are, also beautiful;

but the comparative rarity, with which we regard them as themselves *objects* of contemplation, seems sufficient to explain the association of beauty with external objects.

And secondly (2) it is to be observed that beautiful objects are themselves, for the most part, organic unities, in this sense, that they are wholes of great complexity, such that the contemplation of any part, by itself, may have no value, and yet that, unless the contemplation of the whole includes the contemplation of that part, it will lose in value. From this it follows that there can be no single criterion of beauty. It will never be true to say: This object owes its beauty *solely* to the presence of this characteristic; nor yet that: Wherever this characteristic is present, the object must be beautiful. All that can be true is that certain objects are beautiful, *because* they have certain characteristics, in the sense that they would not be beautiful *unless* they had them. And it may be possible to find that certain characteristics are more or less universally present in all beautiful objects, and are, in this sense, more or less important conditions of beauty. But it is important to observe that the very qualities, which differentiate one beautiful object from all others, are, if the object be truly beautiful, as *essential* to its beauty, as those which it has in common with ever so many others. The object would no more have the beauty it has, without its specific qualities, than without those that are generic; and the generic qualities, *by themselves,* would fail, as completely, to give beauty, as those which are specific.

§II. THE GREATEST GOODS: PERSONAL AFFECTION

It will be remembered that I began this survey of great unmixed goods, by dividing all the greatest goods we know into the two classes of aesthetic enjoyments, on the one hand, and the pleasures of human intercourse or of personal affection, on the other. I postponed the consideration of the latter on the ground that they presented additional complications. In what this additional complication consists, will now be evident; and I have already been obliged to take account of it, in discussing the contribution to value made by true belief. It consists in the fact that in the case of personal affection, the object itself is not *merely* beautiful, while possessed of little or no intrinsic value, but is itself, in part at least, of great intrinsic value. All the constituents which we have found to be necessary to the most valuable aesthetic enjoyments, namely, appropriate emotion, cognition of truly beautiful qualities, and true belief, are equally necessary here; but here we have the additional fact that the object must be not only truly beautiful, but also truly good in a high degree.

It is evident that this additional complication only occurs in so far as there is included in the object of personal affection some of the *mental* qualities of the person towards whom the affection is felt. And I think it may be admitted that, wherever the affection is most valuable, the appreciation of mental qualities must form a large part of it, and that the presence of this part makes the whole far more valuable than it could have been without it. But it seems very doubtful whether this appreciation, by itself, can possess as much value as the whole in which it is combined with an appreciation of the appropriate *corporeal* expression of the mental qualities in question. It is certain that in all actual cases of valuable affection, the bodily expressions of character, whether by looks, by words, or by actions, do form a part of the object towards which the affection is felt, and that the fact of their inclusion appears to heighten the value of the whole state. It is, indeed, very difficult to imagine what the cognition of mental qualities *alone,* unaccompanied by *any* corporeal expression, would be like; and, in so far as we succeed in making this abstraction, the whole con-

sidered certainly appears to have less value. I therefore conclude that the importance of an admiration of admirable mental qualities lies chiefly in the immense superiority of a whole, in which it forms a part, to one in which it is absent, and not in any high degree of intrinsic value which it possesses by itself. It even appears to be doubtful, whether, in itself, it possesses so much value as the appreciation of mere corporeal beauty undoubtedly does possess; that is to say, whether the appreciation of what has great intrinsic value is so valuable as the appreciation of what is merely beautiful.

But further if we consider the nature of admirable mental qualities, by themselves, it appears that a proper appreciation of them involves a reference to purely material beauty in yet another way. Admirable mental qualities do, if our previous conclusions are correct, consist very largely in an emotional contemplation of beautiful objects; and hence the appreciation of them will consist essentially in the contemplation of such contemplation. It is true that the most valuable appreciation of persons appears to be that which consists in the appreciation of their appreciation of other persons; but even here a reference to material beauty appears to be involved, *both* in respect of the fact that what is appreciated in the last instance may be the contemplation of what is merely beautiful, *and* in respect of the fact that the most valuable appreciation of a person appears to *include* an appreciation of his corporeal expression. Though, therefore, we may admit that the appreciation of a person's attitude towards other persons, or, to take one instance, the love of love, is far the most valuable good we know, and far more valuable than the mere love of beauty, yet we can only admit this if the first be understood to *include* the latter, in various degrees of directness.

With regard to the question what *are* the mental qualities of which the cognition is essential to the value of human intercourse, it is plain that they include, in the first place, all those varieties of aesthetic appreciation, which formed our first class of goods. They include, therefore, a great variety of different emotions, each of which is appropriate to some different kind of beauty. But we must now add to these the whole range of emotions, which are appropriate to persons, and which are different from those which are appropriate to mere corporeal beauty. It must also be remembered that just as these emotions have little value in themselves, and as the state of mind in which they exist may have its value greatly heightened, or may entirely lose it and become positively evil in a great degree, according as the cognitions accompanying the emotions are appropriate or inappropriate; so too the appreciation of these emotions, though it may have some value in itself, may yet form part of a whole which has far greater value or no value at all, according as it is or is not accompanied by a perception of the appropriateness of the emotions to their objects. It is obvious, therefore, that the study of what is valuable in human intercourse is a study of immense complexity; and that there may be much human intercourse which has little or no value, or is positively bad. Yet here too, as with the question what is beautiful, there seems no reason to doubt that a reflective judgment will in the main decide correctly both as to what are positive goods and even as to any *great* differences in value between these goods. In particular, it may be remarked that the emotions, of which the contemplation is essential to the greatest values, and which are also themselves appropriately excited by such contemplation, appear to be those which are commonly most highly prized under the name of affection.

THEODOR LIPPS

(1851-1914)

The author who gave currency to the term *Einfühlung,* usually translated "empathy," was a philosopher at several universities, the last of which was Munich. He taught that philosophy ought to be a science of inner experience coordinated with natural science, or, in other words, that it should be virtually identical with psychology. Lipps therefore represents the so-called psychologistic tendency so prominent in German aesthetics at the turn of the century. It is, moreover, not without significance that he was an admirer of Hume, whom he described as "a master in the art of psychological analysis," and whose *Treatise of Human Nature* he helped translate into German.

In the present essay, Lipps unfortunately fails to emulate Hume's notable clarity of expression. He is bound to disappoint us by his difficult and repetitious style. But Lipps's idea, the idea of empathy, is of the greatest consequence in aesthetics and deserves to be considered. If the reader finds the translator's language contorted, he may be assured that it is equally contorted in the original. The difficulty is that Lipps is forcing philosophic language to perform a kind of poetic task for which it is eminently unsuited.

Hume observed "a very remarkable inclination in human nature, to bestow on external objects the same emotions which it observes in itself." Since this inclination (which he thought noticeable only in "children, poets, and the antient philosophers") sometimes hinders the discovery of truth, bestowing our own emotions on external objects, it has frequently been denounced as the pathetic fallacy. The doctrine of empathy denies that it is a fallacy at all, or rather, it confines the inclination to its proper sphere and investigates its rather remarkable workings.

Hume's view of the "necessary connexion" which is part of the idea of causality has a similar explanation. [See footnotes to Subsections 52 and 60 in Selby-Bigge's edition of the *Enquiry Concerning Human Understanding* (New York: Oxford University Press).]

The object of experience, Kant taught, is already deeply infused with concepts of our own devising. We learn in Lipps that the object of aesthetic experience is permeated by our feelings and emotional states. All this is possible because the object of experience is but a *phenomenon*, an appearance.

Though there are several problems for the translator in Lipps's essay, the most difficult is the word *zumuten*. Several equivalents are used here ("summon," "evoke," "elicit," "stimulate," "impute"). All of them, most of all "impute," which is the closest equivalent, seem to do violence to the thought. The subject of this verb is ordinarily a person. But here we have inanimate or impersonal objects—the graceful reed, the laughing meadow, or laughing face—serving as subjects. The effects they work (*zumuten*) in us are not sense-data (though these are also present) but certain activities of the self. Why they stimulate these particular activities Lipps does not fully explain.

The selection that appears here is only a brief introduction to a subject to which Lipps devoted the two large volumes of his *Aesthetik*. He also extended the concept to other subjects, for example, the problems of "other minds," social relations, and obligations in general.

THEODOR LIPPS

Empathy and Aesthetic Pleasure

(Translated by Karl Aschenbrenner)

There are three types, or, more precisely, three directions of enjoyment. First of all, I enjoy a thing or a sensuous object distinct from myself, for example, the taste of a fruit. Second, I enjoy myself, for example, my power or my skill; I am proud of a deed in which I have exhibited such power or skill. Between these two possibilities lies a third which uniquely combines the other two: I enjoy myself in a sensuous object distinct from myself. This type is that of aesthetic enjoyment. It is objectivated self-enjoyment.

That I enjoy myself in a sensuous object presupposes that in it I have, or find, or feel myself. Here we encounter the basic idea of present-day aesthetics, the concept of Empathy.

"Empathy"[1] can be, and is, a much misunderstood term. To begin with, there are many who use the term "feeling"[2] only for the feeling of pleasure or displeasure or who think of the act of feeling[3] as simply that of apprehending pleasure or displeasure and nothing more. Hence, those who illegitimately confine the term "feeling" to this suppose that empathy (which is after all a kind of feeling) does not deserve the name "feeling" at all. What I empathize

From Die Zukunft, *Vol. LIV (1905).*

---

1 [*Einfühlung,* literally "in-feeling" or "feeling into."—TR. NOTE.]

2 [*Gefühl.*—TR. NOTE.]

3 [*Fühlen.*—TR. NOTE.]

is, in the most general sense, life itself. And life is power, inner working, striving, achieving. In one word, life is activity: free or inhibited, easy or arduous, at one with itself or in inner conflict, tense or relaxed, concentrated in a point or scattered and "losing itself" in manifold vital activity.

We have just now associated the concepts of activity and of power, and in fact we can use the second to explicate the first: activity is that in which I experience a manifestation of power. Notice that even the feeling of weakness is a power-feeling, but a feeling of power that is minimal or falling below a certain level. It is a power-feeling in the same sense in which the perception of a soft tone is a perception of loudness or intensity, but one which is minimal or which falls below a certain limit—a less intense intensity. For power need not be concentrated, but remains power even when it is diffused, when within the general frame of inner activity it dissolves or, to use our previous term, "loses itself."

The concept of the will can likewise be fitted into that of activity if one takes "will" in the ordinary sense and equates it with "striving." I can then say that activity is by nature activity of will. It is striving or willing set in motion. Here again we must notice that even "involuntary" surrender is a form of willing. The willing lies precisely in giving oneself. Even in involuntary surrender there is effort.

Finally, one might say metaphorically that activity is an inner breathing or pulsation; or more generally, it is inner motion. By "motion" here we do not mean simply an event within us, but rather the fact that we move. Of course, such motion has nothing to do with space.

But there is more to be said of "life" and "activity." Pleasure and displeasure are not themselves life or activity. They are the immediately experienced color or tone of active or vital feeling. They are, as it were,

the shades and tints of the feeling of life or activity. If I experience pleasure or displeasure, this means, first of all, that I live, that I feel myself to be alive or active. It means that this life or activity has brighter and darker tones. These tones are called pleasure and displeasure. Pleasure and displeasure are thus not actually feelings but feeling-tones, in the sense in which the brighter or darker tone of a color is not the color itself but precisely the tone of it.

What I empathize is not, or is not primarily, pleasure or displeasure, but is life and activity, or a mode of my self-activity. I empathize strong and healthy life, let us say, into the form of a human body. Therefore, I call the body itself strong and healthy. Into a spacious hall I empathize activity which rises and broadens. Or again, I empathize into the words or gestures of another person joy, sorrow, despair. Even these words designate modes of my activity, the activities of myself. Suppose that someone takes it into his head to identify "feeling" with "feeling of pleasure or displeasure." Then all this empathizing is not "empathy" (in-feeling) at all. But now in place of the word "empathy" he has to put some other, perhaps the one already mentioned, "self-objectivation." This, however, in no wise alters the facts.

Another objection is the following. "Empathy" implies that I feel myself into something. And this sounds as if I first of all felt myself, or something in me, power, joy, longing, and then proceeded to remove this and to transfer it to an external object —as if empathy were an act or achievement which transpires when something is empathized into an object.

I intend nothing like that at all. First of all, "empathy" does not mean that that which I empathize, for example, power or joy or longing, is anything visible or audible, or anything outwardly perceptible, but rather that I experience all this within myself. Further, it means that in spite of this, I find this empathic content in what is outside me, that in the storm I seem to find rage and threat. All we need to do is to put these two ideas together and we have the whole meaning of "empathy." If it is the fact that the activity I denote by the words "rage" and "threat" cannot be seen or heard but can only be felt within me, and if I nevertheless find something of that sort in a sensuous object, then I must be finding myself in this sensuous object. I experience or feel myself in it.

That there is empathy in this sense, that what I can feel only within myself I can again find or feel in something other than myself, or in other words, that this kind of thing can "reside" in something else, or can for my consciousness "attach" to or "belong" to something sensuously perceived —this is indeed a remarkable fact. So much so that we cannot afford to glide over it, and what I have already said by no means disposes of the problem of the concept of empathy. I may remark at once that there is a word which seems to mean exactly what the word "empathy" means, namely "expression." A gesture, for instance, expresses joy or sorrow to me. The form of a body expresses to me strength or health. A landscape expresses a mood. Such "expression" says exactly what we intend by the term "empathy."

And yet, the concept of expression is at the same time broader than that of empathy. I also say, a sentence expresses a judgment. But I do not say, I empathize the judgment into the sentence. Of course, I can say this, but the phraseology seems to be somewhat out of place. The reason why this is so is quite easy. A judgment, it is said, is not a matter of feeling. Judgment is a logical act, the act of acknowledging some factual content. No doubt I experience this act when I perform it. But I do not say, "I feel it." I find myself inwardly making this or that judgment, but I do not "feel" myself to be judging as I feel myself

to be passionately stirred up, or intensely interested, and the like. In short, I do not feel the judgment as I feel a passionate stirring.

All this has a sound basis. Such an "act,"[4] or mere acknowledgment of judgment, is of course not an activity,[5] an inner effort or expenditure of energy, nor is it some striving or willing set in motion.

When I feel activity I feel myself: such activity *is* the "self." Activity-feeling, or as I called it earlier, vital feeling, is synonymous with "self-feeling." Therefore, if I do not feel myself to be active in the act of acknowledgment or of judging, neither can I therein have any self-feeling.

This provides the necessary delimitation for the concept of empathy. If I experience any sort of activity which really deserves to be called "activity," if I find some aspect of my life, some inner motion of striving, in a sensuous object, then and there I have felt myself into this object and "objectivated" in it my vital self-feeling. In a sentence that "expresses" a judgment I admittedly find that judgment, but I do not find in it strength, life, activity. That is why I do not speak of empathy in this situation. Yet the fact that a sentence "expresses" a judgment runs parallel to the fact of empathy, that is, the fact that a gesture or an architectural form "expresses" life, activity, or a specific mode of the activity of the self. That is why we can use one of these ideas to help clarify the other.

Let us now ask, what is it that I actually experience when a sentence "expresses" a judgment for me? At first I may say, I know in such a case that he who utters the sentence is making a judgment. I think the speaker's judgment into the sentence, or, uniting myself with the speaker in some unique way, I consider the judgment. But everybody knows this is not enough: the

---

4 [*Akt.*—TR. NOTE.]
5 [*Tätigkeit.*—TR. NOTE.]

sentence elicits from me my own judgment. It elicits from me that act of judgment which is, as it were, contained in it. The sentence asks that I believe it. But if I do so this means simply that I myself assert the judgment which the sentence expresses. This elicitation[6] or evocation or demand I therefore experience when I hear the sentence.

By analogy to what we have when a sentence expresses a judgment, a sensed object expresses life, a gesture expresses pride. "Expression" here is the same fact, but *what* is expressed is in this case something different. It is not a judgment but pride that is expressed, that is to say, a unique inner experience or inner effort.

But let us speak more precisely. Every object of sense evokes in me a certain activity. If it does nothing else, it at least demands of me that I grasp it, that I "apperceive" it in a certain way. A simple line asks to be apprehended as what it is, and this apprehending is a kind of activity. If this activity is consummated I can then even speak of an "act," but this act necessarily presupposes [another] activity. In the end the line is in my mental possession, and this presupposes that I have brought it into my possession. In this there is involved a certain activity.

We must formulate this still more precisely. No matter how a line may be constituted in a given instance, I must in any event grasp it as what it is, must run the length of it with the inner eye, or from the viewpoint of the mind's eye. I must add part to part and gather it all together under this viewpoint. I must extend the inner vision until it grasps all of the line; the inner vision must span the whole. Also I must inwardly set it off and lift it out of its environment. In that extension I need to have a certain goal so that I organize what is found within the sweep of my glance. My apperceptive activity must be bounded within definite limits.

---

6 [*Zumutung.*—TR. NOTE.]

This activity of inner vision, or the viewpoint of the mind's eye, we call apperceptive activity. Every finite line stirs this apperceptive activity in me. In every instance it elicits a twofold movement, one which combines the two movements, of extension and of limitation. Besides this, every line, by virtue of its direction and its form, evokes in me or my apperceptive activity still other more specific responses. But I shall purposely confine myself to the most general one.

The question now arises, how do I behave toward these elicited activities, these modes of self-activity? Here there are two possibilities, namely that I respond with a yes or a no, that I am sympathetic or antagonistic to the call to respond. The question of how I respond is the question of whether or not I let myself go without resisting; whether or not, in response to the stimulus, but yet freely, I bring forth spontaneously from myself that which is being elicited; whether all those tendencies, inclinations, and needs for self-activity in me are in harmony with these elicitations, or whether they are not. We always have a need for self-activity: it is the fundamental need of our being. But the self-activity that is elicited by a sensuous object may be so constituted that by its very nature it cannot be evoked without impediment and friction, without inner conflict. In that event, my own nature, that is, my nature as it is quite apart from this stimulus, will more or less consciously oppose it.

But suppose that the response is achieved without inhibition or friction or inner conflict. Then I experience the stimulated activity just because it has been stimulated, and yet I am quite free, since this has taken place without conflict or friction. I have at the same time a sense of freedom and a feeling of pleasure. The feeling of pleasure is always a feeling of free activity, or self-activity. It is an immediately experienced coloring or toning of the feeling of activity, and it occurs when the activity proceeds without inhibition or friction. The feeling of pleasure in a thing is always the feeling of freedom and unconstricted ease in the activity which the thing elicits from me. It is the conscious symptom of the harmonious relation between the summons to activity and my successful response to it. In a sense the activity is realized in me in a twofold way: first, it is summoned from me or borne in upon me, and second, it is freely taken up by myself —by myself as I am apart from this stimulus. But this is only a theoretical distinction. What I experience in the case in question is simply my activity, not purely spontaneously, but receptively; it is both precipitated by the sensuous object and freely taken up by myself.

We must now consider the following point. The object which I am to grasp or which stimulates my capacity to grasp is in itself, of course, always and only that which it is. For me, however, it does not exist as that which it is (that is, as something whole and complete in itself) without being apprehended in a certain way, its details run through by the survey of the inner eye, and synthesized into a distinct whole. This running through and synthesis, once they have become part of the object, do not thenceforth characterize it forever; as if I could now withdraw from it this "apperceptive" activity, an activity of extending and limiting the inner vision, and direct it to other objects, the previous object remaining meanwhile whole and complete in itself. For the object to remain just this object, whole and complete, that activity of extending and limiting must be continuous and uninterrupted. My activity therefore has its being in this object so long as it exists as this definite thing, as something whole and distinct. The object as it exists for me, is, as is commonly said, the resultant or product of two factors, that is, something sensuously given and my own activity. This activity of mine belongs to it as "my" object just as much as does the sensuous givenness. The latter is merely the material out of which my activity must first con-

struct the object for me. The "object" as it is there for me, is as little the mere sensuous given as a house is a mere heap of stone. Rather, just as both material and form belong to the house, so they both belong also to the "object" which I apprehend as some definite thing. The form is always the being-formed-by me; it is my activity. It is a basic fact of psychology and even more so of aesthetics that there is no such thing, nor can there be such a thing, as a "sensuously given object," strictly considered. To be sure, an object—and here I am speaking always of objects that exist for me—is in some way sensuously given. But it is also something which is permeated by my activity. Activity is life. The word "life" has in fact no other meaning than activity. Everything, therefore, which exists as some particular thing—and other objects simply do not exist for me—is necessarily and self-evidently permeated by my life. This then is the commonest signification of "empathy." It means that when I grasp an object, as it exists and indeed must exist for me, I experience an activity or a kind of self-activity as an attribute of the object. But here one must distinguish between "positive" and "negative" empathy. Whether the empathy be of one sort or the other, in either case I experience a stimulus for activity; some form of self-activity is elicited from me by the object. Here the emphasis must be placed upon the experience.[7]

We must reiterate the two possibilities which we have already distinguished. On one occasion without any effort I experience an activity, and from it I receive a feeling of harmony[8] between what is elicited from me and my own spontaneous activity. On another occasion a conflict ensues between myself, my natural drive[9] toward self-activity, on the one hand, and this other activity elicited from me, entering into me

---

[7] [*Erleben.*—TR. NOTE.]

[8] [*Einklang.*—TR. NOTE.]

[9] [*Bestreben.*—TR. NOTE.]

from without, on the other. I call one of these "positive" and the other "negative" empathy. In both cases the strength of the feeling depends upon the intensity of that "entering into me." And this in turn is conditioned by the degree to which I attend to the stimulant object, by the intensity of my apperceptive surrender to this object. The more I give myself to the object, the more also have I submitted myself to the stimulus, and the more deeply I am absorbed by the activity evoked in me. And if this evocation and my natural drive toward self-activity harmonize, the more noticeable will be the harmony between them. But also, whenever these two are opposed, whenever the drive toward self-activity is contrary to the evoked response, either because of its nature or my own, the more keenly will I feel the conflict between them. The feeling of harmony then is precisely a feeling of pleasure in the object, and the feeling of conflict is a feeling of displeasure in it. Hence the one feeling as well as the other is conditioned by the degree to which I experience or am permeated by the evoked activity. This in turn is conditioned by my sensitivity, by my mental strength and health.

In both cases the activity is experienced as one which is evoked in me. But in the second case, that of conflict, the "evocation" has a special sense. It is inimical, something that enters into me in a hostile way. In the first case, the evocation is freely consonant with me. It may also be described as sympathy, and in fact positive empathy may also be called sympathetic empathy. Negative empathy, on the other hand, is the experience of a stimulus hostile to me, directed against me.

In the foregoing we have described what is evoked in me by the sensuous object, namely a certain mode of apperceptive activity. But there are further possibilities. In a given case, by means of a sensuous object I can be subjected to another more specific stimulus. If we attend carefully to this, we can distinguish several varieties or levels of empathy.

Naturally the first level is characterized by the kind of empathy in which there is only a very general stimulus. We call this "general apperceptive" empathy. In other words, in this only that activity is elicited from me which is necessary for a definite sensuous object to be present to me at all, or for it to be this particular object. Even this stimulus can be of a manifold sort and point toward a multifarious activity. Every new form, of a line for instance, must call up a new and different activity if I am to have a mental grasp of the line, formed just so. Every form of line, or every line with its form evokes a unique creative or re-creative activity. I repeat, this activity lies in the line insofar as it exists for me. It does not exist for me even an instant unless I maintain it by my activity. Every moment it exists it is an interpenetration of the sensuously given and my creative activity.

Insofar as this creative activity lies in the line, the line maintains itself by such activity. It brings itself and its form into existence anew every moment. The activity is at once the vehicle of the powers by which this is done, and of the manner of their operation. It is the vehicle of concentration and discharge, of tension and release of tension, of initiation, continuation, and cessation, and above all of self-extension and self-confinement. For example, empathy into linear forms is of this sort insofar as it is purely "general apperceptive empathy." But even with simple lines we go beyond this kind of empathy. We encounter linear forms as parts of space. This is the same space in which things are found. Here linear forms become objects of that particular kind of empathy which we accord to things. Things, however, do not just present themselves to me to be apperceived. They summon from me an intellectual act of connecting them, of fitting them into a scheme of reality, of incorporating them into a causal order, and thus they evoke the activity of the understanding. This too is action of the will. As in all activity, there is in it striving and fruition, power, tension, release, work, success. And since things evoke this activity in me (or in the process of evoking it), this unique activity, this striving, this power, tension-release, work is likewise "felt into" things. Here again we must repeat: insofar as things belong to the scheme of reality and its spatial context, this kind of connectedness belongs to them, and so also does the activity presupposed by this. Things exist for me as what they are only in just such a context, and my activity is immediately embodied in things as they exist for me. It is there as the activity through which they become for me that which they are. This is the origin of all the "strivings," "tendencies," "activities," and "necessitations," of all the "powers" in nature. I see nothing of what these words designate when I see things—I only feel and "realize" all this within myself. The striving in nature is my striving, the activity in it is my activity, the power is my power; and the degree of effort involved is owing to me. All this is put into things by myself, not arbitrarily but with necessity. In grasping things with the understanding I permeate them with such striving, activity, and power, and these are part of their essence. Insofar as things are my "objects," they are part of my very being.

This kind of empathy I call natural empathy.[10] This means simply that things as grasped by the understanding are necessarily permeated by my activity. This activity is "evoked from" me by things insofar as they stimulate me to connect them intellectually or to grasp them by means of the understanding. Accordingly there is here also the possibility of a "positive" and a "negative" empathy. The question is whether and to what degree there is a correspondence between the striving, ac-

tivity, and power of the empathy on the one hand, and my *need* for self-activity and for power of empathy on the other, and whether and to what degree what is evoked in me runs counter to this need. In particular, this is to ask, whether the striving is consistent with itself, whether the activity approaches its goal without hindrance or is impeded, whether the various activities are harmonious or clash with one another, whether they are vigorous or weak.

The highest evocation of all arises from the sensuous appearance of the human being. We do not know how or why it happens that a glimpse of a laughing face, or a change in that contour of the face, especially the eyes and mouth, which we associate with the phrase "laughing face" should stimulate the viewer to feel gay and free and happy; and to do this in such a way that an inner attitude is assumed, or that there is a surrender to this inner activity or to the action of the whole inner being. But it is a fact. Whenever I see a "laughing face," whenever I see just these spatial changes in a face, I experience a stimulus to grasp them. But remarkably, this stimulus is a stimulus that produces exactly the same kind of inner activity in me. By "remarkably" I mean that there is no further explanation for this. Even if I call it instinctive, nothing is explained thereby. And yet this use of words is quite proper. That the fact in question is so significant and valuable is, we may note in passing, nothing against its instinctive character. What is most important for our existence, nature, wise as she is, has taken into her own hands and made into a matter of instinct removed from our own control. It is precisely because of this instinct that I cannot grasp the laughing face without the evocation of the same kind of inner activity; that is, I cannot grasp even its sheer features without this. I grasp it because a free and joyful inner activity of my being has been evoked.

In the example we have mentioned things

10 [*Natureinfühlung.*—TR. NOTE.]

will not, however, stop merely at evocation. For to this there corresponds on my part an inner longing. That is why in the course of this I will give myself freely to this stimulus or experience it freely. When I do this I feel a certain "harmony," and the feeling of pleasure in this harmony is the feeling of joy at the happy face.

But in this case there may be something more than mere evocation. Perhaps there is something in the laughing face which is mockingly amusing. When this mocking amusement is evoked in me, I am called upon to realize in myself this particular kind of activity. But I cannot give myself so freely to this stimulus. Something in me conflicts with it. This feeling of conflict, of an inner inhibition, friction, or dissonance is one of displeasure. Mocking amusement is unpleasant to me. Perhaps in some fundamental way it grates on me.

Here we have once again a case of negative empathy. This too is empathy. The drive of my own life activity could not be in conflict with the life activity which is stimulated in me by the glimpse of that mocking, amused face, if just this activity were not somehow imputed to me, and if it did not somehow permeate me. The more keenly I feel this, or the more this activity which has been evoked in me begins to take possession of me—and that means, once again, the more I surrender to the impression of this face—the sharper the conflict will be and the more intense the feeling of displeasure.

What we have here said about the laughing face we must now generalize. Every *impression* of the sensuous appearance of a person is based upon its *expression*. That is, the sensuous appearance of a person in all its parts is for me pleasant or unpleasant, beautiful or ugly, because first of all in it there is a kind of life—an evocation of my own experience, an experience of my self, an activity of the inner being, or at least the possibility of this. A certain person is "beautiful." That means, the life which resides in sensuous appearance, enters into me or dwells in me, is taken up by me sympathetically. It is experienced as the fulfillment of a unique vital drive or vital yearning. Or again, the sensuous appearance of some person is "ugly." That means that the life which resides in it is taken up by me but contradicts my own inner drive to live, feel, and act. I experience it as a negation of this drive. Beauty in this case as in all others is an immediately experienced affirmation of life in the contemplation of a sensuous object. Ugliness is the negation of life corresponding to this.

But here an objection may be in order. I see a person who is the victim of poverty, woe, trouble, anxiety, perhaps even despair. I see this in him or hear it in his words as depicted by the artist. And yet, what I see is pleasurable, and I call it beautiful. Here what we have been saying does not seem to hold. Surely I have no "yearning" in me to experience what this person has experienced: inner tension, anxiety, despair. How then in this case can the feeling of joy or the aesthetic pleasure rest upon harmony or sympathy? To this the answer must be that care, anxiety, despair, and the like do not reside somewhere in the blue ether, but only in the mind of man. This is not just a fact in general, but for me. That is, in seeing care, anxiety, despair, I see a person who feels these things in himself, and when I see him or experience him, he introjects himself into my experience. Artistic depiction has evoked an experience of him. I am asked to feel myself as a person who experiences such care and despair. Let us suppose that the care is genuinely human, that the despair is humanly justified, that there is some greatness or strength, some inner power. Then I do not experience just the empty abstractions "care" and "despair," but I experience this person, this revealing instance of real humanity, without inner conflict. He awakens a genuine echo in me. Here there is an inner harmony between my being and the experience or product of my mind's activity which is evoked in me by the object. Thereby a ground is given for a feeling of harmony or of pleasure, in short, for aesthetic enjoyment.

If I see someone suffer and succumb, and if the suffering and defeat bring home to me the fact that it is a human being who suffers, then this means that what is evoked in me is not just this or that mode of my self-activity, but rather that in it I become aware of my being human. I experience myself as a human being in the most general and fundamental sense of the word "human." And this evocation can be realized just because I am human. I feel the harmony between another person and myself; it permeates me; I feel myself as a person in someone else. I have this most joyful and universal feeling of sympathy, which is at the bottom of all other feelings of sympathy. And I have it the more intensely, the more I am touched by the sorrow and defeat of another person, or the more the humanity of another person is brought before my consciousness by his sorrow and defeat. Empathizing is experiencing. It is not just simply *knowing that* somewhere in the outer world there is something mental or inward, some joy, sorrow, woe, or despair, nor is it merely imaging such things.

It has been said that if I experience despair or am myself plunged into despair when I look at a depiction of despair, and if I become angry in looking at a depiction of anger, then aesthetic pleasure is at an end. For this, it is said, is mere pathology. But such reproaches are easily handled. The answer to it has already been given. Just as there are nowhere in the world objectively such things as anger or despair, so there has never been an objective representation of anger, or despair, or the like. What has been depicted has always been a human being. Thus my own experience of the inner depths of some human being as he has been represented (e.g., the depiction of the woe and despair of Faust) is an experiencing of some whole personality with its woe and despair, with its whole power and inner activity, with its effort and

exertion.[11] It is the echo of this human being in me, an inner yea-saying to this being. My enjoyment of such a work of art is an enjoyment that comes from this echoing, this yea-saying. But there is something more in works of art. Where I have earlier spoken of artistic depiction and just now of a particular poetic personality, I have already made the transition from empathy as such to empathy into the work of art, and this is a very special sort of case. Those objections are not very significant which say that if we become angry or despairing in the face of depicted anger or despair, then we are not experiencing aesthetically at all. I become angry when in the course of everyday life I encounter something that stimulates anger. But if anger is artistically presented, nothing actually arouses my anger. Here anger arises not out of experiences which occur to me and wound me, but rather an inner mode of my self-activity is aroused by the artistic depiction. I know at once that the anger is only represented and therefore belongs only to an ideal world. This means that the anger that permeates me lacks the necessary motivating factors of real anger. It is a kind of anger that has nothing in it of a wish or will to react against some inner attack, and it cannot stir me up to some sort of action. For there is here no target toward which it could be directed. Thus artistically depicted anger is, of course, experienced, but the experience is altogether different from what I am referring to when I say, "I'm getting angry." It is being aesthetically experienced. Aesthetic experience is a certain mode of feeling affected when I am paying aesthetic attention, when I give myself up wholly to what has been represented. It is an experiencing which does not affect me as a real individual, as a part of the context of reality, but only as the aesthetic spectator living and moving in a world of aesthetic representation, far removed from actuality.

---

11 [*Strebenden Bemühen,* a reference to *Faust,* Part II, line 878.—TR. NOTE.]

Whoever speaks of empathy and wishes to take part in the controversy about it ought first of all to know what it means to be giving something aesthetic attention, to know how to distinguish aesthetic experiencing from the experiencing of those things that occur in the real world, to know that one must not designate this experiencing with any term that reminds us of the experience which practical life and the context of reality force upon us.

What I am saying is that aesthetic experience, as of anger for example, is a quite unique sort of experience, and in a twofold way: first, the anger that is experienced has a unique origin and has not developed out of an assault on my own being, but has been conveyed to me, and dwells in me, through the medium of the work of art; second, this anger does not stimulate me to practical reaction, nor has it any power to motivate action. To this we must add that represented anger is not real anger. It is the anger of a total personality constructed in just such and such a way, to enable us to experience a human being. In aesthetic representation these things are united. In attending to something aesthetically, I remove it into an ideal realm, or I turn it into a self-contained ideal world. Even the aesthetic inspection of reality, of the real landscape, for example, makes a picture or an image of it. It releases it from the actual, from the context of reality and makes it into an ideal object. I must ignore the fact that it belongs to the humdrum context of reality, which I also inhabit, and that I may be helped or harmed by it. It is quite otherwise for what is represented in the work of art. This inherently and without any effort of mine belongs to an ideal sphere, precisely because it is something represented. It is inherently a picture, an image. Here I can not only initiate aesthetic inspection, but I can do so with a self-evident necessity. The work of art is that which encompasses this necessity. Thereby, the work of art leads me and forces me, the observer, to step out of and beyond myself, and the more it deserves the name of a work of art the more forcibly it does so, immersing me and confining me wholly in an ideal world. To the degree that it does this, the art work leads me and compels me to observe this world, the world of representation, to glimpse in its depths what usually escapes me in the observation of reality. The work of art not only reveals all this but illuminates it brilliantly.

What I mean more precisely by this journey into the depths and the illumination of it is that I gain insight into what is negative, distracting, and odious, and I see what is at bottom positive in it. In the many possible situations of the human being I discern the positive man and the positive ground of his being, the concealed gold of humanity which can be brought to light everywhere, even in wretchedness, evil, and trouble, and perhaps especially there. It allows me to experience and to feel the essentially human even in what is dreadful. Even a dreadful person is still a person. There is no more potent means of making the positive in man apparent or capable of being shared by others than its negation. Such negation is to be found in wretchedness, want, despair, defeat, and even if in a somewhat different way, in evil and horror. This alone is the way in which suffering, want, evil, horror, and gruesomeness which in everyday life we avoid and call hideous, can be beautiful in artistic representation, can be objects of aesthetic pleasure. No art can transform what is the natural object of repudiation or of revulsion into an object in which we take joy. But art can find and help us to feel what is human in all that, the positively human—vitality, strength, power of volition, work, in short, activity. And all of this can find an echo in us and can satisfy a yearning in us. For all the yearning we feel can be comprised in one word: it is the yearning to live.

BERNARD BOSANQUET

(1848-1923)

Bernard Bosanquet and Francis Herbert Bradley were long associated in the minds of philosophers as the two most significant figures in English idealism of the late nineteenth and early twentieth centuries. It is apparent that, of the two, Bradley's name will be the longer remembered in metaphysics and the theory of value, but Bosanquet's place in the history of aesthetics is nonetheless assured. It is curious that, since J. S. Mill, aesthetics in Britain has flourished only among the metaphysicians—notably Bosanquet, Samuel Alexander, Alfred North Whitehead, and R. G. Collingwood. Other significant figures, such as Bertrand Russell, C. D. Broad, and Gilbert Ryle, have expressed either indifference toward, or contempt for, the achievements of aesthetic philosophers. These men seem not to have had an enthusiasm for the arts comparable to their enthusiasm for mathematics, science, or politics. The virtual disappearance of aesthetics from English philosophy during the nineteenth century, at a time when it was undergoing an extraordinary development in Germany, is not easy to explain. Bosanquet's *History of Aesthetic,* published in 1892, marks an important point in the resurgence of aesthetics in the English-speaking world, as does George Santayana's *Sense of Beauty,* which appeared in 1896.

Nothing demonstrates more fully the relevance of aesthetic theory to current and recurrent practice in the arts than Bosanquet's distinction in the present essay between easy and difficult beauty and his discussion of ugliness, for we live in an age in which the artist's product is often "difficult," so difficult that it is often impossible to resist calling it ugly. Certainly it has no "easy" beauty. But, as Bosanquet shows in his discussion of the paradox of expression, such products are anything but aesthetically vacuous. All expression and expressiveness are in some sense or degree beautiful. The ugly cannot be ignored; it is too expressive for that. How then shall we describe or define the indispensable idea of aesthetic failure? This is the question to which Bosanquet finally addresses himself. He closes with a celebrated passage from Goethe, recalling a stunning experience in youth in which the Gothic, long a lamented aesthetic "failure," is suddenly seen in a new light.

The emphasis upon expression in Bosanquet's theory recalls his famed, though somewhat cryptic, definition of the beautiful, on which the reader may wish to reflect—"that which has characteristic or individual expressiveness for sense-perception, subject to the conditions of general or abstract expressiveness in the same medium."

BERNARD BOSANQUET

Three Lectures on Aesthetic

Forms of Aesthetic Satisfaction and the Reverse—Beauty and Ugliness

There must be, so long as ordinary persons continue to exist, a narrower and a wider meaning of beauty, and it has a certain justification in the kinds of beauty.

There must be a general word for what we consider aesthetically excellent. If there is to be any reason in things at all, this, the aesthetically excellent, must have a common property and common rationale, and the only word we can find for this property is the word "beautiful." And, as we shall see, the degrees of its usage, its variations, make it impossible finally to draw a line between what is beautiful and what is not anywhere within this wide range of the aesthetically excellent. I mean, then, that this wide use of the word, "beautiful," is *in the end* the right use.

But again, while ordinary people survive, we shall want a word for what is *prima facie* aesthetically pleasant; or pleasant to the ordinary sensibility; and for this we shall never get the common use of language to abandon the word "beautiful." We shall always find opposition if we say even that the sublime is a form of the beautiful, and when we come to the stern and terrible and grotesque and humorous, if we call them beautiful we shall, as a rule, be in conflict

From Three Lectures on Aesthetic. *London: Macmillan & Co., Ltd., 1931. Reprinted by permission of Macmillan & Co., Ltd. (First published: 1915.)*

with usage. And I take it there is a real *specific* difference between *a* beautiful and the sublime, for instance.

So then, we may say that beauty in the wider sense, which is also the more correct sense, and the sense come to by education, and that preferred I think by persons endowed with much aesthetic insight—beauty in this wider sense is the same as what is aesthetically excellent. But by a justified usage, this wider sense of beauty which equals aesthetically excellent must be taken as containing two classes, that of easy beauty and that of difficult beauty, including the sublime, etc., respectively.

It is dangerous perhaps to give examples, which may offend some one's convictions, but the character of easy or facile beauty is, I think, readily recognisable. It coincides with that which, on grounds which cannot be pronounced unaesthetic, is *prima facie* pleasant to practically every one. A simple tune; a simple spatial rhythm, like that of the tiles in one's fireplace; a rose; a youthful face, or the human form in its prime, all these afford a plain straightforward pleasure to the ordinary "body-and-mind." There is no use in lengthening the list.

Now here there is an interesting and important observation to be met. Surely, it may be urged against our distinction, the very greatest achievements of all in art, and the very most beautiful and splendid things in nature, appeal to everybody, ordinary people and others, so that we must not set down the universality of appeal in beautiful things as a character which implies a trivial or superficial character in them. That is to say, it seems as if some easy beauty were yet beauty of the highest type.

In answer to this, I incline to think we ought to distinguish between the easier types of beauty and what might be called simple victorious or triumphant beauty; between the Venus dei Medici and the Venus de Milo; between the opening of *Marmion* and the first chorus of the *Agamemnon*. I take it that very great works

of art often possess simple aspects which have a very wide appeal, partly for good reasons, partly also for less good ones. We shall see a good reason below.

Thus, I do not think that the existence of triumphant beauty disproves the fact that there is a class of easy beauty.

I believe, therefore, that we cannot dispense with the distinction between the easier and the more difficult beauty. I will pass at once to the latter in order to explain more precisely by contrast what I have in mind.

The difficulty, amounting for some persons to repellence, which belongs to such beauty as makes the rarer appeal, may take different forms. I suggest three. I do not say that they cover all the cases. I will call them: Intricacy, Tension, Width.

The case of *intricacy* is very instructive, because in it you can often show to demonstration that the more difficult aesthetic object has all that the simpler has, and more. You could show this in many conventional patterns, e.g., in the case of the common volutes which are so often found separate, and which are also combined with the palmetto pattern in the design from the ceiling of the treasury at Orchomenus. And I presume that you can show the same thing very completely in music, where the failure of appreciation is often simply the inability to follow a construction which possesses intricacy beyond a certain degree. And, no doubt, there is apt to be a positive revulsion against a difficulty which we cannot solve. It is very noticeable in aesthetic education how the appreciation of what is too intricate for us begins with isolated bits, which introduce us to the pervading beautiful quality of the texture we are trying to apprehend—a lovely face in an old Italian picture, before we are ready to grasp its "music of spaces"; a magnificent couplet in *Sordello*, which has been said to contain the finest isolated distichs in the English language; or a simple melody in a great symphony. When it is demonstrated to one that the texture at every point is exquisitely beautiful, as is always the case in the works which furnish the higher and rarer test of appreciation—we may think of Dante's *Inferno*—it is easier to believe that one's failure to grasp the whole is simply a defect in one's capacity of attention. And the progress of one's education confirms this suggestion. The difficult beauty simply gives you too much, at one moment, of what you are perfectly prepared to enjoy if only you could take it all in.

The same thing is true with the high *tension* of feeling. Aristotle speaks, in a most suggestive phrase, of the "weakness of the spectators," which shrinks from the essence of tragedy. In other words, the capacity to endure and enjoy feeling at high tension is somewhat rare. The principle is the same as that of intricacy, but it is a different case. Such feeling may be embodied in structures, e.g., in words which look very simple. But yet it demands profound effort and concentration to apprehend them.

An exception, within the area of this particular case, may afford an excellent example of what I called triumphant beauty— beauty which, although of the most distinguished quality, is universal in its appeal. I mean when a passage of feeling at high tension, simply and directly expressed, has the mixture of luck and merit which makes it strike on some great nerve of humanity, and thus conquer the suffrages of the world. Great artists, from Plato to Balzac have laid stress on this possibility, and Balzac at least was not the man needlessly to admit anything in derogation of the pure prerogative of art. I have never found the man or woman to whom the Demeter of Knidos failed to appeal, and it surely cannot be set down as facile beauty in the depreciatory sense.

But, in general, one may say that the common mind—and all our minds are common at times—resents any great effort or concentration, and for the same reason resents the simple and severe forms which are often the only fitting embodiment of such a concentration—forms which promise, as Pater says, a great expressiveness, but only on condition of being received with a great attentiveness. The kind of effort required is not exactly an intellectual effort; it is something more, it is an imaginative effort, that is to say, as we saw, one in which the body-and-mind, without resting upon a fixed system like that of accepted conventional knowledge, has to frame for itself as a whole an experience in which it can "live" the embodiment before it. When King John says to Hubert the single word "death," the word is, in a sense, easily apprehended; but the state of the whole man behind the broken utterance may take some complete transformation of mental attitude to enter into. And such a transformation may not be at all easy or comfortable; it may be even terrible, so that in Aristotle's phrase the weakness of the spectator shrinks from it. And this is very apt to apply, on one ground or another, to all great art, or indeed to all that is great of any kind. There is no doubt a resentment against what is great, if we cannot rise to it. I am trying to elucidate the point that in all this difficult beauty, which goes beyond what is comfortable for the indolent or timid mind, there is nothing but a "more" of the same beautiful, which we find *prima facie* pleasant, changed only by being intensified. But this is enough to prevent us from recognising it as beauty, except by self-education or a natural insight.

I suggested yet another dimension of the more difficult beauty, under the name of *width*.

It is a remarkable and rather startling fact that there are genuine lovers of beauty, well equipped in scholarship, who cannot really enjoy Aristophanes, or Rabelais, or the Falstaff scenes of Shakespeare. This is again, I venture to think, a "weakness of the spectator." In strong humour or comedy you have to endure a sort of dissolution of the conventional world. All the serious accepted things are shown you topsy-turvy; beauty, in the narrow and current sense, among them. The comic spirit enjoys itself at the expense of everything; the gods are starved out and brought to terms by the birds' command of the air, cutting off the vapour of sacrifice on which they lived; Titania falls in love with Bottom the weaver; Falstaff makes a fool of the Lord Chief Justice of England.

All this demands a peculiar strength to encompass with sympathy its whole width. You must feel a liberation in it all; it is partly like a holiday in the mountains or a voyage at sea; the customary scale of everything is changed, and you yourself perhaps are revealed to yourself as a trifling insect or a moral prig.

And it is to be noted, that you need strength to cover all this width without losing hold of the centre. If you wholly lost the normal view of all these things which you are to see upside down, the comedy would all be killed dead at once. It is the contrast that makes the humour. If religion is not a serious thing to you, there is no fun in joking about it.

In this region, that of humour, expression is I think inevitably very complex, as is the feeling it embodies. It is a sort of counter-expression—the normal, all of it, plus a further point of view, caricatured, *chargé*, loaded or burdened with an abnormal emphasis.

Thus, here, again, you have the more, as compared with the normal experience of the beautiful; you have a wide range of forms, all of them distinguished by an attitude taken up towards the conventional attitude. And this demands both a complexity of expression and a complexity of mood, departing widely from the lines of the ordinary moods of serious life, and even of serious aesthetic experience. Comedy always shocks many people.

So much for difficult beauty. Now the object of thus insisting on these two grades of beauty was twofold.

First, to defend, as not merely convenient but right, the extension of the term beauty to all that is aesthetically excellent. For the insight of gifted persons regards it all as one; and the recognition of the same nature in it throughout in consequence of sincere self-education is a question of more and less in the way of attentiveness and imaginative effort. There is no constant line to be drawn between easy and difficult beauty. And I think we must all have noticed that the gift of aesthetic appreciativeness has more to do with sincerity of character than with intellectual capacity. In the appreciation of great things, so much depends on teachableness, and the absence of self-absorption and the yearning to criticise.

And, secondly, it was to prepare us to approach the fundamental problem of what we mean by real ugliness. For this account of the degrees and areas of beauty nibbles away to some extent the current antithesis of beauty and ugliness.

Intricacy, tension, and width account for a very large proportion of so-called ugliness, that is to say, of what shocks most people, or else seems to them repellently uninteresting, or overstrained, or fantastic. All this part of ugliness then seems due to the weakness of the spectator, whether his object is nature or art. Note how slowly, e.g., the beauty of old age, I mean of real wrinkled old age, not stately and splendid old age, gains recognition in sculpture; I think not before the Alexandrine period.

Before going further, it will be best to return upon one fundamental point and make it quite clear. We started in the first lecture by describing the aesthetic attitude as involving a pleasant feeling of such and such a kind. But we have now seen that the pleasant feeling which is one with the appreciation of beauty is not a previous condition of beauty. It is not on some other ground a pleasure, and then by being expressed becomes beautiful. It is a pleasantness not antecedent to the appreciation of beauty, but arising in and because of it, in the freedom or expansion which the mind enjoys in and through the act which gives or finds adequate embodiment for its feeling, and so makes the feeling what it is. Therefore, you must not say pleasantness is a condition precedent of beauty; rather, beauty is a condition precedent of pleasantness. Beauty is essentially enjoyed; it lives in enjoyment of a certain kind. But you cannot make it up out of enjoyments of any other kind.

Now about true ugliness. This must mean, if it means anything, invincible ugliness, such as no sane imagination can see as beauty. It must be quite a different thing from difficult beauty.

About this question of true ugliness there is a general paradox, which applies also to the kindred questions of error and moral evil. I will state it first in general language, for the sake of its philosophical interest.

Beauty is feeling become plastic. Now a thing which conflicts with beauty, which produces an effect contrasted with its effect —what we call ugliness—must itself be either plastic (expressive) or not.

If it is not plastic, i.e., has no expressive form by which it embodies anything, then, for aesthetic purposes, it is nothing. But if it *is* plastic, i.e., if it has expressive form, and therefore embodies a feeling, then it itself falls within the general definition of the beautiful as what is aesthetically excellent.

You might be tempted to rejoin—ah, but the ugly expresses only something unpleasant. But we have seen why this will not help us. If an object comes within the definition of beauty, then (supposing the definition is right) its being unpleasant to us would merely be due to our weakness and want of education, and it would come within the limits of difficult beauty.

So we go back to the paradox; if it has no expressive form, it is nothing for aesthetic. If it has one, it belongs to the beautiful. This is no quibble. It is a fundamental difficulty about beauty and truth and goodness; it comes when you try to set up an opposite to anything which depends on being complete. Try love and hate. Hate is to be the opposite of love; well, what do you hate and why? What is your hate directed upon? It cannot be aimed at nothing. It must be directed upon something definite and hold together for some reason, and this reason must be the nature of something which outrages you in some way, violates your purposes and likings. So when you fill it all in and see it in full with what it aims at, your hate has turned to some sort of love; it is a positive passion for something which something else obstructs. There is the same paradox with error.

Thus, you can hardly say that what is ugly is fully expressive of *anything*. For if it were so, it would become *ipso facto* a kind of beauty. And, if you maintain this, you withdraw wholly within the doctrine of the "weakness of the spectator," and you say in effect that there is no such thing as invincible ugliness. I am much inclined to such a view; but there is more to be considered.

For, take the case of mere apparent ugliness itself, such as is due to our weakness of attention or imagination. It seems to be a positive aesthetic effect, and one which must be accounted for as much as if it were fundamental and invincible. When we judge an appearance as ugly, even if ultimately we are wrong, what is it that we mean to indicate?

One might say, an appearance is ugly which has indeed, as everything must have, a form and a self-expression in a sense, but a form such as to convey an impression of formlessness. The German *Unform* is suggestive at this point. Primarily meaning "formlessness," it may also convey the implication of ugliness. We can show the same usage, in saying, for example, "That is a hideous hat, it is perfectly formless." But, *prima facie,* this can only mean that a thing has not the kind of form we expect. Or even if there could be an expression of unexpressiveness, you would, in one sense, have in it the very highest achievements of the sublime and the humorous. For the sublime, take the famous passage in Job, or Milton's description of death. These present to your imagination something whose aesthetic embodiment is that it is too awful to be actually apprehended in a shape. Or, in the region of humour; it is only too easy to tell a story without a point; but it is a very clever and difficult thing to tell a story whose point is that it has no point. Ugliness cannot be merely the expression of what will not go into definite form. Even in the revulsion against difficult beauty, it has a positive quality of discordancy, though perhaps one which we ought to be able to overcome.

We must try again. One might think of a combination of beautiful expressions which should contradict each other so that the whole should be ugly, i.e., incapable as a whole of embodying any single feeling; though the parts were beautiful. This would be in one sense inexpressive, i.e., a conflict or discord of expressions. And this error might be multiplied; there might be an aggregate of beautiful parts which refused to come together as a single embodiment at all. I should suppose that these cases do occur, and one cannot say they are mere absences of beauty. No doubt they would have a positively shocking effect. But we see what they would be. They would be, not something new and alien and brought from somewhere else than beauty. They would consist in a beauty in the wrong place, parallel to conceiving moral badness as a goodness in the wrong place. You can easily fancy a case by misuse of the human form, substituting limbs of the lower animals for its limbs, as in fauns or mediaeval devils. Suppose the beautiful silky ear of a dachshund replacing the ear of a beautiful human

face. It would be, I imagine, a horribly hideous thing. Here we have, in principle, I think, a genuine case of ugliness. But we see how limited its antagonism to beauty is. Then you get again the problem whether in the whole context of what is imagined this discord may not itself be made expressive, and so subordinated to beauty, as in some fairy tale of enchantment. If so, note that it becomes really a part of the whole beauty. It is a half-hearted theory to call it ugly, and treat it as a foil to beauty, like dark to light.

We have then not yet really run down our true or invincible ugliness; though we have approached it so far as we have found something akin to it in a form of "inexpressiveness."

For Croce the ugly is the purely inexpressive. But that we saw is not strictly possible.

The inexpressive, except by self-contradiction, would be nothing. For how can any appearance be inexpressive? Its defect could only be due to our want of insight and sympathy. Put it in another way: if the ugly is the unaesthetic, well then it is not aesthetic at all, and we are not concerned with it. So we seem driven to this. If there is a truly ugly which is aesthetically judged, and which is not merely a failure of our imagination, it must be an appearance which is both expressive and inexpressive at once, aesthetically judged, yet unaesthetic. "The same thing must be looked for that is looked for in the beautiful, and its opposite found" (Solger). That is to say, the appearance must suggest an adequate embodiment of a feeling, and also frustrate it. The imagination must be at once excited in a particular direction and thwarted in it. The pain of a discord in music, it has been said, is like trying to do a sum in your head, and finding the numbers too high. A flickering light is another simple example; if the period of flickering is just enough to begin to satisfy the eye, and then to check its activity, it is exceedingly painful.

Then, going back on our account of the embodiment of feeling and the experience of the rising mountain, we see that any sudden check or break in a pattern, e.g., an obvious want of symmetry, if it is not explained to the imagination, must have this effect of arousing the mind in a certain direction, and then obstructing it in that same direction. This double effect may be brought under the general head of the inexpressive. But of course it is not the merely inexpressive—that, as we have said throughout, would be at least aesthetically nothing at all. It is a form of expression whose intention can be detected, very often a recollection of some other successful and excellent expression, but which in the execution violates its own intention. Thus you have in it the two factors we held necessary; the suggestion of expressiveness and its counteraction by a completion conflicting with it. It must be a story without a point; not the caricature of a pointless story, because in that the defect is made an excellence; but yet a story.

The difference between this and the case of conflicting beautiful expressions, which we spoke of before, is not very wide in principle, because we cannot give up the observation that every form expresses something. The difference is that in this case the suggestion of beauty is baffled by an expression which consists of the interruption and positive undoing or negation of that in which significance for the suggestion consisted. A simple asymmetry, quite unprovoked, is, as we said, a typical case.

Thus we approach the general result that the principal region in which to look for insuperable ugliness is that of conscious attempts at beautiful expression—in a word, the region of insincere and affected art. Here you necessarily have the very root of ugliness—the pretension to pure expression, which alone can have a clear and positive failure. It is possible, I take it, for the appearances of nature to have the same effect, and therefore to be genuinely ugly.

But there is a wide difference of principle between the two provinces, because to nature we can never impute the conscious effort at beautiful expression; and therefore the particular context in which we seem to see such an effort negatived must always be one of our own choosing. The ugly effect must therefore be in some degree imputable to our own mis-selection rather than to the being of nature herself; although, of course, one may argue that just because she has no conscious choice, she must accept discredit for her ugly appearances, as well as credit for her beautiful ones. But one might perhaps rejoin again, "Yes, but in her infinite wealth of contexts and appearances, there is always ample opportunity for the selection of beautiful form, and therefore we have no right to pin her down to an ugliness which does really spring from our limitation." You may reply again that if it is left to us there is just as much room for seeing ugliness as for seeing beauty. But I doubt this. If the intentional attempt at beauty is the main condition of ugliness, then in nature the main condition of ugliness is certainly absent, while immeasurable stores of form and order are as certainly present for those who can elicit them.

And the same applies in great measure to the world of useful objects, so long as they pretend to be nothing more than they are. So long they cannot be fraudulent; and their solid simplicity of purpose may well make it possible to see a beauty in them, due, so to speak, to their single-heartedness, which may make their form a single harmonious expression. On the other hand, any attempt to confer upon them mere decorative beauty inconsistent with their purpose would at once make them positively ugly.

This gives us the clue to a reasonable estimate of the current idea that ugliness is all of man's making and not of nature's. It seems in principle to rest upon the fact we have noted, that man alone has in him the capacity for the attempt to achieve pure expression for its own sake, in other words, beauty, and therefore he is much more likely to produce the appearance of the combined attempt and failure which we have seen to be the essence of the ugly.

One further ambiguity in a common phrase seems worth clearing up. Is beauty the aim of art? Is "art for art's sake" a watchword that conveys a truth?

I hope that the line we have taken shows its value by making it easy to deal with these ideas. Beauty, we have seen, is an ambiguous term. If it means some given ideal which lays restrictions beforehand upon individual expressiveness, something of the nature of the easy beauty, which rules out what is beyond our capacity to grasp at a given moment, then it is very dangerous to say that beauty is the aim of art. It is dangerous, that is, if it means to us that we know beforehand what sort or type of thing our beauty is to be. For beauty is above all a creation, a new individual expression in which a new feeling comes to exist. And if we understand it so, there is not much meaning in saying that it is the aim of art, for we do not know beforehand what that is to be. If we understand it otherwise, as a rule previously prescribed, then it is something which must be hostile to free and complete expression for expression's sake. In that case the aim of art is not the full aim, but only the art in the aim, and that is a fatal separation.

Of "art for art's sake" the same criticism, I think, holds true. It tells you nothing if it only tells you that the aim of art is to do what art truly aims to do. But if it means that art is some limiting conception, some general standard accepted beforehand, then I suggest that it becomes actively mischievous. The aim of art can then no longer be the full self-developing aim which *is* the aim of art, because art as an abstract conception has been thrown into the idea of the aim, carrying with it a fatal and restricting self-consciousness. In applying a method or principle rightly, you do not think of the method or principle. You think of the work,

and live the method or principle. Art, like knowledge, is creative and individual, and you cannot lay down beforehand where either of them will take you. And if you make the attempt, you must be unfaithful to their freedom.

I have not attempted in these lectures to give a systematic account either of the forms of beauty, for example the tragic and the sublime, or of the historical development of art. What I desired was to concentrate upon a single leading conception, the conception of the way in which an object of imagination can be expressive of feeling, and the consequences of this way of expression for the feeling so expressed. And what I should like to have effected, from a negative point of view, so far as it is still necessary in these days, would be to have torn away the gilded veil, the glamour, so to speak, which hangs over the face of beauty and separates it from life. We are not advocating what is miscalled realism; our account of imaginative vision makes that a mere absurdity. But I am trying to prove, and not merely to prove but to help ourselves to realise, how the whole world of beauty, from the Greek key pattern on the one hand and our admiration of the curve of a waterfall on the other, up to the intricacies of the greatest architecture or the tension of Shakespearean tragedy, is the individual operation of a single impulse, the same in spectator and creative artist, and best discerned when we penetrate the heart of strength and greatness under the veil of commonplace destiny or tragic collision, where there is no golden haze to flatter our indolence and luxury. And now as always one's words seem a tale of little meaning, which goes on missing the heart of its own intention. Let me end with a quotation from an early tractate of Goethe, which contains in a few brief strokes all that I have been saying, and the germ, I think, of all that the last hundred years of aesthetic have taught us. Only I must give the warning that he employs the term beautiful sometimes in the sense which he and I alike are working against, the sense of easy beauty.

The passage, however, explains itself:

> When I first went to see the cathedral, my head was full of general conceptions of good taste. I reverenced, from hearsay, harmony of masses and purity of form, and was a sworn foe to the confused caprices of Gothic decoration. Under the rubric "Gothic," like an article in a dictionary, I had collected all the mistaken synonyms that had ever come into my head, "disorderly, unnatural, a heap of odds and ends, patchwork, overloaded."...How unexpected was the feeling with which the sight amazed me, when I stood before the building. My soul was filled by a great and complete impression, which, because it was composed of a thousand harmonious details, I was able to taste and to enjoy, but in no way to understand and explain. How constantly I returned to enjoy this half-heavenly pleasure, to comprehend in their work the giant-spirit of our elder brothers!...How often has the evening twilight interrupted with friendly rest the eye fatigued by its exploring gaze, when the complex parts melted into the complete masses, which, simple and great, stood before my soul, and my powers arose gladly at once to enjoy and to understand.... How freshly it greeted me in the morning brilliance, how gladly I observed the great harmonious masses, vitalised in their numberless minute parts, as in the work of eternal nature, all of it form, and all bearing upon the whole! How lightly the enormous firm-based building rises into the air, how broken it is, and yet how eternal! And so do I not well to be angry when the German art-scholar mistakes his own advantage, and disparages this work with the unintelligible term "Gothic."...
>
> But you, dear youth, shall be my companion, you who stand there in emotion, unable to reconcile the contradictions which conflict in your soul; who now feel the irresistible power of the great totality, and now chide me for a dreamer, that I see beauty where you see only strength and roughness.
>
> Do not let a misconception come between us; do not let the effeminate doctrine of the modern beauty-monger make you too tender to enjoy significant roughness, lest in the end your enfeebled feeling should be able to endure nothing but unmeaning smoothness. They try to make you believe that the fine arts arose from our supposed inclination to beautify the world around us. That is not true. ...
>
> Art is formative long before it is beautiful, and yet is then true and great art, very often truer and greater than beautiful art itself. For man has in him a formative nature, which displays itself in activity as soon as his existence is secure; so soon as he is free from care and from fear, the demigod, active in repose, gropes round him for matter into which to breathe his spirit. And so the savage remodels with bizarre traits, horrible forms, and coarse colours, his "cocos," his feathers, and his own body. And though this imagery consists of the most capricious forms, yet without proportions or shape, its parts will agree together, for a single feeling has created them into a characteristic whole.
>
> Now this characteristic art is the only true art. When it acts on what lies round it from inward, single, individual, independent feeling, careless and even ignorant of all that is alien to it, then, whether born of rude savagery or of cultivated sensibility, it is whole and living. Of this you see numberless degrees among nations and individuals.
>
> The more that this beauty penetrates the being of a mind, seeming to be of one origin with it, so that the mind can tolerate nothing else, and produce nothing else, so much the happier is the artist.[1]

That, ladies and gentlemen, is pretty much what I have been trying to say to you.

[1] [From Goethe's *Von deutscher Baukunst*, written when he was twenty-four. The subject is Strasbourg Cathedral.—ED. NOTE.]

C. K. OGDEN

(1889-1957)

and

I. A. RICHARDS

(1893-   )

Ogden and Richards were educated at Cambridge, where their passionate interest in nearly all aspects of language brought them together and led to several collaborative works. The interests of Richards, who taught at Harvard beginning in 1939, were primarily literary, whereas Ogden's were primarily linguistic. Both, however, had philosophical and psychological interests. Together their names are associated with the system of linguistic analysis and instruction known as Basic English. Their contributions to aesthetics include Richards' influential *Philosophy of Rhetoric* and *Principles of Literary Criticism,* and their volume *The Foundations of Aesthetics,* written in collaboration with James Wood in 1922. In the latter work the schematic representation of the aesthetic theories given earlier in *The Meaning of Meaning* (from which the following selection is taken) is expanded and illustrated with examples from poetry and the visual arts. We say "expanded," even though the *Foundations* is a book of small compass, since the authors have a gift of implying much more than they say, or at least of appearing to do so.

The actual content of their classification of aesthetic theories is less important than their emphasis upon the multiplicity of aspects of art works and of aesthetic situations. They ask why there should be only one subject of investigation called aesthetics and suggest that there are plainly different parts on which emphasis can be laid. Though aesthetic doctrines make much show of polemic, it is unlikely that they conflict as much as their authors suppose. Each of them tends to select a *part* of the subject and to universalize it. But if two doctrines are to conflict, they must first of all deal with the same thing. Aesthetics may make better progress if we look upon it as a large family of subjects rather than as one subject.

In this chapter they also develop the idea of the several functions of language and its consequences for poetry, poetic language, and, especially, the language of criticism and aesthetic response. The cognitive-emotive distinction, which the authors, especially Richards, invented or gave currency to, is the cornerstone of a large literature on value theory in the mid-twentieth century.[1] The development of the distinction between naturalistic and nonnaturalistic moral and value theories has, of course, a bearing on all these issues and also on the issue of the nature of aesthetic theories. Further developments in reference to this subject may be seen in the collection of essays entitled *Aesthetics and Language*[2] and in the writings of numerous authors influenced especially by Ludwig Wittgenstein and J. L. Austin.

---

[1] Cf. Charles L. Stevenson, *Ethics and Language* (New Haven: Yale University Press, 1944), and A. J. Ayer, *Language, Truth and Logic* (New York: Oxford University Press, 1936).

[2] *Aesthetics and Language,* William Elton, ed. (Oxford: B. H. Blackwell, 1954).

C. K. OGDEN

and

I. A. RICHARDS

The Meaning of Meaning

From The Meaning of Meaning. *New York: Harcourt, Brace & World, Inc., 1936. Reprinted by permission of Harcourt, Brace & World, Inc. (First published: 1923.)*

The Meaning of Beauty

This I have here mentioned by the bye to show of what Consequence it is for Men to define their Words when there is Occasion. And it must be a great want of Ingenuity (to say no more of it) to refuse to do it: Since a Definition is the only way, whereby the precise Meaning of moral Words can be known.—LOCKE

Disputes are multiplied, as if everything was uncertain, and these disputes are managed with the greatest warmth, as if everything was certain. Amidst all this bustle 'tis not reason which gains the prize, but eloquence; and no man need ever despair of gaining proselytes to the most extravagant hypothesis, who has art enough to represent it in any favourable colours. The victory is not gained by the men at arms, who manage the pike and sword; but by the trumpeters, drummers, and musicians of the army.—HUME

§ THE PROBLEM OF DEFINING BEAUTY

Many intelligent people have given up aesthetic speculation and take no interest in discussions about the nature or object of Art, because they feel that there is little likelihood of arriving at any definite conclusion. Authorities appear to differ so widely in their judgments as to which things are beautiful, and when they do agree there is no means of knowing *what* they are agreeing about.

What in fact do they mean by Beauty? Prof. Bosanquet and Dr. Santayana, Signor Croce and Clive Bell, not to mention Ruskin and Tolstoi, each in his own way dogmatic, enthusiastic and voluminous, each leaves his conclusions equally uncorrelated with those of his predecessors. And the judgments of experts on one another are no less at variance. But if there is no reason to suppose that people are talking about the same thing, a lack of correlation in their remarks need not cause surprise. We assume too readily that similar language involves similar thoughts and similar things thought of. Yet why should there be only one subject of investigation which has been called Aesthetics? Why not several fields to be separately investigated, whether they are found to be connected or not? Even a Man of Letters, given time, should see that if we say with the poet:

> "Beauty is Truth, Truth Beauty"—that
>   is all
> Ye know on earth, and all ye need to
>   know,

we need not be talking about the same thing as the author who says:

> The hide of the rhinoceros may be admired for its fitness; but as it scarcely indicates vitality, it is deemed less beautiful than a skin which exhibits mutable effects of muscular elasticity.

What reason is there to suppose that one aesthetic doctrine can be framed to include all the valuable kinds of what is called Literature?

Yet, surprising though it may seem, the only author who appears to have expressly admitted this difficulty and recognized its importance is Rupert Brooke. "One of the perils attending on those who ask 'What is Art?' is," he says, "that they tend, as all men do, to find what they are looking for: a common quality in Art....People who

start in this way are apt to be a most intolerable nuisance both to critics and to artists....Of the wrong ways of approaching the subject of 'Art,' or even of any one art, this is the worst because it is the most harmful." He proceeds to point out how "Croce rather naïvely begins by noting that 'aesthetic' has been used both for questions of Art and for perception. So he sets out to discover what meaning it can really have to apply to both. He takes it for the one necessary condition a true answer about 'Aesthetics' must satisfy, that it shall explain how Art and Perception are both included. Having found such an explanation, he is satisfied." The same lively awareness of linguistic pitfalls which enabled Rupert Brooke wisely to neglect Croce also allowed him to detect the chink in Professor G. E. Moore's panoply, and so to resist the inexorable logic of the Cambridge Realists, then at the height of their power. "Psychologically," he says, "they seem to me non-starters. In the first place I do not admit the claims of anyone who says 'There *is* such a thing as Beauty, because when a man says, "This is beautiful," he does not *mean* "This is lovely." '... I am not concerned with what men may *mean*. They frequently mean, and have meant, the most astounding things. It is, possibly, true that when men say, 'This is beautiful' they do not mean 'This is lovely.' They may *mean* that the aesthetic emotion exists. My only comments are that it does not follow that the aesthetic emotion does exist; and that, as a matter of fact, they are wrong."[1]

His own sympathies, at least as they appear in the volume from which we quote, were with views of type XI in the list given

---

[1] *John Webster and the Elizabethan Drama* (New York: Dodd, Mead & Co., 1916), pp. 1–7. Rupert Brooke clearly did not understand that the argument here being refuted professed to supply a proof not of existence but of *subsistence*. Common sense, however, sometimes succeeds where logical acumen overreaches itself.

below, though he does not seem to have considered the matter very deeply, and had no opportunity of following up the promise of his admirable approach.

§ ALTERNATIVE DEFINITIONS OF BEAUTY

Whenever we have any experience which might be called "aesthetic," that is whenever we are enjoying, contemplating, admiring or appreciating an object, there are plainly different parts of the situation on which emphasis can be laid. As we select one or other of these so we shall develop one or other of the main aesthetic doctrines. In this choice we shall, in fact, be deciding which of the main Types of Definition we are employing. Thus we may begin with the object itself; or with other things such as Nature, Genius, Perfection, The Ideal, or Truth, to which it is related; or with its effects upon us. We may begin where we please, the important thing being that we should know and make clear which of these approaches it is that we are taking, for the objects with which we come to deal, the referents to which we refer, if we enter one field will not as a rule be the same as those in another. Few persons will be equally interested in all, but some acquaintance with them will at least make the interests of other people more intelligible, and discussion more profitable. Differences of opinion and differences of interest in these matters are closely interconnected, but any attempt at a general synthesis, premature perhaps at present, must begin by disentangling them.

We have then to make plain the method of Definition which we are employing. The range of useful methods is shown in the following table of definitions, most of which represent traditional doctrines, while others, not before emphasized, render the treatment approximately complete. It should be remarked that the uses of "beautiful" here

tabulated are not by any means fully stated. Any definition is sufficiently explicit if it enables an intelligent reader to identify the reference concerned. A full formulation in each of these cases would occupy much space and would show that the field of the beautiful is for some of them more extensive than that of works of art, while certain restrictions, such as those which would exclude the Police from No. VIII, for example, will readily occur to the reader.

A {
I   *Anything is beautiful—which possesses the simple quality of beauty.*
II *Anything is beautiful—which has a specified Form.*
}

B {
III *Anything is beautiful—which is an imitation of Nature.*
IV   *Anything is beautiful—which results from successful exploitation of a Medium.*
V   *Anything is beautiful—which is the work of Genius.*
VI   *Anything is beautiful—which reveals (1) Truth, (2) the Spirit of Nature, (3) the Ideal, (4) the Universal, (5) the Typical.*
VII *Anything is beautiful—which produces Illusion.*
VIII *Anything is beautiful—which leads to desirable Social effects.*
IX   *Anything is beautiful—which is an Expression.*
}

C {
X   *Anything is beautiful—which causes Pleasure.*
XI   *Anything is beautiful—which excites Emotions.*
XII *Anything is beautiful—which promotes a Specific emotion.*
XIII *Anything is beautiful—which involves the processes of Empathy.*
XIV *Anything is beautiful—which heightens Vitality.*
XV   *Anything is beautiful—which*
}

> *brings us into touch with ex-*
> *ceptional Personalities.*
> XVI *Anything is beautiful—which*
> *induces Synaesthesis.*[2]

It will be noticed that...the definitions in Group C...are all in terms of the effects of things upon consciousness and so are cases of Type 7.[3] Of the two definitions in Group A, the first is a case of simple naming, Type 1. We postulate a quality Beauty, name it, and trust the identification of this mythological referent to the magical efficacy of our name. The discussion of the Beautiful in terms of an intrinsic quality Beauty is in fact an excellent example of the survival of primitive word-superstitions, and of the risks run by any discussion which is symbolically uncritical. The second Definition (II), by Form, is either Spatial or Temporal according to the Art to which it is applied. If any others than these relations seem to be involved on any occasion, we shall find on examination that the definition has had its starting-point surreptitiously changed and has become actually psychological, a change which can easily occur in this field, without any immediately apparent change in the symbolism. As a glaring instance the use of the word "great" in literary and artistic criticism shows this process, the transition, without symbolic indication, from the "objective" to the "subjective" as they used to be called.

The Definitions in Group B are all more or less complex.

Both Imitation (III), and Exploitation

(IV), the definition by reference to the capacities of the medium, are evidently compounded of Causation, Similarity, Cognizing and Willing Relations; Exploitation being in fact as fine an instance as can be found of a complex definition easy to understand in its condensed shorthand form and difficult or impossible to analyse. Few people, however, will suffer any temptation to postulate a special property of being an exploitation, though such devices are the penalty we usually have to pay for convenient short cuts in our symbolization.

The other definitions of Group B offer similar problems in analysis. The degree to which routes of Type 8, mental attitudes of believing (VI and VII) or approving (VIII), appear is an interesting feature, which again helps to account for the tendency of such views to become psychological (Group C). Thus definition XVI tends to absorb and replace VI; and XV in a refined and explicit form often supersedes V. These variations in reference, even for definitions of symbols specially provided to control such inconstancy, serve to remind us of the paramount importance of Canon 4 for all discussion. The use of a symbolic theory of definition lies not in any guarantee which it can offer against ambiguity, but in the insight which it can give as to what, since we are using symbols, will be happening; and in the means provided of detecting and correcting those involuntary wanderings of the reference which are certain in all discourse to occur.

In the case of the above definitions our "starting-points," synaesthesis, specific emotion, desirable social effects, etc., are plainly themselves arrived at by intricate processes of definition. For the particular purposes for which definitions of "beautiful" are likely to be drawn up these starting-points can be assumed to be agreed upon, and the methods by which such agreement can be secured are the same for "emotion" or "pleasure," as for "beautiful" itself.

Equally we can proceed from these defini-

---

[2] A detailed discussion of the views defined in these ways is provided in *The Foundations of Aesthetics* (London: George Allen & Unwin, 1922) by the authors and Mr. James Wood; and a survey of the most recent work in the light of the above classification will be found in the *Encyclopaedia Britannica,* New Volumes (1926) *sub.* "Aesthetics."

[3] [For an explanation of Types and Canons here referred to, see Chapters 5 and 6 of *The Meaning of Meaning.*—ED. NOTE.]

tions or from any one of them, to terms cognate (Ugliness, Prettiness, Sublimity) or otherwise related (Art, Aesthetic Decoration), and to define these in their turn we may take as starting-points either some one of the now demarcated fields of the beautiful and say:—Aesthetics is the study of the Beautiful, or:—Art is the professed attempt to produce Beauty, or we may return to our starting-point for the definition of Beauty and box the compass about it.

The fields indicated by the above definitions may in some cases be co-extensive, e.g., V and XV; or they may partially overlap, e.g., X and XIII; or they may be mutually exclusive, a condition not realized here or indeed in any probable discussion. The question whether two such fields do co-extend, do overlap or do exclude, is one to be decided by detailed investigation of the referents included in the fields. The ranges of overlap between fields, in fact, give rise to the special empirical problems of the sciences. Thus, for instance, we find that beautiful things defined as Imitations of Nature (III) only coincide with beautiful things defined as producers of Illusion (VII) under certain strict conditions among which is to be found the condition that neither shall be included in the range defined by IV. The investigation of such correlations and the conditions to which they are subject is the business of Aesthetic as a science.

The advantage of a grammatically extensional form for the definitions is that, so put, the symbols we use are least likely to obscure the issues raised, by making questions which are about matters of fact into puzzling conundra concerning the interlinking of locutions.

The fields reached by these various approaches can all be cultivated and most of them are associated with well-known names in the Philosophy of Art.

Let us, then, suppose that we have selected one of these fields and cultivated it to the best of our ability; for what reasons was it selected rather than some other? For if we approach the subject in the spirit of a visitor to the Zoo, who, knowing that all the creatures in a certain enclosure are "reptiles," seeks for the common property which distinguishes them as a group from the fish in the Aquarium, mistakes may be made. We enter, for example, Burlington House, and, assuming that all the objects there collected are beautiful, attempt similarly to establish some common property. A little consideration of how they came there might have raised serious doubts; but if, after the manner of many aestheticians, we persist, we may even make our discovery of some relevant common property appear plausible.

. . . Such a respected word as "good" may wander [widely]; and there are good reasons for supposing that "beauty" will not be more faithful to one particular kernel of reference. In discussion we must in fact always bear in mind that there is an indefinitely large number of ways in which any symbol may acquire derivative uses; any similarity, any analogy may provide a sufficient reason for an extension of "meaning," or semantic shift. It no more follows that the two or more symbols which it then becomes will stand for referents with some relevant common property, than it would follow from the common name of a man's step-mother and his daughter-in-law that they share his gout or his passion for the turf.

If, therefore, terms such as Beauty are used in discussion for the sake of their emotive value, as is usually the case, confusion will inevitably result unless it is constantly realized that words so used are indefinable, i.e., admit of no substitution, there being no other equally effective stimulus-word. Such indefinable uses are no doubt what have often led to the assumption of a simple quality of Beauty (Definition I) to account for verbal difficulties; as was also suggested above in the case of Good. If, on the other hand, the term

Beauty be retained as a short-hand substitute, for some one among the many definitions which we have elicited, this practice can only be justified as a means of indicating by a Word of Power that the experience selected is regarded as of outstanding importance; or as a useful low-level shorthand.

§ THE MULTIPLE FUNCTIONS OF LANGUAGE: SYMBOLIC AND EMOTIVE

In addition to providing a test case for any general technique of definition a consideration of the problem of Beauty is perhaps the best introduction to the question of the diverse functions of language. As is well known, those whose concern with the arts is most direct often tend to deprecate a scientific approach as being likely to impair appreciation. This opinion if carefully examined will be found to be a typical symptom of a confusion as to the uses of language so constantly present in all discussions that its general recognition would be one of the most important results which a science of symbolism could yield.

If we compare a body of criticism relating to any of the arts with an equally accredited body of remarks dealing with, let us say, physics or physiology, we shall be struck by the frequency, even in the best critics, of sentences which it is impossible to understand *in the same way* as we endeavour to understand those of physiologists. "Beautiful words are the very and peculiar light of the mind," said Longinus. According to Coleridge "the artist must imitate that which is within the thing, that which is active through form and figure, and discourses to us by symbols—the *Naturgeist,* or spirit of nature." "Poetry," Dr. Bradley writes, "is a spirit. It comes we know not whence. It will not speak at our bidding, nor answer in our language. It is not our servant; it is our master."[4] And Dr. Mac-

kail is even more rhapsodic: "Essentially a continuous substance or energy, poetry is historically a connected movement, a series of successive integral manifestations. Each poet, from Homer to our own day, has been to some extent and at some point, the voice of the movement and energy of poetry; in him poetry has for the moment become visible, audible, incarnate, and his extant poems are the record left of that partial and transitory incarnation.... The progress of poetry...is immortal."[5]

No one who was not resolved to waste his time would for long try to interpret these remarks in the same way as he would, let us say, an account of the circulation of the blood. And yet it would be a mistake to regard them as not worth attention. It is clear that they require a different mode of approach. Whether their authors were aware of the fact or not, the use of words of which these are examples is totally distinct from the scientific use. The point would be made still more plain, if sentences from poetry were used for the experiment. What is certain is that there is a common and important use of words which is different from the scientific or, as we shall call it, the strict *symbolic* use of words.

In ordinary everyday speech each phrase has not one but a number of functions. We shall in our final chapter classify these under five headings; but here a twofold division is more convenient, the division between the *symbolic* use of words and the *emotive* use. The symbolic use of words is *statement;* the recording, the support, the organization and the communication of references. The emotive use of words is a more simple matter, it is the use of words to express or excite feelings and attitudes. It is probably more primitive. If we say "The height of the Eiffel Tower is 900 feet" we are making a statement, we are using symbols in order to record or com-

---

[4] A. C. Bradley, *Oxford Lectures on Poetry* (London: Macmillan & Co., Ltd., 1923), p. 27.

[5] J. W. Mackail, *Lectures on Poetry* (London: Longmans, Green & Company, Ltd., 1911), pp. xi, xiii.

municate a reference, and our symbol is true or false in a strict sense and is theoretically verifiable. But if we say "Hurrah!" or "Poetry is a spirit" or "Man is a worm," we may not be making statements, not even false statements; we are most probably using words merely to evoke certain attitudes.

Each of these contrasted functions has, it will be seen, two sides, that of the speaker and that of the listener. Under the symbolic function are included both the symbolization of reference and its communication to the listener, i.e., the causing in the listener of a similar reference. Under the emotive function are included both the expression of emotions, attitudes, moods, intentions, etc., in the speaker, and their communication, i.e., their evocation in the listener. As there is no convenient verb to cover both expression and evocation, we shall in what follows often use the term "evoke" to cover both sides of the emotive function, there being no risk of misunderstanding. In many cases, moreover, emotive language is used by the speaker not because he already has an emotion which he desires to express, but solely because he is seeking a word which will evoke an emotion which he desires to have; nor, of course, is it necessary for the speaker himself to experience the emotion which he attempts to evoke.

It is true that some element of reference probably enters, for all civilized adults[6] at least, into almost all use of words, and it is always possible to import a reference, if it be only a reference to things in general. The two functions under consideration usually occur together but none the less they are in principle distinct. So far as words are used emotively no question as to their truth in the strict sense can directly arise. Indirectly, no doubt, truth in this strict sense is often involved. Very much poetry consist of statements, symbolic arrangements capable of truth or falsity, which are used not for the sake of their truth or falsity but for the sake of the attitudes which their acceptance will evoke. For this purpose it fortunately happens, or rather it is part of the poet's business to make it happen, that the truth or falsity matters not at all to the acceptance. Provided that the attitude or feeling is evoked the most important function of such language is fulfilled, and any symbolic function that the words may have is instrumental only and subsidiary to the evocation function.

This subtle interweaving of the two functions is the main reason why recognition of their difference is not universal. The best test of whether our use of words is essentially symbolic or emotive is the question— "Is this true or false in the ordinary strict scientific sense?" If this question is relevant then the use is symbolic, if it is clearly irrelevant then we have an emotive utterance.

But in applying this test we must beware of two dangers. There is a certain type of mind which although it uses evocative language itself cannot on reflection admit such a thing, and will regard the question as relevant upon all occasions. For a larger body of readers than is generally supposed poetry is unreadable for this reason. The other danger is more important. Corresponding in some degree to the strict sense of true and false for symbolic statements (True^S), there are senses which apply to emotive utterances (True^E). Critics often use True^E of works of art, where alternative symbols would be "convincing" in some cases, "sincere" in others, "beautiful" in others, and so on. And this is commonly done without any awareness that True^E and

---

[6] It is desirable to make the reservation, if only for educational purposes, for according to some authorities "ninety-nine per cent of the words used in talking to a little child have no meaning for him, except that, as the expression of attention to him, they please him." Moreover, before the age of six or seven children "cannot hold a meaning before their minds without experiencing it in perceptual symbols, whether words or otherwise.... Hence the natural desire of the child to talk or be talked to, if he is asked even for a few minutes to sit still."—W. E. Urwick, *The Child's Mind* (London: E. Arnold & Co., 1907) pp. 95, 102.

True[S] are different symbols. Further there is a purely evocative use of True—its use to excite attitudes of acceptance or admiration; and a purely evocative use of False— to excite attitudes of distrust or disapprobation. When so used these words, since they are evocative, cannot, except by accident, be replaced by others; a fact which explains the common reluctance to relinquish their employment even when the inconvenience of having symbols so alike superficially as True[S] and True[E] in use together is fully recognized. In general that affection for a word even when it is admitted to be ambiguous, which is such a common feature of discussion, is very often due to its emotive efficiency rather than to any real difficulty in finding alternative symbols which will support the same reference. It is, however, not always the sole reason, as we shall see when we come in our final chapter to consider the condition of word-dependence.

This disparity of function between words as supports or vehicles of reference and words as expressions or stimulants of attitudes has, in recent years, begun to receive some attention, for the most part from a purely grammatical standpoint. That neglect of the effects of our linguistic procedure upon all our other activities which is so characteristic of linguists has, however, deprived such studies as have been made of most of their value. G. von der Gabelentz for instance, though he declares that "Language serves a man not only to express something but also to express himself," seems in no way to have considered what extreme consequence this intermingling of functions has for the theory as well as for the form of language. And to take the most recent work upon the subject, Vendryes, in his chapter upon Affective Language, keeps equally strictly to the grammarian's standpoint. "The logical element and the affective element," he says, "mingle constantly in language. Except for technical languages, notably the scientific languages, which are

by definition outside life, the expression of an idea is never exempt from a nuance of sentiment." "These sentiments have no interest for the linguist unless they are expressed by linguistic means. But they generally remain outside language; they are like a light vapour which floats above the expression of the thought without altering its grammatical form," etc. The two chief ways in which the affective side of language concerns the linguist he finds, first in its effect upon the order of words and secondly as determining the vocabulary. Many words are dropped or retained, for affective reasons. "It is by the action of affectivity that the instability of grammars is to a great extent to be explained. The logical ideal for a grammar would be to have an expression for each function and only one function for each expression. This ideal supposes for its realization that the language is fixed like an algebra, where a formula once established remains without change in all the operations in which it is used. But phrases are not algebraic formulae. Affectivity always envelops and colours the logical expression of the thought. We never repeat the same phrase twice; we never use the same word twice with the same value; there are never two absolutely identical linguistic facts. This is due to the circumstances which ceaselessly modify the conditions of our affectivity."[7]

It is perhaps unfair to ask from grammarians some consideration of the wider aspects of language. They have their own difficult and laborious subject to occupy all their attention. Yet from a book the promise of which was the cause of the abandonment by Couturat of his projected "Manual of the logic of language" a more searching inquiry might be expected. It still remains true that linguists, of whom M. Vendryes is one of the most distinguished, abound, but

---

[7] Joseph Vendryes, *Le Langage* (Paris: La Renaissance du Livre, 1921), pp. 163, 165, 182.

investigators into the theory of language are curiously lacking.[8]

From the philosophical side also, the speculative approach to this duality of the symbolic and evocative functions has been made recently under various disguises. All such terms as Intuition, Intellect, Emotion, Freedom, Logic, Immediacy, are already famous for their power to confuse and frustrate discussion. In general, any term or phrase, "élan vital," "purely logical analysis"...which is capable of being used either as a banner[9] or as a bludgeon, or as both, needs, if it is to be handled without disaster, a constant and conscious understanding of these two functions of language. It is useless to try to sterilize our instruments without studying the habits of the bacteria. Not even mathematics is free as a whole from emotive complications; parts of it seem to be, but the ease with which mathematicians turn into mystics ("Even were there no things at all, there would still be the property of being divisible by 107") when they consider its foundations, shows what the true situation is.

One of the best known of these disguised discussions of the emotive function of language centres about the teaching of Bergson on the nature of knowledge. To quote from a recent exposition: "The business of philosophy, according to Bergson, is not to explain reality, but to know it. For this a different kind of mental effort is required. Analysis and classification, instead of increasing our direct knowledge, tend rather to diminish it."[10] As Bergson himself says:

"From the infinitely vast field of our virtual knowledge we have selected, to turn into actual knowledge, whatever concerns our action upon things; the rest we have neglected."[11] And as his expositor continues: "The attitude of mind required for explaining the facts conflicts with that which is required for knowing them. From the point of view simply of knowing, the facts are all equally important and we cannot afford to discriminate, but for explanation some facts are very much more important than others. When we want to explain, therefore, rather than simply to know, we tend to concentrate our attention upon these practically important facts and pass over the rest."[12]

The processes of explanation as described by Bergson bear a close resemblance to what we have called reference when this is supported by symbolism. Owing to his peculiar view of memory, however, he is unable to make the use of mnemic phenomena which, as we have seen, is essential if mysticism, even as regards this kind of "knowledge" is to be avoided.

The other kind of knowledge, "virtual knowledge," the knowledge which is "creative duration," the only kind of knowledge of "really real reality" Bergsonians will allow, is, as he presents it, unavoidably mystical. Not only because any description of it must involve the expositor in self-contradiction—as we have seen, any repudiation of orthodox symbolic machinery has this consequence[13]—but also because it requires an initial act of faith in the existence of a vast world of "virtual knowledge" which is actually unknown. None the less, those who have no such faith, and merely follow the advice of Bergsonians to neglect the actual terms in the descriptions given and to perform instead an "act of syn-

---

8 An exception might be made of Professor Delacroix, who in *Le Langage et la pensée* (Paris: F. Alcan, 1924) devotes considerable space to the subject, but treats the emotive function in a purely academic spirit without regard for its far-reaching effects upon discussion.

9 Cf. Nietzsche's dictum: "Words relating to values are merely banners planted on those spots where a new blessedness was discovered—a new feeling."

10 K. Stephen, *The Misuse of Mind* (London: Routledge & Kegan Paul, Ltd., 1922), p. 19.

---

11 Bergson, *La Perception du changement* (Oxford: The Clarendon Press, 1911), p. 12.

12 K. Stephen, *op. cit.*, p. 22.

13 Mrs. Stephen writes with great lucidity upon this question. Cf. *op. cit.*, especially pp. 57–61.

thesis," can easily become persuaded that they understand what "virtual knowledge" is, and even that they can possess it.

...Knowledge in the sense of reference is a highly indirect affair, and...though we often *feel* an objection to admitting that our mental contact with the world is neither close nor full, but on the contrary distant and schematic, our reluctance might be diminished by a consideration of our non-cognitive contacts. These, too, are for the most part indirect, but they are capable of much greater fullness. The more clear and discriminating reference becomes, the slighter, relatively to similar but cruder reference, is our link with what we are referring to—the more specialized and exquisite the context involved. With all that Bergson has to say about the tendency for precise, discriminating, analytic attention to whittle down our connection with what we are attending to, we can agree. Bergson, moreover, has well emphasized the part played by language in reinforcing and exaggerating this tendency. Thinking casually of conies, the context involved may be of immense complexity, since a large part of our past experience with these animals is operative. Thinking discriminatingly of the same objects as "small deer," our context becomes specialized, and only those features of conies need be involved which they share with their co-members of the class in question. The others *need* not be lost, but we can agree that there is a strong tendency for them to disappear, and in any really difficult feats of discrimination they will certainly be best omitted.

At the extreme of consciousness most removed from analytic and abstract attention we have not one but a variety of possible states, according to the kind and extent of the contexts, to which the experience in question belongs. The state may be comparatively simple, as when we are engaged in some ordinary *perceptual* activity, such as throwing dice; or it may be predominantly emotional: or leaping for our lives from the onrush of motor cyclists we may again experience simple throbs of pure unsophisticated experience. But certain of these concrete, immediate, unintellectualized phases of life have in their own right a complexity and richness which no intellectual activities can equal. Amongst these aesthetic experiences figure prominently. Many to whom Bergson's recommendation of immediacy, and his insistence upon the treasures awaiting those who regain it, make their appeal will admit that this is because he seems to them to be describing what happens when they are most successful in artistic contemplation. We cannot enter here into the details of what, from the standpoint of more or less conventional psychology, may be supposed to happen in these states of synaesthesis.[14] What, however, from this standpoint is indisputable is that the more important of them derive their value from the peculiar fashion in which impulses formed by and representing the past experience of the contemplator are set working.

Thus in a quite precise sense, though one which can only be somewhat elaborately formulated, the states of aesthetic contemplation owe their fullness and richness to the action of memory; not memory narrowed down and specialized as is required in reference, but memory operating in a freer fashion to widen and amplify sensitiveness. In such conditions we are open to a more diffused and more heterogeneous stimulation, because the inhibitions which normally canalize our responses are removed.

Partly because of certain of the felt characters of the states we have been describing, a sense of repose and satisfaction not unlike the repose which follows a successful intellectual effort, though due to quite different causes—partly for other reasons, it is not surprising that these states should have been

---

[14] Those who desire to pursue the matter may be referred to *The Foundations of Aesthetics, op. cit.*

often described as states of knowledge. The temptation to a philosopher when concerned with a subject in which he feels a passionate interest, to use all the words which are most likely to attract attention and excite belief in the importance of the subject is almost irresistible. Thus, any state of mind in which anyone takes a great interest is very likely to be called "knowledge," because no other word in psychology has such evocative virtue. If this state of mind is very unlike those usually so called, the new "knowledge" will be set in opposition to the old and praised as of a superior, more real, and more essential nature. These periodic raids upon aesthetics have been common in the history of philosophy. The crowning instance of Kant, and the attempted annexation of aesthetics by Idealism are recent examples.

The suggestion is reasonable, therefore, that when the pseudo-problems due to cross vocabularies are removed and the illusory promise of a new heaven and a new earth, which Bergsonians somewhat weakly hold out, has been dismissed, the point at issue in the intuitionist-intellectualist controversy will be found to be removable by an understanding of the dual function, symbolic as well as emotive, of the word "knowledge." To deny that "virtual knowledge" is in the symbolic sense knowledge is in no way derogatory to the state (according to the view here maintained, a state, or set of states, of specially free response to stimulation) called by that name. It is merely to apply a rule which all those who are aware of the functions of language will support, namely, that in discussion, where symbolic considerations are supposed to be prior to all others, the evocative advantages of terms are only to be exploited when it is certain that symbolically no disadvantage can result.

But a more general consciousness of the nature of the two functions is necessary if they are to be kept from interfering with one another; and especially all the verbal disguises, by which each at times endeavours to pass itself off as the other, need to be exposed. It ought to be impossible to pretend that any scientific statement can give a more inspiring or a more profound "vision of reality" than another. It can be more general or more useful, and that is all. On the other hand it ought to be impossible to talk about poetry or religion as though they were capable of giving "knowledge," especially since "knowledge" as a term has been so overworked from both sides that it is no longer of much service. A poem—or a religion, though religions have so definitely exploited the confusion of function which we are now considering, and are so dependent upon it, as to be unmistakably pathological growths—has no concern with limited and directed reference. It tells us, or should tell us, nothing. It has a different, though an equally important and a far more vital function—to use an evocative term in connection with an evocative matter. What it does, or should do, is to induce a fitting[15] attitude to experience. But such words as "fitting," "suitable" or "appropriate" are chilly, having little or no evocative power. Therefore those who care most for poetry and who best understand its central and crucial value, tend to resent such language as unworthy of its subject. From the evocative standpoint they are justified. But once the proper separation of these functions is made it will be plain that the purpose for which such terms are used, namely to give a strictly symbolic descrip-

---

15 Instead of "fitting" we might have said "valuable." But since the value of an attitude depends in part upon the other attitudes which are possible and in part upon the degree to which it leaves open the possibility of other attitudes for other circumstances, we use the term "fitting"; not, however, to imply any narrow code of the proper attitudes to be adopted upon all occasions. The term "attitude" should throughout this discussion be understood in a wide sense, as covering all the ways in which impulses may be set ready for action; including those peculiar settings from which no overt action results, often spoken of as the "aesthetic moods" or "aesthetic emotions."

tion of the function of poetry, for many reasons[16] the supreme form of emotive language, cannot conflict with the poetic or evocative appraisal of poetry, with which poets as poets are concerned.

Further, the exercise of one function need not, *if the functions are not confused,* in any way interfere with the exercise of the other. The sight of persons irritated with science because they care for poetry ("Whatever the sun may be, it is certainly not a ball of flaming gas," cries D. H. Lawrence), or of scientists totally immune from the influences of civilization, becomes still more regrettable when we realize how unnecessary

it is. As science frees itself from the emotional outlook, and modern physics is becoming something in connection with which attitudes seem rather *de trop,* so poetry seems about to return to the conditions of its greatness, by abandoning the obsession of knowledge and symbolic truth. It is not necessary to know what things are in order to take up fitting attitudes towards them, and the peculiarity of the greatest attitudes which art can evoke is their extraordinary width. The description and ordering of such attitudes is the business of aesthetics. The evaluation of them, needless to say, must rest ultimately upon the opinions of those best qualified to be judges by the range and delicacy of their experience and their freedom from irrelevant preoccupations.

---

16 Cf. I. A. Richards, *Principles of Literary Criticism,* 2nd ed. (London: Routledge & Kegan Paul, Ltd., 1926), Chapters 33–35.

DAVID WIGHT PRALL

(1886-1940)

D. W. Prall taught English at the University of Texas and philosophy (to which he came rather late in life—but with a vengeance) at the University of California and at Harvard. He published two books, *Aesthetic Judgment* and *Aesthetic Analysis,* together with a long monograph on general theory of value and many articles and reviews on other philosophical subjects. The influence of his aesthetic has been extraordinary.

Prall has a particularly austere and, some might say, narrow conception of aesthetics. The field is to be limited, as the strict etymology of the word "aesthetic" implies, to the immediate data of sense—specifically, data of vision and hearing. Even feeling, the positive or negative response to the object presented, is to be somehow located "out there" on the "aesthetic surface" of things. First of all, these sensory fields are to be analyzed into elements (for example, tones or, more precisely, pitches), orders (such as the pitch continuum), and basic patterns given in nature or selected from these orders (the diatonic scale, which represents a selection from the pitch continuum, will do as an example). We are then to study the possibilities of artistic composition afforded by the combination of these patterns (more exactly, specific configurations, such as melodies selected from them) with patterns (such as rhythms) selected from the natural orders of space and time. Writers who believe that they are more liberal than Prall in their conceptions of aesthetic experience (because they accommodate more in the way of meanings, beliefs, and, in general, the play of the higher faculties) like either to cite his ideas as a contrast to their own or to refute him. He is a fixed pole from which it is possible to measure the distance to any broader and laxer theory.

The brilliant chapter from *Aesthetic Analysis* that we have chosen to present stands by itself and contains views that neither follow from nor presuppose Prall's general aesthetic. Prall does not believe that there can be such a thing as a fixed standard of merit that is applicable to various objects and is a measuring stick of their value. Yet he knows that people do have and do employ standards; and he argues that these standards, though they can readily be abused, can have a limited but useful function in the process of appreciation. To grasp his views on this subject is to advance beyond Hume (and even, in one respect, beyond Kant) and to achieve genuine, though perhaps not complete, enlightenment on the eternally vexing question of critical standards.

DAVID WIGHT PRALL

Aesthetic
Analysis

Apprehension and Critical
Evaluation: Structural and
Qualitative Standards

More or less critical accounts of works of
art make up so large a part of the available
information on the subject, and critical
estimates of the value of works of art have
always held so dominant a place both in
general discussion and in philosophical
aesthetics, that it would not do to give an
outline of aesthetic analysis without showing
its relation to the practice and the so-called
principles of criticism. That general aesthetics is not in the first instance art criticism
theorists would of course avow. But they
would usually add at once that though
aesthetics is some sort of knowledge of a
subject matter, it is not descriptive science,
but normative. On such a view aesthetics
studies not facts but values; and its principles, if it has any, are principles of value
judgment, principles in the light of which
we can see what distinguishes the positive
from the negative, the good from the bad,
the important from the unimportant, in art.
If the theorist subscribes to anything but
a flatly naturalistic theory of value, his
aesthetics is thus a theoretical discipline that
is not natural science made up of generalizations from data, but a set of principles
grounded in something not to be found in
empirical experience. On the basis of this,

From Aesthetic Analysis. *New York: Thomas
Y. Crowell Company, 1936. Reprinted by
permission of Thomas Y. Crowell Company.*

the good and the bad in the realm of art are to be distinguished. It should be clear, however, that any sound account of aesthetic subject matter would, so far as it defines the whole field, apply to the good and the bad alike, and that the distinguishing of them would not be its primary determining function or systematic concern, any more than organic chemistry would base itself systematically on the distinction between food and poison, instead of the general structure of organic compounds as such.

Aesthetic analysis...offers explicitly no critically determining principles. In fact such knowledge of art as analysis would give, so far as its form goes, is like the knowledge that we have in any other science. Its content differs from the content of other fields of knowledge in the nature of the elements that are taken as basic, and the type of relations native to them, or to which they are susceptible. Its purpose differs in being limited to general acquaintance with qualitative presentations instead of with quantitative measures of processes. It is an account of the surface, and the surface structure, of our world, as felt in immediate content, instead of an account of processes conditioning that surface externally and internally, physically, that is, and organically or psychologically.

General aesthetics is a sort of qualitative mathematics. Its application to art is important and proportionately extensive, because in art the qualitative has taken on marked intrinsic significance for human beings. The qualitative is of course also the starting point of the most mathematical and logical aspects of science as well as the point at which all the symbolic calculations and equations of the most developed and successful science return to any application to the actual world that we are acquainted with. Logic itself begins in qualitative distinctions of this from that, presence and absence of content, assertion and denial formulated in abstract relations of implica-

tion, alternation, joint presence, and so on. Mathematics goes further with imaginative construction based on such simple abstractions and formulated in systematic symbolism. The natural sciences use these mathematical forms in an elaborate system of symbolic manipulation, which applies most strikingly to our world, perhaps, in the control of natural processes that scientific engineering has achieved. But in all this, while qualitative starting points are essential and qualitative results the sole possible indication of all consummations—whether in the felt warmth of rooms in winter and coolness in summer, or in immediately apprehended flashes of light of a specific color in electrified gases, or measured deviations of red rays discriminated by the aid of scientific extensions of sensory organs, and formulated by means of elaborate calculations—we do not in natural science seek as our final goal acquaintance with qualities and their own directly felt relations and structures.

We do use aesthetic data in all science; but we use such data as cues to understanding their occurrence, their dynamic relations, and the control of the processes which involve them; whereas in aesthetics we seek as our end a direct general acquaintance with content and structure as actually presented through sense. All this is of very special or of very great importance because in art, and in the aesthetic aspects of nature, such general acquaintance allows a fuller grasp of the character of particular works of art as apprehended, and hence the aesthetic appreciation of nature and art fully and accurately. Since art expresses in clear presentations through sense our feelings and the feelings of artists, the concrete character of the world of nature and life and human experience, it has seemed to men who took it at all seriously to offer us one of the main values of living, a satisfaction too great to be missed— if indeed there is any satisfaction at all that is not on some level aesthetic or artistic. But a science need not pretend to justify itself. If art is not of any great importance to men, then clearly neither is it important to cultivate aesthetics in those developments of it that have to do mainly with art. Only if we wish to have relevant and full knowledge of art in general, and of individual works of art in particular, is aesthetic analysis as so largely concerned with directly experienced qualitative structural content in art, a desirable pursuit.

But one of the most striking facts about art is that men like and dislike works of art with great intensity, so that they dispute fiercely and interminably over the relative values of such works and over the relative greatness of artists. A knowledge of art itself should make it possible to understand this, to see all this excited argument and hyperbolic assertion as grounded in the nature of art, which analysis is supposed to reveal to us. But if we take seriously our theory that art expresses feeling directly, but that it does so with unequivocal relevance to the specific work in question, only if the conditioning discriminatory processes of the organism are capable of ready and full response to the complex surface of the physical object bearing the felt aesthetic quality, then the enormous interest in art that human beings have shown and the violence of their conflicting evaluating judgments become clear. An enormous amount of the conflict is explained by the perfectly obvious fact that organisms differ. And they differ not merely in sensory discriminating powers, both because of natural aptitudes and because of great inequalities in perceptual training, but also in their readiness and range of perceptually controlled emotional correlation.

As we all know in these days, emotional possibilities and emotional clarity depend on a thousand details of individual development, from early infancy through the childhood influences of family, companions and surroundings, on through the manifold perverse possibilities of adolescence, the adjustments of social life, including those of marriage, and the whole range of educating influences, formal and accidental, physical and intellectual. We should not expect like responses to like objects from unlike organisms, any more than we should expect litmus paper to remain blue in an acid solution because it is blue in a solution that is alkaline.

But it is through men's common nature, not through their differences, that they know and serve one another, as Spinoza long ago taught. It is only by their like ways of functioning that communication is possible at all, and hence that science is a general possession. Aesthetics, like all other knowledge, makes its generalizations on the assumption that human organisms in perceptual-affective response are not totally various, but largely alike. Since the one test of communication is response, since response is affective as well as intellectual, affective content in any given case must be for all men sufficiently resembling to be amenable to generalization, if there is any full communication among men at all. Formal symbolic communication itself, whether linguistic or logical or mathematical, rests on this same basis. Hence if no aesthetic generalizations are possible, no scientific knowledge is communicable. The fairly obvious reason for our common view of logic and natural science as the sole fields of demonstrable agreement, compulsory upon men, is that most of science deals with extremely abstract specifications, with aspects of experience narrowly discriminated, unambiguously defined, thoroughly systematized in symbols and tested in operations, where again only these specific abstracted aspects come into question. And that logic itself is tautologous no longer needs remarking.

In aesthetics our objects are relatively concrete wholes, and our feeling of them is complicated by all that enters into a total organic response to the concrete presentation before us. Aesthetics has not reached the point where a fully adequate analysis of a whole concrete experience can be made out, partly because it has not been seriously cultivated, but partly because such an analysis would involve all the findings of all the sciences, a complete knowledge of the organic conditions of the response and a complete knowledge of all that there is to respond to, whether inside the organism or outside it. But so far as aesthetics goes analytically, there is no *a priori* reason why it should fail as scientific knowledge.

And there are theoretical compensations for its inadequacy. What we are concerned with in aesthetic objects is not primarily all the relevant conditions, but the structural whole in which they emerge as determinate content. It is within this field that our systematic analysis applies; if there were not some such boundary for the subject, then aesthetics would simply be science in general. And this is true of every other field of scientific knowledge. Since aesthetic content is by definition consciously present, its qualitative features may at least to a considerable extent be discriminated and analysed, without recourse to laboratory experiment or systematic symbolism. This can certainly be done on the lower levels of spatial configuration, melodic sequence, color design, and rhythmical pattern. In fact, so far as artists use humanly available technical and aesthetic materials and forms in their compositions, so far can other human beings discriminate through the normal exercise of their unaided senses, the concrete structural content presented, and feel its intention as intelligibly expressed.

Whether or not, or how much or how little men *value* what is expressed, will depend on a thousand details of circumstance and the countless complications of organic personality, as well as on accepted standards of value in many fields. But even human valuing is not so violently at cross purposes as the discussion of some theorists and critics suggests. It is a very rare

phenomenon in the world when a reasonably healthy human organism, with ordinarily acute faculties adequately trained in perceptual discrimination, fails to grasp with some satisfaction what artists express in media directly available to such an organism. No two men will put exactly the same emphasis on laying aside some specific sum of money to meet future emergencies and normal expectations in a relatively stable economically systematized society. But this does not mean that no two men can mutually understand one another's financial precautions, though a primitive islander would need some training in a civilized economic community to know what financial precautions were. And it is such general agreement in understanding that we seek in aesthetics, not an impossible identity in degree of approval or disapproval, of liking and disliking in particular cases. Although aesthetics is not primarily concerned with value judgments at all, it is plain enough that, taking as its subject matter the qualitative nature of objects felt directly and hence liked or disliked for their quality, valued in various degrees, it will, in giving an account of the nature of such objects, be relevant to value judgments, in the sense of indicating what conditions them.

Perhaps we have already indicated this relevance; but the matter is important enough for a little more explicit consideration. Aesthetic objects necessarily fulfill two requirements. One of these is that they be coherent enough to be single presentations. Otherwise they are simply not single things at all, not individual works of art, not anything determinate and distinguishable from other things. And coherence in works of art is achieved in many ways by many means. Always, however, it is through some sort of design or pattern, sequence for example, and increasing intensity and rate of occurrence of events to give order and form to a narrative, which reaches a climax, perhaps, and then recedes, by way of diminishing intensity of interest and frequency of new events, to a conclusion. The exhibition of a single character, recognizably a human being with human traits to define it, which may be made out in the most diverse incidents and places and relations to other human beings, will serve as well. Or the whole of a long poem may cohere solely in a particular feeling suggested, and gradually specified to complete determinateness, by the presentation of otherwise disconnected events, persons, places, situations, images of sounds and colors, broken sentences, unconventional speech rhythms, and even apparently perverse punctuation and printing. The most scornful critic of Auden's *Orators,* for example, is too familiarly acquainted with words and language, with sights and sounds and felt experiences expressed by language, to miss the unitary feeling that holds the poem together. And his condemnation of its formlessness, of what he insists upon as its unintelligibility, is wasted, since he himself points out its obvious coherence of intention when he notes this expression of clearly defined feeling in which it effectively culminates.

What we have been pointing out as the instrumentalities of art, and hence of aesthetic analysis, are the elements and the elementary patterns native to all controllable aesthetic material and involved in all artistic composition and in its apprehension. And the contention here is that it is combinations and complexes of such sensuous elements and such spatio-temporal and qualitative orders and patterns as we have surveyed that constitute any coherent form, however elaborate. The distinctive point of our scheme is that it starts with these lower levels, instead of being content to give rather vague literary names to the character of completed works of art, names which sound more adequate than our terms because they suggest the full character instead of defining particular aspects of the structure which has such character. Most of the famous traditional principles of aesthetics are of this large sort. Unity, coherence, a theme in variations, balance, symmetry, hierarchy, climax, simplicity, purity—all these are names for unification for apprehension, and also general characteristics of the apprehended object in its completeness. What we demand in works of art is sufficient coherence, however named and of whatever sort, to make a presentation apprehensible through sense, aesthetically present as some one object of attention.

If we are to have one large term to indicate this demand of human apprehending attention, this required achievement of unity, and to put it in a word that characterizes any or all of the kinds of pattern that could make a presentation structurally apprehensible to men and in this sense intelligible as an object of attention, the term *familiarity* is perhaps more instructive than these others. For what we demand is not merely a pattern or form—in the strict sense nothing perceived would lack some form or other—but pattern or form that is familiar enough to be grasped by us as pattern or form, that is to say, structure composed of discriminable constituents in apprehended relations. Nor will simplicity do, unless simplicity, like intelligibility, is equated with familiarity. Many a configuration difficult to grasp as geometry is eminently simple and clear geometrically, as compared to the pattern of a human face or a human body; but we have become familiar with this extremely complex configuration; we find it an intelligible form because we have learned it and know it.

So of most of the other traditional terms listed above. None of them is of much actual help in gaining a sure acquaintance with works of art and the nature of art in general. What we require is a prior acquaintance with the more fundamental lower-level patterns discriminated and familiarized by perceptual training, elementary spatial, temporal, and qualitative relations and structures out of which all the more complex patterns are composed, to become, under names suggestive of the quality of the whole, its purity, its unity, its thematic consistency in variation, its simplicity and its balanced symmetry.

Apprehensibility, however, based on familiarity is only one aspect of what attention demands in any aesthetic object. The second requirement is that of interest, which amounts in one way or another to the demand for novelty. If unity is to give us satisfaction in art, it will be because it unifies something. It is the variety that is held together in it that gives it any concrete content at all, any actual being. The absolutely unitary is nothing. Nothing actual is unified except as constituted of the various. Abstract order itself, order as such, being by definition the order of nothing, cannot even be present to sense. And aesthetic objects by definition are so present, whether in perceptual or imaginal sensory content. They are the actual being of what is affectively and imaginally perceived. So of the absolutely pure, the absolutely coherent, the absolutely formal under any name. These large terms are meaningless as describing works of art unless they are taken with their complementaries, variety to give content to unity, sensuous richness to make purity not a mere blankness, complexity to give simplicity apprehensibility at all, novelty to give interest to the familiar, to make familiarity anything but inattentively felt dullness, to keep aesthetic content from degenerating into mere cues, aesthetically negligible, though essential to the habitual and scarcely conscious expert response that is characteristic of theoretical and practical activity.

Now different men will be more or less interested in different sorts of content, as well as varying in their capacity for grasping different sorts of form. But all men take satisfaction in clearly apprehensible presented structure, if there is any content in it to interest them. No one can remain alive in the world and not have feelings; and no feelings, as we have perhaps clearly

enough seen, can be fully present and determinately characterized except by their affective-sensory qualitative natures. We might live in the dark regions of incompleted impulse, at the mercy of subconscious organic processes never expressed or possessed, but always possessing us in the disordered flux of what is often taken for spiritual life, though it is coming more and more to be seen as mental-bodily disease, commonly eventuating in melancholia or some other nervous obsession. We might live in this morbid content. Or we might attempt to abandon all sensuous or qualitied content in a habitual activity, not so much like that of full human consciousness as like the perfect social behavior of ants (if ants *do* behave without individual feelings and aesthetic pleasure). We might in our lust for action and control become more and more like the complex and accurate machines that excel scientists and engineers themselves in fineness of discrimination, expertness of operation, and tireless continuity of action. But unless we are to live in one of these inhuman ways, we shall be marked as human by being aesthetically attentive to what interests us in our direct experience, our apprehension of the qualitative affective-sensory surface of our world.

It is only elementary sanity to realize that our interests, of which we are usually not at all consciously aware, and which we never totally control, guide our selection in apprehension. It is equally clear that adequacy of apprehension will be facilitated by such interests, and that interest may also center on formal apprehensibility. It is only natural, then, that in seeing and judging works of art, even the most adequate critic depends largely on his own store of known structural forms, gathered under the guidance of his own interests, and available to his own emotional capacity.

These forms will be not only elements and elementary patterns, but also the complex developed patterns that have become familiar to him in his acquaintance with the art of the past. The intelligible will thus be defined in terms of the forms with which he is familiar, and the interesting in terms of the sort of thing that has already interested him. But of course the only authentic motive for artistic composition is individual feeling, originating in the artist, to be externalized. Unless in the process of externalization, which is the actual constituting of the feeling determinately, the artist uses sensuous elements with a consciousness of their intrinsic relations and their structural possibilities, he cannot even be controlling the aesthetic structure he makes. For these relations, being intrinsic to the elements, will of necessity appear in his work and make up its actual character. But the materials an artist works with include vast ranges of patterns already known through their previous exhibition in works of art, fundamental patterns like that of the scale in music, and the simpler geometrical figures, as well as natural forms selected out of experience at higher levels of structural development. And it is in terms of these, as well as of elements and intrinsic orders, that he works consciously. It is therefore these that apprehension must discern in his work if this work is to be grasped at all as what it actually is.

Thus critics require familiarity with patterns at all levels of complexity if they are to be able even to see what is before them. But no such knowledge will give them the individual character of a genuinely original expression in art; for it is the very nature of such expression to mold instrumentalities to the fulfillment of a unique intention; and important artists are marked by the degree to which such molding of instrumentalities to fresh purposes takes place in their work, as truly as by the individuality and significance of the intention itself. New feeling, really felt, becomes determinate only in new form; for its nature is new and

individual, and this nature is exhibited in the form that its content takes on.

What are called critical standards are very largely the structural patterns of works of art that have become familiar to critics. It is clear that without such standards neither critics nor any one else could apprehend such works in their presented nature. But to apply these standards not for purposes of discerning what is presented, but to judge its value, is clearly misleading. To apply the specific complex elaborated pattern of a Greek play to anything that happens to call itself a play, to find this pattern not exemplified, and upon this finding to condemn the so-called play as either not a play or not a good play, is irrelevant pedantry, not authentic criticism. What it purports to criticize has perhaps not even been discerned. The critic has thought of and mentioned features that are not present in it, and he has also thought of a structural pattern that it does not fit, and that therefore does not fit it. So far he is of course correct. What he says is an account of what has happened to him when he was faced with the play and put his mind on something else. But the irrelevance of his pronouncements to the play itself is patent. And the amount of criticism that is of precisely this sort is very great indeed. The remark that the critic can justly make in such circumstances is that in its general form, or in various particular features, what is before him is not a Greek tragedy. But if it is a modern play, it is hard to suppose that any one would have expected it to be. A modern play is as a matter of course not a Greek tragedy. No modern play could be a Greek tragedy. And if not, then there is no particular feature of it, no general pattern constituting its form, that would sanely be expected to be that of a Greek tragedy.

If it is objected that to be a play at all requires fulfilling the definition of a play, the answer is in the first place that if there is any such definition, it is necessarily in very general terms, only the specific determinations of which in a given case constitute the pattern of any actual play. Individual interest and expressiveness are no more determinately definable in the broad terms of a general definition than is the specific individuality of a painting definable or exhibited in the fact that the main figures in it roughly make out a triangle, or that it consists in a spread of colors over an appreciable area. In the second place, what specifies any aesthetic composition in its individuality is, as we have seen, the unique feeling expressed by it. It is this determinate feeling that is its own peculiar being; and no determinate feeling can possibly be defined in the general terms naming the general characteristics of all plays. In the third place, such general terms taken together make up a definition of a genus or a species, and to suppose that there are any such entities as these, complex universals common to many individuals, not only involves us in an extreme and highly dubious form of ancient and generally repudiated doctrine, but forces us, if the notion is to apply in aesthetics, to consider such a universal present to sense. This is a palpable impossibility, however, since universals of genus or of species could not on any theory be presented sense content. The fact seems rather to be that we distinguish our experiences in the first place by their marked differences from one another, not by an identical common character, and that the various contents experienced differ in widely varying degrees. For convenience we group together things not too greatly different from one another, and then use a general name, which we apply indifferently to any member of the group, but which does not name an identical character to be found in every member of the group or in any one of the members.

Even if the abandonment of such antiquated realism in other fields were too shocking to minds habituated to the convenient fiction of identical common natures

as necessary to give meaning to class names, and so also to general adjectival terms, which are in fact quite another matter, it is plain enough that in aesthetical theory we cannot arrive at the individuality of any particular work of art by any definition that fits anything else. And since this unique individuality not only constitutes the essential character and hence value in works of art, but also furnishes the only authentic guide to relevant analysis, it should be fairly easy to see, not only that the assumption of a common defining nature in them is highly dubious, but that the fact that they exemplified such a common nature— if this *were* a fact—would be quite beside the point, so far as insight into their actual felt character is concerned. So much Croce long ago established beyond any reasonable doubt, even if his more general denial of the significance of species and types in art is less easily acceptable.

Without ready apprehension of a great number of particular forms and patterns, without a knowledge, that is, of the structural constituents of artistic structures, no one is prepared to apprehend what any work of art of the least complexity presents for apprehension. But whether or not a work of art uses one or another sort of constituent pattern, has little to do with its expressive character, except as such constituents do or do not serve to fulfill and specify the artist's individual intention. And the form of the whole, if the work of art is genuinely expressive of anything original, that is, of anything individually felt and intended, can never be experienced and so known to critics, until they have found just this uniqueness. Hence to have a store of definitions and patterns, no matter how structurally adequate these may have proved to be in other cases, and to use their nonoccurrence as constituents, or their nonexemplification in the whole, of any work of art, as a criterion of its value or an account of its presented character, is plainly fatuous. And that this is the very common practice of informed critics—possible to them because of their solid training in materials and technique, and their wide acquaintance with historical examples in the arts—is abundantly proved for us in the abusive caricatures, by way of description, of original works of art in every generation, and the successive condemnation by good taste and authoritative criticism of what have been accepted later as the most significant creative schools of art and the most important works of the greatest individual creative artists.

If, however, critics who have generous knowledge of the arts and an informed interest in the work of artists, reverse one another's judgments or even their own, with the passage of a few years, it is plain that when ordinary mortals put their attention not on apprehending what is before them in works of art, but on expressing their more or less irrelevant feelings in the presence of these works, and then pass on, on the strength of this, to judgments of their relative value, not only do they express conflicting feeling and judgment, but the conflicts that they express have nothing to do with the character, much less the value, of the works of art that are purported to raise these issues.

Such activity helps neither themselves nor any one else. Quite the contrary. For it precludes analytical discrimination of what is there to apprehend, and, if must. be, to judge. It is no help towards acquaintance with the work of art in question or towards greater knowledge of the nature of art in general. Our dominating personal interest in having and expressing feelings of our own, instead of submitting ourselves to the feelings presented to us by others in art, by way of ready apprehension based on perceptual-affective training, stands in the way of our enlarging our range and scope. We actually refuse the proffered communication of other men's feelings, and most violently and abruptly and with least consideration just in those cases where the communication would be of fresh and stimulating content, demanding that greater variety of processes in us that is the development of vitality. We refuse to take on those various rhythms and motions, to achieve the aptness of body and mind that are their increase towards perfection, their only rational happiness. And the confusing conflicts introduced— not into art, of course, but into more or less irrelevant discussion and criticism that purports to concern itself with art—when such self-indulgent and short-sighted egotism is substituted for appreciative apprehension, may well lead a novice to despair altogether of soundness in aesthetic theory or to compensating cynicism. But such cynicism, directed towards art itself or towards aesthetics, has its actual ground in thoroughly irrelevant data, supplied by such professed criticism and such heated and misdirected discussion as we have just been considering. And its object, like that of the criticism of the Christian religion at its lowest ebb in priestly and papal corruption, should be those who furnish the data, not art or religion or aesthetic theory.

To notice such irrelevant use as this of structural patterns, taken as criteria of taste and of value in artists and their work, is not, however, in the least to object to the relevant use of these same structural patterns or standards of composition. And it is very far indeed from a denial of the being or the significant function of standard structural patterns and their absolute necessity to apprehension. It must, on the contrary, have become clear that without such structural patterns to apply as norms, apprehension is helpless either to discriminate structural constituents or to apprehend qualitative structure as a whole and as concretely given. One further example may perhaps make the point more convincing and indicate the literal necessity for elementary patterns, to serve as norms for so much as acquaintance with the actual character of any work of art.

A great deal of what is generally accepted

as the most adequate and satisfying sculpture that has been produced in the course of human civilization uses the human body as its dominant theme. Most of us nowadays do not see the human body regularly as part of our surroundings, unless we live at the seashore and spend most of our hours on the beach. And we have only recently emerged from a dark period, which obscured the body not merely by covering it from physical sight with clothing, but also by erecting a thick screen of fantastically perverse moral sentiment, which averted from it the eyes of the mind as well; so that no full attention to its form was possible in open, untrammeled apprehension. Sculpture in such circumstances was hardly itself, and certainly not adequately seen or appreciated. To the apprehension of a man brought up in the late 'nineties in the United States, the normal, and certainly the only proper, form of a woman from the waist down was a truncated cone spreading to a wide base on the ground. The female nudes of art galleries presented to his eyes forms so strange in respectable public places that he had to get over the sense of an indecent exhibition of nakedness before he could even see what was actually presented to his eyes. Even then the forms seemed distorted and unnatural. That they expressed nothing but the lure of the flesh in highly sophisticated form appeared obvious, as apparently it does still to many an honest and benighted citizen, especially those interested in the moral well-being of the rest of us. And so also of sculpture.

But whether our preconceptions are thus blinding or not, it remains the fact that only the possession in imagination of some pattern of the human body, gathered from experience, can furnish the required preparation for seeing the specific shape of any human form in art. The bare spatial proportions themselves are indeterminate without a pattern by which the eye can measure them, as any one can demonstrate to himself by attempting to name any spatial feature of such a form presented. Is the torso slender? Only, of course, in proportion to the dimensions of other parts of the body. But what is this proportion? Exactly what from experience one has gathered it to be. Such a norm we must possess, if there is to be anything in what we see determinate enough to be describable in any terms. Is the neck short and stocky? Only in proportion to other features in the first place. But any neck is short as compared with the arm of the same figure. Thus we require a set of normal proportions held in mind, if we are even to see the specific features in their determinate character. And without such character they are obviously not the particular features of the form actually to be discerned.

This discernment of spatial form and proportion goes only a little way towards the apprehension of the expressive character of a sculptured figure. But how definitely essential this preliminary seeing is to full apprehension is plain enough. The Greeks clearly realized it. If not, the formulation of a canon such as that of Polyclitus becomes meaningless. But the Greeks were tempted—as the whole Platonic theory of forms shows plainly enough—to look for perfection in the canon itself; and the Egyptians went so far as to reject as not even permissible in art any deviation from their canon, which was sanctified and stabilized by priestly authority. Since no abstract spatial pattern gives the last specification to the determinate contours of a particular figure, there was still room, however, for some degree of imaginative play and for some individual satisfaction, as well as individual expression, in concrete technical completion. When sculpture is free expression, however, what is expressed comes out only by virtue of the underlying structural orientation of parts—head above shoulders, torso above legs, legs tapering downwards, and so on—and the normal proportions of the parts, to give specific felt character to the features and to the whole.

What is thus presented is not only slenderness or delicacy or strength or great stature, but such more complex and emotionally characterizable states or attitudes as breathless excitement, or vitally alive repose, or any one of innumerable other human attitudes and sentiments that may be specified in the modification of the norm to a unique individually expressive sculptured figure.

To feel the abnormally long bodies and faces of El Greco as merely distortion, instead of feeling them as ascetic and in some of his portraits as aristocratic, or as expressive of saintly ecstatic emaciation or intense religious striving or straining, or as whatever more specific and concrete embodiment of feeling any one of them is than is expressible in these indeterminate words, is not only to miss the point of El Greco's painting, but in principle to miss the point of the arts as expressive and not merely representative. It is often equivalent to seeing in art only the attempt to reproduce either a normal pattern or a particular physical object; and sculpture has probably suffered more than any of the other arts from this mistaken notion of its function. Or rather, it is with respect to sculpture that *we* have suffered most, and lost most, by our disingenuous or confused or naïve attempts to find in it something much more obvious and less significant, something much more easily grasped and judged, than any expressive sculpture could be. This is partly due to our lack of familiarity with its underlying norm, so that expressive and sensitive modification of that norm was not even apparent to us, and partly due to the lack of anything but the one theme of the human body in so much sculpture, so that there was no extraneous incidental interest to take our attention, as there is in painting and still more in architecture. In much of the nineteenth century we lost even the discernment of its spatial character as such on account of our irrational refusal to be perceptually acquainted with its underlying norm.

Sculpture is thus a striking case of the way in which the lack of perceptual training in the simplest sorts of discrimination, and in acquaintance with even the most available natural patterns and details of form, results not only in a lack of aesthetic sensibility and relevant appreciation of art, but also in plain sensory blindness and crude ignorance. And this is an ignorance of the actual concrete nature of the world we live in in conscious life, the world at that degree of qualitative differentiation that is apparent from the point of view of the normal human senses. It is this sort of ignorance that the practice of aesthetic analysis might help to dispel, along with the strange delusion that the world from some more microscopic point of view or by way of some more broadly inclusive angelic or divine type of apprehension is more real than the world that we find about us. This involves the fallacy of separating appearance from reality, not as the distinction between one way and another in which whatever there is may appear to beings of different degrees of power and fineness in discrimination, but as the difference between the spurious and the genuine, as if the genuine could be anything but one kind, fully characterized from some point of view in some sort of perspective, as distinguished from some other kind. And to call one point of view real, and others not real, is to deny the obvious fact of the actual variety of perspectives that our own experience acquaints us with.

This sort of ignorance of the actual concrete nature of the world that we live in in conscious life is likely to be condoned, simply because the knowledge that would remove it is so available and potentially so common a possession. But it is a little stupid of us to forget the function of aesthetic theory in enlarging and refining and systematizing every-day knowledge, just because it happens that the word aesthetic has a connotation in which, quite properly, its relevance to art is most emphasized. It is stupid, too, to rest content in such unnecessary ignorance of the actually present features of the world we live in, simply because we are willing to forego any full acquaintance with the arts and their nature, rather than think of ourselves as belonging to a region inhabited by aesthetes and filled with esoteric distortions of no use in a normal, healthy, practical life.

It is our lack of perceptual discrimination and training in general, our superstitious belief in language and symbolism as the sole instruments of knowledge, that so largely turns these instruments into ends and allows us to feel informed and even wise, not to say learned and scholarly, when an enormous proportion of our wise information and our scholarly learning is verbal and symbolic content or some facility in linguistic activity and symbolic manipulation. It is as if training our larynx to the automatic ejaculation of the syllables of some language, preferably a foreign one now no longer in use, were on some ground more genuinely an exhibition of acquaintance with the world of civilization than the automatic fluency of our fingers on a keyboard, running through the phrases of a piece of music. The difference is more likely to be mainly that in one case there is little structural content as sound pattern, with a pretty vague and in all probability unauthentic meaning beyond, whereas in the other the sounds are quite fully structural in themselves and thus constitute the direct presentation of given felt meaning, and so of an actually determinate aspect of the world of civilized experience. And that men should, as we so largely do, think of themselves as tolerably educated when in the whole region of sounds and colors and shapes and forms in general, we are as hopelessly lost as are children of two or three years in the regions of language and mathematical symbolism, is one of the anomalies of our times. Moreover it is not true of the ages that we all extol as great. "Taking the prospect" or following a musical score was as ordinary an occupation for

Evelyn in the seventeenth century as making a financial calculation or operating an electrical device is for us today. And one may suppose that men of education in Greece in Aristotle's day, in Florence of the Renaissance, and in the London of Elizabeth did not avoid elementary acquaintance with the arts as beneath them.

It is not as if there were two worlds, one known through linguistic and scientific symbolism, the other through the sense and indirectly through symbolic systems. These latter are empty and meaningless unless they communicate exactly such discriminated aspects of the sense world, or such sensuous structures, as aesthetic apprehension gives us in the arts. Unless, of course, the linguistic and scientific systematic symbolic forms remain simply such complex structural imaginal content as the symbolism itself directly presents; in which case the symbolic systems and forms are quite obviously the works of one of the more esoteric arts, and acquaintance with them is no more truly knowledge or learning (though of course no *less* truly) than acquaintance with the red of a rose or the sound of the simplest nursery song.

Even the study of the arts themselves is only too easily turned into the cultivation of purely practical skill in manipulation—like so much of laboratory work in the sciences, where we spend hours in learning to seal heavy glass tubing over a gas flame, or to boil liquids without breaking test tubes and glass beakers—or it becomes the sort of verbal expertness and verbal memory that never misplaces the most minor name in the history of painting, never confuses the terms entablature and pediment, can recite a list of artists in any field in the order of their greatness as pronounced upon by the authorities, and so on and on. There is required no necessary feel of the difference between the lines of one draughtsman and another; verbal fluency on the subject of tempera, fresco, and oils and varnishes need never be interrupted by an inkling of the specific effective actuality of the look of any one of them.

These are of course extremes of irrelevance. We have at the opposite extreme such relevant analyses as Mr. Tovey's of musical works and Mr. Barnes's of French painting, though these are at such high levels of both learning and taste that for most of us they offer directly more verbal sophistication than actual acquaintance with the works analysed, unless we are extraordinarily well prepared for them by the elementary knowledge that aesthetic analysis on lower levels would furnish. We have also the lonely devoted teachers of the arts, who refrain in their instruction from exhibitionism even indirectly through performances by their pupils, as well as from verbal emptiness or the imparting of mere operative skill. But there is so little general understanding of the arts in our men of science and learning, and our masters in education itself, that all but the "authorities" in art and aesthetics on the one hand, and the virtuosi on the other, are likely to be quite unknown as forces in education, their competence or incompetence lying in a field where the ignorance of the learned leaves them free play upon helpless younger minds for good or ill. And those who harp upon standards in education are likely to be perfectly ignorant of the nature of the arts; while those critics and theorists who insist upon *critical* standards in the arts themselves, are often contentedly ignorant of the nature and function of the actual structural patterns and forms that constitute these standards.

But critics have another set of standards, not of the structural sort that we have been discussing throughout, which are often explicitly applied for descriptive purposes as well as for the purposes of evaluation. These appear usually as the names of qualities and degrees of qualities.

There are many qualities generally felt as desirable or undesirable, the names for which, even when they are used for description as literally and accurately as possible, have a definite value connotation. To apply to the harmony of Brahms in certain passages the term *thick,* is taken to be a disparaging comment, though thick foundations as such are not necessarily objectionable. The term here is simply a loose characterization of certain aspects of structure that more adequate analysis would put in more determinate form. Many of our critical descriptive terms are like this and are acceptable enough as rough designations at once of structural character and qualitative nature. But many other terms, such as sweet or harsh or brittle or flowing, of music; compact, economical, swift, of style in language; profundity, clarity, and so on indefinitely through a thousand familiar epithets, are used to name as well as may be some general character not primarily of structure but of the felt qualitative nature of the whole. And the most resounding and portentous terms, like universality and probability in Aristotle, unity, grace, the monumental in art, accord with the "laws of nature," classic simplicity, and the rest, are of the same sort, sometimes loosely indicating felt structural character, sometimes naming a quality felt at some time by some critic to be the key to all that is fine or great in art.

If the terms used have a disparaging force, they indicate a more or less condemnatory critical evaluation; if the reverse, they indicate praise or approval. That is, they are collectively, in any given case, a slightly more determinate way of saying *good* or *bad.* Obviously we cannot help employing words with such value connotations. But if our criticism is to be informative, if it is to communicate anything relevant to the work of art criticized, the chief emphasis will not be on our own approval or disapproval, but upon precise specifications and indications of kinds of quality. Here it is plain that any term we may employ will communicate nothing absolute, but only degree, with reference to some selected point on a scale of degrees of the quality named. And the zero point of that scale, or the point of maximum or minimum presence of the quality will have to be defined by the quality as exemplified somewhere in the experience either of other works of art or of events or qualities in nature, and here remembered and applied as a standard.

Compared with Russian novels, for example, English novels are rather mild than intense, whereas compared with one another, English novels vary greatly in emotional intensity, and the term would be positively applicable instead of negatively. The application of this term *intense,* then, amounts to a comparison of the quality of one thing with that of another more or less resembling it in some respect. And in this case it is the comparison of one novel with another, since in other regions of art or experience intensity has the most various meanings. The intensity of sound is a degree of loudness, the intensity of color its brightness or its saturation, depending on our choice of color terms. And there is no distinguishable aspect that is the same in loudness of sound and brightness or saturation of color. In fact loudness in the aesthetic apprehension of sound is an elementary character. From some other point of view than that of aesthetics, that of physics or of physiology, further analysis of this elementary aspect of sound is possible. But for direct discrimination aesthetically, loudness of sound is simply other than brightness and not comparable with it.

Since any intensity actually found as a qualitative aspect of a sense presentation is either such an elementary aspect or the degree of one aspect of a more complex structural qualitative whole, its meaning varies for qualities of structural wholes as clearly as for kinds of elementary aesthetic qualities. And it is not determinate, not

any aspect of experienced quality, except as limited to a more or less homogeneous range, where minimum intensity is a point on a scale of degrees, below which the applicable term would be whatever names the opposite of intensity, dullness instead of brightness, softness instead of loudness—if, that is, we are to use terms in the way in which criticism does actually employ them. So also of any of the vast number of qualitative terms so common in critical appraisals and so obviously necessary even to description.

An adequate and consistent critical standard of this qualitative sort is then—as in informal ordinary critical usage—simply an indifference point on a scale above which it is positively applicable and below which it is negatively applicable. The ordinary critical vocabulary lacks many of the negatives required for such a scheme; but it at least affords the term *lack* itself. And *lack of* prefixed to the positive term will indicate degrees in the negative direction by further modification. We may say *how* lacking a work is in brilliance or swiftness or steadiness or clarity or intelligibility, by saying that it lacks *all* brilliance, or is *somewhat* lacking in steadiness, and so on. Obviously, none of this has definitely applicable meaning unless we have, marked for us somewhere, the indifference point of the critic's own scale. Critical vocabulary is so extremely inadequate in indicating degrees, in fact, that a perfectly honest review of a very ordinary novel in the critic's own opinion, may make use of adjectives that are equally applicable to novels that the critic himself would rank enormously higher in the very aspects indicated. Constant overt comparison is required to other works of the same author or of other authors to indicate any precise meaning for the terms applied. It is this inadequacy of language to the needs of criticism that makes valuable criticism one of the more difficult literary arts, and never merely a matter of learning names of qualitative standards and their degrees, and designating these in specific cases, any more than it is a matter of applying as criteria recognized structural standards.

But if criticism is single-mindedly engaged in telling us what sort of character specific works of art have, and to what degree they have them, it is plain that the adequately functioning critic will have a whole set of such criteria at his disposal to apply. It is equally plain that the standards cited in the history of criticism, when they are not formal structural characteristics but distinguishable qualitative aspects, are still remembered qualities discerned in other works of art as exhibited in various degrees. The critic's standards, in so far as they consist of such qualitative criteria, will have as adequate a basis as the extent and the depth of his experience has furnished. But they will function to communicate the character of specific works of art to others, only if these others have the same basis to relate them to, unless the critic by various means indicates with some precision his own peculiar qualitative scale, the indifference points at which the degrees of any quality attributed by him positively begin to apply. Except in the very few cases where our adjectives—like those for color and pitch—are systematized pretty fully, the available descriptive terms are so extremely indeterminate that their application alone would hardly differentiate in degrees at all, without explicit comparison. Criticism, as we have it, is too vague in its terminology to be taken very seriously as more than roughly descriptive on the one hand, and on the other as expressive of the critic's personal feeling, and this only to the degree to which his literary powers are adequately creative.

As to final evaluating judgments of the good and the bad in art, it must be clear that these are not in the first place relevant to serious aesthetic appreciation or analysis. The degree of satisfaction actually present in any given case is simply what it is, and an honest judgment will record this satisfaction if a record is asked for. It has long been seen that we call things good because they satisfy us; that we do not—*could* not—learn to desire what is somehow in itself good, since good is necessarily dependent upon individual and social human wants and capacities. Thus serious criticism is never primarily evaluation, but intelligent description and comparison, like all other informative discourse. And the two fairly distinct kinds of standard or criterion used in such discourse are terms naming structural characteristics on the one hand and qualities in varying degree on the other.

One further complication arises here, however. Aesthetic elements are aspects of actual artistic media; specific color and texture appear on a statue because they are the color and texture of particular varieties of marble cut and finished in particular ways. All aesthetic elements and structures occur as of and upon physical media technically employed. Hence most of the clearly intelligible terms in both analysis and criticism refer as definitely to matters of medium and technique as to strictly aesthetic content. The aesthetic content, occurring as it does only upon a medium technically used, used that is in the ways of the arts and of artists, is often most clearly seen and appreciated in its technical functioning. The surest approach to understanding the arts is technical instruction in them, the same instruction that would serve the professional artist, not some supposedly intelligible high-road to appreciation in the very kind of verbal form that blurs the necessary distinctions and passes on to a loose literary account of masterpieces quite unapproachable without the elementary training thus neglected. Even strictly aesthetic analysis cannot avoid the technical aspects of the arts, since by definition an artist's technique is the operation on a medium to the artist's ends, and these ends are clearly enough aesthetic, and so in part define the technical functioning itself in terms of aesthetics.

Thus intelligent technical training is very largely aesthetic, and sound aesthetics is largely technical. To consider training for appreciation radically different from technical training, and to be separately cultivated, is one of the obviously misdirected attempts that helps explain the often total lack of intelligent relation to the arts among civilized people who have had what are called fine opportunities. Learning the structure of the scale in its actual heard nature as intervals in relations, will do more for an appreciation of music than all the lectures in the world, even with musical illustrations drawn from classic works. For the lectures will be devoted to the verbal transfer of intelligent powers of musical apprehension, which is, if not a flat impossibility, at least an apparently hopeless enterprise.

It will be plain, then, that the sketch of aesthetic theory that we have followed through is worse than useless unless it is filled out at every point with the actualities it purports to discuss. Aesthetics itself is theory, not appreciative aesthetic experience; but it is in large part a theory of the nature of the arts, and if it tells us anything at all, it is that such knowledge requires direct acquaintance, since its total subject matter is the qualitative nature of things as presented to us directly through our sensory-affective organic functioning.

C. I. LEWIS

(1883-1964)

C. I. Lewis devoted his career to the teaching of philosophy, mainly at the University of California and at Harvard. His books on logic, theory of knowledge, and ethics are held in high esteem throughout the English-speaking world. Although he was not so famous and perhaps not so many-sided and profound a figure as John Dewey, there is no one in his own generation to whom students of philosophy pay greater honor.

The following chapter represents a brave and plausible attempt to bring aesthetic judgments into line with the empirically based judgments of science and common sense. Judgments of taste were, for Lewis, a species of factual judgment—which does not mean that they are not value judgments at the same time. They are that species which deals with a certain kind of aesthetic potentiality, that is to say, with the ability of a work of art to yield, under normal conditions, aesthetic satisfaction to normally constituted observers. Lewis felt that it is possible to be thoroughly bored with *Paradise Lost,* for example, even though the reader sees that it possesses great value and that under other circumstances it could afford intense enjoyment to him and to many others. Thus we have an analysis, quite different from Moore's, of the distinction between liking something and judging it to be beautiful.

One would like to acquiesce in a doctrine which purports that aesthetic judgments are in some degree objective and verifiable. But at least one question ought to be embarrassing to Lewis. The person who makes the judgment of value, the critic, makes it solely on the basis of his scrutiny of the work. While he is absorbed in the work, he has eyes only for what is before him. When the performance is finished or when he turns away from the picture and pronounces the work "beautiful," "great," or "silly," is he thinking of the *capacity* of this work to provide aesthetic pleasure to himself and other men? Does he ask himself which people and how many people would enjoy what he has just seen or heard and under what conditions? Does he not rather, so far as he is careful and reflective, think back to the work again and again to see whether his original impressions are confirmed? We will leave it to the reader to accept or reject the conclusions that are suggested by the series of questions just posed.

C. I. LEWIS

An Analysis of Knowledge and Valuation

From An Analysis of Knowledge and Valuation. *LaSalle, Ill.: The Open Court Publishing Company, 1946. Reprinted by permission of The Open Court Publishing Company.*

Esthetic Judgment

§ ESTHETIC JUDGMENT CONCERNS A PROPERTY OF OBJECTS

We have, so far, been mainly occupied with what might be called the phenomenology of the esthetic; with the nature and conditions of the esthetic in experience. And little has been said, except incidentally, about esthetic *judgment*. Immediate prizings of the directly presented as such, are not judgments. If expression is given to them, then what is expressed is a value-quality of the experience as given, or of the merely phenomenal content of it. The direct finding of positive value-quality may be evidence of an objective value-property in the thing presented; as felt hardness in experience or seen redness may be evidence that the thing presented has the objective property of being hard or being red. And if we pass readily and thoughtlessly from apprehension of the phenomenal qualities of experience-content to a judgment of the objective properties of the thing, that is commonplace and understandable, in the case of value as in these others. It represents a habit of interpretation, due to and in large measure justified by the general character of pertinent experience in the past. But however unmarked and however well warranted this transition from the disclosure of intrinsic value in direct experience to attribution of esthetic or otherwise inherent value in the object, it is one which is validatable only as an inference. The value found in the experience is *evidence* of value in the object; it is even the best possible kind of evidence, since such value-findings represent the ruling confirmations of value in the thing (whereas for non-value properties like hardness, the apprehension of felt hardness upon contact would not constitute such a ruling confirmation). But the single value-finding in experience would never be *conclusive* evidence of objective value in the thing: in any instance, a value-judgment so based may be in error, and it is always subject to possible correction by later experience.

It is precisely at this point that value-theory can so easily go wrong by failing to distinguish between the intrinsic value which lies in the quality of experience itself and the property of inherent value in the object, which consists of a potentiality for such experience in the presence of it. A wrong decision here makes all the difference between the conception of value as subjective and merely relative to particular persons and occasions, and hence of value-predications as merely "emotive," non-cognitive and lacking any objective truth or falsity—between that, and the recognition that evaluations of things are objective and cognitive, and are not relative to particular persons or circumstances or occasions in any fashion which differentiates them from attributions of other properties to objects.

Any property of an object is something determinable through experience, and in that sense definable in terms of the experience which would sufficiently assure it. It could thus be said to be a potentiality in the object for leading to experiences of a specifiable kind under suitable conditions; and could even be said to be relative to experience if one should choose to use this phrase "relative to" in that somewhat dubious fashion. But a property so specified is not relative to any *particular* experience, or to experience of any particular person,

but is an independent character of the thing, inasmuch as any particular experience may fail to be indicative of the character of experience in general to which it is capable of conducing. Further, a property defined as a potentiality of experience is independent and objective in the sense that any potentiality of a thing depends on what it would, could, might, lead to, but not ,necessarily on what it does effect in actual fact. An actual trial of it may happen to be inconclusive or misleading as to the objective potentiality tested; and at best will be confirmation or disconfirmation only and not a final verfication. Furthermore, what potentiality is resident in a thing, is independent of the question whether in point of fact it is tested at all.

Thus the conception of esthetic or inherent value as constituted by the quality of the particular experience in the presence of the object, represents such a value as relative to the individual subject. And failure to distinguish between the quality of the experience and the value-property attributable to the object, must inevitably lead to such subjectivism. But the conception of it as a potentiality for conducing to certain positive value-qualities in experience, represents esthetic or inherent value in an object as an independent property of it; one which, like other properties, is tested by experience, but is not relative to any particular experience or to the value-findings of the individual.

Nor is it any mark of the subjective in esthetic or otherwise inherent value that there are variable conditions on the side of the subject which affect the apprehension of such value. Remarking such conditions is important in the discussion of esthetics because they notably affect the practice of the arts and the necessary discipline of those who would enlarge their capacity for esthetic enjoyment or cultivate that discernment by which they may more surely and accurately judge, from a single inspection, the potentialities of an object for their own further value-findings in the presence of it, and those of other persons. That is, such subjective conditions are important for esthetic evaluation, not because they are conditions of the value in the presented *object,* but precisely because they are conditions of any reliable *test* of a value whose authenticity is still independent of any such single value-finding.

Those who emphasize such "subjective conditions of esthetic value" as if they were peculiar to this particular property of things and to situations in which value is disclosed, would seem to forget that other properties also have their test-conditions in terms of the subject or observing organism. That we cannot reliably determine temperature with cold hands, or judge of shape without reference to our spatial orientation, or tell the weight of things by looking at them without lifting, is not a consideration affecting the independent reality of color or shape or weight in things, or the potentialities of the objects in question for experience in general. And one who should express the fact that we cannot observe colors with our eyes shut by saying that open eyes are an essential condition of those situations in which alone color occurs, would at least be using language in a strange fashion. One who makes the corresponding statement concerning esthetic value in objects, is likely to be similarly misleading. He stands, moreover, in some danger of the fallacy of subjective relativism, which says that beauty is in the eye of the beholder and that concerning tastes there is no disputing.

That value in objects is a potentiality of them for conducing to experience of positive value-quality, has no such relativistic implication: this property of the object remains just what it is regardless of the question whether the further conditions for such value-realization in experience—those on the side of the subject—are met in any particular case or not. It likewise avoids any suggestion that the arithmetic of counting noses has any relevance to an inherent value like the esthetic ones.[1] That a sentimental picture like "The Doctor" is more widely appreciated than "Still Life with Apples," has no bearing on their esthetic rank. And even if the inherent value of tea has no higher significance than that of democratic appreciation (which our Chinese friends will not admit), still there are such people as tea-tasters, whose discrimination affords a better test of the properties in question than others can make. In measure, the same social process which we rely upon to elicit the truths of natural science works also in the assessment of esthetic values: there are those who are especially to be relied upon for judgment, because they have a greater breadth of pertinent experience, and perhaps some higher degree of the requisite powers of discernment, as well as their special place in the continuity of a tradition which represents the social working of a human critical capacity. Their judgment may stand as against any number of contrary votes gathered indiscriminately, because it is something objective which is judged, and not something relative to the particular and perhaps undiscerning experience. If this social process is less essential and works less reliably with respect to the esthetic than in the natural sciences, and the connoisseurs are a less surely distinguished class, that fact too has its explanations: on the one side, the subjective conditions for apprehending the beautiful are somewhat more commonly satisfied than are those for the appreciation of truth in quantum mechanics; and on the other side, there are no crucial experiments in art. In art as in science, there are subjective conditions of the disclosure of the properties of things which are in question; and these conditions of discernment are satisfied in varying degree in different experiences and the experience of different people. But in art as

---

[1] Economic value is peculiar in this respect: being definable in terms of salability, it is thus relative. Certain other social values would also have a similar character.

in science, what these subjective conditions affect is the discovery and discrimination of the properties of things: they have no part in creating the objective character which is to be discerned and assessed. If it were not for this independent status of the esthetic qualities of things, training and cultivation of our capacity to discern them would be pointless, and mistakes in the determination of esthetic value would be impossible. And there can be no implication contrary to this objective character of esthetic value in objects, in the fact that this objective character consists in a potentiality for the disclosure of positive value in the presence of the object. As we have observed above, other properties than value are likewise interpretable as potentialities in the object for leading to experiences of a predictable kind; and for other properties also, there are subjective conditions of such experience which confirms the predication of them to the object.

The contrary conception that subjective conditions exercise some creativity in the case of values, commonly arises from one of two mistakes; either there is confusion as to what it is which is judged in a value-judgment, or this term "value-judgment" (or some synonym) is applied where in fact there is nothing which is judged. If what is to be reported is the value-quality in a present experience, such as our confrontation with an art-object, then no judgment is called for. This value-quality resident in the phenomenal content of the experience itself, is merely found. Applying the term "judgment" to such a direct value-finding is simply a poor and misleading use of the word. This same experience may also have cognitive significance as a clue to or a confirmation of a judgment as to the potentialities of the object for *further* experience. But such predictive judgment based upon this experience must not be confused with the immediate value-finding within the experience itself: the potentiality judged is

a property of the object, and the judgment of it is something calling for confirmation; but the value immediately disclosed belongs to the given experience itself, and the attribution of it neither calls for nor could have any confirmation.

There are, however, certain complicating considerations which require to be observed —even though they do not, in the end, imply any qualification of what is said above. First, there is a certain sense in which the value directly disclosed in given experience may still be said to be *assessed;* and second, there is a further sense in which the *esthetic* quality of an experience may be *judged*. Third, the object of esthetic judgment is oftentimes not a physical thing but something ingredient in it which is easily confused with a quality of experience, or with a mental entity. The first two of these considerations will be taken up in the order mentioned. The third of them is incidental to the larger and more important topic of the laws or specific principles of esthetics.

§ COMPARATIVE EVALUATION OF THE ESTHETIC IN EXPERIENCE

We frequently evaluate experiences as such; because having or not having experiences of a particular character is a matter over which we have partial control, and in which we have a ruling interest. One experience is better than another; characterized by a positive value-quality which is higher in degree; and we are concerned to make such comparisons of different experiences. Such comparative evaluation is clearly an assessment of a particular kind. Whether or not we call it a judgment, will be a matter of no great moment, provided we are clear as to its nature.

Let us first consider an analogue here, which is somewhat simpler. If we are presented with two apples at the same time, we may observe that one is redder than the other; or more accurately, what we may observe directly is that one is redder-*looking* than the other. We may make direct comparison of the phenomenal or presentational quality of apparent redness and assess the degree in which this characterizes one of these presentational items as compared with the other. Whether such assessment should be called a judgment, is doubtful: the comparison being direct, and the items compared being directly given, the decision, "This is more red-looking than that," is subject to no possible error, unless it be one having to do with linguistic expression and not with what is expressed. Perhaps we would best say that no judgment is involved but only recognition of a presentational fact.

The case might, however, be slightly different: the appearance of a presented apple might be compared with that of one seen yesterday. In such a case there definitely would be a judgment, though one of a peculiar sort, because one of the two presentational items to be compared is not now given, and its present memorial surrogate may fail to coincide with the actual character of what it stands for, in the respect which is pertinent. If, then, I decide, "This apple looks redder than the one yesterday," I have made a judgment which is subject to possible error. But the element of judgment in this comparison concerns the *absent* member of the pair compared. The relation of the now-given item to this absent one calls for judgment, not on account of any possible dubiety about the red appearance presently given but only because it is related to something not now given. The redness of this present appearance is indubitable; but its *comparative* redness is something judged because related to something which can be determined only by a judgment.

Or the case may be of a third sort: one apple only may be now presented, and I may assess it as a very red-looking apple— implicitly by comparison with the whole class of apple-appearances in my past ex-

perience. This assessment of a *degree* of redness of the present appearance, is plainly a judgment, or involves a judgment. But again, it is, in an obvious sense, the class of other apple-presentations, mnemonically presented, which is subject of the judgment, and the red character of the given presentation is not judged but is indubitable.

The assessment of a degree of value in a present experience, differs from assessment of the degree of redness in the presentation of an apple, in two respects. First, if we should say that the red-appearance of a presented apple is only *apparent* redness, then we must observe that the *value*-appearance in a present experience is not merely apparent value, but actual and intrinsic value; that kind of value in the light of which all other values are to be determined. And second, while two presentational items within a single given experience might be compared as to their immediate value, the value-quality of one experience cannot be directly compared with that of any other, since no other can be present. When we assess the value-quality of a present experience, we do so in the manner of the second or the third of the above cases. Thus in assigning a *degree* of value-quality to present experience, or to the phenomenal content of it, we make a judgment. Yet in the sense pointed out, it is not the present and indubitable value-quality which is judged, but rather the value-quality of other and absent experience with which, explicitly or implicitly, we compare it, which is the subject of the judgment.

This kind of consideration has its pertinence to assessments of esthetic value. Even in cases where what we wish to judge esthetically is not the directly given presentation but the objectively real thing presented, we may make this judgment of the object mainly or exclusively from the character of our experience in the presence of it. Thus our attribution of esthetic value to the object may be based on and reflect an assessment of comparative value as characterizing our direct experience. And these two somewhat different assessments—of value found in the experience and of value in the real object presented—may fail to be distinguished.

Thus the directly found value-quality disclosed in an experience may, first, be confused with a comparative assessment of it; and second, this comparative assessment of a value in present experience may be further confused with the objective value-property of the presented object; with the result that the value-quality which is found in experience and not judged, comes to be identified with the objective value of the thing observed, which is a property which has to be judged—and may be erroneously judged —because it is not given but only evidenced in some measure by the quality of immediate experience. Perhaps this failure to make distinctions which are required, plays its part in the inappropriate extension of the word "judgment" to direct apprehensions of esthetic quality, as well as in the fallacious supposition that the esthetic character of an object is somehow created by the nature of experience in the contemplation of it, or characterizes the subject-object confrontation only, and cannot be attributed to a presented thing in the same sense as color or shape or other properties.

But one thing at least should remain clear in this whole matter. Wherever there is a judgment of esthetic value in an object, based on the value-character of an immediate experience, or on an assessment of comparative value in the experience itself, it still remains true that the value disclosed in the experience need not be judged. The value directly found need not be assessed in order to be disclosed and enjoyed, nor compared with any other in order to have its own apprehended quality. It is this immediate value-quality which is the fixed and indubitable element in any comparative assessment of it: the dubitable element or elements, by reason of which evaluation of

it may be a judgment, is not the value attributable to this experience which is given but the value attributable to that with which it may be compared.

§ THE ESTHETIC CHARACTER OF EXPERIENCE MAY BE JUDGED

Turning to the second point mentioned above: we may observe that even in the sense in which the value of the phenomenal as such, is one which is found and not judged, the *esthetic* quality of experience may still be a matter of judgment. If our account of the manner in which esthetic experience is marked off from experiences characterized by other intrinsic values should be correct, then there is no purely presentational quality which, for example, is sufficient to distinguish genuinely esthetic experience from the non-esthetic satisfaction of an appetite, or the child's satisfaction in some novel and intriguing noise, or the writer's satisfaction in seeing his name in print. Immediate enjoyments, though various in quality, are still too nearly of one kind to afford any sure indication of the purely esthetic. For that, we must have recourse to criteria which are indirect and reflect, for example, the fact that this kind of experience is one which can be well-maintained instead of exhausting itself soon and leading to dissatisfaction. We learn, in measure, to recognize immediately in experience the signals of such enduring character or the opposite, which admit or rule out an enjoyment from the category of the esthetic; but it is not the enjoyability itself—not the direct value of the given experience— which constitutes this criterion. The artist and the connoisseur doubtless acquire in high degree such ability to determine from directly given clues whether the satisfaction in a painting or a piece of music is the kind that will endure or one which will soon fade; and their apprehension of the enduring ones doubtless is infused with a subtle and derivative immediate quality in their cultivated enjoyment itself. But—to use a comparison—if the tea-taster's experience has developed his capacity to forecast that the tea will soon lose its bouquet, and such tea does not taste quite right to him, still it is the predictable fact signalized and not this subtle immediate signal of it, which marks the tea as not good-quality tea. And if the esthetician's sixth sense of the enduring in art enables him to classify enjoyments as esthetic or non-esthetic by clues which are immediate and immediately affect his own enjoyments, still it remains true that it is not the immediate enjoyability but the signalized endurability of enjoyment which constitutes the sufficient criterion of genuine esthetic character in the experience. Such judgment is directly an assessment of esthetic quality in the *object,* and only indirectly of the genuine esthetic character of the *experience.*

In this sense, the distinctively esthetic character of experience is not simply disclosed but has to be judged. But the judgment in question is one of its classification as esthetic (which calls in some measure for a prediction), and is not the judgment of an immediate value as such. Thus even if, or insofar as, the esthetic quality of experience must be determined by judgment, it still remains true that the directly disclosed value in an experience, whether esthetic or not, calls for no judgment but is indubitable when found. And such values directly disclosable in experience are the final basis and the ultimate referents of all judgments of value.

§ ESTHETICS AND ESTHETIC THEORY

It is no part of our task in this book to attempt any contribution to the science of esthetics. Our concern is with the analysis of esthetic judgments; with the question, "What does it mean to say that *x* has esthetic value?" and with further problems subsidiary to that. The positive science of esthetics concerns a different and a further

question; namely, "By what specific criteria, or by reference to what laws, is the esthetic value of a particular thing to be gauged?"; or "What principles must govern the creative activity of the fine arts, in order that their esthetic purposes may be realized?" As a preliminary let us observe the difference of aim which must govern the attempt at analysis of esthetic judgment and the attempt to determine the specific principles of esthetics, as well as the relation between these two different objectives.

We may help ourselves out on this point by observing the analogous distinction in the case of two other sciences, logic and physics. With respect to the topic of validity in inference, there are similarly two different kinds of questions. First, "What does it mean to say that a piece of reasoning is valid: in what does this character of validity consist?" That question belongs to analysis; to the *theory* of logic. ...We may return to it the answer; "An inference is logically valid if it can be certified by reference to intensional meanings alone." Second, there is the question, "By what specific principles may particular inferences be adjudged valid; by what laws should our procedures of inference be governed in order to attain validity; by what specific criteria may validity be attested in case of doubt?" The answer to that question is to be given by a sufficient canon of inference; by a body of principles belonging to the positive science of logic. The connection between these two different questions lies in the fact that a correct answer to the first, the analytic question or question of theory, determines the underlying and general criterion by reference to which it can be determined whether a particular statement put forward as a rule of logic, is in fact a true law and affords a specific test of valid inference. Any mind which grasped this general nature of the logically valid, would thereby be in position to proceed to solution of the second problem of finding laws of the positive science of logic. However, something more than such grasp of the meaning of "logically valid" would be required for this; namely, acquaintance with more specific meanings in terms of which such positive laws of logic could be formulated.[2]

So too in physics, we have first the general questions of theory, which concern the meanings of attributions of the various essential properties of physical entities: what it means to say that a thing is so long; that a physical particle has a certain position and a certain velocity; that two events are simultaneous; and so on. Such questions belong to physical theory, and are to be answered by analysis; by adequate and accurate explication of physical concepts.[3] It is, implicitly, on the basis of such theory that one can proceed to discovery of the laws of positive physical science (those which are not disguised definitions or merely logical consequences of them). But for this second question of the specific laws of physics, observation of physical phenomena is also requisite. And for the sake of comparison with esthetics we may also note in passing that these positive laws of physics exercise a normative function in engineering and other creative activities which operate with physical things.

However, a fundamental difference is to be observed between logic and physics with respect to the phenomena acquaintance with which is essential for the positive science. The phenomena of logic are themselves phenomena of meaning only, and of relations of meaning. And any meaning is expressible by some statement the truth of which is analytic and *a priori*. No recourse to empirical facts (unless facts of the use of symbols to *express* meanings) is required for the science of logic. Its investigations can be inductive only in the Aristotelian (or Socratic) sense of eliciting from instances something which, when elicited, can be attested "by reason." But assuming correct answers to the questions of physical theory, which call for an analytic answer, the second kind of question, of the positive laws of physics, can only be answered by inductive generalization in the usual sense. Logic is an *a priori* science, and by that fact continuous with logical theory; but physics is an empirical science; though determination of the overall criteria of the various physical properties is analytic and *a priori,* and could not be otherwise, however much it looks to something implicit in the unself-conscious practice of physical science for those meanings which it is called upon to explicate.

In esthetics similarly, there is the first or theoretical question of the meaning of esthetic attributions. The answer to this is to be determined analytically and *a priori,* however essential it may be that, in arriving at it, we should look to and be governed by something which is already implicit in practice and in particular evaluations. But assuming a correct answer to this question of the nature of esthetic value—for example, the answer we have hazarded, that it consists in a quality which solicits contemplative regard and affords a relatively enduring enjoyment for such contemplation—there is the second kind of question also; *"But what particular character or characters of things makes them sources of enduring contemplative enjoyment?"*; "By what marks, universally present in objects which offer such enjoyment and universally absent from those which do not, may we recognize the esthetically valuable in case of doubt?"; "To what specific principles shall we look for guidance in activities directed to crea-

---

[2] There is also a still further question in the case of logic: "What statements capable of attesting validity of inferences are of sufficiently frequent use to be regarded as principles of logic?"; and to this question, there is none but a conventional or pragmatic answer.

[3] As examples of physical theory, in the sense of "theory" here used, one may cite P. W. Bridgman, *The Logic of Modern Physics* (New York: The Macmillan Company, 1927); V. F. Lenzen, *The Nature of Physical Theory* (New York: John Wiley & Sons, Inc., 1931); and the early chapters of A. S. Eddington, *The Philosophy of Physical Science* (New York: The Macmillan Company, 1927).

tion of the esthetically valuable?" And that kind of question can be answered only through induction: it requires generalization from observed instances of the esthetically valuable. The answers to this kind of question belong to the positive science of esthetics.

Here, as in logic or in physics, the definitive explication of what is meant in attributing esthetic value operates as the basic criterion of those phenomena which are pertinent to determination of any specific law, and thus represents the basis from which, either explicitly or implicitly, investigations of the positive science must proceed. But esthetics, like physics, is an empirical science; and the positive laws of it require to be elicited by inductive generalization from particular instances of esthetic phenomena. Thus the nature of esthetic value is a question to be answered by analysis and *a priori*, and constitutes a topic for philosophic investigation. But the laws of the positive science of esthetics are a question which must be left to those who possess sufficiently wide acquaintance with esthetic phenomena and are sufficiently expert to be capable of arriving at trustworthy empirical generalizations in this field.[4]

There are, however, certain generalities in the field of the positive science of esthetics which it will be well for us to consider. Some of these have important bearing upon those epistemological problems with which we are primarily concerned; in particular, upon the distinction between the subjective conditions of esthetic *experience* and the objective conditions of esthetic value in

things. For this reason it will not be out of place here to observe briefly, in conclusion, certain facts having this kind of pertinence, even though full discussion of them would lie outside our province.

§ TYPES OF ESTHETIC OBJECTS

It is an obvious fact—and no criticism of anybody need be read into the observation of it—that the science of esthetics remains largely undeveloped. Subsidiary principles—"principles of composition" in one or another of the fine arts—are available in considerable number and fairly well attested. But these are about the only positive content of it which is presently assured. As has been observed, there is not even as yet any general agreement amongst estheticians as to the categories in terms of which such positive laws of the esthetic should be formulated. This indifferent success is doubtless attributable in part to the marked diversity which obtains amongst objects of esthetic interest, and to the fact that some classes of them at least are phenomena of extreme complexity.

Consider, for example, what entity it is which is termed Beethoven's *Fifth Symphony*. A musical composition is not a physical object: any particular rendition of it is a physical entity of its own complex sort; but between the rendition and the thing itself, there is an obvious difference. The rendition may not, and presumably will not, realize exactly the musical intention of the composer or the esthetic possibilities represented by the composition And in the case of a sonnet or other product of the literary art, there is an even wider gap between the thing itself and the apprehension of it. Here we must ordinarily provide our own rendition; and in so doing we may not only miss a part of the intended meaning but inadvertently introduce certain grace-notes and variations of our own. Also, that most complex of all esthetic things, the drama, is in some of these respects like

---

[4] It is of course true that particular esthetic judgments do not necessarily wait upon the development of the positive science, nor presume command of it. In any field, the development of positive science requires an antecedently determined body of particular truths. There were correct logical judgments before Aristotle, geometrical determinations before Euclid, and attested physical facts before Galileo or Newton. Had there not been, these positive sciences could never have arisen.

music, and in others like poetry; but at least it is clear that a drama cannot be identified with any physical object.

On these points, a painting, a cathedral, or a piece of sculpture seems to differ from a musical composition or a literary product. A picture, edifice or statue may likewise fail to incorporate fully the intention of the creator. But at least esthetic objects of these classes are embodied once for all in physical individuals; and the distinction of any entity so incorporated from the physical embodiment of it seems uncalled for. On second thought, however, this difference can be viewed as one of degree rather than of kind. For example, when we stand before a masterpiece of painting or of sculpture, we may be reminded of something which is common to this physical object and various more or less adequate reproductions of it, some of which we may have observed before. Is it this canvas or this marble which is the object of esthetic contemplation, or is this only the "original" and most adequate incorporation of it; the thing itself being an abstract entity here embodied or approximated to, in these fading pigments or this stone which already shows the marks of time? Even in the case of objects found in nature, the esthetic orientation may be directed upon an ideality not physically present: if the landscape should be intriguing, still the sketcher will at once begin moving this a little in his mind's eye and eliminating that; and in any case the eye of the beholder performs something of the same office. Do such considerations allow the simple identification of any kind of esthetic object with a physical thing; or must we rather say that even the artist's original is an instance and an "imitation" only of an entity which itself is abstract and ideal? And between those physical conditions which qualify presentation of it and those further and psychological conditions which likewise qualify its appearance to any subject, is there any fundamental difference of kind or only one of manner or

degree; the true object being separated from our apprehension by a whole series of accidents of phenomenal appearance, some outward and physical, some inward and psychological?

It seems philistine to lay rude hands of logic on thoughts so edifying. However, there are at least three different kinds of things suggested here: first, the intention of the artist or the ideal which that intention projects; second, the kind of abstract entity which may be instanced in two printings of a poem or two renditions of a piece of music; and third, the physical individual which incorporates this abstraction or approximates to this ideal, and serves on some occasion as the vehicle of its presentation. Each of these requires at least passing attention because any one of them may be taken to represent the basic category of esthetics—*the* esthetic object.

First let us consider the ideality which is aimed at in any purpose of artistic creation, and which might be taken to be the object of our esthetic contemplation in any presentation. Confronting an art object of any kind, one may, and possibly should, seek to penetrate beyond the actual incorporation to the intent of its creator. This is especially important in the case of music and the drama, because a truer rendition may thus be brought about. And a similar attempt in the case of esthetic actualities of any kind may have its value for those who would learn, from the contemplation of past achievements, concerning the possibilities of future ones. Further, it is obvious—or should be—that if we were to discover the completely accurate and adequate laws of esthetics, these would project, as their exemplars, idealities rather than actualities, whether art-produced or natural.

However, neither of the two considerations mentioned reveals any compelling reason for conceiving of esthetic objects as transcendental entities. In other things than the fine arts, it is likewise true that we apprehend on occasion the intentions of another, which he does not fully achieve and may not even envisage adequately. And what it is that he thus fails to actualize, still has its own standing as the object of a purpose and perhaps as realizable though unrealized. Our "interpretation" in such cases, is something rendered possible by an act of empathy and through the use of creative imagination. It is possible because such purposes are capable of being shared. To be sure, such attempts to penetrate beyond the actual thing to an intention behind it—in esthetics as in other matters —lies always in some danger of ending in a romantic deception instead of genuine understanding. And in the case of objects in nature, the setting up of such intentions behind the presented object is sheer pathetic fallacy—either that or a mystic faith the validity of which should not be a question for the science of esthetics. The projected entity ideally realizing any specific attempt at esthetic envisagement or artistic creation is indeed an intelligible kind of thing, subject to esthetic comprehension and to esthetic critique. But there is no need to erect a metaphysical mystery upon the fact that human purposes are marked by a considerable degree of community, enabling us on occasion to pass beyond actualities achieved to the esthetic purpose of them, and—in the case of music and the drama— to recreate from symbols the actualities which will approximate to and convey such intentions. These facts provide no better ground for being transcendentalist about esthetic goals than there is, for example, about economic ones or those of engineering; nor any better reason to invent an empyrean habitat for the esthetically ideal than there is to believe in some New Atlantis as a metaphysical reality.

Nor does the fact that the exemplars of the laws of esthetics would be ideal entities rather than actualities, lend credibility to the transcendentalist point of view in esthetics, or distinguish that science from others. It is likewise true in physics, for example,

that the understanding of its laws projects the conception of certain ideal exemplifications—the perfect vacuum, the frictionless surface, the perfectly elastic solid, the one-hundred percent efficient engine, and so on. Also, in any application of physics—which being practical will be directed to a purpose —those who are concerned with such creative endeavors must look to some projected ideality, though they must also have an eye to the limitations of materials and of human workmanship.

§ THE ESTHETIC ACTUALITY AND
  ITS CONTEXT

It is more important and more profitable to consider that kind of abstraction which may be literally actualized and exemplified by physical occasions—and not merely approximated to or "imitated" by physical things. First, because some esthetic objects definitely are thus abstract, and others may plausibly be so considered. A sonnet, for example, cannot be identified with any physical individual. Not only is it one and the same thing which we and our neighbor may read in different books, but what is essential to the thing presented is not physically there on the printed page, but only conveyed from one mind to another by a pattern of physical symbols. The relevant meanings are associated with this symbol-pattern by a complex and common and strongly enforced social habit. Even the rhythm and cadence of the language used, which lie within the esthetic phenomenon, are not presented to the eye but only associated with what is thus physically present. It is like the score of music rather than the rendition. Yet this poem is actual, as against those as yet undreamt of, solely by the fact that this language-pattern has its concrete and physically occurrent instances, Given the language-habit which makes it possible, these are the presentations of the esthetic object; and without them there would be no poem presented or presentable.

It requires also to be observed that this abstract entity which is the esthetic object itself in the case of literature, is not literally embodied in the physical thing which serves on any occasion as the medium of its presentation. Rather this abstraction, or its instance, is to be located in a context of the physical object—in this case, a mentally associated context. Yet this consideration would be poorly taken as evidence of any subjective character of the esthetic reality in question. What poem it is which is actual, is controlled and to be determined by the factually instanced pattern of language. To be sure, this fact that the esthetic actuality has to be recreated by the subject, in accordance with the conventions of language and other implicit rules of interpretation, leaves the literary object peculiarly liable to subjectivities of apprehension. We might even doubt the possibility of any completely common and perfectly objective interpretation of it. As someone has said, the aged man and the child by his side may both read the same responses from the prayer-book; but these words cannot have the same meaning for the two, because in the one case they are freighted with a lifetime of experience. That kind of consideration has its weight for any language-presented phenomenon; and especially if it be an object of esthetic apprehension, because in that case the meanings conveyed will be predominantly expressive in significance.[5] But that fact does not condone any subjectivistic interpretation of the phenomenon itself. A poem is like a law (a legal enactment), which similarly depends upon community of language for its actuality, but is not thereby open to the wilful interpretation of the individual. What is here implied is, rather, that this actual poem, like any other artistic product, will be better grasped by some than by others; and that it may require experience and capacity in order to understand or judge it. But these conditions on the side of the subject are conditions of the *presentation to him*, not conditions of what is actually there for his apprehension. They are conditions of the esthetic experience but not of the esthetic object.

What needs to be observed here is that the esthetic actuality—the poem—is *physically presented*, when conveyed by the printed page or by a reader's voice, but that this esthetic entity is not, either spatially or in any other appropriate sense, to be located within the physical object or event which serves to present it. Some of the properties of the poem—the language pattern of it—genuinely characterize the print on the page or the temporal sequence of the sounds. In much larger part, however, the "poem itself," being constituted by the meanings thus physically symbolized, lies in the *context associated with* this physical entity which presents it. Second, it needs to be emphasized that what genuinely belongs to the character of the poem but is found in the context of what physically conveys it and not in that physical entity itself, is still not subjective but as fixed as law. And it is fixed in the same general way; that is, by understood conventions governing both the creation of it and its interpretation. Comprehension of it (or miscomprehension) has its conditions on the side of the subject; and the extent of these conditions is the greater according as less of the thing presented is literally disclosed by the physical properties of the physical object which serves to present it. But whatever the subject *must* bring to the presentation, in order correctly to understand the poem presented, belongs to the *poem*. Insofar as he fails to bring this associated context, or brings some other, the esthetic

---

[5] The line of division between *belles lettres* and literature of the more prosaic kind, probably is to be drawn with some reference to the predominance, or the importance in it, of expressive meanings which convey something for the imagination rather than for the intellectual kind of understanding.

object presented fails to be apprehended in its actual esthetic character—is either misapprehended or not apprehended at all.

The poem is an abstraction which is actualized in the instances of its presentation, through the medium of some physical vehicle. It is an entity essentially repeatable in, or common to, different physical events or things which instance it. But it must be observed that this abstractness of it is *not* the kind by which universals like triangularity or honesty or incompatibility stand in contrast to anything which is sensuously qualitative and imaginal. It has the literal character of esthesis: we shall call it an esthetic essence.

It will be fairly obvious that, with respect to the points here in question, not all esthetic objects are like poems. The different classes of them form something like a series, in which products of the literary art represent one extreme. From these we pass on down through drama and music to the pictorial and plastic arts, and finally to esthetic objects found in nature. (Detailed examination of each of these classes would be essential for any full discussion, but must be omitted here.) But though this order suggests itself at once, the principle of ordering does not. A poem is an abstraction, actualized by physical occasions which instance it. But a sunset or a mountain is a physical individuality. And between the abstract and the concrete there can be no intervening stages.

The principle of order here will be found in the extent to which what is esthetically essential is simply the physical characters of the physical vehicle of presentation, and the extent to which this esthetic essence is to be located in an associated context of this physically present thing. In that respect, the objects of esthetic interest can and do differ in degree. Perhaps this can be crudely suggested by a diagram, in which the solid line bounds the esthetic essence and the broken line the physical vehicle:

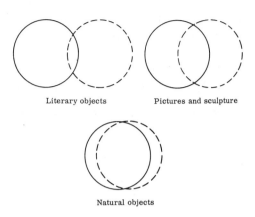

Literary objects   Pictures and sculpture

Natural objects

Further, if we are prone to say that an esthetic object disclosed in nature is wholly concrete, then we must be reminded of two facts. First, there is no natural object which would inevitably solicit and reward esthetic contemplation if we merely open our outward senses to it. *Something* is essential which is not literally a physical property of it but associated with these: it is by that fact that genuinely esthetic values are to be distinguished from inherent values of a "lower" order, like the gratefulness of water to the thirsty man. (We do not say that "lower" values are sheerly physical properties of what presents them, and independent of any context: we do say that esthetic values additionally depend on context.) Second, we must observe that in every physical object of esthetic interest there will be some characters which are irrelevant to the esthetic quality of it, and could be different without in any way affecting its esthetic quality or value. Thus even insofar as the esthetic essence should be contained within the physical object, it is still a literal abstraction from it, and theoretically could be identically presented by some other.

§ THE VARIETY OF THINGS
   ESTHETICALLY VALUED

We can, therefore, say without exception

that the entity contemplated in esthetic experience is actualized by presentation through the instrumentality of a physical object. But the direct object of contemplation is an esthetic essence; an abstraction which theoretically could be identically presented by another physical thing. This esthetic essence includes, in all cases, something not resident in the physical thing which serves to present it but in some context to which it stands related, *in some manner which is not arbitrary or subjective.* And the extent to which such contexts of the physical thing which serves as vehicle of presentation are essential to the esthetic nature and value of what is presented or conveyed, is different for different types of esthetic objects.

When esthetic or any other kind of value is ascribed to anything, it is important to observe just what thing it is which in fact is the subject of the intended attribution. It may be an actual entity of the usual sort: a poem, a drama, a musical composition, a painting, a piece of statuary, a landscape. But also, as has been indicated, it may be the ideal and unactual object projected by a purpose. Or again, it may be a particular *rendition* of a piece of music or a drama. Or it may be the physical object which serves as vehicle of the esthetic presentation. Or it may be the esthetic experience itself to which the value is attributed. When we ask whether what is judged valuable is an abstract or a concrete entity, then the factualities of the intended predication must be observed. When we value a poem, we are not judging any concrete thing, because —typically at least—we are not even thinking of the printed page. If we judge music, then it will have to be decided just what the intention of the valuation is; whether it is directed upon what could be common to or approximated by many physical renditions, or upon the musical content of this particular occasion. Similarly—even if less obviously—when we judge a painting, it will have to become clear whether the in-

tended object is this canvas and the physical pattern on it, or is instead what this canvas could have in common with some reproduction of it. In the case of the landscape or other object disclosed in nature, it may seem fantastic to suggest that what is valued is anything other than just this concrete physical thing. Yet there is that qualitative and abstract essence which is here incorporated, and is theoretically repeatable in some other physical object. Indeed there may be question, for any type of valuation, whether it is the concrete entity or the embodied qualitative abstraction which is the object—e.g., whether it is the apple we are enjoying, or the *flavor* of the apple, which it might share indistinguishably with another. Finally and most important: whatever the kind of thing it is which is presented, we must be careful to consider whether it is some objective entity to which the value is ascribed, or whether the subject of the attribution is the experience itself. Many highly regrettable errors have crept into esthetic theory through ascribing to objects the kind of value which could belong to experiences only. Lumping esthetic judgments all together, as if there were one type of object only, indicated in all of them, can only result in confusion.

That we may evaluate esthetically a concrete physical thing, in no wise contradicts the fact that there can be no physical object the esthetic evaluation of which is altogether independent of its relations to some context. The physical thing may be valued as the *instrument* of esthetic embodiment. *All* values in physically objective things are extrinsic only. The esthetic values attributable to concrete objects are a class of inherent values. But to say that a value is inherent in an object, is not necessarily to locate this value in the physical properties of it. By our definition, a value is inherent if it is one which is realized in experience through the presentation of the object in question, and not through presentation of some other object. Thus a physical thing has esthetic value if it serves to present positive esthetic quality. But if it should be said that, on such conception, no *abstract* entity could have esthetic value; because an abstraction, being incapable of being presented, could not have any kind of inherent value; then it needs to be observed that this reasoning contains a false premise. The kind of abstractions which, like poems and musical compositions, have esthetic value, *can* be presented through the medium of physical things: they are sensuous or imaginal though repeatable in different exemplifications.

What can be said concerning all classes of objects of which esthetic value can be predicated, is that this value of them *depends upon* a complexus of properties constituting an esthetic essence, in some part literally embodied, or capable of being embodied, in some physical thing which is the instrument of presentation, and in some part belonging to a context of this object, which is associated with it in some manner which is not subjective merely. Whatever the nature of the entity which is direct object of the esthetic judgment, this esthetic essence by reason of which it has or lacks

esthetic value, is an abstract entity. This kind of abstraction thus represents the basic category of esthetics.

These hastily summarized suggestions are plainly insufficient to the topic of them, and may be unclear. Still they will serve to indicate the general nature to be expected in any body of specific principles sufficient for the positive science of esthetics. As is independently suggested by such advances as have been made in the direction of this science, the key to the laws of it is probably to be found in what we have referred to as the complexus of properties constituting an esthetic essence; in the character of this as a phenomenal *Gestalt*; in relationships of constituent elements which make it some kind of configurational whole.

The overarching test by which such specific principles are themselves to be elicited, must be the test of a value disclosable as a relatively enduring enjoyment in contemplation. And where the more specific and empirical principles remain undetermined or doubtful, it is directly by that kind of test that correctness in esthetic valuation is principally to be assured.

JEAN-PAUL SARTRE

(1905-   )

Jean-Paul Sartre and Gabriel Marcel are the acknowledged leaders of existentialism in France, as Martin Heidegger and Karl Jaspers have been in Germany. The movement is generally traced to Soren Kierkegaard, the Danish philosopher (1813–1855), who was an antagonist of both the established Protestant church and the regnant Hegelian philosophy. Though perhaps he is better known as a novelist and playwright, Sartre is a philosopher fully trained in the academic sense. He taught in several colleges before World War II, served in the French army up to the fall of France, and was a prisoner of war for a year. His major philosophical work is *L'Etre et le néant* (*Being and Nothingness*), which was published in 1943. He also gives a brief account of some of his philosophical ideas in the popular *Existentialism and Humanism*. His many other works include novels, *Nausea* and others, and a number of plays, for example, *The Flies* and *No Exit*.

Like the Marxists, Sartre believes that philosophers should not merely survey the world at a cool distance but should become involved, or, as he says, engaged, in its painful concerns. In the essay included here he examines the thesis that the literary artist, especially the prose writer, must also be so engaged. If we ask why all artists should not be similarly involved, we immediately raise an aesthetic and philosophical question about the parallelism of the arts. Compare the language of poetry with that of prose literature or everyday life. Are they the same? No, says Sartre. In prose we *utilize* language—turn it into a utensil, an instrument, a prolongation of the body, a "sixth finger, a third leg." Poetry and the other arts have much more in common than poetry and prose.

Although this view is scarcely novel, we cannot be indifferent to Sartre's commitment to present moral concerns or to his verve and contemporaneity. Certainly Sartre exaggerates when in the foreword he says that nobody has ever asked himself what writing is or why one writes. But, written with irony and passion, Sartre's essays on literature lead us to reconsider a problem as old as Plato and as timely as the Communist Party—the place of the artist and the writer in society.

JEAN-PAUL SARTRE

What Is Literature?

(Translated by Bernard Frechtman)

From What Is Literature? *New York: Philosophical Library, Inc., 1949. Reprinted by permission of the Philosophical Library, Inc., and Literary Masterworks, Inc. (First published: 1947.)*

Foreword

"If you want to engage yourself," writes a young imbecile, "what are you waiting for? Join the Communist Party." A great writer who engaged himself often and disengaged himself still more often, but who has forgotten, said to me, "The worst artists are the most engaged. Look at the Soviet painters." An old critic gently complained, "You want to murder literature. Contempt for belles-lettres is spread out insolently all through your review." A petty mind calls me pigheaded, which for him is evidently the highest insult. An author who barely crawled from one war to the other and whose name sometimes awakens languishing memories in old men accuses me of not being concerned with immortality; he knows, thank God, any number of people whose chief hope it is. In the eyes of an American hack-journalist the trouble with me is that I have not read Bergson or Freud; as for Flaubert, who did not engage himself, it seems that he haunts me like remorse. Smart-alecks wink at me, "And poetry? And painting? And music? You want to engage them, too?" And some martial spirits demand, "What's it all about? Engaged literature? Well, it's the old socialist realism, unless it's a revival of populism, only more aggressive."

What nonsense. They read quickly, badly, and pass judgment before they have understood. So let's begin all over. This doesn't amuse anyone, neither you nor me. But we have to hit the nail on the head. And since critics condemn me in the name of literature without ever saying what they mean by that, the best answer to give them is to examine the art of writing without prejudice. What is writing? Why does one write? For whom? The fact is, it seems that nobody has ever asked himself these questions.

What Is Writing?

No, we do not want to "engage" painting, sculpture, and music "too," or at least not in the same way. And why would we want to? When a writer of past centuries expressed an opinion about his craft, was he immediately asked to apply it to the other arts? But today it's the thing to do to "talk painting" in the argot of the musician or the literary man and to "talk literature" in the argot of the painter, as if at bottom there were only one art which expressed itself indifferently in one or the other of these languages, like the Spinozistic substance which is adequately reflected by each of its attributes.

Doubtless, one could find at the origin of every artistic calling a certain undifferentiated choice which circumstances, education, and contact with the world particularized only later. Besides, there is no doubt that the arts of a period mutually influence each other and are conditioned by the same social factors. But those who want to expose the absurdity of a literary theory by showing that it is inapplicable to music must first prove that the arts are parallel.

Now, there is no such parallelism. Here, as everywhere, it is not only the form which differentiates, but the matter as well. And it is one thing to work with color and

sound, and another to express oneself by means of words. Notes, colors, and forms are not signs. They refer to nothing exterior to themselves. To be sure, it is quite impossible to reduce them strictly to themselves, and the idea of a pure sound, for example, is an abstraction. As Merleau-Ponty has pointed out in *The Phenomenology of Perception,* there is no quality of sensation so bare that it is not penetrated with signification. But the dim little meaning which dwells within it, a light joy, a timid sadness, remains immanent or trembles about it like a heat mist; it *is* color or sound. Who can distinguish the green apple from its tart gaiety? And aren't we already saying too much in naming "the tart gaiety of the green apple?" There is green, there is red, and that is all. They are things, they exist by themselves.

It is true that one might, by convention, confer the value of signs upon them. Thus, we talk of the language of flowers. But if, after the agreement, white roses signify "fidelity" to me, the fact is that I have stopped seeing them as roses. My attention cuts through them to aim beyond them at this abstract virtue. I forget them. I no longer pay attention to their mossy abundance, to their sweet stagnant odor. I have not even perceived them. That means that I have not behaved like an artist. For the artist, the color, the bouquet, the tinkling of the spoon on the saucer, are *things,* in the highest degree. He stops at the quality of the sound or the form. He returns to it constantly and is enchanted with it. It is this color-object that he is going to transfer to his canvas, and the only modification he will make it undergo is that he will transform it into an *imaginary* object. He is therefore as far as he can be from considering colors and signs as a *language.*[1]

What is valid for the elements of artistic

---

[1] At least in general. The greatness and error of Klee lie in his attempt to make a painting both sign and object.

creation is also valid for their combinations. The painter does not want to create a thing.[2] And if he puts together red, yellow, and green, there is no reason for the ensemble to have a definable signification, that is, to refer particularly to another object. Doubtless this ensemble is also inhabited by a soul, and since there must have been motives, even hidden ones, for the painter to have chosen yellow rather than violet, it may be asserted that the objects thus created reflect his deepest tendencies. However, they never express his anger, his anguish, or his joy as do words or the expression of the face; they are impregnated with these emotions; and in order for them to have crept into these colors, which by themselves already had something like a meaning, his emotions get mixed up and grow obscure. Nobody can quite recognize them there.

Tintoretto did not choose that yellow rift in the sky above Golgotha to *signify* anguish or to *provoke* it. It is anguish and yellow sky at the same time. Not sky of anguish or anguished sky; it is an anguish become thing, an anguish which has turned into yellow rift of sky, and which thereby is submerged and impasted by the proper qualities of things, by their impermeability, their extension, their blind permanence, their externality, and that infinity of relations which they maintain with other things. That is, it is no longer *readable*. It is like an immense and vain effort, forever arrested half-way between sky and earth, to express what their nature keeps them from expressing.

Similarly, the signification of a melody— if one can still speak of signification—is nothing outside of the melody itself, unlike ideas, which can be adequately rendered in several ways. Call it joyous or somber. It will always be over and above anything you can say about it. Not because its passions, which are perhaps at the origin of the invented theme, have, by being incorporated into notes, undergone a transubstantiation and a transmutation. A cry of grief is a sign of the grief which provokes it, but a song of grief is both grief itself and something other than grief. Or, if one wishes to adopt the existentialist vocabulary, it is a grief which does not *exist* any more, which *is*. But, you will say, suppose the painter does houses? That's just it. He *makes* them, that is, he creates an imaginary house on the canvas and not a sign of a house. And the house which thus appears preserves all the ambiguity of real houses.

The writer can guide you and, if he describes a hovel, make it seem the symbol of social injustice and provoke your indignation. The painter is mute. He presents you with *a* hovel, that's all. You are free to see in it what you like. That attic window will never be the symbol of misery; for that, it would have to be a sign, whereas it is a thing. The bad painter looks for the type. He paints the Arab, the Child, the Woman; the good one knows that neither the Arab nor the proletarian exists either in reality or on his canvas. He offers a workman, a certain workman. And what are we to think about a workman? An infinity of contradictory things. All thoughts and all feelings are there, adhering to the canvas in a state of profound undifferentiation. It is up to you to choose. Sometimes, high-minded artists try to move us. They paint long lines of workmen waiting in the snow to be hired, the emaciated faces of the unemployed, battle-fields. They affect us no more than does Greuze with his "Prodigal Son." And that masterpiece, "The Massacre of Guernica," does any one think that it won over a single heart to the Spanish cause? And yet something is said that can never quite be heard and that would take an infinity of words to express. And Picasso's long harlequins, ambiguous and

---

[2] I say "create," not "imitate," which is enough to squelch the bombast of M. Charles Estienne who has obviously not understood a word of my argument and who is dead set on tilting at shadows.

eternal, haunted with inexplicable meaning, inseparable from their stooping leanness and their pale diamond-shaped tights, are emotion become flesh, emotion which the flesh has absorbed as the blotter absorbs ink, and emotion which is unrecognizable, lost, strange to itself, scattered to the four corners of space and yet present to itself.

I have no doubt that charity or anger can produce other objects, but they will likewise be swallowed up; they will lose their name; there will remain only things haunted by a mysterious soul. One does not paint significations; one does not put them to music. Under these conditions, who would dare require that the painter or musician engage himself?

On the other hand, the writer deals with significations. Still, a distinction must be made. The empire of signs is prose; poetry is on the side of painting, sculpture, and music. I am accused of detesting it; the proof, so they say, is that *Les Temps modernes* publishes very few poems. On the contrary, this is proof that we like it. To be convinced, all one need do is take a look at contemporary production. "At least," critics say triumphantly, "you can't even dream of engaging it." Indeed. But why should I want to? Because it uses words as does prose? But it does not use them in the same way, and it does not even *use* them at all. I should rather say that it serves them. Poets are men who refuse to *utilize* language. Now, since the quest for truth takes place in and by language conceived as a certain kind of instrument, it is unnecessary to imagine that they aim to discern or expound the true. Nor do they dream of *naming* the world, and, this being the case, they name nothing at all, for naming implies a perpetual sacrifice of the name to the object named, or, as Hegel would say, the name is revealed as the inessential in the face of the thing which is essential. They do not speak, neither do they keep still; it is something different. It has been said that they wanted to destroy the "word" by monstrous couplings, but this is false. For then they would have to be thrown into the midst of utilitarian language and would have had to try to retrieve words from it in odd little groups, as for example "horse" and "butter" by writing "horses of butter."[3]

Besides the fact that such an enterprise would require infinite time, it is not conceivable that one can keep oneself on the plane of the utilitarian project, consider words as instruments, and at the same time contemplate taking their instrumentality away from them. In fact, the poet has withdrawn from language-instrument in a single movement. Once and for all he has chosen the poetic attitude which considers words as things and not as signs. For the ambiguity of the sign implies that one can penetrate it at will like a pane of glass and pursue the thing signified, or turn his gaze toward its *reality* and consider it as an object. The man who talks is beyond words and near the object, whereas the poet is on this side of them. For the former, they are domesticated; for the latter they are in the wild state. For the former, they are useful conventions, tools which gradually wear out and which one throws away when they are no longer serviceable; for the latter, they are natural things which sprout naturally upon the earth like grass and trees.

But if he dwells upon words, as does the painter with colors and the musician with sounds, that does not mean that they have lost all signification in his eyes. Indeed, it is signification alone which can give words their verbal unity. Without it they are frittered away into sounds and strokes of the pen. Only, it too becomes natural. It is no longer the goal which is always out of reach and which human transcendence is always aiming at, but a property of each term, analogous to the expression of a face,

---

[3] This is the example cited by Georges Bataille in *Inner Experience,* 5th ed. (Paris: Gallimard, 1943).

to the little sad or gay meaning of sounds and colors. Having flowed into the word, having been absorbed by its sonarity or visual aspects, having been thickened and defaced, it too is a thing, increate and eternal.

For the poet, language is a structure of the external world. The speaker is *in a situation* in language; he is invested with words. They are prolongations of his meanings, his pincers, his antennae, his eyeglasses. He maneuvers them from within; he feels them as if they were his body; he is surrounded by a verbal body which he is hardly aware of and which extends his action upon the world. The poet is outside of language. He sees words inside out as if he did not share the human condition, and as if he were first meeting the word as a barrier as he comes toward men. Instead of first knowing things by their name, it seems that first he has a silent contact with them, since, turning toward that other species of thing which for him is the word, touching them, testing them, palping them, he discovers in them a slight luminosity of their own and particular affinities with the earth, the sky, the water, and all created things.

Not knowing how to use them as a *sign* of an aspect of the world, he sees in the word the *image* of one of these aspects. And the verbal image he chooses for its resemblance to the willow tree or the ash tree is not necessarily the word which we use to designate these objects. As he is already on the outside, he considers words as a trap to catch a fleeing reality rather than as indicators which throw him out of himself into the midst of things. In short, all language is for him the mirror of the world. As a result, important changes take place in the internal economy of the word. Its sonority, its length, its masculine or feminine endings, its visual aspect, compose for him a face of flesh which *represents* rather than expresses signification. Inversely, as the signification is *realized*, the phys-

ical aspect of the word is reflected within it, and it, in its turn, functions as an image of the verbal body. Like its sign, too, for it has lost its pre-eminence; since words, like things, are increate, the poet does not decide whether the former exist for the latter or vice-versa.

Thus, between the word and the thing signified, there is established a double reciprocal relation of magical resemblance and signification. And the poet does not *utilize* the word, he does not choose between diverse acceptations; each of them, instead of appearing to him as an autonomous function, is given to him as a material quality which merges before his eyes with the other acceptation.

Thus, in each word he realizes, solely by the effect of the poetic *attitude,* the metaphors which Picasso dreamed of when he wanted to do a matchbox which was conpletely a bat without ceasing to be a matchbox. Florence is city, flower, and woman. It is city-flower, city-woman, and girl-flower all at the same time. And the strange object which thus appears has the liquidity of the *river,* the soft, tawny ardency of *gold,* and finally abandons itself with *propriety* and, by the continuous diminution of the silent *e,* prolongs indefinitely its modest blossoming.[4] To that is added the insidious effect of biography. For me, Florence is also a certain woman, an American actress who played in the silent films of my childhood, and about whom I have forgotten everything except that she was as long as a long evening glove and always a bit weary and always chaste and always married and misunderstood and whom I loved and whose name was Florence.

---

[4] [This sentence is not fully intelligible in translation as the author is here associating the component sounds of the word Florence with the signification of the French words they evoke. Thus: FL-OR-ENCE, *fleuve* (river), *or* (gold), and *décence* (propriety). The latter part of the sentence refers to the practice in French poetry of giving, in certain circumstances, a syllabic value to the otherwise silent terminal *e.*—TR. NOTE.]

For the word, which tears the writer of prose away from himself and throws him into the midst of the world, sends back to the poet his own image, like a mirror. This is what justifies the double undertaking of Leiris who, on the one hand, in his *Glossary*, tries to give certain words a *poetic definition,* that is, one which is by itself a synthesis of reciprocal implications between the sonorous body and the verbal soul, and, on the other hand, in a still unpublished work, goes in quest of remembrance of things past, taking as guides a few words which for him are particularly charged with affectivity. Thus, the poetic word is a microcosm.

The crisis of language which broke out at the beginning of this century is a poetic crisis. Whatever the social and historical factors, it manifested itself by attacks of depersonalization of the writer in the face of words. He no longer knew how to use them, and, in Bergson's famous formula, he only half recognized them. He approached them with a completely fruitful feeling of strangeness. They were no longer his; they were no longer he; but in those strange mirrors, the sky, the earth, and his own life were reflected. And, finally, they became things themselves, or rather the black heart of things. And when the poet joins several of these microcosms together the case is like that of painters when they assemble their colors on the canvas. One might think that he is composing a sentence, but this is only what it appears to be. He is creating an object. The words-things are grouped by magical associations of fitness and incongruity, like colors and sounds. They attract, repel, and *"burn"* one another, and their association composes the veritable poetic unity which is the *phrase-object.*

More often the poet first has the scheme of the sentence in his mind, and the words follow. But this scheme has nothing in common with what one ordinarily calls a verbal scheme. It does not govern the construction of a signification. Rather, it is comparable to the creative project by which

Picasso, even before touching his brush, prefigures in space the *thing* which will become a buffoon or a harlequin.

> To flee, to flee there, I feel that birds are drunk
> But, oh, my heart, hear the song of the sailors.
> *(Fuir, là-bas fuir, je sens que des oiseaux sont ivres*
> *Mais ô mon coeur entends le chant des matelots.)*

This "but" which rises like a monolith at the threshold of the sentence does not tie the second verse to the preceding one. It colors it with a certain reserved nuance, with "private associations" which penetrate it completely. In the same way, certain poems begin with "and." This conjunction no longer indicates to the mind an operation which is to be carried out; it extends throughout the paragraph to give it its absolute quality of a *sequel.* For the poet, the sentence has a tonality, a taste; by means of it he tastes for their own sake the irritating flavors of objection, of reserve, of disjunction. He carries them to the absolute. He makes them real properties of the sentence, which becomes an utter objection without being an objection *to* anything precise. He finds here those relations of reciprocal implication which we pointed out a short time ago between the poetic word and its meaning; the ensemble of the words chosen functions as an *image* of the interrogative or restrictive nuance, and vice-versa, the interrogation is an image of the verbal ensemble which it delimits.

As in the following admirable verses:

> Oh seasons! Oh castles!
> What soul is faultless?
> *(O saisons! O châteaux!*
> *Quelle âme est sans défaut?)*

Nobody is questioned; nobody is questioning; the poet is absent. And the question involves no answer, or rather it is its own answer. Is it therefore a false question? But it would be absurd to believe that Rimbaud "meant" that everybody has his faults. As Breton said of Saint-Pol Roux, "If he had meant it, he would have said it." Nor did he *mean* to say something else. He asked an absolute question. He conferred upon the beautiful word "soul" an interrogative existence. The interrogation has become a thing as the anguish of Tintoretto became a yellow sky. It is no longer a signification, but a substance. It is seen from the outside, and Rimbaud invites us to see it from the outside with him. Its strangeness arises from the fact that, in order to consider it, we place ourselves on the other side of the human condition, on the side of God.

If this is the case, one easily understands how foolish it would be to require a poetic engagement. Doubtless, emotion, even passion—and why not anger, social indignation, and political hatred?—are at the origin of the poem. But they are not *expressed* there, as in a pamphlet or in a confession. Insofar as the writer of prose exhibits feelings, he illustrates them; whereas, if the poet injects his feelings into his poem, he ceases to recognize them; the words take hold of them, penetrate them, and metamorphose them; they do not signify them, even in his eyes. Emotion has become thing; it now has the opacity of things; it is compounded by the ambiguous properties of the vocables in which it has been enclosed. And above all, there is always much more in each phrase, in each verse, as there is more than simple anguish in the yellow sky over Golgotha. The word, the phrase-thing, inexhaustible as things, everywhere overflows the feeling which has produced them. How can one hope to provoke the indignation or the political enthusiasm of the reader when the very thing one does is to withdraw him from the human condition and invite him to consider with the eyes of God a language that has been turned inside out? Someone may say, "You're forgetting the poets of the Resistance. You're forgetting Pierre Emmanuel." Not a bit! They're the very ones I was going to give as examples.[5]

But even if the poet is forbidden to

engage himself, is that a reason for exempt-

attitude toward language, the following are a few brief indications.

Originally, poetry creates the *myth,* while the prose-writer draws its *portrait.* In reality, the human act, governed by needs and urged on by the useful is, in a sense, a *means.* It passes unnoticed, and it is the result which counts. When I extend my hand *in order to* take up my pen, I have only a fleeting and obscure consciousness of my gesture; it is the pen which I see. Thus, man is alienated by his ends. Poetry reverses the relationship: the world and things become inessential, become a pretext for the act which becomes its own end. The vase is there so that the girl may perform the graceful act of filling it; the Trojan War, so that Hector and Achilles may engage in that heroic combat. The action, detached from its goals, which become blurred, becomes an act of prowess or a dance. Nevertheless, however indifferent he might have been to the success of the enterprise, the poet, before the nineteenth century, remained in harmony with society as a whole. He did not use language for the end which prose seeks, but he had the same confidence in it as the prose-writer.

With the coming of bourgeois society, the poet puts up a common front with the prose-writer to declare it unlivable. His job is always to create the myth of man, but he passes from white magic to black magic. Man is always presented as the absolute end, but by the success of his enterprise he is sucked into a utilitarian collectivity. The thing that is in the background of his act and that will allow transition to the myth is thus no longer success, but defeat. By stopping the infinite series of his projects like a screen, defeat alone returns him to himself in his purity. The world remains the inessential, but it is now there as a pretext for defeat. The finality of the thing is to send man back to himself by blocking the route. Moreover, it is not a matter of arbitrarily introducing defeat and ruin into the course of the world, but rather of having no eyes for anything but that. Human enterprise has two aspects: it is both success and failure. The dialectical scheme is inadequate for reflecting upon it. We must make our vocabulary and the frames of our reason more supple. Some day I am going to try to describe that strange reality, History, which is neither objective, nor ever quite subjective, in which the dialectic is contested, penetrated, and corroded by a kind of antidialectic, but which is still a dialectic. But that is the philosopher's affair. One does not ordinarily consider the two faces of Janus; the man of action sees one and the poet sees the other. When the instruments are broken and unusable, when plans are blasted and effort is useless, the world appears with a childlike and terrible freshness, without supports, without paths. It has the maximum reality because it is crushing for man, and as action, in any case, generalizes, defeat

---

[5] If one wishes to know the origin of this

ing the writer of prose? What do they have in common? It is true that the prose-writer and the poet both write. But there is nothing in common between these two acts of writing except the movement of the hand which traces the letters. Otherwise, their universes are incommunicable, and what is good for one is not good for the other. Prose is, in essence, utilitarian. I would readily define the prose-writer as a man who *makes use* of words. M. Jourdain made prose to ask for his slippers, and Hitler to declare war on Poland. The writer is a *speaker*; he designates, demonstrates, orders, refuses, interpolates, begs, insults, persuades, insinuates. If he does so without any effect, he does not therefore become a poet; he is a writer who is talking and saying nothing. We have seen enough of language inside out; it is now time to look at it right side out.[6]

The art of prose is employed in discourse; its substance is by nature significative; that is, the words are first of all not objects but designations for objects; it is not first of

---

restores to things their individual reality. But, by an expected reversal, the defeat, considered as a final end, is both a contesting and an appropriation of this universe. A contesting, because man *is worth more* than that which crushes; he no longer contests things in their "little bit of reality," like the engineer or the captain, but, on the contrary, in their "too full of reality," by his very existence as a vanquished person; he is the remorse of the world. An appropriation, because the world, by ceasing to be the tool of success, becomes the instrument of failure. So there it is, traversed by an obscure finality; it is its coefficient of adversity which serves, the more human insofar as it is more hostile to man. The defeat itself turns into salvation. Not that it makes us yield to some "beyond," but by itself it shifts and is metamorphosed. For example, poetic language rises out of the ruins of prose. If it is true that the word is a betrayal and that communication is impossible, then each word by itself recovers its individuality and becomes an instrument of our defeat and a receiver of the incommunicable. It is not that there is *another thing* to communicate; but the communication of prose having miscarried, it is the very meaning of the word which becomes the pure incommunicable. Thus, the failure of communication becomes a suggestion of the incommunicable, and the thwarted project of utilizing words is succeeded by the pure disinterested intuition of the word. Thus, we again meet with the description which we attempted earlier in this study, but in the more general perspective of the absolute valorization of the defeat, which seems to me the original attitude of contemporary poetry. Note also that this choice confers upon the poet a very precise function in the collectivity: in a highly integrated or religious society, the defeat is masked by the State or redeemed by Religion; in a less integrated and secular society, such as our democracies, it is up to poetry to redeem them.

Poetry is a case of the loser winning. And the genuine poet chooses to lose, even if he has to go so far as to die, in order to win. I repeat that I am talking of contemporary poetry. History presents other forms of poetry. It is not my concern to show their connection with ours. Thus, if one absolutely wishes to speak of the engagement of the poet, let us say that he is the man who engages himself to lose. This is the deeper meaning of that tough-luck, of that malediction with which he always claims kinship and which he always attributes to an intervention from without; whereas it is his deepest choice, the source, and not the consequence, of his poetry. He is certain of the total defeat of the human enterprise and arranges to fail in his own life in order to bear witness, by his individual defeat, to human defeat in general. Thus, he contests, as we shall

see, which is what the prose-writer does too. But the contesting of prose is carried on in the name of a greater success; and that of poetry, in the name of the hidden defeat which every victory conceals.

[6] It goes without saying that in all poetry a certain form of prose, that is, of success, is present; and, vice-versa, the driest prose always contains a bit of poetry, that is, a certain form of defeat; no prose-writer is *quite* capable of expressing what he wants to say; he says too much or not enough; each phrase is a wager, a risk assumed; the more cautious one is, the more attention the world attracts; as Valery has shown, no one can understand a word to its very bottom. Thus, each word is used simultaneously for its clear and social meaning and for certain obscure resonances—let me say, almost for its physiognomy. The reader, too, is sensitive to this. At once we are no longer on the level of concerted communication, but on that of grace and chance; the silences of prose are poetic because they mark its limits, and it is for the purpose of greater clarity that I have been considering the extreme cases of pure prose and pure poetry. However, it need not be concluded that we can pass from poetry to prose by a continuous series of intermediate forms. If the prose-writer is too eager to fondle his words, the *eidos* of "prose" is shattered and we fall into highfalutin nonsense. If the poet relates, explains, or teaches, the poetry becomes *prosaic*; he has lost the game. It is a matter of complex structures, impure, but well-defined.

all a matter of knowing whether they please or displease in themselves, but whether they correctly indicate a certain thing or a certain notion. Thus, it often happens that we find ourselves possessing a certain idea that someone has taught us by means of words without being able to recall a single one of the words which have transmitted it to us.

Prose is first of all an attitude of mind. As Valéry would say, there is prose when the word passes across our gaze as the glass across the sun. When one is in danger or in difficulty he grabs any instrument. When the danger is past, he does not even remember whether it was a hammer or a stick; moreover, he never knew; all he needed was a prolongation of his body, a means of extending his hand to the highest branch. It was a sixth finger, a third leg, in short, a pure function which he assimilated. Thus, regarding language, it is our shell and our antennae; it protects us against others and informs us about them; it is a prolongation of our senses, a third eye which is going to look into our neighbor's heart. We are within language as within our body. We *feel* it spontaneously while going beyond it toward other ends, as we feel our hands and our feet; we perceive it when it is the other who is using it, as we perceive the limbs of others. There is the word which is lived and the word which is met. But in both cases it is in the course of an undertaking, either of me acting upon others, or the other upon me The word is a certain particular moment of action and has no meaning outside of it. In certain cases of aphasia the possibilities of acting, of understanding situations, and of having normal relations with the other sex, are lost.

At the heart of this apraxia the destruction of language appears only as the collapse of one of the structures, the finest and the most apparent. And if prose is never anything but the privileged instrument of a certain undertaking, if it is only the poet's business to contemplate words in a disinterested fashion, then one has the right to ask the prose-writer from the very start, "What is your aim in writing? What undertakings are you engaged in, and why does it require you to have recourse to writing?" In any case this undertaking cannot have pure contemplation as an end. For, intuition is silence, and the end of language is to communicate. One can doubtless *pin down* the results of intuition, but in this case a few words hastily scrawled on paper will suffice; it will always be enough for the author to recognize what he had in mind. If the words are assembled into sentences, with a concern for clarity, a decision foreign to the intuition, to the language itself, must intervene, the decision of confiding to others the results obtained. In each case one must ask the reason for this decision. And the common sense which our pedants too readily forget never stops repeating it. Are we not in the habit of putting this basic question to young people who are thinking of writing: "Do you have anything to say?" Which means: something which is worth the trouble of being communicated. But what do we mean by something which is "worth the trouble" if it is not by recourse to a system of transcendent values?

Moreover, to consider only this secondary structure of the undertaking, which is what the *verbal moment* is, the serious error of pure stylists is to think that the word is a gentle breeze which plays lightly over the surface of things, which grazes them without altering them, and that the speaker is a pure *witness* who sums up with a word his harmless contemplation. To speak is to act; anything which one names is already no longer quite the same; it has lost its innocence.

If you name the behavior of an individual, you reveal it to him; he sees himself. And since you are at the same time naming it to all others, he knows that he is *seen* at the moment he *sees* himself. The furtive gesture which he forgot while making it, begins to exist beyond all measure, to exist for everybody; it is integrated into the objective mind; it takes on new dimensions; it is retrieved. After that, how can you expect him to act in the same way? Either he will persist in his behavior out of obstinacy and with full knowledge of what he is doing, or he will give it up. Thus, by speaking, I reveal the situation by my very intention of changing it; I reveal it to myself and to others *in order* to change it. I strike at its very heart, I transpierce it, and I display it in full view; at present I dispose of it; with every word I utter, I involve myself a little more in the world, and by the same token I emerge from it a little more, since I go beyond it toward the future.

Thus, the prose-writer is a man who has chosen a certain method of secondary action which we may call action by disclosure. It is therefore permissible to ask him this second question: "What aspect of the world do you want to disclose? What change do you want to bring into the world by this disclosure?" The "engaged" writer knows that words are action. He knows that to reveal is to change and that one can reveal only by planning to change. He has given up the impossible dream of giving an impartial picture of Society and the human condition. Man is the being toward whom no being can be impartial, not even God. For God, if He existed, would be, as certain mystics have seen Him, in a *situation* in relationship to man. And He is also the being Who can not even see a situation without changing it, for His gaze congeals, destroys, or sculpts, or, as does eternity, changes the object in itself. It is in love, in hate, in anger, in fear, in joy, in indignation, in admiration, in hope, in despair, that man and the world reveal themselves *in their truth*. Doubtless, the engaged writer can be mediocre; he can even be conscious of being so; but as one can not write without the intention of succeeding perfectly, the modesty with which he envisages his work should not divert him from constructing it *as if* it were to have the greatest celebrity. He should never say to himself "Bah! I'll be lucky if I have three thousand readers," but rather, "What would happen if everybody read what I wrote?" He remembers what Mosca said beside the coach which carried Fabrizio and Sanseverina away, "If the word Love comes up between them, I'm lost." He knows that he is the man who names what has not yet been named or what dares not tell its name. He knows that he makes the word "love" and the word "hate" *surge up* and with them love and hate between men who had not yet decided upon their feelings. He knows that words, as Brice-Parrain says, are "loaded pistols." If he speaks, he fires. He may be silent, but since he has chosen to fire, he must do it like a man, by aiming at targets, and not like a child, at random, by shutting his eyes and firing merely for the pleasure of hearing the shot go off.

Later on we shall try to determine what the goal of literature may be. But from this point on we may conclude that the writer has chosen to reveal the world and particularly to reveal man to other men so that the latter may assume full responsibility before the object which has been thus laid bare. It is assumed that no one is ignorant of the law because there is a code and because the law is written down; thereafter, you are free to violate it, but you know the risks you run. Similarly, the function of the writer is to act in such a way that nobody can be ignorant of the world and that nobody may say that he is innocent of what it's all about. And since he had once engaged himself in the universe of language, he can never again pretend that he can not speak. Once you enter the universe of significations, there is nothing you can do to get out of it. Let words organize themselves freely and they will make sentences, and each sentence contains language in its entirety and refers back to the whole universe. Silence itself is defined in relationship to words, as the pause in music receives its meaning from the group of notes around it. This silence is a moment of language; being silent is not being dumb; it is to refuse to speak, and therefore to keep on speaking. Thus, if a writer has chosen to remain silent on any aspect whatever of the world, or, according to an expression which says just what it means, to *pass over* it in silence, one has the right to ask him a third question: "Why have you spoken of this rather than that, and—since you speak in order to bring about change—why do you want to change this rather than that?"

All this does not prevent there being a manner of writing. One is not a writer for having chosen to say certain things, but for having chosen to say them in a certain way. And, to be sure, the style makes the value of the prose. But it should pass unnoticed. Since words are transparent and since the gaze looks through them, it would be absurd to slip in among them some panes of rough glass. Beauty is in this case only a gentle and imperceptible force. In a painting it shines forth at the very first sight; in a book it hides itself; it acts by persuasion like the charm of a voice or a face. It does not coerce; it inclines a person without his suspecting it, and he thinks that he is yielding to arguments when he is really being solicited by a charm that he does not see. The ceremonial of the mass is not faith; it disposes the harmony of words; their beauty, the balance of the phrases, *dispose* the passions of the reader without his being aware and orders them like the mass, like music, like the dance. If he happens to consider them by themselves, he loses the meaning; there remains only a boring seesaw of phrases.

In prose the aesthetic pleasure is pure only if it is thrown into the bargain. I blush at recalling such simple ideas, but it seems that today they have been forgotten. If that were not the case, would we be told that we are planning the murder of literature, or, more simply, that engagement is

harmful to the art of writing? If the contamination of a certain kind of prose by poetry had not confused the ideas of our critics, would they dream of attacking us on the matter of form, when we have never spoken of anything but the content? There is nothing to be said about form in advance, and we have said nothing. Everyone invents his own, and one judges it afterward. It is true that the subjects suggest the style, but they do not order it. There are no styles ranged a priori outside of the literary art. What is more engaged, what is more boring than the idea of attacking the Jesuits? Yet, out of this Pascal made his *Provincial Letters*. In short, it is a matter of knowing what one wants to write about, whether butterflies or the condition of the Jews. And when one knows, then it remains to decide how one will write about it.

Often the two choices are only one, but among good writers the second choice never precedes the first. I know that Giraudoux has said that "the only concern is finding the style; the idea comes afterwards;" but he was wrong. The idea did not come. On the contrary, if one considers subjects as problems which are always open, as solicitations, as expectations, it will be easily understood that art loses nothing in engagement. On the contrary, just as physics submits to mathematicians new problems which require them to produce a new symbolism, in like manner the always new requirements of the social and the metaphysical engage the artist in finding a new language and new techniques. If we no longer write as they did in the eighteenth century, it is because the language of Racine and Saint-Evremond does not lend itself to talking about locomotives or the proletariat. After that, the purists will perhaps forbid us to write about locomotives. But art has never been on the side of the purists.

If that is the principle of engagement, what objection can one have to it? And above all *what objection has been made to it*? It has seemed to me that my opponents have not had their hearts in their work very much and that their articles contain nothing more than a long scandalized sigh which drags on over two or three columns. I should have liked to know *in the name of what,* with what conception of literature, they condemned engagement. But they have not said; they themselves have not known. The most reasonable thing would have been to support their condemnation on the old theory of art for art's sake. But none of them can accept it. That is also disturbing. We know very well that pure art and empty art are the same thing and that aesthetic purism was a brilliant maneuver of the bourgeois of the last century who preferred to see themselves denounced as philistines rather than as exploiters. Therefore, they themselves admitted that the writer had to speak about something. But about what? I believe that their embarrassment would have been extreme if Fernandez had not found for them, after the other war, the notion of the *message.* The writer of today, they say, should in no case occupy himself with temporal affairs. Neither should he set up lines without signification nor seek solely beauty of phrase and of imagery. His function is to deliver messages to his readers. Well, what is a message?

It must be borne in mind that most critics are men who have not had much luck and who, just about the time they were growing desperate, found a quiet little job as cemetery watchmen. God knows whether cemeteries are peaceful; none of them is more cheerful than a library. The dead are there; the only thing they have done is write. They have long since been washed clean of the sin of living, and besides, their lives are known only through other books which other dead men have written about them. Rimbaud is dead. So are Paterne Berrichon and Isabelle Rimbaud. The trouble makers have disappeared; all that remains are the little coffins that are stacked on shelves along the walls like urns in a columbarium. The critic lives badly; his wife does not appreciate him as she ought to; his children are ungrateful; the first of the month is hard on him. But it is always possible for him to enter his library, take down a book from the shelf, and open it. It gives off a slight odor of the cellar, and a strange operation begins which he has decided to call reading. From one point of view it is a possession; he lends his body to the dead in order that they may come back to life. And from another point of view it is a contact with the beyond. Indeed, the book is by no means an object; neither is it an act, nor even a thought. Written by a dead man about dead things, it no longer has any place on this earth; it speaks of nothing which interests us directly. Left to itself, it falls back and collapses; there remain only ink spots on musty paper. And when the critic reanimates these spots, when he makes letters and words of them, they speak to him of passions which he does not feel, of bursts of anger without objects, of dead fears and hopes. It is a whole disembodied world which surrounds him, where human feelings, because they are no longer affecting, have passed on to the status of exemplary feelings and, in a word, of *values.* So he persuades himself that he has entered into relations with an intelligible world which is like the truth of his daily sufferings. And their reason for being. He thinks that nature imitates art, as for Plato the world of the senses imitates that of the archetypes. And during the time he is reading, his everyday life becomes an appearance. His nagging wife, his hunchbacked son, they too are appearances. And he will put up with them because Xenophon has drawn the portrait of Xanthippe and Shakespeare that of Richard the Third.

It is a holiday for him when contemporary authors do him the favor of dying. Their books, too raw, too living, too urgent, pass on to the other shore; they become less and less affecting and more and more beautiful. After a short stay in Purgatory they go on to people the intelligible heaven with new values. Bergotte, Swann, Siegfried and Bella, and Monsieur Teste are recent acquisitions. He is waiting for Nathanaël and Ménalque. As for the writers who persist in living, he asks them only not to move about too much, and to make an effort to resemble from now on the dead men they will be. Valéry, who for twenty-five years had been publishing posthumous books, managed the matter very nicely. That is why, like some highly exceptional saints, he was canonized during his lifetime. But Malraux is scandalous.

Our critics are Catharians. They don't want to have anything to do with the real world except eat and drink in it, and since it is absolutely necessary to have relations with our fellow-creatures, they have chosen to have them with the defunct. They get excited only about classified matters, closed quarrels, stories whose ends are known. They never bet on uncertain issues, and since history has decided for them, since the objects which terrified or angered the authors they read have disappeared, since bloody disputes seem futile at a distance of two centuries, they can be charmed with balanced periods, and everything happens for them as if all literature were only a vast tautology and as if every new prose-writer had invented a new way of speaking only for the purpose of saying nothing.

To speak of archetypes and "human nature"—is that speaking in order to say nothing? All the conceptions of our critics oscillate from one idea to the other. And, of course, both of them are false. Our great writers wanted to destroy, to edify, to demonstrate. But we no longer retain the proofs which they have advanced because we have no concern with what they mean to prove. The abuses which they denounced are no longer those of our time. There are others which rouse us which they did not suspect. History has given the lie to some of their predictions, and those which have been fulfilled became true so long ago that

we have forgotten that they were at first flashes of their genius. Some of their thoughts are utterly dead, and there are others which the whole human race has taken up to its advantage and which we now regard as commonplace. It follows that the best arguments of these writers have lost their effectiveness. We admire only their order and rigor. Their most compact composition is in our eyes only an ornament, an elegant architecture of exposition, with no more practical application than such architectures as the fugues of Bach and the arabesques of the Alhambra.

We are still moved by the passion of these impassioned geometries when the geometry no longer convinces us. Or rather by the representation of the passion. In the course of centuries the ideas have turned flat, but they remain the little personal objectives of a man who was once flesh and bone; behind the reasons of reason, which languish, we perceive the reasons of the heart, the virtues, the vices, and that great pain that men have in living. Sade does his best to win us over, but we hardly find him scandalous. He is no longer anything but a soul eaten by a beautiful disease, a pearl-oyster. The *Letter on the Theater* no longer keeps anyone from going to the theater, but we find it piquant that Rousseau detested the art of the drama. If we are a bit versed in psychoanalysis, our pleasure is perfect. We shall explain the *Social Contract* by the Oedipus complex and *The Spirit of the Laws* by the inferiority complex. That is, we shall fully enjoy the well-known superiority of live dogs to dead lions. Thus, when a book presents befuddled thoughts which appear to be reasons only to melt under scrutiny and to be reduced to heart beats, when the teaching that one can draw from it is radically different from what its author intended, the book is called a message. Rousseau, the father of the French Revolution, and Gobineau, the father of racism, both sent us messages. And the critic considers them with equal sympathy. If they were alive, he would have to choose between the two, to love one and hate the other. But what brings them together, above all, is that they are both profoundly and deliciously wrong, and in the same way: they are dead.

Thus, contemporary writers should be advised to deliver messages, that is, voluntarily to limit their writing to the involuntary expression of their souls. I say involuntary because the dead, from Montaigne to Rimbaud, have painted themselves completely, but without having meant to—it is something they have simply thrown into the bargain. The surplus which they have given us unintentionally should be the primary and professed goal of living writers. They are not to be forced to give us confessions without any dressing, nor are they to abandon themselves to the too-naked lyricism of the romantics. But since we find pleasure in foiling the ruses of Chateaubriand or Rousseau, in surprising them in the secret places of their being at the moment they are playing at being the public man, in distinguishing the private motives from their most universal assertions, we shall ask newcomers to procure us this pleasure deliberately. So let them reason, assert, deny, refute, and prove; but the cause they are defending must be only the apparent aim of their discourse; the deeper goal is to yield themselves without seeming to do so. They must first disarm themselves of their arguments as time has done for those of the classic writers; they must bring them to bear upon subjects which interest no one or on truths so general that readers are convinced in advance. As for their ideas, they must give them an air of profundity, but with an effect of emptiness, and they must shape them in such a way that they are obviously explained by an unhappy childhood, a class hatred, or an incestuous love. Let them not presume to think in earnest; thought conceals the man, and it is the man alone who interests us. A bare tear is not lovely. It offends. A good argu-

ment also offends, as Stendhal well observed. But an argument that masks a tear—that's what we're after. The argument removes the obscenity from the tears; the tears, by revealing their origin in the passions, remove the aggressiveness from the argument. We shall be neither too deeply touched nor at all convinced, and we shall be able to yield ourselves in security to that moderate pleasure which, as everyone knows, we derive from the contemplation of works of art. Thus, this is "true," "pure" literature, a subjectivity which yields itself under the aspect of the objective, a discourse so curiously contrived that it is equivalent to silence, a thought which debates with itself, a reason which is only the mask of madness, an Eternal which lets it be understood that it is only a moment of History, a historical moment which, by the hidden side which it reveals, suddenly sends back a perpetual lesson to the eternal man, but which is produced against the express wishes of those who do the teaching.

When all is said and done, the message is a soul which is made object. A soul, and what is to be done with a soul? One contemplates it at a respectful distance. It is not customary to show one's soul in society without an imperious motive. But, with certain reserves, convention permits some individuals to put theirs into commerce, and all adults may procure it for themselves. For many people today, works of the mind are thus little straying souls which one acquires at a modest price; there is good old Montaigne's, dear La Fontaine's, and that of Jean-Jacques and of Jean-Paul and of delicious Gérard. What is called literary art is the ensemble of the treatments which make them inoffensive. Tanned, refined, chemically treated, they provide their acquirers with the opportunity of devoting some moments of a life completely turned outward to the cultivation of subjectivity. Custom guarantees it to be without risk. Montaigne's skepticism? Who can take it seriously since the author of the

Essays got frightened when the plague ravaged Bordeaux? Or Rousseau's humanitarianism, since "Jean-Jacques" put his children into an orphanage? And the strange revelations of *Sylvie,* since Gérard de Nerval was mad? At the very most, the professional critic will set up infernal dialogues between them and will inform us that French thought is a perpetual colloquy between Pascal and Montaigne. In so doing he has no intention of making Pascal and Montaigne more alive, but of making Malraux and Gide more dead. Finally, when the internal contradictions of the life and the work have made both of them useless, when the message, in its imponderable depth, has taught us these capital truths, "that man is neither good nor bad," "that there is a great deal of suffering in human life," "that genius is only great patience,"

this melancholy cuisine will have achieved its purpose, and the reader, as he lays down the book, will be able to cry out with a tranquil soul, "All this is only literature."

But since, for us, writing is an enterprise; since writers are alive before being dead; since we think that we must try to be as right as we can in our books; and since, even if the centuries show us to be in the wrong, this is no reason to show in advance that we are wrong; since we think that the writer should engage himself completely in his works, and not as an abject passivity by putting forward his vices, his misfortunes, and his weaknesses, but as a resolute will and as a choice, as this total enterprise of living that each one of us is; it is then proper that we take up this problem at its beginning and that we, in our turn, ask ourselves: *"Why* does one write?"

ER LIBRAR